MAGILL'S QUOTATIONS
IN CONTEXT
Second Series

———

A-LIV

Magill's
QUOTATIONS
in Context
SECOND SERIES

Edited by
FRANK N. MAGILL

Associate Editor
TENCH FRANCIS TILGHMAN

VOLUME ONE—A-LIV

SALEM PRESS
INCORPORATED
NEW YORK

FIRST EDITION

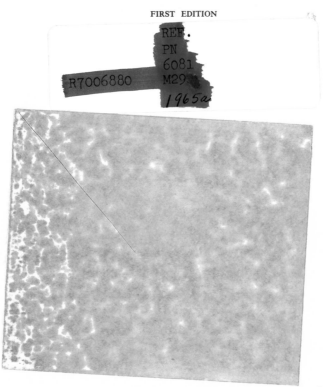

69- 15317

PREFACE

MAGILL'S QUOTATIONS IN CONTEXT, Second Series, is an extension of the original work published in 1965. It contains 1,500 additional quotations handled in the same manner as those in the earlier work except that in most cases the *Context* paragraph is longer and the number of lines quoted from the original source is greater. This change in format is the result of evaluations of comments and suggestions from users, many of whom expressed the desire to have a more extensive background commentary and see more of the original quoted material even if this arrangement meant fewer quotations overall.

In this series we have been concerned not only with familiar aphorisms; we have also included many literary expressions which may not be thought of by most readers as "familiar quotes" but which represent important and well-known sequences from much-esteemed literary works. Many readers will thus encounter expressions that remind them of works previously read, and indeed some may find here opening wedges leading eventually to pleasant discoveries and a broadening literary horizon.

For example, "God tempers the wind to the shorn lamb" (included in an earlier volume) is a lead-in to a delightful and touching sequence from Laurence Sterne's A SENTIMENTAL JOURNEY THROUGH FRANCE AND ITALY, wherein the simpleminded Maria credits the Almighty with showing special mercy to those of His creatures who are flawed through circumstance. Yorick (Sterne) learns that Maria has been wandering about the roads of France on her own. Searching, he comes upon her weeping quietly by the roadside near her home. She tells him of her travels, and he relates her story thus:

> "—She had since that, she told me, stray'd as far as Rome, and
> walk'd round St. Peter's once—and return'd back—that she found
> her way alone across the Apennines—had travell'd over all Lom-
> bardy without money,—and through the flinty roads of Savoy
> without shoes—how she had borne it, and how she had got sup-
> ported, she could not tell—but God tempers the wind, said Maria,
> to the shorn lamb."

Here, then, is a reminder of Sterne's humane approach in his writings—a most attractive characteristic.

Deserving to be remembered, too, are such phrases as "Freedom and not

v

servitude is the cure of anarchy," which can lead one to a full and rewarding study of Edmund Burke's determined efforts at conciliation between Great Britain and the American Colonies. Or, a wry comment such as "A well-written life is almost as rare as a well-spent one" is surely a challenge for one to examine Carlyle's FREDERICK II OF PRUSSIA.

"Simplify, simplify" may not seem striking as a "quote," yet it takes us to Thoreau and thence across the entire spectrum of his philosophy. Consider "The rest is silence." Not dramatic standing alone, yet as a lead-in to the death of Hamlet and indirectly to a review of his moody, turbulent life, the expression becomes noteworthy indeed.

Hence, this work is meant to be more than a book of quotations. There are fifteen hundred opportunities for the reader to travel a path which leads behind the quotation itself and on toward a rapport with the creative sensibility from which it sprang.

Entries in this book are alphabetical by quotation, without regard to author or chronology. There are, however, three complete indexes, enabling the user to find readily any quotation in the book. Two of these indexes appear ahead of the text: The Alphabetical List of Quotations, showing every entry in alphabetical order, and a Key Word Index. The purpose of the latter list is to assist those who may not remember a quotation verbatim but who recall a key word or an identifying phrase. This index, also, is alphabetical, and quotations that contain several key words may appear in this special index several times in different word arrangements. The first word of the true quotation is always given in italics so that the user of the Key Word Index may readily recognize the quotation sought once he has found it in the rearranged form of the line. An Author Index will be found at the end of the book.

It should be pointed out that quotations appearing at the top of an entry do not always agree verbatim with the actual quotation as it appears in the context. Instead, these top lines are treated as *titles* for the entries, a procedure that enabled the editors to take certain minor liberties with the material as it is quoted in the contextual excerpt itself—which is always verbatim. The purpose here was to eliminate archaic spellings or words that have long since disappeared from the quotation as we use it today. Modernization was not attempted in every case, however; who would dare, for example, to disturb "Up roos the sonne, and up roos Emelye"? Inasmuch as our title line need not scan, contractions which may be necessary in a line of poetry as it appears in the context were usually eliminated.

Our hard-working staff joins me in the hope that most of the literary expressions in this book will prove rewarding to readers of all tastes, and that the volume will afford much pleasure to those who use it.

FRANK N. MAGILL

ALPHABETICAL LIST OF QUOTATIONS

ALPHABETICAL LIST OF QUOTATIONS

Jest breaks no bones, A, 559
Joke's a very serious thing, A, 560

Keep up appearances, 561
Keys of the kingdom, The, 562
Kill not the moth nor butterfly, 563
King can do no wrong, The, 564
King may make a nobleman, but he cannot make a gentleman, A, 565
King never dies, The, 566
King of intimate delights, 567
King's a king, do fortune what she can, A, 568
Kissing don't last: cookery do!, 569
Knave's religion is the rottenest thing about him, A, 570
Knock-down argument, A, 570
Know what thou canst work at, 571
Knowledge by suffering entereth, 572
Knowledge enormous makes a God of me, 573

Laboring mountain scarce brings forth a mouse, The, 574
Lady bountiful, 574
Lady in the case, A, 575
Land of scholars and the nurse of arms, The, 576
Language is fossil poetry, 577
Last of all the Romans, fare thee well, The, 578
Last rose of summer, left blooming alone, The, 579
Lasting mansions of the dead, The, 580
Laugh all honesty out of fashion, 581
Laughing queen that caught the world's great hands, The, 582
Laughter is nothing else but sudden glory, 583
Law is a bottomless pit, 584
Laws, like houses, lean on one another, 585
Lead apes in hell, 586
Lean and slippered pantaloon, 587
Lean, hungry, savage, anti-everythings, 587
Leap into the dark, A, 588
Learn'd without sense, and venerably dull, 589
Learning, that cobweb of the brain, 591
Leave Now for dogs and apes! Man has Forever, 592
Leave us leisure to be good, 592
Leper once he lost and gained a king, A, 593
Let dogs delight to bark and bite, 594
Let Grill be Grill and have his hoggish mind, 595
Let him not boast who puts his armor on, 596
Let joy be unconfined, 597
Let them hate, so that they fear, 598
Let there be light, 599
Let us be moral. Let us contemplate existence, 600
Let us hob-and-nob with Death, 601
Let us reason together, 601
Let's have one other gaudy night, 603
Letting I dare not wait upon I would, 604
Letting the rank tongue blossom into speech, 604
Liberty consists in doing what one desires, 605
Liberty must be limited in order to be possessed, 606

Men of culture are the true apostles of equality, 702
Men of few words are the best men, 703
Mighty-mouth'd inventor of harmonies, 704
Milk-soup men call domestic bliss, 704
Mind conscious of virtue may bring to thee suitable rewards, A, 705
Mind quite vacant is a mind distressed, A, 706
Mindful of the unhonored dead, 707
Minister to a mind diseased, 708
Minority is always in the right, The, 709
Minute's success pays the failure of years, A, 709
Miss for pleasure, and a wife for breed, A, 710
Monday is parson's holiday, 711
Moon-struck madness, 712
More an antique Roman than a Dane, 712
More needs she the divine than the physician, 713
More people are flattered into virtue than bullied out of vice, 714
More ways of killing a cat than choking her with cream, 715
Mother and lover of men, the sea, 716
Mother's pride, a father's joy!, A, 717
Motley's the only wear, 718
Mountains of Necessity, 718
Moving finger writes, The, 719
Much malice mingled with a little wit, 720
Muddy ecstasies of beer, The, 721
Multitude is always in the wrong, The, 722
Murmuring poor, who will not fast in peace, The, 723
Music, the greatest good that mortals know, 724
Music, yearning like a God in pain, The, 724
Mutable, rank-scented many, The, 725
Mutilated curtsey, A, 726
My age is as a lusty winter, frosty, but kindly, 726
My banks they are furnished with bees, 727
My dear Lady Disdain, 728
My great taskmaster's eye, 729
My griefs; still am I King of those, 730
My late espoused Saint, 730
My life is like the summer rose, 731
My name is Legion, 732
My nearest and dearest enemy, 733

Nae man can tether time or tide, 734
Naked came I out of my mother's womb, 735
Nation is not governed, which is perpetually to be conquered, A, 736
Nature in him was almost lost in art, 737
Nature never did betray the heart that loved her, 737
Nature of bad news infects the teller, The, 738
Nature's darling, 739
Naught venture, naught have, 740
Nearer the Church the further from God, The, 741
Nest of singing birds, A, 742
Never dares the man put off the prophet, 743
Never did nature say one thing and wisdom say another, 744
Never read any book that is not a year old, 745
Never was patriot yet, but was a fool, 746

Proper man as one shall see in a summer's day, A, 892
Proverb is something musty, The, 893
Public schools 'tis public folly feeds, 893
Publicans and sinners, 895
Pull for the shore, sailor, pull for the shore, 896
Punic faith, 896

Questing beast, The, 897
Quiet to quick bosoms is a hell, 898
Quiet-colored end of evening, The, 899
Quiring to the young-eyed cherubins, 900

Railing at life, and yet afraid of death, 901
Rainbow comes and goes, The, 902
Rare bird, A, 903
Rascally yea-forsooth knave, A, 903
Reading is to the mind what exercise is to the body, 904
Reason is the life of the Law, 905
Recording Angel dropped a tear upon the word, and blotted it out forever, 906
Red fool fury of the Seine, The, 907
Regions Caesar never knew, 908
Religion is by no means a proper subject for conversation in a mixed company, 908
Religion is the opium of the people, 909
Religion of gold, The, 910
Remnant of our Spartan dead, A, 911
Remorse, the fatal egg by pleasure laid, 912
Repentance is but want of power to sin, 914
Republic of Letters, The, 915
Rest is silence, The, 915
Rich beyond the dreams of avarice, 916
Riddles of death Thebes never knew, 918
Ride in triumph through Persepolis, 918
Right of election is the very essence of the constitution, The, 920
Ring in the Christ that is to be, 921
Ringing grooves of change, The, 922
Ripest fruit first falls, The, 923
Roar you as gently as any sucking dove, 924
Roman by a Roman valiantly vanquished, A, 924
Roman holiday, A, 925
Rosebud garden of girls, The, 926
Rose-red city half as old as Time, A, 927
Rude forefathers of the hamlet sleep, The, 928
Rugged the breast that beauty cannot tame, 929
Rule with a rod of iron, 930
Rum, Romanism, and Rebellion, 931
Running a man down, 932

Sable-vested night, eldest of things, 932
Sacrifice to the Graces, 933
Sadness sweeter than a smile, A, 934
Safety of the people shall be their highest law, The, 935
Saint Praxed's ever was the church for peace, 936
Same bright, patient stars, The, 937
Same heart beats in every human breast, The, 937

They'll take suggestion as a cat laps milk, 1077
They're only truly great who are truly good, 1078
Things that love night love not such nights as these, 1079
Think of your forefathers and of your posterity!, 1079
Think only what concerns thee and thy being, 1081
Thinking is the greatest fatigue in the world, 1082
Third among the sons of light, 1083
This and that way swings the flux of mortal things, 1083
This is hell, nor am I out of it, 1084
This is war, 1085
This music crept by me upon the waters, 1086
This night thy soul shall be required of thee, 1086
This submerged tenth, 1088
This weak piping time of peace, 1089
This will never do!, 1090
This world is a comedy to those that think, a tragedy to those that feel, 1091
Those who have much to hope and nothing to lose, will always be dangerous, 1091
Thou art in a parlous state, 1092
Thou didst eat strange flesh, 1093
Thou god of our idolatry, the press, 1093
Thou hast conquered, O pale Galilean, 1094
Thou hast nor youth, nor age, 1095
Thou speakest wiser than thou art ware of, 1096
Though her body die, her fame survives, 1096
Though I be poor, I'm honest, 1097
Though it be a foul great lie: set upon it a good face, 1098
Though poor in gear, we're rich in love, 1099
Thought which saddens while it soothes!, 1100
Three things I never lends—my 'oss, my wife, and my name, 1101
Three-o'clock-in-the-morning courage, 1102
Thrice he routed all his foes; and thrice he slew the slain, 1103
Thy eternal summer shall not fade, 1104
Thy necessity is yet greater than mine, 1104
Thy soul was like a star, and dwelt apart, 1105
Time hath an art to make dust of all things, 1106
Time hath, my lord, a wallet at his back, 1107
Time, not Corydon, hath conquered thee, 1107
Time, the avenger, 1108
Time, thou devourer of all things, 1109
Time will run back, and fetch the age of gold, 1110
Tip me the black spot, 1111
'Tis an awkward thing to play with souls, 1111
'Tis beauty calls, and glory shows the way, 1112
'Tis Death is dead, not he, 1113
'Tis death that makes life live, 1114
'Tis not in mortals to command success, but we'll do more, Sempronius; we'll deserve it, 1115
'Tis not too late to-morrow to be brave, 1116
'Tis not what man does which exalts him, but what man would do!, 1117
'Tis pride that pulls the country down, 1117
'Tis safest in matrimony to begin with a little aversion, 1118
To be constant, in nature were inconstancy, 1119
To Carthage I came, 1120
To compare great things with small, 1121
To die in the last ditch, 1122

To enjoy one's past life is to live twice, 1123
To have great poets, there must be great audiences, too, 1123
To hold the mirror up to nature, 1125
To innovate is not to reform, 1125
To live in hearts we leave behind is not to die, 1126
To lose thee were to lose myself, 1127
To make your children capable of honesty is the beginning of education, 1128
To play billiards well was a sign of an ill-spent youth, 1129
To produce a mighty book, you must choose a mighty theme, 1130
To see her is to love her, 1131
To set a candle in the sun, 1132
To suckle fools, and chronicle small beer, 1133
To tax and to please is not given to men, 1134
To teach the young idea how to shoot, 1135
To the public good private respects must yield, 1136
To the windward of the law, 1137
To whose profit?, 1138
Toes turned up to the daisies!, 1139
Toil, envy, want, the patron, and the jail, 1140
Tomorrow let us do or die!, 1141
Tom's a-cold, 1142
Tonight the American flag floats from yonder hill or Molly Stark sleeps a widow!, 1143
Too much of water hast thou, poor Ophelia, 1144
Too quick a sense of a constant infelicity, 1144
Trade is the golden girdle of the globe, 1145
Tramp! tramp! along the land they rode, 1146
Traveling is the ruin of all happiness, 1147
Tree of life, The, 1148
Triton blowing loud his wreathed horne, 1149
Trodden the winepress alone, 1150
Troilus mounted the Trojan walls, 1151
Trouts are tickled best in muddy water, 1152
Truth is rarely pure and never simple, 1153
Truth lies somewhere, if we knew but where, 1154
Truth never hurts the teller, 1155
'Twas strange, 'twas passing strange, 1156
'Twixt you, me, and the gatepost, 1157
Two of a trade, lass, never agree!, 1158
Two souls with but a single thought, two hearts that beat as one, 1159
Tyranny arises out of democracy, 1159
Tyrants seldom want pretexts, 1161

Ultima Thule, 1161
Under which king, Besonian? Speak, or die, 1162
Undiscovered country, from whose bourn no traveller returns, The, 1163
Unearned increment, 1164
Unfaith in aught is want of faith in all, 1165
Union of hands and hearts, The, 1166
Unmissed but by his dogs and by his groom, 1167
Unplumbed, salt, estranging sea, The, 1168
Unpremeditated lay, The, 1169
Unreturning brave, The, 1170
Unwept, unhonored, and unsung, 1171
Up roos the sonne, and up roos Emelye, 1172

Well roared, Lion, 1217
We'll pluck a crow together, 1218
Well-written Life is almost as rare as a well-spent one, A, 1219
What a genius I had when I wrote that book!, 1220
What a goodly outside falsehood hath!, 1221
What a man needs in gardening is a cast-iron back, with a hinge in it, 1221
What a piece of work is a man, 1222
What! all this for a song?, 1223
What avails the sceptered race, 1224
What dire effects from civil discord flow, 1225
What, frighted with false fire!, 1225
What have kings, that privates have not too, 1226
What her eyes enthralled her tongue unbound, 1227
What I tell you three times is true, 1228
What I want is, Facts, 1229
What ills from beauty spring, 1230
What is past my help is past my care, 1231
What man has made of man, 1232
What millions died that Caesar might be great!, 1232
What news on the Rialto?, 1233
What scourge for perjury?, 1234
What shelter to grow ripe is ours, what leisure to grow wise?, 1235
What so wild as words are?, 1236
What song the Sirens sang, or what name Achilles assumed, 1236
What was he doing, the great god Pan, 1237
What you desire is not mortal, 1238
Whatever gods may be, 1239
Whatever happens at all happens as it should, 1240
Whatever is, is in its causes just, 1240
Whatever you have, spend less, 1241
When a heroine goes mad, she always goes into white satin, 1242
When faith is lost, when honor dies, the man is dead!, 1243
When Freedom from her mountain height, 1244
When he leaves our houses, let us count our spoons, 1244
When I give, I give myself, 1245
When I was a child, I spake as a child, 1246
When, in disgrace with Fortune and men's eyes, 1247
When Music, heavenly maid, was young, 1248
When Rome falls—the World, 1249
When the fight begins within himself, a man's worth something, 1250
When the liquor's out, why clink the cannikin?, 1251
When we build, let us think we build forever, 1251
When we think we lead, we are most led, 1252
When you have nothing to say, say nothing, 1254
Where are the songs of Spring?, 1255
Where freedom broadens slowly down, 1255
Where my heart lies, let my brain lie also, 1257
Where mystery begins, religion ends, 1257
Where wilt thou find their like again?, 1258
Whiff of grapeshot, A, 1259
While listening senates hang upon thy tongue, 1260
Whispering "I will never consent,"—consented, 1261
Whispering tongues can poison truth, 1262
Whistle and she'll come to you, 1263

Yet still we hug the dear deceit, 1310
You can make better use of iron than forging it into chains, 1312
You carry Caesar and his fortune, 1313
You come most carefully upon your hour, 1314
You might prove anything by figures, 1315
You must not kiss and tell, 1316
You never know what life means till you die, 1317
You roll my log, and I will roll yours, 1319
You shall comprehend all vagrom men, 1319
You would find a tale in everything, 1320
Young boys and girls are level now with men, 1321
Young man married is a man that's marred, A, 1322
Younger generation will come knocking at my door, The, 1322
Your sin will find you out, 1323
Your true lover of literature is never fastidious, 1325
Your wit's too hot, it speeds too fast, 'twill tire, 1326
Youth on the prow, and Pleasure at the helm, 1327
Youth will be served, 1328
You've a darned long row to hoe, 1329

KEY WORD INDEX

(The *italicized* word indicates the beginning of a quotation)

xxxvii

Exalts him, but what man would do!, *'Tis* not what man does which, 1117
Excess are wrong, The, *Best* things carried to, 89
Exercise is to the body, *Reading* is to the mind what, 904
Expressive to be blue, too lovely to be grey, *Eyes* too, 267
Extinction of unhappy hates, *Endless,* 244
Eye, in a fine frenzy rolling, The, *Poet's,* 875
Eye of the beholder, *Beauty* is in the, 81
Eyes, The, *Cynosure* of neighboring, 183

Face is a letter of recommendation, A, *Good,* 359
Faces like a flint, *Set* your, 952
Factions are volcanoes burnt out, *Old* religious, 812
Facts, *What* I want is, 1229
Fair, *Divinely* tall, and most divinely, 221
Fair, whatever you do!, *Drink,* 233
Fairies!, *Farewell,* rewards and, 280
Fairy Lilian, *Airy,* 14
Faith in all, *Unfaith* in aught is want of, 1165
Faith is lost, when honor dies, the man is dead!, *When,* 1243
Faith, *O* thou of little, 794
Faith, *Punic,* 896
Faith; vain faith, and courage vain, *Courage* and, 174
Faith's absurd, A, *Scientific,* 943
Falchions in fair hands, *Fans* turn into, 279
False fire!, *What,* frighted with, 1225
False man, *Man:,* 663
Falsehood hath!, *What* a goodly outside, 1221
Falsehood to the heart, *Who* speaks the truth stabs, 1270
Fame survives, *Though* her body die, her, 1096
Fame while woman wakes to love, *Man* dreams of, 662
Families last not three oaks, *Old,* 811
Famous, *I* awoke one morning and found myself, 471
Fancy bred, *Tell* me where is, 1041
Fancy, *Chewing* the food of sweet and bitter, 140
Fancy-free, *Maiden* meditation, 658
Fancy's child, *Sweetest* Shakespeare, 1029
Far from home, The, *Night* is dark, and I am, 748
Fashion, *After* the high Roman, 11
Fashion, The, *Glass* of, 339
Father's business, *I* must be about my, 490
Fathom five, *Full,* 320
Fatigue in the world, *Thinking* is the greatest, 1082
Fault, and honesty is his, *Every* man has his, 256
Fault, *Clever* to a, 151
Faults is to be conscious of none, The, *Greatest* of, 381
Fault's with time, The, *Only,* 830
Fear thou not at all, *Hope* thou not much, and, 454
Feast!, *Liberty's* a glorious, 607
Feather for each wind that blows, *I* am a, 463
Feathers, An, *Upstart* crow, beautified with our, 1173
Feeling, a woman as old as she looks, A, *Man* is as old as he's, 671
Fell who fell, *Freely* they stood who stood, and, 313
Fester smell far worse than weeds, *Lilies* that, 620
Few words are the best men, *Men* of, 703

Fight another day, *He* who turns and runs away, lives to, 417
Figures, *You* might prove anything by, 1315
Files of time, The, *Heir* of all the ages, in the foremost, 427
Finds himself, loses his misery, *Who,* 1268
Finger touched him and he slept, *God's,* 352
Finger writes, The, *Moving,* 719
Fish-like smell, A, *Very* ancient and, 1180
Fish ye're buying—it's men's lives, *It's* no, 556
Fitful fever he sleeps well, *After* life's, 9
Flaming bounds of place and time, *He* passed the, 405
Flattered into virtue than bullied out of vice, *More* people are, 714
Flatters I abhor the most, The, *Lie* that, 610
Fleeting years!, *Alas!* the, 16
Flesh and blood so cheap!, *Oh!* God! that bread should be so dear, and, 804
Flim-flam, A, *Pretty,* 886
Fling, *I'll* have a, 518
Flower enjoys the air it breathes, *Every,* 254
Flummery, *Down* on, 230
Flutters least is longest on the wing, The, *Bird* that, 96
Flux of mortal things, *This* and that way swings the, 1083
Foam, The, *Cruel* crawling, 179
Foes; and thrice he slew the slain, *Thrice* he routed all his, 1103
Fool, but at a cheaper rate, *Play* the, 869
Fool, *Fortune's,* 309
Fool may ask more than the wisest man can answer, The, *Greatest,* 380
Fool than to be dead, *It* is better to be a, 544
Fools, The, *Paradise* of, 846
Foot, *Hercules* is not only known by his, 431
Forbearance ceases to be a virtue, *There* is a limit at which, 1053
Forbid, *God,* 344
Forefathers of the hamlet sleep, The, *Rude,* 928
Foresters, gentlemen of the shade, minions of the moon, *Diana's,* 213
Forgetting, by the world forgot, The, *World,* 1301
Forks, *Fingers* were made before, 292
Fortune and men's eyes, *When,* in disgrace with, 1247
Fortune what she can, A, *King's* a king, do, 568
Forty, *Fair,* fat, and, 282
Fossil poetry, *Language* is, 577
Fought the better fight, *Well* hast thou, 1215
Foxes, that spoil the vines, The, *Little,* 623
Fox-hunter, and I loves him at once, *Tell* me a man's a, 1039
Frailty of the mind, *Love's* the noblest, 650
Frailty of the mind, *Wit's* the noblest, 1291
France, *That* sweet enemy, 1044
Free country, *Parties* must ever exist in a, 849
Freedom broadens slowly down, *Where,* 1255
Freedom from her mountain height, *When,* 1244
Freeman whom the truth makes free, *He* is the, 404
Fresh as is the month of May, *As,* 56
Friend, *Death:* the last, best, 199
Friend in need, nor a bottle to give him, *May* we never want a, 689
Friends, The, *Wretched* have no, 1308
Friendship ever ends in love, A, *Woman's* 1295
Frost, *Fell* death's untimely, 287

Horne, *Triton* blowing loud his wreathed, 1149
Horrors, hail!, *Congenial,* 166
Horse amble true, *Hard* is to teach and old, 391
Hottentot, *Consider* him as a respectable, 171
Hour, *You* come most carefully upon your, 1314
How a man dies, but how he lives, *It* matters not, 554
Hub of the solar system, *Boston* State House is the, 109
Human for being devout, *I* am not the less, 468
Humanities of old religion, The, *Fair,* 272
Humour, A, *Holiday,* 447
Hung upon his lips, *Persuasion,* 857
Husband, A, *Light* wife doth make a, 617
Husband than the best of men, *No* worse a, 762

Iago, the pity of it, *O,* 789
Idealistic nation in the world, *America* is the only, 37
Idols, *God* keeps a niche in heaven to hold our, 349
Ignorance, *O!* more than Gothic, 791
Ills from beauty spring, *What,* 1230
Ill-spent youth, *To* play billiards well was a sign of an, 1129
Image of death, *In* every parting there is an, 523
Impeachment, *I* own the soft, 493
Imperator, those about to die salute thee, *Hail,* 386
Impotently great, *Ignobly* vain, and, 514
Impunity a rose, *Any* nose may ravage with, 45
Impure what God declares pure, *Defaming* as, 204
Inconstancy, *To* be constant, in nature were, 1119
Increment, *Unearned,* 1164
Incurable disease, *Life* is an, 611
Indictment against a whole people, *I* do not know the method of drawing up an, 477
Indifference, *Nothing* is so fatal to religion as, 779
Indifferent to me, *Nothing* human is, 776
Industry, *Captains* of, 130
Infelicity, *Too* quick a sense of a constant, 1144
Infinite spaces terrifies me, The, *Eternal* silence of these, 250
Injured they also hate, *Whom* they have, 1275
Inn, *No* room in the, 759
Inn, The, *World,* I count it not an, 1301
Innocence but sin, *Ignorance* is not, 514
Innovate is not to reform, *To,* 1125
Institution, It's more than a game. *It's* an, 556
Instructor, Time, The, *Grand,* 365
Insult, An, *Injury* is much sooner forgotten than an, 533
Insult to injuries, *Adding,* 6
Intoxication, The, *Best* of life is but, 88
Invisible, The, *Choir,* 144
Iron enter into his soul, *I* saw the, 495
Iron pokers into true-love knots, *Wreathe,* 1307
Iron than forging it into chains, *You* can make better use of, 1312
Island, *No* man is an, 755
Ivory, *Gates* of, 325

Jangled out of tune, *Sweet* bells, 1024
Jargon of the schools, *All,* 20
Jargon of their Babylonian pulpits, The, *Confused,* 165

1

Mind in a sound body, A, *Sound,* 998
Mind is slow, The, *March* of the human, 683
Mind, *Years* steal fire from the, 1309
Minds, *As* many men, so many, 60
Minds, The, *Marriage* of true, 686
Mind's height by the shade it casts!, *Measure* your, 690
Mine own, An, *Ill-favoured* thing sir, but, 520
Mine, *Vengeance* is, 1178
Mine, The, *World* is, 1302
Minions of the moon, *Diana's* foresters, gentlemen of the shade, 213
Minutes; for hours will take care of themselves, *Take* care of the, 1031
Miracles are past, *They* say, 1072
Mirror up to nature, *To* hold the, 1125
Mischief, The, *Devil's* in the moon for, 211
Mob, *Our* supreme governors, the, 839
Moderns without contempt, and of the ancients without idolatry, *Speak* of the, 1001
Modesty—no more, *She* just wore enough for, 959
Molly Stark sleeps a widow!, *Tonight* the American flag floats from yonder hill or, 1143
Moment, *Eternity* was in that, 252
Money, heigh ho!, *How* pleasant it is to have, 460
Moneybag, *Aristocracy* of the, 50
Monk who shook the world, The, *Solitary,* 989
Monster which the world never saw, A, *Faultless,* 285
Montezuma, *Every* schoolboy knows who imprisoned, 260
Monument, *Patience* on a, 851
Moon for mischief, The, *Devil's* in the, 211
Moon, *I* had had an affair with the, 480
More, *Please,* sir, I want some, 870
Mores!, *O* tempora! O, 793
Morning, *He's* for the, 434
Morning shows the day, The, *Childhood* shows the man as, 142
Mortal coil, *Shuffled* off this, 965
Mortal, *What* you desire is not, 1238
Most wise, are greatest fools, *Who* think themselves, 1271
Moth nor butterfly, *Kill* not the, 563
Mountain scarce brings forth a mouse, The, *Laboring,* 574
Mouse, The, *Laboring* mountain scarce brings forth a, 574
Mouth, *Down* in the, 229
Mouth water, *Made* his, 655
Mouths, to steal away their brains, *That* men should put an enemy in their, 1043
Mud, *Homesickness* for the, 451
Muddy water, *Trouts* are tickled best in, 1152
Murder will out, *Love* and, 641
Murder, will out, *Vanity,* like, 1175
Murmur of a summer's day, *All* the live, 27
Music crept by me upon the waters, *This,* 1086
Music, heavenly maid, was young, *When,* 1248
Music lie, *Such* sweet compulsion doth in, 1018
Musical than any song, *Silence* more, 969
Musty, The, *Proverb* is something, 893
Mute inglorious Milton, *Some,* 993
Myself, *When* I give, I give, 1245
Mystery begins, religion ends, *Where,* 1257

Naiad of the strand, The, *Guardian,* 383

liv

Piety more prone, The, *Weaker* sex, to, 1213
Pink of courtesy, The, *Very,* 1182
Pit, *Law* is a bottomless, 584
Pity of it, *O* Iago, the, 789
Plaything for an hour, A, *Child's* a, 143
Pleasing consists in being pleased, The, *Art* of, 52
Pleasure afterwards, *Business* first;, 123
Pleasure, and a wife for breed, A, *Miss* for, 710
Pleasure laid, *Remorse,* the fatal egg by, 912
Pleasure, *No* sterner moralist than, 760
Pleasure, *Variety* is the soul of, 1176
Pleasure was his business, *Business* was his aversion;, 124
Ploughshare as well as soldiers of the sword, *Soldiers* of the, 988
Pluck a crow together, *We'll,* 1218
Plunder, but pitied the man, *He* shared in the, 408
Poet, *God* is the perfect, 347
Poets are mad, *All,* 24
Poke, *Pig* in a, 861
Politics, and politics present history, *History* is past, 446
Poniards, *She* speaks, 961
Poor Child!, *If* I were dead, you'd sometimes say, 510
Poor, *He* found it inconvenient to be, 399
Poor, I'm honest, *Though* I be, 1097
Poor man, An, *Honest* exceeding, 452
Poor man's dearest friend, *Death,* the, 200
Poor, who will not fast in peace, The, *Murmuring,* 723
Posterity, but I would fain see posterity do something for us, *We* are always doing something for, 1197
Posterity!, *Think* of your forefathers and of your, 1079
Poverty depressed, *Slow* rises worth, by, 979
Power, the more dangerous the abuse, The, *Greater* the, 378
Praise any man that will praise me, *I* will, 503
Praise, *Damn* with faint, 185
Praxed's ever was the church for peace, *Saint,* 936
Praying, it spoils business, *No,* 758
Preached to death by wild curates, *Deserves* to be, 206
Preaching is like a dog's walking on his hind legs, A, *Woman's,* 1296
Precepts for the teacher's sake, *We* love the, 1205
Presbyter is but old priest writ large, *New,* 746
Presence, and no land beside, *Lord* of thy, 637
Present, *No* time like the, 761
Press, *Thou* god of our idolatry, the, 1093
Pretexts, *Tyrants* seldom want, 1161
Price, *Peace* at any, 852
Pride, a father's joy!, A, *Mother's,* 717
Pride that pulls the country down, *'Tis,* 1117
Princes have great playthings, *Great,* 376
Principality in Utopia, An, *Acre* of Middlesex is better than a, 5
Privates have not too, *What* have kings, that, 1226
Privilege of human nature, *Death* is the, 197
Prodigal of ease, *Bankrupt* of life, yet, 72
Profane, and impiously gay, *Coldly,* 158
Profession, An, *Ornament* to her, 834
Profit?, *To* whose, 1138

Right, The, *Minority* is always in the, 709
Right, A, *Noisy* man is always in the, 765
Rivalry, *With* the dead there is no, 1288
Roar, *Melancholy,* long, withdrawing, 694
Rock, *Founded* upon a, 309
Rocks among which she sits, *Older* than the, 814
Rod, and spoil the child, *Spare* the, 1000
Rod of iron, *Rule* with a, 930
Roman citizen, *I* am a, 465
Roman holiday, *Butchered* to make a, 125
Roman style, *If* you are in Rome, live in the, 513
Romans, fare thée well, The, *Last* of all the, 578
Rome, *Everyone* soon or late comes round by, 264
Rome falls—the World, *When,* 1249
Room in the inn, *No,* 759
Rose of summer, left blooming alone, The, *Last,* 579
Rose of youth upon him, *He* wears the, 416
Row to hoe, *You've* a darned long, 1329
Ruin in himself, *He* bears the seed of, 398
Ruin of all happiness, *Traveling* is the, 1147
Ruin swallow all, *One* prodigious, 826
Run, *I* do not choose to, 476
Runs away, lives to fight another day, *He* who turns and, 417
Runs away with his head, *His* heart, 439

Saddens while it soothes!, *Thought* which, 1100
Safety, *I* would give all my fame for a pot of ale, and, 504
Sands of time, *Footprints* on the, 302
Sassy, *I'm* sickly but, 521
Satire by my song, *Fools* are my theme, let, 301
Savage, anti-everythings, *Lean,* hungry, 587
Savage, The, *Noble,* 765
Save charges, *Die* to, 213
Scandals form good subjects for dissection, *Dead,* 193
Scarecrow of the law, *We* must not make a, 1206
Sceptered race, *What* avails the, 1224
Sceptered sovereigns, *Dead* but, 192
Scholar among rakes, *He* was a rake among scholars and a, 415
School of mankind, *Example* is the, 265
Schools 'tis public folly feeds, *Public,* 893
Science, The, *Dismal,* 217
Scotched the snake, not killed it, *We* have, 1204
Scoundrels, A, *Healthy* hatred of, 420
Scourge of God, must die, *Tamburlaine,* the, 1037
Sea-scented beach, *Warm,* 1195
Sea-mark standing every flaw, *Like* a great, 618
Sea, *Mother* and lover of men, the, 716
Seas of thought, *Voyaging* through strange, 1192
Seas over, *Half,* 387
Secret of life, *Digestion* is the great, 214
See her is to love her, *To,* 1131
Seed of the Church, The, *Blood* of the martyrs is the, 102
Seems beforehand, *Nothing* is so good as it, 779
Seine, The, *Red* fool fury of the, 907

Sleep! thou flatterer of happy minds, *O*, 791
Sleeping hound to wake, *It* is nought good a, 549
Slowly up this way, *Spring* comes, 1003
Sluggard, The, *Voice* of the, 1190
Small voice, A, *Still*, 1011
Smile, A, *Sadness* sweeter than a, 934
Smith was the first murderer's son, The, *First*, 297
Sneezed at, *Not* to be, 772
Soar, *Ambition* can creep as well as, 34
Sober as a judge, *As*, 63
Sober life, A, *Godly* righteous and, 350
Soda-water, *Sermons* and, 949
Soldier be he, *God's*, 353
Solemn creed with solemn sneer, *Sapping* a, 940
Somewhere, if we knew but where, *Truth* lies, 1154
Son, my son, *Absalom*, my, 1
Song?, *What!* all this for a, 1223
Songs are those that tell of saddest thought, *O* 'r sweetest, 840
Sons of light, *Third* among the, 1083
Sophist-led, but be a man!, *Be* neither saint no , 76
Sorrows, A, *Man* of, 674
Sought in vain that sought the Lord aright!, *They* never, 1071
Soul shall be required of thee, *This* night thy, 1086
Soul was like that, A, *White* bird his own, 1264
Souls, *'Tis* an awkward thing to play with, 1111
Souls with but a single thought, two hearts that beat as one, *Two*, 1159
Spain, *Castles* in, 132
Spartan dead, A, *Remnant* of our, 911
Spartans, *Go,* tell the, 344
Spend less, *Whatever* you have, 1241
Spider to the Fly, *"Will* you walk into my parlor?" said the, 1282
Spires, *That* sweet city with her dreaming, 1044
Spoke among your wheels, *I'll* put a, 519
Sport, that owes its pleasures to another's pain, *Detested,* 208
Spot I damn him, *He* shall not live; look, with a, 407
Spring, ethereal mildness, come, *Come,* gentle, 159
Spring?, *Where* are the songs of, 1255
Spur of all great minds, *Danger,* the, 187
Spur of industry, *Avarice,* the, 66
Squad, The, *Awkward,* 67
Stakes were thrones, *Whose* game was empires and whose, 1277
Stalking-horse to error, *They* make truth serve as a, 1069
Star, and dwelt apart, *Thy* soul was like a, 1105
Star-Chamber matter of it, *I* will make a, 502
Stars, oft stumbles at a straw, *He* that strives to touch the, 413
Stars, The, *Same* bright, patient, 937
Stoic fur, *Budge* doctors of the, 121
Stones, *Sermons* in, 950
Stood who stood, and fell who fell, *Freely* they, 313
Strain, The, *Dorian* pipe, the Dorian, 226
Strange capers, *We* that are true lovers run into, 1211
Strange faces, other minds, *Among* new men, 41
Strange flesh, *Thou* didst eat, 1093
Strange gods, *After,* 10

MAGILL'S QUOTATIONS
IN CONTEXT
Second Series

———

A-LIV

Absalom, my son, my son

Source: II SAMUEL 18:33
Author: Unknown
First transcribed: 1100-400 B.C.
Type of work: Religious history

Context: Absalom, the son of David, plots against his father, the king. When men from all over Israel flock to Absalom's side, David says to his people that for safety they must flee Jerusalem with him, and go into the wilderness. Absalom moves into the city upon David's departure, even taking over King David's concubines, as a sign that he has become the ruler. Ahithophel, one of Absalom's counselors, asks to be allowed to pursue the forces of David and destroy them, but Hushai, who is a secret agent of King David, advises differently. When Ahithophel sees that his counsel is not taken, he goes to his home and hangs himself. Following the advice of Hushai, Absalom takes a force to go out and crush David's loyal followers. But David and his people meet Absalom and his force in battle in the wood of Ephraim and defeat them. Absalom loses twenty thousand men in the battle. Absalom himself is caught in the branches of a great oak tree when his mule passes beneath; there he hangs, alive, till found by David's men. Joab, one of David's lieutenants, stabs Absalom with three darts, and his men then beat Absalom to death, despite King David's injunction to his followers not to harm Absalom. Ahimaaz and Cushi are sent as runners to tell David of the victory; Ahimaaz does not reveal Absalom's death, but Cushi does. King David, who loves Absalom dearly, despite the son's great treachery, is saddened beyond measure by Absalom's death, and the victory over the rebel and his men becomes a day of mourning. The king is distraught over his son's death:

> And the king was much moved, and went up to the chamber over the gate, and wept: and as he went, thus he said, O my son **Absalom, my son, my son** Absalom! would God I had died for thee, O **Absalom, my son, my son!**
>
> • • •
>
> And the people gat them by stealth that day into the city, as people being ashamed steal away when they flee in battle.
> But the king covered his face, and the king cried with a loud voice, O my son Absalom, O **Absalom, my son, my son!**

The absent are always in the wrong

Source: L'OBSTACLE IMPRÉVU (Act I, sc. vi)
Author: Philippe Néricault Destouches (1680-1754)
First published: 1717
Type of work: Dramatic comedy

Context: As Jean Baptiste Poquelin (1622–1673) took the pen name of Molière, to publish his plays, so Philippe Néricault became known as the popular playwright Destouches, being especially remembered for his comedy of interclass marriage, *Le Glorieux* (1732) in which the pride of a haughty nobleman takes a fall. *L'Obstacle imprévu ou L'Obstacle sans obstacle* (The Unforeseen Obstacle or the Obstacle without an Obstacle) achieved popularity when first performed in Paris in 1717. It was later condensed by L. Monrose into three acts. Following the usual classical formula, it observes the unities, taking place in the home of Lisimon, an elderly man. Valère is his foppish son. He is also guardian of Julie, his niece. She and Leandre are in love. Again, according to formula, each of them has a servant who is a friendly adviser, like the *gracioso* in Spanish comedies. Julie has her confidante Nérine. Leandre has Crispin, and Valère is served by Pasquin. The comedy opens with a discussion between Valère and Pasquin. The son is complaining about his inability to get along with his father, and the servant is trying to stop such talk. If Valère will cease behaving foolishly, there will be no trouble. To push home his point, Pasquin acts out that morning's discussion between father and son about the way the young man had spent the previous evening among a lot of over-dressed dandies, when he should have been thinking about Angelique, to whom his father had arranged a marriage. There is another love complication, one between Julie and Leandre. She has the idea that there is an obstacle to their marriage, and she intends to enter a convent. Nérine, down-to-earth like all classical comedy servants, suggests that if Julie cannot marry Leandre, she look for another sweetheart. Crispin comes to report in a mixed-up speech an overheard and puzzling conversation about confusion between two daughters of an Italian in Paris and some skullduggery between Julie's guardian and her uncle. In Scene vi, Lisimon shows that he intends to marry Julie himself. Her mother is dead. She has been left in his care by her supposed father, now in the Indies, who also gave him power to marry her off. Now he tries to persuade Nérine to work on her mistress to give her consent to marry him. The servant knows the situation and refuses to coöperate, saying that Julie could never love a bilious and choleric old man who wants her only for her inheritance, about which she is ignorant. Julie loves Leandre. All that prevents their marriage is that for the moment neither of them has money. He is trying to keep her from taking her vows until he can earn a living, which he says he will do or die. In Nérine's conversation with Lisimon, she tells him the situation. Here is a translation of the French original.

NÉRINE

They wanted to get married, but when he had to come to the point, Leandre learned that Julie hadn't a centime and that she was living on an allowance from her uncle, ever since her mother had left her in Paris without telling anybody where she was going.

2

Was the young man rich?

NÉRINE

His riches, present and future, amounted to a large sum of tenderness and beautiful sentiments.

. . .

LISIMON

They could hardly establish a home on that!

NÉRINE

He had a servant, too, named Crispin, who was a nice young
man.

LISIMON

Did you like him?

NÉRINE

Must you ask? A maid always yearns for the servant of the man
who comes courting her mistress. That's the way it always is, in
plays.

LISIMON

Tell me, is your mistress still in love with that Leandre?

NÉRINE

Of course! She's no fickle girl. She's not like me. I was sort of in
a hurry, and since **the absent are always in the wrong,** and Pasquin
was on hand, why, I went ahead and married him.

Abstract liberty is not to be found

Source: SPEECH ON MOVING HIS RESOLUTIONS FOR RECONCILIATION WITH THE
     COLONIES
Author: Edmund Burke (1729-1797)
First published: 1775
Type of work: Political Speech

Context: Burke was the greatest and
the most articulate defender of the
American Colonies in the English
Parliament. He foresaw the great
loss England would suffer if the colonies were alienated and lost as a result of harsh suppression. He pleaded
desperately with Parliament not to
take the strong measures of taxation
and military aggression, which, he
admitted, were strictly legal measures, but he begged instead for an act
of redress, for which the acts of redress toward Ireland and Wales were

3

valid historical precedents. He fully realized the intensity of the sense of freedom and liberty in the colonies and knew that revolution would result from repression:

> . . . This fierce spirit of liberty is stronger in the English colonies probably than in any other people of the earth; and this from a great variety of powerful causes; . . .
>
> First, the people of the colonies are descendants of Englishmen. England, Sir, is a nation, which still I hope respects, and formerly adored, her freedom. The colonists emigrated from you when this part of your character was most predominant; and they took this bias and direction the moment they parted from your hands. They are therefore not only devoted to liberty, but to liberty according to English ideas, and on English principles. **Abstract liberty,** like other mere abstractions, **is not to be found.** Liberty inheres in some sensible object; and every nation has formed to itself some favourite point, which by way of eminence becomes the criterion of their happiness. It happened, you know, Sir, that the great contests for freedom in this country were from the earliest times chiefly upon the question of taxing.

Accurst be he that first invented war

Source: TAMBURLAINE THE GREAT (Part I, Act II, sc. iv, l. 664)
Author: Christopher Marlowe (1564-1593)
First published: 1590
Type of work: Dramatic tragedy

Context: Mycetes, King of Persia, finds his kingdom menaced by the forces of Tamburlaine, a former Scythian shepherd. Anxious to rid his crown and his lands of this threat, Mycetes sends Theridamas at the head of a thousand richly armed cavalrymen to subdue Tamburlaine and his few hundred foot soldiers. But Theridamas, impressed by Tamburlaine at a parley, decides to join forces with him. Mycetes' brother, Cosroe, meanwhile, plots to become king, disdaining Mycetes as a weak monarch. He joins forces with Tamburlaine, expecting to use Tamburlaine to defeat Mycetes and thus win the crown of Persia. During the ensuing battle Mycetes leaves the field to hide his crown. He is found alone by Tamburlaine, who tells Mycetes he may keep the crown till Tamburlaine can pull it publicly from his head. Mycetes makes his comment about war just before meeting Tamburlaine:

MYCETES
Accurst be he that first invented war,
They knew not, ah, they knew not simple men,
How those were hit by pelting Cannon shot,
Stand staggering like a quivering Aspen leaf,

Fearing the force of *Boreas* boisterous blasts.
In what a lamentable case were I,
If Nature had not given me wisedomes lore?
For Kings are clouts that every man shoots at,
Our Crown the pin that thousands seek to cleave.
Therefore in pollicy I think it good
To hide it close: a goodly Strategem,
And far from any man that is a fool.
So shall I not be knowen, or if I be,
They cannot take my crown from me.
Here will I hide it in this simple hole.

An acre of Middlesex is better than a principality in Utopia

Source: LORD BACON
Author: Thomas Babington Macaulay (1800-1859)
First published: July, 1837
Type of work: Biographical essay and book review

Context: The essays of Lord Macaulay, based on wide reading and a memory that seemed never to forget a fact, made him a welcome magazine contributor. His reviews of biographical volumes usually turned out to be more biographies than reviews. He could provide interesting parallels and illustrations. The fact that his knowledge did not extend to art or science and was superficial was not important to his readers. Like them, he judged everything from the viewpoint of a liberal Whig. When asked to review Basil Montagu's sixteen-volume *The Works of Francis Bacon, Lord Chancellor of England* (London: 1825–34), Macaulay substituted for an opinion of the merits of this lengthy work, an essay on Lord Bacon, that was published in the *Edinburgh Review,* in July, 1837, declaring that while the aim of the philosophy of Plato was to exalt man into a god, something noble, Bacon's philosophic aim was the more obtainable one of supplying man's vulgar (i.e., ordinary) wants. Tennyson was to write in *Locksley Hall* (1842): "Better fifty years of Europe than a cycle of Cathay" (that is, a long while in China). Macaulay localizes the idea to England. Utopia refers to an imaginary and idealistic island described by Sir Thomas More (1478–1535) in a Latin romance of the same name, written in 1516.

. . .

An acre of Middlesex is better than a principality in Utopia.
The smallest actual good is better than the most magnificent promises of impossibilities. The wise man of the Stoics would, no doubt, be a grander object than a steam-engine. But there are steam-engines. And the wise man of the Stoics is yet to be born. A philosophy which should enable a man to feel perfectly happy while in agonies of pain, may be better than a philosophy which assu-

ages pain. But we know that there are remedies which will assuage pain; and we know that the ancient sages liked the tooth-ache just as little as their neighbors.

        .   .   .

Adding fuel to the flame

Source: SAMSON AGONISTES (Line 1351)
Author: John Milton (1608-1674)
First published: 1671
Type of work: Dramatic tragedy

Context: The play opens with the last phase of the life of Samson, the Old Testament hero. The Philistines have blinded him and hold him prisoner in Gaza. The play, structured as a Greek tragedy, depicts the restoration of the fallen Samson to the grace of God. Samson has already been tested by God and failed the test. Having been punished and having repented his sin, he now undergoes trials of his will and integrity to prove that he is worthy to be tested a second time. The last of these trials comes when Harapha, a strong man of Gath, taunts Samson for his blindness and helplessness. Samson makes a humble admission of his sins and finds his punishment just. He still hopes for God's pardon. Samson challenges Harapha to single combat that they might find whose god is strongest, but the champion from Gath declines. Samson is then summoned to entertain the nobles at the feast of the god Dagon, but he refuses. As the officer leaves to report his refusal, the Chorus warns:

> Consider, Samson; matters now are strain'd
> Up to the highth, whether to hold or break;
> He's gone, and who knows how he may report
> Thy words by **adding fuel to the flame?**
> Expect another message more imperious,
> More Lordly thund'ring then thou well wilt hear.

Adding insult to injuries

Source: THE FOUNDLING (Act V, sc. ii)
Author: Edward Moore (1712-1757)
First published: 1748
Type of work: Dramatic comedy

Context: Edward Moore began his writing career as an author of fables, offering to the public *Fables for the Female Sex,* in 1744. They have been compared to the earlier fables by John Gay, better known for *The Beggar's Opera.* Like his predecessor, Moore also turned to the theater, and in 1748 offered to the actor David Garrick, then manager of Theatre Royal in Drury Lane, his first attempts, *The Foundling*. Its reception was mixed. Some critics applied to it a couplet Garrick had meant as a general comment on comedies, written as Epilogue for the performance:

"From such dull stuff, what profit can you reap?
You cry:—' 'Tis very fine!' and fall asleep."

Henry Brooke in his preface to the printed edition damned it with faint praise. Some of the audience found revolting the character of Faddle, and said he had a mind too deformed for public exhibition. His friend, young Belmont, the play's hero, is only a step above him in baseness, and that because he does possess courage. But the great Mrs. Cibber put life into the insipid character of "The Foundling," and the play continued to be performed, and was even translated into French. Out of it all, the dramatist found a wife. A poetic spinster, falling in love with him, sent a letter in verse to her young cousin:

"Would you think it, my coz, for the fault I must own,
Your Jenny, at last, is quite covetous grown:
Though millions, if fortune should lavishly pour,
I still should be wretched, if I had not More."

The poem circulated. Moore got the message, and out of curiosity sought out Jenny. Liking what he saw, he gambled on his luck, married her, and wrote a greatly improved tragedy, *The Gamester*. In the plot of *The Foundling*, Sir Charles Raymond has a son, Colonel Raymond, in love with Rosetta Belmont. Her father, Sir Robert, has another child, young Belmont. Rosetta has a passion for William Faddle, unprincipled but full of fun. Rosetta has made friends with Fidelia, about whose parentage little is known, and so young Belmont thinks he can enjoy her without marrying her, with Faddle's help. He puts out the story that she is an heiress, but will not comment on her family. His sister backs his love affair in hopes the girl can redeem him from his wildness. The situation is cleared at the end. Fidelia is really Harriet, the lost daughter of Sir Charles. While he was in France, her nurse stole her, announcing that the girl was dead, and then putting out the story that she had discovered a foundling at her steps. Having brought her up, she sells her at the age of twelve to Villiard, who now claims to be her guardian. But the repentent nurse confesses, Sir Charles welcomes his missing daughter, and marries her to a reformed young Belmont. Colonel Raymond marries Rosetta for a general pairing-up. At the beginning of Act V, Fidelia and Belmont are trying to clarify their situation when the two parents and Villiard appear, the latter accusing young Belmont of stealing his ward.

7

VILLIARD

My doors were broken open at midnight by this gentleman, my-self wounded, and Fidelia ravished from me. He ran off with her in his arms. Nor, till this morning, in a coach which brought her hither, have my eyes ever beheld her.

SIR ROBERT

A very fine business, truly, young man! [*To his son.*]

FIDELIA

He has abused you, sir. Mr. Belmont is noble—

BELMONT

No matter, Fidelia. Well, sir, you have been robbed, you say? [*To Villiard.*]

VILLIARD

And will have justice, sir.

BELMONT

Take it from this hand then. [*Drawing.*]

SIR CHARLES

Hold, sir. This is **adding insult to injuries.** Fidelia must be re-stored, sir.

SIR ROBERT

Ay, sir, Fidelia must be restored.

FIDELIA

But not to him. Hear but my story. . . .

Adventure brave and new

Source: RABBI BEN EZRA (Stanza 14)
Author: Robert Browning (1812-1889)
First published: 1864
Type of work: Dramatic monologue

Context: Rabbi Ben Ezra was a distinguished Jewish philosopher, physician, astronomer, and poet of the twelfth century. The ideas found in this poem are drawn largely from the Rabbi's own writings and correspond closely to Browning's own philosophy of life. The Rabbi's monologue opens on the optimistic, almost exultant, note as he declares: "Grow old along with me! / The best is yet to be, / The last of life, for which the first was made," He does not grieve for the past hopes and fears of youth. He

8

finds hope in the philosophic doubt which assails him. This doubt he sees as evidence of the spark of God within each man. Man is exalted by what he aspires to be rather than by what he actually becomes. The Rabbi declares that the Maker's plan is perfect, and that we should be thankful to be men. "For pleasant is this flesh; / Our soul, in its rose-mesh / Pulled ever to the earth, still yearns for rest." All that is past is ever with us. Our experiences and our desires are God's potter's wheel on which our souls are shaped. The Rabbi expectantly approaches old age and the life after death:

> Therefore I summon age
> To grant youth's heritage,
> Life's struggle having so far reached its term!
> Thence shall I pass, approved
> A man, for aye removed
> From the developed brute—a God, though in the germ.
> And I shall thereupon
> Take rest, ere I be gone
> Once more on my **adventure brave and new;**
> Fearless and unperplexed,
> When I wage battle next,
> What weapons to select, what armor to indue.

After life's fitful fever he sleeps well

Source: MACBETH (Act III, sc. ii, l. 23)
Author: William Shakespeare (1564-1616)
First published: 1623
Type of work: Dramatic tragedy

Context: Advised by three witches that he will be king, Macbeth gives way to his ambition, murders King Duncan, and usurps the throne. In his hasty grab for power, Macbeth has lost something more precious, peace, which, ironically, he has given to the slain king. The new king addresses Lady Macbeth.

MACBETH
. . .

> . . . Better be with the dead,
> Whom we, to gain our peace, have sent to peace,
> Than on the torture of the mind to lie
> In restless ecstasy. Duncan is in his grave.
> **After life's fitful fever he sleeps well,**
> Treason has done his worst; nor steel, nor poison,
> Malice domestic, foreign levy, nothing,
> Can touch him further.

LADY MACBETH
Come on.
Gentle my lord, sleek o'er your rugged looks,
Be bright and jovial among your guests to-night.

MACBETH
So shall I, love, and so I pray be you. . . .

After strange gods

Source: DEUTERONOMY 31:16
Author: Unknown
First transcribed: 1000-300 B.C.
Type of work: Homiletic religious law and history

Context: When the book of Deuteronomy begins, Moses has arrived with his people at the threshold of the promised land. Behind them lie forty years of wandering, to which they were condemned by the Lord for their lack of faith. Moses recites the history of these years for them: their deliverance from Egypt and from the pursuit by Pharaoh, their idolatry in the encampment at Sinai, their sojourn in the deserts. He reminds them of the miracles by which they were fed, and of the angel they have followed. The Amorites, whom they once refused to attack when commanded to do so, have been defeated. So has Og, king of Bashan: much territory east of the Jordan now belongs to the Israelites. Now they must cross to the west bank of the river and destroy all who dwell there. At this point Moses preaches to his followers, setting forth a long and detailed code of laws by which they must live. Some of these laws deal with sanitation and the prevention of disease, and more than one present-day writer has found them remarkably sound in the light of modern discoveries. Again and again Moses warns his people away from any form of heathenism, and it is clear that this is his chief concern. Forty years of wandering have eliminated the older generation, that would always be likely to return to Egyptian ways; the few survivors will not be allowed to cross the Jordan. But even the younger ones, raised up under the laws of Moses, cannot be depended upon. They are like children, difficult to manage and forever running after some novelty. More than twenty times during his discourse, Moses reminds them of the Lord's promise to punish them severely if they take up with other gods. He reminds them at the same time that they are God's chosen people and will flourish if they abide by his commandments. Moses is now one hundred and twenty years of age; he will not live to cross the river and is ready to hand over the command to Joshua. He warns his people again and again, once angrily:

And the LORD said unto Moses, Behold, thy days approach that

10

thou must die: call Joshua, and present yourselves in the tabernacle of the congregation, that I may give him a charge. And Moses and Joshua went, and presented themselves in the tabernacle of the congregation.

And the LORD appeared in the tabernacle in a pillar of a cloud: and the pillar of the cloud stood over the door of the tabernacle.

And the LORD said unto Moses, Behold, thou shalt sleep with thy fathers; and this people will rise up, and go a whoring **after the gods of the strangers** of the land, whither they go to be among them, and will forsake me, and break my covenant which I have made with them.   .

Then my anger shall be kindled against them in that day, and I will forsake them, and I will hide my face from them, and they shall be devoured, and many evils and troubles shall befall them; so that they will say in that day, Are not these evils come upon us, because our God is not among us?

And I will surely hide my face in that day for all the evils which they shall have wrought, in that they are turned unto other gods.

Now therefore write ye this song for you, and teach it the children of Israel: put it in their mouths, that this song may be a witness for me against the children of Israel.

For when I shall have brought them into the land which I sware unto their fathers, that floweth with milk and honey; and they shall have eaten and filled themselves, and waxen fat; then will they turn unto other gods, and serve them, . . .

After the high Roman fashion

Source: ANTONY AND CLEOPATRA (Act IV, sc. xv, l. 87)
Author: William Shakespeare (1564-1616)
First published: 1623
Type of work: Dramatic tragedy

Context: Dissension and struggle for power mark the rule of the Roman Empire by the triumvirate, Antony, Octavius Caesar, and Lepidus. Antony loses influence to young Caesar when he becomes romantically entangled with Cleopatra, the betwitching queen of Egypt. When the forces of Caesar and Antony finally meet in battle, Antony is defeated. Accusing Cleopatra of double-crossing him and causing his downfall, Antony vows to kill the queen. Cleopatra dispatches word to Antony that she is dead, hoping to bring her lover to repentance. Antony, distraught, falls upon his sword and is taken to die in the arms of Cleopatra. Cleopatra faints with her dead lover in her arms, but quickly recovers and commands Charmian and her other attendants to put aside their sorrow and to prepare a noble funeral befitting the noble Roman who has died:

CLEOPATRA
. . . How do you do, women?

11

What, what, good cheer! Why how now Charmian!
My noble girls! Ah women, women, look
Our lamp is spent, it's out. Good sirs, take heart.
We'll bury him. And then, what's brave, what's noble,
Let's do it **after the high Roman fashion,**
And make death proud to take us. Come, away.
This case of that huge spirit now is cold.
Ah women, women! Come, we have no friend
But resolution, and the briefest end.
                    [*Exeunt, bearing off* ANTONY'S *body.*]

After the scole of Stratford atte Bowe

Source: THE CANTERBURY TALES (Prologue, l. 125)
Author: Geoffrey Chaucer (1343?-1400)
First transcribed: c. 1387-1392
Type of work: Collection of tales

Context: The Canterbury pilgrims, a diverse group, having lodged by chance at the Tabard Inn in Southwark, decide to travel together to the shrine of Thomas à Becket at Canterbury and to tell tales to alleviate the tedium of the journey. In the Prologue, which establishes the framework for the pilgrimage and introduces the tale-tellers, Chaucer describes the physical appearance and gives the background of each of the pilgrims. Among them is a prioress whom the poet, although he respects her greatly, may be satirizing very gently. The school at Stratford at Bow, for example, could hardly compare its French with that of Paris.

Ther was also a Nonne, a PRIORESSE,
That of hir smylying was ful symple and coy;
Hire gretteste ooth was but by Seinte Loy;
And she was cleped madame Eglentyne.
Ful weel she song the service dyvyne,
Entuned in hir nose ful semely,
And Frenssh she spak ful faire and fetisly,
After the scole of Stratford atte Bowe,
For Frenssh of Parys was to hire unknowe.

The age of chivalry is gone

Source: REFLECTIONS ON THE REVOLUTION IN FRANCE
Author: Edmund Burke (1729-1797)
First published: 1790
Type of work: Political treatise

Context: Burke was a believer in law and order, and all that contributed to the preservation of law and order he admired. He was equally a lover of liberty, and he saw in the French Revolution a threat to law and order, and to liberty, throughout the European world, as well as in his beloved England. He saw the Revolution's leaders use abstract theories to produce chaos and bloodshed in the name of liberty, and the sight led him to continue his advocacy of slow change in government and equally slow change in the bounds of liberty. He was particularly struck by the mistreatment of the French royal family during the Revolution, as he was impressed by what he termed "the serene patience" with which Marie Antoinette, the Queen of France, endured her mistreatment. In writing about her and her fate he says he would have expected ten thousand Frenchmen to have leaped to her defense with their swords if she had been even looked at insultingly, but, he remarks:

. . . the age of chivalry is gone. That of sophisters, economists, and calculators, has succeeded; and the glory of Europe is extinguished for ever. Never, never more shall we behold that generous loyalty to rank and sex, that proud submission, that dignified obedience, that subordination of the heart, which kept alive, even in servitude itself, the spirit of an exalted freedom. The unbought grace of life, the cheap defence of nations, the nurse of manly sentiment and heroic enterprise, is gone! It is gone, that sensibility of principle, that chastity of honor, which felt a stain like a wound, which inspired courage whilst it mitigated ferocity, which ennobled whatever it touched, and under which vice itself lost half its evil, by losing all its grossness.

Ah Christ! if only I had known, known, known

Source: THE DEFENCE OF GUENEVERE (Line 41)
Author: William Morris (1834-1896)
First published: 1858
Type of work: Narrative poem

Context: William Morris, who was highly interested in everything medieval, wrote a number of poems utilizing materials from the Arthurian legends. This poem is based upon the famous story, puzzling and disturbing to the British in the age of Queen Victoria, of King Arthur's queen, Guenevere, who fell in love after her marriage with one of the greatest, some legends say the greatest, of the Knights of the Round Table, Sir Lancelot. In this poem Queen Guenevere is called upon, after charges have been made, particularly by Sir Gauwaine, to defend her conduct, which for a queen involves treason, not merely adultery. Guenevere loves Lancelot and does not pretend otherwise, but she compares herself to a dying man who is presented with cloths of two colors by an angel and asked to choose which is the color of Hell and which of Heaven. With no

13

one, nor anything, to help, the dying man must choose between the red and the blue cloths held by the angel —making his choice for eternity. Choosing the blue, as the color of the heavens, the dying man unwittingly chooses Hell. Guenevere says to the court that the judges should try to envision themselves in the dying man's place, as she feels she has a similar decision:

"After a shivering half-hour you said,
'God help! heaven's color, the blue;' and he said, 'Hell.'
Perhaps then you would roll upon your bed,

"And cry to all good men who loved you well,
'Ah Christ! if only I had known, known, known;'
Lancelot went away, then I could tell,

"Like wisest man how all things would be, moan,
And roll and hurt myself, and long to die,
And yet fear much to die for what was sown."

Airy, fairy Lilian

Source: LILIAN (Stanza 1)
Author: Alfred, Lord Tennyson (1809-1892)
First published: 1830
Type of work: Lyric poem

Context: In this early poem by Tennyson, the speaker is fascinated by Lilian's "black-beaded eyes," "lightning laughters," and "gaiety without eclipse." She is light and frivolous and only teases him. Yet this very light and flitting quality "wearieth" her admirer as time passes and she fails to return his love. Her coyness and laughter soon irritate him to the point that in the final stanza he asserts that "If prayers will not hush thee,/ Airy Lilian,/ Like a rose-leaf I will crush thee."

Airy, fairy Lilian
Flitting, fairy Lilian,
When I ask her if she loves me,
Claps her tiny hands above me,
Laughing all she can;
She'll not tell me if she love me,
Cruel little Lilian.

Airy tongues that syllable men's names

Source: COMUS (Line 207)
Author: John Milton (1608-1674)
First published: 1637
Type of work: Masque

Context: When *Comus* was presented at Ludlow Castle to celebrate the installation of the Earl of Bridgewater as the President of Wales, the earl's daughter and two sons had leading roles in the production. The three, making their way to Ludlow, are benighted in a forest inhabited by the vile enchanter Comus and his rabble rout of followers. The Lady, becoming separated from her brothers, who left her, too weary to proceed further into the tangled wood, to find fruits and berries to refresh her, hears the wild, tumultuous music that accompanies a dance by Comus's crew. She is filled with misgiving at the sound of the riotous and ill-managed merriment, as it is the kind of music that stirs up the loose, unlettered rustics when they celebrate the harvest season. She reflects that she would be loath to encounter the rudeness and insolence of a band of midnight drinkers, but her situation is such that she is compelled to seek any sort of aid that offers itself. She is afraid that her brothers have wandered so far away that they will not be able to find her again. She makes her way to where the revelry was, but finds no one. She says:

> This is the place, as well as I may guess,
> Whence even now the tumult of loud mirth
> Was rife and perfect in my listening ear,
> Yet nought but single darkness do I find.
> What might this be? A thousand fantasies
> Begin to throng into my memory
> Of calling shapes, and beckoning shadows dire,
> And **airy tongues, that syllable men's names**
> On sands and shores and desert wildernesses.
> These thoughts may startle well, but not astound
> The virtuous mind, that ever walks attended
> By a strong-siding champion conscience.—
> O welcome, pure-eyed faith, white-handed hope,
> Thou hovering angel, girt with golden wings,
> And thou unblemished form of chastity,
> I see ye visibly, and now believe
> That he, the supreme good, t'whom all things ill
> Are but as slavish officers of vengeance,
> Would send a glistering guardian, if need were,
> To keep my life and honor unassailed.

Alas! the fleeting years!

Source: ODES (Book II, Ode 14, l. 1)
Author: Horace (65-8 B.C.)
First transcribed: 23-13 B.C.
Type of work: Ode

Context: Inevitably death comes to every man, says the poet, in a short poem filled with allusions familiar to his contemporaries. Pluto, God of the Underworld and Death, unappeased by righteousness or by elaborate sacrifice, comes to both rich and poor, and all, though they may have escaped the wrath of Mars, God of War, or the fierce waves of the Adriatic Sea, must finally gaze upon Cocytus, the underworld river of lamentation and the dead of Rome, leaving behind those they hold dear—wives, children—and their possessions. In one translation, the passage reads:

> **Alas,** my Postumus, **our years**
> **Glide silently away.** No tears,
> No loving orisons repair
> The wrinkled cheek, the whitening hair
> That drop forgotten to the tomb.
> Pluto's inexorable doom
> Mocks at thy daily sacrifice.
> Around his dreary kingdom lies
> That fatal stream whose arms infold
> The giant race accurst of old:
> All, all alike must cross its wave,
> The king, the noble, and the slave.

All art constantly aspires towards the condition of music

Source: THE RENAISSANCE ("The School of Giorgione")
Author: Walter Pater (1839-1894)
First published: 1873
Type of work: Aesthetic criticism

Context: In *The Renaissance,* Pater is concerned with a discussion of the artists whose work best reflects the essential qualities of the era, an age which he describes not merely as a revival of classical antiquity but as a period of general excitement and enlightening of the human mind. He traces its beginnings far back into the Middle Ages, "with its motives already clearly pronounced, the care for physical beauty, the worship of the body, the breaking down of the limits which the religious system of the middle age imposed on the heart and on the imagination." But he finds in Italy the dominant Renaissance expression—in the concrete works of art and its prominent personalities. One of the essays, "The School of

Giorgione," describes the fervid artistic activity in Venice at the turn of the sixteenth century, with the experimentation in light, the harmonious and splendid color, the large and free design. Giorgione was an accomplished musician, and his canvases can aptly be termed symphonies in paint. It is this symphonic quality with which Pater is concerned in the opening paragraphs in which he discusses the separate, yet similar, aspects of art. There is rhythmic design in canvas painting, just as there is body and color in music; all art is but a translation "into different languages of one and the same fixed quantity of imaginative thought":

> **All art constantly aspires towards the condition of music.** For while in all other kinds of art it is possible to distinguish the matter from the form, and the understanding can always make this distinction, yet it is the constant effort of art to obliterate it. That the mere matter of a poem, for instance, its subject, namely, its given incidents or situation—that the mere matter of a picture, the actual circumstances of an event, the actual topography of a landscape—should be nothing without the form, the spirit, of the handling, that this form, this mode of handling, should become an end in itself, should penetrate every part of the matter: this is what all art constantly strives after, and achieves in different degrees.

All by my own-alone self

Source: BROTHER WOLF FALLS A VICTIM
Author: Joel Chandler Harris (1848–1908)
First published: 1883 in *Nights with Uncle Remus*
Type of work: Short story

Context: Joel Chandler Harris, always referred to by his full name, made his reputation by a series of animal stories, supposedly told by an elderly Negro ex-slave, Uncle Remus. He published the first one in *The Atlanta Constitution* with which he was associated from 1876 to 1900. The stories attribute human traits to Brer (Brother) Rabbit and to other animals, and are told in the Negro dialect of middle Georgia. In Europe it was the Fox, not the Rabbit, who was the trickster hero of folk tales. But in Chapter 36 of Harris's second book, as the title declares, "Brother Wolf Falls a Victim" (to Brother Rabbit). In the conversation, the little boy who is listening asks whether Uncle Remus ever saw the Witch-Rabbit, Mammy-Bammy Big-Money. The elderly Negro replies that if he has ever run across her, she disappeared so fast he never caught a glimpse of her.

The result of this good-humored explanation was that the child didn't know whether Uncle Remus had ever seen the Witch-Rabbit or not, but his sympathies led him to suspect that the old man was

17

thoroughly familiar with all her movements.

"Uncle Remus," the little boy said after a while, "If there's another story about Mammy-Bammy Big-Money, I wish you would tell it to me **all by my own-alone self.**"

All have not the gift of martyrdom

Source: THE HIND AND THE PANTHER (Part II, l. 59)
Author: John Dryden (1631-1700)
First published: 1687
Type of work: Religious allegory

Context: Having been converted in 1686 to Catholicism, Dryden championed his new Church in a long poem, *The Hind and the Panther.* In his allegory, animals represented England's various religious groups. The hares were the Quakers; the apes, the freethinkers; the boar, the Anabaptists; the fox, the Unitarians; the wolf, the Presbyterians. "The milk white Hind" was the Roman Catholic Church, in danger of being attacked by the Panther (The Church of England), but defended by the British Lion (King James II). In the second part, the Panther accompanies the Hind through the woods, and they talk together. The Panther congratulates her at having escaped the hunter's snares. The Hind retorts that the snares were laid for the Panther, who twisted out of them. Some people are born to be martyrs, she tells her companion, while others are unwilling to suffer for a just cause. Instead, from fear and selfishness, they do everything to escape. The use of the word "gift" shows the poet's admiration of those who suffer for righteousness' sake.

. . .

"Long time you fought, redoubled batt'ry bore,
But, after all, against yourself you swore:
Your former self; for ev'ry hour your form
Is chopp'd and chang'd, like winds before a storm.
Thus fear and int'rest will prevail with some;
For **all have not the gift of martyrdom.**"
　The Panther grinned at this, and thus replied:
"That men may err was never yet denied.
But if that common principle be true,
The cannon, dame, is level'd full at you." . . .

All heiresses are beautiful

Source: KING ARTHUR OR THE BRITISH WORTHY (Act I, sc. i)
Author: John Dryden (1631-1700)
First published: 1691
Type of work: Dramatic opera

Context: Henry Purcell (1659–1695) provided the music for this play as he and other famous composers did for the many songs by Dryden, so popular in late seventeenth century drawing rooms. As the curtain rises on *King Arthur or The British Worthy,* Conon, Duke of Cornwall, Albanact, Captain of Arthur's Guards, and Aurelius, a friend of the king, discuss the coming battle that will determine whether Arthur or the invading Saxons will rule Britain. Oswald, King of Kent, the Saxon leader, had come earlier to Conon's court seeking to marry the duke's daughter, Emmeline. Because she was in love with Arthur, his suit was refused. Determined to marry her, he began the present war. The soldiers ponder Oswald's motives, since the princess is blind, but one of them remarks that her wealth is bound to make her attractive. The man who marries her will not get a "blind bargain." He knows well how advantageous it will be. Conon then describes Oswald, as he seemed to be at the court of Cornwall.

CONON

Revengeful, rugged, violently brave; and once resolved,
is never to be moved.

ALBANACT

Yes, he's a valiant dog, pox on him!

CONON

This was the character he then maintained,
When in my court he sought my daughter's love,
My fair, blind Emmeline.

ALBANACT

I cannot blame him for courting the heiress of Cornwall;
All heiresses are beautiful; and, as blind as she is, he
Would have no blind bargain of her.

All is gas and gaiters

Source: NICHOLAS NICKLEBY (Chapter 49)
Author: Charles Dickens (1812-1870)
First published: 1838-1839
Type of work: Novel

Context: At a gathering in the Nickleby residence in London are Mrs. Nickleby and her daughter, Kate; Miss La Creevy, the artist; Mr. Linkinwater, who professes to admire Miss La Creevy; and Frank Cheeryble, who, with his brother Charles, employs Nicholas Nickleby. While the company is engaged in conversation, a muffled voice singing in melancholy tones issues from a neighboring room. The company, upon investigation,

19

finds a pair of legs in coarse gray stockings dangling from the chimney, and when they are sharply pulled a gentleman in small clothes, that is, tight-fitting knee breeches, appears. Kate says that he is a madman who has escaped from the neighboring house, but Mrs. Nickleby insists that he is the victim of a plot to rob him of his wealth. His demanding bottled lightning, a thunder sandwich, a fricassee of boot-tops with goldfish sauce rather substantiates Kate's opinion of him. He greets Miss La Creevy as his lost love and says that all is gas and gaiters, by which expression he seems to mean that now everything is all right:

"Aha!" cried the old gentleman, folding his hands, and squeezing them with great force against each other. "I see her now; I see her now! My love, my life, my bride, my peerless beauty. She is come at last—at last—and **all is gas and gaiters!**"

Mrs. Nickleby looked rather disconcerted for a moment, but immediately recovering, nodded to Miss La Creevy and the other spectators several times, and frowned, and smiled gravely; giving them to understand that she saw where the mistake was, and would set it all to rights in a minute or two.

"She is come!" said the old gentleman, laying his hand upon his heart. "Cormoran and Blunderbore! She is come! All the wealth I have is hers if she will take me for her slave. Where are grace, beauty, and blandishments, like those? In the Empress of Madagascar? No. In the Queen of Diamonds? No. In Mrs. Rowland, who every morning bathes in Kalydor for nothing? No. Melt all these down into one, with the three Graces, the nine Muses, and fourteen biscuit-bakers' daughters from Oxford-street, and make a woman half as lovely. Pho! I defy you."

All jargon of the schools

Source: ON EXODUS 3:14 (Stanza vi)
Author: Matthew Prior (1664-1721)
First published: 1707
Type of work: Philosophic poem

Context: English poet and diplomat, Matthew Prior is known chiefly for his epigrams, satires, and society verse. With his Tory party affiliation, he was thrown into close literary association with Alexander Pope and John Arbuthnot. In his public life, he took part in several important European treaty negotiations, including the Treaty of Ryswick and the Treaty of Utrecht. "On *Exodus* 3:14: I am That I am: An Ode," written in 1688, originated as an exercise at St. John's College, Cambridge. In many ways it anticipates in a limited fashion Pope's *An Essay on Man.* Prior berates "foolish man," who scarce knows himself, for his presumptuous curiosity—his "daring Pride and insolent Delight"—which would attempt to fathom the mysteries of God's universe. He avers that God's laws will never submit to "Reason's Batteries, or the Mines of Wit." The perspective of faith is man's only recourse; as Pope was to describe it: "Whatever is, is right." At one point Prior takes to task the petty knowledge of the schools and laboratories, always claiming the answers to some enigma of the universe or of human nature, yet ever replacing the "answers" of yesterday with the new hypotheses and theories of today:

> Man does with dangerous Curiosity
> These unfathom'd Wonders try:
> With fancy'd Rules and arbitrary Laws
> Matter and Motion he restrains;
> And study'd Lines and fictious Circles draws:
> Then with imagin'd Soveraignty
> Lord of his new Hypothesis he reigns.
> He reigns: How long? 'till some Usurper rise;
> And he too, mighty Thoughtful, mighty Wise,
> Studies new Lines, and other Circles feigns.
> From this last Toil again what Knowledge flows?
> Just as much, perhaps, as shows,
> That all his Predecessor's Rules
> Were empty Cant, **all Jargon of the Schools;**
> That he on t'other's Ruin rears his Throne;
> And shows his Friend's Mistake, and thence confirms
> his own.

All men would be cowards if they durst

Source: A SATYR AGAINST MANKIND (Line 158)
Author: John Wilmot (Second Earl of Rochester, 1647–1680)
First published: 1675
Type of work: Verse satire

Context: In this verse satire Rochester expresses a general and cold contempt for human life as he saw and lived it. He begins, as does Boileau in his eighth satire, with a picture of the contempt in which man is held by the beasts for his supposed reason, or "common sense." A clergyman interrupts for a brief dialogue, protesting Rochester's slander of "Blest glorious Man, to whom alone kind Heav'n / An everlasting Soul hath freely giv'n;" a gift which enables him to reason. The poet responds that it is "This super-nat'ral Gift, that makes a Mite / Think he's the Image of the Infinite." Reason, in Rochester's philosophy, is useful only when leagued with knavery and hypocrisy. Concerning man's martial accomplishments, the poet observes that animals kill out of necessity but man from wantonness and lust for power "for the which alone he dares be brave:"

> Look to the bottom of his vast Design,
> Wherein Man's Wisdom, Pow'r, and Glory join;

21

The Good he acts, the Ill he does endure,
'Tis all for Fear, to make himself secure.
Merely for safety, after Fame we thirst;
For **all Men would be Cowards if they durst:**
And Honesty's against all common sense—
Men must be Knaves; 'tis in their own defence,
Mankind's dishonest; if you think it fair,
Amongst known Cheats, to play upon the square,
You'll be undone—
Nor can weak Truth, your Reputation save;
The Knaves will all agree to call you Knave.
Wrong'd shall he live, insulted o'er, opprest,
Who dares be less a Villain than the rest.

All places are distant from Heaven alike

Source: ANATOMY OF MELANCHOLY (Partition II, sec. 3, memb. 4)
Author: Robert Burton (1577-1640)
First published: 1621-1651
Type of work: Essays

Context: As an early forerunner of Freud, the vicar Burton, who dabbled in every field of learning, spent much of his life writing a thick book that might be called "An Analysis of Morbid Psychology." But there was no body of applied science on which Burton could draw, so he took from every sort of source to produce a series of informal essays on ways of curing man's dissatisfaction with the universe. In the first two of his three Partitions, he considered first the causes and then the cures of melancholy. Section 3 of Partition II concerns remedies for discontent. No one should be unhappy at servitude, for everybody is subservient to some one: nobles to their king, lovers to their mistresses, and rich men to their gold. Imprisonment is not sufficient cause for discontent, since all life is a prison. Nor should one who is banished or forced to change his residence feel himself a slave at the orders of a master. His new place of residence is attractive to some one who considers the newcomer lucky to be there. A man can travel as quickly to Heaven from one place as from another.

. . . There is a base Nation in the north (saith Pliny), called Chauci, that live amongst rocks and sands by the seaside, feed on fish, drink water: and yet these base people account themselves slaves in respect, when they come to Rome . . . so it is. Fortune favors some to live at home to their further punishment: 't is want of judgment. **All places are distant from Heaven alike,** the Sun shines happily as warm in one city as in another, and to a wise man there is no difference of climes, . . .

22

All places shall be hell that are not heaven

Source: THE TRAGICAL HISTORY OF DOCTOR FAUSTUS (Scene V, l. 27)
Author: Christopher Marlowe (1564-1593)
First published: 1604
Type of work: Dramatic tragedy

Context: The death of the greatest of Elizabethan dramatists, next to Shakespeare, "Stab'd with a dagger" by a drinking companion, Ingram Frizer, at the age of twenty-nine, has been ascribed to a plot by the Puritans because of the playwright's atheistic and heretical religious principles. Yet how could any heretic write such a Puritanical sermon as the struggle of Dr. Faustus with his conscience, his final awful soliloquy, and the terrifying climax of this play, where amid thunder and lightning the devils carry him off to hell? The German scholar brings his punishment on himself. Reviewing the vast knowledge he possesses, Dr. John Faustus pronounces it futile. He decides to take up magic and with a spell conjures up Mephostopilis with whom he signs a pact: his soul in return for twenty-four years of service from Lucifer's chief minister. Receiving the signed document, the Minister of Hell speaks:

MEPHOSTOPHILIS
Now, Faustus, ask me what thou wilt.

FAUSTUS
First will I question with thee about hell.
Tell me, where is the place that men call hell?

MEPHOSTOPHILIS
Under the Heavens.

FAUSTUS
Aye, so are all things else, but whereabout?

MEPHOSTOPHILIS
Within the bowels of these elements,
Where we are tortured and remain forever.
Hell hath no limits, nor is circumscribed
In one self place, for where we are is hell,
And where hell is, there must we ever be:
And, to be short, when all the world dissolves
And every creature shall be purified,
All places shall be hell that are not heaven.

FAUSTUS
I think hell's a fable.

23

MEPHOSTOPHILIS
Ay, think so still, till experience change thy mind.

All poets are mad

Source: ANATOMY OF MELANCHOLY: DEMOCRITUS JUNIOR TO THE READER
Author: Robert Burton (1577-1640)
First published: 1621-1651
Type of work: Essays

Context: The seventeenth century was a time of intellectual ferment when scholars tried to master all they could of human knowledge. Burton called himself Democritus Junior, after the Greek philosopher of the fifth and fourth centuries B. C. who, besides studying the physical world and theorizing about atoms, held that the true end of life was happiness achieved through inner tranquility. Burton's book has no special theme or thesis, but into it he poured his immense sum of learning. A lengthy introduction, "Democritus Junior to the Reader," is a satirical catalog of the follies of mankind. Parts sound very modern: the injustice of a system where a lawyer gets more money in a day than a philosopher in a year, and where wise men are degraded and fools preferred. He gives his recipe for a New Utopia. Quoting Tully (Cicero), he writes: "I prefer silent Wisdom to talkative Folly," He gives his own opinions, sometimes footnoting them by references to ancient writers, many of whom are no longer mentioned in the most minute biographical volumes. Frascatorious (1483–1553) was an Italian physician and poet whose long poem about Syphilis gave that disease its name. Scaliger (1484–1558) wrote *Poetics* (published in 1561).

> . . . I esteem a man wise, not according to his words but to his deeds. Make the best of him, a good orator is a turn-coat, an evil man, his tongue is set to sale, he is a mere voice, as he said of a nightingale, gives a voice without thought, an hyperbolical liar, a flatterer, a parasite, and as Amnianus Marcellinus will, a corrupting cozener, one that doth more mischief by his fair speech, than he that bribes by money; for a man may with more facility avoid him that circumvents by money, than he that deceives by glozing terms; which made Socrates so much abhor and explode them. Frascatorius, a famous poet, freely grants all Poets to be mad; so doth Scaliger, and who doth not? Either mad or making verses (saith Horace); (saith Virgil) it pleases one to be mad, i.e., to make verses; So Servius interprets it, **all Poets are mad.** . . .

All service ranks the same with God

Source: PIPPA PASSES (Part IV, "Night")
Author: Robert Browning (1812-1889)
First published: 1841
Type of work: Dramatic poem

Context: Pippa Passes is the first of a series of little pamphlets which Browning called *Bells and Pomegranates.* It did not achieve immediate recognition; a previous poem, *Sordello,* had done him considerable harm because of its obscurity, and some time elapsed before *Pippa Passes* began to receive the attention it deserved. It eventually became one of Browning's most popular poems. This story of an innocent little girl and her love of life reflects one of his basic beliefs—that life and intensity are the same thing and that they are good. His religious conviction was that the right would always triumph in the end, and that the Divine love he found manifested through nature and intellect could have no other effect. To Browning, love is not a passion dedicated to human perfection; it is instead a Divine tolerance of imperfect humanity. Pippa is unaware that she is an instrument of Divine love and justice—she is just a child who loves life and sings because of it. All the same, when she passes by and people hear her song, their lives are affected dramatically. A very poor child, she works the year round at a silk mill in Asolo, Italy. On her one holiday, New Year's day, she goes about the town to see the homes of four people she admires and considers the happiest in the city. In the first house she passes, an adulterer and murderer hears her song, is conscience-stricken, and expiates his crime with poison; in the second, a sculptor enmeshed in the world's complexities receives new inspiration and resolves to go elsewhere rather than kill a man; in the third house, an unstable youth duped by others musters his courage and goes forth to destroy an evil at its source. Pippa passes the fourth house in time to prevent an evil man from selling a child into prostitution—and the child she saves is herself. Pippa returns home unaware that she has influenced anyone; she is content with her lot and not envious, but she has enjoyed imagining herself in the places of these high and happy people. Regretting that her holiday is over, she prepares to sleep:

> Now, one thing I should like to really know:
> How near I ever might approach all these
> I only fancied being, this long day:
> —Approach, I mean, so as to touch them, so
> As to . . . in some way . . . move them—if you please,
> Do good or evil to them some slight way.
> For instance, if I wind
> Silk tomorrow, my silk may bind
> > [*Sitting on the bedside.*]
> And border Ottima's cloak's hem.

Ah me, and my important part with them,
This morning's hymn half promised when I rose!
True in some sense or other, I suppose.
[*As she lies down.*]
God bless me! I can pray no more tonight.
No doubt, some way or other, hymns say right.
All service ranks the same with God—
With God, whose puppets, best and worst,
Are we; there is no last nor first.
[*She sleeps.*]

All silent, and all damned

Source: PETER BELL (Part I, Original Edition)
Author: William Wordsworth (1770-1850)
First published: 1819
Type of work: Narrative poem

Context: As the author explains in his preface to this long, unsuccessful poem, "the Imagination . . . does not require for its exercise the intervention of supernatural agency"; quite the contrary, the poet can stimulate his readers' imaginations by faithfully adhering to "the humblest departments of daily life." The story of the poem, an attempt to illustrate everyday occurrences, earned the laughing scorn of practically all of Wordsworth's major contemporaries: a potter named Peter Bell is a sinful man who not only has a dozen wives but also is so insensitive that he does not appreciate nature. One day he comes upon a starving ass that has remained where its master died, and from the patient loyalty of the animal (as well as from his own guilt) he learns the wickedness of his ways and repents. The quotation occurs near the end of the first part of the original poem: Peter Bell, discovering that the ass is dying, loses his temper and begins to beat the poor beast, but as he maltreats it, he is seized with irrational fear and thinks that he hears noises such as demons might make:

Is it a party in a parlour?
Cramm'd just as they on earth were cramm'd—
Some sipping punch, some sipping tea,
But, as you by their faces see,
All silent, and all damn'd!

All taxes must, at last, fall upon agriculture

Source: THE DECLINE AND FALL OF THE ROMAN EMPIRE (Chapter 8)
Author: Edward Gibbon (1737-1794)
First published: 1776-1788
Type of work: History

Context: In Chapter 8 of his narrative of Roman history, Edward Gibbon leaves the chronicle of the Roman Empire itself to inform his reader of the nature of Rome's enemies from without, the tribes which were to invade the outer provinces of the Empire at first and, later, overrun the Empire as a whole and sack the city of Rome itself. These invaders Gibbon calls "the nations who avenged the causes of Hannibal and Mithridates." He first tells of the Persians, including in his narrative a succinct, but clear, account of their religion, Zoroastrianism. He then relates how Artaxerxes wrested the control of the Near East from the Parthians and established his own vigorous administration throughout Persia by subduing each of the under-kings who had ruled under his predecessor. The quotation about taxes and agriculture is credited to Artaxerxes by Gibbon, who notes that it can be found in D'Herbelot's *Bibliothèque Orientale,* under the entry "Ardshir," another form of Artaxerxes' name. The quotation appears in a paragraph in which Gibbon praises the Persian ruler for his intelligent and effective rule:

> The reign of Artaxerxes . . . forms a memorable era in the history of the East, and even in that of Rome. His character seems to have been marked by those bold and commanding features that generally distinguished the princes who conquer, from those who inherit, an empire. Till the last period of the Persian monarchy his code of laws was respected as the ground-work of their civil and religious policy. Several of his sayings are preserved. One of them in particular discovers a deep insight into the constitution of government. "The authority of the prince," said Artaxerxes, "must be defended by a military force; that force can only be maintained by taxes; **all taxes must, at last, fall upon agriculture;** and agriculture can never flourish except under the protection of justice and moderation. . . .

All the live murmur of a summer's day

Source: THE SCHOLAR-GYPSY (Stanza 2)
Author: Matthew Arnold (1822-1888)
First published: 1853
Type of work: Philosophical poem

Context: Arnold's poem is derived from a passage in Joseph Glanvil's *Vanity of Dogmatizing* (1661) which tells of a scholar who, for lack of money, abandoned his studies at Oxford and joined a band of gypsies. The scholar was admitted to the confidence of the gypsies, who communicated to him the secrets of their knowledge and philosophy. After he had been with them for several years, two of his fellow students at Oxford chanced upon him, and to them he said that the gypsies have the power to bind the imagination of others with their own. He asserted that when he was perfect in the knowledge he would communicate it to the world.

Arnold's poem begins with the poet's telling the shepherd to go to the hills to release the sheep from the fold, but in the evening, when tired men and dogs have gone to rest, the shepherd is to renew his quest for knowledge. The poet sits in a corner of the field where the reaper stored his basket of food, his jug of drink, and his coat while he was working. The poet will sit and wait for country sounds to come to him—the bleating of sheep, the cries of the reapers, and all the live murmur of a summer's day.

> Here, where the reaper was at work of late—
> In this high field's dark corner, where he leaves
> His coat, his basket, and his earthen cruse,
> And in the sun all morning binds the sheaves,
> Then here, at noon, comes back his stores to use
> Here will I sit and wait,
> While to my ear from uplands far away
> The bleating of the folded flocks is borne,
> With distant cries of reapers in the corn—
> **All the live murmur of a summer's day.**

All the perfumes of Arabia will not sweeten this little hand

Source: MACBETH (Act V, sc. i, ll. 56-57)
Author: William Shakespeare (1564-1616)
First published: 1623
Type of work: Dramatic tragedy

Context: Lady Macbeth receives a letter from her husband telling her of the prophetic words of three witches that he will become king. When the chance comes to kill King Duncan as he sleeps, an overnight visitor in Macbeth's castle, Lady Macbeth urges Macbeth to murder his liege and cousin and to usurp the throne. The deed is done, Macbeth is crowned king, and yet the queen does not enjoy her new estate. Finally insane, Lady Macbeth is obsessed with the murder of Duncan and the idea that his blood would not wash off her hands after she had smeared it upon the grooms who slept by their king.

LADY MACBETH
Here's the smell of the blood still: **all the perfumes of Arabia will not sweeten this little hand.** Oh, oh, oh!

DOCTOR
What a sigh is there! The heart is sorely charged.

GENTLEWOMAN
I would not have such a heart in my bosom for the dignity of the whole body.

DOCTOR

Well, well, well.

GENTLEWOMAN

Pray God it be sir.

DOCTOR

This disease is beyond my practice. Yet I have known those which have walked in their sleep who have died holily in their beds.

All things that love the sun

Source: RESOLUTION AND INDEPENDENCE (Stanza 2)
Author: William Wordsworth (1770–1850)
First published: 1807
Type of work: Didactic poem

Context: Although the second half of this poem has been made famous by two parodies of it (Edward Lear: "Incidents in the Life of My Uncle Arly" and Lewis Carroll: "The White Knight's Ballad"), it remains an important work from the author's early period when his inspiration was still at its height. The poem, twenty stanzas in length, shows that the author, who had so often declared his faith in nature as a guide, a teacher, and a friend, was also aware that nature could at times be very unkind. The subject arose from an actual experience that Wordsworth encountered in the Lake District: that of meeting, during one of his walks, an old man, badly crippled by an accident and yet struggling to make some kind of a living. The old man's fortitude amidst these reverses of fortune compelled the poet's admiration but reminded him that all men—especially poets—are subject to these same reverses. The poem breaks into two parts: the first describes the beauty of the moors early in the morning after a heavy storm; the second recounts the poet's meeting with the old leech-gatherer and the conversation that ensued. It was this second section that inspired the parodies of Lear and Carroll, and it must be admitted that Wordsworth's questions and his inattention to the old man's replies are fit subjects for parody. But in the early part of the poem, Wordsworth expresses his usual view of his kinship with nature and his attribution of human qualities to all of her manifestations:

There was a roaring in the wind all night;
The rain came heavily and fell in floods;
But now the sun is rising calm and bright;
The birds are singing in the distant woods:
Over his own sweet voice the stock-dove broods;
The jay makes answer as the magpie chatters;
And all the air is filled with pleasant noise of waters.

29

All things that love the sun are out of doors;
The sky rejoices in the morning's birth;
The grass is bright with raindrops;—on the moors
The hare is running races in her mirth;
And with her feet she from the plashy earth
Raises a mist, that, glittering in the sun,
Runs with her all the way wherever she doth run.

All things work together for good

Source: ROMANS 8:28
Author: Paul
First transcribed: c.50-60
Type of work: Religious epistle

Context: Romans is a letter which Paul wrote to his fellow-Christians in Rome; it is a letter to strangers, because he had never been to Rome and had no part in founding the church there. For this reason his epistle is more a treatise on the principles and practice of Christianity than a letter. It is evident that he wishes to offer his readers encouragement and reassurance in their faith; at the same time, he is anxious to furnish as many arguments as possible which can be used by them in gaining converts to Christianity. His principal concern is for the Jews; most of his work has been done among these people, and it has been his habit as a missionary to go to the synagogue whenever he arrives in a community. There he begins his effort by arguing scripture and preaching. He has found the Jews very resistant to conversion. In the first eight chapters of this epistle he draws upon his long experience and enumerates all the objections to Christianity that members of the Jewish faith are likely to raise. For each of the objections he provides an answer. Paul begins the epistle with a statement of his qualifications; he then blesses his readers and states his gospel for them, reminding them that God offers salvation through it to all men regardless of their origin. He adds that all men are sinners and that to satisfy the outward requirements of faith is useless unless one's belief is genuine. To observe the law is good, but its observance without faith is vain: belief in man's redemption through Christ transcends the law. At this point Paul turns to a discussion of sin and its nature, adding the reassurance that ancient sins are wiped out by baptism. He then returns to his discussion of the law; no earthly law has power over us after death. The true Christian is dead to sin because his law is Christ. In Chapter 8 Paul goes back to an earlier point, that to be one with Christ is to be pure and free from condemnation. He elaborates his theme of the transcendency of spiritual things over material:

For we are saved by hope: but hope that is seen is not hope: for
what a man seeth, why doth he yet hope for?

But if we hope for that we see not, then do we with patience wait for it.

Likewise the Spirit also helpeth our infirmities: for we know not what we should pray for as we ought: but the Spirit itself maketh intercession for us with groanings which cannot be uttered.

And he that searcheth the hearts knoweth what is the mind of the Spirit, because he maketh intercession for the saints according to the will of God.

And we know that **all things work together for good** to them that love God, to them who are the called according to his purpose.

For whom he did foreknow, he also did predestinate to be conformed to the image of his Son, that he might be the firstborn among many brethren.

Moreover whom he did predestinate, them he also called: and whom he called, them he also justified: and whom he justified, them he also glorified.

What shall we then say to these things? If God be for us, who can be against us?

He that spared not his own Son, but delivered him up for us all, how shall he not with him also freely give us all things?

Who shall lay any thing to the charge of God's elect? It is God that justifieth.

All this and heaven too

Source: THE LIFE AND DEATH OF THE REV. PHILIP HENRY (Chapter V)
Author: Matthew Henry (1662-1714)
First published: 1696-1697?
Type of work: Biography

Context: Matthew Henry writes the life of his father, Philip Henry (1631 –1696), a non-conformist minister whose entire existence lay in preaching the gospel. After a pleasant and tranquil beginning to his career as a minister, he was, during much of the reign of King Charles II, barred from preaching in public and was subjected to various other harassments because his conscience forbade his conforming to the church regulations set up by parliament at the instigation of the king. Although he was deprived of his pulpit, he was, because he had married a woman of some wealth, never in want for the necessities of life. He contrived to lead a useful and pleasant life, although he was several times imprisoned for short terms for his lack of conformity. As, however, other ministers of the gospel were incarcerated at the same time as he was, he rather enjoyed the experience, as it gave him the opportunity to discuss religion with his peers, an opportunity he did not have while at liberty. He was always charitable and used to season his gifts to the poor with wholesome advice and gentle admonitions for erring conduct. He always took great pleasure in being able to contribute to the poor, believing that anything material he gave would be returned to him in gifts of the spirit:

. . . though he did not delight himself in the abundance of wealth; yet, which is far better, he delighted himself in the "abundance of peace." . . . All that he had and did, observably prospered, so that the country oftentimes . . . called his family, "a family which the Lord had blessed." And his comforts of this kind were (as he used to pray they might be) "oil to the wheels of his obedience," and in the use of these things he served the Lord his God with "joyfulness and gladness of heart"; yet still mindful of and "grieved for, the afflictions of Joseph." He would say sometimes, when he was in the midst of the comforts of this life, as that good man who exclaimed, **"All this and heaven too!** surely then we serve a good Master." Thus did the Lord bless him, and make him a blessing; and this abundant grace, through the thanksgiving of many, redounded to the glory of God.

An allegory on the banks of Nile

Source: THE RIVALS (Act III, sc. iii)
Author: Richard Brinsley Sheridan (1751-1816)
First published: 1775
Type of work: Dramatic comedy

Context: In this scene of Sheridan's play, Captain Absolute appears to Lydia Languish as "Ensign Beverley," which is a fictitious identity he has taken on to woo the fanciful, but beautiful, young heiress. He knows that with her romantic notions she wants to marry the penniless "ensign" for love, rather than the real Captain Absolute, who is heir to wealthy Sir Anthony Absolute. The situation is complicated further by the fact that Mrs. Malaprop, the girl's guardian, knows the suitor for Lydia is Captain Absolute, but she does not know that he is also the fictitious "ensign," whom she despises. During the interview between the young people Mrs. Malaprop enters unseen to eavesdrop. Hearing Lydia say that she will never marry Captain Absolute, Mrs. Malaprop comes forward to berate the headstrong girl. As usual when she speaks, Mrs. Malaprop uses wrong words, here saying "allegory" for "alligator":

MRS. MALAPROP
[*Aside.*] Ay, poor young man!—down on his knees entreating for pity!—I can contain no longer.—[*Coming forward.*] Why, hussy! hussy! I have overheard you.

CAPT. ABSOLUTE
[*Aside.*] Oh, confound her vigilance!

MRS. MALAPROP
Captain Absolute, I know not how to apologize for her shocking rudeness.

32

CAPT. ABSOLUTE

[*Aside.*] So all's safe, I find.—[*Aloud.*] I have hopes, madam, that time will bring the young lady—

MRS. MALAPROP

Oh, there's nothing to be hoped for from her! She's as head-strong as **an allegory on the banks of Nile.**

All's love, yet all's law

Source: SAUL (Line 242)
Author: Robert Browning (1812-1889)
First published: 1855
Type of work: Dramatic monologue

Context: David, the shepherd boy, has cured King Saul of his melancholic despair of pleasure in all things. It is now the next morning, and David recounts, step by step, the events of the previous evening in Saul's camp: his meeting with Abner, his entry into Saul's darkened tent, and his first glimpse of the king "erect as that tent prop, both arms stretched out wide / On the great cross-support in the center, that goes to each side." There is then a catalogue of all the good things of the earth for which Saul should thank heaven. On his harp, David tells of the God-given signs of order in all creatures and of men working together as a society. A moan breaks from Saul's lips, a sign that the melancholy is somewhat broken. David sings of the joys of living and of the king's great worth. Slowly, Saul regains his kingly habits and bearing. It is through David's deep love and desire to help that the boy suddenly attains a mystical glimpse of Truth. He breaks off singing to speak aloud:

I have gone the whole round of creation; I saw and I spoke;
I, a work of God's hand for that purpose, received in my brain
And pronounced on the rest of his handwork—returned him again
His creation's approval or censure; I spoke as I saw;
Reported as man may of God's work—**all's love, yet all's law.**
. . .
I but open my eyes—and perfection, no more and no less,
In the kind I imagined, full-fronts me, and God is seen God
In the star, in the stone, in the flesh, in the soul and the clod.

Am I no a bonny fighter?

Source: KIDNAPPED (Chapter 10)
Author: Robert Louis Stevenson (1850-1894)
First published: 1886
Type of work: Novel

33

Context: David Balfour, a Scots lad, is sent by a rascally uncle to enforced service in the American colonies. While aboard the ship bound to America, he becomes the cabin-boy for the "Covenant." Shortly afterward the ship runs down a small boat; one man is saved after the accident, a Jacobite adventurer named Alan Breck, a Highlander with a price on his head. Alan Breck demands that the "Covenant's" master set him ashore in Scotland; the captain agrees to put the new passenger on land, but plots to deliver the man to the authorities so he may receive the bounty for turning Breck in. David Balfour overhears the captain and the second officer plotting against the Highlander and warns the man of his peril. Breck and the lad take refuge in the ship's roundhouse, where they hold off the ship's crew, who endeavor to capture them by force. Breck with his sword, and David Balfour with pistols, drive off the crew, killing the second officer and three other men, as well as wounding the captain and several others. Having driven the survivors below decks, Breck returns to the roundhouse, now described by young Balfour:

> The roundhouse was like a shambles; three were dead inside, another lay in his death agony across the threshold; and there were Alan and I victorious and unhurt.
>
> He came to me with open arms. "Come to my arms!" he cried, and embraced and kissed me upon both cheeks. "David," said he, "I love you like a brother. And O, man," he cried in a kind of ecstasy, **"am I no a bonny fighter?"**
>
> Thereupon he turned to the four enemies, passed his sword clean through each of them, and tumbled them out of doors one after the other. As he did so, he kept humming and singing and whistling to himself, like a man trying to recall an air; only what *he* was trying to do was to make one. All the while the flush was on his face, and his eyes were as bright as a five-year-old child's with a new toy. . . .

Ambition can creep as well as soar

Source: LETTERS ON A REGICIDE PEACE (Letter III)
Author: Edmund Burke (1729-1797)
First published: 1796-1797
Type of work: Open letter

Context: As Burke's life approached its end so did the life of the French Revolution. In Paris horror succeeded horror, culminating in the execution of the king and queen; the Army moved in, and under the command of Napoleon, protected what was of permanent value in the increasing shambles of the disintegrating Revolution. To the astonishment of many, France, wracked by violent internal conflicts and collapsing credit, was able to break up the European coalition arrayed against her. In England a movement was afoot to make peace with the Revolutionary government, and peace talks were actually opened at one point. Burke, ever a firm and stanch enemy of the French Revolution, was equally firmly opposed to this peace movement. In a series of four open letters he argued his case for France as a menace to all of Europe. In this third letter Burke insisted that France had at one time contemplated an invasion of England and that the peace terms offered to England by the Directory were positively humiliating; he derided and cast suspicion on those who encouraged peace as an apology for England's military actions against France:

> There is one thing in this business which appears to be wholly unaccountable, . . . I cannot help asking, Why all this pains to clear the British nation of ambition, perfidy, and the insatiate thirst of war? At what period of time was it that our country has deserved that load of infamy of which nothing but preternatural humiliation in language and conduct can serve to clear us? If we have deserved this kind of evil fame from anything we have done in a state of prosperity, I am sure that it is not an abject conduct in adversity that can clear our reputation. Well is it known that **ambition can creep as well as soar.** The pride of no person in a flourishing condition is more justly to be dreaded than that of him who is mean and cringing under a doubtful and unprosperous fortune. . . .

Ambition's debt is paid

Source: JULIUS CAESAR (Act III, sc. i, l. 83)
Author: William Shakespeare (1564-1616)
First published: 1623
Type of work: Dramatic tragedy

Context: Following his stirring victories over Pompey, Julius Caesar has returned to Rome and is swept up in the plaudits of "the common herd." In the rush of this popular acclaim, there is rumor that Caesar is on the verge of allowing himself to be crowned emperor. Such a period of political instability is the season of discontent both for those who, fed by personal ambition, see their own opportunities for power thwarted and also for those who are apprehensive lest the law of the land is to be subordinated to the individual and the freedom of the Republic lost forever. These two kinds of individuals are, of course, philosophies apart, but rebellion makes strange bedfellows. Thus it is that the ambitious aristocrats Cassius, moved by envy in his hatred of Caesar and possessed of "an itching palm," and Casca, who holds in high disdain the "tag-rag" multitude which heaps accolades upon Caesar, are joined in rebellion against their Roman leader. As for Brutus, he is as idealistic as his compatriots are practical. His love of Caesar is great, but his love for Rome greater. In the desperate efforts which he is convinced are necessary to save

35

the Republic, he becomes a part of that which, were it for personal gain, he would loathe. Following the mo-

ment of Caesar's murder, he attempts to quiet the distracted populace:

CAESAR
Et tu Brute? Then fall Caesar.

CINNA
Liberty! Freedom! Tyranny is dead.
Run hence, proclaim, cry it about the streets.

CASSIUS
Some to the common pulpits, and cry out,
Liberty, freedom, and enfranchisement!

BRUTUS
People and senators, be not affrighted,
Fly not, stand still. **Ambition's debt is paid.**

. . .

METELLUS
Stand fast together, lest some friend of Caesar's
Should chance—

BRUTUS
Talk not of standing. Publius, good cheer,
There is no harm intended to your person,
Nor to no Roman else: so tell them Publius.

America is the country of young men

Source: SOCIETY AND SOLITUDE (Chapter 12, "Old Age")
Author: Ralph Waldo Emerson (1803-1882)
First published: 1870
Type of work: Moral essay

Context: Emerson begins this essay by relating how the appearance of former President Josiah Quincy of Harvard at the annual Phi Beta Kappa Society dinner there in 1861 as the oldest living Phi Beta Kappan and oldest living alumnus of Harvard, had caused him to return home to look again at Cicero's famous essay on old age, and to write down his own comments about it. Emerson notes that the trappings of old age are often an illusion, that a gray head of hair, or a bald head, can make a person seem older than he really is. The real value is in what a person has learned —so that some men are old, in a good sense, while still very young in years. He adds that the experience of age is important, pointing out, "Life and art are cumulative; and he who has accomplished something in any department alone deserves to be heard on that subject." He notes that as one approaches old age another advantage is the sense of relief one can enjoy at having escaped so many dangers, even fates. There is also, Emerson says, yet another capital advantage to age, that as one gains years a success more or less signifies not as much to one's self and to those about one. A third benefit or felicity of age is that it has already found the expression that youth so badly wants. And, lastly, Emerson suggests that old age sets its house in order by completing secular affairs. The essayist then notes, as if in contrast:

America is the country of young men, and too full of work hitherto for leisure and tranquillity; yet we have robust centenarians, and examples of dignity and wisdom. I have lately found in an old notebook a record of a visit to ex-President John Adams, in 1825, soon after the election of his son to the Presidency. It is but a sketch, and nothing important passed in the conversation; but it reports a moment in the life of a heroic person, who, in extreme old age, appeared still erect and worthy of his fame.

America is the only idealistic nation in the world

Source: ADDRESS AT SIOUX FALLS (September 8, 1919)
Author: Woodrow Wilson (1856-1924)
First published: 1919
Type of work: Speech

Context: On January 8, 1918, long before World War I was over, Woodrow Wilson delivered an address in which he presented the "Fourteen Points" under which he hoped a lasting peace could be established. When the Germans proposed an armistice, the Allied Powers named Wilson their common spokesman; he accordingly went to Paris to aid in peace negotiations. The previous Congressional election had resulted in a Republican Congress hostile to Wilson's ideals of peace, and there was other opposition to the Fourteen Points, which would commit all men to open diplomacy, freedom of the seas, self-determination of peoples, free trade, free access to harbors, disarmament, and—most important to Wilson—a League of Nations that would settle disputes and guide the world. In spite of the veneration accorded Wilson abroad, it was soon apparent that his ideals represented more self-sacrifice than any nation cared to undertake. He fought for his Fourteen Points but was forced to make concessions. During a brief trip home, he warned his opposition that the League and the Treaty would be so closely interwoven that either both or none would be the choice. He did succeed in his principal goal at Paris; the League of Nations was made a part of the Treaty of Peace. The concessions he made had weakened his position, however, and when he at length presented a completed Treaty to the Senate on July 10, 1919, he met with violent opposition. He continued to fight for his work and his dreams; he made a speaking tour of the country in order to tell the American public, in person, what he was trying to achieve. The grueling schedule sometimes involved several lengthy addresses in one day, and the result was a collapse from which he never really recovered. The following extract, taken from an address given in the Coliseum at Sioux Falls, illustrates both his idealism and his concept of America:

> . . . You cannot establish freedom, my fellow citizens, without force, and the only force you can substitute for an armed mankind is the concerted force of the combined action of mankind through the instrumentality of all the enlightened Governments of the world. . . . Your choice is between the League of Nations and Germanism. I have told you what I mean by Germanism—taking care of yourselves, being armed and ready, having a chip on your shoulder, thinking of nothing but your own rights and never thinking of the rights of anybody else, thinking that you were put into this world to see that American might was asserted and forgetting that American might ought never to be used against the weak, ought never to be used in an unjust cause, ought never to be used for aggression; ought to be used with the heart of humanity beating behind it.
>
> Sometimes people call me an idealist. Well, that is the way I know I am an American. America, my fellow citizens—I do not say it in disparagement of any other great people—**America is the only idealistic Nation in the world.** When I speak practical judgements about business affairs, I can only guess whether I am speaking the voice of America or not, but when I speak the ideal purposes of history I know that I am speaking the voice of America, because I have saturated myself since I was a boy in the records of that spirit, and everywhere in them there is this authentic tone of the love of justice and the service of humanity. . . .

America! thou half-brother of the world!

Source: FESTUS (Scene VIII)
Author: Philip James Bailey (1816-1902)
First published: 1839
Type of work: Philosophical poetic dialogue

Context: Festus is a dialogue between Lucifer and Festus, a character who evidently derives from Christopher Marlowe's Faustus, in that he has a craving to find answers to all the philosophical questions that have vexed the mind of man from the beginning of time. In Scene VIII Lucifer provides two horses, Ruin and Darkness, upon which the pair of speakers ride over the world to perceive the characters of the various lands that they pass. In rapid succession they view France, Spain, Italy,

Greece, Switzerland, Germany, Poland, Russia, Hindustan, and Egypt. They then plunge into the depths of the sea to make their way to America, which is characterized as a compound of something good and something evil found in all of the countries on earth; this compounding of qualities makes America the half-brother of the world. Festus is much concerned that America is a slave-holding country; he prophesies that eventually the slaves will be freed, and then there will be no blot upon the stars of the flag of the country that is dedicated to freedom. In the quotation below the two travelers have just emerged on their horses from the depths of the sea:

LUCIFER

There! now we stand
On the world's-end-land!
Over the hills
Away we go!
Through fire, and snow.
And rivers, whereto
All others are rills.

FESTUS

Through the lands of silver,
The lands of gold;
Through lands untrodden.
And lands untold.

.   .   .

LUCIFER

By strait and bay
We must away;
Through swamp, and plain,
And hurricane;

FESTUS

And that dark cloud of slaves
Which yet may rise;—
Though nought shall blot the bannered stars
From Freedom's skies.
America! thou half-brother of the world!
With something good and bad of every land;
Greater than thee have lost their seat—
Greater scarce none can stand.
Thy flag now flouts the skies,
The highest under Heaven. . . .

39

An amiable weakness

Source: THE SCHOOL FOR SCANDAL (Act V, sc. i)
Author: Richard Brinsley Sheridan (1751-1816)
First published: 1777
Type of work: Dramatic comedy

Context: Sheridan's contemporaries called him "The modern Congreve," after the Restoration master of the comedy of manners, William Congreve (1670–1729). Others, thinking of *Tom Jones* called the characters Joseph and Charles, "the Blifil and Tom Jones of the comedy." Its screen scene has been termed "the best one-act play in the English language." Many pirated editions appeared, but no authorized version was published in England during Sheridan's lifetime. The expression "an amiable weakness" can be found in *Tom Jones* (1749) (X, viii): "The too inordinate fondness of a father . . . must be allowed the name of an amiable weakness," and in Gibbon, *Decline and Fall of the Roman Empire* (1776), where in Chapter XIV the author speaks of "the amiable weakness of human nature." In Sheridan's play, it occurs in the last act when Sir Oliver Surface, returning after fifteen years abroad, is trying to decide which of his two nephews is the more deserving to be his heir. He visits Joseph in the guise of Mr. Stanley, a poor relative, to ask for charity. He has already made a generous present of cash to each of his nephews. The comment of his nephew, Joseph Surface, shows Sir Oliver how little gratitude the young man has, for he lies about his uncle's gifts. He also boasts falsely about his own generosity toward his brother. "Congou tea" is an excellent quality of black tea; avadavats are oriental birds of the finch family; pagodas were Indian gold coins of the period.

JOSEPH

. . . Sir Oliver is a worthy man—a very worthy man; but avarice, Mr. Stanley, is the vice of age. I tell you, my good sir, in confidence, what he has done for me has been a mere nothing—though people, I know, have thought otherwise, and for my part I never chose to contradict the report.

SIR OLIVER

What! has he never transmitted you bullion—rupees—pagodas?

JOSEPH

O, dear sir, nothing of the kind!—No, no—a few presents now and then—china, shawls, congou tea, avadavats, and Indian crackers—little more, believe me.

SIR OLIVER [*aside.*]

Here's gratitude for twelve thousand pounds! Avadavats and Indian crackers!

Then, my dear sir, you have heard, I doubt not, of the extravagance of my brother: There are very few who would credit what I have done for that unfortunate man.

SIR OLIVER [*aside.*]

Not I, for one!

JOSEPH

The sums I have lent him!—Indeed I have been exceedingly to blame; it was **an amiable weakness,** however, I don't pretend to defend it,—and now I feel it doubly culpable since it has deprived me of the pleasure of serving you, Mr. Stanley, as my heart dictates.

SIR OLIVER [*aside.*]

Dissembler! . . .

Among new men, strange faces, other minds

Source: IDYLLS OF THE KING ("The Passing of Arthur," Line 406)
Author: Alfred, Lord Tennyson (1809-1892)
First published: 1869
Type of work: Narrative poem

Context: Sir Bedivere, the last surviving knight of the Round Table, relates the final scenes of the life of King Arthur. First comes the ghost of Gawain, warning of the hollowness of delight and of Arthur's impending death. Second, Modred's forces are pressed back to the western boundary of Lyonesse. Third, is the great battle, fought on winter solstice in a chill white mist in which friend and foe seem like shadows. Only Arthur, Bedivere, and Modred survive the battle. In the last act of his kingship, Arthur slays Modred and receives, himself, a mortal wound. Bedivere bears Arthur to a nearby chapel which has, symbolically, a broken chancel and a broken cross. Arthur, realizing that death is near, asks Bedivere to return his sword, Excalibur, to the water from whence it came. Bedivere, his sense of right and wrong clouded, twice lies to Arthur. The third time, however, he throws the sword into the water and sees it caught by a white hand, which brandishes it three times before taking it down into the mere. Arthur asks to be taken to the edge of the lake. Standing under the winter moon, amid the icy caves, frosty chasms, and bare, black cliffs, they see a dusky barge bearing three black-hooded queens. Arthur is taken aboard. As the barge prepares to cast off, Bedivere asks:

"Ah! My Lord Arthur, whither shall I go?
Where shall I hide my forehead and my eyes?

For now I see the true old times are dead,
When every morning brought a noble chance,
And every chance brought out a noble knight.

· · ·

But now the whole Round Table is dissolved
Which was an image of the mighty world;
And I, the last, go forth companionless,
And the days darken round me, and the years
Among new men, strange faces, other minds."
And slowly answered Arthur from the barge:
"The old order changeth, yielding place to new,
And God fulfills himself in many ways,
Lest one good custom should corrupt the world."

· · ·

And lo! Ben Adhem's name led all the rest

Source: ABOU BEN ADHEM AND THE ANGEL (Last time)
Author: Leigh Hunt (1784-1859)
First published: 1844
Type of work: Lyric poem

Context: As editor of *The Examiner,*
Leigh Hunt recognized and encouraged the poetic ability of Shelley and
Keats. For a slighting comment on
the fat "Adonis of fifty," later George
IV, Hunt was imprisoned for two
years (1813–1815), during which
time his cell was a meeting place for
young radicals. He is chiefly remembered, however, for his light essays
and his delightful autobiography
(1850), though he also wrote and
published many short poems, of
which "Jennie Kissed Me" and
"Abou Ben Adhem" are those best
remembered today. They show his
efforts, as leader of the "Cockney
School of Poetry," toward a colloquial style. In his *Bibliothèque Orien-*
tale (1781), D'Herbelot told the legend of Abou-Ishak Ben Adhem. Hunt
gave it poetic form, perhaps for Mrs.
S. C. Hall's album, though it was first
published in her husband's *Books of
Gems,* Vol. III. It underscores the
idea that a man can show his love of
God and receive His blessing by loving his fellow-men. Abou Ben (son
of) Adhem awakens one night to see
an angel writing in a book of gold. He
asks what the vision is doing, and receives the answer: "Writing the
names of those who love the Lord."
Asked whether Abou's name is there,
the angel replies, "No." "Well, at
least write down my name as one who
loves his fellow-men," Abou insists.

The Angel wrote, and vanished. The next night
It came again with a great wakening light,
And showed the names whom love of God had blessed,
And lo! Ben Adhem's name led all the rest.

42

Another race hath been, and other palms are won

Source: ODE. INTIMATIONS OF IMMORTALITY FROM RECOLLECTIONS OF EARLY CHILDHOOD (Stanza 11)
Author: William Wordsworth (1770-1850)
First published: 1807
Type of work: Ode

Context: In the earlier stanzas of his celebrated ode, Wordsworth has written of his awareness of a loss of freshness and radiance in living and of his temporary grief over the loss. (See "The rainbow comes and goes.") But though he is now in middle age and will not know again "the hour/ Of splendour in the grass, of glory in the flower," he will not grieve but rather find strength in what remains: in "primal sympathy" and compassion for man, in faith, and in the development of a philosophical view. As he concludes his ode, he weighs his losses and his gains and finds himself richer than before. The earth still shows its beauties, and because of what has happened in the growth of his heart and mind, he may still win palms in the remaining race of life:

> I love the Brooks which down their channels fret,
> Even more than when I tripped lightly as they;
> The innocent brightness of a new-born Day
>   Is lovely yet;
> The Clouds that gather round the setting sun
> Do take a sober colouring from an eye
> That hath kept watch o'er man's mortality;
> **Another race hath been, and other palms are won.**
> Thanks to the human heart by which we live,
> Thanks to its tenderness, its joys, and fears,
> To me the meanest flower that blows can give
> Thoughts that do often lie too deep for tears.

Answer came there none

Source: THE BRIDAL OF TRIERMAIN (Canto III, x)
Author: Sir Walter Scott (1771-1832)
First published: 1813
Type of work: Narrative poem

Context: During the early nineteenth century Walter Scott, known for his ballads, narrative poems, and historical novels, captured the Romantic interest in the medieval past. The descendant of a family related to the old Scotch clan of Buccleuch, he cherished the ambition to become a landed aristocrat and attempted to recapture the flamboyancy and magnificence of the past through the construction of the mansion of Abbotsford

43

on the banks of the Tweed. He was known to his readers as "The Wizard of the North" and, until the sudden advent of Byron on the literary scene with the publication of *Childe Harold,* was the most popular writer of his day. One of Scott's later poems, "The Bridal of Triermain," is the first of a long series of nineteenth century treatments of the "Matter of Arthur." Around the Arthurian characters he winds the legend of Sleeping Beauty, thus creating a tone of the marvelous and supernatural which is commonplace to the metrical romance. Lord Roland de Vaux, motivated by a strange and inexplicable sound of the harp, undertakes a perilous journey both to test his chivalry and to search for a bride for Triermain. At one point he must pass through a forbidding valley which, following sunset, takes on a ghastly hue and is filled with strange and shrieking sounds. Dauntless, Roland rushes from his cave-shelter to do battle with whatever adversary there may be, only to find the sounds and the sight a phantasy of the enchanted mind:

> He paused perforce, and blew his horn,
> And on the mountain-echoes borne
> Was heard an answering sound,
> A wild and lonely trumpet-note;
> In middle air it seem'd to float
> High o'er the battled mound;
> And sounds were heard, as when a guard
> Of some proud castle, holding ward,
> Pace forth their nightly round.
> The valiant Knight of Triermain
> Rung forth his challenge-blast again,
> But **answer came there none;**
> And 'mid the mingled wind and rain,
> Darkling he sought the vale in vain,
> Until the dawning shone; . . .

Antony should conquer Antony

Source: ANTONY AND CLEOPATRA (Act IV, sc. xv, ll. 16-17)
Author: William Shakespeare (1564-1616)
First published: 1623
Type of work: Dramatic tragedy

Context: Battling against Octavius Caesar for the right to rule the Roman Empire, Mark Antony is twice defeated, once at the Battle of Actium and again later, near Alexandria. Antony's defeats are caused by his love for Cleopatra. Twice she deserts him in battle, leaving the scene with her forces, and twice he loses a victory because of her defection. Realizing that his love for Cleopatra has cost him victory, the empire, and even his honor, Antony vows revenge, despite his love. But when

44

Cleopatra learns of his anger she sends him the false news of her suicide. These tidings persuade Antony that Cleopatra truly loved him, and in remorse he falls upon his sword, fatally wounding himself. Before he dies, however, members of his guard carry him to the monument where Cleopatra has taken refuge. The dying Antony assures Cleopatra that he dies of his own will, personally unconquered by Octavius Caesar. That he should slay himself is proper, replies Cleopatra.

ANTONY

                                    Peace!
Not Cæsar's valour hath o'erthrown Antony,
But Antony's hath triumph'd on itself.

CLEOPATRA

So it should be, that none but **Antony**
Should conquer Antony, but woe 'tis so!

ANTONY

I am dying, Egypt, dying; only
I here importune death a while, until
Of many thousand kisses the poor last
I lay upon thy lips.

Any nose may ravage with impunity a rose

Source: SORDELLO (Book VI)
Author: Robert Browning (1812-1889)
First published: 1840
Type of work: Narrative poem

Context: The story of Sordello, the forerunner of Dante, is a painful history of a man of imagination born in the midst of civil war and political confusion. As a young man, Sordello tries to change the history of poetry but miserably fails, yet as he grows older, he finds that failure may be success, and turning from his deeply subjective vision joins the political disputes. However, the clash of personal vision and public involvement turns his mind into a feverish mass of contradictions that prevent any peace or happiness. Only when he realizes that there is a life after death can he reconcile himself to his apparent failure; he realizes that earthly fame is pallid beside immortal joy, and he accepts the fact that his vision, however great, was unfulfilled but will inspire others. Having told his painful tale, Browning directly addresses the reader to remind him that a story is more than the immediate reaction it calls up in the reader's mind; in fact, the poem is written so that the revelations of the poet do not come immediately but only after the reader has thought much about the surface story and has come to see that in the poem's obscurity lies the clarity of profound psychological insight.

> Wake up! The ghost's gone, and the story ends
> I'd fain hope, sweetly; seeing, peri or ghoul,
> That spirits are conjectured fair or foul,
> Evil or good, judicious authors think,
> According as they vanish in a stink
> Or in a perfume. Friends, be frank! ye snuff
> Civet, I warrant. Really? Like enough!
> Merely the savor's rareness; **any nose**
> **May ravage with impunity a rose;**
> Rifle a musk-pod and 't will ache like yours!
> I'd tell you that same pungency ensures
> An after-gust, but that were overbold.
> Who would has heard Sordello's story told.

Anybody can be good in the country

Source: THE PICTURE OF DORIAN GRAY (Chapter 19)
Author: Oscar Wilde (1856-1900)
First published: 1891
Type of work: Novel

Context: The relationship between young Dorian Gray and his older friend Lord Henry Wotton resembles that of Faust and his tempter Mephistopheles. Through the influence of Lord Henry, Dorian lives for some years a life that on the surface is filled with sensation and pleasure but that at the same time is destroying his soul. His pleasures bring pain, suffering, and even death to others. At his country home Dorian is hunting one day with a friend who accidentally shoots and kills a man. When Dorian discovers that the dead man is James Vane, who had been pursuing him because he had caused the suicide of Vane's sister eighteen years earlier, he is at first pleased and relieved to be safe from Vane's revenge. Afterward, however, he determines to give up his evil ways, and Lord Henry mocks him:

> . . . "My dear boy," said Lord Henry, smiling, **"anybody can be good in the country.** There are no temptations there. That is the reason why people who live out of town are so absolutely uncivilized. Civilization is not by any means an easy thing to attain to. There are only two ways by which man can reach it. One is by being cultured, the other by being corrupt. Country people have no opportunity of being either, so they stagnate."

The apparel oft proclaims the man

Source: HAMLET (Act I, sc. iii, l. 72)
Author: William Shakespeare (1564-1616)
First published: 1603
Type of work: Dramatic tragedy

Context: With much fatherly advice, Polonius, Lord Chamberlain in the court of Denmark and a tedious old man, sends his son Laertes, returned to Denmark for the coronation of the king, back to Paris, where he has been in school. The main body of the speech follows:

> POLONIUS
> . . . There—my blessing with thee.
> And these few precepts in thy memory
> Look thou character. Give thy thoughts no tongue,
> Nor any unproportioned thought his act.
> Be thou familiar, but by no means vulgar.
> . . .
> Give every man thy ear, but few thy voice;
> Take each man's censure, but reserve thy judgement.
> Costly thy habit as thy purse can buy,
> But not expressed in fancy; rich, not gaudy,
> For **the apparel oft proclaims the man;**
> And they in France of the best rank and station,
> Or of the most select and generous, chief in that.
> . . .
> This above all, to thine own self be true,
> And it must follow, as the night the day,
> Thou canst not then be false to any man.
> Farewell, my blessing season this in thee.

Applaud the hollow ghost which blamed the living man

Source: GROWING OLD (Stanza 7)
Author: Matthew Arnold (1822-1888)
First published: 1867
Type of work: Lyric poem

Context: With a definite note of melancholy and irony, this poem discusses the physical and emotional developments characteristic of the aging process. Growing old is characterized by loss of vitality and strength as well as of a vision for the future. Feeling and sensitivity fade into nothingness. "Ah, 'tis not what in youth we dream'd 'twould be!" The days stretch out into meaningless hours. But, as the final lines tell us, when an old person does die, the world finally remembers he has been a living man and commemorates him with a funeral. The irony lies in the fact that the world that gave the old person no praise, only blame, while he was living lavishes attention upon him after he has no need of it.

It is—last stage of all—
When we are frozen up within, and quite
The phantom of ourselves,
To hear the world **applaud the hollow ghost**
Which blamed the living man.

Apples of gold for the king's daughter

Source: THE KING'S DAUGHTER (Line 4)
Author: Algernon Charles Swinburne (1837-1909)
First published: 1866
Type of work: Literary ballad

Context: In their search for inspiration that might give poetry a new foundation, the Romantic poets frequently turned to the Middle Ages where they discovered the almost forgotten traditional ballad. The ballad was adopted as a medium through which the nineteenth century poet could create a literature of mysteriously enchanting beauty such as Keats' "La Belle Dame sans Merci" or Coleridge's "Ancient Mariner." Swinburne, more than any other British poet, came to the ballad tradition with an ear for the rhythm and an eye for the form; as a result, he created literary ballads that are unique in English poetry, for they capture the primitivism of the traditional ballad as well as their form and brevity of expression. This poem, one of his most successful ballads, is a chant in which nine sisters give their gifts to the daughter of the king, their niece; the unlimited jealousy that the women still have because they were not chosen by the king's son slowly unfolds as the gifts become more and more curses.

We were ten maidens in the green corn,
    Small red leaves in the mill-water:
Fairer maidens never were born,
    Apples of gold for the king's daughter.

We were ten maidens by a well-head,
    Small white birds in the mill-water:
Sweeter maidens never were wed,
    Rings of red for the king's daughter.

48

The appropriate title of "agnostic"

Source: SCIENCE AND CHRISTIAN TRADITION (Chapter 7)
Author: Thomas Henry Huxley (1825-1895)
First published: 1889 (Chapter 7)
Type of work: Essay

Context: Huxley was an English biologist and teacher who became famous through his defense of Darwin's evolutionary theories. He lectured widely and wrote a number of works designed to popularize science. In addition he produced a number of writings in which he examines Scripture critically and with some effort at scientific detachment. He once engaged in a controversy with Gladstone, the British statesman, in which theories of evolution were compared with Biblical tradition. Huxley's opinions are elaborated in a group of essays written from 1887 to 1892; these were collected and published in one volume under the title, *Science and Christian Tradition.* Huxley considered himself an agnostic, and in his essay on agnosticism, which forms Chapter 7, he explains how he came to invent the term. Before doing so, however, he retraces the history of his thinking in regard to Christian Scripture, particularly the Gospels. This essay was written primarily in reply to Dr. Wace, Principal of King's College, who had stated flatly that an agnostic and an infidel are one and the same. Huxley's reply is to the effect that he does not know the truth but is searching for it in a scientific manner. He notes that the Gospels were written some time subsequent to the death of Jesus, and that variant texts all reveal additions and elaborations by their transcribers; that it is therefore difficult to determine precisely what Jesus actually said and did; and that early Christian rites and customs differed greatly from those of our own time. He can prove nothing either way; and if he must be faithful, then to which of the many Christian doctrines? Huxley then tells his readers how the term "agnostic" originated:

When I reached intellectual maturity and began to ask myself whether I was an atheist, a theist, or a pantheist; a materialist or an idealist; a Christian or a freethinker; I found that the more I learned and reflected, the less ready was the answer; until, at last, I came to the conclusion that I had neither art nor part with any of these denominations, except the last. The one thing in which most of these good people were agreed was the one thing in which I differed from them. They were quite sure they had attained a certain "gnosis,"—had, more or less successfully, solved the problem of existence; while I was quite sure I had not, and had a pretty strong conviction that the problem was insoluble. . . .

This was my situation when I had the good fortune to find a place among the members of that remarkable confraternity of antagonists, long since deceased, but of green and pious memory, the Metaphysical Society. Every variety of philosophical and theological opinion was represented there, and expressed itself with entire openness; most of my colleagues were -*ists* of one sort or another; and, however kind and friendly they might be, I, the man without a rag of a label to cover himself with, could not fail to have some . . . uneasy feelings . . . So I took thought, and invented what I conceived to be **the appropriate title of "agnostic."** It came into my head as suggestively antithetic to the "gnostic" of Church history, who professed to know so much about the very things of which I was ignorant. . . . To my great satisfaction, the term took, . . .

That is the history of the origin of the terms "agnostic" and "agnosticism. . . ."

Aristocracy of the Moneybag

Source: THE FRENCH REVOLUTION (Vol. II, Book IX, chapter 7)
Author: Thomas Carlyle (1795-1881)
First published: 1837
Type of work: History

Context: Carlyle was determined to be a historian. Frustrated in his purpose to enter the clergy according to the wishes of his parents, and by a revulsion against eighteenth century rationalism, he shifted to the study of law. However, he found it dull reading in the office of an Edinburgh lawyer. Frustration brought on illness and a breakdown which he cured with a new interest. He learned German and began delving into German philosophy and literature that gradually introduced him to the idea of an orderly universe and an immanent and friendly God, postulated by Fichte and Goethe. He capitalized on his experiences in his spiritual autobiography, *Sartor Resartus,* appearing first in a magazine in 1835, as an attack on the materialization of his era. Carlyle's knowledge of German led to assignments as book reviewer for several magazines. Generally each book served as text for a biographical essay on its subject. The success of *Sartor Resartus* permitted him and his wife

to move to London, where they found a house near the British Museum, and he began reading and note-taking for his most ambitious work, *The French Revolution: A History.* His tragedy with the first draft is literary history. Having completed his Volume I, he took his only copy to get the opinion of his friend, John Stuart Mill (1806 –1873) philosopher and economist, with special interest in France. A stupid maid, seeing a pile of scribbled papers in her employer's study, burned them. However, Carlyle started his task again and by 1837 had completed the two volumes. In his essays and lectures, Carlyle frequently expressed the opinion that great men were the causes of great movements and human progress. He saw the French Revolution as evidence of man's divinity exemplified by the deeds of its great leaders. And so his history is actually a series of portraits of those involved. But added to them, to give brilliancy to his story, are graphic recreations of great scenes of

50

the Revolution, the assassination of Marat by Charlotte Corday, the execution of Marie Antoinette, the capture of the Bastille, so exciting that occasional distortions of history pass unnoticed. For the writing of *Sartor Resartus,* Carlyle devised a Teutonic sort of English; for his French Revolution, his style is more vivacious French-English, with exclamations, questions, comments to the reader, quotations in French, and an abundance of footnotes that show the extent of his preparatory reading. His thesis that the aristocracy of blood and documents was wiped out by an aristocracy of money appears early in his history. In Chapter 7 of Book VII, the author declares: ". . . (Demoiselle) Thèroigne had bags of money, which she distributed over Flandre:—furnished by whom? Alas, with money-bags, one seldom sits on insurrectionary cannon. Calumnious Royalism!" In the last book of his second volume, Carlyle reverts to this idea:

> . . . Confused wreck of a Republic of Poverties, which ended in Reign of Terror, is arranging itself into such composure as it can. Evangel of Jean-Jacques, and most other Evangels, become incredible, what is there for it but to return to the old Evangel of Mammon? *Contrat-Social is true or untrue.* Brotherhood is Brotherhood or Death, but money always will buy money's worth; in the wreck of human dubitations, this remains indubitable, that Pleasure is pleasant. Aristocracy of Feudal Parchment has passed away with a mighty rushing; and now, by a natural course, we arrive at **Aristocracy of the Moneybag.** . . . Apparently a still baser sort of Aristocracy? An infinitely baser; the basest yet known.

Aroint thee witch the rump-fed ronyon cries

Source: MACBETH (Act I, sc. iii, l. 6)
Author: William Shakespeare (1564-1616)
First published: 1623
Type of work: Dramatic tragedy

Context: Macbeth and Banquo, generals in the army of King Duncan of Scotland, pass along a heath near Forres as they return home from a battle in which they have successfully put down a rebellion against the king. Three witches await their approach to pronounce the words of prophecy that Macbeth, who is Thane of Glamis, will bear the titles of Thane of Cawdor and finally king, and that the heirs of Banquo will ascend the throne. As the witches wait, they discuss their day's adventures, the first witch filling her sisters with indignation as she tells them of the way a despicable, mangy (ronyon) sailor's wife, fat-bottomed from eating refuse (rump-fed) refused to share with her the chestnuts she is eating, yelling at her to be gone.

51

A sailor's wife had chestnuts in her lap,
And munched, and munched, and munched.
  Give me, quoth I.
Aroint thee witch the rump-fed ronyon cries.
Her husband's to Aleppo gone, master o'th' Tiger;
But in a sieve I'll thither sail,
And like a rat without a tail,
I'll do, I'll do, and I'll do.

Art never expresses anything but itself

Source: THE DECAY OF LYING
Author: Oscar Wilde (1856-1900)
First published: 1889
Type of work: Literary essay

Context: To support a wife, Oscar Wilde became editor of *The Woman's World,* a position that kept him in funds and allowed him to indulge in his favorite sport of talking. The loss of that job drove him to the writing of magazine articles, usually *résumés* of his monologues. One was "The Decay of Lying," later included in *Intentions* (1891). In it he pleaded for imagination and the *beau ideal* instead of the crude and raw life of the realists. While the essay established his reputation among critics, it seemed to the average Englishman more like a cynical defense of mendacity. Its form is a Plantonic dialogue between Vivian and Cyril, in a country house in Nottinghamshire. Vivian reads his unfinished essay, while Cyril interrupts and objects. Vivian sees Art not as holding a mirror up to Nature, but as revealing Nature's imperfections and lack of design. To him, Art does not imitate Life; Life imitates Art. His arguments almost convince Cyril.

CYRIL—You have proved it to my dissatisfaction. But even admitting this strange imitative instinct in Life and Nature, surely you would acknowledge that Art expresses the temper of its age, the spirit of its time, the moral and social conditions that surround it, and under whose influence it is produced.

VIVIAN—Certainly not! **Art never expresses anything but itself.** This is the principle of my new aesthetics; and it is this, more than that vital connection between form and substance, on which Mr. Pater dwells, that makes Music the type of all the arts. . . .

The art of pleasing consists in being pleased

Source: THE ROUND TABLE ("On Manner")
Author: William Hazlitt (1778-1830)
First published: 1817
Type of work: Essay

52

Context: Hazlitt was very much an individualist, and his free-ranging style is essentially his own. His lack of formal education and the narrow limits of his reading furnished ammunition to his enemies, of whom he had many; he admitted the truth of their charges but was not cowed by them. A lover of art in all its forms, he felt that his function as a critic was to sense what is good in art and to furnish reasons for the faith he had in it. Thus his critical opinions depended less on knowledge than on his "depth of taste," as his friend Keats evaluated it. This faculty seldom went astray; Hazlitt's judgements of his contemporaries usually anticipate those of posterity. As an essayist he commands a respectable place in English literature. *The Round Table,* similar to a number of other volumes by him, is a collection of essays on a variety of subjects. Hazlitt's usual method is to begin with a specific idea and then to follow it with a rapid series of examples and associations; this, together with his terseness and clarity, gives the writing a sense of excitement. He does not usually end with a definite conclusion. In the essay, "On Manner," Hazlitt begins by noting that Lord Chesterfield believed manner was more important than matter; and he adds that the practice of the world seems to bear this opinion out. He then defines his terms: "What any person says or does is one thing; the mode in which he says or does it is another. The last of these is what we understand by *manner*." He then presents a rush of examples. Manner is involuntary or incidental, betraying our sincerity or lack of it; the way we confer a favor is often far more valuable than the favor itself; the difference between a good actor and bad one is the manner in which the part is played. He then discusses humor:

. . . The same story told by two different persons shall, from the difference of the manner, either set the table in a roar, or not relax a feature in the whole company. We sometimes complain (perhaps rather unfairly) that particular persons possess more vivacity than wit. But we ought to take into the account, that their very vivacity arises from their enjoying the joke; and their humouring a story by drollery of gesture or archness of look, shews only that they are acquainted with the different ways in which the sense of the ludicrous expresses itself. It is not the mere dry jest, but the relish which the person himself has of it, with which we sympathise. For in all that tends to pleasure and excitement, the capacity for enjoyment is the principal point. One of the most pleasant and least tiresome persons of our acquaintance is a humourist, who has three or four quaint witticisms and proverbial phrases, which he always repeats over and over; but he does this with just the same vivacity and freshness as ever, so that you feel the same amusement with less effort than if he had startled his hearers with a succession of original conceits. Another friend of ours, who never fails to give vent to one or two real *jeu-d'esprits* every time you meet him, from the pain with which he is delivered of them, and the uneasiness he seems to suffer all the rest of the time, makes a much more interesting than comfortable companion. If

53

you see a person in pain for himself, it naturally puts you in pain for him. **The art of pleasing consists in being pleased.** To be amiable is to be satisfied with one's self and others. Good-humour is essential to pleasantry.

Art remains the one way possible of speaking truth

Source: THE RING AND THE BOOK (Book XII, "The Book and the Ring," Line 842)
Author: Robert Browning (1812-1889)
First published: 1868-1869
Type of work: Dramatic monologue

Context: It is fitting that Browning concludes his longest work with one of his favorite observations about art. Because men live in a world that they experience only through their senses and because the senses are not always reliable, no two men will agree about the world. The differences in opinion about the most trivial experiences are, therefore, essentially the same as the controversies between philosophers or theologians. Art, unlike the disputers, speaks obliquely, addressing all men so that, while there may remain disagreement, the underlying truth of the human condition is apparent. In *The Ring and the Book* Browning has illustrated this belief by telling the story of the Roman murder trial from different, often divergent, points of view, leaving to the reader the responsibility of sifting the evidence to reach a conclusion. Like the human condition, the truth of the murder case is hidden within the differing reports, and only the skillful mind has the ability of figuring out the truth.

So, British Public, who may like me yet,
(Marry and amen!) learn one lesson hence
Of many which whatever lives should teach:
This lesson, that our human speech is nought,
Our human testimony false, our fame
And human estimation words and wind.
Why take the artistic way to prove so much?
Because, it is the glory and good of Art,
That **Art remains the one way possible
Of speaking truth,** to mouths like mine at least.

Arts to rule as they desired

Source: THE SCHOLAR-GYPSY (Stanza 5)
Author: Matthew Arnold (1822-1888)
First published: 1853
Type of work: Philosophical poem

Context: As in many of his works, Arnold in this poem is trying to teach the people of his age. He wanted men to have a better view of life, to understand the futility of meanness of mind, to understand the glory of living an enlightened life. In this poem he begins by having the narrator imagining himself on a hill above Oxford, on a summer day, looking down from a corner of a field to the towers of the university. Beside the speaker of the poem is a book, identifiable as Joseph Glanvil's *Vanity of Dogmatizing* (1661), in which is found the story of an Oxford student forced by his poverty to leave the university, whereupon he joins a band of gypsies. Arnold transforms the young man of Glanvil's tale into an ideal, a young man who rejects his own time and seeks higher goals. The fifth stanza of the poem relates how two of the scholar-gypsy's former fellow students met him in a country lane, how they asked him of his new life, and how he replied to them.

> But once, years after, in the country-lanes,
> Two scholars, whom at college erst he knew,
> Met him, and of his way of life enquired;
> Whereat he answered, that the gypsy-crew,
> His mates, had **arts to rule as they desired**
> The workings of men's brains,
> And they can bind them to what thoughts they will.
> "And I," he said, "the secret of their art,
> When fully learn'd, will to the world unpart;
> But it needs heaven-sent moments for this skill."

As far as angel's ken

Source: PARADISE LOST (Book I, l. 59)
Author: John Milton (1608-1674)
First published: 1667
Type of work: Epic poem

Context: Milton asks his epic question, who seduced our original parents into disobeying God? The answer is, the infernal serpent, whose pride had cast him out of heaven; with him there fell a host of rebel angels. Satan, motivated by envy of God and by the desire to be revenged on Him for what he considered injustice, deceived Eve, the mother of all mankind. For his revolt, God hurled him and his cohorts out of heaven, down to bottomless perdition, there to dwell in adamant chains and penal fire. Milton here was probably drawing on the classical account of Zeus's hurling of the defeated Titans into the underworld, where they were perpetually imprisoned. Milton, however, quickly abandons the idea of the unbreakable chains—if he ever had it—as the devils are free to travel through the universe, especially up to the earth. But for nine days the devils lie stunned on a fiery lake. "Ken," usually "knowledge," is here "range of view."

Nine times the space that measures day and night
To mortal men, he with his horrid crew
Lay vanquished, rolling in the fiery gulf,
Confounded though immortal: but his doom
Reserved him to more wrath; for now the thought
Both of lost happiness and lasting pain
Torments him; round he throws his baleful eyes
That witnessed huge affliction and dismay,
Mixed with obdúrate pride and steadfast hate:
At once **as far as angel's ken** he views
The dismal situation waste and wild,
A dungeon horrible, on all sides round
As one great furnace flamed, yet from those flames
No light, but rather darkness visible
Served only to discover sights of woe,
Regions of sorrow, doleful shades, where peace
And rest can never dwell, hope never comes
That comes to all; . . .

As fresh as is the month of May

Source: THE CANTERBURY TALES (Prologue, l. 92)
Author: Geoffrey Chaucer (1343?-1400)
First transcribed: c. 1387-1392
Type of work: Collection of tales

Context: Little is known with certainty about the life of Geoffrey Chaucer. He was probably born in London, but when? In 1386, while a witness concerning a coat of arms, he testified that he was "forty years of age and more," which would make his birthyear nearer 1343 than the traditional date of 1340. He also said he had "born arms for twenty-seven years." Part of this service included his year in France with the English army, in 1359–1360, during the Hundred Years War. It was not a very important campaign, but in one of the skirmishes, at Réthal, near Rheims, he was captured. The amount of his ransom, £16, amounting to about $2,400 today, indicates Chaucer's importance, when common soldiers were freed for a pound or two. After a gap of six years, Chaucer's history can be picked up again, as a yeoman in the household of King Edward III. In 1368, he was an esquire; and in 1369, in the army of John of Gaunt, he took part in a raid on Picardy, along with 600 men at arms and 150 other members of the king's household. This part of his life may well have been in his mind when he included a squire among those on the Pilgrimage from London to Canterbury. The Squire, too, had been on a military expedition in Flanders, Artois, and Picardy. There are thirty in the group, twenty-eight Pilgrims, the host of the Tabard Inn at Southward, across the Thames River from London, and the author. To entertain themselves on the journey to the tomb of Thomas à Becket, each agrees to tell two stories, and two more on the return trip. Actually only twenty-two of the proposed 120 appear in Chaucer's volume, set down in iambic pentameter. The Prologue, introducing the members of the company, declares that in April when the showers wake up nature, birds sing, the crops begin growing, and people like to go on pilgrimages. By his selection of pilgrims, Chaucer gave a complete panorama of the English social classes of his day, from the clergy and knights to the humble plowman. The Knight, though the highest in rank of all the pilgrims, is modest and prudent. Chivalry was on the decline in the fourteenth century, but Chaucer makes his Knight an ideal character, untouched by satire. Though veteran of wars for king and religion all over the known world, he is dressed in sober garb and accompanied by only two retainers, a yeoman clad in green, and his son of about twenty, who had also fought in several campaigns. His duty as Squire is to attend his father and carry his lance. His dress is the height of fashion, and he has the courtly accomplishments. He can sing and play the flute. Though he loves the ladies so passionately that at night he sleeps no more than a nightingale does, he is as fresh as May, that month of beauty and flowers used by many poets in their similes. Tennyson in his *Idylls of the King,* commands: "Blow, Trumpet, for the world is white with May." Many poets have written of the "Merry month of May," and only an occasional cynic like Lowell declares: "May is a pious fraud of the almanac." Chaucer says about the Squire:

With hym ther was his sonne, a yong SQUIER,
A lovyere and a lusty bacheler
With lokkes crulle, as they were leyd in presse.
Of twenty yeer of age he was, I gesse.
Of his stature he was of evene lengthe,
And wonderly delyvere and of greet strengthe.
And he hadde been somtyme in chivachye
In Flaundres, in Artoys, and Pycardie,
And born hym weel, as of so litel space,
In hope to stonden in his lady grace.
Embrouded was he, as it were a meede,
Al full of fresshe floures, whyte and rede.
Syngynge he was or floytynge, al the day
He was **as fressh as is the monthe of May.**

As fresh as paint

Source: FRANK FAIRLEGH (Chapter 41)
Author: Francis Edward Smedley (1818-1864)
First published: 1850
Type of work: Novel

Context: Smedley was just one of the   many writers of the Victorian era who produced a vast number of exceedingly sentimental novels which were quickly bought up by a sentimental reading public and as quickly forgotten. Since, says the author of this novel, many volumes have appeared concerned with " 'Schoolboy Days' and 'College Life,' " but none concerned with "the mysteries of that paradise of public-school-fearing mammas—a 'Private Tutor's,' " this novel was produced to fill that void.

It chronicles the adventures in the life of a private pupil. In Chapter 41, Oaklands, a friend of the hero, laments that Fairlegh's sister seems very apathetic and lacking in interest in anything and asserts that he shall raise her spirits by having her ride horseback every day. Oaklands, who has been very ill, is overheard by Lawless, who has entered unperceived and misunderstands the context:

"Horseback, eh!" exclaimed Lawless, who had entered the cottage without our perceiving him. "Ay, that's a prescription better than all your doctor's stuff; clap her on a side-saddle, and a brisk canter for a couple of hours every day across country will set the old lady up again in no time, if it's your mother that's out of condition, Frank. Why, Oaklands, man, you are looking **as fresh as paint**; getting sound again, wind and limb, eh?"

As full of valor as of kindness

Source: KING HENRY THE FIFTH (Act IV, sc. iii, l. 15)
Author: William Shakespeare (1564-1616)
First published: 1600
Type of work: Historical drama

Context: The English army begins battle at Agincourt against the forces of France in a contest in which King Henry of England eventually gains the crown of France. Some of the English leaders, speaking briefly before going into battle, note that the French have three thousand troops, or five to each English soldier. The Duke of Bedford and the Earl of Exeter bid farewell to the Earl of Salisbury as he leaves for battle:

BEDFORD
Farewell good Salisbury, and good luck go with thee.

EXETER
Farewell kind lord; fight valiantly to-day.
And yet I do thee wrong, to mind thee of it,
For thou art framed of the firm truth of valor.
[*Exit* SALISBURY.]

BEDFORD
He is **as full of valour as of kindness;**
Princely in both.

58

As hardy as the Nemean lion's nerve

Source: HAMLET (Act I, sc. iv, l. 83)
Author: William Shakespeare (1564-1616)
First published: 1603
Type of work: Dramatic tragedy

Context: In the frosty night before the castle at Elsinore, Hamlet encounters the ghost of his father. He is bursting with impatience to know what the purpose of the apparition is: "What may this mean. . . . What should we do?" But the ghost wishes to speak to Hamlet in private, and since others are present—the sentinels and Hamlet's friend, Horatio—the spirit beckons Hamlet away. However, no one knows, at this point, whether the spirit is the ghost of Hamlet's father or a demon in his father's shape; therefore, the prince's companions warn Hamlet against following. But Hamlet insists that he will follow. He hears his destiny calling, and every artery in his body feels as bold as the great lion whose slaying was the first of the Twelve Labors of Hercules, and he insists that he will create another ghost of anyone who hinders—"lets"—him:

> HAMLET
> It waves me still.
> Go on; I'll follow thee.
>
> MARCELLUS
> You shall not go my lord.
>
> HAMLET
> Hold off your hands.
>
> HORATIO
> Be ruled, you shall not go.
>
> HAMLET
> My fate cries out,
> And makes each petty artery in this body
> **As hardy as the Nemean lion's nerve.**
> Still am I called. Unhand me gentlemen—
> By heaven I'll make a ghost of him that lets me.
> I say, away!—Go on, I'll follow thee.
> *[Exeunt* GHOST *and* HAMLET.]

As he who, seeking asses, found a kingdom

Source: PARADISE REGAINED (Book III, l. 242)
Author: John Milton (1608-1674)
First published: 1671
Type of work: Epic poem

Context: Christ in the wilderness is tempted by Satan, first with great luxury and second with wealth and earthly power that will provide fame. Christ resists both of these temptations and points out that both Job and Socrates achieved great glory by entirely peaceful means; military conquerors, He says, are mere destroyers. He says that he seeks not his own glory but the glory of Him that sent him. But Satan does not easily give up the chance to seduce Christ with the prospect of glory, which, he says, God the Father himself receives, but Christ rebuts this argument by pointing out that God's glory is a by-product of His goodness, for which He desires only thanks. This argument strikes Satan dumb, as he had fallen from heaven through his desire for glory. Recovering his presence of mind, he urges that Christ assume the kingdom that he is to inherit. Christ says that that is no concern of Satan's, and His assuming of His kingdom will be Satan's destruction. Satan, however, says that perhaps Christ hesitates because of a lack of worldly experience; after all, He has hardly seen the towns that neighbor his own home. The wisest, he says, will be fearful to act if they lack experience: Saul, a simple country boy, hunted asses and found a kingdom. (I Samuel, 9) Satan says:

> The world thou hast not seen, much less her glory,
> Empires, and monarchs, and their radiant courts,
> Best school of best experience, quickest in sight
> In all things that to greatest actions lead.
> The wisest, unexperienced, will be ever
> Timorous and loth, with novice modesty,
> **(As he who seeking asses found a kingdom)**
> Irresolute, unhardly, unadventurous:
> But I will bring thee where thou soon shalt quit
> Those rudiments, and see before thine eyes
> The monarchies of earth, their pomp and state,
> Sufficient introduction to inform
> Thee, of thyself so apt, in regal arts,
> And regal mysteries; that thou mayst know
> How best their opposition to withstand.

As many men, so many minds

Source: PHORMIO (Act III, sc. iii)
Author: Terence (Publius Terentius Afer, c. 190-159 B.C.)
First transcribed: Second century, B.C.
Type of work: Dramatic comedy

Context: Demipho, an aged Athenian, goes abroad, leaving his grown son at home in Athens. During the father's absence, the son, named Antipho, marries Phanium without his father's consent, an act unheard of in classical times. Upon Demipho's return he is righteously angry about his son's marriage, and becomes even angrier when Antipho refuses to come

60

to explain the matter to him. In his anger and his anxiety, Demipho turns to his three legal advisers—Hegio, Crito, and Cratinus—for their opinions on what to do in the matter, hoping they can give him advice about what action to take. When Hegio speaks in his turn, he makes the comment about the diversity of men's opinions. The comment has been translated variously, although always with the same meaning.

DEMIPHO

You see how matters stand? What shall I do? Tell me, Hegio.

HEGIO

I? I think Cratinus ought to give his opinion, if you have no objection.

DEMIPHO

Tell me, Cratinus.

. . .

CRATINUS

Well, I think you should do what is best; what this son of yours has done in your absence should be undone. In that way you will secure justice. . . .

DEMIPHO

Now you, Hegio.

HEGIO

I believe that Cratinus has spoken with good sense. But it's a fact that **"As many men, so many minds"**: each man after his own fashion. Now, it doesn't seem to me that what has been done by law can be undone; and it's wrong to try to change it.

As savage as a bear with a sore head

Source: THE KING'S OWN (Chapter 26)
Author: Frederick Marryat (1792-1848)
First published: 1830
Type of work: Novel

Context: Twenty-six volumes are included in the standard edition of works by Captain Marryat. Son of a member of Parliament, young Frederick several times ran away from school until finally at the age of fourteen, he was allowed to join the British navy. There he served against Napoleon and in the Burmese War, and reached the rank of Commander. However, his articles attacking the system of recruiting by press gangs lost him favor, and he resigned in 1829, to spend the rest of his life as a writer. *The King's Own* is his only tragic novel; and it has a more artful plot than his other books. Its hero is drawn from the novelist's second and favorite son, William, who died at the age of seven. Captain M——is a portrait of his first commander, Lord Cochrane, later admiral of Chile's navy during its struggle for independence. The book was completed on shipboard, during a six weeks' charting expedition in the Atlantic. The novelist's variety of interests may explain its many digressions. The book's most famous scene, the sea fight and shipwreck, is patterned on a naval battle between the French and English in 1797. Though the novel will never be as popular as Marryat's *Peter Simple* or *Mr. Midshipman Easy,* many critics consider it his best work. Chapter 26 contains one of the digressions, a story told by the coxswain Marshall, to Surgeon Macallan. On a previous ship, a pet cat had made dirt on the master's sextant case. Though usually even-tempered, the captain has ordered the crew to kill the cat. None of the sailors is willing, but finally, under the captain's eye and in order to keep the ship's deck clean, the cat is thrown overboard and shot while in the water.

"Well, sir, I never seed a ship's company in such a farmant, or such a nitty kicked up 'tween decks, in my life . . . all agrees that no good would come to the ship a'ter that, and very melancholy they were, and couldn't forget it.

"Well, sir, our sailing orders come down the next day, and the first cutter is sent on shore for the captain, and six men out of ten leave the boat, and I'm sure that it warn't for desartion, but all along of that cat being hove overboard and butchered in that way —for three on 'em were messmates of mine, . . . and if they had had a mind to quit the sarvice, I should have know'd it. The captain was **as savage as a bear with a sore head,** and did nothing but growl for three days afterwards, and it was well to keep clear on him, for he snapped right and left, like a mad dog."

As she would catch another Antony in her strong toil of grace

Source: ANTONY AND CLEOPATRA (Act V, sc. ii, ll. 350-351)
Author: William Shakespeare (1564-1616)
First published: 1623
Type of work: Dramatic tragedy

Context: The love of Antony, one of the reigning triumvirs of the Roman Empire, and Cleopatra, voluptuous Queen of Egypt, has run its course, with Antony, dead from his own sword and Cleopatra from a poisonous snake. Caesar, in Egypt to carry its mighty queen back to Rome as a display for his own grandeur, views the bodies of Cleopatra and her attendants, unmarred by the venom of the asp.

62

CAESAR

O noble weakness!
If they had swallowed poison, 'twould appear
By external swelling; but she looks like sleep,
As she would catch another Antony
In her strong toil of grace.

DOLABELLA

Here on her breast,
There is a vent of blood, and something blown.
The like is on her arm.

FIRST GUARD

This is an aspic's trail, and these fig-leaves
Have slime upon them, such as the aspic leaves
Upon the caves of Nile.

CAESAR

Most probable
That so she died; for her physician tells me
She hath pursued conclusions infinite
Of easy ways to die. . . .

As sober as a judge

Source: DON QUIXOTE IN ENGLAND (III, xiv)
Author: Henry Fielding (1707-1754)
First published: 1734
Type of work: Dramatic comedy

Context: Fielding began this comedy in 1728, then was dissuaded from completing it by his actor friends Booth and Cibber. However, when Drury Lane actors needed a play in a hurry, he resurrected it, completed it, and saw it performed at the New Theatre. Sancho Panza and Don Quixote enter an English inn where they find people as mad as they are. Each scene ends with a song by one of the actors. As in the Cervantes' novel, Don Quixote believes that since he is a knight-errant, the world owes him a living. The point of the play is expressed in one of its songs:

"The more we see of human kind,
The more deceits and tricks we find,
    In every land as well as Spain."

Squire Badger is important in the coming elections; also being rich, he is sought as husband for Dorothea, the daughter of Sir Thomas Loveland, though she in turn loves Fairlove. Don Quixote also loves her. In this scene of Act III, Sir Thomas goes to Badger to arrange a marriage, but the squire reveals himself as such a bore that Dorothea's father agrees to let his daughter marry her true love, Fairlove. "Oons" and " 'sbud"

63

are euphemisms for the oaths "God's Wounds," and "God's Blood!" A be- wigged judge sitting in court certainly gives the impression of being sober.

SQUIRE BADGER

Oons! what's the matter with you all? Is the devil in the inn, that you won't let a man sleep? I was as fast on the table, as if I had been in a feather bed. 'Sbud, what's the matter? Where's my Lord Slang?

SIR THOMAS LOVELAND

Dear squire, let me entreat you would go to bed; you are a little heated with wine.

SQUIRE BADGER

Oons, sir, do you say that I am drunk? I say, sir, that I am **as sober as a judge;** and if any man say that I am drunk, sir, he's a liar.

As sure as death

Source: EVERY MAN IN HIS HUMOUR (Act II, sc. i, l. 119)
Author: Ben Jonson (1573?-1637)
First published: 1598
Type of work: Dramatic comedy

Context: In the title *Every Man in his Humour,* the word humour means whim or quirk of behavior; consequently, the play is filled with characters who consistently pursue courses of action in accordance with their ruling follies. Some of the characters are Old Knowell, who has the confidence of action produced by the belief that he knows everything; Edward Knowell, his son, around whom most of the action centers; Brainworm, a mad, rascally servant who is a prime mover of the action; Master Stephen, a loutish country cousin of Edward Knowell who has the humour to be a city dandy; Master Matthew, a city gull, or fool, who wishes to be a gentleman poet; Captain Bobadill, a braggart soldier who is at heart a coward; Wellborn, a city sophisticate, companion of Edward Knowell; Kitely, a cowardly merchant; and Squire Downright, a forthright and plain-speaking, no-nonsense fellow. In Act I, scene i of the play, Kitely is complaining to Downright of the way in which his lodger, Wellborn, acts; he has turned Kitely's house into a tavern or a stews by introducing into it his ritous companions. They mock Kitely and say that he is jealous in his behavior because he has recently married a young and pretty wife and lodges her attractive sister in his house also—as sure as death they say it!

64

Whilst they, sir, to relieve him in the fable,
Make their loose comments upon every word,
Gesture, or look, I use; mock me all over,
From my flat cap unto my shining shoes;
And, out of their impetuous rioting phant'sies,
Beget some slander that shall dwell with me.
And what would that be, think you? marry, this:
They would give out, because my wife is fair,
Myself but lately married, and my sister
Here sojourning a virgin in my house,
That I am jealous!—nay, **as sure as death,**
That they would say: and how that I had quarelled
My brother purposely, thereby to find
An apt pretext to banish them my house.

At the feet of Gamaliel

Source: ACTS 22:3
Author: Unknown (traditionally Luke)
First transcribed: 60-150 (probably c. 80-90)
Type of work: Religious history and tradition

Context: The Acts of the Apostles is the only contemporary account of the early Christian Church and its beginnings which remains to us. Its author may or may not have been Luke the physician; in any case he evidently wrote both Luke and Acts, and it is probable that Luke supplied much of the material. Acts begins with the Resurrection and the commission Jesus laid upon His apostles, then tells the story of their missionary activities. It is an inspiring record of struggle and of moral courage, and of the growth of an institution. Chapters 15 through 28 cover the efforts of Paul. The story of his career as wandering evangelist is eloquent testimony of the difficulties these early missionaries had to face. His travels took him through Syria, Greece, and into Asia Minor. It was his custom to enter the synagogues in cities which had them, and there to argue scripture with the Jews. He preached publicly, labored when necessary to sustain life, and persevered with great singlemindedness in the face of hardship and widespread hostility. To be an evangelist in the time of the apostles was to accept persecution and strife, and to thrive on it if possible. In Thessalonica, Paul was the center of a riot when ruffians were persuaded, or hired, to break up the activities of the Christians; the agitators followed him to Berea. Much later, in Ephesus, he was again the focal point of a riot started by silversmiths who feared his success at winning converts would stop the sale of figurines representing Diana, and thus wreck their business. After he leaves Ephesus Paul insists, in spite of warnings, on going to Jerusalem. Here he is recognized and accused in the temple by persons who have seen him in Asia Minor; he is dragged from the temple by a mob and the centurions arrive to conduct him to prison. He gains permission to tell the people how he became a Christian; they are not appeased by his words; only the fact that he is a Roman citizen saves him from a scourging.

Men, brethren, and fathers, hear ye my defence which I make now unto you.

(And when they heard that he spake in the Hebrew tongue to them, they kept the more silence: and he saith,)

I am verily a man which am a Jew, born in Tarsus, a city in Cilicia, yet brought up in this city **at the feet of Gamaliel,** and taught according to the perfect manner of the law of the fathers, and was zealous toward God, as ye all are this day.

And I persecuted this way unto the death, binding and delivering into prisons both men and women.

As also the high priest doth bear me witness, and all the estate of the elders: from whom also I received letters unto the brethren, and went to Damascus, to bring them which were there bound unto Jerusalem, for to be punished.

And it came to pass, that, as I made my journey, and was come nigh unto Damascus about noon, suddenly there shone from heaven a great light round about me.

And I fell unto the ground, and heard a voice saying unto me, Saul, Saul, why persecutest thou me?

And I answered, Who art thou, Lord? And he said unto me, I am Jesus of Nazareth, whom thou persecutest.

And they that were with me saw indeed the light, and were afraid; but they heard not the voice of him that spake to me.

Avarice, the spur of industry

Source: ESSAYS (XII "Of Civil Liberty")
Author: David Hume (1711–1776)
First published: 1752
Type of work: Political essay

Context: The Scottish philosopher David Hume, described as having a face broad and fat with an expression of imbecility, with wide mouth and eyes vacant and spiritless, and who was further handicapped by a body "to communicate the idea of a turtle-eating alderman," stirred his era by essays whose determined skepticism was practically unanswerable on empirical grounds. Most of Hume's devastating essays were completed before he was forty, his *Essays Moral and Philosophical,* in 1741, and his *Philosophical Essays,* in 1748. He also wrote an exhaustive History of England (1754–1761) whose errors in fact, especially in flattering the Stuarts, were compensated for by its style; its readability kept it a standard text for years. Surprisingly, not until 1817 did an edition of his Essays appear in the United States, and then Dr. Thomas Ewell of Virginia edited

Hume's Essays in two volumes, dedicated to President Monroe. Dr. Ewell enters a defense of the supposed atheism of Hume. Perhaps the author's stand on miracles is objectionable, but the physician maintains that the essays should be read by every clergyman as training in thought and reflection that will increase the ability to preach convincingly. On many points, the apologist insists, Hume showed himself benevolent, with a universal love of mankind. Hume's "Essay of Civil Liberty" includes most of the qualities that made him admired and feared. He laments that the world is too young to have determined general truths in politics. Not only is the art of reasoning still imperfect, but sufficient facts are lacking. Machiavelli's reasoning produced many maxims about the Prince that can be completely refuted, especially in regard to absolute government. Trade, too, is just beginning to be esteemed as an affair of state. Only the modern maritime nations see the importance of an extensive commerce, which was neglected by the ancients. So, too, in comparing civil liberty and absolute government, Hume fears that what he writes may be refuted by further experience and rejected by posterity. However, he sees that Greece, the home of culture, lost that culture when it lost its liberty and when learning was transported to Rome, the only free nation at the time in the world. However, the idea that arts and sciences flourish only in a free government can be refuted by a look at France, which scarcely ever enjoyed any established liberty. Commerce, however, does fix its seat in free government.

> . . . there is something hurtful to commerce inherent in the very nature of absolute government, and inseparable from it, though the reason I should assign for this opinion is somewhat different from that which is commonly insisted on. Private property seems to me almost as secure in a civilized European monarchy as in a republic; nor is danger much apprehended in such a government, from the violence of the sovereign; more than we commonly dread harm from thunder or earthquakes, or any accident the most unusual and extraordinary. **Avarice, the spur of industry,** is so obstinate a passion, and works its way through so many real dangers and difficulties, that it is not likely to be scared by an imaginary danger. . . . Commerce, therefore, in my opinion, is apt to decay in absolute governments, not because it is there less secure, but because it is less honorable. . . .

The awkward squad

Source: WORKS OF BURNS; WITH HIS LIFE (Volume I, p. 344, 1834 ed.)
Author: Allan Cunningham (1784-1842)
First published: 1834
Type of work: Biography

Context: Allan Cunningham, Scottish poet and man of letters, was well acquainted with many of the writers of his native land, including the Ettrick Shepherd, James Hogg (1770–1835). Cunningham wrote three original novels and many songs, one of them "A Wet Sheet and a Flowing Sea" (1825). His imitations of old Scotch ballads, published in Cromek's *Remains of Nithsdale and Galloway Song* (1810), seemed so authentic that they attracted the attention of Sir Walter Scott and led to a lifelong friendship. Cunningham was also a biographer. He began with a six-volume *Lives of the Most Eminent British Poets, Sculptors, and Architects* (1829–1834), and a three-volume life of the Scottish genre and portrait painter, Sir David Wilkie (1785–1841), who began his work in a humble Scotch home and ended painting kings. However, the works for which Cunningham will be longest remembered are his accounts of his friendship with another humble Scotsman, Robert Burns (1759–1796). Burns was one of the most prolific and varied of lyric poets. He sent 160 songs to Johnson's Museum. For his friend Thomson, he wrote at least a hundred more, some of them recasting old and imperfect songs of his country. Not until the very end of Burns's life, when he realized he had little time to live, did he write to Johnson to beg that his poems—or copies of them—be returned to him to allow them to be put into perma-

nent shape for publishing, but by then it was too late, and he was too ill. So it was left to his young friend, Allan Cunningham, to collect the prose and verse scattered around the country at random. At least a third of these works had never been published. He edited them in an eight volume *Works of Robert Burns; With his Life* (London; James Cochrane, 1834), with a second edition the following year. The first volume, of 380 pages, is devoted to the life. In the final section, describing Burns' last days, Cunningham tells of the poet's trip to the seashore where Dr. John Maxwell, his physician, hoped salt water bathing would be beneficial. He returned home late in July, 1796, knowing that his end was near. In 1794, at the possibility of an invasion by France, Burns had enlisted in the Dumfriesshire Volunteers. Though he never saw military service, he knew he would receive a military funeral, and joked about it. In describing the funeral, Cunningham wrote: "When the first shovelfull of earth sounded on the coffin-lid, I looked up and saw tears on many cheeks where tears were not usual. The Volunteers justified the surmise of Burns by three ragged and straggling volleys: the earth was heaped up, and the vast multitude melted silently away." Earlier in the account, Cunningham wrote:

> Though Burns now knew he was dying, his good humor was unruffled, and his wit never forsook him. When he looked up and saw Dr. Maxwell at his bed-side,—"Alas!" he said, "what has brought you here? I am but a poor crow, and not worth plucking." He pointed to his pistols and desired that Maxwell would accept them, saying they could not be in worthier keeping, and that he should never more have need of them. This relieved his proud heart from a sense of obligation. Soon afterward he saw Gibson,

one of his brother-volunteers, by the bedside with tears in his eyes. He smiled and said,—"John, don't let **the awkward squad** fire over me!"

An ax to grind

Source: WHO'LL TURN GRINDSTONE?
Author: Charles Miner (1780-1865)
First published: 1810
Type of work: Essay

Context: Charles Miner, editor of *The Gleaner and Luzerne Advertiser,* of Wilkes-Barre, Pennsylvania, wrote for his paper a number of short essays which were collected into book form in 1815 as *Essays from the Desk of Poor Robert the Scribe, Containing Lessons in Manners, Morals, and Domestic Economy.* The essay *Who'll Turn Grindstone?* tells of an incident in the author's early boyhood. One cold winter morning a smiling stranger with an ax over his shoulder accosted him and asked permission to grind his ax on the boy's grandfather's grindstone. The stranger had the lad get some hot water for the stone and then flattered him into turning the crank. Then, patting the lad on the head, he called him "my man" and "one of the finest lads I have ever seen." It was a new ax and took a great deal of grinding. Time to go to school came and went, and still the little boy toiled and tugged away until his hands were blistered:

> The school bell rung, and I could not get away;—my hands were blistered, and it was not half ground. At length, however, the axe was sharpened, and the man turned to me, with "Now you little rascal, you've played the truant—scud to school, or you'll buy it." Alas, thought I, it was hard enough to turn grindstone, this cold day; but now to be called "little rascal" was too much. It sunk deep in my mind, and often have I thought of it since.
> When I see a merchant, overpolite to his customers—begging them to taste a little brandy, and throwing half his goods on the counter—thinks I—That man has **an axe to grind.**

Babbled of green fields

Source: KING HENRY THE FIFTH (Act II, sc. iii, 1. 17)
Author: William Shakespeare (1564-1616)
First published: 1600
Type of work: Historical drama

Context: In a street in Eastcheap, London, in front of the Boar's Head Tavern, Pistol announces to his cronies the death of Sir John Falstaff, the roguish and lewd knight who has whiled away many hours at the

69

Boar's Head Tavern and has been a favorite drinking companion of Prince Hal before his coronation as King Henry V. Bardolph says he wishes he were with Falstaff whether he be in heaven or in hell, but the hostess says that Falstaff is in Arthur's bosom and proceeds to give the particulars of the death and last words of the merry knight:

HOSTESS

Nay sure, he's not in hell; he's in Arthur's bosom, if ever man went to Arthur's bosom. 'A made a finer end, and went away an it had been any christom child; 'a parted ev'n just between twelve and one, ev'n at the turning o' th' tide: for after I saw him fumble with the sheets, and play with flowers, and smile upon his finger's end, I knew there was but one way; for his nose was as sharp as a pen, and 'a **babbled of green fields.** . . .

Back and side go bare, go bare

Source: GAMMER GURTON'S NEEDLE (Act II, Song)
Author: William Stevenson (Sixteenth century)
First published: 1575
Type of work: Dramatic comedy

Context: Gammer Gurton's Needle, which dates from about 1553, is one of the first regular English comedies. In five acts, it follows the classic Latin pattern; but it is completely English in all other respects. The author, a "Mr. S.," has been identified with William Stevenson, M.A. of Christ's College, Cambridge, where the play was originally performed. The setting is an English village; the characters are likeable and morally upright, though their speech is earthy enough to have a certain shock value even today. The plot is complex. Gammer Gurton has lost her precious needle, an article of great value upon which many villagers depend. She was putting a patch on the breeches of Hodge, her servant (the entire seat had fallen out of them), when she saw Gib, her cat, in the milk pan. Throwing down her mending, she chased Gib out of the house. When she returned, the needle had vanished. Gammer, Tib her maid, and Hodge are equally upset when the play opens. Hodge is recounting the tragedy to Diccon, an eccentric who has been released from Bethlehem Hospital (Bedlam) and who now wanders harmlessly around the village. Diccon proceeds to the tavern where he hopes to beg some ale, while Hodge goes home to help in the search. The fire is out, and he sifts through the ashes; Gib has taken refuge at the back of the hearth, and Hodge sees her eyes glowing. She dashes up the stairs; Hodge, thinking the glowing eyes are sparks in her fur and fearing she will fire the thatched roof, charges up the stairway in pursuit. He is rewarded with two cracked shins. (The needle will not be found until the last act, when Hodge puts on his breeches and sits down on it). Diccon, meanwhile, arrives at the tavern in time to hear a robust drinking song; it is rendered by Dame Chat, tavern keeper and friend of Gammer Gurton:

Back and side go bare, go bare,
Both foot and hand go cold;
But belly, God send thee good ale enough,
Whether it be new or old.

I cannot eat but little meat,
My stomach is not good;
But sure I think that I can drink
With him that wears a hood.
Though I go bare, take ye no care,
I am nothing a-cold;
I stuff my skin so full within
Of jolly good ale and old.
　　Back and side go bare, go bare, . . .
　　　　. . .
Now let them drink till they nod and wink,
Even as good fellows should do;
They shall not miss to have the bliss
Good ale doth bring men to;
And all pour souls that have scoured bowls,
Or have them lustly trolled,
God save the lives of them and their wives,
Whether they be young or old.
　　Back and side go bare, go bare, . . .

Bad laws are the worst sort of tyranny

Source: SPEECH AT BRISTOL PREVIOUS TO THE ELECTION, 1780
Author: Edmund Burke (1729-1797)
First published: 1780
Type of work: Political speech

Context: Edmund Burke faced an election at the time he made this speech at the guildhall in Bristol, which he had been representing in Parliament for six years. The speech is a bid for re-election and also a defense of his conduct as a member of the House of Commons. He notes that he is accused of neglecting his constituents by not visiting Bristol, of being wrong in his stand upon the Irish trade acts, of being wrong in his opinions and mode of proceeding on Lord Beauchamp's debtors' bills, and of voting wrongly on bills having to do with religious freedom for Roman Catholics. He defends himself against these charges one by one. In answering the last-named accusation, he describes how laws against Roman Catholics came into existence during the seventeenth century, especially how one law had been passed ironically in 1699. This particular law had been intended to seem so harsh that it could not pass, but it did. And, says Burke, "The effects of the act have been as mischievous as its origin was ludicrous and shameful. From that time every person of that communion, lay and ecclesiastic, has been obliged to fly from the face of day." Burke shows specific examples of the cruel effects of this law, the repeal of which he had worked for. After challenging his hearers, "Let him stand forth that disapproves what we have done!" Burke comments on bad laws:

> Gentlemen, **bad laws are the worst sort of tyranny.** In such a country as this they are of all bad things the worst, worse by far than anywhere else; and they derive a particular malignity even from the wisdom and soundness of the rest of our institutions. For very obvious reasons you cannot trust the crown with a dispensing power over any of your laws. However, a government, be it as bad as it may, will, in the exercise of discretionary power, discriminate times and persons; and will not ordinarily pursue any man, when its own safety is not concerned. A mercenary informer knows no distinction. Under such a system, the obnoxious people are slaves, not only to the government, but they live at the mercy of every individual; they are at once the slaves of the whole community, and of every part of it; and the worst and most unmerciful men are those on whose goodness they most depend.

Bankrupt of life, yet prodigal of ease

Source: ABSALOM AND ACHITOPHEL (Part I, l. 168)
Author: John Dryden (1631-1700)
First published: 1681
Type of work: Satiric poem

Context: Absalom and Achitophel is generally regarded as the finest political satire in the English language. Though it appeared anonymously, everyone recognized Dryden's acid pen. He finally acknowledged his authorship in his *Discourse Concerning Satire* (1692), though no published version during his lifetime carried his name as author. The use of a Scriptural story for satirical purposes was not a new idea. Absalom, weak and misguided, but full of good intentions, represents the Duke of Monmouth. Achitophel, who by his counsel guided Absalom into rebellion, was the Earl of Shaftesbury, and in the poem there are excellent portraits of other contemporary politicians. There is some basis for the rumor that Dryden began the poem at the urging of King Charles II. Many editions followed, to weaken the already declining influence of Shaftesbury. Part II appeared in 1692. Shaftesbury was small in stature, but had an active brain. To describe his son, a man of little capacity, the poet rephrases Plato's definition of a man. Cataloguing the conspirators in the "Popish Plot," Dryden reminds readers of the belief that there is only a

72

thin division between genius and insanity. The intelligent Shaftesbury must have slipped over the edge, or he would never, in his declining years and having already achieved honor and wealth, have continued to punish his body that had so little life left, just to help a worthless son. Why not be wasteful of the leisure that he possessed in abundance?

> Of these the false Achitophel was first;
> A name to all succeeding ages curst:
> For close designs and crooked counsels fit;
> Sagacious, bold, and turbulent of wit;
>
>   .   .   .
>
> A fiery soul, which, working out its way
> Fretted the pigmy body to decay,
>
>   .   .   .
>
> Great wits are sure to madness near allied,
> And thin partitions do their bounds divide;
> Else why should he, with wealth and honor blest,
> Refuse his age the needful hours of rest?
> Punish a body which he could not please;
> **Bankrupt of life, yet prodigal of ease?**
> And all to leave what with his toil he won,
> To that unfeather'd two-legg'd thing, a son?

Bare ruined choirs, where late the sweet birds sang

Source: SONNET 73 (Line 4)
Author: William Shakespeare (1564-1616)
First published: 1609
Type of work: Sonnet

Context: A mood of melancholy is sustained in this sonnet, in which the poet, likening his estate to the end of the autumn, to the end of the day after the sunset, and to the final dying embers of the fire, reckons yet that his beloved must count him dearer because of the nearness of the time of separation. A forceful image is created in the likening of the bare branches of the trees to the arches of a ruined cathedral, both deserted by their choirs. The entire sonnet reads:

> That time of year thou mayst in me behold,
> When yellow leaves, or none, or few, do hang
> Upon those boughs which shake against the cold,
> **Bare ruin'd choirs, where late the sweet birds sang.**
> In me thou seest the twilight of such day,
> As after sunset fadeth in the west,
> Which by and by black night doth take away,
> Death's second self, that seals up all in rest.
> In me thou seest the glowing of such fire,

That on the ashes of his youth doth lie,
As the death-bed whereon it must expire,
Consum'd with that which it was nourish'd by.
    This thou perceiv'st, which makes they love more strong,
    To love that well which thou must leave ere long.

Battering the gates of heaven with storms of prayer

Source: SAINT SIMEON STYLITES (Line 7)
Author: Alfred, Lord Tennyson (1809-1892
First published: 1842
Type of work: Dramatic monologue

Context: The darkness of the human mind that leads to guilt and the frenzied, practically insane, drive and the means men use to purge themselves of this guilt are here explored through the dying speech of a Christian saint who does not want to be sainted. Obsessed with his guilt yet unable to determine its source, Simeon follows the route of the medieval saints who so hated their bodies that they tortured themselves in the hopes of earning heaven. He has tied coarse ropes around his loins until the ulcers be- trayed his penance; he has lived for three years with his leg chained to a mountain crag; but, for most of his life, he has lived on the tops of great columns where, exposed to all kinds of weather, he has suffered privation, starvation, and the pains of exposure. After such a lifetime, he believes that he is about to die; still obsessed with his guilt, he prays for the last time, begging for forgiveness and hoping that his pain will allow him to enter heaven.

Altho' I be the basest of mankind,
From scalp to sole one slough and crust of sin,
Unfit for earth, unfit for heaven, scarce meet
For troops of devils, mad with blasphemy,
I will not cease to grasp the hope I hold
Of Saintdom, and to clamor, mourn, and sob,
Battering the gates of heaven with storms of prayer,
Have mercy, Lord, and take away my sin! . . .

Be bold, be bold—but not too bold

Source: THE FAERIE QUEENE (Book III, Canto 11, stanza 54)
Author: Edmund Spenser (c. 1552-1599)
First published: 1590
Type of work: Allegorical poem

Context: The exemplification of love's aspects is the major theme of Book III. Britomart, the lady-knight of Active Chastity, is fervently seeking her love, Sir Artigall, the knight of Justice. While on this quest, she finds Scudamore, the Shield of Love, weeping on the ground because Busirane has held Amoret captive for seven months by means of black magic. Busirane, who represents the negation of Chastity and of the will of love, is Lust. Britomart accompanies Scudamore to Busirane's castle where the entrance is guarded by a sulphurous smoking flame. Britomart, alone, is able to penetrate the flame. Inside the castle, she passes through three rooms, each of which teaches her something of the transforming nature of love. In the first, she sees a tapestry depicting the many disguises under which Jove made love, showing that even gods can debase themselves and become bestial in the search for love. Britomart passes through a door capped with Busirane's motto: *Be bold*. She finds herself in a room of pure gold hung with Cupid's "warlike spoils" which show the destructive effect of love on personal and political power. These two rooms have portrayed graphicly the boldness of love: desire, pursuit, victory. Over the centuries, Spenser's lines have undergone a change in the popular memory.

And as she lookt about, she did behold
How over that same dore was likewise writ,
Be bold, be bold, and every where Be bold,
That much she muz'd, yet could not construe it
By any ridling skill, or commune wit.
At last she spyde at that roomes upper end,
Another yron dore, on which was writ,
Be not too bold; whereto though she did bend
Her earnest mind, yet wist not what it might intend.

Be it ever so humble, there's no place like home

Source: HOME, SWEET HOME (from the opera, *Clari, or, The Maid of Milan*)
Author: John Howard Payne (1791-1852)
First published: 1823
Type of work: Lyric

Context: Payne was an itinerant actor and dramatist; he left his home in Easthampton, Long Island, at the age of fifteen and spent several years in New York City, where he worked for a counting-house by day and edited a theatrical paper at night. After two years of college he made his first appearance on the stage (1809). He then went to London and spent a number of years there, writing several dramas and adapting others; all are forgotten now. He wrote a highly successful tragedy, *Brutus,* in which he had intended to play the leading role; however, Kean took the part and was made famous by it. In addition to producing several other popular works, Payne wrote a number of critical reviews. He returned to the United States in 1832 and in spite of a substantial income from his plays was in financial difficulties most of the time. He was United States Consul at Tunis, Algeria, from 1841 to 1845 and again in 1851 to 1852, dying there. While in London in 1823, Payne had written the lyric for an operatic aria; it is for this that he is still remembered. Henry R. Bishop, on a commission by the manager of Covent Garden Theatre, adapted a French play into an opera. Its title is *Clari, or, The Maid of Milan.* The song, "Home, Sweet Home," is presented several times in the course of the opera—in the overture, as an aria by Clari during the first act, as a song by peasants in the third act, and finally as a chorus. According to Bishop, the melody is partly founded on a Sicilian air. In the lyrics Payne, a homeless wanderer himself, expresses all the heartfelt longing for home that strikes us—either with pain or with nostalgia—at some time in the course of our lives. This yearning for a stability he could never have has touched the sentiments of millions over nearly a century and a half of time. The first and last stanzas are given below:

'Mid pleasures and palaces though we may roam,
Be it ever so humble, there's no place like home;
A charm from the sky seems to hallow us there,
Which, seek through the world, is ne'er met with elsewhere.
 Home, Home, sweet, sweet Home!
There's no place like Home! there's no place like Home!
   . . .
To thee I'll return, overburdened with care;
The heart's dearest solace will smile on me there;
No more from that cottage again will I roam;
Be it ever so humble, there's no place like home.
 Home! Home! sweet, sweet, Home!
There's no place like Home! there's no place like Home!

Be neither saint nor sophist-led, but be a man!

Source: EMPEDOCLES ON ETNA (Act I, sc. ii, 1. 136)
Author: Matthew Arnold (1822-1888)
First published: 1852
Type of work: Poetic drama

Context: Empedocles, the poet and philosopher, is an exile on Mount Etna. Disillusioned, because he has questioned until the glory of life and the splendor of nature are dead; and hopeless, because he is torn between the blind faith of religion and the critical logic of philosophy, he can understand neither the young poet nor the physician. Callicles, the poet, advocates a romantic escape into idyllic beauty, but Empedocles cannot stop asking the questions that make such escape impossible. Pausanias, the physician, is interested only in the magic of healing people in a civilized society, but Empedocles cannot escape the lure of poetry that promises,

76

however feebly, the hope of beauty. In one of his moods, Empedocles breaks off his conversation with Pausanias to listen to Callicles, seizes his harp, and in a long monologue characterizes the dilemma that drives men from youthful hope to the adult despair. The quotation occurs in the part of the monologue where Empedocles describes how differences in opinions make the individual sink into his own subjectivity.

> And we feel, day and night,
> The burden of ourselves—
> Well, then, the wiser wight
> In his own bosom delves,
> And asks what ails him so, and gets what cure he can.
> The sophist sneers: Fool, take
> Thy pleasure, right or wrong.
> The pious wail: Forsake
> A world these sophists throng.
> **Be neither saint nor sophist-led, but be a man!**

Be wise today; 'tis madness to defer

Source: THE COMPLAINT: OR, NIGHT THOUGHTS ("Night the First," l. 390)
Author: Edward Young (1683-1765)
First published: 1742
Type of work: Philosophical poem

Context: The poet awakes from uneasy, dream-ridden sleep in the middle of the night and in the darkness and silence reflects upon man's place on earth and in the future life. Man is a wonderful creature, midway in the great chain of being between mere nothing and the deity—a worm and yet a god. His true place is in the infinite with God, but he spends his time here on earth busying himself with trivial concerns. Because man is a selfish creature, he pays attention to his own wants and desires here on earth, but by so doing he stores up woes in the future life. Man is really a petty creature, without vision; he tries to gain deceptive earthly joys, and ambition leads him towards what he foolishly believes are worthy goals. When he has almost reached them, death, whose hungry maw demands millions of human lives every day, consumes him. No one is ever ready for death; man never prepares for it: he should be wise and to-day be waiting for his long journey—it is madness to delay so important an activity. But procrastination is the thief of time.

> Not e'en Philander had bespoke his shroud:
> Nor had he cause; a warning was denied;
> How many fall as sudden, not as safe!
> As sudden, though for years admonished home.
> Of human ills the last extreme beware,

Beware, Lorenzo! a slow sudden death.
How dreadful that deliberate surprise!
Be wise to-day; 'tis madness to defer;
Next day the fatal precedent will plead;
Thus on, till wisdom is pushed out of life.
Procrastination is the thief of time;
Year after year it steals, till all are fled,
And to the mercies of a moment leaves
The vast concerns of an eternal scene.
If not so frequent, would not this be strange?
That 'tis so frequent, this is stranger still.

Be your oriflamme today the helmet of Navarre

Source: IVRY: A SONG OF THE HUGUENOTS (Line 30)
Author: Thomas Babington Macaulay (1800-1859)
First published: 1824
Type of work: Ballad

Context: The original Huguenot was "one who took an oath." It comes from the earlier French *eiguenot,* changed because of a fancied resemblance to the name Hugh, and was applied to the sixteenth and seventeenth century French Protestants. Though Henry IV (1553–1610) of France, was brought up as a Protestant, he wavered back and forth toward Catholicism. His claim to the French throne was recognized by Coligny, chief of the Huguenots, in 1569. When he was named to the throne, the Catholic League, to force him to abjure Protestantism, waged the War of the Three Henrys. The League was defeated at the Battle of Ivry, in northern France, where Henry IV issued his gallant order: "If you lose your standards, follow my white plume." Later, with the explanation, "Paris is worth a Mass," he permanently became a Roman Catholic. Navarre lies across the Pyrenees Mountains and was formerly an independent kingdom. Now the southern part forms Spain's Basque region, while the northern section is part of France. In one of his miscellaneous poems, Macaulay tells of the Battle of Ivry. The oriflamme was the ancient royal standard of France, with flame-shaped streamers.

The king is come to marshal us, in all his armor drest,
And he has bound a snow-white plume upon his gallant
      crest.
He looked upon his people, and a tear was in his eye;
He looked upon the traitors, and his glance was stern and
      high.
Right graciously he smiled on us, as rolled from wing to
      wing,
Down all our line, a deafening shout, "God save our Lord
      the King!"

78

"And if my standard-bearer fall, as fall full well he may,
For never saw I promise yet of such a bloody fray,
Press where ye see my white plume shine, amidst the ranks
    of war,
And **be your oriflamme to-day the helmet of Navarre.**"

A beauteous evening, calm and free

Source: IT IS A BEAUTEOUS EVENING, CALM AND FREE (Line 1)
Author: William Wordsworth (1770-1850)
First published: 1807
Type of work: Sonnet

Context: This beautiful sonnet was composed on the beach near Calais in the autumn of 1802. The girl walking with Wordsworth is Caroline, his natural daughter by Annette Vallon. The father is deeply moved by the beauty of the evening and the sound of the sea, but the child seems indifferent. Yet, says Wordsworth, you have a divinity in you and a worshipful spirit, even though you appear untouched. "Abraham's bosom" is the place where souls rest in heaven after death. Luke 16:22: "And it came to pass, that the beggar died, and was carried by the angels into Abraham's bosom." The sonnet follows:

It is **a beauteous evening, calm and free,**
The holy time is quiet as a Nun,
Breathless with adoration; the broad sun
Is sinking down in its tranquillity;
The gentleness of heaven broods o'er the Sea:
Listen! the mighty Being is awake,
And doth with his eternal motion make
A sound like thunder—everlastingly.
Dear Child! dear Girl! that walkest with me here,
If thou appear untouched by solemn thought,
Thy nature is not therefore less divine:
Thou liest in Abraham's bosom all the year;
And worshipp'st at the Temple's inner shrine,
God being with thee when we know it not.

The beautiful uncut hair of graves

Source: SONG OF MYSELF (Canto 6)
Author: Walt Whitman (1819-1892)
First published: 1855
Type of work: Lyric poem

Context: After experiences as printer, journalist, and newspaper editor, during which he published a few poems and articles, Walt Whitman, under an abbreviated first name that he used for the rest of his life, published at his own expense a small volume, *Leaves of Grass,* containing twelve lyric poems, among them "Song of Myself." The book was largely ignored except by Ralph Waldo Emerson, who wrote him a congratulatory letter. In subsequent years through commercial publishers, Whitman issued ten editions, each radically different. At first Whitman was criticized for his daring subject matter and for his long, rhythmical, but unrhymed lines. Readers thought he well characterized himself when he wrote about his "barbaric yawp." Today, however, critics recognize the greatness of some poems, amid the false greatness and mediocrity of the rest. Some of the best of Whitman appeared in its longest poem, "Song of Myself," in 52 cantos. It shows the poet as a mystic, a pantheist, and a lover of humanity. In Canto 6, he combines two of his favorite themes: death and democracy.

A child said *What is the grass?* fetching it to me with
full hands;
How could I answer the child? I did not know what it
was any more than he . . .

Or I guess it is the handkerchief of the Lord,
A scented gift and remembrance designedly dropt,
Bearing the owner's name someway in the corner, that
we may see and remark, and say *Whose?* . . .

Or I guess it is a uniform hieroglyphic,
And it means, Sprouting alike in broad zones and narrow
zones,
Growing among black folk as among white,
Kanuck, Tuckahoe, Congressman, Cuff, I give them the
same, I receive them the same.

And now it seems to me **the beautiful uncut hair of graves.**

Beauty in distress

Source: TO FLORENCE (Stanza 7)
Author: George Gordon, Lord Byron (1788-1824)
First published: 1812
Type of work: Lyric poem

Context: On Byron's first trip to Europe, he and his companion, John Hobhouse, spent some time in Malta where they met Spencer Smith and his wife Constance. Hers was a fantastic story, quite apart from her adventures with the Marquis de Salvo. In 1806 she incurred the enmity of Napoleon and was imprisoned. She escaped down a rope ladder in male disguise.

80

Byron was immediately taken with her, perhaps because of her near-sightedness and habit of looking at men with bewildered vagueness, like a romantic lady in distress. But she was realist enough to defraud the poet of a costly yellow diamond. Byron wrote to his mother that he was in love with a German lady with fat arms, though his references to her in *Childe Harold's Pilgrimage* II, 30–35, do not make him appear very much infatuated with her. Her actual name was Constance, but in his narrative the poet gives her the more romantic name of Florence. Thomas Moore, who used Byron's Memoirs in writing the poet's biography, declared —and Byron's friend Hobhouse agreed—that Byron's references to her were cold. With the passing of time, however, Byron idealized her in a number of short poems, and made passionate references to their relationship. The poems include "Stanzas Composed during a Thunderstorm," "Stanzas written in Passing the Ambracian Gulf," and "To Florence," of which the first, seventh, eighth, and final stanzas are here given. He tells her he loves her and wants her to look on him as a friend, and he will think of her when he sees her birthplace, Stamboul.

Oh Lady! when I left the shore,
  The distant shore which gave me birth,
I hardly thought to grieve once more,
  To quit another spot on earth: . . .
      •   •   •
And who so cold as look on thee,
  Thou lovely wand'rer, and be less?
Nor be, what man should ever be,
  The friend of **Beauty in distress?**

Ah, who could think that form had past
  Through Danger's most destructive path,
Had braved the death-winged tempest's blast,
  And 'scaped a tyrant's fiercer wrath? . . .
      •   •   •
And though I bid thee now farewell,
  When I behold that wondrous scene,
Since where thou are I may not dwell,
  'T will soothe to be, where thou hast been.

Beauty is in the eye of the beholder

Source: MOLLY BAWN (Chapter XII)
Author: Margaret Wolfe Hungerford (c. 1855-1897)
First published: 1878
Type of work: Novel

Context: Molly Bawn is the nick-name Philip Massereene has given his pretty step-sister Eleanor. Philip, a poor but honest gentleman of Victorian England, owns a small homestead south of London where he lives with his wife, Letitia, and Molly. Molly has a fierce old grandfather who disowned her mother when she married beneath her and who has never seen his granddaughter, but as he becomes ill in his old age he sends for her. In the meantime, however, Molly has fallen in love with Teddy, a friend of her brother. The two cannot marry because Teddy, whose full name is Tedcastle, has an inadequate income. Molly, interrupting her courtship to visit her wealthy but ill-natured grandfather, meets her cousin Marcia, a scheming but beautiful girl. One evening soon after Molly's arrival, several neighbors come to visit, including Lady Stafford, who is met at the door by Marcia. Lady Stafford inquires concerning the arrival of the other guests:

"One moment, Marcia. Many people come yet? Tedcastle?"

"Yes, and Captain Mottie, with his devoted attendant, and the Darleys."

"Maudie? Is she as fascinating as ever? I do hope, Marcia, you have got her young man for her this time, as she was simply unbearable last year."

"I have not," laughing: "it is a dead secret, but the fact is, he *wouldn't come*."

"I like that young man. Though I consider he has sold us shamefully. Any one else?"

"My cousin, Eleanor Massereene."

"*The* cousin! I am so glad. Anything new is such a relief. And I have heard she is beautiful: is she?"

"Beauty is in the eye of the beholder," quotes Marcia, in a low tone, and with a motion of her hand towards the open door inside which sits Molly, that sends Lady Stafford up-stairs without further parley.

Beauty is the lover's gift

Source: THE WAY OF THE WORLD (Act II, sc. ii)
Author: William Congreve (1670-1729)
First published: 1700
Type of work: Dramatic comedy

Context: Mrs. Millamant, attended by her admirer Witwoud, joins Mrs. Fainall and Mirabell, whom she loves. Mrs. Millamant has been late in arriving for this rendezvous and gropes for an explanation for her tardiness. She finally says that she had been reading a batch of just-arrived letters. She loathes letters, which serve only one useful purpose—to pin up one's hair. It seems that those in prose are useless; she tried some once and her hair was in such a wretched condition that her maid, Mincing, had to work all morning in an effort to rectify matters. Letters in poetry, however, make the hair sit properly the next day. It then develops that

82

Mrs. Millamant loves to inflict pain, as when one parts with her cruelty she parts with her power; when one parts with her power she is old and ugly. Mirabell, however, says that if a woman destroys her lover she destroys herself. She is no longer beautiful when she has lost her lover, because her beauty dies in the instant of losing him. It is the lover who bestows beauty on the beloved; the old and ugly, who cannot bear to look in their mirrors, can be flattered, for the mirror reflects men's praises—what they say about their ladies—rather than accurate reflections of the faces.

MIRABELL

Ay, ay, suffer your cruelty to ruin the object of your power, to destroy your lover—and then how vain, how lost a thing you'll be! Nay, 'tis true: you are no longer handsome when you've lost your lover; your beauty dies upon the instant; for **beauty is the lover's gift;** 'tis he bestows your charms—your glass is all a cheat. The ugly and the old, whom the looking-glass mortifies, yet after commendation can be flattered by it, and discovers beauties in it; for that reflects our praises, rather than your face.

Beauty unadorned

Source: THE ROVER; OR, THE BANISH'D CAVALIERS, PART TWO (Act IV, sc. i)
Author: Aphra Behn (1640-1689)
First published: 1681
Type of work: Dramatic comedy

Context: The Rover, a Cavalier named Willmore, is an Englishman, a soldier of fortune since his banishment from England for supporting the crown during the civil wars. He comes to Madrid, where he falls in love with La Nuche, a Spanish courtesan, who also loves him. Their love affair is complicated in several ways. There is, of course, La Nuche's reputation as a courtesan. Also, Ariadne, a young lady of quality, bids for Willmore's love, as a rival to La Nuche, even though she is engaged to marry Beaumond, Willmore's friend. La Nuche, truly in love with Willmore, grumbles from time to time about being a courtesan and finding it difficult to prove to Willmore that she really loves him. One of the persons to whom she complains is Petronella Elenora, her bawd, who is herself a worn-out courtesan. Petronella tries, as she does in this passage, to persuade La Nuche that she ought not to worry about love in general or Willmore, a penniless man, in particular. She admonishes La Nuche that wealth is everything:

LA NUCHE
. . .
Oh give me Love: I will be poor and love.

PETRONELLA

She's lost—but hear me—

LA NUCHE

I won't, from Childhood thou hast trained me up in Cunning,
read Lectures to me of the use of Man, but kept me from the
knowledge of the Right; taught me to jilt, to flatter and deceive:
and hard it was to learn th' ungrateful Lessons. But oh how soon
plain Nature taught me Love, and shew'd me all the cheat of thy
false Tenents—No—give me Love with any other Curse.

PETRONELLA

But who will give you that when you are poor? when you are
wretchedly despis'd and poor?

LA NUCHE

Hah!

PETRONELLA

Do you not daily see fine Clothes, rich Furniture, Jewels and
Plate are more inviting than **Beauty unadorn'd?** be old, diseas'd,
deform'd, be any thing, so you be rich and splendidly attended,
you'll find your self lov'd and ador'd by all. . . .

Begin with the beginning

Source: DON JUAN (Canto I, stanza 7)
Author: George Gordon, Lord Byron (1788-1824)
First published: 1819 (Cantos I-II)
Type of work: Satirical poem

Context: In the literary world, the
Spanish Don Juan Tenorio is the
symbol of the great lover, the profli-
gate libertine, with feudal power but
without feudal obligation. One is not
sure how much Byron knew of the
Spanish play that introduced this
character to the literary world, the
Golden Age *El Burlador de Sevilla*
(The Mocker of Seville) by Tirso de
Molina (1584?–1648). *Don Juan
Tenorio* (1844) by the romantic
dramatist José Zorrilla (1817–1893)
did not appear until later. Certainly
Byron did not know how to pronounce the Spaniard's name, for instead of Don Hwahn (to rhyme with
"John"), he rhymed it with "ruin."
But then, he rhymed Cádiz with "ladies" and the three-syllable "capote"
with "boat." Nor did he follow the
story line of the Spanish original.
Started out like a bedroom farce, it
let him indulge his talent for insults
and ridicule. Its dedication insults
Wordsworth, Coleridge, and "Sir
Laureate" Robert Southey, who lives
to sing about kings "very ill." About
Coleridge, Byron remarks that the
poet explained metaphysics to the na-

tion, then adds: "I wish he would explain his explanation." Wisely, the publisher, Murray, who published Cantos I and II in July, 1819, and Cantos III, IV, and V in August, 1821, issued them without mentioning either his name or the name of the author. Of course the authorship was quickly guessed, and upon Byron fell a storm of obloquy for their voluptuousness and skepticism. Consequently Murray refused to publish any later cantos. They were printed in sets of three by John Hunt in 1823 and 1824. Byron was writing Canto XVII when he died of a fever in Greece. Byron announced that he intended to write an epic of modern life; however, the poem fails to follow the epic tradition, since the poet departs from the story with frequent digressions, as he does in *Childe Harold's Pilgrimage*. He refers to many people and things, as well as indulging in bitter tirades against England,

society, wealth, and power. So the adventures of the Don are incidental to a satire that is, in the opinion of many critics, the greatest in English, as well as the poem above all others of his pen into which are gathered the most outstanding traits of his genius. It is written largely in ottava rima, an Italian meter: eight lines of ten syllables with the first six rhyming alternately, and a rhymed couplet at the end. As an example, see the stanza quoted here. In the opening lines of the first canto, Byron remarks: "I want a hero," and therefore he takes Don Juan, familiar as a figure in the pantomime, sent to the devil before his time. Then the author digresses to list some of the heroes of the present and past, all of whom he finds unfit for his poem. He also comments on the usual way of plunging somewhere into the middle of the action in an attempt to seize attention at once. But as he comments:

That is the usual method, but not mine—
   My way is to **begin with the beginning;**
The regularity of my design
   Forbids all wandering as the worst of sinning,
And therefore I shall open with a line
   (Although it cost me half an hour in spinning)
Narrating somewhat of Don Juan's father,
And also of his mother, if you'd rather.

Believing where we cannot prove

Source: IN MEMORIAM (Prologue, stanza 1)
Author: Alfred, Lord Tennyson (1809-1892)
First published: 1850
Type of work: Elegy

Context: When Arthur Henry Hallam, Tennyson's beloved friend, suddenly died in Vienna at the age of twenty-two years, Tennyson composed in his honor one of the great elegies in the English language. He begins his work with a prologue addressed to Love, the son of God. We have not seen Love face to face; we accept its existence on faith alone, believing something that we cannot prove. In this passage Tennyson is echoing the conclusion of the gospel of *John* (20:24–29): the disciple Thomas said that he would not believe that Christ had risen from the dead until he had put his finger into the print of the nails in Christ's hands and thrust his hand into the wound in his side. Christ invites him to do what he demanded and then said, "Thomas, because thou hast seen me, thou hast believed; blessed are they that have not seen and yet have believed." Tennyson, following Christ, is saying in different form that belief grounded on proof is inferior in merit to the accepting of what cannot be proved, which is true faith.

> Strong Son of God, immortal Love,
>   Whom we, that have not seen thy face,
>   By faith, and faith alone, embrace,
> **Believing where we cannot prove;**
>
> Thine are these orbs of light and shade;
>   Thou madest Life in man and brute;
>   Thou madest Death; and lo, thy foot
> Is on the skull which thou has made.
>
> Thou wilt not leave us in the dust:
>   Thou madest man, he knows not why,
>   He thinks he was not made to die;
> And thou hast made him: thou art just.

Beneath the Good how far—but far above the Great

Source: PROGRESS OF POESY (Last line)
Author: Thomas Gray (1716-1771)
First published: 1757
Type of work: Pindaric ode

Context: Gray wrote poetry for his friends. He had little but scorn for the intellectual qualities and knowledge of the general public. Therefore, he declared, concerning the lines and references in his poem that traced the history of poetry from the Greek Pindar to the great English figures, that they were "vocal to the intelligent; for the many they need interpreters." However, many of its footnotes were in Greek that would be of little help to the general reader. Most of the names mentioned in the ode are familiar today. After the poet's tribute to Shakespeare (see, "Nature's darling") and to Milton (see, "He pass'd the flaming Bounds"), Gray lauds the greatness of Dryden. However, now that Dryden is dead, Gray asks who will inherit the lyre of the Theban Eagle (Pindar). Perhaps some one still a child will one day prove how far goodness can outshine greatness.   (See, "They're only truly great").

> Yet oft before his infant eyes would run
> Such forms as glitter in the Muse's ray,
> With orient hues, unborrowed of the Sun;
> Yet shall he mount, and keep his distant way
> Beyond the limits of a vulgar fate;
> **Beneath the Good how far—but far above the Great.**

The best in this kind are but shadows

Source: A MIDSUMMER NIGHT'S DREAM (Act V, sc. i, l. 213)
Author: William Shakespeare (1564-1616)
First published: 1600
Type of work: Dramatic comedy

Context: As the wedding festivities of Theseus and Hippolyta draw to a close, Philostrate, Master of Revels, is commanded to bring a dramatic performance before the royal group. Various selections are rejected as inappropriate for the nuptial occasion: the eunuch reciting the battle with the centaurs, the riot of the tipsy Bacchanals, the thrice three muses mourning for the death of learning. Instead, Theseus prefers the Athenian handicraftsmen's production of *The Most Lamentable Comedy, and Most Cruel Death of Pyramus and Thisbe.* Philostrate is quick to caution the duke that the quality of performance leaves much to be desired, but Theseus replies that "never anything can be amiss,/ When simpleness and duty tender it." He informs his bride of the honesty and sincerity of such a group in comparison with the finely polished performances of deceit. Moreover, if the rustics confuse line, meter, and meaning in their delivery, it will be no worse than "great clerks" who have come to me with "premeditated welcome," but who "shiver and look pale," making "periods in the midst of sentences" and throttling "their practis'd accent in their fears." Following the duke's example, the courtiers attempt to receive the performance with graceful pleasure, but, when the character representing Wall informs the crowd his part is concluded and stalks off stage, the farce is more than Hippolyta can bear. Again Theseus reminds her that all players are but shadows of the mind which must be fitted to proper form by the imagination:

WALL
Thus have I, Wall, my part discharged so;
And, being done, thus Wall away doth go. [*Exit.*]

THESEUS
Now is the Moon to see between the two neighbours.

87

DEMETRIUS

No remedy my lord, when walls are so wilful, to hear without warning.

HIPPOLYTA

This is the silliest stuff that e'er I heard.

THESEUS

The best in this kind are but shadows; and the worst are no worse, if imagination amend them.

HIPPOLYTA

It must be your imagination then, and not theirs.

THESEUS

If we imagine no worse of them than they of themselves, they may pass for excellent men.

The best of life is but intoxication

Source: DON JUAN (Canto II, stanza 179)
Author: George Gordon, Lord Byron (1788-1824)
First published: 1819 (Cantos I and II)
Type of work: Satiric poem

Context: The young Don Juan, as punishment for an amorous scrape that has resulted in a divorce and a scandal which has all Spain talking, has been banished from his homeland and packed off to sea on his pious mother's assumption that the salt air will somehow bring about a change of heart and a return to innocence. Who knows but that her scheme might have worked had not a great storm come up, battering the ship to pieces, killing all of Juan's fellow voyagers, and depositing him, half-drowned, on an island coast. Two ladies, the beautiful Haidée, "The greatest heiress of the Eastern Isles," and her companion, find the unconscious and emaciated youth lying on the sand, carry him to a cave, and nurse him back to health and alas! to love. As the lovely Haidée accompanies the handsome Juan on his first venture from the cave since his rescue, the poet describes the "wild and breaker-beaten coast" along which the lovers stroll. He then digresses a bit and speaks up in favor of old wine!

> And the small ripple spilt upon the beach
>   Scarcely o'erpassed the cream of your champagne,
> When o'er the brim the sparkling bumpers reach,
>   That spring-dew of the spirit! the heart's rain!
> Few things surpass old wine; and they may preach
>   Who please,—the more because they preach in vain,—

Let us have wine and women, mirth and laughter,
Sermons and soda-water the day after.

Man, being reasonable, must get drunk;
   The best of life is but intoxication:
Glory, the grape, love, gold, in these are sunk
   The hopes of all men, and of every nation;
Without their sap, how branchless were the trunk
   Of life's strange tree, so fruitful on occasion!
But to return,—Get very drunk; and when
You wake with headache, you shall see what then.

The best things carried to excess are wrong

Source: THE ROSCIAD (Line 1039)
Author: Charles Churchill (1731-1764)
First published: 1761
Type of work: Satiric poem

Context: A dissipated clergyman, Churchill won both fame and notoriety as a satiric poet during the last four years of his life. He was associated with and defended John Wilkes, the unscrupulous editor of the *North-Briton.* Much of the harsh and vitriolic nature of Churchill's satire seems to have been formed by this association. In *The Rosciad,* his first important poem, Churchill attacked a number of theatrical personalities with such witty satire that it was at one time regarded as the most important satiric work between those of Pope and Byron. Near the end of the poem, after a long catalogue of contemporary stage personalities, all subjected to biting attack, came the famous actor David Garrick, followed by a train of critics. The first critic accuses Garrick of being too short to play a hero because "Your Hero always should be tall, you know":

   Another can't forgive the paltry arts,
By which he makes his way to shallow hearts;
Mere pieces of finesse, traps for applause.—
"Avaunt, unnat'ral start, affected pause."

   For me, by Nature form'd to judge with phlegm,
I can't acquit by whosesale, nor condemn.
The best things carried to excess are wrong:
The start may be too frequent, pause too long;
But, only us'd in proper time and place,
Severest judgment must allow them Grace.

Better be courted and jilted than never be courted at all

Source: THE JILTED NYMPH (Stanza 3)
Author: Thomas Campbell (1777-1844)
First published: 1842
Type of work: Humorous poem

Context: Thomas Campbell took more pride in having founded the University of London than in his poetry, even his heroic and patriotic poetry that stirred Great Britain between 1800 and 1840. That is well, because the university continued and grew, while Campbell's reputation as a poet diminished until he is now almost forgotten. One section of his collected poems is headed "Songs, chiefly Amatory," and contains thirty poems to almost as many ladies. He started with two "To Caroline" poems, written in 1795, just after he left the University of Glasgow. He was eighteen and Caroline, seventeen. He wrote "Ode to Content" in 1800, dedicated to Matilda Sinclair, whom he later married. Then came poems to Julia, to Florine who married one of his best friends, to Margaret, a lovely table maid, and to three celebrated Scottish beauties: Jemima, Rosa, and Eleanore. Many of the poems were trite, but Campbell could turn a phrase and incorporate humor, as he did when one young lady in 1840 begged him for something original for her album. His response was: "An original something, fair maid, you will win me/ To write—but how shall I begin?/ For I fear I have nothing original in me—/ Excepting Original Sin." How many times he loved, he was too much the gentleman to boast. How many times he lost, he was too proud to confess. But like Samuel Butler in *The Way of All Flesh* (Chapter 77), and Tennyson in *In Memoriam,* Campbell agreed " 'Tis better to have loved and lost/Than never to have loved at all." In his song, "The Jilted Nymph," he phrased it differently. It was written to be sung to the Scots tune of "Woo'd and married and a'." The first, part of the third, and the last stanzas are given here. In the lines omitted, the nymph tells of her sad experiences with various temporary suitors.

I'm jilted, forsaken, outwitted;
   Yet think not I'll whimper or brawl—
The lass is alone to be pitied
   Who ne'er has been courted at all;
Never by great or small
Wooed or jilted at all;
   Oh, how unhappy's the lass
Who has never been courted at all!

   • • •

What though at my heart he has tilted,
   What though I have met with a fall?
Better be courted and jilted
   Than never be courted at all . . .

   • • •

90

But lately I've met with a suitor
   Whose heart I have gotten in thrall,
And I hope soon to tell you in future
   That I'm wooed and married and all.
Wooed and married and all,
   What greater bliss can befall?
   And you all shall partake
    Of my bridal cake,
When I'm woo'd and married, and all.

The better day the worse deed

Source: AN EXPOSITION OF THE OLD TESTAMENT (Genesis 3:6)
Author: Matthew Henry (1662-1714)
First published: 1708-1710
Type of work: Biblical commentary

Context: Matthew Henry was an English noncomformist clergyman whose father, Philip Henry, was a clergyman before him and was persecuted for his beliefs. Matthew became minister of a Presbyterian church in Chester in 1687, remaining there until 1712. In the latter year he moved to Hackney, and two years later he died suddenly at Nantwich. He wrote a number of doctrinal works and a moving biography of his father, but he is best remembered for his commentaries on the Bible. These represent a truly monumental achievement and were published under the title *Expositions of the Old and New Testaments.* To many, this lengthy and exhaustive work still holds first place for general usefulness in its field. The lessons which Henry draws from his text are both sound and sensible, and he presents them in memorable fashion. Much use is made of metaphor, analogy, and illustration; the language is direct and simple, homely and warm without loss of dignity. His writing abounds with pithy observations and quotable expressions, and his reflective statements give evidence that his work was a labor of devotion. It is obvious to the reader that Henry had a warm understanding of the world and of man, that he was deeply pious, and that his knowledge of scripture was keen and searching. His commentaries are practical and devotional in nature; they are expositions and explanations of the material and do not undertake to criticize it. In his discussion of the third chapter of Genesis, he describes the transgression of Eve when she partook of the forbidden fruit, and the transgression of Adam when he joined her in surrendering to the wiles of the Serpent. Then he explains the enormity of Adam's guilt in no uncertain terms:

. . . In neglecting the tree of life which he was allowed to eat of, and eating of the tree of knowledge which was forbidden, he plainly shewed a contempt of the favours which God had be-

91

stowed on him, and a preference given to those God did not see fit for him. He would be both his own carver, and his own master; would *have* what he pleased, and *do* what he pleased; his sin was, in one word, *disobedience* . . . to a plain, easy, and express command, which, probably, he knew to be a command of trial. He sins against great knowledge, against many mercies, against light and love, the clearest light, and the dearest love, that ever sinner sinned against. He had no corrupt nature within him to betray him; but had a freedom of will, not enslaved, and was in his full strength, not weakened or impaired. He *turned aside quickly.* Some think he fell the very same day on which he was made: though I see not how to reconcile that with God's pronouncing all *very good,* in the close of that day: others suppose he fell on the sabbath day; **the better day the worse deed:** however, it is certain that he kept his integrity but a very little while; being in honour, he *continued not.* But the greatest aggravation of his sin, was, that he *involved all his posterity* in sin and ruin by it. God having told him that his race should replenish the earth, surely he could not but know that he stood as a public person, and that his disobedience would be fatal to all his seed; and if so, it was certainly the greatest treachery as well as the greatest cruelty that ever was.

Better one suffer than a nation grieve

Source: ABSALOM AND ACHITOPHEL (Part I, l. 416)
Author: John Dryden (1631-1700)
First published: 1681
Type of work: Satiric poem

Context: In his poetical rewriting of the Biblical story of the revolt of Absalom against King David (II Samuel, 13–18) Dryden, England's leading poet of his time, incorporated a thinly disguised allegory of the frustrated attempts of the Whigs to make the illegitimate James Stuart, Duke of Monmouth, the successor of Charles II. If Dryden thought to conceal his authorship by publishing it anonymously, he failed. The rhymed couplets, handled in a way none of his contemporaries could match, were as good as a signature. When another James, the Roman Catholic Duke of York, brother of Charles II, loomed as heir to the English throne, the Earl of Shaftesbury headed a plot to legitimatize Monmouth. When details were made public, in 1678, the attempt became known as "The Popish Plot." At the start of this satire, Shaftesbury, as Achitophel, is attempting, by saying that the right of succession sometimes brings harm to a nation, to persuade Absalom (Monmouth) to appeal to the people to dethrone King David and give him the throne. Rather than the "right of kings," he argues, there is such a thing as the "right of people" to decide how they shall be governed. The "right of succession," when it would bring harm to a country, should be abrogated. Perhaps the heir to the throne would suffer, but what is the unhappiness of one person in compar- ison to that of a whole nation?

> . . . the people have a right supreme
> To make their kings; for kings are made for them.
> All empire is no more than pow'r in trust,
> Which, when resum'd, can be no longer just.
> Succession, for the general good design'd,
> In its own wrong a nation cannot bind;
> If altering that the people can relieve.
> **Better one suffer than a nation grieve.**

Between craft and credulity, the voice of reason is stifled

Source: LETTER TO THE SHERIFFS OF BRISTOL
Author: Edmund Burke (1729-1797)
First published: 1777
Type of work: Political treatise

Context: Burke's letter was written to John Farr and John Harris, the sheriffs of Bristol, about the state of affairs between Great Britain and the American Colonies. Burke was elected to the House of Commons in 1774, as the representative of Bristol, whose citizens had broad commercial interests which made them sympathetic to Burke's liberal views on the war between Great Britain and the colonists. Burke was not a man to adhere blindly to abstract principles in the way of many of his fellow countrymen; he cared nothing for his country's right to coerce the Colonies or its so-called dignity. He asked always what was the humane action and what was in Great Britain's best interests in the long run. In his letter to the sheriff he writes to them about the most recent acts of Parliament with respect to the Colonies and what he calls the civil war then going on. He recounts how one of the acts brands men aboard American privateers and warships as buccaneers, to be tried and hanged as pirates when they are captured. Such action, along with the insistence upon trying Americans for treason only in Great Britain, Burke feels to be wholly unjustified. He also comments on the fact that New York, Long Island, and Staten Island should have been restored, but have not, to trade when they submitted voluntarily to British rule. Burke then comments:

> . . . But we see well enough to what the whole leads. The trade of America is to be dealt out in *private indulgences and graces;* that is, in jobs to recompense the incendiaries of war. They will be informed of the proper time in which to send out their merchandise. From a national, the American trade is to be turned into a personal monopoly; and one set of merchants are to be rewarded for the pretended zeal of which another set are the dupes; and

93

thus, **between craft and credulity, the voice of reason is stifled,** and all the misconduct, all the calamities of the war are covered and continued.

Beware of those who are homeless by choice

Source: THE DOCTOR (Chapter 34)
Author: Robert Southey (1774-1843)
First published: 1834-1847)
Type of work: Literary miscellany

Context: In his own time, Robert Southey was a literary innovator and leader; he explored new areas in writing, pioneered in a number of styles, and was the only "entire man of letters" in his day. He supported and helped to found the romantic movement, experimented with a number of departures from eighteenth century rigidity, and established paths for others to follow. These include the ballad, the reintroduction of blank verse, the epic, and the exotic oriental setting. He wrote voluminously in all fields; in addition to his poetry, he proved himself a competent historian, essayist, biographer, and critic. He was named poet laureate of England in 1813 and held the post for thirty years. A tireless scholar and a conscientious craftsman whose mind eventually failed from overwork, Southey now appears to have been far inferior in genius to his friends Coleridge, Wordsworth, and Scott; to present-day critics, his importance is almost purely historical and he is remembered for a handful of minor poems —and a nursery classic, "The Three Bears." It is generally agreed that his talents were not equal to his ambitions; and the epics, which he was certain would ensure his lasting reputation, are now considered failures. Nonetheless there is much of interest in his writings, and much of the unusual. *The Doctor* is an example of his prose; a lengthy and curious work which Southey wrote for amusement in his leisure time, it is a collection of nearly everything: fantasy, fiction, whimsy, opinion, criticism, lore of all sorts, anecdotes, and an overriding facetiousness. The last quality seems labored to a modern reader, whose attention is nonetheless held by the endless variety of the book. Many of his comments are sound and perceptive; for example, his distrust of the "world citizen" who acknowledges no ties, owes no allegiances, accepts no responsibilities, and cannot be involved in life:

Whatever strengthens our local attachments is favorable both to individual and national character. Our home,—our birth place, —our native land,—think for a while what the virtues are which arise out of the feelings connected with these words; and if thou hast any intellectual eyes thou wilt then perceive the connection between topography and patriotism.
Shew me a man who cares no more for one place than another,

and I will shew you in that same person one who loves nothing but himself. **Beware of those who are homeless by choice!** You have no hold on a human being whose affections are without a tap-root. The laws recognize this truth in the privileges which they confer upon freeholders; and public opinion acknowledges it also, in the confidence which it reposes upon those who have what is called a stake in the country. Vagabond and rogue are convertible terms; and with how much propriety any one may understand who knows what are the habits of the wandering classes, such as gypsies, tinkers, and potters.

Beware the fury of a patient man

Source: ABSALOM AND ACHITOPHEL (Part I, l. 1005)
Author: John Dryden (1631-1700)
First published: 1681
Type of work: Satiric poem

Context: According to warnings supplied to the British government by Titus Oates in August, 1678, conspirators were plotting the murder of King Charles, who would be replaced by James Duke of York, acting as an agent of the Jesuits. The French would then play a role to suppress the Protestants. Dryden satirized what was called "The Popish Plot," in the guise of retelling the Biblical story of Absalom's plot against his father, King David. Anthony Cooper, Earl of Shaftesbury, who at first sided with the king, later changed sides and became a strong supporter of the Exclusion Bill, whose purpose was to deprive the Duke of York of right of succession. He is cast in the poem as Achitophel. Absalom represents Monmouth, illegitimate son of Charles II. David is Charles II. Though the details of the plot reported by Oates were largely false, there was enough truth in them so that an investigation did reveal an actual conspiracy. King Charles II was forced to take action against Parliament (called "The Sanhedrin" in Dryden's allegory). James went into temporary exile; and in 1681, the year of the appearance of Dryden's poem, Shaftesbury was arrested for treason. In the lament of King David, close to the conclusion of the poem, one is reminded of Maxim Number 289 by Publilius Syrus of the first century, B.C.: "An overtaxed patience gives way to fury," as well as of the colloquial: "Even a worm will turn." Here David (Charles II) is sorry that the conspirators had mistaken his merciful treatment of them for fear. Now that his patience has been overtaxed, he will be forced to act cruelly and decisively.

. . .

Must I at length the sword of justice draw?
O curst effect of necessary law!
How ill my fear they by my mercy scan,
Beware the fury of a patient man.

95

Law they require, let Law then show her face;
They could not be content to look on Grace,
Her hinder parts, but with a daring eye
To tempt the terror of her front and die.

. . .

Big-Endians and Little-Endians

Source: GULLIVER'S TRAVELS (*Voyage to Lilliput,* Chapter IV)
Author: Jonathan Swift (1667-1745)
First published: 1726
Type of work: Satirical fiction

Context: Lemuel Gulliver, shipwrecked off the coast of Lilliput and captured by its tiny inhabitants, is exhibited before the Lilliputians, including their emperor. Instructed in the language, Gulliver is brought to the chief city, Mildendo, and into the court, where he discusses politics with a leading official. He is informed that a controversy over which end of an egg is to be broken has led to the formation of two political parties, the Big-Endians and the Little-Endians, with a result that Lilliput has been at war for thirty-six moons with the neighboring land of Blefescu. The author first recounts the historical episode, and scholars explain the meaning in a footnote:

> . . . It began upon the following occasion. It is allowed on all hands, that the primitive way of breaking eggs before we eat them, was upon the larger end: but his present Majesty's grandfather, while he was a boy, going to eat an egg, and breaking it according to the ancient practice, happened to cut one of his fingers. Whereupon the Emperor his father published an edict, commanding all his subjects, upon great penalties, to break the smaller end of their eggs.[3] . . .

---

[3] The **Big-Endians and Little-Endians** are no doubt the Roman Catholics and Protestants. But here, as elsewhere, the analogy must not be strained too far. The King who cut his finger is Henry VIII, the father of Edward VI.

The bird that flutters least is longest on the wing

Source: THE TASK (Book VI, ll. 930–931)
Author: William Cowper (1731-1800)
First published: 1785
Type of work: Meditative poem in blank verse

Context: This quotation is taken from that section, or book, of *The Task* entitled "The Winter Walk at Noon." The poet intersperses meditations on many topics with descriptions of the English countryside during a winter noon when snow blankets all the earth, except the places beneath the forest trees. Toward the end of this book, which is the last section of the poem, he meditates upon the end of creation and invokes the aid of God, Who will bring the end and the restoration of man. The poet, having been forced out of an active life by severe mental illness, seeks to vindicate the life, in spiritual terms, of the human being who has lived a life of retirement from the usual activities and pace of the world. He notes that the world scorns the pleasures of the retired person, as he overlooks the world's pleasures for what is beyond. The poet then explains why the spiritual man is not interested in the usual activities of this world.

> He seeks not hers, for he has proved them vain.
> He cannot skim the ground like summer birds
> Pursuing gilded flies, and such he deems
> Her honours, her emoluments, her joys;
> Therefore in contemplation is his bliss,
> Whose pow'r is such, that whom she lifts from earth
> She makes familiar with a heav'n unseen,
> And shows him glories yet to be reveal'd.
> Not slothful he, though seeming unemploy'd,
> And censured oft as useless. Stillest streams
> Oft water fairest meadows; and **the bird**
> **That flutters least is longest on the wing.**
> Ask him, indeed, what trophies he has raised,
> Or what achievements of immortal fame
> He purposes, and he shall answer—None.
> His warfare is within.

A bitter heart, that bides its time and bites

Source: CALIBAN UPON SETEBOS (Line 167)
Author: Robert Browning (1812-1889)
First published: 1864
Type of work: Dramatic monologue

Context: This poem, although subtitled "Natural Theology in the Island," is an attack upon such deterministic religious sects as Calvinism, which picture a God who saves or damns human beings, punishes or rewards them, wholly according to whim. The speaker of the poem is Caliban, the brutish monster-slave of Prospero in Shakespeare's *Tempest.* Caliban speculates upon his god, Setebos, who may be all-powerful or who may be under another god called the Quiet. Setebos is strong but devoid of any feelings of affection for the thing that he has created, man, although he may feel envy and spite. He is all alone in the cold, since to

97

have made a mate would have been like making himself. Caliban says that Setebos is like what he himself would be if he could give life to creatures he might make of clay. He might make a bird that would break its leg; when the poor creature cried out in pain, Caliban might pluck off its remaining leg, or, on the other hand, he might give it two more legs. Whichever he did, he would feel pleasure at the display of his power. As a line of crabs marched past him, he might smash one now and then— or give one a special reward. And again the whimsical display of power would be pleasing. Setebos has made things that are better than he is, but they must submit to his power. Setebos, however, looks up to the Quiet and envies it; then he looks down and makes imitations of a world and creatures that he can never reach. It is as though he had captured a sea beast which he had penned, blinded and with the webs of its feet split, in a pool. The creature, powerless as it is, yet has bitterness in its mind and bites at its master.

And hath an ounce sleeker than youngling mole,
A four-legged serpent he makes cower and couch,
Now snarl, now hold its breath and mind his eye,
And saith she is Miranda and my wife:
'Keeps for his Ariel a tall pouch-bill crane
He bids go wade for fish and straight disgorge;
Also a sea-beast, lumpish, which he snared,
Blinded the eyes of, and brought somewhat tame,
And split its toe-webs, and now pens the drudge
In a hole o' the rock and calls him Caliban;
A bitter heart, that bides its time and bites,
'Plays thus at being Prosper in a way,
Taketh his mirth with make-believes: so He.

The bivouac of the dead

Source: THE BIVOUAC OF THE DEAD (Stanza 1)
Author: Theodore O'Hara (1820-1867)
First published: 1847
Type of work: Ode

Context: Theodore O'Hara was primarily a soldier, exemplifying in his career the colorful reputation of the Irish. He was a Kentuckian by birth and during his checkered lifetime held numerous responsible posts in civilian life. But the world of the military evidently had first call upon him. After receiving his college education he was for a time Professor of Greek; he then practiced law and was later employed by the U.S. Treasury Department. When the Mexican War broke out, he served throughout the campaign and was brevetted for gallantry. After the war he practiced law again in Washington, D.C., but apparently could not settle down to the humdrum routines of peacetime. Becoming interested in the struggles for independence of patriots in other nations, he abandoned his law practice and led a regiment at Cardenas in support of Lopez for the liberation of Cuba. He returned severely wounded from this adventure, and as soon as he had recovered he joined Walker's filibustering expedition. Following this adventure, he resumed a peacetime existence and was connected editorially with several newspapers until the outbreak of the Civil War. During this conflict he served in the Confederate Army, first as Commander of the fort at Mobile Bay and later as Chief of Staff for General Breckenridge. O'Hara's devotion to military life and his understanding of the soldier give his poem "The Bivouac of the Dead" a certain personal quality that lifts it above many sentimental tributes of its time to those killed in the nation's wars. These are men he knew, men who fought beside him and shared the rigors of the campaign. The poem is one which O'Hara read at the dedication of a monument to the soldiers of Kentucky who were killed in the Mexican War; it enjoyed considerable popularity, and lines from it appeared frequently on monuments and gates in the various national cemeteries during the last half of the nineteenth century. The first two stanzas are given below:

> The muffled drum's sad roll has beat
> The soldier's last tattoo;
> No more on life's parade shall meet
> That brave and fallen few.
> On Fame's eternal camping-ground
> Their silent tents are spread,
> And glory guards with solemn round
> **The bivouac of the dead.**
>
> No rumor of the foe's advance
> Now swells upon the wind—
> No troubled thought at midnight haunts
> Of loved ones left behind;
> No vision of the morrow's strife
> The warrior's dream alarms;
> No braying horn or screaming fife
> At dawn shall call to arms.

The blind hysterics of the Celt

Source: IN MEMORIAM (Part CIX, stanza 4)
Author: Alfred, Lord Tennyson (1809-1892)
First published: 1850
Type of work: Elegy

Context: This elegy was written as a monument to Arthur Henry Hallam, a young man of extraordinary promise and an intimate friend of Tennyson's, who died suddenly in Vienna at the age of twenty-two. The poem records the slow, spiritual progress of Tennyson from his initial depth of personal sorrow to the gradual healing of grief through a sense of spiritual contact with Hallam in a wider love of God and humanity. Through intuition rather than reason, Tennyson has achieved a certainty that the spirit exists divorced from the body, that the spirit survives death. In Part CIX, the poet dwells on the completeness of Hallam's character, analyzing the characteristics of this ideal man. Hallam was original, yet critical; logical and forceful in "impassion'd logic;" a lover of good, yet not ascetic; a passionate, yet pure lover. Hallam had:

> A love of freedom rarely felt,
>   Of freedom in her regal seat
>   Of England; not the schoolboy heat,
> **The blind hysterics of the Celt;**
>   . . .
> All these have been, and thee mine eyes
>   Have look'd on: if they look'd in vain,
>   My shame is greater who remain,
> Nor let thy wisdom make me wise.

Bliss was it in that dawn to be alive, but to be young was very Heaven!

Source: THE PRELUDE (Book XI, ll. 108-109)
Author: William Wordsworth (1770-1850)
First published: 1850
Type of work: Autobiographical poem

Context: When still a young man, Wordsworth, like many of the British liberals, believed that the French Revolution marked the inauguration of a new age of political equality and freedom from tyranny; the old ways that had enslaved men were being changed by Reason, and dreams were coming true because people were concentrating on the problem of how to make life on earth pleasant rather than on how to earn an eternal life of joy. After he had grown apart from nature and momentarily accepted the rationalistic doctrine that man could form a perfect society on earth, Wordsworth was blinded to the full implications of the Revolution. In fact, he believed so strongly in the power of Reason that the Reign of Terror and the execution of the royal family came as a disillusioning shock to him and threw him into such a quandary that for a while he could find nothing solid upon which to build his life. The quotation comes from his account of the dreams of his youth before the period of disillusionment began.

Bliss was it in that dawn to be alive,
But to be young was very Heaven! O times,
In which the meagre, stale, forbidding ways
Of custom, law, and statute, took at once
The attraction of a country in romance!
When Reason seemed the most to assert her rights,
When most intent on making of herself
A prime enchantress—to assist the work
Which then was going forward in her name!

Blond beast

Source: A GENEALOGY OF MORALS (First Essay, section 11, as translated by
William A. Hausemann)
Author: Friedrich Wilhelm Nietzsche (1844-1900)
First published: 1887
Type of work: Philosophy

Context: The influence of Nietzsche upon certain areas of twentieth century thought has been considerable. Although students of his work have divided his development into three periods, his underlying ideas remained much the same and his changes lay in his consideration of them. His third, or ethical, period is usually considered most important; in it he seeks to define the ultimate good. To Nietzsche there are two standards of good and evil, one for the masters and one for the slaves. According to the first standard, whatever expresses the will of the individual or forms a part of him is good; all else is evil. Under the second standard, anything painful is bad and whatever makes life more endurable is good. Western standards are at present those of the slaves; Nietzsche blames this state of affairs on a plot by the Jews. Self-assertion is his moral ideal: the will to power lies at the root of all things, and power is the sole good which can be gained. In connection with this idea may be mentioned the concept most often associated with him—the doctrine of the superman. Nietzsche believed that man will evolve into a higher species. He also believed in External Recurrence, an old theory that history is a great cycle and repeats itself in every detail. To it he added the idea that life is good because of suffering, not in spite of it. He believed the ultimate good in art is a mixture of dream and intoxication evoking an underlying truth, a goal most nearly achieved in Wagnerian opera. A number of his ideas were incorporated into the ideology of Adolf Hitler and Nazi Germany. Nietzsche's writing style is somewhat incoherent; much of his life was spent in a struggle against the insanity which destroyed his mind in 1889. In the following selection Nietzsche, who has been discussing the cramped and cowardly outlook of the servile mentality, contrasts with it his ideal man—the lusty and amoral young savage:

101

. . . those very men, who by manners, reverence, usage, gratitude, and still more by mutual superintendence, by jealousy *inter pares* are rigorously held within bounds, and who, on the other hand, in their conduct among one another prove themselves so inventive in regardfulness, self-restraint, delicacy, faith, pride and friendship,—these same men are towards that which is without, which to them is foreign, a foreign land, not much better than so many disengaged beasts of prey. Here they enjoy liberty from all social restraint; the wilderness must compensate them for the tension produced by a long incarceration and impalement in the "peace" of society; they step *back* into the innocence of the conscience of the beast of prey, as exultant monsters, which, perhaps, walk away from an abominable sequence of murder, burning down, violation, torture, with such wantonness and equanimity, as if merely some student-trick had been accomplished; with the conviction, that now for a long time again the poets will have something to celebrate and sing of. At the ground of all these noble races, the beast of prey, the splendid, **blond beast,** lustfully roving in search of spoils and victory, cannot be mistaken. An outlet is necessary from time to time for this hidden ground; the animal must come out again, must go back into wilderness: Roman, Arabian, Germanic, Japanese nobility, Homeric heroes, Scandinavian vikings—in this need they all are *one.* It is the noble races, that left the concept "barbarian" on every trace, wherever they passed; even in their highest civilisation the consciousness of this fact is visible and even a certain pride in it. . . .

The blood of the martyrs is the seed of the Church

Source: APOLOGETICUS (50)
Author: Tertullian (c.155-c.220)
First transcribed: c.197
Type of work: Religious philosophy

Context: Educated in his native Carthage and in Rome in law and in rhetoric, Tertullian was well prepared for the position he holds as ablest of the early defenders of the Christian faith. Among his writings are *De Carne Christi,* a rebuttal to Marcion and other heretics, and a number of treatises on morality and the discipline of the Church. His *Apologeticus* points out the guilt of many non-Christians of the very acts of immorality for which Christians are falsely accused and for which they suffer martyrdom. Ironically *"the blood of the martyrs is the seed of the Church,"* contends Tertullian, for Christian believers multiply with each incidence of martyrdom:

. . . Nor does your cruelty, however exquisite, avail you; it is rather a temptation to us. The oftener we are mown down by you, the more in number we grow; **the blood of Christians is seed.** Many of your writers exhort to the courageous bearing of pain and death, as Cicero in the *Tusculans,* as Seneca in his *Chances,* as Diogenes, Pyrrhus, Callinicus. And yet their words do not find so many disciples as Christians do, teachers not by words, but by their deeds. . . .

Blood will have blood

Source: MACBETH (Act III, sc. iv, l. 122)
Author: William Shakespeare (1564-1616)
First published: 1623
Type of work: Dramatic tragedy

Context: Macbeth orders Banquo and his son, Fleance, murdered the night of his feast. The murderers kill Banquo, but Fleance escapes. One of the murderers comes to tell Macbeth what has happened just as the celebration is beginning. Macbeth, knowing full well Banquo is dead, wishes for his presence and is confronted by his wounded and gory ghost sitting in the place of honor. Shocked almost into madness, Macbeth babbles of blood and murders. Lady Macbeth hastily excuses him on grounds of an old infirmity, but when the ghost returns a second time, Macbeth is completely unnerved. Lady Macbeth asks the guests to leave immediately. Macbeth is sure the ghost is a horrible omen of things to come.

LADY MACBETH
I pray you speak not; he grows worse and worse.
Question enrages him. At once, good night.

·   ·   ·

MACBETH
It will have blood, they say; **blood will have blood.**
Stones have been known to move, and trees to speak.
Augurs and understood relations have
By maggot-pies and choughs and rooks brought forth
The secret'st man of blood. What is the night?

Blow winds, and crack your cheeks

Source: KING LEAR (Act III, sc. ii, l. 1)
Author: William Shakespeare (1564-1616)
First published: 1608
Type of work: Dramatic tragedy

Context: King Lear, old and foolish, has attempted to rid himself of the responsibilities of kingship by dividing his realm among his three daughters

103

on the condition that each daughter declare her love for him. When the youngest daughter, Cordelia, refuses to indulge in the effusive love of her sisters, she is disinherited. Lear, however, soon discovers the seeming love of Goneril and Regan, his oldest daughters, and when Regan puts

Kent, the king's courtier, into stocks and Goneril refuses to take the part of the aged monarch, he calls his daughters "unnatural hags" and rushes into the stormy night. On the heath with his faithful fool, he cries out against the elements:

LEAR
Blow winds, and crack your cheeks. Rage, blow,
You cataracts, and hurricanoes, spout
Till you have drenched our steeples, drowned the cocks.
You sulphurous and thought-executing fires,
Vaunt-couriers of oak-cleaving thunderbolts,
Singe my white head. And thou all-shaking thunder,
Strike flat the thick rotundity o' th' world,
Crack nature's moulds, all germens spill at once,
That makes ingrateful man.

The bonded warehouse of my knowledge

Source: HANDLEY CROSS (Chapter 27, 1843 edition; Chapter 32, 1854 edition)
Author: Robert Smith Surtees (1803-1864)
First published: 1843
Type of work: Novel

Context: Robert Surtees, as editor of *The New Sporting Magazine,* established a place in literature for himself with a long series of humorous sketches which he contributed to its pages. The principal character which he developed as humorist and chronicler of the hunting field is that of John Jorrocks, a wholesale grocer in London whose greatest ambition is to become a Master of Foxhounds. These sketches were first collected in book form in *Jorrocks' Jaunts and Jollities* (1838); another collection entitled *Handley Cross* was published in 1843. A second edition of *Handley Cross,* greatly enlarged with additional characters and episodes, appeared in 1854. The sleepy little vil-

lage of Handley Cross, located in the Vale of Sheepwash, has experienced a sudden burst of prosperity and become a flourishing community. Now approaching urban status, it desires more formality in its social institutions. The hunt is one of these. Jorrocks has become widely known by this time because of his frequent country excursions, during which he combines business with pleasure by taking orders for groceries while riding with the huntsmen. This is the reason the Committee of Management, seeking a likely candidate for Master of the Handley Cross Hunt, sends its invitation to Jorrocks. His dreams come true, Jorrocks arrives in a state of great agitation; he delivers an impassioned acceptance speech to the townspeople and nearly breaks down in the middle of it. He describes the ideal M.F.H., and assures his listeners he is prepared to meet those qualifications; furthermore, he intends to deliver a series of "lectors" on various matters pertaining to the hunt. It is soon evident that whenever Jorrocks allows himself to dwell upon the joys of the chase, his emotions get the best of him. In his first lecture, he instructs novices in the art of acquiring a horse; in the second, he takes up another important matter:

"Frinds and fellow-countrymen! Lend me your ears. That's to say, listen to wot I'm a goin' to say to you. This night I shall enlighten you on the all-important ceremony of takin' the field." (Loud applause.)

"TAKIN' THE FIELD!" repeated he, throwing out his arms, and casting his eyes up at the elegant looping of his canopy. "TAKIN' THE FIELD! glorious sound! wot words can convey anything 'alf so delightful?

"In my mind's eye I see the 'ounds in all their glossy pride a trottin' around Arterxerxes, who stamps and whinnies with delight at their company. There's old Pristess with her speckled sides, lookin' as wise as a Christian, and Trusty, and Tuneable, and Warrior, and Wagrant, and Workman, and Wengence, and all the glorious comrades o' the chase.

"But to the pint. Ingenious youth, having got his 'oss, and learned to tackle him, let me now, from **the bonded warehouse of my knowledge,** prepare him for the all-glorious ceremony of the 'unt.

"How warious are the motives," continued Mr. Jorrocks, looking thoughtfully, "that draw men to the kiver side. Some come to see, others to be seen; some for the ride out, others for the ride 'ome; some for happetites, some for 'ealth, some to get away from their wives, and a few to 'unt. Ah! give me the few. . . ."

The bone of manhood

Source: SPEECH ON MOVING HIS RESOLUTIONS FOR RECONCILIATION WITH THE COLONIES
Author: Edmund Burke (1729-1797)
First published: 1775
Type of work: Political speech

Context: As a member of Parliament, Burke defied George III, who was attempting to overthrow established political traditions and centralize governmental power, and he strongly urged that Parliament should not suppress the American Colonies, citing the acts of redress for both Ireland and Wales as precedent. Not only, he argued, would justice and right be served by a reconciliation between the colonies and the mother

105

country, but such action would also be profitable for England as a result of the many imports, exports, and in- dustries of the colonies, especially their whaling and fishing activities:

> . . . No sea but what is vexed by their fisheries. No climate that is not witness to their toils. Neither the perseverance of Holland, nor the activity of France, nor the dexterous and firm sagacity of English enterprise, ever carried this most perilous mode of hard industry to the extent to which it has been pushed by this recent people; a people who are still, as it were, but in the gristle, and not yet hardened into **the bone of manhood.** When I contemplate these things; when I know that the colonies in general owe little or nothing to any care of ours, and that they are not squeezed into this happy form by the constraints of watchful and suspicious government, but that, through a wise and salutary neglect, a generous nature has been suffered to take her own way to perfection; . . . when I see how profitable they have been to us, I feel all the pride of power sink, and all presumption in the wisdom of human contrivances melt and die away within me. My rigour relents. I pardon something to the spirit of liberty.

A book in breeches

Source: A MEMOIR OF THE REVEREND SYDNEY SMITH BY HIS DAUGHTER LADY HOLLAND (Chapter 11)
Author: Sydney Smith (1771-1845)
First published: 1855
Type of work: Biographical memoir

Context: A considerable part of Saba, Lady Holland's, biography of her father, the Reverend Sydney Smith, is devoted to quotations from his general conversation, in Combe Florey where he preached. Begun in 1843, the biography was not published until ten years after his death. Most of his quips and comments appear in unconnected paragraphs. One of the longest paragraphs reports his comment about Thomas Babington Macaulay (1800–1859). Many people have been called "a walking encyclopedia." Here is a more original description of a well-informed man, "like a book in breeches." Macaulay read widely and voraciously, and many have testified to his retentive memory.

> Some one speaking of Macaulay: "Yes, I take great credit to myself; I always prophesied his greatness from the first moment I saw him, then a very young and unknown man, on the Northern Circuit. There are no limits to his knowledge, on small subjects as well as on great; he is like **a book in breeches.** . . . Yes, I agree, he is certainly more agreeable since his return from India. His en-

emies might perhaps have said before (though I never did so) that he talked rather too much; but now he has occasional flashes of silence that make his conversation perfectly delightful. . . ."

Books are not seldom talismans and spells

Source: THE TASK (Book VI, l. 98)
Author: William Cowper (1731-1800)
First published: 1785
Type of work: Meditative poem in blank verse

Context: This quotation is from the sixth book, or section, of the poem, entitled "The Winter Walk at Noon." As in the other books of the poem, Cowper here mingles meditations on many subjects with descriptions of nature. In this book, as in the one preceding, the descriptions are of the English countryside in the winter-time. One also finds in this section the poet's thoughts on a wide variety of subjects: bells ringing in the distance, the origin of cruelty to animals, the difference between lawful and unlawful destruction of animals, man's extravagant praise of himself, and, among other topics, the effect the spring season has upon the shrubbery. The particular quotation is taken from the section containing Cowper's commentary on meditation, in which he opines that meditation is better for man than the study of books. Walking in the silent woods of winter, the poet says, "Meditation here may think down hours to moments." He says also that he believes the heart must give lessons to the head, that knowledge and wisdom often have little or nothing in common. He goes on to compare knowledge and wisdom:

> Knowledge dwells
> In heads replete with thoughts of other men;
> Wisdom in minds attentive to their own.
> Knowledge, a rude unprofitable mass,
> The mere materials with which wisdom builds,
> Till smooth'd and squared and fitted to its place,
> Does but encumber whom it seems t'enrich.
> Knowledge is proud that he has learn'd so much;
> Wisdom is humble that he knows no more.
> **Books are not seldom talismans and spells**
> By which the magic art of shrewder wits
> Holds an unthinking multitude enthrall'd.

Books are the legacies that a great genius leaves to mankind

Source: THE SPECTATOR (Number 166)
Author: Joseph Addison (1672-1719)
First published: September 10, 1711
Type of work: Essay

Context: The Spectator, a periodical issued by Joseph Addison and his friend and classmate Richard Steele, amused and enlightened the English public by telling, among other matters, of the conversation of a small club meeting at a coffee house. The members of the club included a country gentleman, Sir Roger de Coverley, the author, known as Mr. Spectator, and several other members representative of the general populace. In issue Number 166, Addison discusses the concept of Aristotle that the world is a transcript of the mind of the first being and that the ideas of men are transcripts of the world. Following this logic, says Addison, books are the legacies left by geniuses to mankind:

> There is no other method of fixing those thoughts which arise and disappear in the mind of man, and transmitting them to the last periods of time; no other method of giving a permanency to our ideas, and preserving the knowledge of any particular person, when his body is mixed with the common mass of matter, and his soul retired into the world of spirits. **Books are the legacies that a great genius leaves to mankind,** which are delivered down from generation to generation, as presents to the posterity of those who are yet unborn.

Books, clad in black and red

Source: THE CANTERBURY TALES (Prologue, l. 294)
Author: Geoffrey Chaucer (1343?-1400)
First transcribed: c. 1387-1392
Type of work: Collection of tales

Context: Chaucer, to bind together his collection of tales, establishes the framework of a group of pilgrims traveling from the Tabard Inn in Southwark to the shrine of Thomas à Becket at Canterbury and telling tales to make the trip less tiresome. In the Prologue, the pilgrims are introduced and described in sharp detail. Among the most memorable of the travelers is a poor clerk, or student, who would choose from the world's riches a mere collection of books.

> A CLERK ther was of Oxenford also,
> That unto logyk hadde longe ygo.
> As leene was his hors as is a rake,
> And he nas nat right fat, I undertake,
> But looked holwe, and therto sobrely.
> Ful thredbare was his overeste courtepy;
> For he hadde geten hym yet no benefice,
> Ne was so worldly for to have office.
> For hym was levere have at his beddes heed
> Twenty **bookes, clad in blak or reed,**

Of Aristotle and his philosophie,
Than robes riche, or fithele, or gay sautrie.

Boston State House is the hub of the solar system

Source: THE AUTOCRAT OF THE BREAKFAST-TABLE (Chapter 6)
Author: Oliver Wendell Holmes (1809-1894)
First published: 1858
Type of work: Essay

Context: Chapter Six of *The Autocrat of the Breakfast Table* opens with a discussion of famous sayings by men of Boston, starting with Benjamin Franklin's comment, "He that has once done you a kindness will be more ready to do you another than he whom you yourself have obliged." This is followed by a comment attributed to the Autocrat's friend, the Historian, "Give us the luxuries of life, and we will dispense with its necessaries." The Autocrat adds a third, "Good Americans, when they die, go to Paris." A stranger at the boarding-house table, a young "jaunty-looking" chap, says he has heard a fourth saying, about Boston and its views. Under some prodding from the other guests, the young man gives the quotation above. It is followed by a discussion of the parochialism that one finds in every city. The people of Boston, suggests the Autocrat, are no different in their attitudes toward their native city from those of other towns, large or small. He goes on to comment, "Boston is just like the other places of its size;—only, perhaps, considering its excellent fish-market, paid fire-department, superior monthly publications, and correct habit of spelling the English language, it has some right to look down on the mob of cities."

A jaunty-looking person, who had come in with the young fellow they call John,—evidently a stranger,—said there was one more wise man's sayings that he had heard; it was about our place, but he didn't know who said it.—A civil curiosity was manifested by the company to hear the fourth wise saying. I heard him distinctly whispering to the young fellow who brought him to dinner, *Shall I tell it?* To which the answer was, *Go ahead!*—Well,—he said,—this was what I heard:—

"Boston State-House is the hub of the solar system. You couldn't pry that out of a Boston man, if you had the tire of all creation straightened out for a crowbar."

Bottled lightning

Source: NICHOLAS NICKLEBY (Chapter 49)
Author: Charles Dickens (1812-1870)
First published: 1838-1839
Type of work: Novel

Context: After the great success of *Pickwick Papers* and *Oliver Twist* had established his reputation, Dickens looked around for a new subject to which he could direct his humanitarian and reforming zeal. As a child, he had heard of the notorious "Yorkshire schools," the name given to a type of school, many of them located in that county, which, while masquerading as educational institutions, were in reality only places to which unwanted children could be sent to be kept out of the way. They were run by ignorant and often brutal men, and the ill-treatment to which the helpless boys were subjected had become a byword. Dickens traveled to Yorkshire under an assumed name and with the pretext of being a parent in search of such a school. He soon assembled his material and created the figure of Wackford Squeers, headmaster of Dotheboys Hall, one of his most loathsome scoundrels. To develop the complicated and melodramatic type of plot at which he excelled, Dickens interwove the story of Squeers and his school with that of the usurer Ralph Nickleby, uncle of the naïve hero of the novel. Around the main characters Dickens grouped a supporting cast of the humorous and eccentric minor figures that his inexhaustible imagination produced. One of these is Mrs. Nickleby, the verbose, rattle-brained, and totally impractical mother of the hero. In one of the comic side episodes of the story, Mrs. Nickleby and her daughter Kate are entertaining some callers, when their attention is attracted by strange noises from the next room. The group rushes to investigate and discovers that a man is climbing down the chimney; his feet and legs are already visible. When he is pulled out, he is revealed as "the gentleman in small-clothes" (that is, tightly-fitting knee breeches), a harmless lunatic living in the next house who fancies himself in love with Mrs. Nickleby. His first demand, after a rambling speech by that lady, in which she expresses her inability to accept his attentions, has given us a phrase still applied to liquor of unusual strength:

. . . He did not appear to take the smallest notice of what Mrs. Nickleby said, but when she ceased to speak he honoured her with a long stare, and inquired if she had quite finished.

"I have nothing more to say," replied that lady modestly. "I really cannot say anything more."

"Very good," said the old gentleman, raising his voice, "then bring in the **bottled lightning,** a clean tumbler, and a corkscrew."

Nobody executing this order, the old gentleman, after a short pause, raised his voice again and demanded a thunder sandwich. This article not being forthcoming either, he requested to be served with a fricassee of boot-tops and goldfish sauce, . . .

Bowels of compassion

Source: I JOHN 3:17
Author: Unknown (traditionally John the Apostle)
First transcribed: c.95-100
Type of work: Pastoral epistle

Context: The author of this epistle was a man of great authority in early Church matters, and it is probable that he was also the author of the fourth Gospel. It is not known with certainty that he was John the Apostle; but if not, he was apparently either an eyewitness to much of Jesus' ministry or knew those who were. The present epistle forms part of a battle of the early Church to preserve its identity. Gnosticism was a growing religious movement of the time which sought to combine all religions and to embrace all religious systems and philosophies under a universal method. There were some able thinkers connected with it, and it offered something of a synthesis, capable of endless adaptation, and having some philosophical basis. It offered a kind of pantheism in which the various gods were represented by spiritual essences, and all manner of ceremonies were connected with it. Being more a method or system than a result, it could include both puritanical fanatics and debased libertines. There were early Christians who wished for such a tolerant arrangement; but John and his contemporaries saw a very real danger in it. If Christianity should be absorbed into such a system, its entire meaning and identity would cease to be important and would soon be destroyed. Too, there were opponents of Christianity who were promoting the Gnostic adoption of Christianity, probably for that very reason. This was a time when sects were proliferating, and most of the Gnostic-Christian groups had already withdrawn from the parent Church. John's epistle represents an effort on his part to strengthen those who remain faithful to it; he sets forth Christian principles simply and clearly for them, that they may not be tempted to abandon the Church in favor of a debased substitute.

Whosoever is born of God doth not commit sin; for his seed remaineth in him: and he cannot sin, because he is born of God.

In this the children of God are manifest, and the children of the devil: whosoever doeth not righteousness is not of God, neither he that loveth not his brother.

For this is the message that ye heard from the beginning, that we should love one another.

Not as Cain, who was of that wicked one, and slew his brother. And wherefore slew he him? Because his own works were evil, and his brother's righteous.

Marvel not, my brethren, if the world hate you.

We know that we have passed from death unto life, because we love the brethren. He that loveth not his brother abideth in death.

Whosoever hateth his brother is a murderer: and ye know that no murderer hath eternal life abiding in him.

Hereby perceive we the love of God, because he laid down his life for us: and we ought to lay down our lives for the brethren.

But whoso hath this world's good, and seeth his brother have need, and shutteth up his **bowels of compassion** from him, how dwelleth the love of God in him?

My little children, let us not love in word, neither in tongue; but in deed and in truth.

The bravest are the tenderest, the loving are the daring

Source: A SONG OF THE CAMP (Stanza 11)
Author: Bayard Taylor (1825-1878)
First published: 1860
Type of work: Lyric poem

Context: A Song of the Camp relates an incident in the Crimean War. The English, Irish, and Scottish troops have temporarily ceased from bombarding the enemy forts when a guardsman, announcing that they are to storm the forts tomorrow, calls for a song. The songs the soldiers sing are of love, not of Britain's glory. All sing "Annie Laurie," but each soldier thinks of a different name as he sings. Voice after voice catches up the song, until it rises like an anthem, and many a soldier has the powder stains washed off his face by tears of honest emotion. The next day the battle resumes:

> Beyond the darkening ocean burned
> The bloody sunset's embers,
> While the Crimean valleys learned
> How English love remembers.
>
> And once again a fire of hell
> Rained on the Russian quarters,
> With scream of shot, and burst of shell,
> And bellowing oɪ the mortars!
>
> And Irish Nora's eyes are dim
> For a singer, dumb and gory;
> And English Mary mourns for him
> Who sang of "Annie Laurie."
>
> Sleep, soldiers! still in honored rest
> Your truth and valor wearing:
> **The bravest are the tenderest,—**
> **The loving are the daring.**

Brazil, where the nuts come from

Source: CHARLEY'S AUNT (Act I)
Author: Brandon Thomas (1849-1914)
First published: 1892
Type of work: Dramatic comedy

Context: Brandon Thomas, British dramatist, is best remembered today for his comedy "Charley's Aunt;" it was tremendously popular and its initial run lasted four years. It is still frequently revived, and over the past three-quarters of a century has moved millions to tears of laughter. Jack Chesney and Charles Wykeham, undergraduates at Oxford, are both in love—Jack with Kitty Verdun and Charles with Amy Spettigue. Neither has found himself able to declare the fact. Charley's aunt, Donna Lucia d'Alvadorez, is coming to pay him a visit. She is from Brazil, is wealthy and is a widow; but Charley has never seen her and knows nothing about her beyond these basic facts. Jack's father drops by to leave his son an allowance check, and while there informs Jack that their fortune is in difficulties; Jack tells him about the impending visit of Charley's aunt and suggests that his father try to win her hand. The boys invite Kitty and Amy to their lodgings for luncheon, since all will be chaperoned by the aunt— but a message arrives from that lady, saying she will be delayed. Jack and Charley are determined to have their luncheon anyway, but must not compromise the girls. A solution to this dilemma occurs in the form of a fellow undergraduate, Lord Fancourt Babberley, who is to impersonate an old lady in some amateur theatricals. The boys force him into his costume and pass him off as Charley's aunt. Kitty and Amy make a great fuss over him when they arrive, to his obvious delight. Presently Amy's uncle appears, bent on breaking up the party; Lord Fancourt scolds him and sends him on his way, unaware that both Spettigue and Jack's father will be competing for Charley's Aunt's vast fortune and her hand in marriage. As Spettigue leaves, Lord Fancourt shies a book at him and knocks off his hat. Spettigue exits, muttering to himself. As soon as he is gone, Jack and Charley and the two girls come back into the room.

KITTY [*to* LORD FANCOURT.]
It was sweet of you!

AMY
You darling!
[*One on each side of* LORD FANCOURT, *they kiss him.*]

CHARLEY
Look at him, Jack!

JACK [*to* CHARLEY.]
I'll punch his head if he does it again!
Here's my father!

JACK [*to* LORD FANCOURT.]
Donna Lucia!
[*Aside.*] Take care, here's my father.

LORD FANCOURT
Look here, am I any relation to him?

113

JACK

No; You're *Charley's* Aunt, from **Brazil.**

LORD FANCOURT

Brazil! Where's that?

JACK

You know—er—**where the nuts come from.**

The bread of life

Source: JOHN 6:35
Author: Unknown (traditionally John the Apostle)
First transcribed: By 130
Type of work: Gospel

Context: In Chapter 6 of his Gospel, John describes the miracle of the loaves and fishes, in which Jesus miraculously feeds an audience of five thousand persons with five barley loaves and two small fish. He gives these to his disciples to distribute among the crowd, and after everyone is fed all he can eat there are twelve baskets of food left over. According to Matthew, this incident occurs while Jesus is sorrowing for the brutal execution of John the Baptist; but the writer of this Gospel does not connect the two. Both Gospels record that Jesus afterward sends the disciples ahead by ship and asks the multitudes to return to their homes; and thus excusing Himself, He ascends into a mountain to pray. The implication in Matthew is that He wishes to be alone because of His grief concerning the Baptist; according to John, Jesus retires to the mountain to pray for another reason: the people wish to make Him king. An excellent case could be made that the two accounts do not conflict with each other, and that if the two were combined a fuller and probably more accurate rendering of the event would result. Such an assumption does much to emphasize those trials of the spirit that Jesus was continually beset with. It is the belief of some scholars that John's intention was to supplement the other Gospels with information and events which they do not include. His description of the miracle which followed that of the loaves and fishes is in substantial agreement with Matthew: after Jesus' disciples have embarked, they are caught in a storm, and Jesus walks to them across the water. He reassures them, the storm dies, and they reach port safely. John does not mention Peter's test of faith, when he tried to walk on the water and partially succeeded. John relates that the multitude, on the following day, goes in search of Jesus; and when they find Him He obliges them with a sermon.

Jesus answered them and said, Verily, verily, I say unto you, Ye seek me, not because ye saw the miracles, but because ye did eat of the loaves and were filled.

Labour not for the meat which perisheth, but for that meat which endureth unto everlasting life, which the Son of man shall give unto you: for him hath God the Father sealed.

Then said they unto him, What shall we do, that we might work the works of God?

Jesus answered and said unto them, This is the work of God, that ye believe on him whom he hath sent.

They said therefore unto him, What sign shewest thou then, that we may see, and believe thee? what dost thou work?

Our fathers did eat manna in the desert; as it is written, He gave them bread from heaven to eat.

Then Jesus said unto them, Verily, verily, I say unto you, Moses gave you not that bread from heaven; but my Father giveth you the true bread from heaven.

For the bread of God is he which cometh down from heaven, and giveth life unto the world.

Then said they unto him, Lord, evermore give us this bread.

And Jesus said unto them, I am **the bread of life:** he that cometh to me shall never hunger; and he that believeth on me shall never thirst.

Bred en bawn in a brier patch

Source: HOW MR. RABBIT WAS TOO SHARP FOR MR. FOX
Author: Joel Chandler Harris (1848-1908)
First published: 1880 in *Uncle Remus: His Songs and His Sayings*
Type of work: Short story

Context: The feud between Brer (Brother) Fox and Brer Rabbit is the origin of a number of tales, supposedly told by old Uncle Remus, on a plantation in middle Georgia. Their author, always known by his full name, Joel Chandler Harris, wrote them for *The Atlanta Constitution,* on which he advanced from reporter to editor between 1876 and 1900. In 1880 he gathered 34 of his animal fables into *Uncle Remus, His Songs and His Sayings.* The best known story of them begins in Chapter 2, "The Wonderful Tar-Baby Story," and continues in Chapter 4, "How Mr. Rabbit Was Too Sharp for Mr. Fox." To capture his annoying enemy, Brer Rabbit, Brer Fox mixes tar with "turkentine," and models a Tar-Baby. Along comes the Rabbit. Angry because the creature will not answer his greeting, the Rabbit punches its head, and his fist sticks in the sticky mess. In a second attempt to punch it, the Rabbit's other fist sticks tight. So do his feet, when he tries to kick the Tar-Baby. Now he cannot move. At this point, Uncle Remus interrupts the story. He looks at the little boy and sees that "Old Man Nod wuz ridin' on his eyelids." In Chapter 4, he finishes the tale. To all the cruel threats made by Brer Fox about what he is going to do with his victim, Brer Rabbit has only one reply: "I don't keer what you do wid me, Brer Fox, so you don't fling me in dat brier-patch." Deciding to punish the Rabbit in the way he feared most, Brer Fox:

> cotch 'im by de behinn legs en slung 'im right in de middle er de brier-patch . . . Brer Fox sorter hang 'roun' fer ter see w'at wuz gwine ter happen. Bimeby he hear somebody call 'im, en way up de hill he see Brer Rabbit settin' cross-legged on a chinkapin log koamin' de pitch out'n his ha'r wid a chip. Den Brer Fox know dat he been swop off mighty bad. Brer Rabbit wuz bleedzd fer ter fling back some er his sass, en he holler out:
> **"Bred en bawn in a brier-patch,** Brer Fox!" . . . en wid dat he skip out des ez lively ez a cricket in de embers.

Bright Apollo's lute, strung with his hair

Source: LOVE'S LABOUR'S LOST (Act IV, sc. iii, l. 343)
Author: William Shakespeare (1564-1616)
First published: 1598
Type of work: Dramatic comedy

Context: The Court of Navarre shall become "a little Academe" pledge King Ferdinand and his lords, Berowne, Longaville, and Dumaine, as they vow for three years to forsake women, to fast, and to study. The arrival of the Princess of France and three attractive attendants on a diplomatic mission upsets the academicians, who fall in love with the ladies, forsake their former vows, and pledge themselves to pursue love and happiness. Love, says Berowne, which enhances the senses, is "as sweet and musical" as the golden lyre of Apollo, a favorite god of the Greeks associated with light, truth, and beauty:

BEROWNE
. . .

Love's feeling is more soft and sensible
Than are the tender horns of cockled snails.
Love's tongue proves dainty Bacchus gross in taste.
For valour, is not Love a Hercules,
Still climbing trees in the Hesperides?
Subtle as Sphinx, as sweet and musical
As **bright Apollo's lute, strung with his hair.**
And when Love speaks, the voice of all the gods
Make heaven drowsy with the harmony.
Never durst poet touch a pen to write
Until his ink were tempered with Love's sighs.
O then his lines would ravish savage ears
And plant in tyrants mild humility.
. . .

The bright face of danger

Source: ACROSS THE PLAINS, WITH OTHER MEMORIES AND ESSAYS ("The Lantern-Bearers," Part IV)
Author: Robert Louis Stevenson (1850-1894)
First published: 1892
Type of work: Literary essay

Context: In his essay *The Lantern-Bearers,* Stevenson investigates the poetic impulse which he feels to be universal in man. Painting a vivid word picture of his youth in a sea-coast village, he describes a local custom among the boys: in autumn they bought tin bull's-eye lanterns of the type once worn by policemen. These had a shutter which cut off the dim light they produced and were called dark-lanterns. They were sometimes used also by burglars, but the boys were imitating neither. Each wearing his lantern concealed under his top-coat, the boys would sally forth and foregather in the early darkness to talk of the things they felt at their age to be serious. "But the talk, at any rate," says Stevenson, "was but a condiment; and these gatherings themselves only accidents in the career of the lantern-bearer. The essence of this bliss was to walk by yourself in the black night; the slide shut, the top-coat buttoned; not a ray escaping, whether to conduct your footsteps or to make your glory public . . . and to exult and sing over the knowledge."

It is said that a poet has died young in the breast of the most stolid. It may be contended, rather, that this (somewhat minor) bard in almost every case survives, and is the spice of life to his possessor. Justice is not done to the versatility and the unplumbed childishness of man's imagination. His life from without may seem but a rude mound of mud; there will be some golden chamber at the heart of it, in which he dwells delighted; and for as dark as his pathway seems to the observer, he will have some kind of a bull's-eye at his belt. . . .

The average man . . . is just like you and me, or he would not be average . . . this harping on life's dulness and meanness is a loud profession of incompetence; it is one of two things: the cry of the blind eye, *I cannot see,* or the complaint of the dumb tongue, *I cannot utter.* To draw a life without delights is to prove I have not realised it. . . .

For to miss the joy is to miss all. In the joy of the actors lies the sense of any action. That is the explanation, that the excuse. To one who has not the secret of the lanterns, the scene . . . is meaningless. And hence the haunting and truly spectral unreality of realistic books . . . in each, life falls dead like dough . . . ; each is true, each inconceivable; for no man lives in the external truth, among salts and acids, but in the warm, phantasmagoric chamber of his brain. . . .

In nobler books we are moved with something like the emotions of life. . . . These are notes that please the great heart of man.

Not only love, and the fields, and **the bright face of danger,** but sacrifice and death and unmerited suffering humbly supported, touch in us the vein of the poetic. We love to think of them, we long to try them, we are humbly hopeful that we may prove heroes also.

A bright particular star

Source: ALL'S WELL THAT ENDS WELL (Act I, sc. i, l. 97)
Author: William Shakespeare (1564-1616)
First published: 1623
Type of work: Dramatic comedy

Context: Helena, daughter of the late physician of great renown Gerard de Narbon, has been taken into the household of the Countess of Rousillon, where she is loved and treated as a daughter. As the play begins, Bertram, the Countess' son, is commanded to attend the king at his court and takes sorrowful leave of his mother and the strangely reticent Helena. Upon Bertram's departure, Helena in soliloquy pours out her secret love for him and thus explains her melancholy silence. Not of noble birth, she has held her love within her heart alone rather than embarrass the Countess, for whom she has great affection. Later in the act, the Countess will discover Helena's secret, encouraging her to take active pursuit by traveling to the king's court in order to be near Bertram and in order to attempt to cure the king of a fistula by a rare prescription which her father has left her. In this present soliloquy, however, she assumes her love to be futile and foolish; her love for a star in the heavens far above would be just as hopeless. As long as Bertram was physically present, she could observe him every hour, but now in his absence the pangs of undeclared love grow unbearable:

> . . . My imagination
> Carries no favour in't but Bertram's.
> I am undone, There is no living, none,
> If Bertram be away. 'Twere all one
> That I should love **a bright particular star,**
> And think to wed it, he is so above me.
> In his bright radiance and collateral light
> Must I be comforted, not in his sphere.
> The ambition in my love thus plagues itself;
> The hind that would be mated by the lion
> Must die for love. 'Twas pretty, though a plague,
> To see him every hour, to sit and draw
> His arched brows, his hawking eye, his curls,
> In our heart's table: heart too capable
> Of every line and trick of his sweet favour.
> But now he's gone, and my idolatrous fancy
> Must sanctify his reliques.

118

Britannia rules the waves

Source: ALFRED, A MASQUE (Finale: "Ode in Honour of Great Britain")
Author: James Thomson (1700-1748)
First published: 1740
Type of work: Song lyric

Context: James Thomson's reputation as a poet rests solidly on his long poem *The Seasons,* the first poetic work of such length (well over 5000 lines) devoted primarily to the description of nature and scenery. His best-known work, however, is a song. In 1740 Thomson, in collaboration with David Mallet, wrote the words for a patriotic masque entitled *Alfred.* The music for this production was composed by Dr. Thomas Augustine Arne (1710–1778), contemporary of Handel and one of England's finest native composers. The masque, an art form long popular in England, was a type of pageant combining spectacle, drama, and music; it was frequently allegorical or symbolic, and often very elaborately staged. The shorter masques were frequently inserted into plays as diversions or interludes. The more spectacular forms, however, were produced as separate works. *Alfred* is one of the latter. Replete with splendor, it culminated in a triumphant anthem for full orchestra and chorus which was instantly popular and has remained so to this day: the song now universally known as "Rule, Britannia." The anthem has, of course, undergone a certain amount of evolution over the years; the more difficult passages have been modified to accommodate untrained voices, and in its most frequently-quoted line the word *rule* was changed in use to *rules.* Thus, what was originally a sacred command soon became a statement of fact. In any case, "Rule, Britannia" has those vital ingredients which any great national anthem must have—a happy combination of spirited, soaring melody and words of rousing patriotic inspiration. Three of the six stanzas are given below as they first appeared.

> When Britain first, at Heaven's command,
>   Arose from out the azure main,
> This was the charter of the land,
>   And guardian angels sang this strain:
>   Rule, **Britannia, rule the waves!**
>   Britons never will be slaves!
>
> The nations not so blest as thee,
>   Must in their turns to tyrants fall,
> Whilst thou shalt flourish great and free,
>   The dread and envy of them all.
>   Rule, **Britannia, rule the waves!**
>   Britons never will be slaves!
>   •   •   •
> The Muses, still with freedom found,
>   Shall to thy happy coast repair;
> Blest isle, with matchless beauty crowned,

119

And manly hearts to guard the fair!
Rule, **Britannia, rule the waves!**
Britons never will be slaves!

The brother of death exacteth a third part of our lives

Source: ON DREAMS
Author: Sir Thomas Browne (1605-1682)
First published: 1836
Type of work: Philosophy

Context: As physician, philosopher, and amateur theologian, Browne produced a number of literary works on a variety of subjects. This short essay concerning seventeenth century dream psychology survived, with a number of Browne's other works, in manuscript until the nineteenth century. Dreams, says Browne, are in part the result of the day's thoughts and actions; virtuous men have pleasant and peaceful sleep while vicious men are troubled and tormented by their dreams. What we dream is influenced not only by our character, however, but may also be determined by the foods we eat. The images appearing in dreams, he continues, are often symbolic and require subtle interpretation; this theory he illustrates by citation of classical examples. Some dreams contain useful intelligence, but others may delude and mislead us if we do not interpret them with care. Since we spend one-third of our lives asleep, we should give due attention to the dreams that come to us during that period:

Half our days we pass in the shadow of the earth, and **the brother of death exacteth a third part of our lives.** A good part of our sleeps is pieced out with visions, and phantastical objects wherin we are confessedly deceived. The day supplyeth us with truths, the night with fictions and falsehoods, which uncomfortably divide the natural account of our beings. And therefore having passed the day in sober labours and rational enquiries of truth, we are fain to betake ourselves unto such a state of being, wherin the soberest heads have acted all the monstrosities of melancholy, and which unto open eyes are no better than folly and madness.

A brotherhood of venerable trees

Source: MEMORIALS OF A TOUR IN SCOTLAND, 1803: SONNET COMPOSED AT —————CASTLE (Line 6)
Author: William Wordsworth (1770-1850)
First published: 1807
Type of work: Sonnet

Context: This sonnet is addressed   to William Douglas (1724–1810),

120

fourth Duke of Queensbury, a celebrated rake of the time. Douglas had the ancient plantations of trees felled at Neidpath, or Nidpath, Castle, referred to in the poem, to provide a dowry for Maria Fagniani, whom he supposed to be his daughter. Another notable of the time also provided her with a dowry for the same reason; historians of the period believe that both of them might have been mistaken in their beliefs about their relationship to the lady; at least one certainly was. Wordsworth arrived at Nidpath in time to see the trees lying scattered on the ground; he wrote the sonnet that same night. The act of felling the trees met with considerable resistance in the neighborhood. The poet says that the traveler will gaze with pain at such an outrage, but nature, which has a multitude of sheltered places, nooks, bays, mountains, and the gentle River Tweed, hardly seems to notice such acts of vandalism.

Degenerate Douglas! oh, the unworthy Lord!
Whom mere despite of heart could so far please,
And love of havoc, (for with such disease
Fame taxes him,) that he could send forth word
To level with the dust a noble horde,
A brotherhood of venerable trees,
Leaving an ancient dome, and towers like these,
Beggared and outraged!—Many hearts deplored
The fate of those old Trees; and oft with pain
The traveler, at this day, will stop and gaze
On wrongs, which Nature scarcely seems to heed:
For sheltered places, bosoms, nooks, and bays,
And the pure mountains, and the gentle Tweed,
And the green silent pastures, yet remain.

Budge doctors of the Stoic fur

Source: COMUS (Line 707)
Author: John Milton (1608-1674)
First published: 1637
Type of work: Masque

Context: Milton wrote the masque *Comus* to celebrate the installation of the Earl of Bridgewater as President of Wales; parts were acted by the earl's daughter and two sons. The three endeavor to reach Ludlow Castle, where the masque was presented; they pass at night through a wild wood in which the wicked enchanter, son of Bacchus and Circe and a symbol of license and debauchery, holds sway. Comus meets the earl's daughter, known as the Lady, who has become separated from her brothers; he offers to show her the way through the wood, but instead of doing so, takes her to his palace, the scene of his immoral revels. He threatens to deprive the Lady of physical motion by waving his magic wand, but, as she

121

says, he cannot touch the freedom of her mind, which is dedicated to virtue. She further says that in spite of all of Comus's promises of the good that will befall her if she succumbs to his blandishments, only good people can bestow good on others. To this Comus replies that people are foolish to listen to moralists who preach abstinence. Stoic moralists in doctor's gowns preach things contrary to nature. In the quotation, budge meant a fur used to trim doctoral gowns during the time that Milton was a student at Cambridge; he seems to have had unpleasant memories of his professors. The hair-splitting scholastic philosophers who preached a degraded Stoicism were especially the objects of Milton's scorn.

LADY

. . .

And wouldst thou seek again to trap me here
With lickerish baits fit to ensnare a brute?
Were it a draught for Juno when she banquets,
I would not taste thy treasonous offer; none
But such as are good men can give good things,
And that which is not good, is not delicious
To a well-governed and wise appetite.

COMUS

O foolishness of men! that lend their ears
To those **budge doctors of the Stoic fur,**
And fetch their precepts from the Cynic tub,
Praising the lean and sallow abstinence.
Wherefore did Nature pour her bounties forth
With such a full and unwithdrawing hand,
Covering the earth with odors, fruits, and flocks,
Thronging the seas with spawn innumerable,
But all to please and sate the curious taste?

. . .

Bulls of Bashan

Source: PSALMS 22:12
Author: Unknown
First transcribed: c.400-200 B.C.
Type of work: Religious poetry

Context: The poet, in a psalm prophetic of the passion of the sorrowful Christ, weeps because he is forsaken by God, unlike his forefathers who were delivered from exile. The plight of the poet is so overwhelming that he describes himself as being surrounded by roaring bulls of Bashan (a region of the northern kingdom of Israel between Gilead and Hermon, originally assigned to the tribe of Manasseh):

Many bulls have compassed me: strong **bulls of Bashan** have beset me round.

They have gaped upon me with their mouths, as a ravening and a roaring lion.

I am poured out like water, and all my bones are out of joint: my heart is like wax; it is melted in the midst of my bowels.

My strength is dried up like a potsherd; and my tongue cleaveth to my jaws; and thou hast brought me into the dust of death.

For dogs have compassed me: the assembly of the wicked have inclosed me: they pierced my hands and my feet.

I may tell all my bones: they look and stare upon me.

They part my garments among them, can cast lots upon my vesture.

Business first; pleasure afterwards

Source: THE ROSE AND THE RING, OR THE HISTORY OF PRINCE GIGLIO AND PRINCE BULBO (Chapter 1)
Author: William Makepeace Thackeray (1811-1863)
First published: 1854
Type of work: Christmas story

Context: In his "Prelude" to this story, Thackeray tells how at one Christmas in a foreign city he drew a set of Twelfth-Night characters for the English children and then composed *The Rose and the Ring* as a story to accompany the pictures and serve as a Christmas pantomime for the English children and their parents. Chapter I of the story, entitled "Shows How the Royal Family Sate Down to Breakfast," introduces King Valoroso XXIV of Paflagonia; his queen, humorously called by her husband Mrs. V; and their daughter, Princess Angelica. The king, left alone when his wife and daughter finish breakfast, falls to drinking many egg-cupfuls of brandy to raise up his courage for his conscience bothers him. He is really a villain, despite his kind treatment of his queen and daughter in matters of gifts and allowances for parties and dresses, for he has usurped the throne from Prince Giglio upon the death of the late king, Valoroso's older brother and Giglio's father. Following his consumption of several draughts of brandy, King Valoroso sits down at the table again, to complete his breakfast and read the newspapers. The queen, meanwhile, wonders whether she should go visit Prince Giglio, who is convalescing from an illness; she considers the matter to herself:

". . . Not now. **Business first; pleasure afterwards.** I will go and see dear Giglio this afternoon; and now I will drive to the jeweller's, to look for the necklace and bracelets." The Princess went up into her own room, and made Betsinda, her maid, bring out all her dresses; and as for Giglio, they forgot him as much as I forget what I had for dinner last Tuesday twelvemonth.

123

Business was his aversion; pleasure was his business

Source: THE CONTRAST (Chapter 1)
Author: Maria Edgeworth (1767-1849)
First published: 1804
Type of work: Didactic short story

Context: While seldom read today except by scholars or literary historians, Maria Edgeworth was once the leading best-seller of England and enjoyed such fame that she was praised by the writers of America and Europe. What these men found in her short stories was a remarkable ability to describe character within a short space. Although her stories are primarily didactic — or "moral," as she would have said it — she seldom fell back on the stereotyped characters that are often the backbone and the fault of the sermonizing story. Quite the contrary, as she shows in the description of Philip Folingsby, one of the minor characters in this story, she could pinpoint a man's personality with a few choice words that so strike the reader that the character is unforgettable.

. . . he was a man whose head was at this time entirely full of gigs, and tandems, and unicorns: **business was his aversion; pleasure was his business.** Money he considered only as the means of pleasure; and tenants only as machines, who make money. He was neither avaricious nor cruel; but thoughtless and extravagant.

The busy trifler

Source: EXPOSTULATIONS (Line 322)
Author: William Cowper (1731-1800)
First published: 1782
Type of work: Essay in verse

Context: William Cowper, frequently suffering from a sense of wrong-doing and several times confined in an insane asylum for religious mania, remonstrates in 734 lines with his country for her ungodly ways. "Why weeps the Muse for England?" he queries in his opening line. Everything looks attractive and successful in the land, yet things are wrong. He reminds his readers that, before its downfall, prophets wept for Israel even when it seemed favored by God. And he goes still farther into antiquity to Assyria, called upon to repent, then to Greece and Rome, whose glories faded. At the conclusion, he calls on his country to take stock of itself and not be over-proud or seek comfort in the feeling that other nations are just as guilty of wrong-doing. God, not man, is responsible for the present blessings of the world. Man is only a busy trifler, making much ado about nothing. The poet uses a similar phrase, "important trifler," in *Conversations* (line 250).

Know, then, that heavenly wisdom on this ball
Creates, gives birth to, guides, comsummates all;
That, while laborious and quick-thoughted man
Snuffs up the praise of what he seems to plan,
He first conceives, then perfects his design,
As a mere instrument in hands divine:
Blind to the workings of that secret power,
That balances the wings of every hour,
The busy trifler dreams himself alone,
Frames many a purpose, and God works his own.

Butchered to make a Roman holiday

Source: CHILDE HAROLD'S PILGRIMAGE (Canto IV, stanza 141)
Author: George Gordon, Lord Byron (1788-1824)
First published: 1818 (Canto IV)
Type of work: Narrative poem

Context: In Canto IV of Byron's long poem, Childe Harold (Byron) visits Venice, Florence, and Rome. His pilgrimage ends at Rome, the goal toward which all his journeying has tended. The title "Childe" is one which candidates for knighthood bore, in the days of chivalry, until their pilgrimage was done and knighthood was conferred upon them. The poem's title thus symbolizes Byron's wanderings over Europe, seeking an escape from himself and from the world that wearies him. His love and admiration for Rome, the eternal city, "lone mother of dead empires," is such that he declares it his country. Saddened by the ruins of its former glory and conscious of its past greatness, he calls the roll of famous men who made the city what it was. Some of them were tyrants; Byron considers the nature of tyranny and despairs of the achievement of true freedom by mortal men. Byron's passionate devotion to freedom is not merely rhetorical: at the age of thirty-six he will die of a fever contracted while fighting in the name of Greek liberty. Now he visits ancient tombs, wondering about the lives of those who were buried there. In the ruins he sees "the moral of all human tales" retraced: "First Freedom and then Glory—when that fails, / Wealth, vice, corruption,—barbarism at last." Byron ponders the sequence as Rome experienced it: the greatness which passed into softness, indulgence and orgy—until, too fat and corrupt to resist, the great empire fell before hordes of barbarians. Contemplating the vastness of the Colosseum, Byron envisages the bloody spectacles that were staged there for the excitement and entertainment of bored and sated crowds—part of that degeneracy which led to the nation's fall:

I see before me the Gladiator lie:
He leans upon his hand—his manly brow
Consents to death, but conquers agony,
And his dropp'd head sinks gradually low—

125

And through his side the last drops, ebbing slow
From the red gash, fall heavy, one by one,
Like the first of a thunder-shower; and now
The arena swims around him—he is gone,
Ere ceased the inhuman shout which hail'd the wretch who won.

He heard it, but he heeded not—his eyes
Were with his heart and that was far away;
He reck'd not of the life he lost nor prize,
But where his rude hut by the Danube lay,
There were his young barbarians all at play,
There was their Dacian mother—he, their sire,
Butcher'd to make a Roman holiday—
All this rush'd with his blood.—Shall he expire
And unavenged?—Arise! ye Goths, and glut your ire!

A button-hole lower

Source: LOVE'S LABOUR'S LOST (Act V, sc. ii, 1. 706)
Author: William Shakespeare (1564-1616)
First published: 1598
Type of work: Dramatic comedy

Context: Don Adriano de Armado, Costard, a clown, and several others are presenting a play for the Princess of France and her court with King Ferdinand of Navarre and his nobles. In this play Costard plays the part of Pompey. While Armado, who plays Hector, delivers his lines, Berowne—an attendant lord to the king—whispers to Costard some alarming information about Jaquenetta and Armado. And then, while Armado is still playing the part of Hector, Costard—with his newly gained knowledge—confronts him with the fact that Jaquenetta, a country "wench" is "two months on her way" with his child. Armado challenges Costard to a duel because of this public charge, and the two are led on by the onlookers who keep referring to them as Pompey and Hector. Then Moth, page to Armado, steps in to remind his master of his position and to head off a duel not worthy of his master's fighting. He reminds Armado that his position is not that of the play hero, Hector, being challenged by a lofty antagonist; rather, the challenge is from Costard the clown concerning a mere country wench. Thus, Moth's desire is to bring Armando "a button-hole lower," out of the play and back into reality.

MOTH

Master, let me take you **a button-hole lower.** Do you not see Pompey is uncasing for the combat? What mean you? You will lose your reputation.

126

By night an atheist half-believes in God

Source: THE COMPLAINT: OR, NIGHT THOUGHTS ("Night the Fifth," 1. 176)
Author: Edward Young (1683-1765)
First published: 1742
Type of work: Philosophical poem

Context: The poet excoriates the use of "wit" in poetry, which too often is used to exalt sensuality and not virtue. The bulk of the poetry of sensuality far exceeds that of virtue, which should be the true subject of poetry. The poet goes on to say that night is the time for thought; during daylight, virtue, a frail and fair thing, suffers in the crowd. Few people bring back to their homes at evening the manners they possessed in the morning; their thoughts are blotted by the corruption of the world, their good resolutions are shaken, their thoughts tainted. The example of others is a bad thing; people see vain ambition and are stimulated to pursue their own ambitions. The riot, pride, and perfidy everywhere evident undermine otherwise good and virtuous people and set them upon wrong courses. A single glance can carry infection. Safety lies only in remaining remote from the crowd. At night, freed from the fevers and distractions of the day, we are close to the deity; we realize our faults and vice loses its allurements and looks as black as the night itself. At night even the atheist has doubts about his spiritual questionings and almost believes in God.

> This sacred shade, and solitude, what is it?
> 'Tis the felt presence of the deity.
> Few are the faults we flatter when alone,
> Vice sinks in her allurements, is ungilt,
> And looks, like other objects, black by night.
> **By night an atheist half-believes in God.**

By thunders of white silence overthrown

Source: HIRAM POWERS' GREEK SLAVE (Line 14)
Author: Elizabeth Barrett Browning (1806-1861)
First published: 1850
Type of work: Sonnet

Context: As a poet of the mid-nineteenth century, Mrs. Browning was influenced by the school of idealism, especially in terms of her understanding of the nature and role of art; according to this school, a work of art transcends reality and lifts the spectator into the realm of ideas wherein the anguish and pain of life are harmonized into cosmic order. Accepting this didactic and elevated view of art, Mrs. Browning was always interested in social reform and in the lamentable conditions of the lower classes; to her, poetry and the fine arts were instruments for the amelioration of so-

127

ciety. In the 1840's and 1850's there was much talk against the slave trade, especially in relationship to the United States since England had already outlawed slavery; as a social reformer, Mrs. Browning, horrified by attempts to rationalize the practice, turned to art as a means of lifting men's minds to a universal truth. By drawing her readers' attentions to the statue of the Greek Slave, she hopes to uplift their spirits to the point that art and universal truth will triumph and thus end slavery. Hiram Powers was an American sculptor working in Italy during the time of the Brownings' residence there. His "Greek Slave" (1843) was one of the most famous sculptures of this period.

Pierce to the centre,
Art's fiery finger! and break up ere long
The serfdom of this world! appeal, fair stone,
From God's pure heights of beauty against man's wrong!
Catch up in thy divine face, not alone
East griefs, but west, and strike and shame the strong,
By thunders of white silence overthrown.

Call me early, mother, I'm to be Queen of the May

Source: THE MAY QUEEN (Stanzas 1 and 11)
Author: Alfred, Lord Tennyson (1809-1892)
First published: 1832
Type of work: Lyric poem

Context: "The May Queen" is filled with vain young Alice's joyous anticipation of her one-day reign as Queen of the May. Other girls are fair and black-eyed, but none, she exults, "so fair as little Alice in all the land they say." She will "sleep so sound all night" that her mother must wake her with a loud call, to "gather knots of flowers, and buds and garlands gay." She boasts of the sharp look she gave Robin, who must have thought her a ghost, "for I was all in white." She knows her reputation for cruelty, "but I care not what they say." Though Robin is not dying of love, as reported, his heart may be breaking, but "what is that to me?" Many a bolder lad will woo her "any summer day." Her mother, her little sister Effie, and shepherd lads from far away will come to see her crowned. Honeysuckle, cuckoo-flowers, a n d marsh-marigolds are all in bloom. Night-winds b l o w and seem to brighten the stars above, and Alice predicts, "There will not be a drop of rain the whole of the livelong day." All the valley will be "fresh and green and still," cowslip and crowfoot will cover the hillside, and the rivulet in the dale below will "merrily glance and play," for Alice is to be Queen of the May. Thus she ends as she began, exulting, and reminding her mother:

128

So you must wake and call me early, **call me early, mother
dear,**
To-morrow 'ill be the happiest time of all the glad New-year:
To-morrow 'ill be of all the year the maddest merriest day,
For I'm to be Queen o' the May, mother, **I'm to be Queen o'
the May.**

Calm's not life's crown

Source: YOUTH AND CALM (Line 23)
Author: Matthew Arnold (1822-1888)
First published: 1852
Type of work: Lyric poem

Context: Never a genuinely happy person, Arnold developed a view of life that fully accepted the harsh facts of existence and the torment of human anguish; however, he was not a man to luxuriate in misery, unwilling to make a compromise with his world. Slowly learning that the promises of youth are seldom fulfilled, he came to accept life on its own terms: man's responsibility was to seek calm, not joy. Such stoicism gradually led to a mature serenity, freed from the passions and romantic dreams of youth; this serenity enabled him to rise above his own suffering into a state of calm detachment wherein he achieved his fame as a man who had found the compromise with life that preserves sanity without despair. This quotation comes from a passage in which he makes one of the clearest statements of his view of life:

> Youth dreams a bliss on this side death.
> It dreams a rest, if not more deep,
> More grateful than this marble sleep;
> It hears a voice within it tell:
> **Calm's not life's crown,** though calm is well.
> 'Tis all perhaps which man acquires,
> But 'tis not what our youth desires.

Calumnies are answered best with silence

Source: VOLPONE (Act II, sc. ii, l. 20)
Author: Ben Jonson (1573?-1637)
First published: 1607
Type of work: Dramatic comedy

Context: Volpone, the Fox, a wealthy Venetian, pretends to be upon his death's bed in order to extort rich presents from a crew of legacy-hunters, each member of which believes that he is to be Volpone's heir. Volpone is aided in his masquerade by a servant as unprincipled as himself,

Mosca, the Fly. After a visit by Corvino, the Crow, Mosca describes the charms of Corvino's young, beautiful, and virtuous wife, Celia, whom Corvino keeps under lock and key, so great is his jealousy and his fear that she will find a lover. Volpone decides that he must see this paragon and has Mosca set up a bench upon which he can stand to sell his medicines, as he is announced to the public as Scoto of Mantua, a famous mountebank, or traveling seller of remedies for all kinds of diseases. A naïve and credulous English knight, Sir Politick Would-be, who believes that he sees deep meanings in events that strike others as unimportant commonplaces, takes it upon himself to tell a gentleman traveler, Peregrine, all about Scoto of Mantua. Mountebanks, according to Sir Politick, are the only knowing men in Europe, scholars, physicians, statesmen, and counsellors to states. Peregrine replies that he has heard they are mere lewd imposters, but Sir Politick, pitying his ignorance, tells him that one does well to disregard such attacks upon character and refuse to say a word, for calumnies are answered best with silence.

SIR POLITICK
Pity his ignorance.
They are the only knowing men of Europe!
Great general scholars, excellent physicians.
Most admired statesmen, professed favorites,
And cabinet counsellors to the greatest princes;
The only languaged men of all the world!

PEREGRINE
And, I have heard, they are most lewd imposters;
Made all of terms and shreds; no less beliers
Of great men's favors, than their own vile med'cines;
Which they will utter upon monstrous oaths;
Selling that drug for twopence, ere they part,
Which they have valued at twelve crowns before.

SIR POLITICK
Sir, **calumnies are answered best with silence.** . . .

Captains of Industry

Source: PAST AND PRESENT (Book IV, chapter 4, chapter title)
Author: Thomas Carlyle (1795-1881)
First published: 1843
Type of work: Book of essays on economics and society

Context: Carlyle was something of a romanticist about the past. Like others in the Victorian period, both in England and in the United States, he looked to the past to see only what was good; he therefore believed it to

130

be superior to his own age and exaggerated its glories. But he also acquired the truth which the great historian always learns: by studying the past we can learn, if we will, how to avoid the mistakes of the generations of mankind who have preceded us. In this particular essay Carlyle looks at nineteenth century industrialists in Great Britain and finds them wanting, seeing them merely as men who are busy gathering up thousand-pound notes as American Indians were alleged to gather scalps, as trophies giving visible evidence of prowess over one's enemies and fellowmen. But Carlyle expresses hope that the pursuit of money, Mammonism, as he calls it, will not always be the end for which the leaders of industry strive. He hopes for the improvement, he says, to come from the industrialists themselves. Government, he says, can help, but government cannot do it all, if for no other reason than that the government merely reflects the people. The remedies, he says, must be found "by those who stand practically in the middle of it; by those who themselves work and preside over work"—in short, by the men he calls captains of industry. Carlyle issues a ringing challenge to these men:

. . . *Captains of Industry* are the true Fighters, henceforth recognizable as the only true ones: Fighters against Chaos, Necessity and the Devils and Jotuns; and lead on Mankind in that great, and alone true, and universal warfare; the stars in their courses fighting for them, and all Heaven and all Earth saying audibly, Well done! Let the **Captains of Industry** retire into their own hearts, and ask solemnly, If there is nothing but vulturous hunger for fine wines, valet reputation and gilt carriages, discoverable there? Of hearts made by the Almighty God I will not believe such a thing. . . .

Carthage must be destroyed

Source: PARALLEL LIVES ("Cato the Censor")
Author: Plutarch (c.45-c. 125)
First transcribed: c. 105-115
Type of work: Biography

Context: Marcus Portius (234–149 B.C.), called Cato the Censor and Cato the Elder to distinguish him from his grandson, the Stoic philosopher, was given the name of Cato, or Wise Man, because of the admiration of his fellow citizens. He was a soldier who when he was only seventeen fought against Hannibal. Rising in the political world, he was consul in 195 B.C., and in 187, censor, the official with rights to inquire into the lives and morals of Rome's citizens, and punish disorders and immorality. He spent his life trying to restore what he thought were the morals and simplicity of the old days. Sent on a diplomatic mission to Carthage, he returned convinced that that city-state was a danger to Rome and

131

should be destroyed. Carthage, near modern Tunis, was supposedly built by Dido on the site of old Utica. By the fifth century B.C. it was gaining power in the Mediterranean and, under Hannibal, it became very strong. Rome challenged it in the third century in the Punic Wars, so-called because Rome called the Phoenicians "Poeni." The First Punic War ended with Carthage's loss of Sicily. In the Second Punic War, Fabio and Scipio Africanus defeated Hannibal at the Battle of Zama (202 B.C.). Still because of its commercial power, many Romans felt it should be razed and its streets sprinkled with salt. Chief advocate was Cato the Censor, who ended all his speeches in the Senate, regardless of their topic, with the words: "Ceterum, censeo, Carthaginem esse Delendam" (For the rest, I vote that Carthage should be destroyed). Plutarch repeats Cato's demands in slightly different words. Plutarch, the biographer, was born in Greece, but after study in Athens visited Rome, where he probably wrote most of his works. One was *Parallel Lives,* in which he linked twenty-three great Greeks with their Roman counterparts, then added other biographies, including that of Cato. Plutarch was a moralist. His interest in noteworthy men of the past was in what they could teach about morality. By their deeds, rather than by the social and historical period in which they were involved, he wanted them judged, and he was not above occasional distortion of history to prove his point. Ethics ranked high in his thoughts: "Generosity brings reward as arrogance earns punishment." Did he have Cato's hatred of Carthage in mind when he wrote that "no beast is more savage than a man possessed with power added to his rage?" Cato, by continually preaching the destruction of Carthage, brought on the Third Punic War (149–146 B.C.) that completely ended its existence at the hands of an army under the command of the son of the Scipio who had proclaimed his belief that it should be left standing. Speaking of Cato the Censor, said Plutarch:

It is said that at the conclusion of his speech he shook the lap of his gown, and purposely dropped some Libyan figs; and when he found that the Senators admired them for their size and beauty, he told them, that the country where they grew was but three days' sail from Rome. But what was a stronger instance of his enmity to Carthage, he never gave his opinion in the Senate upon any other point whatever, without adding DELENDA EST CARTHAGO, **Carthage must be destroyed.** Scipio made a point to mention the contrary, and concluded his speeches: "And my opinion is, that Carthage should be left standing."

Castles in Spain

Source: THE ROMAUNT OF THE ROSE (Fragment B, l. 2573)
Author: Geoffrey Chaucer (1343?-1400), translator of part of the *Roman de la Rose* by Guillaume de Lorris (died c. 1235)
First transcribed: 1360?-1372
Type of work: Allegorical romance

Context: The English translation of Guillaume de Lorris's and Jean de Meun's *Roman de la Rose* exists in three fragments, A, B, and C, and comprises but a fraction of the French poem. Some critical opinion holds that Fragment B was not translated by Chaucer. The poet says that the lover should set his thoughts on loving and place his heart in but one place and never remove it. He should give his heart freely and gladly, but never show it to the world. When his beloved is absent he will mourn; he will constantly try to catch a sight of her. When he fails to see her, he will be in great sadness; when he does see her, his spirits will be immeasureably quickened. When he comes into her presence, he will be dumb, and afterwards he will reproach himself for not having spoken. Finally, night will come and the lover will have to make his sad way to his lonesome bed, there to dream he has her at his side, a situation as imaginary as building a Castle in Spain.

> Thanne shall thee come a remembraunce
> Of hir shap and hir semblaunce,
> Whereto non other may be pere.
> And wite thou wel, withoute were,
> That thee shal seme, somtyme that nyght,
> That thou hast hir, that is so bright,
> Naked bitwene thyne armes there,
> All sothfastnesse as though it were.
> Thou shalt make **castels** thanne **in Spayne,**
> And dreme of joye, all but in vayne,
> And thee deliten of right nought,
> While thou so slombrest in that thought,
> That it so swete and delitable,
> The which, in soth, nys but a fable;
> For it ne shall no while laste.

A cat may look at a king

Source: ALICE'S ADVENTURES IN WONDERLAND (Chapter 8)
Author: Lewis Carroll (Charles Lutwidge Dodgson, 1832-1898)
First published: 1865
Type of work: Imaginative tale for children

Context: The English proverb, "A cat may look at a king," was already old when John Heywood (1497–1580) included it in his collection of English colloquial sayings, *Proverbes.* This was the first volume of its kind and was published in 1546. The meaning of the proverb is that there is safety in insignificance: an inferior may do certain things in the presence of a superior without fear, simply because he is beneath the latter's notice. The most delightfully memorable use of this saying is undoubtedly that which occurs in Lewis Carroll's dream-tale, *Alice's Adventures in Wonderland.* After a series of strange experiences, Alice finds herself lost in a forest and uncertain which way she should go. The Cheshire Cat appears in a tree and counsels her in such a way that she is more confused than ever. He has the pleasant ability to appear and disappear at will; normally the process is gradual, and his fixed grin is the first and last part of him which is visible. As he vanishes, he informs Alice that he will see her later at the Queen's croquet-match. In time Alice does find herself part of this festive event, in which the mallets are flamingoes, the hoops are soldiers bent double, and the balls are hedgehogs. This arrangement does not make the game easy to play, and the Queen's ferocious disposition is upsetting. "The players all played at once, without waiting for turns, quarrelling all the while, and fighting for the hedgehogs; and in a very short time the Queen was in a furious passion, and went stamping about, and shouting, 'Off with his head!' or 'Off with her head!' about once in a minute." Alice wonders that there is anyone left alive. At this point the cat reappears, though it halts the process while only its head is visible.

"How do you like the Queen?" said the Cat in a low voice.

"Not at all," said Alice: "she's so extremely—" Just then she noticed that the Queen was close behind her, listening: so she went on "—likely to win, that it's hardly worth while finishing the game."

The Queen smiled and passed on.

"Who *are* you talking to?" said the King, coming up to Alice, and looking at the Cat's head with great curiosity.

"It's a friend of mine—a Cheshire Cat," said Alice: "allow me to introduce it."

"I don't like the look of it at all," said the King: "however, it may kiss my hand, if it likes."

"I'd rather not," the Cat remarked.

"Don't be impertinent," said the King, "and don't look at me like that!" He got behind Alice as he spoke.

"A cat may look at a king," said Alice. "I've read that in some book, but I don't remember where."

"Well, it must be removed," said the King very decidedly; and he called to the Queen, who was passing at the moment, "My dear! I wish you would have this cat removed!"

The Queen had only one way of settling all difficulties, great or small. "Off with his head!" she said without even looking round.

"I'll fetch the executioner myself," said the King eagerly, and he hurried off.

Caterpillars of the commonwealth

Source: KING RICHARD THE SECOND (Act II, sc. iii, 1. 166)
Author: William Shakespeare (1564-1616)
First published: 1597
Type of work: Historical drama

Context: Henry Bolingbroke, banished from England on charge of treason, hears that King Richard II has confiscated his inheritance upon the death of John of Gaunt, Duke of Lancaster, his father and uncle of the king. While the king is in Ireland to oversee his wars, and the affairs of state are left in the hands of another uncle, the Duke of York, Bolingbroke returns and finds that York will not stand in the way of his claim to his title and inheritance. When the Duke of York proposes that Bolingbroke spend the night at Bristol Castle, Bolingbroke quickly accepts, confessing that he has sworn to rid the castle of the low companions of the king:

BOLINGBROKE

An offer uncle, that we will accept,
But we must win your Grace to go with us
To Bristol Castle, which they say is held
By Bushy, Bagot, and their complices,
The **caterpillars of the commonwealth,**
Which I have sworn to weed and pluck away.

YORK

It may be I will go with you—but yet I'll pause,
For I am loth to break our country's laws.
Nor friends, nor foes, to me welcome you are.
Things past redress are now with me past care.

[*Exeunt.*]

Caverns measureless to man

Source: KUBLA KHAN (Line 4)
Author: Samuel Taylor Coleridge (1772-1834)
First published: 1816
Type of work: Narrative-lyric poem

Context: By his poetry, Wordsworth put magic into ordinary situations. His friend Coleridge tried to make exotic and supernatural situations sound real. They collaborated in *Lyrical Ballads* (1798–1800), a work that ushered in the English Romantic Movement. Coleridge needed to be pressured into writing. The sight of Wordsworth's activity did serve as a spur, and most of his poetry was produced while he lived near Wordsworth and his sister Dorothy in the lovely Lake Region of England. Coleridge's greatest work was "The Ancient Mariner" included in *Lyrical Ballads.* The story of another of his poems has often been told. One day in 1797, he had taken a dose of the opium to which he had become accustomed for his pain. Then while endulging in his other opiate, reading, he fell asleep. He had been reading *Purchas, His Pilgrimage* (1613), into which an English clergyman named Samuel Purchas (1577–1626) had gathered stories of peoples and religions of the world. He had finished a

135

chapter dealing with the Mongol Emperor Kublai Khan (1215?–1294), grandson of Jenghiz Khan, and the palace he had built at Cambaluc, now Peiping, which Marco Polo saw and described. Sleeping profoundly, Coleridge dreamed out a long poem, as John Masefield reported he had seen in a dream and set down later one of his masterpieces. However, Coleridge did not have the same good fortune. He opened his eyes and began feverishly to write down all he could remember. While working, he was interrupted by a caller from the town of Porlock, probably a creditor. By the time Coleridge could send him away, the rest of the poem had slipped from his mind. Only the fragment that he had put onto paper remained. Critics ever since have raged against the interruptor. Yet in its present state, the fifty-four lines of "Kubla Khan" make one of the most magical poems in the English language, full of exquisite music and haunting phrases. Byron used one of the lines: "And woman wailing for her Demon Lover," as the motto for his *Heaven and Earth* (1823). Perhaps it is even two poems, because after the pause at line 35, the poet is reminded of a vision he once had of an Abyssinian maid playing her dulcimer. He cries that if he could only re-create within himself her music, he could rebuild that ancient pleasure-dome and cave of ice to be so real that people would be frightened and believe him some spirit come from Paradise. Scholars have found the inspiring paragraph that supplied some of Coleridge's phrases. It occurs in the 1626 edition, Book IV, chapter xiii, p. 418: "In Xamdu did Cublai Can build a stately palace encompassing sixteene miles of plaine ground with a wall, wherein are fertile meadowes, pleasant Springs, delightful Streams, and all sorts of beasts of chase and game, and in the middest thereof a sumptuous house of pleasure." This is the way Coleridge transmuted the prose into poetic beauty:

In Xanadu did Kubla Khan
A stately pleasure-dome decree;
Where Alph, the sacred river, ran
Through **caverns measureless to man**
    Down to a sunless sea.
So twice five miles of fertile ground
With walls and towers were girdled round:
And here were gardens bright with sinuous rills,
Where blossomed many an incense-bearing tree;
And here were forests ancient as the hills,
Enfolding sunny spots of greenery.

Chaos is come again

Source: OTHELLO (Act III, sc, iii, 1. 92)
Author: William Shakespeare (1564-1616)
First published: 1622
Type of work: Dramatic tragedy

136

Cassio, friend and former lieutenant to Othello, the Moor of Venice, is out of favor with his lord because of a drunken brawl engineered by Iago, the jealous ensign who had hoped for the position to which Cassio has been appointed. At the suggestions of Iago, who intends to destroy Cassio, the repentant offi-cer pleads with Desdemona, wife of the valiant Moor, to speak for him. She consents, but, in the course of her persistent pleading, becomes mildly annoying to Othello, who loves her so much that he cannot really find fault with her. He compares life without her love to the disorder before the creation of the world.

DESDEMONA
. . . What, Michael Cassio,
That came a-wooing with you; and so many a time,
When I have spoke of you dispraisingly,
Hath ta'en your part; . . .
. . .

OTHELLO
I will deny thee nothing.
Whereon, I do beseech thee, grant me this,
To leave me but a little to myself.

DESDEMONA
Shall I deny you? No. Farewell my lord.
. . .

OTHELLO
Excellent wretch! Perdition catch my soul
But I do love thee; and when I love thee not,
Chaos is come again.

Chapter of accidents

Source: LETTERS TO HIS FRIENDS (To Solomon Dayrolles, No. LXXIX, February 16, 1753)
Author: Philip Dormer Stanhope, Lord Chesterfield (1694-1773)
First published: 1777
Type of work: Personal letters

Context: To his friend and protégé, Solomon Dayrolles (d. 1786), the Earl of Chesterfield writes that he has been silent for a long time (the last previous letter to Dayrolles was written two months before this one). He complains that he constantly grows deafer and consequently more isolated from people. He can now say, what is he to the world, or the world to him. He is discouraged about the prospect of regaining his hearing, as he has tried a thousand remedies, but all have been ineffective. But although knowledge is severely limited, chance is vast, and perhaps a lucky accident will be able to do more than knowledge has been able to accomplish, and he will find a remedy for his deafness.

I grow deafer, and consequently more *isolé* from society, every day. I can now say of the world, as the man in Hamlet, *What is Hecuba to me, or I to Hecuba?* My best wishes, however, will attend my friends, though all my hopes have left me. I have in vain tried a thousand things that have done others good in the like case, and will go on trying, having so little to lose, and so much to get. The chapter of knowledge is a very short, but the **chapter of accidents** is a very long one. I will keep dipping in it, for sometimes a concurrence of unknown and unforeseen circumstances, in the medicine and the disease, may produce an unexpected and lucky hit. But no more of myself, that self, as now circumstanced, being but a disagreeable subject to us both.

Charlie is my darling, the young Chevalier

Source: CHARLIE IS MY DARLING
Author: Carolina Oliphant, Baroness Nairne (1766-1845)
First published: c. 1846
Type of work: Lyric poem

Context: One critic notes that "only Shakespeare, Burns and Carolina Oliphant could claim that they wrote so many as three lyrics which after a hundred years or more are still known to everybody. . . ." Baroness Nairne was born in Scotland at Gask, Perthshire, the daughter of an ardent Jacobite who named her Carolina in memory of "Bonnie Prince Charlie." In 1745 Prince Charles Edward, the "Young Pretender," aided by a French declaration of war on England, landed in Scotland in an attempt to lead an uprising which would culminate in his accession to the throne of England. It was a pathetic if heroically romantic attempt, doomed to failure from the start, but for a brief span the Bonnie Prince rode through Scotland raising hearts and hopes for the "good old cause." This lyric commemorates his arrival:

'Twas on a Monday morning,
  Right early in the year,
When Charlie came to our toun,
  The young Chevalier.
    Oh, Charlie is my darling,
    My darling, my darling;
  Oh, **Charlie is my darling,**
    The young Chevalier.
As he came marching up the street,
  The pipes play'd loud and clear,

And a' the folk came running out
To meet the Chevalier.
Oh, Charlie is my darling. . . .

Chaucer, well of English undefiled

Source: THE FAERIE QUEENE (Book IV, Canto 2, stanza 32)
Author: Edmund Spenser (c.1552-1599)
First published: 1590
Type of work: Allegorical poem

Context: Sir Blandamour, riding in company with Paridell, comes upon Sir Ferraugh, who is in the company of the counterfeit Florimell. Sir Blandamour vanquishes Sir Ferraugh in combat and takes Florimell from him. After a time the situation of Florimell's being Sir Blandamour's love irritates Paridell, as Paridell and Blandamour had an agreement to share any prizes they might take. They engage in a fight for the lady, and when both are bleeding freely from their wounds, they are joined by the Squire of Dames, who tells them that there is to be a tournament, the prize to be Florimell's girdle, which Satyran had found and worn until the jealousy of other knights forced him to arrange the contest. As they therefore all go towards the place of the tourney, they are met by the two fast friends, Cambell and Triamond, and their ladies, Canacee and Cambine. There then ensues the stanza in the poem in which Spenser refers to Chaucer as the well of English undefiled. It was a popular Elizabethan idea that Chaucer was the founder of the English language, but Spenser does not say so: what he does say is that Chaucer wrote pure and unblemished English. The stanza containing Spenser's reference to him is as follows (a "beadroll" is a list):

Whylome, as antique stories tellen vs,
Those two were foes the fellonest on ground,
And battell made the dreddest daungerous,
That euer shrilling trumpet did resound;
Though now their acts be no where to be found,
As that renowmed Poet them compyled,
With warlike numbers and Heroicke sound,
Dan **Chaucer, well of English vndefyled,**
On Fames eternall bea(d)roll worthie to be fyled.

Bur wicked Time, that all good thoughts doth waste,
And workes of noblest wits to nought out weare,
That famous moniment hath quite defaste,
And robd the world of threasure endlesse deare,
The which mote haue enriched all vs heare.

· · ·

139

Chewing the food of sweet and bitter fancy

Source: AS YOU LIKE IT (Act IV, sc. iii, 1. 102)
Author: William Shakespeare (1564-1616)
First published: 1623
Type of work: Dramatic comedy

Context: In the Forest of Arden, Orlando, suitor of Rosalind, discovers and kills a lion ready to attack his cruel brother, Oliver, with whom he becomes reconciled because of this act of bravery and compassion. Wounded, Orlando dispatches Oliver to explain his delay in an appointment with the shepherd lad who instructs him in how to win the hand of Rosalind (actually Rosalind disguised as a shepherd lad as she searches for her father, an exiled Duke).

OLIVER

When last the young Orlando parted from you,
He left a promise to return again
Within an hour, and pacing through the forest,
Chewing the food of sweet and bitter fancy,
Lo what befell. He threw his eye aside,
And mark what object did present itself.
Under an old oak, whose boughs were mossed with age,
And high top bald with dry antiquity,
A wretched ragged man, o'ergrown with hair,
Lay sleeping on his back; about his neck
A green and gilded snake had wreathed itself,
Who with her head, nimble in threats, approached
The opening of his mouth; but suddenly,
Seeing Orlando, it unlinked itself,
And with indented glides did slip away
Into a bush, under which bush's shade
A lioness, with udders all drawn dry,
Lay couching head on ground, with catlike watch
When that the sleeping man should stir; for 'tis
The royal disposition of that beast
To prey on nothing that doth seem as dead.
This seen, Orlando did approach the man,
And found it was his brother, his elder brother.

A chiel's amang you, taking notes

Source: ON THE LATE CAPTAIN GROSE'S PEREGRINATIONS THROUGH SCOTLAND (Stanza 1)
Author: Robert Burns (1759-1796)
First published: 1789
Type of work: Humorous poem

Context: Captain Grose was an antiquarian and friend of Robert Burns, who had published many of his findings on the cultural history of Scotland, including *Antiquities of Scotland* and his *Treatise on Ancient Armor and Weapons.* Burns comments humorously on both the man and his work: of the man, he says it would be better had he fallen in battle than left the army. For his work, Burns has humorous ridicule, commenting that Captain Grose has porridge pots dating from before Noah's Flood, a cinder from Eve's first fire, Tubalcain's fire-shovel and fender, and the Witch of Endor's brass-bound broomstick. Burns even suggests that the antiquary is a colleague of the devil, a man to make ghosts, warlocks, and witches all "quake at his conjuring hammer." In the first stanza the poet warns his fellow Scots that no one is safe from Grose's inquisitive mind, that he takes notes on everything, great or small, significant or of no consequence, in order to get it into print:

> Hear, Land o' Cakes, and brither Scots,
> Frae Maidenkirk to Johnny Groats;—
> If there's a hole in a' your coats,
>   I rede you tent it;
> **A chiel's amang you, taking notes,**
>   And faith, he'll prent it.

Child of misery, baptized in tears

Source: THE COUNTRY JUSTICE, PART ONE, APOLOGY FOR VAGRANTS
Author: John Langhorne (1735-1779)
First published: 1774
Type of work: Didactic poem

Context: The Reverend John Langhorne, D.D., was selected by Dr. Samuel Johnson for a place in his anthology of English poets from Chaucer to Cowper. Langhorne's clergyman father died when the boy was only four; a tender poem commemorates his mother's loving care in his upbringing. Poverty, however, prevented him from continuing his education beyond grammar school. He became first a tutor, then a schoolteacher, always using his spare time writing poetry and studying to become a minister. He continued his religious education as curate to a clergyman. Finally for religious writings, especially his *Genius and Valor: A Scotch Pastoral* he was supposedly given an honorary Doctor of Divinity by the University of Edinburgh in 1766. Some of Langhorne's poetry and prose appeared in *The Monthly Review.* Adding more criticism and fanciful prose, he published a two-volume *Effusions of Friendship and Fancy,* in a flippant style in which critics saw the influence of Sterne. He and his brother published their translation of Plutarch in 1770. Sir Walter Scott and Tobias Smollet were among his admirers. Most of his writing lay in what his son called "the lighter provinces of literature," when he collected his father's verse into two elegant volumes in 1804, twenty-five years after the poet's death. He and his writing are largely forgotten today. Langhorne was never very well off financially, so in 1772 he accepted appointment as Justice of the Peace in Blagdon, Somerset. After carefully considering the duties of his new office, he wrote a three part didactic and satirical poem, called *The Country Justice, a poem by one of Her Majesty's Justices of the Peace for the county of Somerset.* Part I was published in 1774, and the other two parts followed later, a year apart. In the Introduction, the poet praises British laws from King Richard to his own time. The early Saxon serfs gained liberty only by flight, but Edward III did manage to achieve some law and order, and established a system of rural justice. Langhorne describes the ancient Hall of Justice. The stanzas of rhymed couplets that follow are headed by phrases descriptive of their content. In "The Character of a County Justice," the poet writes: "His featur'd soul display'd Honor's strong beam, and Mercy's melting shade." The section "General Motives for Lenity" pleads "Be this, ye rural Magistrates, your plan: / Firm be your justice, but be friends to man." Before sentencing, the magistrate is urged to discover whether vice or nature prompts the deed, and he is adjured to consider "the strong temptations and the need." Bringing up a specific case, Langhorne offers his "Apology for Vagrants."

> For him who, lost to ev'ry hope of life
> Has long with fortune held unequal strife,
> Known to no human love, no human care,
> The friendless, homeless object of despair;
> For the poor vagrant, feel, while he complains,
> Nor from sad freedom sent to sadder chains . . .
>
>   · · ·
>
> Perhaps on some inhospitable shore
> The houseless wretch a widow'd parent bore,
> Who, then, no more by golden prospects led,
> Of the poor Indian begg'd a leafy bed,
> Cold on Canadian hills, or Minden's plain
> Perhaps that parent mourn'd her soldier slain;
> Bent o'er her babe, her eye dissolv'd in dew,
> The big drops mingling with the milk he drew,
> Gave the sad presage of his future years,
> The **child of misery, baptiz'd in tears!**

The childhood shows the man as morning shows the day

Source: PARADISE REGAINED (Book IV, ll. 220-221)
Author: John Milton (1608-1674)
First published: 1671
Type of work: Epic poem

Context: In offering temptations to Christ, Satan takes Him to the top of a mountain and shows Him all the kingdoms of the world and urges Him to free the tribes of Israel. Christ replies that Jews brought down their own destruction on themselves by departing from the one true God. Satan then shows Him Rome, which spreads its rule over all the earth. With Satan's help, Christ could depose the depraved Tiberius and become the Emperor of Rome, a more exalted position than he would gain by assuming David's throne, which He is prophesied to ascend. Christ scorns the idea, as Rome, although of great magnificence, is also the seat of a wicked, debauched, cruel, blood-thirsty people. Of His kingdom Christ says there is no end. Satan replies that he can give Him any kingdom, as they had all been given to him. He then suggests that Christ should fall down and worship him; this Christ refuses to do. Satan may have tempted Eve but he cannot tempt Christ. Satan then says that perhaps in His disregard for worldly things, Christ is more addicted to contemplation and debate than to the acquisition of material things; when He was only twelve years of age He went to the temple, where He argued learnedly with the priests, and one can tell what a man will be by what he is as a child. Satan says:

> And thou thyself seemst otherwise inclined
> Than to a worldly crown, addicted more
> To contemplation and profound dispute,
> As by that early action may be judged,
> When slipping from thy mother's eye thou went'st
> Alone into the temple; there was found
> Among the gravest rabbis disputant
> On points and questions fitting Moses' chair,
> Teaching, not taught; **the childhood shows the man**
> **As morning shows the day.** Be famous then
> By wisdom; as thy empire must extend,
> So let extend thy mind o'er all the world,
> In knowledge, all things in it comprehend.

A child's a plaything for an hour

Source: PARENTAL RECOLLECTIONS
Author: Mary Ann Lamb (1764-1847)
First published: 1809
Type of work: Children's poem

Context: If it had not been for a writer and publisher disliked by the Lamb family, William Godwin (1756–1836), Mary Lamb might have gone silent to the grave. Her brother Charles Lamb (1775–1834) earned his name in literature by his *Essays of Elia* published in the *London Magazine* between 1820 and 1825, observations on life set down in familiar language and delightful style. His plans for marriage were disrupted by his sister's spell of madness in which she attacked her father and killed her mother. Lamb spent the rest of his life acting as her guardian. He, too, became unbalanced and spent the years 1795–1796 in an asylum, but recovered. So did she, but their acquaintance, Godwin, suggested that to occupy Mary's mind, Charles and she should join in writing children's books for his "Juvenile Library." At that time, most books for children were simple and stupid tales, sure to bore any bright child. Mary Lamb was especially critical of them, so they began writing as a kind of protest, first *King and Queen of Hearts* (1805) and then the volume for which they are best remembered, *Tales from Shakespear* (1807), a prose retelling of his best known plays. Next came a simplified version of the *Adventures of Ulysses* (1808). Since both of the Lambs had written poetry, they collected eighty of their products as *Poetry for Children* (1809). Only internal evidence indicates which author wrote any given poem. One, called "Parental Recollections," is generally attributed to Mary, though some scholars ascribe the authorship to Charles, possibly because he quoted the first line in his Elia essay "The Old and the New Schoolmaster," and because his "Dream Children," is correlated to the whole poem.

A child's a plaything for an hour;
Its pretty tricks we try
For that or for a longer space;
    Then tire, and lay it by.

But I know one, that to itself
    All seasons could controul;
That would have mock'd the sense of pain
    Out of a grievèd soul.

Thou, straggler into loving arms,
    Young climber up of knees,
When I forget thy thousand ways,
    Then life and all shall cease.

The choir invisible

Source: O MAY I JOIN THE CHOIR INVISIBLE (Line 1)
Author: George Eliot (1819-1880)
First published: 1867
Type of work: Lyric poem

Context: Known primarily as a great novelist, George Eliot was also a poet; although it is true that most of her poems are highly personal, she at times touches upon themes and sentiments that are universal. Like many of her more intellectual contemporaries, George Eliot quite early faced the dilemma of Christianity's confrontation with skeptical science. Not only did she radically disagree with the traditional interpretation of Christ, she also translated and made accessible to the English, Straus's *Leben Jesu,* a liberal version of the life of Jesus. But George Eliot was not content to rest with skepticism. Torn by the desire to find a meaningful faith, she came more and more to exalt the basic goodness of man, a humanism that transcended individuals. In this brief poem, she tells of her desire to be a part of the company of men who have made earthly life better; hers was no fuzzy otherworldliness—she searched for a community in which the best of human endeavor formed the highest religion.

> O may I join **the choir invisible**
> Of those immortal dead who live again
> In minds made better by their presence: live
> In pulses stirred to generosity,
> In deeds of daring rectitude, in scorn
> For miserable aims that end with self,
> In thoughts sublime that pierce the night like stars,
> And with their mild persistence urge man's search
> To vaster issues. . . .

The Christless code, that must have life for a blow

Source: MAUD (Part II, sec. i, 11. 26-27)
Author: Alfred, Lord Tennyson (1809-1892)
First published: 1855
Type of work: Narrative poem

Context: When the narrator of this long poem (which Tennyson called a "monodrama") was a small boy, he heard his father and the father of an as yet unborn child agree that, should the baby be a girl, the children shall marry each other when they are grown. But a few years later the narrator's father loses all of his money and dies, perhaps a suicide. Maud's father, on the other hand, grows richer; and the narrator is discarded as a possible husband for Maud because of his poverty—a favorite theme with Tennyson. Maud's brother has found what he considers a better match for her in the person of a newly-made lord, an overdressed, supercilious, and proud young man. The brother, who is politically ambitious, gives a large dinner and ball for his constituents, from which the narrator is pointedly excluded. He and Maud, however, plan that she will meet him in the garden of her house at the conclusion of the dance. But hardly has she entered the garden, in all the splendor of her ballgown and jewels, than her brother arrives, bringing with him the "babefaced lord," and pours out "terms of disgrace" on his sister. The narrator replies with equal anger, until the brother strikes him in the face. This

145

act, according to the code still prevailing as late as the 1850's, demands a challenge, which the narrator immediately gives; and in the duel which takes place within an hour, he kills Maud's brother. Tennyson uses this episode to express his detestation of the code of dueling.

And he struck me, madman, over the face,
Struck me before the languid fool,
Who was gaping and grinning by;
Struck for himself an evil stroke;
Wrought for his house an irredeemable woe;
For front to front in an hour we stood,
And a million horrible bellowing echoes
     broke
From the red-ribb'd hollow behind the wood,
And thunder'd up into Heaven **the Christless code,**
     That must have life for a blow.
Ever and ever afresh they seem'd to grow.

Christmas comes but once a year

Source: FIVE HUNDRED POINTS OF GOOD HUSBANDRY (Chapter 12, "The Farmer's Daily Diet")
Author: Thomas Tusser (c.1525-1580)
First published: 1557
Type of work: Didactic poem

Context: Thomas Tusser was a gentleman of good birth and a graduate of Eton and Cambridge, who forsook the world of the court and took up farming. He evidently did not prosper at it, for he moved several times and finally died in a debtor's prison; but he nonetheless became the poet of early Elizabethan farm life. His works are composed largely of practical instructions to farmers and housewives, and are written in verse. Much of this material is doggerel, but it is vivid and possesses a homely charm. The result is a faithful and realistic picture of rural England during the middle of the sixteenth century. The first eleven chapters of *Five Hundred Points of Good Husbandry* are short verses which describe husbandry and offer general recommendations; beginning with Chapter Thirteen, Tusser covers the farmer's year month by month, discussing the various activities peculiar to each. Each month is preceded by a brief summary of the matters to be discussed, and various comments on weather, planets and climate are interspersed from time to time. The book is an early forerunner of the farmers' almanacs. Chapter Twelve is entitled "The Farmer's Daily Diet," and describes the plain but solid and substantial fare of the period. Fish is an important staple in the diet, both fresh and salted, as is salt meat. The first three stanzas of the chapter refer

146

to Lent and Easter. "Martilmas beef" is beef dried and smoked in the chimney after the manner of bacon. The couplets which follow refer to Midsummer (St. John's Day), Michaelmas, Hallowmass, and Christmas; these in turn are followed by moral reflections and references to special days. The second and third stanzas and the first five couplets are given below:

> Let Lent, well kept, offend not thee,
> For March and April breeders be:
> Spend herring first, save salt-fish last,
> For salt-fish is good, when Lent is past.
>
> When Easter comes, who knows not than
> That veal and bacon is the man;
> And Martilmas beef doth bear good tack,
> When country folks do dainties lack.
>
> When Mackrell ceaseth from the seas,
> John Baptist brings grass-beef and pease.
>
> Fresh herring plenty, Mitchell brings,
> With fatted crones [old ewes], and such old things.
>
> All Saints do lay for pork and souse,
> For sprats and spurlings for their house.
>
> At Christmas play, and make good cheer,
> For **Christmas comes, but once a-year.**
>
> Though some then do, as do they would,
> Let thrifty do, as do they should.

The Cincinnatus of the West

Source: ODE TO NAPOLEON BONAPARTE (Stanza 19)
Author: George Gordon, Lord Byron (1788-1824)
First published: 1814
Type of work: Satiric ode

Context: Napoleon, in his years of glory, seemed to the British and to many others a supremely dangerous man, and his empire a great shadow into which all Europe would shortly disappear. By the beginning of 1814, however, the tide had turned; and Napoleon's disastrous Russian campaign was the turning point. He invaded Russia with an army of 640,-000 men; the Russians retreated, laying waste the countryside as they retired. When Napoleon entered Moscow it was set afire and burned for

147

five days; his troops had to take refuge in the open, devastated countryside and could not live off the land. It was October, and Napoleon had to retreat. His men, continually harassed by mounted Cossacks, died of hunger, cold, disease, and exhaustion. When the army entered its own territory at last there were but 25,000 men left. No longer thought invincible, Napoleon found all Europe ready to fight him. He still had an army in Germany, and undertook another campaign. A series of victories was followed by utter defeat in the "Battle of the Nations," and his retreat from the Rhine was almost as disastrous as that from Moscow. From Paris he sallied forth once more, but the defeat this time was decisive; Napoleon abdicated on April 6, 1814, and retired to the Island of Elba. Byron was editing a paper called *The Corsair* at the time and had announced his intention to give up the writing of poetry. However, when word was received concerning Napoleon's abdication, Byron broke his resolution and wrote an ode to Bonaparte. In it he excoriates the emperor, who has strewn all Europe with blood and bones and whose only work has been destruction. If Napoleon had been truly great, says Byron, he would have stepped down as soon as France's greatness had been restored. The last portion of the poem is given below; in the final stanza Byron makes an interesting comparison between a leader he deplores and one he admires.

There was a day—there was an hour—
    While earth was Gaul's—Gaul thine—
When that immeasurable power
    Unsated to resign,
Had been an act of purer fame
Than gathers round Marengo's name,
    And gilded thy decline
Through the long twilight of all time,
Despite some passing clouds of crime.

But thou forsooth must be a king . . .
Vain forward child of empire! say,
Are all thy playthings snatch'd away?

Where may the wearied eye repose,
    When gazing on the Great;
Where neither guilty glory glows,
    Nor despicable state?
Yes—one—the first—the last—the best—
The Cincinnatus of the West,
    Whom envy dared not hate,
Bequeath'd the name of Washington,
To make man blush there was but one!

Civility costs nothing and buys everything

Source: LETTER TO THE COUNTESS OF BUTE (30 May 1756)
Author: Lady Mary Wortley Montagu (1689-1762)
First published: 1763
Type of work: Personal letter

Context: The eighteenth century is remembered in part for the excellency of its letter writers such as the Earl of Chesterfield, Thomas Gray, Horace Walpole, and above all Lady Mary Wortley Montagu. The wife of an ambassador, she was provided not only the opportunity for extensive travel but also the access to many of the events which an ordinary traveler would never experience. Her letters, unusually detailed and frank in tone, were written for the most part to her daughter, her sisters, and her intimate friends. Apparently at home in France, Italy, Spain, Germany, Holland, Austria, or Turkey, Lady Mary recorded a vivid and intimate record of the nations and their political institutions. In a letter of May 30, 1756, to her daughter, the Countess of Bute, Lady Mary describes her sorrow upon hearing of the death of an old friend—Sir William Lowther—and, in turn, her anger at the way his estate has been devoured by ravenous inheritors. In this respect she asserts that he died "fortunately," believing "himself blessed in many friends, whom a short time would have shown to be worthless, mercenary, designing scoundrels." The letter is typical of those to her daughter in that it is imbued with moral counsel and earnestness of purpose. In the opening paragraph she urges the countess to be discreet and gracious in her associations with a certain Mr. Prescot who had previously taken offense at her haughty demeanor:

> I sent you a long letter very lately, and enclosed one to Lady Jane, and also a second bill for fifty pounds, which I hope you have received, though I fear I cannot prevail on Mr. Prescot to take care of my letters; if he should do it, I beg you would be very obliging to him; remember, **civility costs nothing and buys everything;** your daughters should engrave that maxim in their hearts.

Clean hands and a pure heart

Source: PSALMS 24:4
Author: Unknown
First transcribed: c.400-200 B.C.
Type of work: Religious poetry

Context: Psalm 24 embodies the liturgy for Jehovah's entrance into the Temple. The first two verses are a quiet affirmation of faith, acknowledging God's universal dominion. The next four verses are a liturgy for those who come to worship in Jerusalem, the holy place. In them the need for purity is emphasized: the worshiper must be clean physically and spiritually, he must be humble, and honesty is required of him. Such a person will receive the blessing of the Lord. The serene faith in these lines echoes that in Psalm 23 and is a reflection of the same deep religious feeling. The liturgy ends with a verse stating that the people are spiritually ready to enter the temple. Here there is a gathering sense of anticipation, of a pause before the next act in this sacred drama. The last four verses fulfill that expectation; they celebrate the entrance of Jehovah, as symbolized by the Ark of the Covenant, into the Temple. It is carried in by a procession; members of the procession are singing praises to the Lord, who will be present in the Temple so long as the Ark remains there. This jubilant hymn is a demand that the gates of the Temple may be opened so that the Lord can enter. In accordance with custom, the demand is made twice; twice the identity of "this King of glory" is demanded in return; and twice there is the joyous reply that this King is none other than Jehovah. This brief hymn of four verses is one of the most majestic passages in Scripture; Handel drew upon it for some of the exalted portions of his *Messiah,* giving it music which, in dignity and grandeur, is worthy of it.

The earth is the LORD's, and the fulness thereof; the world, and they that dwell therein.

For he hath founded it upon the seas, and established it upon the floods.

Who shall ascend into the hill of the LORD? or who shall stand in his holy place?

He that hath **clean hands, and a pure heart;** who hath not lifted up his soul unto vanity, nor sworn deceitfully.

He shall receive the blessing from the LORD, and righteousness from the God of his salvation.

This is the generation of them that seek him, that seek thy face, O Jacob. Selah.

Lift up your heads, O ye gates; and be ye lift up, ye everlasting doors; and the King of glory shall come in.

Who is this King of glory? The LORD strong and mighty, the LORD mighty in battle.

Lift up your heads, O ye gates; even lift them up, ye everlasting doors; and the King of glory shall come in.

Who is this King of glory? The LORD of hosts, he is the King of glory. Selah.

Cleave ever to the sunnier side of doubt

Source: THE ANCIENT SAGE (Line 68)
Author: Alfred, Lord Tennyson (1809-1892)
First published: 1885
Type of work: Philosophical poem

Context: A venerable sage a thousand years before the time of Christ speaks to a follower. He points to a gushing spring of water and says that its source is not here, but high up—not merely in the hills, nor yet in the clouds, but in the heavens where the clouds are moulded. The follower has a scroll in which is written a poem, the essence of which is that the things of this earth owe their existence to a nameless power that is never seen nor heard. The Nameless, says the sage, is in all things; if he removed himself, everything would vanish, even though he had never spoken to man. The follower cannot prove the existence of the Nameless; he cannot prove the existence of the world in which he lives; he cannot prove that he is a body, soul, or a combination of the two; he cannot prove that he is either mortal or immortal; he cannot prove that the sage is not another part of himself, holding a dialogue with himself. In fact, since nothing worthy of being proved can be either proved or disproved, he will do well to cleave to the better side of things that he doubts, because faith always sees the best in the world, even though it may be cloaked with the worst.

> Thou canst not prove the Nameless, O my son,
> Nor canst thou prove the world thou movest in,
> Thou canst not prove that thou art body alone,
> Nor canst thou prove that thou art spirit alone,
> Nor canst thou prove that thou art both in one:
> Thou canst not prove thou art immortal, no
> Nor yet that thou art mortal—nay, my son,
> Thou canst not prove that I, who speak with thee,
> Am not thyself in converse with thyself,
> For nothing worthy proving can be proven,
> Nor yet disproven: wherefore thou be wise,
> **Cleave ever to the sunnier side of doubt,**
> And cling to Faith beyond the forms of Faith!

Clever to a fault

Source: BISHOP BLOUGRAM'S APOLOGY (Line 420)
Author: Robert Browning (1812-1889)
First published: 1855
Type of work: Dramatic monologue

Context: Bishop Blougram and a literary acquaintance, Gigadibs, discuss religion over their wine, following Corpus Christi Day supper. Gigadibs, a thirty-year-old magazine writer, appears as a representative of mid-nineteenth century philosophical thought. The bishop, a person with "a soul and body that exact/ A comfortable care in many ways," dominates the discussion with his self-defense. The talk centers on whether it is better to live a life of faith diversified by doubt, as does the bishop, or of doubt diversified by faith, as does Gigadibs. In a skeptical age, the bishop finds his

151

inner-core of faith confronted by his intellectual doubt. He attempts to rationalize his position of a doubting believer whose faith has been questioned by his contemporary intellectuals. His unique position, he claims, is a historical accident. Had he been born three hundred years earlier, no one would have questioned his faith; seventy years later, no one would question his doubt:

> It's through my coming in the tail of time,
> Nicking the minute with a happy tact.
> Had I been born three hundred years ago
> They'd say, "What's strange? Blougram of course believes";
> And, seventy years since, "disbelieves of course."
> But now, "He may believe; and yet, and yet
> How can he?"—All eyes turn with interest.
> Whereas, step off the line on either side—
> You, for example, **clever to a fault,**
> The rough and ready man who writes apace,
> Read somewhat seldomer, think perhaps even less—
> You disbelieve! Who wonders and who cares?

Close thy Byron; open thy Goethe

Source: SARTOR RESARTUS (Book II, chapter 9)
Author: Thomas Carlyle (1795-1881)
First published: 1833-1834
Type of work: Spiritual autobiography

Context: In an involved work with the subtitle "The Life and Opinions of Herr Teufelsdröckh," and written at his wife's farm where they had moved to economize, Carlyle continued his censorship of the highly praised Victorian Era. The title of the work, *Sartor Resartus* (The Tailor Reclothed) was taken from a figure used by Swift in a *Tale of a Tub* (1704). As the father, in Swift's satire, gave garments to his three sons, representing three branches of religion with stipulations that they should not alter the garments, only to have each son change the clothing to suit his ideals, so Carlyle expounded that the material world was merely clothing for the spiritual world. Swift had asked: "What is man himself but a microcoat," living amid surroundings that are like a "large suit of clothes which invests everything?" Carlyle put into the work his own social criticism and transcendental philosophy. And, of course, he worked into it his basic ideas on duty, work, and silence that appear in almost everything he wrote. At the age of 24, Carlyle had begun to study German at a time when few of his countrymen were interested in its philosophy or literature. He translated a number of works not previously available for English readers, such as his 1824 translation of Goethe's *Wilhelm Meister's Apprenticeship and Travels*. He also wrote a biography of Goethe and essays on his works. Not blinded by Romanticism like so many of his contemporaries, he believed that Byron's poetic works were frothy in comparison with the writing of Goethe. In his book, he quotes the imaginary professor and philosophic author Teufelsdröckh, as he utters his "Everlasting No," his bitter and sweeping denunciation of the structure of society. Two chapters later, one entitled "The Everlasting Yea," voices what he does believe: that clothes, and human institutions, and religions of the past should be considered only as an expression of the continuing life of the Soul. Man has the power to design the clothes that he will wear. In urging Englishmen to stop living in the exotic, rebellious world of Byron and Romanticism, and to turn against the love intrigues and irreverent frivolities of *Don Juan* and *Childe Harold,* Carlyle quotes the Professor's stern command: "Love not pleasure; love God. This is the EVERLASTING YEA, wherein all contradiction is solved."

"I asked myself: What is this that, ever since earliest years, thou hast been fretting and fuming, and lamenting and self-tormenting, on account of? Say it in a word: is it not because thou art not HAPPY? Because the THOU (sweet gentleman) is not sufficiently honored, nourished, soft-bedded, and lovingly cared for? Foolish soul! What Act of Legislature was there that *thou* shouldst be Happy? . . . Art thou nothing other than a Vulture, then, that fliest through the Universe seeking after somewhat to *eat;* and shrieking dolefully because carrion enough is not given thee? **Close thy Byron; open thy Goethe."**

Close-lipped patience

Source: THE SCHOLAR-GYPSY (Stanza 20)
Author: Matthew Arnold (1822-1888)
First published: 1853
Type of work: Philosophical poem

Context: The poem is centered around just what its title suggests—a scholar who became a gypsy after being disillusioned with Oxford. This scholar began to learn how gypsies "had arts to rule as they desired/ the workings of men's brains." As time passed, the scholar's great mission in life became to learn this gypsy art completely and then "impart the art" to the world. The scholar-gypsy goes on to say that he must have "heaven-sent moments" to master this skill. Using this legend of the scholar-gypsy and his central mission, the poet Arnold contrasts the gypsy's life with the lives of most men. He says that modern men go first one direction then another, never really knowing what their goal is. And finally after wearing themselves out with their daily insignificant struggles, they wait with "close-lipp'd patience" for death. This in contrast with the scholar-gypsy who waits "for the spark from heaven" so he can carry out his great purpose in life.

153

. . . and we others pine,
And wish the long unhappy dream would
    end,
And waive all claim to bliss, and try to
    bear;
With **close-lipp'd patience** for our only
    friend,
Sad patience, too near neighbor
    to despair—
But none has hope like thine!

Coat of many colors

Source: GENESIS 37:23
Author: Unknown
First transcribed: c.1000-300 B.C.
Type of work: Religious history and law

Context: Israel has many sons by his wives, Bilhah and Zilpah, but he loves best his son Joseph, because Joseph is the child of his old age. When the other sons see that their father loves Joseph the best, they hate the boy and speak evil of him. Joseph tells his brothers of dreams he has, and these dreams increase their hatred. He tells them that in one dream their sheaves of grain make obeisance to his sheaf and that in another dream "the sun and moon and the eleven stars" make obeisance to him. Later Israel's other sons take their father's flocks to graze in Shechem. While they are away, Israel sends Joseph to ascertain their well-being. Joseph finds they have left Shechem and wandered on with the flocks to Dothan, and he follows them there. When Joseph arrives in their midst, the brothers conspire against him. Lest Joseph be killed, Reuben suggests to the others that Joseph be stripped of the coat their father has given him and be placed in a pit, for Reuben hopes that he may rescue Joseph and return him to their father. But while Reuben is away, the other brothers follow Judah's suggestion to sell Joseph into slavery. To hide their deed they dip Joseph's coat in a kid's blood and send it to Israel, who then believes that a wild beast has killed the boy:

And it came to pass, when Joseph was come unto his brethren, that they stript Joseph out of his coat, his **coat of many colours** that was on him:
And they took him, and cast him into a pit: and the pit was empty, there was no water in it.

· · ·

And they took Joseph's coat, and killed a kid of the goats, and dipped the coat in the blood;
And they sent the **coat of many colours,** and they brought it to their father. . . .

154

And he knew it, and said, It is my son's coat; an evil beast hath devoured him; Joseph is without doubt rent in pieces.

Cock and bull story

Source: THE LIFE AND OPINIONS OF TRISTRAM SHANDY, GENT. (Book IX, chapter 33)
Author: Laurence Sterne (1713-1768)
First published: 1759-1767
Type of work: Novel

Context: Laurence Sterne's novel displays his whimsical nature as an author throughout. He uses such tricks of typography as blank pages, black pages, pointing fingers, and a large assortment of dots, dashes, and asterisks. Even the Preface is at an unusual place, not being found by the reader till he reaches the twentieth chapter of Book III. The very end of the novel is as whimsical as the portions that precede it. The final chapter begins with Mr. Walter Shandy, Tristram's father, discoursing upon idiosyncrasies of man's attitudes toward sex, as compared to those we have about the honor attached to the killing of men, especially in war. While he is speaking he is interrupted by one of his tenants, who has come with a complaint about the bull that Walter Shandy keeps to serve the cows of the parish. The tenant's wife has been brought to bed with a child some six weeks before, but the man's cow, which should have calved at the same time, has not produced an offspring. At the end of the conversation which follows, about the bull and his paternal abilities, Mrs. Shandy asks what the story is all about. Parson Yorick comments to her about the story of the bull, but the ambiguity of his comment goes further, being a statement as well about the novel which Laurence Sterne has laid before the reader.

—Most of the townsmen, an' please your worship, quoth Obadiah, believe that 'tis all the Bull's fault—
—But may not a cow be barren? replied my father, turning to Dr. Slop.
—It never happens: said Dr. Slop, but the man's wife may have come before her time naturally enough—Prithee has the child hair upon his head?—added Dr. Slop—
—It is as hairy as I am; said Obadiah.—Obadiah had not been shaved for three weeks—Wheu—u——u————cried my father; beginning the sentence with an exclamatory whistle—and so, brother Toby, this poor Bull of mine, who is as good a bull as ever p-ssed, and might have done for Europa herself in purer times—had he but two legs less, might have been driven into Doctors' Commons and lost his character—which to a town Bull, brother Toby, is the very same thing as his life—

155

L—d! said my mother, what is this story all about?—
A **Cock and a Bull,** said Yorick—and one of the best of its kind, I ever heard.

Coiner of sweet words

Source: SOHRAB AND RUSTUM (Line 458)
Author: Matthew Arnold (1822-1888)
First published: 1853
Type of work: Narrative poem

Context: In this long poem, based on an episode in the Persian epic *Shah Namah,* Sohrab, a young Tartar warrior, had been reared by his mother in a province of Persia; because she did not want him to be a warrior, she told his father that the child was a girl. Now, however, Sohrab has grown to manhood and in hopes of finding his father, the famous war chieftain Rustum, challenges the Persian army to send its greatest warrior to fight him in a single combat. Without knowing that the challenger is his son, Rustum comes out of retirement to fight the youth. Although Sohrab at first thinks that the Persian defender is his father, Rustum, who fights incognito, thinks that the hesitant boy wants to back from his challenge and forces him to begin the combat. Just before the quotation, Sohrab again asks the unknown defender if he is Rustum; when Rustum angrily rebukes him, the battle is renewed with such fury that he forgets himself, shouts his battlecry and kills his son, who was too shocked by the cry to defend himself. Early in the combat, Rustum is enraged that the youth has so much skill in arms.

> His breast heaved, his lips foam'd, and twice his voice
> Was choked with rage; at last these words broke way:—
> "Girl! nimble with thy feet, not with thy hands!
> Curl'd minion, dancer, **coiner of sweet words!**
> Fight, let me hear thy hateful voice no more! . . .
> Speak not to me of truce, and pledge, and wine!
> Remember all thy valour; try thy feints
> And cunning! all the pity I had is gone; . . ."

The cold charities of man to man

Source: THE VILLAGE (Line 245)
Author: George Crabbe (1754-1832)
First published: 1783
Type of work: Satiric poem

Context: The poet begins by saying that the usual pastoral poem bears not the faintest resemblance to reality; instead of being based on observation of the country and its folk, it is wholly derived from classical writers, such as Virgil. He gives a description of the land, which is evidently that along the English Channel, in which region Crabbe was born and bred. He finds the soil sandy, thin, and sterile, and covered with the plants that grow only on barren ground. And the people are far different from those in the pastoral idyls. Instead of devoting themselves to happy rural sports and piping gaily, they sweat the long day through in back-breaking toil. Their pains are not the amorous ones of the poets, but actual physical pains of bones, muscles, and sinews. Nor do they sit down to the plain but plentiful repasts of the songs: their diet is sparse and pinching and those who sing of it would not deign to touch it. As a result of what they have to live on, they are highly susceptible to disease. When a man grows old, his miseries increase; he can be useful only in some sedentary labor such as herding sheep. Or he can resort to the poorhouse, truly the dwelling place of misery, where the most enviable inmates are the idiots who do not feel hardships. It is here that the cold charities of man to man are dispensed amidst scenes of unimaginable squalor.

> Here too the sick their final doom receive,
> Here brought, amid the scenes of grief, to grieve,
> Where the loud groans from some sad chamber flow,
> Mix'd with the clamours of the crowd below;
> Here, sorrowing, they each kindred sorrow scan,
> And **the cold charities of man to man:**
> Whose laws indeed for ruin'd age provide,
> And strong compulsion plucks the scrap from pride;
> But still that scrap is bought with many a sigh,
> And pride embitters what it can't deny.

The cold neutrality of an impartial judge

Source: PREFACE TO THE ADDRESS OF M. BRISSOT
Author: Edmund Burke (1729-1797)
First published: 1794
Type of work: Political essay

Context: M. Brissot had addressed the French Constituent Assembly concerning the deterioration of French diplomatic relations with several European nations following the decline into violence of the French Revolution and the attempts of the Concordat to export revolutionary ideas. As a revolutionary himself, he described the horrors in very vivid terms. This address was translated into English by William Burke, a relative and close friend of Edmund. In presenting this *Address* to English readers Edmund Burke prefaced it with an essay in which he described it as the testimony of a revolutionary against his own revolution and therefore of greater force than the opinions of those who opposed the Revolution:

157

They who are inclined to think favorably of that event will undoubtedly object to every state of facts which comes only from the authority of a royalist. Thus much must be allowed by those who are the most firmly attached to the cause of religion, law, and order, (for of such, and not of friends to despotism, the royal party is composed,)—that their very affection to this generous and manly cause, and their abhorrence of a Revolution not less fatal to liberty than to government, may possibly lead them in some particulars to a more harsh representation of the proceedings of their adversaries than would be allowed by **the cold neutrality of an impartial judge.** This sort of error arises from a source highly laudable; but the exactness of truth may suffer even from the feelings of virtue. History will do justice to the intentions of worthy men, but it will be on its guard against their infirmities; it will examine with great strictness of scrutiny whatever appears from a writer in favour of his own cause. . . .

Coldly profane and impiously gay

Source: THE LIBRARY (Line 265)
Author: George Crabbe (1754-1832)
First published: 1781
Type of work: Satiric poem

Context: The poet begins by saying that books are a refuge for the despondent, as the pains in books are less than those of real life; or they may be so much greater than our own that we are reconciled to our lot. He describes how the books are arranged in the library: first, noble folios, followed by quartos, octavos, and duodecimos. They are also grouped by subject, the first being divinity. These books, however, do not give us the great and important truths by which we could live; instead, they are mainly concerned with religious controversy and hair-splitting distinctions. The writers have been motivated more by spleen than by desire to inform. Sect contends against sect, from the Athanasians against the Arians down to the controversies of modern times. Next to the works on divinity are those on skepticism, which are for the most part of the modern period. The writers of these works lack deep learning, genius, and grace. But what they lack in depth of learning they make up in numbers. Some are serious in their dubious claims; others are more flippant, coldly profane, and impiously gay.

> Near to these seats, behold yon slender frames,
> All closely fill'd and mark'd with modern names;
> Where no fair science ever shows her face,
> Few sparks of genius, and no spark of grace;
> There sceptics rest, a still-increasing throng,
> And stretch their widening wings ten thousand strong;
> Some in close fight their dubious claims maintain;

158

Some skirmish lightly, fly and fight again;
Coldly profane, and impiously gay,
Their end the same, though various in their way.

Come, gentle Spring, ethereal mildness, come

Source: THE SEASONS: SPRING (Line 1)
Author: James Thomson (1700-1748)
First published: 1728
Type of work: Nature poem

Context: Despite the fact that at the beginning of each new year James Thomson burned what he considered his inferior poetry of the previous year, critics consider his early work inferior to that of most poets, and preserved only because of the excellence of such later efforts as *The Seasons*. After studying theology in Edinburgh, he moved to London where "Winter," the first of his *Seasons,* was published in 1726, followed by "Summer," and, in 1728, by "Spring," dedicated to Frances, Countess of Hertford. Poetry was not a paying profession, and Thomson spent time in a debtors' prison until friends paid the debt. As his poetry became better known, his financial status improved. Yet he always claimed he was too poor to marry, and died a bachelor at forty-eight, boasting "no line which dying he could wish to blot." Part One of the *Seasons,* "Spring," describes the effect of that time of the year on everything from inanimate matter and vegetables to man, and contrasts wild, passionate love with the purer and gentler kind. It begins:

> **Come, gentle Spring, ethereal mildness come;**
> And from the bosom of yon dropping cloud,
> While music wakes around, veil'd in a shower
> Of shadowing roses, on our plains descend.
>   O HERTFORD, fitted or to shine in court
> With unaffected grace, or walk the plain
> With innocence and meditation join'd,
> In soft assemblage, listen to my Song,
> Which thy own season paints; where Nature all
> Is blooming, and benevolent, like thee.
>   And see where surly WINTER passes off,
> Far to the north, and calls his ruffian Blasts;
> While softer gales succeed, at whose kind touch,
> Dissolving snows in livid torrents lost,
> The mountains lift their green heads to the sky.

159

Come into the garden, Maud

Source: MAUD (Part I, section 22, stanza 1)
Author: Alfred, Lord Tennyson (1809-1892)
First published: 1855
Type of work: Narrative poem

Context: Maud, in its day one of Tennyson's most disputed works, has for many readers lost the appeal which it once had for some. Nonetheless, it is still one of the most readable of all his poems. In form it is a "monodrama"—an extended dramatic monologue divided into episodes, each of which is a soliloquy. The plot, typical of the era in which *Maud* was written, concerns a poor young man; his poverty is a source of great pain to him, for he is proud. He falls in love with the beautiful Maud and struggles to win her in spite of her wealthy family and the rival of their choice; the end is despair, madness, and death. In his first soliloquy the narrator reveals an unstable, or unsettled, mind: he recalls the tragic death of his father, who probably committed suicide; he considers the evils of the world, and says bitterly that war is the best remedy for them. He raves, as his father used to do. In the meantime he notes that the Hall is being refurbished; he has heard of the beauty of Maud, who will live there; he had known her as a child and is eager to see her again. When he does so, his first impression is that she is cold as a stone. After a second meeting, he thinks about her and about the barrier of wealth that lies between them. Later, he hears her sing. Gradually they are drawn together. But the narrator is suddenly convulsed with jealousy: there is a rival, a haughty new-made lord with little to commend him save his money and his title. Maud returns the narrator's love, but he knows he has little chance against Maud's family and the supercilious competitor they have chosen for her. Her love has improved the narrator's mental health, and his nightmare thoughts no longer persecute him. One night there is a huge dinner and dance given at the Hall; Maud will slip away and meet the narrator afterward. He, anticipating her arrival, indulges in a passionate love-song—little dreaming that they will be discovered and that he will kill her brother in a duel:

Come into the garden, Maud,
> For the black bat, night, has flown,
Come into the garden, Maud,
> I am here at the gate alone;
And the woodbine spices are wafted abroad,
> And the musk of the rose is blown.

For a breeze of morning moves,
> And the planet of Love is on high,
Beginning to faint in the light that she loves
> On a bed of daffodil sky,

To faint in the light of the sun she loves,
To faint in his light, and to die.

. . .

She is coming, my own, my sweet;
Were it ever so airy a tread,
My heart would hear it and beat,
Were it earth in an earthy bed;
My dust would hear her and beat,
Had I lain for a century dead;
Would start and tremble under her feet,
And blossom in purple and red.

Come lovely and soothing death

Source: WHEN LILACS LAST IN THE DOORYARD BLOOM'D (Line 135)
Author: Walt Whitman (1819-1892)
First published: 1865
Type of work: Elegy

Context: Walt Whitman wanted to write down-to-earth poetry, unrhymed and with lines of varying length, in order to appeal to the workers. Ironically, few of the common people in his own country knew his works. However, poets all over the world have been influenced by him to experiment with meter and subject matter. Stirred by the Civil War, he wrote patriotic poetry. He traveled to Washington in December, 1862, to look after his brother, wounded in battle; there following the slaughter at Fredericksburg, he found much to do as a volunteer nurse. In Washington he saw President Lincoln many times and was especially moved by his death at the moment of victory. The result was "When Lilacs Last in the Dooryard Bloom'd." Its appearance under such tragic circumstances made over-praise easy. Closer study, however, shows that while the poem contains many lines of rich poetic imagery, much of the poetry is conventional, with stock phrases. The references to Lincoln are so few that the poem might serve as a lament for almost any great man. Actually, Whitman's poem "O Captain! My Captain!" is much more concerned with the national calamity. However, the carol of death, sung by the gray-brown bird, is a poetic statement of Whitman's own attitude toward death. It begins with an echo of Shakespeare's "O amiable lovely death!" (*King John,* III, iv).

Come lovely and soothing death,
Undulate round the world, serenely arriving, arriving,
In the day, in the night, to all, to each,
Sooner or later delicate death.

Prais'd be the fathomless universe,
For life and joy, and for objects and knowledge curious,

161

And for love, sweet love—but praise! praise! praise!
For the sure-enwinding arms of cool-enfolding death.

Come the three corners of the world in arms

Source: KING JOHN (Act V, sc. vii, l. 116)
Author: William Shakespeare (1564-1616)
First published: 1623
Type of work: Historical drama

Context: It is a dark hour in the history of England: the crown is worn by John, a king sadly lacking in grace and grandeur; King Philip of France demands the throne for his nephew, Arthur, son of the deceased older brother of John; the pope excommunicates the king for his refusal to accept the papal choice for the Archbishop of Canterbury; and several powerful English noblemen rebel against their king and join forces with the French. Ironically, though, when the English lords, "her princes," have returned their support to their king, when the breach with the Church has been healed, and when finally the forces of the French have been turned back, it is discovered that King John is dying of poison given to him by a villainous monk. Nevertheless, England has been brought to a firm stand. Henry, the son of King John, receives the crown, and the play ends in a speech of patriotic triumph delivered by Philip Faulconbridge, bastard nephew of King John:

BASTARD
. . .
This England never did, nor never shall
Lie at the proud foot of a conqueror,
But when it first did help to wound itself.
Now these her princes are come home again,
Come the three corners of the world in arms,
And we shall shock them. Naught shall make us rue,
If England to itself do rest but true.

A coming shower your shooting corns presage

Source: A DESCRIPTION OF A CITY SHOWER (Line 9)
Author: Jonathan Swift (1667-1745)
First published: 1710
Type of work: Descriptive poem

Context: Swift's poem realistically describing the coming of a rain shower to eighteenth century London was written in 1710 and published that year in No. 238 of the famous periodical *The Tatler*. Swift describes,

162

in his first verse paragraph, the portents of the coming storm; the second portion of the poem describes people's reactions to the falling rain and their activities during the storm; and the third part describes how the rain, having fallen, runs through the gutters of the London streets to empty into the River Thames. The poem ends with the highly realistic, if somewhat unpoetic, lines that tell what the waters carry away with them: ". . . from butchers' stalls, dung, guts, and blood,/ Drown'd puppies, stinging sprats, all drench'd in mud,/ Dead cats, and turnip-tops, come tumbling down the flood." Readers familiar with Swift's poetry will recognize the technique of this poem, as well as the subject matter, to be akin to his "Description of the Morning," which appeared earlier in *The Tatler*. The quotation above appears in the first verse paragraph, which tells how the approaching storm may be predicted:

Careful observers may foretell the hour
(By sure prognostics) when to dread a show'r.
While rain depends, the pensive cat gives o'er
Her frolics, and pursues her tail no more.
Returning home at night, you'll find the sink
Strikes your offended sense with double stink.
If you be wise, then go not far to dine;
You'll spend in coach-hire more than save in wine.
A coming show'r your shooting corns presage,
Old aches throb, your hollow tooth will rage:
Saunt'ring in coffee-house is Dulman seen;
He damns the climate, and complains of spleen.

Commit the oldest sins the newest kinds of ways

Source: KING HENRY THE FOURTH: PART TWO (Act IV, sc. v, ll. 125-126)
Author: William Shakespeare (1564-1616)
First published: 1600
Type of work: Historical drama

Context: Struck by a fit of apoplexy, King Henry IV is placed on a bed by his courtiers, who have little hope he can survive. Beside him they place the crown, symbol of his kingship. Prince Hal, who has led a riotous life, but who will prove to be one of England's great kings, comes to the sickroom. Dismissing the courtiers, he sits to watch by his father's side. Thinking the old king has died, Hal falls to meditating on the burdens which have come to him. He reaches for the crown, places it upon his head, and, vowing nothing shall keep him from his rightful heritage, steps into another room, to weep. His father, rousing and missing the crown, recalls the young prince to him. Prince Hal defends his action, but the king speaks bitterly of his son and his early, riotous life. He accuses the prince of foolishly stealing what shall be rightfully his within a few hours;

163

and he complains that Hal has never loved him: "Thy life did manifest thou loved'st me not,/ And thou wilt have me die assur'd of it." The dying king continues his complaints, believing that he is leaving England in the hands of a son who will be the ruin of the kingdom. He fears that once he is dead, Hal will dismiss the good officials and repeal all the good decrees. It will be a question when Hal is crowned, laments the king, of elevating vanity and destroying the royal dignity. He fears that England will become "a wilderness again." He prophesies that from every kingdom the worst men will flock to England and his son's court:

HENRY
And to the English court assemble now,
From every region, apes of idleness!
Now, neighbour confines, purge you of your scum.
Have you a ruffian that will swear, drink, dance,
Revel the night, rob, murder, and **commit**
The oldest sins the newest kinds of ways?
Be happy, he will trouble you no more.
England shall double gild his treble guilt,
England shall give him office, honour, might;
For the fifth Harry from curbed license plucks
The muzzle of restraint, and the wild dog
Shall flesh his tooth on every innocent.
O my poor kingdom, sick with civil blows!

Conduct is three-fourths of our life

Source: LITERATURE AND DOGMA (Chapter I, section 3)
Author: Matthew Arnold (1822-1888)
First published: 1873
Type of work: Religious and literary essay

Context: English poet, literary critic, and classical scholar, Matthew Arnold—like John Ruskin—felt himself called as a kind of prophet to the Victorian scene. Son of the Headmaster of Rugby, he had grown up in a stanchly religious, if liberal, home, and he himself had experienced the frustration and spiritual dislocation which resulted from the scientific theories and discoveries of the mid-century. He could not, however, become a convert to science, for science in the final analysis would merely explain the systems under which life exists; it would not replace the inherent psychological needs for the religion it was destroying. Clearly then, to Arnold, with the old religion no longer feasible, a new kind of religion had to be found if man's personality was to remain meaningfully oriented to the principles of human dignity and the value of life. His solution was culture—"the best that has been said and thought in the world." Through education which would inculcate into the new generations the inherent human values as they have been articulated in the great aesthetic creations of the past, man could be taught to respect and sanctify the traditions of his civilization which have been inspired and crystallized under the impetus of religious worship. The Scriptures themselves, for example, quite apart from any divine record, possess valuable human instruction:

> The Old Testament, nobody will ever deny, is filled with the word and thought of righteousness. "In the way of righteousness is life, and in the pathway thereof is no death;" "Righteousness tendeth to life;" "He that pursueth evil pursueth it to his own death;" "The way of transgressors is hard;"—nobody will deny that those texts may stand for the fundamental and ever-recurring idea of the Old Testament. No people ever felt so strongly as those people of the Old Testament, the Hebrew people, that **conduct is three-fourths of our life** and its largest concern. No people ever felt so strongly that succeeding, going right, hitting the mark in this great concern, was the way of peace, the highest possible satisfaction. . . .

The confused jargon of their Babylonian pulpits

Source: REFLECTIONS ON THE REVOLUTION IN FRANCE
Author: Edmund Burke (1729-1797)
First published: 1790
Type of work: Political treatise

Context: Edmund Burke's essay was called "a letter intended to have been sent to a gentleman in Paris." Actually, it was an answer, carefully worked out, from a conservative viewpoint, to the sympathy for the French Revolution which was being expressed in England, written by a man who knew how much he could influence the opinions of his times. As a conservative, and as a man who appreciated the manner by which the history and traditions of Great Britain had evolved as a means to good government, Burke took exception to a suggestion, which he notes, that kings ought to be styled, and to think of themselves, as the servants of the people. That such a notion should be taken seriously, Burke notes, is evidence of a movement to displace solid government in England with the kind of misrule to be found in France during the French Revolution. Burke observes, answering specifically a sermon by Dr. Price, an English clergyman:

> Kings, in one sense, are undoubtedly the servants of the people, because their power has no other rational end than that of the general advantage; but it is not true that they are, in the ordinary sense (by our constitution at least), anything like servants; the essence of whose situation is to obey the commands of some other,

165

and to be removable at pleasure. But the king of Great Britain obeys no other person; all other persons are individually, and collectively too, under him, and owe to him a legal obedience. The law, which knows neither to flatter nor to insult, calls this high magistrate, not our servant, as this humble divine calls him, but *"our sovereign Lord the king;"* and we, on our parts, have learned to speak only the primitive language of the law, and not **the confused jargon of their Babylonian pulpits.**

Congenial horrors, hail!

Source: THE SEASONS: WINTER (Line 6)
Author: James Thomson (1700-1748)
First published: 1726 (*Winter*)
Type of work: Pastoral poem

Context: The first long-sustained poem in English devoted primarily to the description of nature and its changing moods, *The Seasons* broke new ground in several directions. Thomson, a forerunner of the Romantic period, used a number of ideas new at the time—sensuous imagery, fantasy, and a love of nature. He also brought blank verse back into use as a poetic medium, and re-established Milton as a major force in the development of English poetry. He founded the tradition of nature poetry in England. The four parts of *The Seasons* were published over a period of time, from 1726 to 1730, *Winter* being the first; after all the parts were issued they were published with the seasons in their natural order, beginning with spring. *Winter* begins solemnly; Thomson describes the storms, the gloom, the wind, the swelling rivers. But he makes it plain that he enjoys their sublimity to the utmost: "Nature! great parent! whose unceasing hand/ Rolls round the Seasons of the changeful year,/ How mighty, how majestic, are thy works!"

Throughout the scenes of tempest, piled one upon the other, one hears the blast; Thomson's descriptive powers almost provide winter in its actuality. Then the calm descends momentarily; life's vanities are considered a moment; and the storms rage again. We have glimpses of wild creatures and beasts of burden suffering from the elements, and of a belated wanderer lost and freezing in the snow. Thomson dwells for a moment on winter famine and the lot of all who suffer; then he introduces his own snug retreat, "where ruddy fire and beaming tapers join/ To cheer the gloom. There studious let me sit,/ And hold high converse with the mighty Dead. . . ." He considers at some length these great thinkers of the past and the joys they bring the reader. Then he returns to the outside world once more, where at long last the iron grip of winter is gradually relaxing and there are signs of spring. In spite of all its rigors, one is left with the certainty that when another year is past, Thomson will welcome winter once again:

166

See, Winter comes to rule the varied year,
Sullen, and sad, with all his rising train;
Vapours, and *Clouds,* and *Storms.* Be these my theme,
These, that exalt the soul to solemn thought,
And heavenly musing. Welcome, kindred glooms!
Congenial horrors, hail! with frequent foot,
Pleas'd have I, in my chearful morn of life,
When nurs'd by careless solitude I liv'd,
And sung of Nature with unceasing joy,
Pleas'd have I wander'd thro' your rough domain;
Trod the pure virgin-snows, myself as pure;
Heard the winds roar, and the big torrent burst;
Or seen the deep fermenting tempest brew'd
In the grim evening sky. Thus pass'd the time,
Till thro' the lucid chambers of the south,
Look'd out the joyous Spring, look'd out, and smil'd.

Conscience avant; Richard's himself again

Source: THE TRAGICAL HISTORY OF KING RICHARD III, ALTER'D FROM SHAKE-
SPEARE (Act V, sc. v)
Author: Colley Cibber (1671-1757)
First published: 1699
Type of work: Historical tragedy

Context: Scholars acknowledge that *Richard III,* first performed in 1592 or 1593, is not one of Shakespeare's greatest plays. The dramatist distorted the handsome prince of history into a heartless hunchback, and turned out a "tragedy of blood," so much to the tastes of Elizabethan theater-goers. It deals with Richard's attempt to gain the throne of England, following the death of Edward IV. By craft he gets rid of most of his rivals, then persuades the citizens of London, through their Lord Mayor, to beg him to ascend the throne. However, retribution follows. Henry Tudor, Earl of Richmond and later King Henry VII, invades England. Richard sees the ghosts of his victims appearing on the eve of battle to prophesy his defeat. On Bosworth Field, after having his horse killed from under him and offering his ill-gotten kingdom in exchange for another, he is killed by Richmond. A century after Shakespeare wrote the tragedy, another playwright-actor, Colley Cibber (both of whose names were generally pronounced with a hard "C" during his lifetime), decided he could improve on Shakespeare. Cibber was short, thin, and with a piercing voice, born to be a comic actor, and first achieving recognition in a comedy by Congreve. He was also one of the best comic writers of his age and author of a dozen hits. But he yearned for fame in tragedy. His first attempt, *Xerxes* (1699), lasted one performance; next he decided to "alter" *Richard III.* He changed the order of scenes, cut out scenes where Richard did not appear, brought in lines from other plays by Shakespeare, and

167

added many of his own. The result was a version so much more actable than the original that for nearly two centuries, Cibber's play replaced Shakespeare's. It had fifteen printed editions between 1700 and Cibber's death in 1757. It was the first "Shakespearean" play seen in America, when Edwin Forest toured the colonies with it in 1750. The great Edmund Kean brought it to the independent United States. Even in the twentieth century, it was preferred by Walter Hampton and Robert Mantell. Charles Macready tried to restore Shakespeare in 1821, but in view of audience apathy, had to retreat to Cibber. Not till the time of Sir Henry Irving in the 1870's did the version by Shakespeare make its return to the stage. Audiences complained that Cibber played the sly Richard by slinking about the stage like a pick-pocket. He also used the trick of delivering his lines very slowly and deliberately, while the rest of the lines raced with melodramatic speed. But it was effective. And one of the most effective moments closed Act IV, when Catesby (as Cibber renamed Ratcliff) announces the capture of Buckingham. "Off with his head!" cries the king. "So much for Buckingham!" Close to the end of the play, after the ghosts of Richard's victims appear in the dark to curse him, Cibber introduced into Shakespeare's Scene III, what he called Scene V. Of the three speechs quoted, Shakespeare wrote the first; Cibber rearranged words originally written by Shakespeare, in the second; and Cibber was the author of the third dramatic speech that closes the scene.

RICHARD
. . . , shadows to-night
Have struck more terror to the Soul of Richard
Than can the substance of ten Thousand Soldiers
Arm'd all in Proof, and led by shallow Richmond.

CATESBY
Be more your self, my Lord: consider, sir,
Were it but known a dream had frighted you,
How wou'd your animated Foes Presume on't?

RICHARD
Perish that thought: No, never be it said,
That Fate it self could awe the soul of *Richard*.
Hence, Babling dreams, you threaten here in vain:
Conscience avant; Richard's himself again.
Hark! the shrill Trumpet sounds, to Horse: Away!
My Soul's in Arms, and eager for the Fray.

168

Conservatism is adherence to the old and tried against the new and untried

Source: ADDRESS AT COOPER UNION, NEW YORK CITY (February 27, 1860)
Author: Abraham Lincoln (1809-1865)
First published: 1860
Type of work: Political speech

Context: John Brown's raid on Harper's Ferry, which the old man hoped would start a general uprising among slaves in the South, was a failure; but it crystallized opinion on both sides of the slavery issue and brought the Civil War a step closer. Brown's raid was a source of embarrassment to the Republican Party. Some abolitionists, feeling that it came closer than any other party to representing their views, flocked to its ranks. The Democrats noted this movement and naturally tried to make the Republicans responsible for the raid. The Republicans went out of their way to deny any connection with John Brown and abolitionism. Lincoln, as leader of the Republican Party, repeated this disavowal in his Cooper Union address. This is not only the most important speech Lincoln had made up to this time but was and is considered one of his greatest. In it he set forth a course and a policy for his party, made his name known throughout the East, and paved his way to the Presidency. The address is basically a reply to the assertion by Stephen A. Douglas that the writers of the Constitution had forbidden the Federal Government to exercise any control over slavery in the territories. Lincoln as Republican spokesman departs from the middle-of-the-road policy his party has hitherto pursued and calls on it to resist strongly any aggressive move by the South to establish slavery in places where it does not yet exist. "Wrong as we think slavery is," says Lincoln, "we can afford to let it alone where it is;" but he does not feel it can be allowed to spread. Denouncing Southern talk of secession from the Union, he concludes with a ringing declaration of purpose: "Neither let us be slandered from our duty by false accusations against us, nor frightened from it by menaces of destruction to the government, nor of dungeons to ourselves. Let us have faith that right makes might, and in that faith let us to the end dare to do our duty as we understand it." It is interesting to note that in replying to the various charges which had been leveled against his party by the Democrats, Lincoln provided what many conservatives still consider the best definition of their viewpoint:

But you say you are conservative—eminently conservative—while we are revolutionary, destructive, or something of the sort. What is **conservatism? Is** it not **adherence to the old and tried, against the new and untried?** We stick to, contend for, the identical old policy on the point in controversy which was adopted by "our fathers who framed the government under which we live;" while you with one accord reject, and scout, and spit upon that old policy, and insist on substituting something new. . . .

169

Consider anything, but don't cry

Source: THROUGH THE LOOKING-GLASS (Chapter 5)
Author: Lewis Carroll (Charles Lutwidge Dodgson, 1832-1898)
First published: 1871
Type of work: Imaginative tale for children

Context: How a lecturer in mathematics at Christ Church College, Oxford University, could turn into a writer of fantastic stories for children is as hard to explain as how his pen name "Lewis Carroll," was derived from Lutwidge, Charles. Obviously he had to provide some sort of disguise for a sober mathematician whose college students reported his class lectures as extremely dull; but figuring out the nom de plume by which he is now almost universally known is another sort of problem. He had played with words before. In 1855, while studying Anglo-Saxon poetry, he wrote his famous "Jabberwocky" poem, beginning: " 'Twas brillig, and the slithy toves/ Did gyre and gymble in the wabe." In 1865, he had published *Alice's Adventures in Wonderland,* a work that made him well known. Naturally one success demands another. Queen Victoria, charmed with Alice, had hinted that she would be pleased to have Mr. Dodgson dedicate his next book to her. Unfortunately for Her Majesty, his next book was a mathematical volume with the title *An Elementary Treatise on Determinants.* Not until seven years after the publication of *Alice's Adventures in Wonderland* did he get around to its sequel, *Through the Looking-Glass and What Alice Found There.* It begins with the same sort of illogical logic that is to be found in the original story of Alice. Playing one day with her kitten in the living room, she holds the animal up to the mirror over the fireplace. The game is "Let's Pretend," and Alice is talking about her ideas of what might be in a Looking-glass House, when the mirror turns into mist and she can pass through and jump down on the other side. Here she meets the White Queen, most untidily dressed, who envies Alice.

". . . You must be very happy, living in this wood, and being glad whenever you like!"

"Only it's so very lonely here!" Alice said in a melancholy voice; and at the thought of her loneliness, two large tears came rolling down her cheeks.

"Oh, don't go on like that!" cried the poor Queen, wringing her hands in despair. "Consider what a great girl you are. Consider what a long way you've come today. Consider what o'clock it is. **Consider anything, but don't cry!"**

Alice could not help laughing at this, even in the midst of her tears. "Can you keep from crying by considering things?" she asked.

"That's the way it's done," the Queen said with great decision: "Nobody can do two things at once, you know. . . ."

Consider him as a respectable Hottentot

Source: LETTERS TO HIS SON (Letter 132)
Author: Philip Dormer Stanhope, Lord Chesterfield (1694-1773)
First published: 1774
Type of work: Personal letters

Context: Chesterfield was a proud man and a brilliant one. That he makes a fetish of social graces can be explained in terms of the age in which he lived. Success—that is, statesmanship and a high place in the social and political hierarchy—was dependent upon mastery of all the niceties of etiquette and social behavior. Chesterfield had perfected himself in these matters and had achieved the success he desired. Some critics have accused him, because of his calculating approach to his world, of lacking a heart. This charge is not quite fair to him; he loved his family and had numerous friends he loved and admired. But it is true that he considered the impression one created to be of primary importance. On the other hand, he despised those who possessed the graces and had nothing with which to back them up. His life's ambition, never fully realized, was to make his illegitimate son the finished figure of a polished English gentleman; and his voluminous correspondence with Philip was largely directed toward this end. Although Chesterfield had little use for anyone who had merely acquired the veneer of culture without any solid foundation, he would have probably considered such a person preferable to one who had the good basic qualities and no refinement whatever. To Chesterfield the latter was a mere savage. He might respect and even admire the man, but could not love him: he would lack the sophistication and urbanity Chesterfield considered essential. Chesterfield would never be comfortable in his company. In a letter to Philip written February 28, 1751, Chesterfield makes clear the extent to which he is irked by crudity:

How often have I, in the course of my life, found myself in this situation, with regard to many of my acquaintance, whom I have honored and respected, without being able to love. I did not know why, because, when one is young, one does not take the trouble, nor allow one's self the time, to analyze one's sentiments and trace them up to their source. But subsequent observation and reflection have taught me why. There is a man, whose moral character, deep learning, and superior parts, I acknowledge, admire, and respect; but whom it is so impossible for me to love, that I am almost in a fever whenever I am in his company. His figure (without being deformed) seems made to disgrace or ridicule the common structure of the human body. His legs and arms are never in the position which, according to the situation of his body, they ought to be in, but constantly employed in committing acts of hostility upon the Graces. He throws anywhere, but down his throat, whatever he means to drink, and only mangles what he means to carve. Inattentive to all the regards of social life, he mis-

171

times or misplaces everything. He disputes with heat, and indiscriminately, mindless of the rank, character and situation of those with whom he disputes; absolutely ignorant of the several gradations of familiarity or respect, he is exactly the same to his superiors, his equals, and his inferiors; and therefore, by a necessary consequence, absurd to two of the three. [The person to whom Chesterfield refers is Dr. Samuel Johnson.] Is it possible to love such a man? No. The utmost I can do for him, is to **consider him as a respectable Hottentot.**

A consummation devoutly to be wished

Source: HAMLET (Act III, sc. i, ll. 63-64)
Author: William Shakespeare (1564-1616)
First published: 1603
Type of work: Dramatic tragedy

Context: Hamlet, the meditative, melancholy Prince of Denmark, finds himself with a father dead and a mother taken in an incestuous marriage by his uncle, declared by the Ghost of his father to be the murderer. In his most famous soliloquy, Hamlet, faced with the necessity for revenge, considers his course of action. The idea of the cessation of life through suicide pleases him, but the consequences of the act do not.

HAMLET

To be, or not to be, that is the question—
Whether 'tis nobler in the mind to suffer
The slings and arrows of outrageous fortune,
Or to take arms against a sea of troubles,
And by opposing end them. To die, to sleep—
No more; and by a sleep to say we end
The heart-ache, and the thousand natural shocks
That flesh is heir to; 'tis **a consummation
Devoutly to be wished.** To die, to sleep—
To sleep, perchance to dream, ay there's the rub,
For in that sleep of death what dreams may come
When we have shuffled off this mortal coil,
Must give us pause; . . .

The cool flowery lap of earth

Source: MEMORIAL VERSES: APRIL, 1850 (Line 49)
Author: Matthew Arnold (1822-1888)
First published: 1850
Type of work: Elegy

172

Context: In this poem Arnold laments the deaths of the three greatest poets of the early nineteenth century. Byron, who died in 1824, taught little but enabled men to feel "the strife . . . Of passion with eternal law." Goethe, however, was "Europe's sagest head," and his death in 1832 deprived men of the vision of suffering that might lead to happiness. But Wordsworth, unlike the others, was a healer. Byron and Goethe showed what human life was like and that misery was inescapable; they can be replaced. But after Wordsworth's death in 1850, there can be no other poet to soothe the misery of "doubts, disputes, distractions, fears"; this ability was Wordsworth's greatness—he had neither force nor wisdom, only the ability to make men forget their misery and be young again.

> He found us when the age had bound
> Our souls in its benumbing round;
> He spoke, and loosed our hearts in tears.
> He laid us as we lay at birth
> On **the cool flowery lap of earth.** . . .
> Our youth return'd; for there was shed
> On spirits that had long been dead,
> Spirits dried up and closely furl'd,
> The freshness of the early world.

The coquetry of public opinion

Source: LETTER TO THOMAS BURGH
Author: Edmund Burke (1729–1797)
First published: 1780
Type of work: Open letter

Context: During the mid-eighteenth century Ireland was granted considerable economic concession by England as well as extensive legislative independence. The result was a surge of economic prosperity unprecedented in Irish history. The executive branch of the Irish government remained an English appointment, however, and the millions of Irish Catholics remained subordinated to an Anglican Establishment. Both of these latter conditions displeased Burke, and he worked and hoped consistently for a peaceful reconciliation on all points. Burgh had written to Burke to inform him of the misrepresentation of his Parliamentary position in Ireland, and this letter, which constitutes Burke's reply, was one of his numerous public comments on this issue:

> . . . If I had sought popularity in Ireland, when, in the cause of that country, I was ready to sacrifice, and did sacrifice, a much nearer, a much more immediate, and a much more advantageous popularity here, I should find myself perfectly unhappy, because I should be totally disappointed in my expectations, . . . But I

acted then, as I act now, and as I hope I shall act always, from a strong impulse of right, and from motives in which popularity, either here or there, has but a very little part.

With the support of that consciousness I can bear a good deal of **the coquetry of public opinion,** which has her caprices, and must have her way. . . . I, too, have had my holiday of popularity in Ireland. . . .

Courage and faith; vain faith, and courage vain

Source: EPITAPH ON A JACOBITE
Author: Thomas Babington Macaulay (1800-1859)
First published: 1845
Type of work: Elegy

Context: Those who sought to restore Roman Catholic James Stuart to the throne of England, after the revolution of 1688 gave it to William III and Mary, were called Jacobites, after the Latin form of James's name, Jacobus. In the struggle for power against the Protestants, some of the Jacobites were imprisoned and killed; others fled to exile on the continent. The movement did not die out with that generation, but had occasional flurries until 1746 when "The Young Pretender," "Bonny Prince Charlie" invaded England on behalf of his father and was defeated at Culloden Moor. The line of Stuarts did not die out, however, until Henry Stuart died in 1807. This brief poem was supposed to have been written for the gravestone of one Jacobite who died in exile in Italy. His "one dear hope" was probably to live in England under a Catholic Stuart ruler, though the romantic reader will suspect it refers to a sweetheart.

To my true king I offered free from stain
Courage and faith; vain faith, and courage vain.
For him, I threw lands, honors, wealth, away,
And one dear hope, that was more prized than they.
For him I languished in a foreign clime,
Grey-haired with sorrow in my manhood's prime;
Heard on Lavernia Scargill's whispering trees,
And pined by Arno for my lovelier Tees;
Beheld each night my home in fevered sleep,
Each morning started from the dream to weep;
Till God who saw me tried too sorely, gave
The resting place I asked, an early grave.
Oh thou, whom chance leads to this nameless stone,
From that proud country which was once mine own,
By those white cliffs I never more must see,
By that dear language which I spake like thee,
Forget all feuds, and shed an English tear
O'er English dust. A broken heart lies here.

174

Courage mounteth with occasion

Source: KING JOHN (Act II, sc. i, l. 82)
Author: William Shakespeare (1564-1616)
First published: 1623
Type of work: Historical drama

Context: Chatillion is sent to John to press the suit of Arthur, John's nephew, for the throne of England. John, at his mother Elinor's urging, tells Chatillion to report to Arthur and his allies, Austria and King Philip of France, that he will fight. Arthur, Philip, and Austria have been fighting against Angiers and are hardly prepared to face John and his forces who arrive practically at Chatillion's heels. Austria, however, urges courage and action.

. . .

CHATILLION

. . .

. . . they are at hand,
To parley or to fight, therefore prepare.

PHILIP
How much unlooked for is this expedition.

AUSTRIA
By how much unexpected, by so much
We must awake endeavour for defence,
For **courage mounteth with occasion.**
Let them be welcome then, we are prepared.

Courtesy is the true Alchemy

Source: THE SONG OF COURTESY (Stanza 4)
Author: George Meredith (1828-1909)
First published: 1859
Type of work: Lyric poem

Context: In this simple little lyric, George Meredith turns to the stories of King Arthur's knights for inspiration and likewise, at least in part, to Chaucer's *Tale of the Wife of Bath.* Sir Gawain, hated by the others because of his purity, is forced to marry an old hag who "was yellow and dry as a snake's old skin," and being the knight of courtesy, a title that roughly means "a perfect gentleman," he cannot hurt the hag's feelings by showing his disgust. Alone with her in the bed chamber, he takes the route of honor: he ignores her loathsomeness and covers her with kisses. Such courtesy, however, is well rewarded, for the hag is miraculously transformed into a beautiful maiden. The quotation occurs in the last stanza of the poem:

175

Of gentle Sir Gawain they had no sport,
When it was morning in Arthur's court;
What think you they cried?
　　　Now, life and eyes!
This bride is the very Saint's dream of a prize,
　　　Fresh from the skies!
　　　See ye not, **Courtesy**
　　　Is the true Alchemy,
Turning to gold all it touches and tries?

　　　·　·　·

Cowardly dogs bark loudest

Source: THE WHITE DEVIL (Act III, sc. 1, l. 163)
Author: John Webster (1580?-1625?)
First published: 1612
Type of work: Dramatic tragedy

Context: Paulo Giordano Ursini, Duke of Brachiano, falls in love with Vittoria Corombona and, with the help of her brother, his secretary, the duke pursues her; and she proves willing for the suit to take place. The duke's wife, Isabella, a sister of Francisco de Medicis, Duke of Florence, is thus deserted by her husband; and her brother, with the help of Cardinal Monticelso, seeks to patch up the rift between the married couple. In order to aid his master in having Vittoria Corombona as his mistress, Flamineo, Duke Brachiano's secretary and Vittoria's brother, kills Camillo, Vittoria's husband, making the death look like an accident, giving out that the husband broke his neck jumping a vaulting-horse. At a hearing following Camillo's death, Cardinal Monticelso deals harshly with Vittoria, accusing her of killing her husband that she might more easily have an affair with the Duke of Brachiano. Having had no part in the crime, she asserts her innocence; but the cardinal treats her all the more harshly in his questioning. He asks if she had any visitors the night of her husband's death, and she replies truthfully that she was visited by the duke. The Duke of Brachiano, an observer at the hearing, though uninvited, interferes on her behalf, interrupting the cardinal to say that he had gone to her home to see if he could help her pay off a debt to the cardinal, fearful that the churchman might cheat her. Monticelso then turns on Brachiano:

MONTICELSO
Who made you overseer?

BRACHIANO
Why, my charity, my charity, which should flow
From every generous and noble spirit
To orphans and to widows.

MONTICELSO

Your lust.

BRACHIANO

Cowardly dogs bark loudest: sirrah priest,
I'll talk with you hereafter. Do you hear?
The sword you frame of such an excellent temper
I'll sheathe in your own bowels.
There are a number of thy coat resemble
Your common post-boys.

MONTICELSO

Ha!

BRACHIANO

Your mercenary post-boys:
Your letters carry truth, but 'tis your guise
To fill your mouths with gross and impudent lies.

Cows are my passion

Source: DOMBEY AND SON (Volume I, chapter 21)
Author: Charles Dickens (1812-1870)
First published: 1846-1848
Type of work: Novel

Context: Mr. Dombey, the wealthy London merchant, is at Leamington for a holiday. His hanger-on, Major Joseph Bagstock, has taken him under his wing to acquaint him with the town and to inform him about the current scandals. As they walk down the street, they meet a wheeled chair, in which reclines a faded ancient coquette named Mrs. Skewton. Beside her walks her scornful but beautiful daughter, Mrs. Edith Granger. Mrs. Skewton, who could very well be walking, as there is nothing wrong with her health, invariably rides in one fixed position. Fifty years earlier, when she was a beauty of about twenty years of age, a fashionable artist had sketched her picture as she sat in this posture in a barouche; he had labeled the work "Cleopatra," because the Egyptian queen had taken the same position in her galley. The beauty and the carriage had both disappeared, but the attitude persisted. Mrs. Skewton asks Mr. Dombey if he is fond of nature and explains that she has a passion for seclusion, but society will not permit her to indulge it. She is really an Arcadian at heart, with a burning desire for rural solitude; she is thrown away on society and cows are her passion. What she would like to do is retire to a Swiss farm where she could live entirely surrounded by cows—and china.

". . . There is only one change, Mr. Dombey," observed Mrs. Skewton, with a mincing sigh, "for which I really care, and that I

177

fear I shall never be permitted to enjoy. People cannot spare one. But seclusion and contemplation are my what's-his-name—"

"If you mean Paradise, mamma, you had better say so, to render yourself intelligible," said the younger lady.

"My dearest Edith," returned Mrs. Skewton, "you know that I am wholly dependent upon you for those odious names. I assure you, Mr. Dombey, Nature intended me for an Arcadian. I am thrown away in society. **Cows are my passion.** What I have ever sighed for, has been to retreat to a Swiss farm, and live entirely surrounded by cows—and china."

This curious association of objects, suggesting a remembrance of the celebrated bull who got by mistake into a crockery shop, was received with perfect gravity by Mr. Dombey, who intimated his opinion that Nature was, no doubt, a very respectable institution.

Crocodile's tears

Source: ANATOMY OF MELANCHOLY (Part III, sec. 2, memb. 2, subsec. 4)
Author: Robert Burton (1577-1640)
First published: 1621-1651
Type of work: Essays

Context: At about the middle of the introduction to a remarkable book, the author, the Reverend Robert Burton, as "Democritus, Junior," ponders on what his fifth century namesake Democritus would say about behavior in the contemporary world. Burton lists the way man "turns himself into all shades like a chameleon, or as Proteus transforms himself into all that is monstruous." He fawns like a spaniel, rages like a lion, barks like a cur, fights like a tiger, stings like a serpent, grins like a tiger, and weeps like a crocodile. The idea that anything as big and thick-skinned as a crocodile could be so moved by tender emotions as to shed tears from its tiny, deep-sunken eyes, is absurd.

Chapman and Ben Jonson in their 1605 *Eastward Ho!,* and many others who came after Burton, used this phrase. Burton himself used the figure again in Partition III of his anatomical study of morbid psychology. Continuing with a consideration of the causes of Heroical Love, which flourishes most during the conjunction of certain planets, he likewise blames the climate of some places, as well as rich diet and idleness. As more direct causes of the growth of love, he quotes Lucian about the effect of the sight of beauty. Love can also be provoked by artificial stimulants, and increased by opportunity and importunity, including sweet sounds, kisses, dancing, and tears.

. . . When nothing else will serve, the last refuge is their tears. 'Twixt tears and sighs I write this (I take love to witness), saith Chelidonia to Philonius. Those burning torches are now turned to floods of tears. Aretine's Lucretia, when her sweetheart came to

Town, wept in his bosom, that he might be persuaded those tears were shed for joy of his return. . . . To these **crocodile's tears,** they will add sobs, fiery sighs, and sorrowful countenance, pale color, leanness, and if you do but stir abroad, these fiends are ready to meet you at every turn, . . .

The cruel crawling foam

Source: ALTON LOCKE, TAILOR AND POET (Chapter 26)
Author: Charles Kingsley (1819-1875)
First published: 1850
Type of work: Novel

Context: The Reverend Charles Kingsley was deeply interested in the workingman and in the labor movement. Labor's militant spirits in the 1840's were the Chartists; this group demanded a Charter which would guarantee certain basic rights to labor. A number of the reforms they agitated for actually took place, and the group then split into the two movements which ensued: coöperatives and trade-unionism. Kingsley supported the Chartist movement, and wrote a number of articles for various radical labor papers. He believed that in order for any labor movement to succeed, it must be based on Christian motives; and he exhorted labor accordingly. In addition to these activities, he wrote one of the first labor novels, *Alton Locke.* This is the story of a young Cockney whose place in society is to be a tailor, but who is determined to surmount all obstacles and become a poet. He is befriended by a Scot, Sandy Mackaye, who is a Chartist and becomes as a father to him. Alton's mother is a strong Calvinist who does not want him to read anything but Scripture; when he disagrees with her doctrine she casts him out. The story, told in the first person, follows Alton through his encounters with the Chartists, his experiences in the sweatshops, his studies and his trials. He at length goes to an old cathedral town, where he is befriended by Dean Winnstay and falls in love with the Dean's daughter Lillian. At last the long struggle to write poetry while he lives as a hack writer is rewarded: the list of subscribers for his book is complete. Lillian and her father invite Alton to a party where he can meet various literary personages. During the party Lillian plays a haunting air on the piano and asks Alton to write her some verses for it. He obliges with "The Sands o' Dee," which in the novel is untitled:

"O Mary, go and call the cattle home,
    And call the cattle home,
    And call the cattle home,
    Across the sands o' Dee";
The western wind was wild and dank wi' foam,
    And all alone went she.

179

The creeping tide came up along the sand,
    And o'er and o'er the sand,
    And round and round the sand,
    As far as eye could see;
The blinding mist came down and hid the land—
    And never home came she.

"Oh, is it weed, or fish, or floating hair—
    A tress o' golden hair,
    O' drowned maiden's hair,
    Above the nets at sea?
Was never salmon yet that shone so fair,
    Among the stakes on Dee."

They rowed her in across the rolling foam,
    The cruel crawling foam,
    The cruel hungry foam,
    To her grave beside the sea:
But still the boatmen hear her call the cattle home,
    Across the sands o' Dee.

The cruelest lies are often told in silence

Source: VIRGINIBUS PUERISQUE ("Truth of Intercourse")
Author: Robert Louis Stevenson (1850-1894)
First published: 1881
Type of work: Familiar essay

Context: In "The Truth of Intercourse," Stevenson begins by saying that, despite the currency of a proverb to the opposite effect, it is easier to tell a lie than to tell the truth, inasmuch as truth is so hard to ascertain. He notes that "The habitual liar may be a very honest fellow, and live truly with his wife and friends; while another man who never told a formal falsehood in his life may yet be himself one lie—heart and face, from top to bottom." Later in the essay Stevenson tries to show that truth is "something more difficult than to refrain from open lies." For example, one may avoid falsehood and yet not tell the truth; we can speak the truth or avoid it: on the one hand, a man can speak so pithily as to avoid truth; on the other, he can speak at such length as to avoid it:

> **The cruelest lies are often told in silence.** A man may have sat in a room for hours and not opened his teeth, and yet come out of that room a disloyal friend or a vile calumniator. And how many loves have perished because, from pride, or spite, or diffidence, or that unmanly shame which withholds a man from daring to betray emotion, a lover, at the critical point of the relation, has but hung his head and held his tongue? And again, a lie may be told by a

180

truth, or a truth conveyed through a lie. Truth to facts is not always truth to sentiment; and part of the truth, as often happens in answer to a question, may be the foulest calumny. . . .

A cup of hot wine, with not a drop of allaying Tiber in it

Source: CORIOLANUS (Act II, sc. i, ll. 52-53)
Author: William Shakespeare (1564-1616)
First published: 1623
Type of work: Dramatic tragedy

Context: The renowned Roman general Caius Martius, dubbed Coriolanus for his victory at Corioles, is nevertheless hated by the mobs of Rome, already disgruntled because of famine. Menenius, a popular patrician and friend of Coriolanus, chides Sicinius and Brutus, elected tribunes of the people, for their condemnation of Coriolanus for his pride while they, too, are proud and with little reason. Menenius, dismissing Sicinius and Brutus as "a brace of unmeriting, proud, violent, testy magistrates, alias fools," is told by Sicinius that his reputation is also known in Rome. Menenius then sums up his own reputation:

> MENENIUS
> I am known to be a humorous patrician, and one that loves **a cup of hot wine, with not a drop of allaying Tiber in't;** said to be something imperfect in favouring the first complaint, hasty and tinderlike upon too trivial motion; one that converses more with the buttock of the night than with the forehead of the morning. What I think I utter, and spend my malice in my breath. . . .

Curse on his virtues! They've undone his country

Source: CATO (Act IV, iv, 35)
Author: Joseph Addison (1672-1719)
First published: 1713
Type of work: Dramatic tragedy

Context: Cato of Utica (95 B.C.–46 B.C.), great-grandson of Cato the Elder, is a symbol of probity in public life. Violently opposed to Julius Caesar and fiercer against the conspiring Cataline than was Cicero, he supported Pompey in his break with Caesar, and even after defeat at Pharsala, fled to Africa to continue resistance. After Caesar crushed Scipio at Thapsus, in 46 B.C., Cato decided on suicide. Addison's excellent classical tragedy in blank verse, following the rules of Aristotle, is only one of many dramatizations of the story. Performed in 1713 and interpreted by the Whigs as an attack on the dominant Tory party, it was a great suc-

181

cess on the stage because of its political implications. It also went through seven printed editions that same year. Throughout Latin America in the nineteenth century, when Spain prohibited local plays about revolution, a Spanish translation of *Cato* was widely used to whip up resistance to Spain. Here is the scene when Cato announces his decision to commit suicide.

LUCIUS

While pride, oppression, and injustice reign,
The world will still demand her Cato's presence.
In pity to mankind, submit to Caesar
And reconcile thy mighty soul to life.

CATO

Would Lucius have me live to swell the number
Of Caesar's slaves, or by a base submission
Give up the cause of Rome, and own a tyrant?

LUCIUS

The victor never will impose on Cato
Ungenerous terms. His enemies confess
The virtues of humanity are Caesar's.

CATO

Curse on his virtues! they've undone his country.
Such popular humanity is treason.

* * *

Custom is the great guide of human life

Source: AN INQUIRY CONCERNING HUMAN UNDERSTANDING (Section V, part 1, 36)
Author: David Hume (1711-1776)
First published: 1748
Type of work: Philosophy

Context: There is a danger, says Hume, that a passion for philosophy, like a passion for religion, may lead us astray; the passion for philosophy may, instead of correcting our manners and relieving our vices, push us toward the very selfishness we are trying to avoid. But nature, maintains Hume, has a means of prevailing upon us, a principle which helps us to avoid our undermining the understanding of common life, that principle being custom, or habit. To judge the happenings about us on the basis of custom enables us to avoid trying to answer the *how* of the happenings and to limit ourselves to that which we know from experience. Reason alone, says Hume, is incapable of variation, but experience tells us there

182

can be variation; so Hume concludes, "All inferences from experience, therefore, are effects of custom, not of reasoning." He continues, in a discussion of custom:

> **Custom, then, is the great guide of human life.** It is that principle alone which renders our experience useful to us; and makes us expect, for the future, a similar train of events with those which have appeared in the past. Without the influence of custom, we should be entirely ignorant of every matter of fact beyond what is immediately present to the memory and senses. We should never know how to adjust means to ends, or to employ our natural powers in the production of any effect. There would be an end at once of all action, as well as of the chief part of speculation.

Cut is the branch that might have grown full straight

Source: THE TRAGICAL HISTORY OF DOCTOR FAUSTUS (Final chorus)
Author: Christopher Marlowe (1564-1593)
First published: 1604
Type of work: Dramatic tragedy

Context: Dr. Faustus, illustrious scholar in divinity, the liberal arts, medicine, and law, in seeking a new field of study succumbs to the fascination of metaphysics and, in a deal with the Devil, sealed with his own blood, sells his soul to Lucifer in exchange for black wisdom, the assurance of twenty-four more years of life, the constant attendance of the demon Mephistophilis, and a life of voluptuousness. The degeneration of Faustus is complete by the end of the years of the bargain; and, amid thunder and the tolling of the midnight bell, devils bear him off to hell, as a final chorus philosophizes for the audience on the tragical fall of Faustus:

CHORUS
Cut is the branch that might have grown full straight,
And burnèd is Apollo's laurel-bough
That sometime grew within this learnèd man.
Faustus is gone: regard his hellish fall,
Whose fiendful fortune may exhort the wise
Only to wonder at unlawful things,
Whose deepness doth entice such forward wits
To practice more than heavenly power permits.

The cynosure of neighboring eyes

Source: L'ALLEGRO (Line 80)
Author: John Milton (1608-1674)
First published: 1645
Type of work: Lyric poem

183

Context: The poet, bidding Melancholy depart, beseeches blithe and buxom Mirth, daughter perhaps of Venus and Bacchus or perhaps, suggests Milton, of the West Wind and the Dawn, to stay with him, while together they spend the hours from the awakening sights and sounds of morning, through the activities of the day and finally, evening come, through the frolicking tales of the shepherds, the theatrical entertainment of learned Jonson and fanciful Shakespeare, and the sweet sounds of music. The eye of the poet, during the early hours of the morning, would notice the fields with grazing sheep, mountain peaks imbedded in clouds, meadows filled with daisies, and the flowing streams. Looking up, his eye might behold towers above the trees, a source of both beauty and direction for those in the neighborhood:

Towers and battlements it sees
Bosomed high in tufted trees,
Where perhaps some beauty lies,
The cynosure of neighboring eyes.

Daffodils, that come before the swallow dares

Source: THE WINTER'S TALE (Act IV, sc. iv, ll. 118-119)
Author: William Shakespeare (1564-1616)
First published: 1623
Type of work: Tragi-comedy

Context: Banished by her father, King Leontes of Sicilia, Perdita, her mother falsely imprisoned for adultery with King Polixenes of Bohemia and supposedly dead, is reared by a shepherd in a remote section of Bohemia. Since Florizel, son of Polixenes, has fallen in love with the shepherdess (now sixteen), Polixenes and his trusted aide Camillo go disguised to the shepherd's cottage to see and pass judgment on the object of Florizel's affection. With Arcadian charm Perdita pretends she is giving appropriate flowers to her guests and, coming to Florizel, wishes for him daffodils, violets, primrose, oxlips, and lilies:

PERDITA
. . . Now my fair'st friend,
I would I had some flowers o' th' spring that might
Become your time of day; and yours, and yours,
That wear upon your virgin branches yet
Your maidenheads growing. O Proserpina,
For the flowers now, that frighted thou let'st fall
From Dis's wagon; **daffodils,**
That come before the swallow dares, and take
The winds of March with beauty; violets, dim,
But sweeter than the lids of Juno's eyes,

184

Or Cytherea's breath; pale primroses,
That die unmarried, ere they can behold
Bright Phoebus in his strength . . .

Damn with faint praise

Source: EPISTLE TO DR. ARBUTHNOT (Line 201)
Author: Alexander Pope (1688-1744)
First published: 1735
Type of work: Satire

Context: Pope's poetical epistle was written in the form of a dialogue between the poet and his good friend, Dr. Arbuthnot, a physician and contemporary literary figure. The poem is a vehicle for the poet's mordant comments upon other writers of the time, with whom, by his own admission, he found little favor himself. The "Atticus" of the section in which this quotation occurs is Joseph Addison, a quiet and workmanlike man of letters of the period. Pope, however, felt that he had more than one grievance against Addison; in this poem he complains, not quite fairly, that his critic, not being able to stand competition, causes others to sneer at Pope's work to which Addison himself gives less praise than it deserves:

> But were there one whose fires
> True genius kindles and fair fame inspires;
> Blest with each talent and each art to please,
> And born to write, converse, and live with ease:
> Should such a man, too fond to rule alone,
> Bear, like the Turk, no brother near the throne,
> View him with scornful, yet with jealous eyes,
> And hate for arts that caus'd himself to rise;
> **Damn with faint praise,** assent with civil leer,
> And without sneering teach the rest to sneer;
> Willing to wound, and yet afraid to strike,
> Just hint a fault, and hesitate dislike;
> . . .
> Who but must laugh, if such a man there be?
> Who would not weep, if Atticus were he?

Damned if you do and damned if you don't

Source: REFLECTIONS ON THE LOVE OF GOD (VI, 30, or Chain of Lorenzo)
Author: Lorenzo Dow (1777-1834)
First published: 1836
Type of work: Religious meditation

Context: Lorenzo Dow was an itinerant preacher, one of the most remarkable men of his age for his zeal and labor in the cause of religion. A native of Coventry, Conn., he early became impressed with the truths of the Gospel and felt irresistably impelled to devote his life to the preaching of the Word in various parts of the world. He tells about his life between 1777 and 1816 in a four-volume *Journal,* first published in 1836. A fifth edition, published at Wheeling, Va., by John Martin in 1845, includes a number of reflections, sermons, and the "Journey of Life" by his wife, Peggy Dow, telling of their existence together and apart. At the age of four, as Dow testifies in his *Journal,* while playing with a companion, he "fell into a muse about God and heaven and hell," about which he had heard his parents talk. Suddenly he asked his playmate: "Do you ever say your prayers?" When the boy replied: "No," little Lorenzo exclaimed, "You are wicked, and I shall not play with you," and ran into his house. The first chapter records other episodes that served to convince him of his mission in life. At twelve, during a bout with the fever, he had a vision of the prophet Nathan, who told him that he would die at the age of 22. After several more dreams and visions, the arrival of a group of Methodists crystallized Dow's determination, and he made up his mind to become a circuit rider and camp-meeting preacher. Though never formally connected with the society, he was a Methodist in principle. In the beginning of 1796, he did his first preaching. His uncle gave him a horse, and his parents their blessing, and off he went. His eccentric clothes and his forceful sermonizing were both effective. His shrewdness and quick discernment of character gave him considerable influence over the multitudes that attended his ministry. After preaching for several years in the eastern and southern United States, he made the first of two journeys to England and Ireland, where he was just as successful. He then returned to America, and United States. Being a public preacher for more than thirty-five years, Dow probably brought the gospel to more people than any other individual since the days of the Calvinistic preacher George Whitefield (1714–1770). His *Journal* ended with the entry for October 4, 1818, when he was 39; but after that time, on his journeys he rode along jotting down his thoughts and reflections which were published in a number of books such as *The Dealings of God, Man, and the Devil* (Norwich, 1833). In his writings were revealed his purity, integrity, and benevolence. A wanderer through life, he was a sincere Christian Pilgrim in search of a heavenly home. He finally found rest in Georgetown, D.C., on February 2, 1834. As an example of his dramatic style, he wrote concerning "Particular Election" in his "Reflections on the Love of God," an attack on preachers who select for their hearers conflicting opinions and Bible verses, criticizing:

. . . those who preach it up, to make the Bible clash and contradict itself by preaching somewhat like this:
"You can and you can't—You shall and you shan't—
You will and you won't—

And you will be **damned if you do**—
And you will be **damned if you don't."**

Dance an antic hay

Source: THE TROUBLESOME REIGN AND LAMENTABLE DEATH OF EDWARD THE
SECOND (Act I, sc. i, l. 60)
Author: Christopher Marlowe (1564-1593)
First published: 1594
Type of work: Historical drama

Context: Gaveston, banished from court by old King Edward I because of his bad influence on his son, receives word from King Edward II, the new monarch and his friend, that the old king has died, that he has been crowned, and that he desires the immediate return of his favorite. Returning, Gaveston schemes to control the king by appealing to the weakness of his nature with "wanton poets," musicians, and players:

GAVESTON
Therefore I'll have Italian masks by night,
Sweet speeches, comedies, and pleasing shows.
And in the day, when he shall walk abroad,
Like sylvan nymphs my pages shall be clad;
My men, like satyrs grazing on the lawns,
Shall with their goat-feet **dance an antic hay.**
. . .
Such things as these best please his majesty,
My lord.

Danger, the spur of all great minds

Source: THE REVENGE OF BUSSY D'AMBOIS (Act V, sc. i, l. 78)
Author: George Chapman (1559-1634)
First published: 1613
Type of work: Dramatic tragedy

Context: Clermont, the brother of the dead Bussy D'Ambois, and the Duke of Guise enter. The duke tells Clermont of a voice that spoke to him in the heat of a battle. Clermont says that it was only a waking dream, as the imaginary power of the mind or the vapors of humors present illusions so convincingly that they seem real. Guise, however, is of the opinion that such things are portents of weighty and secret events to come. The news he has received from abroad convinces him that his plot for the furtherance of Catholicism will prove to be bloody. Upon Clermont's advising him to abandon the plot if there will be so much blood-

187

shed, he replies that to do so would be the abandoning of France. Clermont says to let fall everything that is unlawful and do not in the name of religion indulge in vice. By being virtuous and religious the duke can accumulate grace without running into danger. At this point the ghost of Bussy D'Ambois appears to Clermont alone and remains invisible and inaudible to Guise. He speaks so that only Clermont can hear him:

GHOST

Danger, the spur of all great minds, is ever
The curb to your tame spirits; you respect not,
With all your holiness of life and learning,
More than the present, like illiterate vulgars.
Your mind, you say, kept in your flesh's bounds,
Shows that man's will must ruled be by his power,
When by true doctrine you are taught to live
Rather without the body than within,
And rather to your God still than yourself;
To live to Him is to do all things fitting
His image, in which like Himself we live:
To be His image is to do those things
That make us deathless, which by death is only
Doing those deeds that fit eternity;
And those deeds are the perfecting that justice
That makes the world last, which proportion is
Of punishment and wreak for every wrong,
As well as for right a reward as strong.

• • •

Dangers by being despised grow great

Source: SPEECH ON THE PETITION OF THE UNITARIANS
Author: Edmund Burke (1729-1797)
First published: 1808
Type of work: Parliamentary address

Context: In May, 1792, a motion was made in the House of Commons to repeal and alter certain acts of Parliament respecting religious opinions. The motion was grounded chiefly upon a petition presented by the Unitarian Society. This motion caused Edmund Burke to make this well-known address in the House of Commons on May 11, 1792. Proclaiming at the beginning of his speech that he is, as always, looking to circumstances, as well as principles, Burke goes on to point out that in a Christian country the church and state are really one, being composed of the same persons; in such a situation, he believes, the magistracy has religion as a part of their care. Burke states as his view, "A reasonable, prudent, provident, and moderate coercion may be a means of preventing acts of extreme ferocity and rigour; for by propagating excessive and extrava-

188

gant doctrines, such extravagant disorders take place, as require the most perilous and fierce corrections to oppose them." Burke is careful to say that he is looking only at the Unitarians, not at other religious groups, when he says that they represent a danger to the state. He maintains that they are a political faction at that time, as well as a theological sect. He says that they are sympathetic to the French, at a moment when the French Revolution appears as a real threat to the peace of every country in western Europe, including Great Britain. Burke expresses his fear that Unitarians, because of their expressed beliefs, are a danger that cannot be overlooked:

. . . **Dangers by being despised grow great;** so they do by absurd provision against them. . . . Whether an early discovery of evil designs, an early declaration, and an early precaution against them, be more wise than to stifle all inquiry about them, for fear they should declare themselves more early than otherwise they would, and therefore precipitate the evil—all this depends on the reality of the danger. Is it only an unbookish jealousy, as Shakespeare calls it? It is a question of fact. Does a design against the constitution of this country exist? If it does, and if it is carried on with increasing vigour and actively by a restless faction, and if it receives countenance by the most ardent and enthusiastic applauses of its object in the great council of this kingdom, by men of the first parts which this kingdom produces, perhaps by the first it has ever produced, can I think that there is no danger? . . .

Dare to be unhappy

Source: TAMERLANE, A TRAGEDY (Act IV, sc. i, l. 95)
Author: Nicholas Rowe (1674-1718)
First published: 1702
Type of work: Dramatic tragedy

Context: As the play opens, Bajazet, the pagan and dishonorable Emperor of the Turks, has attacked and overrun Greece in violation of a thrice-sworn treaty. In the course of the invasion, Moneses, a Grecian prince and a Christian, and his bride of a few hours, Arpasia, are captured; as a protective device they pretend to be brother and sister. Bajazet, holding Arpasia as hostage, forces Moneses to act as guard to his daughter, Selima, and to conduct her away from the scene of battle. Tamerlane, the pagan but honorable ruler of Asia, has taken the field with his armies to force Bajazet to honor his treaties and restore freedom to Greece; in a preliminary skirmish one of Tamerlane's generals captures Moneses and Selima. After the battle in which the forces of Bajazet are defeated, Moneses is reunited with Arpasia, but she informs him that during their separation Bajazet had forced her into marriage and a consummation of it. She can, therefore, no longer consider herself to be the wife of Moneses but

189

to her great sorrow must remain the wife of the despicable Emperor of the Turks. In the first scene of the fourth act she contemplates suicide, reflects on several classical heroines who preferred death to dishonor, and concludes that as a Christian this course of action is not open to her:

ARPASIA

Oh! Death! thou gentle end of human Sorrows,
Still must my weary Eye-lids vainly wake
In tedious Expectation of thy Peace:
Why stand thy thousand Doors still open,
To take the Wretched in? if stern Religion
Guards every Passage, and forbids my Entrance?—
Lucrece could bleed, and Porcia swallow Fire,
When urg'd with Griefs beyond a mortal Sufferance;
But here it must not be. Think then, Arpasia,
Think on the Sacred Dictates of thy Faith,
And let that arm thy Virtue, to perform
What *Cato's* Daughter durst not,—Live Arpasia,
And **dare to be unhappy.**

Darkness quieted by hope

Source: SORDELLO (Book I, l. 370)
Author: Robert Browning (1812-1889)
First published: 1840
Type of work: Narrative poem

Context: Long noted for its obscurity, *Sordello,* a study of "the incidents in the development of a soul," is based on the troubadour poet's spiritual growth and the maturation of his poetic genius. The historical background, the Italian civil wars of the late Middle Ages, is so confusing that Browning, who otherwise ignores his audience's lack of historical training, spends several hundred lines describing the political dispute between the Ghibellins and the Guelfs. He places the young Sordello in this world of violence and struggle so that his problems as a poet will take on greater meaning. The quotation occurs toward the end of this long introduction and just before the young poet is first seen as he turns the dreary, war-torn world into a realm of unequalled splendor. As Sordello is presented, Browning compares him to his great follower Dante and points out that, while Dante described the worlds of Hell, Purgatory, and Heaven, Sordello's world was that of ordinary men and women; Browning hopes to bring Sordello from the obscurity into which Dante's greater vision cast him.

. . . what if I approach the august sphere
Named now with only one name, disentwine

190

That under-current soft and argentine
From its fierce mate in the majestic mass
Leavened as the sea whose fire was mixt with glass
In John's transcendent vision,—launch once more
That lustre? Dante, pacer of the shore
Where glutted hell disgorgeth filthiest gloom,
Unbitten by its whirring sulphur-spume—
Or whence the grieved and obscure waters slope
Into a **darkness quieted by hope;**
Plucker of amaranths grown beneath God's eye
In gracious twilights where his chosen lie,—
I would do this! If I should falter now!

The days of our youth are the days of our glory

Source: STANZAS WRITTEN ON THE ROAD BETWEEN FLORENCE AND PISA (Line 2)
Author: George Gordon, Lord Byron (1788-1824)
First published: 1830
Type of work: Lyric poem

Context: The cult of Romanticism is the cult of youth. Too soon young people acquire world weariness. They have seen and experienced all, and there is nothing left to live for. But in their passage through life, they must achieve glory. Of course, the movement had other facets, since each country interpreted Romanticism differently, and there was even a different norm for romantic prose and poetry. Revolt and search for liberty were other characteristics. One of the definitions of Romanticism is "a revolt against everything that Classicism stands for." In English literature, the first generation of Romantic poets, Wordsworth, Coleridge, and Southey, while friends of revolution in their youth, became conservatives by the time the bulk of their work appeared. The second generation of Romantic poets, Byron, Shelley, and Keats, all rebelled so fiercely that their passions wore them out. All died young, before any tendency toward conservatism could develop. It seems unbelievable today, when Byron's poetic gift is considered secondary to that of the other two, that he was formerly widely and admiringly read by people to whom Shelley and Keats were practically unknown. Byron took joy in his youth, and dreaded the approach of old age— which he never knew because when he died of malaria while preparing to help the Greeks in their struggle for liberty against the Turks, he was only thirty-six years old. From the mature age of thirty-three, one day while riding from Florence to Pisa in Italy, he meditated on the significance of Fame and Glory. Probably the resulting poem is a pose, since most Romanticists maintained some sort of pose, but he declares in the four stanzas that he is not ambitious for a name in some future history of literature. He is happy with the lesser crown achieved by a twenty-two-year-old; the more honorable laurel crown is

191

not bestowed until the recipient is too elderly and wrinkled for it to become him. For Byron, the only use of Fame is to realize how it makes him more attractive to the girl beside him, and the sight of love for him in her eyes is his real joy. The final stanza is addressed to Fame.

Oh, talk not to me of a name great in story;
The days of our youth are the days of our glory:
And the myrtle and ivy of sweet two-and-twenty
Are worth all your laurels, though ever so plenty.

What are garlands and crowns to the brow that is wrinkled?
'T is but as a dead-flower with May-dew besprinkled.
Then away with all such from the head that is hoary!
What care I for the wreaths that can *only* give glory! . . .

. . .

There chiefly I sought thee, *there* only I found thee;
Her glance was the best of the rays that surround thee;
When it sparkled o'er aught that was bright in my story,
I knew it was love, and I felt it was glory.

Dead but sceptered sovereigns

Source: MANFRED (Act III, sc. iv, l. 40)
Author: George Gordon, Lord Byron (1788-1824)
First published: 1817
Type of work: Dramatic tragedy

Context: Manfred has been called the perfect expression of Byron's temperament. The first two acts were written during the poet's residence in Switzerland with the Shelleys in 1816. The early lines of incantation over the unconscious Manfred were composed immediately after Byron's unsuccessful attempts at reconciliation with his wife, and are filled with thoughts of her. The final act, completed in Venice the next year, was so adversely criticized by the publisher, that the poet rewrote most of it before publication. However, he explained in the covering letter that he had been ill with a fever when he wrote the original version, and that while he thought the speech of Manfred to the Sun contained some passable writing, the new version offered some pretty good poetry. He noted that he had changed his characterization of the Abbot and made him a good man. He also brought back the Spirits to be there at Manfred's death. A reader, comparing the two versions, will agree that the changes improved the play, though like most "closet drama," it would be impossible to stage. In this first great poem of revolt by Byron, the parallel to Goethe's *Faust* is obvious. He said he had never read Marlowe's version, but had heard a reading of a translation of the German tragedy. However, he gave his drama originality, and in its field it is excellent, as the

192

story of an individual who cannot find in any external social machinery a remedy for his feeling of isolation. Therefore, he must work out his own solution. Like Dr. Faustus, Manfred is a lonely magician, meditating in his Gothic gallery at midnight about his life. He calls repeatedly upon the spirits of the universe to appear before him, but they do not obey until he commands them in the name of his accursed soul. He demands their aid to help him forget his guilt-haunted past, a former love whose details he will not reveal. They cannot help him. As he falls senseless, there is heard a mysterious, despairing incantation. In the next scene, wandering alone in the Alps, Manfred is befriended by a chamois hunter who suggests he seek the consolation of the Church. A witch offers help in return for obedience to her. Refusing, Manfred returns to his castle where the Abbot of St. Maurice arrives, to save his soul. However, the Abbot confesses he cannot help so noble a man. Later he makes a second attempt, and finds Manfred remembering his thoughts of the past when he stood in the Coliseum, where those who are dead still command. The Abbot, told that a dangerous Spirit is approaching, offers to confront it. Manfred refuses to go with the Spirit to Hell, to which he has no obligation. And so he dies alone and lonely. Nothing except death could conquer him. In his soliloquy in the tower he says:

I do remember me, that in my youth . . .
I stood within the Coliseum's wall,
Midst the chief relics of almighty Rome . . .
And thou didst shine, thou rolling moon, upon
All this, and cast a wide and tender light . . .
Leaving that beautiful which still was so,
And making that which was not, till the place
Became religion, and the heart ran o'er
With silent worship of the great of old,—
The **dead but sceptred sovereigns,** who still rule
Our spirits from their urns. . . .

Dead scandals form good subjects for dissection

Source: DON JUAN (Canto I, stanza 31)
Author: George Gordon, Lord Byron (1788-1824)
First published: 1819 (Cantos I and II)
Type of work: Satiric poem

Context: Don Jóse and Donna Inez, proud parents of Don Juan, young hero of Lord Byron's satiric epic, have quarrelled—precisely *why* no one can guess "Though several thousand people chose to try." They live respectably as man and wife while showing to the world a well-bred calm, until at last pent-up anger flares and leaves the world in no doubt as to the true state of affairs between them. Donna Inez tries first to prove that

193

Don Jóse is *mad;* failing this, that he is merely *bad.* When asked on what evidence she is moved to treat him so, she replies only that her conduct is required by her duty to God and man; and, while hinting that she has journals, books and letters which *could* be used should occasion demand, she falls serenely and magnanimously silent. "And then she had all Seville for abettors,/ The hearers of her case became repeaters." Old gossip is dredged up, old rumors brought to life; to the amusement of some, the requital of others, the entertainment of all.

> And then this best and meekest woman bore
>   With such serenity her husband's woes,
> Just as the Spartan ladies did of yore,
>   Who saw their spouses kill'd, and nobly chose
> Never to say a word about them more—
>   Calmly she heard each calumny that rose,
> And saw *his* agonies with such sublimity,
> That all the world exclaim'd, "What magnanimity!"
>
>   .   .   .
>
> And if our quarrels should rip up old stories,
>   And help them with a lie or two additional,
> *I'm* not to blame, as you well know—no more is
>   Any one else—they were become traditional;
> Besides, their resurrection aids our glories
>   By contrast, which is what we just were wishing all:
> And science profits by this resurrection—
> **Dead scandals form good subjects for dissection.**

Deaf as a door

Source: THE WIL OF WITS (Part IV, "Miseries of Mauillia," The Fifth Miserie)
Author: Nicholas Breton (1545?-1626?)
First published: c.1580
Type of work: Melancholy fiction

Context: Nicholas Breton, from an ancient Essex family, was long believed to have been born in 1555 until modern scholars found a document setting his age at 64 in 1609. Since much of his work was published at Oxford, his wealthy father may have sent him there to study. In his writing, he was influenced by his stepfather, George Gascoigne, from whom he copied his out-of-date verse technique and poetic diction. His *Wil* of *Wits, Wits Will, or Wils Wit, chuse you whether* was first published in 1580 or 1582, but all copies have been lost, and the earliest surviving edition is 1599. Breton was not as fortunate as some of his contemporaries in choice of patrons; so much of his writing, largely pious tracts, has disappeared. *The Wil of Wits* contains five discourses: 1. A Pretie and Wittie Discourse between Wit and Will; 2. The Authors Dreame; 3.

The Scholler and the Souldiour; 4. The Miseries of Mauillia; 5. The Praise of Vertuous Ladies. In all of them, Breton's fondness for proverbs is apparent. Discourse 4, "The Miseries of Mauillia, the most unfortunate Ladie that ever lived," is divided into five miseries. She begins her suffering when not yet five years old by seeing both her parents stabbed by "bloudie fellowes" pillaging her city. At the child's cries, a poor laundress picks her up, and is rewarded with freedom, since the child pleads for her to one of the captains. However, in the second Miserie Mauillia is kept to sew and clean for him until he decides to send her to a new home, only to have her and her escort attacked by robbers. This time a boy rescues her, and she helps him without bettering her own lot. The author, on the first page, provides a brief biography of poor Mauillia.

A sweet young soule, in time of tender yeeres,
In souldiours hands, eskapéd killing neere:
And growing on, did run through many breers,
As in the booke, do plainly follow heere.
Long wandering, in a world of miseries:
Loathing her life, she lamentably dies.

Her miseries, in number are but five.
Yet in those five, five thousand haps of hate:
Which she endurde. whiles that she was alive,
And dide at last, in miserable state:
What need more words, the rest here followes on:
For mourning minds, to sit and muze upon.

The final miserie finds the melancholy narrator in possession of some money, and courted for her wealth, for herself, and for her love. She describes the least attractive suitor, not only (as we say) "deaf as a post," but "an elderly foole who having lately buried his olde Jone, would now fain play the young gentleman." Of him she says:

. . . the foole will be kissing, and the stubble of his olde shaven beard new come up so pricks mee and tickles my lippes, that I am ready to scratch them after every kisse: but yet his nose is so great that hee hath much a do to kisse kindly; besides, hee hath a stinking breath and a hollow eye.
Further, I feare by his complexion, hee hath bene a traveller in some lowe countreys. where hee hath been infected with some unholesome ayre: I gesse it the more by his speaking in the nose, and never a good tooth in his head. Hee is as **deafe as a doore;** I must tell him a tale in his eare, that all the town must be privie to, or else hee cannot heare mee.

Dear to maidens are their rivals dead

Source: AMELIA (Line 135)
Author: Coventry Patmore (1823–1896)
First published: 1878
Type of work: Irregular ode

Context: Writing as a man well used to elevate the charms of married love and quite opposed to the lack of sexual restraint that he found in many of his contemporaries, Patmore tells in this poem about the first time he went out alone with his beloved Amelia. Amelia's mother had carefully sheltered her and begs the speaker to remember the girl's honor; with this single warning, she allows her daughter to accompany him to the grave of Millicent, the woman he had once loved. The quiet atmosphere of the cemetery and the speaker's praise of the almost divine Millicent cause Amelia to show her love, but the speaker, being older and recalling the mother's plea, preserves the girl's honor. By restraining himself, he discovers that he will reach the epitome of joy after marriage; thus he finds the hope for a future marriage by taking his sweetheart to the grave of his last love and watching her reactions to his eulogy upon the "rival's" beauty.

> But all my praise
> Amelia thought too slight for Millicent,
> And on my lovelier-freighted arm she leant,
> For more attent;
> And the tea-rose I gave,
> To deck her breast, she dropp'd upon the grave.
> "And this was her's," said I, decoring with a band
> Of mildest pearls Amelia's milder hand.
> "Nay, I will wear it for *her* sake," she said:
> For **dear to maidens are their rivals dead.**

Death has done all death can

Source: AFTER (Line 4)
Author: Robert Browning (1812-1889)
First published: 1855
Type of work: Lyric poem

Context: After is a companion piece to *Before.* In *Before* we see two men in a deadly quarrel because one has wronged the other. The question is, however, who is the wronged and who the wronger? There is no solution for the problem except to fight it out: if the culprit wins, life will take its toll of him; if the wronged man ' loses, he will have his reward as a martyr in heaven. There can be no question of forgiveness by the wronged man, because wrong must always be resisted and evil not be

196

crowned on earth; God will be the judge. The wronger, obdurate until the end, refuses to admit his wrong, and so the duel takes place. In *After* the winner of the contest looks at the corpse of the victim: death has done all that it can do to him. He is now in a new life in which his wrong and the survivor's vengeance are alike inconsequential. It is only at this place in the poem that the reader learns the victor in the duel is the wronged man: God has shielded the protector of right and has vindicated him, as in the ancient trials by combat. The speaker in the poem concludes by wishing that the two of them were again boys: the victim's outrage, God's patience, and man's scorn would then be easy to bear.

> Take the cloak from his face, and at first
>   Let the corpse do its worst.
>
> How he lies in his rights of a man!
>   **Death has done all death can:**
> And, absorbed in the new life he leads,
>   He recks not, he heeds
> Nor his wrong nor my vengeance—both strike
>   On his senses alike,
> And are lost in the solemn and strange
>   Surprise of the change.
>
> Ha, what avails death to erase
>   His offence, my disgrace?
> I would we were boys as of old
>   In the field, by the fold:
> His outrage, God's patience, man's scorn
>   Were so easily borne.
>
> I stand here now, he lies in his place:
>   Cover the face.

Death is the privilege of human nature

Source: THE FAIR PENITENT (Act V, sc. i, l. 133)
Author: Nicholas Rowe (1674-1718)
First published: 1703
Type of work: Dramatic tragedy

Context: The plot of the first of Rowe's "she-tragedies," concerns Sciolto, a nobleman of Genoa, who has just promised his lovely daughter, Calista, to Altamont, a youth he has befriended since the death of Altamont's parents. Calista secretly loves and has been seduced by Altamont's bitter enemy, "gay Lothario." Lothario forces Calista to meet him on the day of her marriage by threatening to make her shame public. Altamont discovers Lothario and Calista in conference and, having learned their

197

secret, kills Lothario. Sciolto enters and, upon learning of his daughter's shame, attempts to kill her. Altamont prevents this murder, and Sciolto leaves still insisting on justice. In the final act Rowe presents to his audience a scene of appalling melancholy and horror with Calista keeping a deathwatch over the corpse of Lothario. When her father enters, she expresses her wish for death, and he offers his dagger. As she takes the weapon, he announces that his duty as a judge is done and expresses his love for her as a father:

SCIOLTO

I could curse nature and that tyrant, honor,
For making me thy father and thy judge;
Thou art my daughter still.

CALISTA

          For that kind word
Thus let me fall, thus humbly to the earth;
Weep on your feet and bless you for this goodness;
Oh! 'tis too much for this offending wretch,
This parricide, that murders with her crimes,
Shortens her father's age and cuts him off
E'er little more than half his years be numbered.

SCIOLTO

Would it were otherwise!—but thou must die.—

CALISTA

That I must die—it is my only comfort;
Death is the privilege of human nature,
And life without it were not worth our taking;
Thither the poor, the pris'ner, and the mourner
Fly for relief and lay their burdens down.
Come then, and take me now to thy cold arms,
Thou meagre shade; here let me breathe my last,
Charmed with my father's pity and forgiveness
More than if angels tuned their golden viols
And sung a requiem to my parting soul.

Death is the veil which those who live call life

Source: PROMETHEUS UNBOUND (Act III, sc. iii, l. 113)
Author: Percy Bysshe Shelley (1792-1822)
First published: 1820
Type of work: Lyric drama

Context: Bound by Jupiter to a rock in the mountains because he refuses to tell the tyrant when he would be overthrown, Prometheus has learned that love is superior to hate, but he still heroically refuses to aid the evil king of the gods. However, the time that Jupiter fears finally comes, and Demogorgon overthrows the monarch, leaving the throne vacant because if any deity seizes it, he might become a tyrant. This heavenly revolt is the sign of a new age of peaceful anarchy during which happiness will come to gods and men alike. Following the fall of Jupiter, Hercules releases Prometheus, who plans to discover how he can further help his beloved race of men, how he can help them escape misery and despair. After he concludes his speech of unlimited love, Asia, the spirit of love and universal brotherhood, and Earth, the great mother, talk of death, the major cause of man's unhappiness. Earth tells why men should not fear it by using the Platonic notion that what men call life is really death, because the body enslaves the soul:

ASIA

Oh, mother! wherefore speak the name of death?
Cease they to love, and move, and breathe, and speak,
Who die?

THE EARTH

It would avail not to reply:
Thou art immortal, and this tongue is known
But to the uncommunicating dead.
Death is the veil which those who live call life:
They sleep, and it is lifted: . . .

Death: the last, best friend

Source: CARMEN NUPTIALE ("The Dream," Stanza 87)
Author: Robert Southey (1774-1843)
First published: 1817
Type of work: Epithalamium

Context: Because he was poet laureate, Southey was called upon to write a commemorative poem to honor Princess Charlotte's royal marriage; however, he was, as he says in the proem to *Carmen Nuptial,* at a loss. He well understood that his talent was limited to themes of vengeance and violence and showed to greatest advantage in poems of epic length. Thus he turned for inspiration to Edmund Spenser and wrote "The Dream," a long poem in the style of his Elizabethan master but lacking both the organization and charm of his source. Southey presents a catalogue of men and personifications who greet the princess and give her gifts. Naturally the last speaker is Death:

"Hear me, O Princess!" said the shadowy form:
"As, in administering this mighty land,

199

Thou with thy best endeavor shalt perform
The will of Heaven, so shall my faithful hand
Thy great and endless recompense supply:
My name is **DEATH: THE LAST, BEST FRIEND AM I!**"

Death, the poor man's dearest friend

Source: MAN WAS MADE TO MOURN (Stanza 11)
Author: Robert Burns (1759-1796)
First published: 1786
Type of work: Dirge

Context: Robert Burns was rarely a happy man. All his life he knew suffering and disappointment. His youth was harsh and painful. Born on a farm whose tenant farmer, his father, was always in debt because of the poor soil and high rent, Robert spent his early life in a series of moves from one poor farm to another. He tried to better his lot by learning to dress flax, only to have the flax shop burn down. His father's death, when Robert was twenty-five, started the poet on a period of four years of intense labor with his younger brothers in a vain attempt to wrest a living from the soil. In his search for love, he had also been unfortunate. The father of one sweetheart, Jean Armour, refused to consent to their marriage even though the girl was mother of his child. Another girl, Mary Campbell, died while at home preparing to marry him. So Burns could hardly be blamed for writing melancholic poetry. A reader can only admire his spirit when poems of wild fun, satire, and delightful descriptions reveal his fine sense of humor. But certainly "Man Was Made to Mourn" is not of this kind. The poet describes himself walking one chill November evening along the banks of Ayr. He comes upon an eighty-year-old man, with white hair and a face furrowed with care. He inquires of the poet the reason for his roaming, whether it is in search of wealth or fun, or perhaps to join with him in mourning the miseries of mankind. Then he expounds his own philosophy. Every returning winter's sun adds only more proof that most of the inhabitants of the moor toil to support some haughty lord. There is nothing in their future except mourning. Indeed, each stanza of the eleven ends with the melancholic statement that mourning is the lot of most men. Even the major part of those who seem favored by fate, the rich and the great, are not really happy. "Man's inhumanity to man/ Makes countless thousands mourn." The "rev'rend sage" cannot understand why, if designed by Nature to be a slave, he was endowed with ability to form independent desires. His consolation, with which the poem closes, is the most melancholic thought of all: because of his oppressed existence, he has escaped one fear that terrifies so many people. Life for him is so bad that he does not fear Death.

200

The poor, oppressèd, honest man
Had never, sure, been born,
Had there not been some recompense
To comfort those who mourn!

O **Death! the poor man's dearest friend,**
The kindest and the best!
Welcome the hour my agéd limbs
Are laid with thee at rest!

The great, the wealthy, fear thy blow,
From pomp and pleasure torn;
But, Oh! a blest relief to those
That weary-laden mourn!

The deceiving mirror of self-love

Source: THE PARLIAMENT OF LOVE (Act I, sc. v)
Author: Philip Massinger (1583-1640)
First published: 1805
Type of work: Tragi-comic drama

Context: As the text of *The Parliament of Love* is defective, what we have of the play begins in scene iv of the first act, with Chamont conjuring his former ward, the noble Bellisant, to live a quieter and more decorous life. She is associating herself with unworthy persons, and as a result of her behavior, her reputation will suffer. Bellisant spurns Chamont's advice and says that, since she is entirely virtuous, she will pursue the course that gives her the most amusement; she says that she will disprove the generally accepted idea that chastity can live only in a cottage by living a pure life in the center of court activity. In Act I, scene v, Charles VIII of France returns to his court from his successful military campaign in Italy and finds a universal dullness prevailing. When a courtier attributes the lack of gaity to the cruel behavior of the court ladies, Bellisant says that the fault lies with the courtiers. Formerly, when they desired to woo a lady, they were careful to have to their credit a series of gallant exploits, deep wisdom, and service to the state, and men such as those the ladies could treat with favor. But now, anyone who has traveled enough in Italy to learn a little of the language and can make fashionable grimaces, dance lavoltas, and be rude and saucy and see himself as his self-love would like him to be, thinks there is hardly a woman worthy of him. Bellisant speaks:

"Ere they durst
Presume to offer service to a lady,
In person they perform'd some gallant acts
The fame of which prepared them gracious hearing,

201

Ere they made their approaches: what coy she, then,
Though great in birth, not to be parallel'd
For nature's liberal bounties, both set off
With fortune's trappings, wealth; but, with delight,
Gladly acknowledged such a man her servant,
To whose heroic courage, and deep wisdom,
The flourishing commonwealth, and thankful king,
Confess'd themselves for debtors? Whereas, now,
If you have traveled Italy, and brought home
Some remnants of the language, and can set
Your faces in some strange and ne'er-seen posture,
Dance a lavolta, and be rude and saucy;
Protest, and swear, and damn, (for these are acts
That most think grace them,) and then view yourselves
In **the deceiving mirror of self-love,**
You do conclude there hardly is a woman
That can be worthy of you."

A deed without a name

Source: MACBETH (Act IV, sc. i, l. 49)
Author: William Shakespeare (1564-1616)
First published: 1623
Type of work: Dramatic tragedy

Context: Macbeth and Banquo are told by three witches that Macbeth will be king and that the descendants of Banquo will be crowned. Driven by his own wicked ambition and that of his wife, Macbeth murders King Duncan and usurps the throne. Worried because the sons of Duncan remain safe in exile and Fleance, son of the recently murdered Banquo, has escaped his assassins, Macbeth visits the den of the weird sisters.

SECOND WITCH
By the pricking of my thumbs,
Something wicked this way comes.
Open locks,
Whoever knocks.

[*Enter* MACBETH.]
MACBETH
How now, you secret, black, and midnight hags?
What is't you do?

ALL
A deed without a name.

MACBETH

I conjure you, by that which you profess,
Howe'er you come to know it, answer me.
Though you untie the winds, and let them fight
Against the churches; though the yesty waves
Confound and swallow navigation up;
Though bladed corn be lodged, and trees blown down;
Though castles topple on their warders' heads;
. . .
Even till destruction sicken—answer me
To what I ask you.

The deep damnation of his taking off

Source: MACBETH (Act I, sc. vii, l. 20)
Author: William Shakespeare (1564-1616)
First published: 1623
Type of work: Dramatic tragedy

Context: In a well-known soliloquy, Macbeth, forewarned by the prophecy of three witches that he will be "King hereafter" and spurred on by the determination of Lady Macbeth, debates murdering King Duncan, his kinsman, his king, and, this night, his guest.

MACBETH
    . . . He's here in double trust;
First, as I am his kinsman, and his subject,
Strong both against the deed; then, as his host,
Who should against his murderer shut the door,
Not bear the knife myself. Besides, this Duncan
Hath borne his faculties so meek, hath been
So clear in his great office, that his virtues
Will plead like angels, trumpet-tongued against
The deep damnation of his taking-off.
. . .
            . . . I have no spur
To prick the sides of my intent, but only
Vaulting ambition, which o'erleaps itself,
And falls on th'other—

Defaced, deflowered, and now to death devote

Source: PARADISE LOST (Book IX, l. 901)
Author: John Milton (1608-1674)
First published: 1667
Type of work: Epic poem

203

Context: Eve, deceived by Satan disguised as a serpent, eats the forbidden fruit of the tree of the knowledge of good and evil. The immediate effect upon her is a feeling of intoxication. She soliloquizes that to tell Adam what she has done and to share the fruit with him will be to sacrifice the superiority that she has gained by her daring act. She believes that her new superiority will enhance her charms in Adam's eyes. She then thinks that death, which has not yet appeared, may actually be the result of eating the fruit, and she cannot stand the thought of herself dead and Adam living happily in the garden with a new Eve. She then resolves that Adam will have to eat the fruit and so share her fate, whatever it is to be. When she approaches him, she says that what they had heard about the fruit was not true; it is a remarkable stimulant which made the serpent almost human and her almost a god. Adam is appalled at what she has done, as he fully realizes the immensity of her crime. He drops the garland he had woven for her, and all the roses in it fade and drop their petals. He speaks:

> O fairest of creation, last and best
> Of all God's works, creature in whom excelled
> Whatever can to sight or thought be formed,
> Holy, divine, good, amiable, or sweet!
> How art thou lost, how on a sudden lost,
> **Defaced, deflowered, and now to death devote?**
> Rather how hast thou yielded to transgress
> The strict forbiddance, how to violate
> The sacred fruit forbidden! some cursèd fraud
> Of enemy hath beguiled thee, yet unknown,
> And me with thee hath ruined, for with thee
> Certain my resolution is to die;
> How can I live without thee, how forgo
> Thy sweet converse and love so dearly joined,
> To live again in these wild woods forlorn?
>   •   •   •

Defaming as impure what God declares pure

Source: PARADISE LOST (Book IV, ll. 746-47)
Author: John Milton (1608-1674)
First published: 1667
Type of work: Epic poem

Context: Adam and Eve finish their day's work of cultivating the garden. The time for rest has come, and all the beasts and birds seek repose except the nightingale, which sings throughout the night. Adam explains to Eve that man is dignified by having duties to perform; the lower animals are idle throughout the day. Eve indicates that whatever Adam commands is law to her. She comments on the beautiful evening, the fragrance of the air, and the glittering of the stars. She asks why the stars shine when all are asleep. This question leads Adam into explaining that millions of unseen spirits walk the earth in the starlight. With this explanation, they pass into their blissful bower, which is adorned with flowers; it is closed to the entry of any of the lower creatures. Adam praises the Omnipotent who created all things, and mentions that He has promised them that there will come a race from them to fill the earth, which shall extol the infinite goodness of God.

> This said unanimous, and other rites
> Observing none, but adoration pure
> Which God likes best, into their inmost bower
> Handed they went; and eased the putting off
> These troublesome disguises which we wear,
> Straight side by side were laid, nor turned, I ween,
> Adam from his fair spouse, nor Eve the rites
> Mysterious of connubial love refused:
> Whatever hypocrites austerely talk
> Of purity and place and innocence,
> **Defaming as impure what God declares**
> **Pure,** and commands to some, leaves free to all.
> Our Maker bids increase, who bids abstain
> But our destroyer, foe to God and man?
> Hail, wedded love, mysterious law, true source
> Of human offspring, sole propriety,
> In paradise of all things common else.
> · · ·

The demi-Atlas of this earth

Source: ANTONY AND CLEOPATRA (Act I, sc. v, l. 23)
Author: William Shakespeare (1564-1616)
First published: 1623
Type of work: Dramatic tragedy

Context: Once the greatest of generals, Antony has ceased to concern himself with affairs of empire because of his passion for Cleopatra. As one of his friends disgustedly notes, "His captain's heart" "is become the bellows and the fan/To cool a gypsy's lust." But now rebellion and invasion have recalled Antony to Rome, where the other members of the ruling triumvirate—Lepidus and Octavius Caesar—are in great need of his soldierly qualities. In Alexandria, meanwhile, Cleopatra awaits the return of her lover, writing letter after letter to her "demi-Atlas," for if Atlas bore the globe on his shoulders, Antony bears half of it (the other half being borne by Octavius, Lepidus being too ineffectual to matter). As a general, moreover, Antony is the protecter of men, their armor—"arm," and helmet—"burgonet." Thus, the intensity of the conflict within Antony—be-

205

tween his passion for Cleopatra and his Roman sense of duty—is sug- gested unwittingly by Cleopatra her- self:

CLEOPATRA

O Charmian.
Where think'st thou he is now? Stands he, or sits he?
Or does he walk? Or is he on his horse?
O happy horse to bear the weight of Antony!
Do bravely horse, for wot'st thou whom thou mov'st,
The demi-Atlas of this earth, the arm
And burgonet of men? He's speaking now,
Or murmuring Where's my serpent of old Nile—
For so he calls me.

.   .   .

Deserves to be preached to death by wild curates

Source: A MEMOIR OF THE REVEREND SYDNEY SMITH BY HIS DAUGHTER LADY
HOLLAND (Chapter 11)
Author: Sydney Smith (1771-1845)
First published: 1855
Type of work: Biographical memoir

Context: A volume of 268 pages, written by his daughter, Saba (1802–1866), wife of Lord Holland, tells of the life of the Reverend Sydney Smith, and recounts some of the witty sayings for which he was famous. The witticisms are set down one after another, without connection or explanation, rather like the Joe Miller joke book, a volume published in 1739 and many times reprinted, containing jokes supposed to have originated with a famous English comedian, Josiah Miller (1684–1738). Most of the contents was actually invented by its publisher, John Mottley. In contrast, the amusing comments in Lady Holland's book were the genuine products of her clergyman father's quick mind. The first one obviously originated through a clever twist of the phrase: "trampled to death by wild horses."

Oh, the Dean of——**deserves to be preached to death by wild curates.**

.   .   .

"The advice I sent to the Bishop of New Zealand, when he had to receive the cannibal chiefs there, was to say to them, 'I deeply regret, Sirs, to have nothing on mye own table suited to your tastes, but you will find plenty of cold curate and roasted clergyman on the sideboard;' and if, in spite of this prudent provision, his visitors should end their repast by eating him likewise, why I should only add, 'I sincerely hope he would disagree with them!' " . . .

206

Destructive, damnable, deceitful woman!

Source: THE ORPHAN (Act III, l. 586)
Author: Thomas Otway (1652-1685)
First published: 1680
Type of work: Domestic tragedy

Context: The leading Restoration writer of comedies was Thomas Otway. One of his best was *The Orphan or The Unhappy Marriage,* a domestic tragedy, distantly following the plot of Shakespeare's *Cymbeline.* Its simple and direct language fits the action. Its psychology is convincing, and its pathos does not distract. It shows Otway's tendency to leave behind the heroic bombast of the Elizabethan period in the direction of pathos and sentimentality. Monimia, an orphan, has been left under the guardianship of Acasto, a Bohemian nobleman, retired from court and living in the country. Both his sons, Castalio and Polydore, love her. She prefers the older Castalio and gives him a password to let him enter her chamber. However, Polydore, overhearing the conversation, arrives first, and when Castalio comes the servant says the lady will not admit him. That news causes Castalio to embark, at the end of Act III, on a tirade to an elderly servant, Ernesto, about all the evil caused by such women as Cleopatra, Helen of Troy, and others:

CASTALIO
My thoughts are full of woman; thou poor wretch, art past 'em.

ERNESTO
I hate the sex.

CASTALIO
Then I'm thy friend, Ernesto.
I'd leave the world for him that hates a woman.
Woman the fountain of all humane frailty!
What mighty ills have not been done by woman?
Who was't betrayed the Capitol? A woman.
. . .
Who was the cause of a long ten years war,
And laid at last old Troy in ashes? Woman.
Destructive, damnable, deceitful woman!
Woman to man first as a blessing giv'n,
When innocence and love were in their prime.

207

Detested sport, that owes its pleasures to another's pain

Source: THE TASK (Book III, ll. 326-327)
Author: William Cowper (1731-1800)
First published: 1785
Type of work: Meditative poem in blank verse

Context: Cowper, descendant of John Donne, was the last English poet to belong to what has been called the cult of simplicity. He began his adult career in the legal profession and was called to the bar in 1754; however, he was forced into early retirement by attacks of insanity. The first of these made it impossible for him to marry the girl he loved. Another, brought on by the strain of preparing for an examination in 1763, led him to attempt suicide. His convalescence lasted for some time; he then retired to the country and settled eventually at Olney, where he turned to poetry as a serious avocation. He was then fifty years of age. The first volume, *Poems,* was published in 1782; his greatest work, *The Task,* was completed two years later. Its ready sale was ensured by the inclusion of a few other poems to round out the volume, notably his popular humorous ballad *John Gilpin's Ride.* *The Task,* widely praised, brought him lasting renown. It is a lengthy poem in blank verse and explores, quietly and meditatively, the life of seclusion that Cowper leads. He describes the beauty of the countryside, the simple pleasures and routines of the day, and considers the outside world that he has renounced. He dwells at some length on the nature of human existence and upon moral and spiritual problems; his strong Calvinism, a factor in his recurrent periods of depression, encourages him to moralize. The poem is a task given him by his friend Lady Austen, who suggested he write about a sofa. He begins with the sofa and then describes his morning walk and his accompanying thoughts. In the second book he discusses at some length his view of the outside world and its problems. In Book III he takes up the subject of his garden and the pleasure it gives him; but he prefaces this description with some remarks concerning people who visit the country only to disturb the peace and serenity of it: holiday-seekers, hunters, and fishermen. To the mild and gentle Cowper, such people are vandals, utterly lacking in sensibility:

> We persecute, annihilate the tribes
> That draw the sportsman over hill and dale
> Fearless, and rapt away from all his cares;
> Should never game-fowl hatch her eggs again,
> Nor baited hook deceive the fish's eye;
> Could pageantry, and dance, and feast, and song
> Be quell'd in all our summer-months' retreats;
> How many self-deluded nymphs and swains,
> Who dream they have a taste for fields and groves
> Would find them hideous nurs'ries of the spleen,
> And crowd the roads, impatient for the town!

They love the country, and none else, who seek
For their own sake its silence and its shade;
Delights which who would leave, that has a heart
Susceptible of pity, or a mind
Cultured and capable of sober thought,
For all the savage din of the swift pack,
And clamours of the field? **Detested sport,**
That owes its pleasures to another's pain,
That feeds upon the sobs and dying shrieks
Of harmless nature. . . .

The devil watches all opportunities

Source: THE OLD BACHELOR (Act II, sc. ii)
Author: William Congreve (1670-1729)
First published: 1693
Type of work: Dramatic comedy

Context: Araminta teases Belinda for being in love with Bellmour; Belinda strenuously denies the allegation, as loving a man would be unfitting for a lady of quality. The maid announces that Bellmour and Vainlove, with whom Araminta is in love, are waiting on the ladies. Belinda says that she will not stay to receive the gentlemen and calls for her hood, preparatory to leaving the house. Araminta urges the maid, Betty, to put Belinda's hood on her so that she can go, but Belinda takes it off, saying that she has changed her mind and will stay. When Araminta says that Belinda has decided not to let Araminta have all the company to herself, Belinda replies that she is of such a charitable nature that she will not trust Araminta. The devil watches all occasions so as to seize the opportunity to do mischief, and Araminta might be tempted, if alone, to be indiscreet. So Belinda will stay only to protect Araminta's reputation; she contends that she is willing to remain out of pure affection.

BELINDA

. . . Here, take 'em all again, my mind's changed, I won't go.

[*Exit* BETTY *with hoods.*]

ARAMINTA

[*Aside.*] So, this I expected.—[*Aloud.*] You won't oblige me then, cousin, and let me have all the company to myself?

BELINDA

No; upon deliberation, I have too much charity to trust you to yourself. **The devil watches all opportunities;** and, in this favorable disposition of your mind, Heaven knows how far you may be tempted: I am tender of your reputation.

209

ARAMINTA

I am obliged to you. But who's malicious now, Belinda?

BELINDA

Not I; witness my heart, I stay out of pure affection.

ARAMINTA

In my conscience, I believe you.

Devils are not so black as they be painted

Source: A MARGARITE OF AMERICA
Author: Thomas Lodge (1558?-1625)
First published: 1596
Type of work: Prose romance

Context: Thomas Lodge was a many-sided man. Son of a Lord Mayor of London, he graduated from Oxford in 1577, for which reason he is believed to have been born about 1558. He went on to study law and to make a name for himself in literature with several plays and with euphuistic tales in the style of John Lyly, told in a mingling of extravagant prose and poetry. Shakespeare borrowed from his *Scillaes Metamorphosis* (1589) for *Venus and Adonis,* and from Lodge's best-known *Rosalynde* (1590) for *As You Like It.* Both were planned and partly written during Lodge's voyages to Terceiras and the Canaries in 1588. Later, in 1591–1593, Lodge accompanied Thomas Cavendish on an expedition to South America. During the voyage, he read a Spanish manuscript in a Jesuit library in Santos, Brazil, that he adapted into *A Margarite of America, the Ladies delight and the Ladies honor.* The "America" part of the title came because it was written while passing through the Straits of Magellan. As he indicates in a foreword "To the Gentlemen Readers," he found seasickness interfering with composition, so he craved charity from those who perused it. Its elegant and exaggerated style may be traced to Antonio de Guevara (1480–1545) who helped to father Spanish Gongorism. After its completion, Lodge became interested in medicine in which he took two degrees, in Avignon, France, (1598) and at Oxford (1602), after which he practiced medicine for the rest of his life. *A Treatise on the Plague* was one product of his new career. The complicated story of Margarita begins with a flowery description of "blushing morning," as armies under Emperor Protomachus of Mosco and Artofago of Cuzco prepare for combat. Before they join in battle, however, "an old man whose sober looks betokened his severe thoughts and mournful garments shadowed his melancholy mind" takes a position between the armies and delivers a two page speech quoting Plutarch and Plato in a plea not to destroy mankind. He suggests that Arasdachus, heir to the Empire of Cuzco, visit Princess Margarita of Mosco with a view to matrimony.

210

The emperor greets the suitor with a joust. Earl Asaphus gives a party for the knights and ladies. The Cuzcan Prince is a gay deceiver and, as Lodge put it in the 1596 edition:

"Margarita (poore princesse) thinking all that golden which glisters, trusted too long." In reporting the earl's speech, Lodge writes (in modernized spelling):

. . . Since therefore (my subjects) you are at my obedience, and upon my direction are to do homage to love, I give you free license to discourse, free liberty to look, the sweets whereof, after you have gathered, come to me, and after the priest hath hand-fasted you, come touch and spare not, you shall have my patent to take your pleasure. It is a dangerous matter (said Arsadachus) to enter those lists where women will do what they list. Well (said Margarita) **devils are not so black as they be painted** (My Lord), nor women so wayward as they seem. . . . With that they brake up the assembly, for it was supper time, and the prince entreated them to sit down, where they merrily passed the time, laughing heartily at the pleasant and honest mirth wherein they had passed that afternoon.

The devil's in the moon for mischief

Source: DON JUAN (Canto I, stanza 113)
Author: George Gordon, Lord Byron (1788-1824)
First published: 1819 (Cantos I and II)
Type of work: Satiric poem

Context: Don Juan, now growing up, is "Tall, handsome, slender, but well knit: . . ." Since his father's death he has been in the charge of his mother, who, remembering her late lord's frailties, has provided, as his sole companions, the households ancient maids, his tutors and confessor, and, (alas! for ". . . a breeding . . . strictly moral") her lovely friend, Donna Julia, a young wife of twenty-three, who, when Juan was younger ". . . saw, and, as a pretty child,/ Caress'd him often— . . ." But now the pretty child is suddenly sixteen, and a subtle change takes place. Donna Julia is blushingly self-conscious, while Juan broods in the "lonely wood,/ Tormented with a wound he [cannot] know, . . ." One summer's day toward evening, the two find themselves together in a sequestered bower, Donna Julia full of honor, virtue, and resolve never to disgrace the marriage ring she wears; Juan, as is love's way when it is new, tremblingly fearful lest he do wrong as in gratitude he kisses the little hand so carelessly placed on his. And then the moon comes up.

The sun set, and up rose the yellow moon:
The devil's in the moon for mischief; they
Who call'd her CHASTE, methinks, began too soon
Their nomenclature; there is not a day,

211

The longest, not the twenty-first of June,
   Sees half the business in a wicked way,
On which three single hours of moonshine smile—
   On them she looks so modest all the while.

There is a dangerous silence in that hour,
   A stillness, which leaves room for the full soul
To open all itself, without the power
   Of calling wholly back its self-control;
The silver light which, hallowing tree and tower,
   Sheds beauty and deep softness o'er the whole,
Breathes also to the heart, and o'er it throws
A loving languor, which is not repose.

The Devil's most devilish when respectable

Source: AURORA LEIGH (Book VII, l. 105).
Author: Elizabeth Barrett Browning (1806-1861)
First published: 1857
Type of work: Romance in blank verse

Context: Marian Erle, a poor but virtuous girl who has had a wretched, poverty-stricken childhood, becomes engaged to marry Romney Leigh, the wealthy, socially conscious cousin of the teller of the tale, Aurora Leigh. A wealthy and beautiful widow, Lady Waldemar, asks Aurora to help her break off Romney's marriage, but Aurora refuses to do so and forms a friendship with Marian. On the wedding day, Marian does not appear at the church, but sends a letter saying that she will not marry Romney. Romney unavailingly searches for Marian for months; finally, he gives up the quest and becomes engaged to marry Lady Waldemar. Later, Aurora, on her way to take up residence in Italy, finds Marian in Paris. Marian is now possessed of a baby boy; the situation at first shocks the some-what priggish Aurora. According to Marian, Lady Waldemar, under the guise of being Marian's fast friend, convinced her that marriage with Romney would be a mistake. She therefore sent her off with a woman who was supposed to conduct her to Australia to set her up in a new life. Instead, she takes her to France, drugs her, and has her raped. After a period of madness, Marian regains her sanity and gets a position as a lady's maid to a married coquette who is another man's mistress. When the lady finds that Marian is about to give birth to a baby, she disdainfully dismisses her, saying that it would not be reputable to retain her. Aurora meditates that such women are far worse than actual street-walkers— they are most devilish when they put on a cloak of respectability.

For my part,
I'd rather take the wind-side of the stews
Than touch such women with my finger-end!

212

They top the poor street-walker by their lie
And look the better for being so much worse:
The Devil's most devilish when respectable.

Diana's foresters, gentlemen of the shade, minions of the moon

Source: KING HENRY THE FOURTH: PART ONE (Act I, sc. ii, ll. 25-27)
Author: William Shakespeare (1564-1616)
First published: 1598
Type of work: Historical drama

Context: Sir John Falstaff, jolly old reprobate and friend of Prince Hal, heir to the throne, asks the prince the time of day. Hal, in a jovial mood, declares that, since his old companion spends his life only in napping, eating, and drinking, the hours of the day mean nothing to him. Falstaff, confessing that as a highwayman the night is his time, begs the future king's protection for the men of the night:

> FALSTAFF
> Marry then sweet wag, when thou art King let not us that are squires of the night's body be called thieves of the day's beauty; let us be **Diana's foresters, gentlemen of the shade, minions of the moon,** and let men say we be men of good government, being governed as the sea is, by our noble and chaste mistress the moon, under whose countenance we steal.

Die to save charges

Source: ANATOMY OF MELANCHOLY (Partition I, sec. 2, memb. 3, subsec. 12)
Author: Robert Burton (1577-1640)
First published: 1621-1651
Type of work: Essays

Context: Some have called this lengthy volume "a literary cosmos, a compendium of everything that caught the fancy of a fine and lusty scholar who lived in an unspecialized age." Science and pseudo-science, history, theology, philosophy, poetry, and politics mingle in this work by a seventeenth century vicar and mathematician whose humor is sly, broad, or earthy by spells. While by his divisions into Partitions, Sections or Paragraphs, Members, and Subsections, he seems to promise a logical development of thought, his continual digressions into any field that comes to his mind make summarization impossible. Partition I begins with a contrast between Adam in Eden and the present-day man who, because of the forbidden fruit, has suffered a universal malady, a melancholy that affects his religion and his knowledge. Burton's idea of this effect of "the humors" is, of course, long out of date, but the mind as a cause of melancholy, the topic of Member 3, is still current. Its twelfth division, Subsection 12, deals with covetousness or miserliness. Burton pictures men as afraid of everything, since anything might impoverish them. They will not spend, for fear of becoming poor, and would hang themselves to avoid poverty, except that ropes cost money. Some even die because of the high cost of remaining well.

> . . . They are afraid of . . . thieves, lest they rob them; they are afraid of war and afraid of peace, afraid of rich and afraid of poor; afraid of all. Last of all, they are afraid of want, that they shall die beggars, which makes them lay up still, and dare not use what they have; (what if a dear year comes, or dearth, or some loss?) and were it not that they are loth to lay out money on a rope, they would be hanged forthwith, and sometimes **die to save charges,** and make away themselves, if their corn and cattle miscarry, though they have abundance left. . . . Valerius makes mention of one that in a famine sold a mouse for 200 pence, and famished himself; such are their cares, griefs, and perpetual fears. . . .

Digestion is the great secret of life

Source: A MEMOIR OF THE REVEREND SYDNEY SMITH BY HIS DAUGHTER LADY HOLLAND
Author: Sydney Smith (1771-1845)
First published: 1855
Type of work: Biographical memoir

Context: Arthur Kinglake probably sent to his neighbor, the Reverend Sydney Smith, a copy of *A Dissertation on Gout* (1804), by his doctor brother, Robert Kinglake (1765–1842). Its idea of the therapeutic value of foods must have fitted in with the dean's own ideas of the effect of diet, in addition to environment, on the life and acts of men, often expressed in his own writing. At any rate, it occasioned one of the witty minister's many letters, full of references from his abundant learning and theories. Timotheus was the famous Court minstrel of Alexander the Great. The letter was sent from Smith's parish.

> Dear Sir,   Combe Florey, Sept. 30, 1837
>   I am much obliged by the present of your brother's book. I am convinced **digestion is the great secret of life;** and that character, talents, virtues, and qualities are powerfully affected by beef, mutton, pie-crust and rich soups. I have often thought I could feed or starve man into many virtues and vices, and affect them more

214

powerfully with my instruments of cookery than Timotheus could formerly do with his lyre.

Ever yours, very truly   Sydney Smith

Discords make the sweetest airs

Source: HUDIBRAS (Part III, Canto I, l. 919)
Author: Samuel Butler (1612-1680)
First published: First and second parts, 1663; third part, 1678
Type of work: Burlesque poem

Context: The first six cantos of *Hudibras* had been published by 1664. They contained a sarcastic attack upon the enemies of Charles II, ridiculing the Puritans who had beheaded his father. Surely out of gratitude, the Merry Monarch would show the author some sort of favor. Rumor had it that he carried a copy of the poem in his pocket and frequently quoted from it. But the story that Charles settled an annual pension of £100 on the poet must not be true. Butler scribbled in his Common-place Book: "To think how Spenser died, how Crowley mourn'd,/ How Butler's faith and service were return'd." That remark probably explains the lapse of fourteen years between the publication of the Second and Third Parts, and the lack of interest that can be detected in the final section. Two years after it appeared in print, the poet died. If he had had future plans for *Hudibras,* still incomplete, they were never carried out. The poem contains a minimum of action. Actually there are only four episodes: Hudibras' victory over Crowdero; Trulla's victory over Hudibras; Hudibras' victory over Sidrophel, an astrologer; and the Widow's unmasking of Hudibras and his escape through the window. Then the poem drops into religious exposition and attack on the Presbyterians and Independents, whose rivalry had opened the way for the restoration of the throne to Charles II. To parallel the magic scenes in *Don Quixote,* Butler provides one in the first canto of Part III. At the end of the previous canto the angry bickering of the knight and his squire is interrupted by a traveling antique show and violence over a henpecked husband. Hudibras once more tries to attack the sinful crowd until a well-thrown egg discourages him. To discover their future, Ralpho suggests a visit to Sidrophel—under whose name a famous astrologer, William Lilly, is satirized. The episode brings up talk of famous dealers in Black Arts of the past. Hudibras is soon convinced that the conjurer is a fake and sends his servant for a constable while he holds the man and his servant. Afraid that the police will arrest his master for Black Art, Ralpho goes instead to the Widow, confessing his master's trickery. Hudibras, when his prisoners get away, also heads for his lady love. She will not marry him. There are no marriages in Heaven, and she adds: "That's the reason, as some guess,/ There is no heav'n in marriages." But he does not object to quarrels. "The bad in marriages only improves the good."

215

And hearts have been as oft with sullen
As charming looks surpris'd and stolen;
Then why should more bewitching clamor
Some lovers not so much enamour?
For **discords make the sweetest airs,**
And curses are a kind of prayers;
Two slight alloys for all those grand
Felicities by marriage gain'd; . . .

Disease of admiration

Source: WILLIAM PITT, EARL OF CHATHAM
Author: Thomas Babington Macaulay (1800-1859)
First published: January, 1834
Type of work: Biographical essay and book review

Context: Macaulay was well prepared to review an 1827 *History of the Right Honorable William Pitt, Earl of Chatham* by the Reverend Francis Thackeray (1793–1842). Macaulay had long been interested in Parliamentary history and was sympathetic to the spirit of the eighteenth century dominated by Pitt (1708–1778). Like others, he believed Pitt's famous first administration the most glorious in Parliament's history. And so his essay on the Earl of Chatham is one of his best. He drew little upon the two volumes he was supposed to be reviewing. Even in his time, this biography was considered pompous and prolix. Much of his material came from Horace Walpole's *Letters* and his *Memoirs of the Reign of King George the Second.* As a critic, Macaulay speaks, in the very beginning of his essay, of Francis Thackeray's dullness in contrast to his talented nephew, William M. Thackeray (1811–1863), author of *Vanity Fair.* James Boswell (1740–1795) was the admiring biographer of Dr. Samuel Johnson (1709–1784). Macaulay's essay begins:

Almost every mechanical employment, it is said, has a tendency to injure some one or other of the bodily organs of the artisan. Grinders of cuttlery die of consumption; weavers are stunted in their growth; smiths become blear-eyed. In the same manner almost every intellectual employment has a tendency to produce some intellectual malady. Biographers, translators, editors, all, in short, who employ themselves in illustrating the lives or the writings of others, are peculiarly exposed to the *Lues Boswelliana,* or **disease of admiration.** But we scarcely remember ever to have seen a patient so far gone in this distemper as Mr. Thackeray. He is not satisfied with forcing us to confess that Pitt was a great orator, a vigorous minister, an honorable and high-spirited gentleman. He will have it that all virtues and all accomplishments met in his hero. . . .

The Dismal Science

Source: LATTER-DAY PAMPHLETS (*The Present Time*)
Author: Thomas Carlyle (1795-1881)
First published: 1850
Type of work: Political essay

Context: These essays on the political problems of his time exhibit Carlyle at his most vehement. He is alarmed by the wave of upheaval that shook all Europe in 1848 with riot and revolution, and by the unrest in England. To Carlyle, the growing trend toward democracy is an evil that must somehow be met and turned into sanity and order. He excoriates the hereditary aristocracy, which he considers least qualified by nature to govern anything; he believes man must be ruled, but that some other group must rule. As for democracy, he considers it no more than "Constituted Anarchy." America cannot serve as a successful example of democracy in action, he points out: with a small population and half a continent to subdue, it could get along with no government at all. When enough time has passed to reverse these conditions, the boasted freedoms will vanish. Here Carlyle pokes fun at suffrage: one cannot change a law of nature, he observes, by voting otherwise. He then turns to one of the great problems of his time, which has also contributed greatly to the revolutionary movements of Europe: the large masses of unemployed and indigent people. The government is spending vast amounts of money keeping these persons alive; some want employment and cannot secure it, others avoid it. Clearly, they and their country cannot be helped in this fashion. They must be put to work, and must be led. The hereditary leaders have already proven themselves incapable of the task; Carlyle suggests that the newly-developed "Captains of Industry" may be better qualified. He then presents an imaginary speech by a hypothetical Prime Minister to these multitudes, pointing out the labor that must be undertaken if all Britain is to be made productive, and the fact that it is better to pay them for work than to pay them for rotting where they sit. At this point there is an interruption from the political and social scientists—"all manner of Economists, Emancipationists, Constitutionalists," and other practitioners of political and social theory; but the Prime Minister quiets them:

"Respectable Professors of **the Dismal Science,** soft you a little. Alas, I know what you would say. For my sins, I have read much in those inimitable volumes of yours,—really I should think, some barrowfuls of them in my time,—and, in these last forty years of theory and practice, have pretty well seized what of Divine Message you were sent with to me. Perhaps as small a message, give me leave to say, as ever there was such a noise made about before. Trust me, I have not forgotten it, shall never forget it. Those Laws of the Shop-till are indisputable to me; and practically useful in certain departments of the Universe, as the multiplication-table itself. Once I even tried to sail through the Immensities with them, and to front the big coming Eternities with them; but I found it would not do. As the Supreme Rule of Statesmanship, or Government of Men,—since this Universe is not wholly a Shop,—no. You rejoice in my improved tariffs, free-trade movements and the like, on every hand; for which be thankful, and even sing litanies if you choose. But here at last, in the Idle-Workhouse movement, —unexampled yet on Earth or in the waters under the Earth,—I am fairly brought to a stand; and have had to make reflections, of the most alarming, and indeed awful, and as it were religious nature! Professors of **the Dismal Science,** I perceive that the length of your tether is now pretty well run. . . ."

Dispatch is the soul of business

Source: LETTERS TO HIS SON (Letter 104)
Author: Philip Dormer Stanhope, Lord Chesterfield (1694-1773)
First published: 1774
Type of work: Personal letters

Context: In Chesterfield's day it was not possible to become a great statesman or a socially and politically successful person unless one cultivated to perfection the attitudes and graces of the polished gentleman. Chesterfield made every effort to train his son in these attributes; many of his admonitions are simply sound common sense and worth-while advice to anyone. Again, many of them are more applicable to the age in which he lived: great attention to manner, rigid adherence to the many social graces and forms of etiquette, and a carefully calculated and rather cold approach to social relationships. For all the careful training Chesterfield bestowed, Philip never really lived up to his father's expectations. He spent most of his life in Europe, serving the British government; plagued by ill health, he died at thirty-six. Chesterfield corresponded faithfully with him and seldom failed to give him advice. In a letter written February 5, 1750,

he discusses the need to be economical, both of time and money. Quoting the saying, "Take care of the pence, and the pounds will take care of themselves," he points out that the same maxim can be equally well applied to time. The minutes we waste, says Chesterfield, do not amount to much; but if we add them up at the end of a year, it is a different story. One should neglect no opportunity to improve one's time; for example, rather than squandering an idle hour in a coffee-house, it is better to read a good book—not, he hastens to add, "frivolous and idle books, such as the absurd romances . . . where characters, that never existed, are insipidly displayed, and sentiments that were never felt, pompously described." Rather, one should stick to the best established books in any language. Chesterfield then touches on the evils of procrastination and the value of budgeting one's time:

218

Many people lose a great deal of their time by laziness; they loll and yawn in a great chair, tell themselves that they have not time to begin anything then, and that it will do as well another time. This is a most unfortunate disposition, and the greatest obstruction to both knowledge and business. At your age, you have no right nor claim to laziness; I have, if I please, being *emeritus*. You are but just listed in the world, and must be active, diligent, indefatigable. If ever you propose commanding with dignity, you must serve up to it with diligence. Never put off till tomorrow what you can do today.

Dispatch is the soul of business; and nothing contributes more to dispatch than method. Lay down a method for everything, and stick to it inviolably, as far as unexpected incidents may allow. Fix one certain hour and day in the week for your accounts, and keep them together in their proper order; by which means they will require very little time, and you can never be much cheated. Whatever letters and papers you keep, docket and tie them up in their respective classes, so that you may instantly have recourse to any one. Lay down a method also for your reading. . . .

The divine discontent

Source: HEALTH AND EDUCATION ("The Science of Health")
Author: Charles Kingsley (1819-1875)
First published: 1874
Type of work: Essay

Context: The Reverend Charles Kingsley was a high-minded man whose novels and essays were vehicles for his idealism. In them he tried to work for various kinds of social reform, and he gained a large following. He expressed, among other ideas, his admiration for strength, courage, and good health; and he did so with such effectiveness that these qualities began to be cultivated. An ideal grew up in Victorian England which some persons have since referred to as "muscular Christianity;" its principle was that the youth of England should have the bodies of vikings, with the souls of saints. One of Kingsley's efforts in this direction is his volume of essays, *Health and Education*. In the first essay he observes that the Brit-ish people appear to be less stalwart than they formerly were; and he points out that the reason is that the high mortality rate of earlier times weeded out all but those best equipped to survive. Now that the industrial age is here and advances in human survival have been made, the population is increasing and much of it is less rugged physically. Kingsley adds that instead of longing for a heroic past that was not really so desirable, we must accept the new age and seek to make it better. One factor that has lessened the number of robust Englishmen is the warfare of recent centuries. "War is, without doubt, the most hideous physical curse which fallen man inflicts upon himself; and for this simple reason,

219

that it reverses the very laws of nature, and is more cruel even than pestilence. For instead of issuing in the survival of the fittest, it issues in the survival of the less fit; and therefore, if protracted, must deteriorate generations yet unborn." He then describes the living and working conditions of the poor, noting that these cannot produce healthy children unless they are improved. Intelligence cannot grow properly in an unhealthy body. He then answers those who would rather ignore the problem, or who fear the poor may be made discontented:

> . . . But are not people discontented already, from the lowest to the highest? And ought a man, in such a piecemeal, foolish, greedy, sinful world as this is, and always has been, to be anything but discontented? If he thinks that things are going all right, must he not have a most beggarly conception of what going right means? And if things are not going right, can it be anything but good for him to see that they are not going right? Can truth and fact harm any human being? I shall not believe so, as long as I have a Bible wherein to believe. For my part, I should like to make every man, woman, and child whom I meet discontented with themselves, even as I am discontented with myself. I should like to awaken in them, about their physical, their intellectual, their moral condition, that divine discontent which is the parent, first of upward aspiration and then of self-control, thought, effort to fulfil that aspiration even in part. For to be discontented with **the divine discontent,** and to be ashamed with the noble shame, is the very germ and first upgrowth of all virtue. Men begin at first, as boys begin when they grumble at their school and their schoolmasters, to lay the blame on others; to be discontented with their circumstances. . . . But that way no deliverance lies. That discontent only ends in revolt and rebellion, social or political; and that, again, still in the same worship of circumstances—but this time desperate—which ends, let it disguise itself under what fine names it will, in what the old Greeks called a tyranny; in which . . . all have become the voluntary slaves of one man, because each man fancies that the one man can improve his circumstances for him.

Divine tobacco

Source: THE FAERIE QUEENE (Book, III, Canto 5, stanza 32)
Author: Edmund Spenser (c.1552-1599)
First published: 1590
Type of work: Allegorical poem

Context: The bold and virtuous squire, Timias, pursues a wicked foster, or forester, who had attempted an assault upon the person of the beautiful damsel, Florimell. The foster, knowing the woods, escapes from the pursuit and makes his way to his two brothers, who are as wicked and de-

220

praved as he; the three band together to go to meet Timias, with whom they do battle. He finally slays all three of them, but not before he is severely wounded in the thigh by an arrow. The wound and the resultant loss of blood cause him to fall in a faint, almost dead, upon the ground. In the meanwhile the beautiful Belphoebe is ranging the forest in search of a wild beast that she has wounded in the chase. Instead of finding her prey, she comes upon the unconscious Timias, who lies weltering in his blood. Tenderly she removes his armor, and at the sight of his face she falls completely in love with him. She tries for a while unsuccessfully to revive him to consciousness, and then decides that medicines are called for:

Into the woods thenceforth in hast she went,
To seeke for hearbes, that mote him remedy;
For she of hearbes had great intendiment,
Taught of the Nymphe, which from her infancy
Her nourced had in trew Nobility;
There, whether it **diuine Tobacco** were,
Or *Panachaea*, or *Polygony*,
She found, and brought it to her patient deare
Who al this while lay bleeding out his hartbloud neare.

Divinely tall, and most divinely fair

Source: A DREAM OF FAIR WOMEN (Lines 87-88)
Author: Alfred, Lord Tennyson (1809-1892)
First published: 1833
Type of work: Narrative poem

Context: A Dream of Fair Women, in its imagery, shows a certain affinity with Keats. In it the poet tells us he has been reading Chaucer's *Legend of Good Women;* "for a while, the knowledge of his art/ Held me above the subject, as strong gales/ Hold swollen clouds from raining, tho' my heart,/ Brimful of those wild tales,/ Charged both mine eyes with tears. In every land/ I saw, wherever light illumineth,/ Beauty and anguish walking hand in hand/ The downward slope to death." Through his mind there passes a phantasmagoria of scenes occurring throughout the ages in which women have suffered and men have fought over them and for them. There are glimpses of duels and wars, insults, pillage, ruined shrines, dungeons and seraglios. Then the poet falls asleep and finds himself in an ancient forest, where he presently meets a group of beautiful women. These are the famed beauties of legend and history; he sees, among others, Helen of Troy, Cleopatra, and Joan of Arc. Some tell him their stories. The poet is dazzled by these creatures, for some of whom whole armies died; he finds that at least a few wish they had not been born beautiful and that they had not altered the course of empire or of history. Their punishment seems to be that they are forever set aside from

221

men; as Cleopatra expresses it, "I govern'd men by change, and so I sway'd/ All moods . . ./ I have no men to govern in this wood:/ That makes my only woe." The poet, waking, finds himself plunged in melancholy. "With what dull pain/ Com-pass'd, how eagerly I sought to strike/ Into that wondrous track of dreams again!/ But no two dreams are like." The passage in which the poet finds himself in the forest is remarkable for its evocation of stillness and heavy foliage:

> At last methought that I had wander'd far
> In an old wood: fresh-washed in coolest dew,
> The maiden splendours of the morning star
> Shook in the steadfast blue.
>
> Enormous elm-tree-boles did stoop and lean
> Upon the dusky brushwood underneath
> Their broad curved branches, fledged with clearest green,
> New from its silken sheath.
> . . .
> I knew the flowers, I knew the leaves, I knew
> The tearful glimmer of the languid dawn
> On those long, rank, dark wood-walks drench'd in dew,
> Leading from lawn to lawn.
> . . .
> The smell of violets, hidden in the green,
> Pour'd back into my empty soul and frame
> The times when I remember to have been
> Joyful and free from blame.
> . . .
> At length I saw a lady within call,
> Stiller than chisell'd marble, standing there;
> A daughter of the gods, **divinely tall,**
> **And most divinely fair.**

Do as you would be done by

Source: LETTERS TO HIS SON (Letter 17)
Author: Philip Dormer Stanhope, Lord Chesterfield (1694-1773)
First published: 1774
Type of work: Personal letters

Context: In Lord Chesterfield's letters to his illegitimate son there is a constant emphasizing of the rules by which a young man rises in the world. Due attention is directed to intelligence and ability, but the most important quality a young man can have, according to the earl, is the ability to please. He therefore begins the letter of October 16, 1747, by telling his son to pay constant attention to pleasing; he says that the best way to do so is by observing the Golden Rule. He begins the letter thus:

Dear Boy: The art of pleasing is a very necessary one to possess; but a very difficult one to acquire. It can hardly be reduced to rules; and your own good sense and observation will teach you more of it than I can. **Do as you would be done by,** is the surest method that I know of pleasing. Observe carefully what pleases you in others, and probably the same thing in you will please others. If you are pleased with the complaisance and attention of others to your humors, your tastes, or your weaknesses, depend upon it the same complaisance and attention, on your part to theirs, will equally please them. Take the tone of the company that you are in, and do not pretend to give it; be serious, gay, or even trifling, as you find the present humor of the company; this is an attention due from every individual to the majority. . . .

Do other men, for they would do you

Source: MARTIN CHUZZLEWIT (Chapter 11)
Author: Charles Dickens (1812-1870)
First published: 1843-1844
Type of work: Novel

Context: Jonas Chuzzlewit calls upon the Pecksniff sisters, in residence at Todgers', a London boarding house catering to commercial gentlemen, to conduct them to his home for dinner. He walks them until they are thoroughly fatigued and finally brings them to the house occupied by his father, Anthony, and himself. The residence is part of a moldy old office building; the living quarters are strewn with odds and ends of old fabrics and other bits of discarded merchandise; the combination of living room and dining room is filled with office equipment. During the dinner an old retainer, Chuffey, whose wits have been addled, is the target of insulting remarks by Jonas. Even Anthony is not spared, but he seems to enjoy the bitter remarks, as they show that his son is a sharp fellow. In alluding to Mr. Pecksniff, Anthony says that his hypocrisy can be overdone. Jonas replies that a thing not easily overdone is a bargain; one should always try to outdo others:

"There's another thing that's not easily overdone, father," remarked Jonas, after a short silence.

"What's that?" asked the father, grinning already in anticipation.

"A bargain," said the son. "Here's the rule for bargains—'**Do other men, for they would do you.**' That's the true business precept. All others are counterfeits."

The delighted father applauded this sentiment to the echo, and was so much tickled by it, that he was at the pains of imparting the same to his ancient clerk, who rubbed his hands, nodded his palsied head, winked his watery eyes, and cried in his whistling tones, "Good! good! Your own son, Mr. Chuzzlewit!" with every feeble demonstration of delight that he was capable of making. But this old man's enthusiasm had the redeeming quality of being felt in sympathy with the only creature to whom he was linked by ties of long association, and by his present helplessness. . . .

Dog in the manger

Source: FIVE HUNDRED POINTS OF GOOD HUSBANDRY (Chapter 29, "Against Fantastical Scrupleness")
Author: Thomas Tusser (c.1525-1580)
First published: 1557
Type of work: Didactic poem

Context: The expression "dog in the manger" refers of course to Aesop's fable of the dog who, although he had no use for straw, would not allow the ox to have any. Throughout the ages since Aesop this term has been used to describe our common human reluctance to share things we cannot or will not put to use ourselves. Tusser probably did more than any other person to make this expression a popular household saying. His book, *Five Hundred Points of Good Husbandry,* enjoyed a wide and lasting popularity and served to perpetuate many of the proverbs and old sayings contained in it. An early version of the farmer's almanacs, it is made up of verses which give all manner of practical instruction to the farmer. These rhymes also incorporate moral advice, maxims, and observations upon the climate, the planets, and weather. Each month is taken up in its turn, beginning with September, and the work proper to it described at some length. The book thus provides us with an excellent insight into early Elizabethan rural life and farming methods. Tusser was a gentleman of good birth and education who retired to a farm; he obviously had a wide knowledge of husbandry but was unable to make a success of it. After several moves in an effort to improve his condition he at length died in a debtor's prison. In Chapter 29, entitled "Against Fantastical Scrupleness," he encourages hospitality. This chapter is appended to the material for December and refers to the Christmas season. Tusser does not feel that Christmas is a time to be stingy or in any way lacking in generosity. It is easy to see, too, that he prefers a merry soul to a grave one: he is deeply suspicious of the stern and disapproving nature.

At this time and that time, some make a great matter;
Some help not, but hinder the poor with their clatter.
Take custom from feasting, what cometh then last?
Where one hath a dinner, a hundred shall fast.

To **dog in the manger,** some liken I could,
That hay will eat none, nor let other that would.
Some scarce, in a year, give a dinner or two,
Nor well can abide any other to do.

Play thou the good fellow! seek none to misdeem;
Disdain not the honest, though merry they seem;
For oftentimes seen, no more very a knave,
Than he that doth counterfeit most to be grave.

Done those things which we ought not to have done

Source: THE BOOK OF COMMON PRAYER (Page 6)
Author: Traditional; translated and arranged by Archbishop Cranmer (1489–1560)
First published: 1549
Type of work: Prayer of confession

Context: The Order for Daily Morning Prayer is the first service in the Book of Common Prayer and is a direct descendent of a system of worship in practise during the Middle Ages known as the Canonical Hours, which in turn were developed out of Apostolic times from customs of daily instruction, praise, and prayer in use in the early Church. Morning Prayer, evolved principally from the longest of the Canonical Hours, the service of *Matins*, begins in a penitential mood. After a series of opening sentences which set the theme and tone of the service, there follows the *Exhortation* in which the congregation is reminded that no converse with God can be fitting or profitable until the worshiper, in all honesty, lays bare his disobediences to God's Holy Will, and, in all sincerity, seeks reconciliation with His Love. The minister urges the people to accompany him, with pure hearts and humble voices to the very "throne of the heavenly grace" and join with him in a confession of their sins. There follows then the *General Confession,* called "general" because it is said by the minister and all the people and is a confession not only of individual shortcomings but of the corporate guilt of the whole community of worshipers, who have "strayed . . . like lost sheep" from God's holy ways.

Almighty and most merciful Father; We have erred, and strayed from thy ways like lost sheep. We have followed too much the devices and desires of our own hearts. We have offended against thy holy laws. We have left undone those things which we ought to have done; And we have **done those things which we ought not to have done;** And there is no health in us. But thou, O Lord, have mercy upon us, miserable offenders. Spare thou those, O God, who confess their faults. Restore thou those who are penitent; According to thy promises declared unto mankind In Christ Jesus our Lord. And grant, O most merciful Father, for his sake; That we may hereafter live a godly, righteous, and sober life, To the glory of thy holy Name. Amen.

The Dorian pipe, the Dorian strain

Source: THYRSIS (Line 97)
Author: Matthew Arnold (1822-1888)
First published: 1866
Type of work: Elegy

Context: "Thyrsis" was written to commemorate Arnold's close friend Arthur Hugh Clough. The poem is composed in the traditional pastoral form for elegies; shepherds are brought into it, and references to the Doric past are prominent. Arnold brings in the "Dorian" or "Sicilian" by first reminding the reader that ". . . when Sicilian shepherds lost a mate,/ Some good survivor with his flute would go," and of course lament his friend with lyric music. This lovely music would be played directly to Proserpine, daughter of the goddess of vegetation and growth and queen of the world of the dead, who had often "trod Sicilian fields." The goddess cherished the beauty of the countryside and thus also "She loved the Dorian pipe, the Dorian strain."

> O easy access to the hearer's grace
> When Dorian shepherds sang to Proserpine!
> For she herself had trod Sicilian fields,
> She knew the Dorian water's gush divine,
> She knew each lily white which Enna yields,
> Each rose with blushing face;
> She loved **the Dorian pipe, the Dorian strain.**

A double glass o' the inwariable

Source: THE PICKWICK PAPERS (Chapter 33)
Author: Charles Dickens (1812-1870)
First published: 1836-1837
Type of work: Novel

Context: Mr. Pickwick, president of the Pickwick Club, and several companions have agreed to travel to various areas of England, such as Bath and Rochester, and to report of their adventures and travels to the other club members. In the meantime, Mr. Pickwick has an unsolicited adventure: when he rented his present quarters, Mrs. Bardell, his landlady, misunderstood him and concluded that he intended to marry her, and now is suing him for breach of promise. Old Mr. Weller, father of Sam Weller, servant of Mr. Pickwick, meets his son at the Blue Boar to pass along some advice for Mr. Pickwick as he faces trial. As he enters, Mr. Weller is disturbed to find Sam composing a Valentine, this being the thirteenth of February, but, reassured that Sam has no intentions of matrimony, he says in his cockney accent to the waitress:

. . . **"A double glass o' the inwariable,** my dear."

"Very well, Sir," replied the girl; who with great quickness appeared, vanished, returned, and disappeared.

"They seem to know your ways here," observed Sam.

"Yes," replied his father, "I've been here before in my time. . . ."

Doubt is Devil-born

Source: IN MEMORIAM (Part XCVI, stanza 1)
Author: Alfred, Lord Tennyson (1809-1892)
First published: 1850
Type of work: Elegy

Context: This elegy was written as a monument to Arthur Henry Hallam, a young man of extraordinary promise and an intimate friend of Tennyson's, who died suddenly in Vienna at the age of twenty-two. The poem records Tennyson's slow spiritual progress from his initial depth of personal sorrow to the gradual healing of grief through a sense of spiritual contact with Hallam in a wider love of God and humanity. Preceding section XCVI, Tennyson describes having fleetingly achieved the reunion in spirit with his friend which he had so earnestly desired. This union in section XCV is one of the climaxes of the elegy. After this mystical experience, Tennyson comes out of his trance and begins to doubt the validity of his experience. In spite of his intellectual doubts, he affirms the certainty of intuitive powers. At the close, he sees darkness and light no longer as two opposing powers but united in a single image of dawn, symbolic of a new faith. Section XCVI is an occasional poem designed to illustrate the change within the poet's mind and soul caused by his experience. Tennyson affirms the value of honest doubting in the search for a stronger faith:

> You say, but with no touch of scorn
> Sweet-hearted, you, whose light-blue eyes
> Are tender over drowning flies,
> You tell me, **doubt is Devil-born.**
>
> I know not: one indeed I knew
> . . .
> Perplext in faith but pure in deeds,
> At last he beat his music out.
> There lives more faith in honest doubt,
> Believe me, than in half the creeds.

227

Doubtless God could have made a better berry,
but doubtless God never did

Source: THE COMPLEAT ANGLER (Part I, chapter 5)
Author: Izaak Walton (1593–1683)
First published: 1653
Type of work: Dialogue on fishing

Context: From the third century A.D. Roman rhetorician Claudius Aelianus who first mentioned fly fishing, and Dame Juliana Barnes who first treated the subject in English in her fifteenth century *Treatyse of Fysshynge wyth an Angle* to the present, thousands of fishermen have written of their craft, but few have produced a more enjoyable book than Izaak Walton's *The Compleat Angler.* The first edition appeared in 1653 in a small octavo volume that could be tucked into a fisherman's bulging pocket. It sold for eighteen pence. Previous to that, Walton had written biographies of the Reverend John Donne and Sir Henry Wotton, his friends. "I write not for money but for pleasure," Walton declared. He did not need money, for he had retired after a career in London as ironmonger or hardware merchant. He found in his birthplace of Stafford a refuge from the turmoil of civil war with Royalists and Parliamentarians killing each other. Now aloof from politics, a representative of the seventeenth century search for relief from the world's woes in Nature and the works of God, Walton became a champion for the Christian virtues of friendship and goodness, and for the country joys as opposed to the money-grubbing life of the city. At his age of sixty, when the book appeared, he confessed he was a gentle man wielding "a mild pen, not used to upbraid the world." He wove into its pages anecdotes, poetry, descriptions of nature, and an uncritical choice of quotations from even Pliny with his unnatural *Natural History.* The result may not be a completely trustworthy guide to fishing practices; indeed its author declared that it is hard "to make a man that was none to be an Angler by a book." But the book provides delightful reading for even non-fishermen. The first edition contained thirteen chapters that were later increased to twenty-one, and in the fifth edition of 1676, the last printed during his lifetime, a second part on fly-making and casting was added by his poet friend Charles Cotton (1630–1687). Walton himself preferred "bottom fishing" with worms, grasshoppers, or frogs, using a fifteen-foot pole, a "trembling quill," and a hook tied on by hair leaders. Not until Samuel Pepys (1633–1703) was there mention of the use of gut leaders. Chapter V of *The Compleat Angler* contains a conversation between Piscator (The Fisherman, representing W a l t o n) and Venator (Hunter), who in the first edition, was the scholarly wayfarer, Viator. On their walk in the early dawn to a fishing spot along the river Piscator discourses on the relative merits for trout fishing of flies, worms, caterpillars, and real and artificial minnows; but as he proves by catching fish when his companion is unsuccessful, it is the skill of the fisherman and not the lure that fills the basket. As they walk and later fry their fish under a tree, they discuss Nature. Piscator recites several poems. He also quotes, in modern spelling, from "Dr. Bote-ler," Doctor William Butler (1535–1618), the Cambridge-trained court physician of King James I, among whose writings was an article on foods and diets.

> . . . No life, my honest Scholar, no life so happy and so pleasant as the life of a well governed Angler; for when the Lawyer is swallowed up with business, and the Statesman is preventing or contriving plots, then we sit on Cowslip-banks, hear the birds sing, and possesse ourselves in as much quietnesse as these Silent silver streams, which we now see glide so quietly by us. Indeed my good Scholar, we may say of Angling, as Dr. Boteler said of Strawberries; **Doubtlesse God could have made a better berry, but doubtlesse God never did:** And so (if I might be Judge) God never did make a more calm, quiet, innocent recreation than Angling.

Down in the mouth

Source: THE OLD BACHELOR (Act IV, sc. iv)
Author: William Congreve (1670-1729)
First published: 1693
Type of work: Dramatic comedy

Context: Araminta and Belinda meet at St. James Park, a favorite gathering place for people of fashion in the seventeenth and eighteenth centuries. Araminta, in love with Vainlove, hopes to meet him on the Mall nearby. She and her beloved have had a disagreement, and she hopes to be able to settle their differences. As they walk along, the two women put on their masks, as women in public often did at the time. As they stroll through the park they are seen by Sir Joseph Wittol, a stupid and cowardly knight, and his favorite companion, Captain Bluffe, a cowardly soldier who pretends to be a bully. Having drunk a bit, the two men approach Araminta and Belinda, hoping to be attractive to them. The two women know the men for what they are and repulse their advances. The reaction of the women causes Captain Bluffe to make his comment.

BLUFFE
Ladies, by these hilts you are well met.

ARAMINTA
We are afraid not.

BLUFFE [*to Belinda.*]
What says my pretty little knapsack carrier?

229

BELINDA

O monstrous filthy fellow! Good slovenly Captain Huffe, Bluffe, (what is your hideous name?) be gone: you stink of brandy and tobacco, most soldier-like. Foh! [*Spits.*]

BLUFFE [*aside.*]

Now I am slap dash **down in the mouth,** and have not one word to say!

Down on flummery

Source: SKETCHES NEW AND OLD ("The Undertaker's Chat")
Author: Mark Twain (1835-1910)
First published: 1875
Type of work: Humorous anecdote

Context: Samuel Langhorne Clemens, more familiarly known to readers as Mark Twain, had many gifts; one of the greatest was his ability to depict character and human feeling through the words of people he created. Another was his mastery of dialect. Combining these with his insight into human nature, he filled his tales with persons who are natural and entirely believable; they seem alive, and we feel that we not only know them, but know them well. All are individuals. Much of Twain's humor derives from the same aspects of his deep understanding: his characters express emotions which are universal, but do so in picturesque and at times outlandish terms. We understand the character, like him, and sympathize with him; at the same time, the humor of the scene is inescapable. Tragedy is sometimes masked with laughter to make it bearable. A brief sketch, "The Undertaker's Chat," provides, a good example. The old undertaker is engaged in readying the body of a friend for burial. He has known and admired this man for many years, and in his conversation reveals deep affection for him. We learn that the dead man was a humble person who deplored ostentation and that he was loved by all. His relatives all wanted to buy him a ruinously expensive coffin, but he refused; he also declined a silver nameplate, observing that "he judged that wher' he was going to a body would find it considerable better to attract attention by a picturesque moral character than a natty burial case with a swell doorplate on it." In his eulogy the undertaker endeavors to camouflage his grief with far-fetched expressions and thereby renders it even more obvious; his apparent irreverence is strangely touching:

"Splendid man, he was. I'd druther do for a corpse like that 'n any I've tackled in seven year. There's some satisfaction in buryin' a man like that. You feel that what you're doing is appreciated. . . .

"Well, the relations they wanted a big funeral, but corpse said he was **down on flummery**—didn't want any procession—fill the hearse full of mourners, and get out a stern line and tow *him* behind. He *was* the most down on style of any remains I ever struck. A beautiful simple-minded creature—it was what he was, you can depend on that. He was just set on having things the way he wanted them, and he took a solid comfort in laying his little plans. He had me measure him and take a whole raft of directions; then he had the minister stand up behind a long box with a table-cloth over it, to represent the coffin, and read his funeral sermon, saying 'Angcore, angcore!' at the good places, and making him scratch out every bit of brag about him, and all the hifalutin; and then he made them trot out the choir so's he could help them pick out the tunes for the occasion, and he got them to sing 'Pop Goes the Weasel,' because he'd always liked that tune when he was down-hearted, and solemn music made him sad; and when they sung that with tears in their eyes (because they all loved him), and his relations grieving around, he just laid there as happy as a bug, and trying to beat time and showing all over how much he enjoyed it; and presently he got worked up and excited, and tried to join in, for, mind you, he was pretty proud of his abilities in the singing line; but the first time he opened his mouth and was just going to spread himself his breath took a walk."

A dream itself is but a shadow

Source: HAMLET (Act II, sc. ii, l. 266)
Author: William Shakespeare (1564-1616)
First published: 1603
Type of work: Dramatic tragedy

Context: As Hamlet probes further the story told him by his father's ghost—that his father was murdered by his Uncle Claudius, the present king, and that his mother had committed adultery with Claudius—the young prince feigns madness and is himself probed by others eager to discover the cause of his madness. The king and queen send for two of Hamlet's youthful companions, Rosencrantz and Guildenstern, who agree to scout the melancholy Dane. The quick-witted Hamlet spars with his old friends—who wonder whether ambition may be at the root of his trouble, that is, disappointment at not being made king after his father's death—and manages to keep them interested while avoiding any definite commitment. Hamlet calls Denmark a prison; Rosencrantz and Guildenstern protest:

HAMLET

Why then 'tis none to you; for there is nothing either good or bad but thinking makes it so. To me it is a prison.

231

Why then your ambition makes it one; 'tis too narrow for your mind.

HAMLET
O God, I could be bounded in a nutshell, and count myself a king of infinite space, were it not that I have bad dreams.

GUILDENSTERN
Which dreams indeed are ambition, for the very substance of the ambitious is merely the shadow of a dream.

HAMLET
A dream itself is but a shadow.

Dream of London, small, and white, and clean

Source: THE EARTHLY PARADISE ("Prologue: The Wanderers," Line 5)
Author: William Morris (1834-1896)
First published: 1868-1870
Type of work: Narrative poem

Context: English painter, poet, and prose writer, Morris was associated with the Pre-Raphaelite aesthetic movement of the late nineteenth century, an attempt to revive greater freedom of expression for artist and writer alike. This demand for individuality he carried to the production of household furniture, tapestry, and carpet through the foundation of Morris, Marshall, Faulkner, and Company. Later he headed a similar movement in founding the Kelmscott Press to meet the need for quality printing and illustration. As a poet, Morris was primarily interested in the Nordic and Grecian legends, and, in *The Earthly Paradise,* he recounts the tales of a group of Norwegian pilgrims who set sail to find the legendary "earthly paradise" of which they have heard so much. After many years they arrive at a "Western land" where, highly honored by the natives, they pass their remaining years. In establishing his scene at the outset, the author recalls a land unbesmirched by the industrial trade of Victorian England, a land reminiscent of what he imagines Chaucer's England to have been:

Forget six counties overhung with smoke,
Forget the snorting steam and piston stroke,
Forget the spreading of the hideous town;
Think rather of the pack-horse on the down,
And **dream of London, small, and white, and clean,**
The clear Thames bordered by its gardens green;
Think, that below bridge the green lapping waves
Smite some few keels that bear Levantine staves,

232

Cut from the yew-wood on the burnt-up hill,
And pointed jars that Greek hands toiled to fill,
And treasured scanty spice from some far sea. . . .

A nameless city in a distant sea,
White as the changing walls of faerie,
Thronged with much people clad in ancient guise
I now am fain to set before your eyes; . . .

Drink down all unkindness

Source: THE MERRY WIVES OF WINDSOR (Act I, sc. i, l. 203)
Author: William Shakespeare (1564-1616)
First published: 1602
Type of work: Dramatic comedy

Context: Early in the first act of *The Merry Wives of Windsor,* the reader learns that several injustices have been committed against Robert Shallow, Esquire, by Sir John Falstaff and his followers. Master Page, Sir John, and his followers soon enter the scene, and Shallow confronts Falstaff hotly with his list of grievances, which Falstaff acknowledges. When Slender, cousin of Shallow, begins enumerating more in detail what happened to him during his drinking with Falstaff and his men, Sir John calls on his associates to answer the accusations. The words become more heated as Bardolph, Pistol, and Nym deny Slender's charges. The ladies enter the scene, appropriately causing the heated discussion to cease momentarily. Page then urges his wife and the other ladies to invite all the gentlemen inside their house for drink and dinner. He says he hopes that drink will soothe the atmosphere of hostility among them.

PAGE

Wife, bid these gentlemen welcome. Come, we have a hot venison pasty to dinner. Come, gentlemen, I hope we shall **drink down all unkindness.**

Drink fair, whatever you do!

Source: MARTIN CHUZZLEWIT (Chapter 49)
Author: Charles Dickens (1812-1870)
First published: 1843-1844
Type of work: Novel

Context: Dickens was often the conscience of Victorian England, and the theme of *Martin Chuzzlewit* is hypocrisy and selfishness, as exemplified by the various characters; the character of Mrs. Gamp, Sairey she calls her-

233

self, is no exception; nor is her erstwhile partner in sickroom care (one cannot call it nursing), Betsey Prig, an exception. On one occasion Mrs. Gamp invites Betsey Prig to tea, hoping to persuade Mrs. Prig to work with her in caring for Mr. Chuffey, a weak-minded man who will require someone's attention twenty-four hours of the day. Since Betsey Prig is difficult to deal with, and does not really like Mrs. Gamp, the latter is careful in her preparations. The little apartment is made neat as it can be, two whole pounds of highly pickled salmon are purchased, and the tea things are laid out carefully. The teapot contains spirits, rather than tea, and the two irascible women make frequent application to its contents. Betsey Prig is not much interested in Mrs. Gamp's proposal and reaches frequently for the tea-pot, too frequently to please her hostess. Mrs. Gamp is finally moved to remonstrate with her guest for taking more than her share:

> Here Mrs. Prig, without any abatement of her offensive manner, again counterfeited abstraction of mind, and stretched out her hand to the tea-pot. It was more than Mrs. Gamp could bear. She stopped the hand of Mrs. Prig with her own, and said, with great feeling:
> "No, Betsey! **Drink fair, whatever you do!**"
> Mrs. Prig, thus baffled, threw herself back in her chair, and closing the same eye more emphatically, and folding her arms tighter, suffered her head to roll slowly from side to side, while she surveyed her friend with a contemptuous smile.

A drop of a bucket

Source: ISAIAH 40:15
Author: Isaiah
First transcribed: c.800-200 B.C.
Type of work: Religious prophecy and exhortation

Context: The fortieth chapter of Isaiah is justly considered one of the finest passages in Scripture. Isaiah was both an inspired prophet and a great poet; this chapter is a song of joy resulting from a vision in which he has glimpsed the deliverance of his people. Rejoicing in the greatness of God, he tells his audience that their long suffering is destined to end; and the picture he paints is one of spiritual triumph. Many of these verses were set to music by Handel and incorporated into *Messiah;* the result is a remarkable fusion of genius, in which sublime poetry is enhanced by music of great power and majesty. Chapter 40 forms a prelude to Isaiah's later prophecies, particularly those in chapters 42, 49, 50, 52, and 53, which foretell the coming of the Messiah; Isaiah refers to this figure as the Servant. The early fathers of the Christian Church felt certain, reading these lines, that Isaiah had prophesied the coming of Christ. Later scholars puz-

234

zled over the poet's words and considered a number of Jewish leaders, contemporary with Isaiah, who might have fitted the role of deliverer. Later opinion has concluded, however, that a Messiah was precisely what Isaiah had in mind. He begins by saying that the Lord has at last pardoned Israel and that all things shall be made right, and that all men shall see the glory of the Lord. All flesh comes from grass, and men wither away as the grass does, but the word of God endures forever. Men will behold God on earth; and he will rule them, caring for his flock as a shepherd does. Isaiah then emphasizes the greatness of the Lord, beside which the works of man are nothing.

O Zion, that bringest good tidings, get thee up into the high mountain; O Jerusalem, that bringest good tidings, lift up thy voice with strength; lift it up, be not afraid; say unto the cities of Judah, Behold your God!

Behold, the Lord GOD will come with strong hand, and his arm shall rule for him: behold, his reward is with him, and his work before him.

He shall feed his flock like a shepherd: he shall gather the lambs with his arm, and carry them in his bosom, and shall gently lead those that are with young.

Who hath measured the waters in the hollow of his hand, and meted out heaven with the span, and comprehended the dust of the earth in a measure, and weighed the mountains in scales, and the hills in a balance?

Who hath directed the Spirit of the LORD, or being his counselor hath taught him?

With whom took he counsel, and who instructed him, and taught him in the path of judgment, and taught him knowledge, and shewed to him the way of understanding?

Behold, the nations are as **a drop of a bucket,** and are counted as the small dust of the balance: behold, he taketh up the isles as a very little thing.

And Lebanon is not sufficient to burn, nor the beasts thereof sufficient for a burnt offering.

The dust of creeds outworn

Source: PROMETHEUS UNBOUND (Act I, l. 697)
Author: Percy Bysshe Shelley (1792-1822)
First published: 1820
Type of work: Lyric drama

Context: The Titan Prometheus, chained to a precipice in the Indian Caucasus, is tortured by the evil Jupiter because he refused to tell who will overthrow the tyranny of heaven; however, he has suffered so long that he has lost his bitterness and no longer hates his tormenter. Panthea and Ione are seated at his feet when the Phantasm of Jupiter reminds the

235

Titan of his awful curse, and they hear Prometheus repent of his rash anger, but when Mercury comes with the Furies and offers him a life of ignoble ease if he will reveal his dread secret, he refuses to coöperate with evil. As a result, the Furies unleash their worst, but Prometheus, who has learned the secret of suffering love, is able to withstand them until they show him a vision of "a youth/ With patient looks nailed to a crucifix." Such a vision tortures him more than any physical pain could, and as he writhes in agony, Earth calls up the spirits of human thought to comfort him. The quotation is from the First Spirit's song:

> On a battle-trumpet's blast
> I fled hither, fast, fast, fast,
> 'Mid the darkness upward cast.
> From **the dust of creeds outworn,**
> From the tyrant's banner torn,
> Gathering 'round me, onward borne,
> There was mingled many a cry—
> Freedom! Hope! Death! Victory!
> Till they faded through the sky;
> And one sound, above, around,
> One sound beneath, around, above,
> Was moving; 'twas the soul of Love, . . .

Dwindle into a wife

Source: THE WAY OF THE WORLD (Act IV, sc. i)
Author: William Congreve (1670-1729)
First published: 1700
Type of work: Dramatic comedy

Context: Millamant, a beautiful and witty young heiress, falls in love with Mirabell, a gentleman of fashion, who loves her equally. In talking about marriage, Millamant reveals what she expects in matrimony, and as she does, satirizes the views of marriage held by many courtiers at the time. She tells her lover that she could only hate a man who became too assured of her, and that she wants to be assured herself of both her will and pleasure in marriage. She says, too, that she does not want to be called by pet names, as she thinks they are hypocritical. Nor does she want to be openly affectionate or familiar; as she says, "Let us be as strange as if we had been married a great while; and as well bred as if we were not married at all." Mirabell then asks her if she has any other conditions to offer, observing that her demands up to this point seem reasonable. Millamant says more:

MILLAMANT
Trifles—as liberty to pay and receive visits to and from whom

236

I please; to write and receive letters, without interrogatories or wry faces on your part. To wear what I please; and choose conversation with regard only to my own taste; to have no obligation upon me to converse with wits that I don't like, because they are your acquaintance; or to be intimate with fools, because they may be your relations. Come to dinner when I please, dine in my dressing-room when I'm out of humour, without giving a reason. To have my closet inviolate; to be sole empress of my tea-table, which you must never approach without first asking leave. And lastly, wherever I am, you shall always knock at the door before you come in. These articles subscribed, if I continue to endure you a little longer, I may by degrees **dwindle into a wife.**

Each age is a dream that is dying

Source: ODE (Last stanza)
Author: Arthur William Edgar O'Shaughnessy (1844-1881)
First published: 1874
Type of work: Lyric poem

Context: Arthur William Edgar O'Shaughnessy was himself a man who dreamed a dream; although he was vitally interested in literature and wanted a career as a poet and scholar, he spent his adult life in the natural history department of the British Museum, earning a living by the preserving of fish. Yet from that unpoetic work he emerged as a poet, albeit a minor one, of the Victorian era. Dead at the age of thirty-seven, he did not live long enough to come to grips with great themes in poetry, but he did prove in his short career as a poet that he had a real lyric talent; the *Ode* testifies to that talent. In the poem he tells the reader that he sees history as belonging to men who dream dreams and make music; these men, he says, "are the movers and shakers/ Of the world forever, it seems." One man, he writes, with a dream can conquer a crown; three others with a song can "trample a kingdom down." And he writes in the third and last stanza:

We, in the ages lying
    In the buried past of the earth,
Built Nineveh with one sighing,
    And Babel itself with our mirth;
And o'erthrew them with prophesying
    To the old of the new world's worth;
For **each age is a dream that is dying,**
    Or one that is coming to birth.

237

Each alike was Greek, alike was free

Source: TO VICTOR HUGO (Line 3)
Author: Algernon Charles Swinburne (1837-1909)
First published: 1866
Type of work: Eulogy

Context: Few major English poets have the power to hypnotize the reader into a state wherein he accepts obscenities because they are given intoxicating rhythms, but Swinburne, a master at turning ugliness into beauty, has just that ability and uses it to create some of the most unforgettable poems in British literature. Perhaps one reason why he was such a shock to his contemporaries was that he learned quite young how to lift his readers into the sound of his verse; such knowledge, of course, came in part, from the other poets he read and loved. A brilliant, searching intellect, he was not content to read only the literature in his own language; in fact, the strongest influences on his style and thought came from French literature of both the Middle Ages and the nineteenth century. Among the French poets that he loved were the romantic writers of the emotional and sensational poetry of the senses—the poetry of men like Victor Hugo, whom he praises in this eulogy. Hugo, like the German and English Romantics, was instrumental in giving the emotions a primary place in poetry that was a mixture of melodious words and sensual content. Such poetry seemed to Swinburne to have the spirit of Greek verse:

> In the fair days when God
> By man as godlike trod,
> And **each alike was Greek, alike was free,**
> God's lightning spared, they said,
> Alone the happier head
> Whose laurels screened it; fruitless grace for thee,
> To whom the high gods gave of right
> Their thunders and their laurels and their light.

Each of us suffers his own hell

Source: THE AENEID (Book VI, as translated by John Jackson)
Author: Virgil (Publius Vergilius Maro, 70-19 B.C.)
First transcribed: c.29-19 B.C.
Type of work: Epic poem

Context: Written with patriotic inspiration, *The Aeneid* attempts to give Rome an origin worthy of her greatness. Aeneas, the son of Venus and a hero of the Trojan War, sails from Troy to Italy, encountering perils reminiscent of those of Ulysses. Upon his arrival in Italy, Aeneas is conducted by a Sybil to the land of the dead where his father Anchises reveals to him his destiny as founder of the Roman Empire, showing him the grandeur of their mutual heirs awaiting their earthly sojourns. Anchises explains to Aeneas that all men bear the taint of guilt and that for this reason *each of us suffers his own hell* before reaching the rewards of the blessed Elysian Fields, or in the translation of Jackson:

> . . . Some are hung outspread to the substanceless winds: from others the stain of guilt is washed clean under the waste of waters, or burnt away by fire. **We suffer, each in his proper spirit;** then are sent to the spacious plains of Elysium, where some few abide in the blissful fields; till at length the hoary ages, when time's cycle is run, purge the incarnate stain, and leave but the purified ethereal sense and the unsullied essential flame. . . .

An eagle mewing her mighty youth

Source: AREOPAGITICA
Author: John Milton (1608-1674)
First published: 1644
Type of work: Printed speech

Context: Although Milton had long been one of the most passionate and articulate defenders of Puritanism, he could not agree when the revolutionary Puritan Parliament, on June 14, 1643, ordered that no book, pamphlet, or paper should be printed without a license from the proper authorities. Milton believed implicitly in the individual nature of the search for truth and in the necessity for freedom of speech and conscience. He recognized that such freedoms would, of course, produce differences of opinion. This speech, addressed to Parliament and cast into the form of a classical oration, is Milton's response to the Parliamentary order and is a world-famous defense of freedom of the press. He first demonstrates that none of the great classical states had engaged in such repressive measures and then shows that censorship was invented by the Catholic Church, to the Puritans the greatest symbol of error and heresy. To the often repeated argument that difference of opinions breeds the dangers of sect and schism Milton replies that in their very ability to tolerate such differences and resolve them into truth lies the strength of the English people:

> . . . when the cheerfulness of the people is so sprightly up, as that it has not only wherewith to guard well its own freedom and safety, but to spare, and to bestow upon the solidest and sublimest points of controversy and new invention, it betokens us not degenerated, nor drooping to a fatal decay, but casting off the old and wrinkled skin of corruption to outlive these pangs, and wax young again, entering the glorious ways of truth and prosperous

virtue, destined to become great and honorable in these latter ages. Methinks I see in my mind a noble and puissant nation rousing herself like a strong man after sleep, and shaking her invincible locks: methinks I see her as **an eagle mewing her mighty youth,** and kindling her undazzled eyes at the full midday beam; purging and unscaling her long-abused sight at the fountain itself of heavenly radiance; while the whole noise of timorous and flocking birds, with those also that love the twilight, flutter about, amazed at what she means, and in their envious gabble would prognosticate a year of sects and schisms.

Earth, with her thousand voices, praises God

Source: HYMN BEFORE SUNRISE, IN THE VALE OF CHAMOUNI (Last line)
Author: Samuel Taylor Coleridge (1772-1834)
First published: 1802
Type of work: Lyric poem

Context: Coleridge, in the Vale of Chamonix, or Chamouni, stands at early dawn before the great mass of Mont Blanc and is so mightily affected by the scene that he is moved to hymn the glory of God, Whose handwork the mountain is. The rivers Arve and Arveiron roar ceaselessly at the base of the mountain, which rises in silence so profound as to make him raise his voice in praise. The wonder of the mighty foundations of the mass, sunk deep into the earth; its face snow-covered, bathed with the rosy light of early morning; its parentage of many streams that perpetually gush forth from its caves of ice; its ice falls, like silent cataracts; all speak to the poet of God. The brilliant blue gentians that flourish up to the edge of the ice, the wild goats leaping upon the crags, the eagles sporting with the mountain storm, and the lightning, like arrows, also proclaim the reality of God. The avalanche that plunges unheard by human ears into the clouds that sometimes veil the mountain, and above all, the great mountain itself, like a kingly spirit enthroned amid the encircling hills, is conjured by the poet to tell the sky, the stars, and the rising sun that the earth in all its forms praises God.

Thou too, hoar Mount with thy sky-pointing peaks,
Oft from whose feet the avalance, unheard,
Shoots downward, glittering through the pure serene
Into the depth of clouds, that veil thy breast—
Thou too again, stupendous Mountain! thou
That as I raise my head, awhile bowed low
In adoration, upward from thy base
Slow travelling with dim eyes suffused with tears,
Solemnly seemest, like a vapory cloud,
To rise before me—Rise, O ever rise,
Rise like a cloud of incense from the Earth!

240

Thou kingly Spirit throned among the hills,
Thou dread ambassador from Earth to Heaven,
Great Hierarch! tell thou the silent sky,
And tell the stars, and tell yon rising sun
Earth, with her thousand voices, praises God.

East of the sun, west of the moon

Source: THE EARTHLY PARADISE ("September")
Author: William Morris (1834-1896)
First published: 1868-1870
Type of work: Narrative poem

Context: In this section of *The Earthly Paradise,* Morris, who is frequently called the last and most excessive of the romantics, tells the tragic love story of a peasant and a queen. Although John, the peasant, loves the queen, he betrays her by telling who she really is. As in the Cupid and Psyche tale, upon which this story is based, John does penance for his betrayal and finally wins back the beautiful queen. However much Morris may have been the romantic, he was also the realist. Where an inferior poet might have ruined the tale, he carefully places the lovers in a world of hard facts and crushing responsibilities so that the reader is never able to wallow in mere sentimentality. The first appearance of the oft-repeated quotation occurs in the queen's speech to her lover, who still sleeps, as she leaves him; as a crushing reminder that the world is indeed real, it is a fitting antidote to the romance of escape.

Dream not then
Of named lands, and abodes of men!
Alas, alas, the loneliest
Of all such were a land of rest
When set against the land where I
Unhelped must note the hours go by! . . .

.   .   .

My feet, lost Love, shall wander soon
East of the Sun, West of the Moon!
Tell not old tales of love so strong,
That all the world with all its wrong
And heedlessness was weak to part
The loving heart from loving heart?

Education has for a chief object the formation of character

Source: SOCIAL STATICS (Part II, chapter 17, section 4)
Author: Herbert Spencer (1820-1903)
First published: 1850
Type of work: Scientific treatise

Context: Herbert Spencer, the English social scientist and philosopher, declined the opportunity for a university education. A self-educated man, he was engaged in engineering from 1837–1845, and from 1848–1853 was sub-editor of the *Economist*. His subsequent compositions on psychology, sociology, and ethics did much to apply the Darwinian principles of evolution to philosophy. His first significant title, originally published as *Social Statics: or, the Conditions essential to Human Happiness specified and the first of them developed,* contained various observations on the fundamental purposes and goals of education and the desirability of the state's maintaining and controlling a national educational system. He defends formal education, not as the sole means of proper maturation, but as a system to exercise properly the sentiments through which the savage instincts are checked. At one point he roundly condemns the practice of physical punishment as an inducement to proper behavior. He calls on advocates of "the stern will and the strong hand" to visit Hanwell Asylum and observe the effects of the tolerance practiced by the present management. "Let them contrast (with these horrors) the calmness, the contentment, the tractability, the improved health of mind and body, and the not unfrequent recoveries, that have followed the abandonment of the strait-jacket *regime:* and then let them blush for their creed." And the same principles should be applied to discipline in the classroom:

Education has for a chief object the formation of character. To curb restive propensities, to awaken dormant sentiments, to strengthen the perceptions and cultivate the tastes, to encourage this feeling and repress that, so as finally to develop the child into a man of well-proportioned and harmonious nature—this is alike the aim of parent and teacher. . . . But the power of self government, like all other powers, can be developed only by exercise. Whoso is to rule over his passions in his maturity, must be practised in ruling over his passions during youth. Observe, then, the absurdity of the coercive system. Instead of habituating a boy to be a law to himself, as he is required in after-life to be, it administers the law for him.

Either be wholly slaves, or wholly free

Source: THE HIND AND THE PANTHER (Part II, l. 857)
Author: John Dryden (1631-1700)
First published: 1687
Type of work: Religious allegory

Context: Celebrating his conversion to Roman Catholicism in 1686, England's most noted poet of this period played his part in the quarrel between Protestantism and Catholicism by composing a long allegorical poem about animals, in which the Hind represents the Catholics, the Panther the

Church of England, and the Lion, King James II. Part II of the poem contains a dialogue between the chief animals over religious practices. The Hind upholds church authority and Purgatory, and refuses to concede that everyone should follow "his particular judgment." After the struggle to establish authority of the Bible, it is folly to accept an unauthorized interpretation of it, or argue for a personal hell. Dryden's poetry is superior to his religious exegesis, but he was writing for partisan readers whom he hoped would maintain traditions.

. . .

"Did we a lawful tyranny displace,
To set aloft a bastard of the race?
Why all these wars to win the Book, if we
Must not interpret for ourselves, but she?
Either be wholly slaves, or wholly free.
For *purging* fires traditions must not fight,
But they must prove episcopacy's right.
Thus those led horses are from service freed;
You never mount 'em but in time of need.
Like mercenaries, hir'd for home defense,
They will not serve against their native prince."

. . .

Embarrassment of riches

Source: L'EMBARRAS DES RICHESSES
Author: Abbé Leonore d'Allainval (1700–1753)
First published: 1726
Type of work: Dramatic comedy

Context: To us the expression "An embarrassment of riches" means "Too much to choose from"; that is, the more alternatives we have, the more difficult is our choice. Although a literal translation from the French, it is one in which the meaning does not survive the transition: in its original form it refers to the burden of wealth. Its first appearance in print seems to have been as the title of d'Allainval's comedy, usually given as *L'embarras des richèsses*. The play was popular in France, and an English translation by John Ozell opened at the Haymarket Theater October 9, 1738. In it Harlequin, the stock comic character of French drama, is a gardener. His singing irritates Mr. and Mrs. Midas; Midas is a financier who worships Plutus, the god of wealth. Plutus answers their prayers, and punishes Harlequin by giving him a treasure. Harlequin is utterly corrupted by this gift; he puts on airs, abandons the pastoral Chloe, who loves him, gives himself over to vanity and display, and is in continual terror lest his treasure be stolen from him. He finally gives it up after he has become utterly miserable; the lovers are then reunited, and Harlequin becomes his old self again. The implication here is that wealth is a burden, especially to those who are not born to it; and the play's title had probably become a commonly used figure of speech by the time Voltaire used it in its context in another comedy, *Le Droit du Seigneur,* which was given in Paris in 1762 in five acts under the title *L'Ecueil du Sage* (*The acquisition of wisdom*), and revived in 1778, after the author's death. In it Mathurin, a farmer who has come into some money, abandons the pastoral Colette and pursues Acante, who is obviously too good for him. Her foster parents agree to let Mathurin marry her, and Acante is desperate. She wishes to take refuge with friends in a ruined château. The lord will be arriving soon, and Acante will appeal to him; she is unaware of "Le droit du seigneur." This "right of the lord" is an old French custom whereby the lord, when one of his vassals marries, spends the wedding night with the bride. In Act II, scene vi, the cavalier is telling Champagne, a servant, that he has been sent ahead by the marquis; his mission is to see that Mathurin does not get to Acante first. He suggests they take advantage of the great man's dignity, gravity, and slowness: they will abduct Acante and take her to a ruined château nearby. Champagne reminisces about the old lady who lives there:

CHAMPAGNE
The old girl was young once.
I remember your madcap of a father
Had a certain affair with her,
Wherein each of them made a poor bargain
Faith, he was a debauched master,
Exactly like you, drinking, loving the girls,
Carrying them off, and then making fools of them;
He devoured everything and left you nothing.

LE CHEVALIER
I have a marquis, and that is a good thing.
With no worries of my own, I live off his bounty.
I want nothing to do with the **responsibility of riches:**
He who can always play is rich enough.
The first good, believe me, is pleasure.

Endless extinction of unhappy hates

Source: MEROPE (Line 102)
Author: Matthew Arnold (1822-1888)
First published: 1858
Type of work: Dramatic tragedy

Context: Twenty years have passed since Polyphontes, now tyrant of Messenia, murdered Cresphontes, the proper king, and forced Merope, the

244

widow of the murdered monarch, to marry him; however, Polyphontes did not kill Merope's youngest son, Aepytus, who mysteriously disappeared. The drama opens as Aepytus, now an adult, returns to Messenia to take vengeance on his father's murderer; he comes with his uncle, Laias, who shows him the kingdom that belongs to him. His plan is to enter the palace as an unknown guest bringing word of his own death; in this way he will be able to kill Polyphontes when he least expects danger. But no sooner does he relate his plan than Merope and Polyphontes enter; she has come to Cresphontes' tomb to honor the twentieth anniversary of his death, but Polyphontes wants her to stop such mourning because her behavior is making the people uneasy. The quotation comes from Polyphontes' speech requesting Merope to stop her mourning:

All this I bear, for, what I seek, I know:
Peace, peace is what I seek, and public calm;
Endless extinction of unhappy hates,
Union cemented for this nation's weal.
And even now, if to behold me here,
This day, amid these rites, this black-robed train,
Wakens, O Queen! remembrance in thy heart
Too wide at variance with the peace I seek—
I will not violate thy noble grief,
The prayer I came to urge I will defer.

Enough to make a deacon swear

Source: THE BIGLOW PAPERS (Second Series, No. 2)
Author: James Russell Lowell (1819-1891)
First published: 1867
Type of work: Satirical poem

Context: This poem, written in the New England dialect, ostensibly by "Squire Biglow," is a commentary on the famous Mason and Slidell incident of the recent Civil War, with a "frame" letter from Homer Wilber, A. M., a fictional person who supposedly forwards the poem from the little town of Jaalam, in Middlesex County, to the editors of the *Atlantic Monthly,* in Boston. Mason and Slidell, appointed by Jefferson Davis as diplomatic representatives of the Confederacy at London and Paris, respectively, had been seized from a British steamer by an American war vessel; this act was of the kind the United States had objected to when England had committed it against Americans prior to the War of 1812. Lowell has Squire Biglow begin by telling how he likes to take a walk in the evening, after the chores are done, "to shake the kinkles out o' back and legs." On one such walk, "round the whale's-back o' Prospect Hill," the squire begins a reverie in which he seems to hear the Concord Bridge, site of the famous battle in the American Revolution, talking to the monument at

Bunker Hill. The bridge, noting that the ghosts of the dead British soldiers buried nearby have been restless in the previous night, asks the Bunker Hill monument what is bothering the long-dead men. The monument says it is Mason and Slidell, the men Captain Wilkes took off the "Trent." The bridge replies that it hopes the authorities have not hanged the two and thus made "a goose a swan." The monument tells the bridge that the English want the release of the two men sent by the Confederacy, to which the bridge replies, thinking the United States has been insulted:

THE BRIDGE

Hev they? Wal, by heaven,
Thet's the wust news I've heered since Seventy-seven!
By George, I meant to say, though I declare
It's 'most **enough to make a deacon swear.**

Envy keeps no holidays

Source: THE ADVANCEMENT OF LEARNING (Book VI, chapter 3, antitheses, 16)
Author: Sir Francis Bacon (1561-1626)
First published: 1605
Type of work: Philosophy

Context: Sir Francis Bacon was trained in the legal profession and spent much of his active life in politics. He was a member of Parliament for many years, and was careful to associate himself with various royal favorites; one of these was the unfortunate Essex, whom Bacon helped to convict after his fall. Another was George Villiers, Duke of Buckingham. His cultivation of the latter earned for Bacon a series of royal favors which lasted until Buckingham's fall from grace; Bacon was then charged with accepting bribes from various persons who had appeared in his court. Bacon did not deny the truth of these charges, although he insisted that he had not actually perverted justice. He was fined heavily and imprisoned for a brief period, then pardoned. He was forbidden to take part in politics again, however, and entered upon his retirement. His last years were devoted to the voluminous literary and philosophical works for which he is famous; in these writings Bacon concentrated most heavily on the promotion and explanation of his intellectual ideals, and most of them were intended to become a part of *The Great Instauration.* This was planned as a vast work which would reorganize all systems of knowledge along what we would consider more scientific lines. The introduction to it, and a full-length work in itself, is entitled *De Degnitate et Augmentis Scientiarium (Of the Dignity and Advancement of Learning).* Its title is usually shortened. A synopsis and summary of all learning and knowledge current in Bacon's time, it stresses his ideals of objectivity, sound observation, and a critical approach. Its influence upon later philosophical and scientific thought was considerable. Book VI is a discussion of rhetoric, discourse, and argument; in Chapter 3 Bacon gives several examples of fallacious reasoning (sophisms), following with a number of "antitheses"—neatly arranged epigrammatic arguments for and against specific things. An example follows:

XVI. ENVY

FOR	AGAINST
It is natural for a man to hate that which reproaches to him his own fortunes.	**Envy keeps no holidays.** Nothing but death can reconcile envy to virtue.
Envy in commonwealths is a wholesome kind of ostracism.	Envy puts virtues to laborious tasks, as Juno did Hercules.

Envy, ye great, the dull unlettered small

Source: TRUTH (Line 375)
Author: William Cowper (1731-1800)
First published: 1782
Type of work: Meditative poem

Context: Cowper, a descendant of John Donne, was primarily a poet of rural life; he was the last English poet who belonged to the "cult of simplicity." A deeply religious man, he drew both comfort and despair from his Calvinism: in his writings he moralizes frequently, and most of his poems are to some extent moral essays. His mother died when he was a child, and his life in the public schools was a bitterly unhappy one. He was trained in the legal profession and called to the bar in 1754, but recurring attacks of insanity forced him to abandon his career. His first attack made it impossible for him to marry the cousin he loved; during the second he tried to commit suicide. He suffered from these periods of melancholia, in which his religion played a major role, throughout his later years. Retiring to the country, he eventually settled at Olney. Here, at fifty years of age, he turned to poetry as a serious avocation. The first volume, *Poems,* was published in 1782. His humorous poem, *John Gilpin's Ride,* was published the same year and gained wide popularity. *The Task,* his greatest work, appeared in 1785 and ensured his lasting fame. Typical of Cowper at his best, it is a quiet picture of rural life: the beauty of the countryside in winter, the simplicity and the pleasures of his daily routine are vividly and tranquilly presented. He considers, at some length, the nature of life and of moral responsibility; and he examines the world from a comfortable distance. *Truth,* one of the poems in his first volume, is a good example of those works in which Cowper produces a moral commentary akin to a sermon. In it he examines man's moral and spiritual responsibilities and the consolations afforded by Scripture. He concludes that the world and its many activities serve only to alienate man from God, that riches merely compound the problem, and that those who possess little are in reality the   most fortunate:

> Oh bless'd effect of penury and want,
> The seed sown there, how vigorous is the plant!
> No soil like poverty for growth divine,
> As leanest hand supplies the richest wine.
> Earth gives too little, giving only bread,
> To nourish pride, or turn the weakest head;
> To them, the sounding jargon of the schools
> Seems what it is, a cap and bells for fools;
> The light they walk by, kindled from above,
> Shows them the shortest way to life and love:
> They, strangers to the controversial field,
> Where deists always foil'd, yet scorn to yield,
> And never check'd by what impedes the wise,
> Believe, rush forward, and possess the prize.
> **Envy, ye great, the dull unletter'd small;**
> Ye have much cause for envy—but not all;
> We boast some rich ones whom the Gospel sways,
> And one who wears a coronet and prays:
> Like gleanings of an olive-tree they show,
> Here and there one upon the topmost bough.

Ercles' vein

Source: A MIDSUMMER NIGHT'S DREAM (Act I, sc. ii, l. 36)
Author: William Shakespeare (1564-1616)
First published: 1600
Type of work: Dramatic comedy

Context: In Athens the festivities have commenced in celebration of the marriage of Duke Theseus and the fair captive, Hippolyta, Queen of the Amazons. To honor the royal couple, a group of craftsmen rehearse a play based upon the legend of Pyramus and Thisbe. The talkative weaver, Bottom, assigned the role of Pyramus, the lover who gallantly kills himself for love, comments, that, though the part of Pyramus will require acting skill, he would prefer to enact the part of the tyrant familiar to the Elizabethan stage, Hercules:

> BOTTOM
> That will ask some tears in the true performing of it. If I do it, let
> the audience look to their eyes. I will move storms. I will condole
> in some measure. To the rest. Yet my chief humour is for a tyrant.
> I could play Ercles rarely, or a part to tear a cat in, to make all
> split.
>> The raging rocks,
>> And shivering shocks,
>> Shall break the locks

248

Of prison gates,
And Phibbus' car
Shall shine from far,
And make and mar
The foolish Fates.
This was lofty. Now name the rest of the players. This is **Ercles'
vein,** a tyrant's vein. A lover is more condoling.

Erred and strayed like lost sheep

Source: THE BOOK OF COMMON PRAYER (Page 6)
Author: Traditional; translated and arranged by Archbishop Cranmer (1489–
    1560)
First published: 1549
Type of work: Prayer of confession

Context: The Order for Daily Morning Prayer is the first service in the Book of Common Prayer and is a direct descendent of the system of services used during the Middle Ages and known as the Canonical Hours. This system of daily worship was regarded not only as a means of personal edification but as a part of the Church's "bounden duty and service" in a continual offering to God of a corporate act of praise and thanksgiving. Morning Prayer begins with a series of opening sentences which set the theme and tone of the service to come. The Exhortation which follows reminds the worshiper that no converse with God can be fitting or profitable until his sins are laid bare and he has sought reconciliation with God's Love. The minister beseeches the people to accompany him "with a pure heart, and humble voice, unto the throne of heavenly grace," and there to confess their sins unto Almighty God. There follows a General Confession of all the faithful in which they compare themselves to wandering and rebellious sheep the essence of whose sin is self-assertion: the following after their own wills rather than of God's holy ways. The inevitable result of this straying is the loss of the spiritual health which only their merciful and loving shepherd can restore to them.

Almighty and most merciful Father; We have **erred, and strayed** from thy ways **like lost sheep.** We have followed too much the devices and desires of our own hearts. We have offended against thy holy laws. We have left undone those things which we ought to have done; And we have done those things which we ought not to have done; And there is no health in us. But thou, O Lord, have mercy upon us, miserable offenders. Spare thou those, O God, who confess their faults. Restore thou those who are penitent; According to thy promises declared unto mankind In Christ Jesus our Lord. And grant, O most merciful Father, for his sake; That we may hereafter live a godly, righteous, and sober life, To the glory of thy holy Name. Amen.

249

The eternal silence of these infinite spaces terrifies me

Source: PENSÉES (Section III, number 206)
Author: Blaise Pascal (1623-1662)
First published: 1670
Type of work: Philosophical commentary

Context: Pascal, a French author and religious thinker, is known for his defenses of the religious reform movement known as Jansenism, named for Cornelius Jansen, who taught the doctrines of original sin, irresistible grace, and man's helplessness before God; in many ways the sect he founded resembled Calvinism. Before his conversion to Jansenism, Pascal was chiefly interested in mathematics; he invented a calculating-machine, did work in probability theory, and is believed by some to have originated the system of calculus. After his religious conversion, he gave most of his attention to theology. His writings are notable for objectivity and rationality, insight, and a graceful style which is at times ironic. *Pensées* (Thoughts) is probably his best-known work today. Found among his belongings after his death, it was considered too unorthodox for publication and did not see the light of print in its entirety until 1844. A collection of religious thoughts and observations, *Pensées* is actually the accumulated notes for an Apologia, or justification, of the Christian religion—a book which Pascal had intended to write. In Section III of *Pensées*, Pascal takes up the subject of eternity and man's relationship to it. Beginning with the ironic comment that "Men despise religion; they hate it and fear it is true," he considers the man who is concerned only with the things of this life. He feels there must be some strange confusion in man's nature that allows him so to concern himself with daily trifles and at the same time remain indifferent to things of vastly greater importance:

> For it is not to be doubted that the duration of this life is but a moment; that the state of death is eternal, whatever may be its nature; and that thus all our actions and thoughts must take such different directions, according to the state of that eternity, that it is impossible to take one step with sense and judgement, unless we regulate our course by the truth of that point which ought to be our ultimate end.
>
> ⋅ ⋅ ⋅
>
> . . . That passion may not harm us, let us act as if we had only eight hours to live.
> If we ought to devote eight hours of life, we ought to devote a hundred years.
> When I consider the short duration of my life, swallowed up in the eternity before and after, the little space which I fill and even can see, engulfed in the immensity of spaces of which I am ignorant and which know me not, I am frightened and am astonished at being here rather than there; for there is no reason why here rather than there, why now rather than then. Who has put me

250

here? By whose order and direction have this place and time been allotted to me? . . .
The eternal silence of these infinite spaces terrifies me.

Eternity! thou pleasing, dreadful thought!

Source: CATO (Act V, sc. i, l. 10)
Author: Joseph Addison (1672-1719)
First published: 1713
Type of work: Dramatic tragedy

Context: Marcius Porcius Cato (95–46 B.C.) is the hero of Addison's play. Having fought long against Caesar's despotism and espoused the cause of republicanism, Cato is saddened and defeated by the course of events. He has even lost one of his sons in the struggle. He advises Portius, his remaining son, to retire from public life to the Sabine hills, there to live on the land where their great ancestor, Cato the Censor, the present Cato's great-grandfather, had lived. At the beginning of the fifth act of the play Cato is found sitting by a table on which lie a sword and what Addison calls "Plato's Book on the Immortality of the Soul," probably the *Phaedo.* Cato considers what death may bring if he commits suicide, as he later does. He notes that man longs after immortality and shrinks from believing that death is but oblivion. And he asks why man fears death so greatly.

CATO
             Why shrinks the soul
Back on herself, and startles at destruction?
'Tis the divinity that stirs within us;
'Tis heaven itself, that points out an hereafter,
And intimates eternity to man.
Eternity! thou pleasing, dreadful thought!
Through what variety of untried being,
Through what new scenes and changes must we pass!
The wide, th' unbounded prospect lies before me;
But shadows, clouds, and darkness, rest upon it.
Here will I hold. If there's a pow'r above us,
(And that there is all nature cries aloud
Through all her works) he must delight in virtue;
And that which he delights in must be happy.
But when! or where!—This world was made for Caesar.
I'm weary of conjectures—This must end 'em.
                        [*Laying his hand on his sword.*]

251

Eternity was in that moment

Source: THE OLD BACHELOR (Act IV, sc. iii)
Author: William Congreve (1670-1729)
First published: 1693
Type of work: Dramatic comedy

Context: Old Fondlewife, married to the young and beautiful Laetitia, is, as an impotent husband, jealous of the virtue of his lusty wife. He is compelled to be absent on a business matter of £500, and to insure his wife's good behavior, purposes to have a one-eyed Puritanical minister, Tribulation Spintext, sit with her while he is absent. Laetitia had written to Vainlove, whose mistress she had formerly been, and had said that she would so arrange matters that Spintext would not be at her house. Vainlove, who has tired of Laetitia, turns the affair over to his friend, Bellmour, who procures a long black cloak, a broad hat, and an eye-patch and visits Laetitia after her husband departs. At first she is startled to find a stranger in her home, but Bellmour speedily makes an impression upon her with his excellent appearance and bold manners. It is only a matter of moments before she gives him, in return for his importunities, a passionate kiss. As the two part, he says that eternity was in that moment. She admires his agreeable impudence and accedes to his request.

LAETITIA

I hope you are a gentleman;—and since you are privy to a weak woman's failing, won't turn it to the prejudice of her reputation. You look as if you had more honor—

BELLMOUR

And more love, or my face is a false witness, and deserves to be pilloried. No, by Heaven I swear—

LAETITIA

Nay, don't swear if you'd have me believe you; but promise—

BELLMOUR

Well, I promise—A promise is so cold!—give me leave to swear— by those eyes, those killing eyes; by those healing lips.—Oh! press the soft charm close to mine—and seal 'em up for ever.

LAETITIA

Upon that condition.   [*He kisses her.*]

BELLMOUR

Eternity was in that moment! One more upon any condition.

252

Even God cannot change the past

Source: NICHOMACHEAN ETHICS (Book VI, chapter ii)
Author: Agathon (c.477-401 B.C.), attributed by Aristotle (384-322 B.C.)
First transcribed: Fourth century, B.C.
Type of work: Philosophical treatise

Context: Aristotle, in discussing morality, says that in all moral states there is some object which the rational man keeps in view in intensifying or relaxing his activity: this object should be the mean, or the state between two extremes. The intellect, Aristotle says, is divided between the speculative intellect and practical intellect; the function of the speculative intellect is to apprehend truth in conformity with right reason. Thus moral purpose is the origin of action, which implies reason. It then follows that moral purpose is intellectual desire, and it is this intellectual desire which makes a man. Anything that is desired must be something in the future, as it is impossible to desire things in the past. Aristotle explains it thus:

> But nothing which is done and past can be the object of moral choice; for instance, no man chooses to have sacked Troy; because, in fact, no one ever deliberates about what is past but only about that which is future and which may therefore be influenced, whereas what has been cannot not have been: and so Agathon is right in saying,
> **Even God cannot change the past.**

The evening star, love's harbinger

Source: PARADISE LOST (Book XI, ll. 588-589)
Author: John Milton (1608-1674)
First published: 1667
Type of work: Epic poem

Context: Michael, sent down from Heaven by God to instruct Adam in preparation for his expulsion from the garden, takes him to the top of a hill from which can be seen much of the earth and there shows him various forms of death that will kill men as a result of Adam and Eve's wickedness in eating the forbidden fruit. Adam wants to know why man, made in the divine similitude, must suffer these loathesome forms of death. Michael replies that the Maker's image forsook man when his ungoverned appetite led him astray. Man can live a temperate life and drop off easily in old age, but to do so he will have to outlive his youth, his beauty, and his strength. Man should live his life well, whether for a long or a short time, as Heaven decrees. Michael then shows Adam a new sight: a broad plain with tents and grazing cattle; the people are miners and work all sorts of metals. These people are the sons of Lamech: Jabal, Jubel,

253

and Tubal-Cain. The scene then shifts to some dwellers in the hills, just people who worship God in a proper manner. They may be the sons of Seth, who tradition holds were the mysterious "sons of God" (Genesis 6: 2) who took wives of the daughters of men:

> They on the plain
> Long had not walked, when from the tents behold
> A bevy of fair women, richly gay
> In gems and wanton dress; to the harp they sung
> Soft amorous ditties, and in dance came on:
> The men though grave, eyed them, and let their eyes
> Rove without rein, till in the amorous net
> Fast caught, they liked, and each his liking chose;
> And now of love they treat till **the evening star,**
> **Love's harbinger,** appeared; then all in heat
> They light the nuptial torch, and bid invoke
> Hymen, then first to marriage rites invoked;
> With feast and music all the tents resound.
> . . .

Every flower enjoys the air it breathes

Source: LINES WRITTEN IN EARLY SPRING (Lines 11-12)
Author: William Wordsworth (1770-1850)
First published: 1798
Type of work: Lyric poem

Context: Reclined in a grove, the poet hears "a thousand blended notes" which lead him to the thought that in the world of external Nature there is a joy in merely being. By contrast, his heart is grieved "to think/ What man has made of man." Whether his belief is heaven-sent, whether it is "Nature's holy plan" that flowers enjoy the air they breathe, the birds their playing, and the twigs their spreading to the air— he knows not. But if it is true, then "Have I not reason to lament/ What man has made of man?" Stanzas 3 and 6 read:

> Through primrose tufts, in that green bower,
> The periwinkle trailed its wreaths;
> And 'tis my faith that **every flower**
> **Enjoys the air it breathes.**
> . . .
> If this belief from heaven be sent,
> If such be Nature's holy plan,
> Have I not reason to lament
> What man has made of man?

254

Every good servant does not all commands

Source: CYMBELINE (Act V, sc. i, l. 6)
Author: William Shakespeare (1564-1616)
First published: 1623
Type of work: Tragi-comedy

Context: Posthumus orders his servant, Pisanio, in a letter, to slay Imogen, the wife from whom he has been forcibly separated and whom he believes to be untrue to him because of the lies of an Italian, Iachimo. Pisanio, who could not bring himself to kill the lovely and virtuous Imogen, has actually sent her, disguised as a man, to do service as a page to the Roman ambassador. In order to convince Posthumus that he has killed her, however, he sends Posthumus her bloody handkerchief. Posthumus has repented and wishes Pisanio had not followed his orders, for even good servants do not always do as told.

> POSTHUMUS
> Yea, bloody cloth, I'll keep thee, for I wished
> Thou shouldst be colored thus. You married ones,
> If each of you should take this course, how many
> Must murder wives much better than themselves
> For wrying but a little. O Pisanio,
> **Every good servant does not all commands.**
> No bond but to do just ones. Gods, if you
> Should have ta'en vengeance on my faults, I never
> Had lived to put on this; so had you saved
> The noble Imogen to repent, and struck
> Me, wretch, more worth your vengeance. . . .

· · ·

Every hero becomes a bore at last

Source: REPRESENTATIVE MEN (Chapter I, "Uses of Great Men")
Author: Ralph Waldo Emerson (1803-1882)
First published: 1850
Type of work: Moral essay

Context: Emerson believed in the importance of great men, and this volume, a collection of seven lectures he gave during the 1840's, illustrates his views on the subject. As representative men he selected Plato, as philosopher; Swedenborg, as mystic; Montaigne, as skeptic; Shakespeare, as poet; Napoleon, as man of the world; and Goethe, as writer. Each of these was, for Emerson, representative of a kind of greatness, and greatness was, for Emerson, a necessary ingredient of the nature of mankind. He says in his opening statement in *Representative Men,* "It is natural to believe in great men." He goes on to comment, "Nature seems to exist for

255

the excellent. The world is upheld by the veracity of good men." And he notes a little later in "Uses of Great Men," "The search after the great man is the dream of youth and the most serious occupation of manhood." But Emerson also warns that we must learn to think for ourselves, that the domination of a great man over others' minds can degenerate into idolatry, and then the influence of the great man becomes evil, rather than good. Nature, suggests Emerson, is a help to us, as she, through death, provides a necessary rotation of great men, so that one is replaced by another of a different kind. The best kind of great man that lives in our own time, suggests Emerson, is one from whom we learn "almost through the pores of our skin, pulling ourselves up to the level, or trying to, of the great one." But though a great man is an indemnification for a whole population of lesser men, there is always some danger from him:

> . . . a new danger appears in the excess of influence of the great man. His attractions warp us from our place. We have become underlings and intellectual suicides. Ah! yonder in the horizon is our help;—other great men, new qualities, counterweights and checks on each other. We cloy of the honey of each peculiar greatness. **Every hero becomes a bore at last.** Perhaps Voltaire was not badhearted, yet he said of the good Jesus, even, "I pray you, let me never hear that man's name again." They cry up the virtues of George Washington,—"Damn George Washington!" is the poor Jacobin's whole speech and confutation. But it is human nature's indispensable defense. The centripetal augments the centrifugence. We balance one man with his opposite, and the health of the state depends on the see-saw.

Every man has his fault, and honesty is his

Source: TIMON OF ATHENS (Act III, sc. i, ll. 28-29)
Author: William Shakespeare (1564-1616)
First published: 1623
Type of work: Dramatic tragedy

Context: Timon, wealthy and generous Athenian nobleman, finally realizing that his indebtedness has become much greater than his wealth, dispatches Flaminius, a trusted servant, to borrow some money to meet the demands of his creditors, from Lucullus, a friend and frequent recipient of Timon's largesse. The refusal of assistance by Lucullus and his condemnation of Timon for too much honesty is typical of the responses Timon receives from his friends. When Flaminius presents the request of his master, "nothing doubting your present assistance therein," Lucullus replies:

LUCULLUS
La, la, la, la! Nothing doubting, says he? Alas good lord! A noble

256

gentleman 'tis, if he would not keep so good a house. Many a time and often I ha' dined with him, and told him on't, and come again to supper to him of purpose to have him spend less, and yet he would embrace no counsel, take no warning by my coming. **Every man has his fault, and honesty is his.** I ha' told him on't, but I could ne'er get him from't.

Every man loves what he is good at

Source: A TRUE WIDOW (Act V)
Author: Thomas Shadwell (1640-1692)
First published: 1679
Type of work: Dramatic comedy

Context: Lady Cheately, a widow with very little capital, comes to London to marry off herself and her two daughters. That each one may marry a rich man, the widow puts on a great show of business affairs, with the aid of a scoundrelly steward. This show is designed to lure wealthy suitors, of course. When the steward threatens to reveal how his mistress is cheating both suitors and business clients, Lady Cheately has one of her suitors, Prig, who thinks of nothing but gaming and sports, act as a clergyman for a mock-marriage. The steward is taken in by the trick and believes he is really married to his employer. Lady Cheately, anxious to be rid of him, tries to have him lured aboard ship and sent out of the country to indentured servitude. But the steward escapes from the ship in time and returns to threaten his "wife." This situation, plus the seduction of her empty-headed daughter, Gertrude, by a fool named Selfish, has Lady Cheately quite disturbed; it seems as though all her planning is to go for nothing. She decides to ask help from Mr. Maggot, another of her suitors, who loves the affairs of business for their own sake:

LADY CHEATELY

. . . Oh Mr. *Maggot!* I have business to communicate to you, of the greatest concernment to me that ever hapned.

MAGGOT

Gad, Madam, do! If any Man in *England* understands Business, or loves it better than I do, I'll be burnt.

LADY CHEATELY

Every Man loves what he is good at; give me a Man of Business for my Friend: the fine Gentlemen of the Town, are like Fidlers, only good at idle hours.

Every man meets his Waterloo at last

Source: SPEECHES, FIRST SERIES (Harper's Ferry: Speech delivered at Brooklyn, November 1, 1859)
Author: Wendell Phillips (1811-1884)
First published: 1859
Type of work: Political speech

Context: Wendell Phillips was a confirmed abolitionist and an orator of wide renown. A Harvard graduate and a lawyer, he abandoned the legal profession to identify himself with William Lloyd Garrison's fight against slavery. Forceful, dynamic, pleasant, he abandoned the high-flown oratory of other great speakers and cultivated a natural, familiar style. He soon became one of the country's leading voices in the abolitionist movement. When, in 1859, John Brown and his followers captured the arsenal at Harper's Ferry, Virginia, in an effort to spark a general slave uprising throughout the South, all abolitionists applauded. But Brown's raid was a failure; he and his men were taken after a brief siege, and the revolt failed to materialize. On the evening of November 1, Phillips spoke on "the lesson of the hour" in Henry Ward Beecher's church. "The lesson of the hour," says Phillips, "is insurrection. . . .

Insurrection of thought always precedes insurrection of arms. The last twenty years have been an insurrection of thought. We seem to be entering on a new phase of the great American struggle. . . ." He contrasts Europe with America: "The Old World . . . has always distrusted the average conscience—the common sense of the millions." To Phillips, law is nothing unless public opinion is behind it. And he is not an advocate of passive resistance; "let me say, in passing," he says, "I think you can make a better use of iron than forging it into chains. If you must have the metal, put it into Sharpe's rifles." (The gun made famous by John Brown and his men was invented by Christian Sharpe). Adding that the American public must be made to see things as they are, Philipps praises Brown highly and likens him to the patriots of the Revolution. Though he failed, Brown is no less a hero:

. . . Harper's Ferry is the Lexington of to-day. Up to this moment, Brown's life has been one unmixed success. Prudence, skill, courage, thrift, knowledge of his time, knowledge of his opponents, undaunted daring,—he had all these. He was the man who could leave Kansas, and go into Missouri, and take eleven men, give them liberty, and bring them off on the horses which he carried with him, and two which he took as tribute from their masters in order to facilitate escape. Then, when he had passed his human *protégés* from the vulture of the United States to the safe shelter of the English lion, this is the brave, frank, and sublime truster in God's right and absolute justice, who entered his name in the city of Cleveland, "John Brown, of Kansas," advertised there two horses for sale, and stood in front of the auctioneer's stand, notifying all bidders of—what some would think—the defect in the title. . . . This is the man who, in the face of the nation, avowing his right, and laboring with what strength he had in behalf of the wronged, goes down to Harper's Ferry to follow up his work. Well, men say he failed. Every man has his Moscow. Suppose he did fail, **every man meets his Waterloo at last.** There are two kinds of defeat. Whether in chains or in laurels, LIBERTY knows nothing but victories. Soldiers call Bunker Hill a defeat; but Liberty dates from it, though Warren lay dead on the field. Men say the attempt did not succeed. No man can command success. . . .

Every man's hand against him

Source: GENESIS 16:12
Author: Unknown
First transcribed: c.1000-300 B.C.
Type of work: Religious history and law

Context: One of the famous stories in the Book of Genesis is the story of Hagar and her child, Ishmael. At the time Abram is more than eighty years old, his wife, Sarai, has not given him any children. She gives her maid, Hagar, to Abram, as his concubine, hoping that Hagar will bear children for Abram. Hagar, an Egyptian girl, conceives a child; in her pride at having bested her mistress, she openly despises Sarai. When the wife complains, Abram tells her to deal as she will with the prideful maiden. When Hagar is given harsh treatment for her despising of Sarai, she runs away into the wilderness, where she is visited by an angel of God, who bids the girl return and submit to Sarai. The angel also promises that Hagar shall be rewarded, for her seed will multiply exceedingly. The angel bids Hagar to name her first-born, who will be a son, Ishmael, which means "God hears." But the angel also tells Hagar that her son will be an outcast among men:

And the angel of the LORD said unto her, I will multiply thy seed exceedingly, that it shall not be numbered for the multitude.

And the angel of the LORD said unto her, Behold, thou art with child, and shall bear a son, and shalt call his name Ishmael; because the LORD hath heard thy affliction.

And he will be a wild man; his hand will be against every man, and **every man's hand against him;** and he shall dwell in the presence of all his brethren.

. . .

And Hagar bare Abram a son: and Abram called his son's name, which Hagar bare, Ishmael.

259

Every schoolboy knows who imprisoned Montezuma

Source: LORD CLIVE
Author: Thomas Babington Macaulay (1800-1859)
First published: January, 1840
Type of work: Biographical essay and book review

Context: An essay on Milton, published in the influential *Edinburgh Review* in 1825, brought Macaulay a reputation as an essayist and biographer. Its smooth elegance and clear prose, with each topic sentence logically developed, made easy reading. The parallels he provided, drawn from the wide scope of his reading, and his phenomenal memory, blinded readers to the real shallowness and sweeping judgments about everything. So Macaulay was frequently assigned books to review, and the result would be very readable and enlightening literary and biographical essays. Since he had become a specialist on Indian affairs, having served in India on the Supreme Council between 1834 and 1838, he was the natural one to review Major-General Sir John Malcolm's three-volume *Life of Robert Lord Clive,* of

1836. While that work is now rarely read, Macaulay's review of it is still the best-known brief account of the early days of the British in India. His review starts with the accusation that the British people know more about the Aztec Emperor Montezuma and Hernán Cortés in sixteenth century Mexico, and about the Inca Emperor Atahualpa and Francisco Pizarro of the same period in Peru than of events in eighteenth century India. Macaulay puts a series of questions to his readers to make them realize how ignorant they are about people and happenings in their wealthiest colony. Still less do the people today know that the British won at Buxar in 1764; Meer Cossim ordered the massacre of 200 British prisoners at Patna; Sujah Dowlah ruled in Oude; and Holkar was a Hindu.

We have always thought it strange that, while the history of the Spanish empire in America is familiarly known to all the nations of Europe, the great actions of our countrymen in the East should, even among ourselves, excite little interest. **Every schoolboy knows who imprisoned Montezuma,** and who strangled Atahualpa. But we doubt whether one in ten, even among English gentlemen of highly cultivated minds, can tell who won the battle of Buxar, who perpetrated the massacre of Patna, whether Sujah Dowlah ruled in Oude or in Travancore, or whether Holkar was a Hindoo or a Mussulman.

   .   .   .

Everyone as they like, as the good woman said when she kissed her cow

Source: POLITE CONVERSATION (Dialogue I)
Author: Jonathan Swift (1667-1745)
First published: 1738
Type of work: Dialogue

Context: Under the title *A Complete Collection of Genteel and Ingenious Conversation according to the Most Polite Mode and Method,* and with the author's name given as Simon Wagstaff, Esq., Swift published three dialogues in 1738 from both London and Dublin. The first is in the form of a play with eight characters. Two of them meet in the Mall, from where they go to dine with Lady Smart. Later they have tea and play quadrille (a game for four players and forty cards) until 3 A.M. The expression here quoted is, of course, nonsense. It is sometimes expressed, "There is no accounting for tastes, as the old lady said, . . ." It is merely part of the humor of Dean Swift. At the beginning of the dialogue, Lord Sparkish meets Colonel Atwit in St. James's Park. Mr. Neverout joins them. His protest is humorously taken as a challenge to a duel.

COLONEL

Tom, you must go with me to Lady Smart's for breakfast.

NEVEROUT

Must? Why, Colonel, must's for the King. [*The Colonel offers in jest to draw his sword.*]

COLONEL

Have you spoken with all your friends?

NEVEROUT

Colonel, as you're stout, be merciful.

SPARKISH

Come, agree, agree; the law's costly. [*Colonel taking his hand from the hilt.*]

COLONEL

Well, Tom, you are never the worse man to be afraid of me. Come along.

NEVEROUT

What, do you think I was born in a wood, to be afraid of an owl? I'll wait on you. I hope Miss Notable will be there; 'egad, she's very handsome, and has a wit at will.

Why, **every one as they like; as the good woman said, when she kissed her cow.**

Everyone can master a grief but he that has it

Source: MUCH ADO ABOUT NOTHING (Act III, sc. ii, ll. 28-29)
Author: William Shakespeare (1564-1616)
First published: 1600
Type of work: Dramatic comedy

Context: The principal comic device of this play is an elaborate intrigue in which Don Pedro, Claudio, and Leonato attempt to provoke romantic interest between Benedick and Beatrice, the mocking anti-lovers. By arrangement, each while eavesdropping overhears a declaration of the other's love, and each in turn feels an attraction for the other which he erstwhile has refused to admit to himself, let alone to others. One of the great comic moments comes with this public admission. After all, the jeerers at love have a reputation for barbed wit and cynical jests—directed especially at each other—and difficult indeed is the admission that they who were love's mockers are now love's victims. The comic anticipation is high, then, as Benedick comes on stage for the first time since the eavesdropping scene. His friends, primed for lighthearted taunting, wait to see how he will face down his change of attitude. Ironically, the gallant who has always been the first to accept the gage of verbal combat now finds himself unable to compete, unable even to defend himself against their jibes concerning his cleanshaven, washed face and his well-kempt hair:

DON PEDRO
. . . I will only be bold with Benedick for his company, for from the crown of his head to the sole of his foot, he is all mirth. . . .

BENEDICK
Gallants, I am not as I have been.

LEONATO
So say I, methinks you are sadder.

CLAUDIO
I hope he be in love.

• • •

BENEDICK
I have the toothache.

DON PEDRO
Draw it.

BENEDICK
Hang it.

CLAUDIO
You must hang it first, and draw it afterwards.

DON PEDRO
What? Sigh for the toothache?

LEONATO
Where is but a humour or a worm?

BENEDICK
Well, **every one can master a grief but he that has it.**

CLAUDIO
Yet say I, he is in love.

Everyone lives by selling something

Source: ACROSS THE PLAINS ("Beggars," Section III)
Author: Robert Louis Stevenson (1850-1894)
First published: 1892
Type of work: Familiar essay

Context: Part IX of Stevenson's *Across the Plains* is entitled "Beggars." It opens with reminiscences of two consumptive beggars whom Stevenson had met in his rambles about Scotland. One, an ex-soldier, loved "the romance of language," Keats and Shelley were his favorite poets, and the only books he would borrow from Stevenson—and always return —were volumes of poetry. Recalling this simple lover of literature, Stevenson is led to some random comments on beggars and men who follow other callings. Among the comments are these:

Everyone lives by selling something, whatever be his right to it. The burglar sells at the same time his own skill and courage and my silver plate (the whole at the most moderate figure) to a Jew receiver. The bandit sells the traveller an article of prime necessity: that traveller's life. And as for the old soldier, . . . he dealt in a specialty; for he was the only beggar in the world who ever gave me pleasure for my money. He had learned a school of manner in the barracks and had the sense to cling to it, accosting strangers with a regimental freedom, thanking patrons with a merely

263

regimental difference, sparing you at once the tragedy of his position and the embarrassment of yours. . . .

Everyone soon or late comes round by Rome

Source: THE RING AND THE BOOK (Book V, "Count Guido Franceschini," Line 296)
Author: Robert Browning (1812-1889)
First published: 1868-1869
Type of work: Dramatic monologue

Context: Count Guido Franceschini, the smooth-tongued murderer of his wife and her parents, tells the court about his family's honor and service to the church and state. Arguing that the murder was done with God's blessing, he attempts to create a favorable impression; however, as he speaks, his greed and duplicity frequently creep into his statements so that the reader more and more distrusts his defense. When he describes how his friends advised him to go to Rome in order to live off the corruption in the church, his defense reaches one of its peaks of hypocrisy: he claims that he was too honest to do such a dishonorable thing; instead, he sought a wife who had a large dowry. In effect, he says that the result of his honesty was his marriage to a girl whose "parents" had purchased her from a prostitute and who was not really an heir to the fortune he needed to redeem his family's honor and that he had the right to murder the people who had deceived him.

> I waited thirty years, may it please the Court:
> Saw meanwhile many a denizen o' the dung
> Hop, skip, jump o'er my shoulder, make him wings
> And fly aloft,—succeed, in the usual phrase.
> **Every one soon or late comes round by Rome:**
> Stand still here, you'll see all in turn succeed.
> Why, look you, so and so, the physician here,
> My father's lacquey's son we sent to school,
> Doctored and dosed this Eminence and that,
> Salved the last Pope his certain obstinate sore,
> Soon bought land as became him, names it now: . . .

The evil that men do lives after them

Source: JULIUS CAESAR (Act III, sc. ii, l. 80)
Author: William Shakespeare (1564-1616)
First published: 1623
Type of work: Dramatic tragedy

Context: Julius Caesar has been stabbed to death before the Capitol of

264

Rome by a group of conspirators. Later, in the Forum, the citizens of Rome are addressed first by Brutus, a friend of Caesar and a conspirator, who explains that the hero has been killed because of his ambition which would lead to the enslavement of free Romans; and then by Mark Antony, who, pretending to agree with Brutus, subtly enrages the throng against the conspirators. Antony speaks:

ANTONY

Friends, Romans, countrymen, lend me your ears.
I come to bury Caesar, not to praise him.
The evil that men do, lives after them,
The good is oft interred with their bones;
So let it be with Caesar. The noble Brutus
Hath told you Caesar was ambitious;
If it were so, it was a grievous fault,
And grievously hath Caesar answered it.
Here, under leave of Brutus, and the rest—
For Brutus is an honourable man,
So are they all, all honourable men—
Come I to speak in Caesar's funeral.

．　．　．

Example is the school of mankind

Source: LETTERS ON A REGICIDE PEACE (Letter I)
Author: Edmund Burke (1729-1797)
First published: 1796-1797
Type of work: Open letter

Context: As Burke's life approached its end so did the life of the French Revolution. In Paris horror succeeded horror, culminating in the execution of the king and queen; the Army moved in, and under the command of Napoleon, protected what was of permanent value in the increasing shambles of the disintegrating Revolution. To the astonishment of many, France, wracked by violent internal conflicts and collapsing credit, was able to break up the European coalition arrayed against her. In England a movement was afoot to make peace with the Revolutionary government, and peace talks were actually opened at one point. Burke, ever a firm and stanch enemy of the French Revolution, was equally firmly opposed to this peace movement. In a series of four open letters he argued his case for France as a menace to all of Europe. Near the end of this first letter he insisted that those led to accept a French monarch's overthrow would soon accept the overthrow of other monarchs:

And is, then example nothing? It is everything. **Example is the school of mankind,** and they will learn at no other. This war is a

265

war against that example. It is not a war for Louis the Eighteenth, or even for the property, virtue, fidelity of France. It is a war for George the Third, for Francis the Second, and for all the dignity, property, honor, virtue, and religion of England, of Germany, and of all nations.

An eye like Mars, to threaten and command

Source: HAMLET (Act III, sc. iv, l. 57)
Author: William Shakespeare (1564-1616)
First published: 1603
Type of work: Dramatic tragedy

Context: Hamlet, Prince of Denmark, robbed by his uncle of a father by murder, of a mother by an incestuous marriage, and a throne by usurpation, confronts his mother and reproaches her in her chamber. Inviting her to compare pictures of her noble first husband and her base second husband, he assesses the two men.

HAMLET

Look here upon this picture, and on this,
The counterfeit presentment of two brothers.
See what a grace was seated on this brow,
Hyperion's curls, the front of Jove himself,
An eye like Mars, to threaten and command,
A station like the herald Mercury,
New lighted on a heaven-kissing hill,
A combination and a form indeed,
Where every god did seem to set his seal
To give the world assurance of a man.
This was your husband, look you now what follows.
Here is your husband like a mildewed ear,
Blasting his wholesome brother. Have you eyes,
Could you on this fair mountain leave to feed,
And batten on this moor? Ha, have you eyes? . . .

Eye of newt

Source: MACBETH (Act IV, sc. i, l. 14)
Author: William Shakespeare (1564-1616)
First published: 1623
Type of work: Dramatic tragedy

Context: Macbeth and Banquo are advised by three witches that Macbeth will become king and that the descendants of Banquo will be monarchs. Macbeth, driven by his own evil ambition and that of his wife, murders Duncan, his king, his cousin, and his over-night guest. Though the crown is given to Macbeth, the new king is worried because the two sons of Duncan remain in exile, and, though Banquo has been murdered, Fleance, his son, has escaped Macbeth's hired assassins. Macbeth prepares to visit the oracles who gave him the former prophecy. In the meantime, the witches fix a charm by preparing a boiling caldron, taking turns casting hideous and venomous objects into the stew and muttering incantations.

SECOND WITCH

Fillet of a fenny snake,
In the caldron boil and bake;
Eye of newt, and toe of frog,
Wool of bat, and tongue of dog,
Adder's fork, and blind-worm's sting,
Lizard's leg, and howlet's wing;
For a charm of powerful trouble,
Like a hell-broth boil and bubble.

ALL

Double, double toil and trouble;
Fire burn, and caldron bubble.

Eyes too expressive to be blue, too lovely to be grey

Source: FADED LEAVES ("On the Rhine," Lines 19-20)
Author: Matthew Arnold (1822-1888)
First published: 1852
Type of work: Lyric poems

Context: Perhaps no other English poet has written with greater serenity and calm about the end of love and the misery of unrequited love than Matthew Arnold; many of his most famous lyrics open with a lovers' quarrel and develop into a speaker's plea for a renewal of the now thwarted love. In these poems he repeats that it is only through the beloved's eyes that the momentarily locked up love can be released. Staring silently into the beloved's eyes causes a bolt deep inside the lover to be thrown back, and he escapes from his sorrow by discovering his true self which has been buried. The group of lyrics in which this quotation appears are descriptive of a romance that has ended because the beloved does not return the poet's love; hoping that if he can gaze into her lovely eyes his sorrow will cease and the romance will again return, he begs his beloved to grant him this final wish. The poem is addressed to Frances Lucy Wightman, his courtship of whom was interrupted because of his poor financial prospects.

So let me lie, and, calm as they,
Let beam upon my inward view
Those eyes of deep, soft, lucent hue—
Eyes too expressive to be blue,
Too lovely to be grey.

Face-flatterer and backbiter are the same

Source: IDYLLS OF THE KING ("Merlin and Vivien," Line 822)
Author: Alfred, Lord Tennyson (1809-1892)
First published: 1859
Type of work: Narrative poem

Context: Vivien, the beautiful, wily, and malignant daughter of a man killed fighting against King Arthur, leaves Tintagel, the court of Mark of Cornwall, to go to Camelot. There she intends to sow seeds of suspicion concerning the honor and purity of Lancelot's devotion to Guinevere. While in Camelot, she sets out to win the heart of the aging wizard, Merlin. Even while doubting Vivien's honesty, Merlin "felt the flattery and at times/ Would flatter his own wish in age for love." Foreseeing the doom poised to fall on Camelot, Merlin leaves the court, consumed with melancholy. Vivien accompanies him to Broceliande where she attempts to extract from him a charm which en- snares its victim forever. Merlin agrees that he owes her a boon for breaking his melancholy, but he as- serts that this particular charm should not be shared. He fears that Vivien might, in a sudden fit of anger or jeal- ousy, use the charm against him or one of the Round Table. Mention of the knights irritates Vivien; she ac- cuses them of breaking their vows of chastity. In her spite, she even says Arthur is cowardly and foolishly self- deceived. Merlin proves her accusa- tions to be groundless slander. As a result of Vivien's fit of anger, Merlin swears not to tell her the secret of the charm, in spite of all her previous flattery. He says:

I know the Round Table, my friends of old;
All brave, and many generous, and some chaste.
She cloaks the scar of some repulse with lies.
I will believe she tempted them and failed,
Being so bitter. . . .
. . .
I will not let her know; nine tithes of times
Face-flatterer and backbiter are the same.
And they, sweet soul, that most impute a crime
Are pronest to it, and impute themselves,
Wanting the mental range, or low desire
Not to feel lowest makes them level all; . . .
. . .

Facts are facts

Source: THE RING AND THE BOOK (Book II, "Half-Rome," l. 1049)
Author: Robert Browning (1812-1889)
First published: 1868-1869
Type of work: Dramatic monologue

Context: The speaker, defending Guido who has murdered his wife and her parents, sarcastically relates the events that led to the murder. Not believing Pompilia's story of her husband's cruelty and her own innocence, he says that her flight from her husband was an obvious sign of her guilt, especially since she went with a very handsome priest who was not wearing his clerical clothes. That flight had ended in Castelnuovo, just outside Rome, when Guido came upon the pair and demanded the priest's punishment; the court at Rome had disciplined the priest but not as severely as Guido thought it should. The speaker, moreover, agrees with Guido: all of the evidence insinuates that he was grossly wronged, and if future husbands are to have any peace, he must be rewarded for defending his honor. The quotation occurs right after the speaker has described the circumstances under which Guido discovered his wife and the priest in Castlenuovo.

> But **facts are facts** and flinch not; stubborn things,
> And the question "Prithee, friend, how comes my purse
> I' the poke of you?"—admits of no reply.
> Here was a priest found out in masquerade,
> A wife caught playing truant if no more;
> While the Count, mortified in mien enough,
> And, nose to face, an added palm in length,
> Was plain writ "Husband" every piece of him:
> Capture once made, release could hardly be.
> Besides, the prisoners both made appeal,
> "Take us to Rome!"

Faint heart ne'er wan a lady fair

Source: TO DR. BLACKLOCK (Stanza 8)
Author: Robert Burns (1759-1796)
First published: 1789
Type of work: Epistle in verse

Context: Burns, the oldest of seven children of a terribly poor farmer, was encouraged by his father to take up literature. From his mother, he inherited wit and an ability to rhyme. So endowed, at the age of sixteen he wrote his first song, "O, once I loved a bonie lass." But though in subsequent years he added other poems to the manuscripts collected in a table drawer, he did nothing with them until, in 1786, he needed money for passage to Jamaica, where he had been offered a job on a plantation. Then he shipped off the bundle to a publisher who issued them as *Poems, Chiefly in the Scottish Dialect,* in an edition of 600 copies that brought Burns £20. Before he could sail for the West Indies, however, a letter from a certain Dr. Thomas Blacklock reached him, complimenting him on the volume and encouraging him to consider a second edition. From then on, Dr. Blacklock was one of Burns' best friends. A number of Burns' letters to Blacklock have been preserved. However, one, telling how he planned to legitimatize his relationship with Jean Armour by marrying her, was lost in transit. From Edinburgh, on August 24, 1789, Black-

lock wrote a rhymed letter beginning "Dear Burns, thou brother of my heart." It inquired about the health of Jean and their children. To this graceful letter, so full of interest and good wishes, Burns replied with another in verse that begins in a light mood, but turns bitter before its conclusion. It is dated at Ellisland Farm, 21st Oct., 1789, and for it the poet used the rhyme scheme now known as "Burns's stanza." It begins: "Wow, but your letter made me vauntie!" In it he apologizes for the non-arrival of the earlier letter. Then Burns mentions his "wife and twa wee laddies," and hopes to provide well for them because it is man's duty to maintain a happy fireside for "weans" (children) and wife. The final three stanzas declare:

Come, Firm Resolve, take thou the van,
Thou stalk o' carl-hemp in man!
And let us mind, **faint heart ne'er wan**
 A lady fair;
Wha does the utmost that he can,
 Will whyles do mair.

But to conclude my silly rhyme,
(I'm scant o' verse, and scant o' time,)
To make a happy fireside clime
 To weans and wife,
That's the true pathos and sublime
 Of human life.

My compliments to sister Beckie;
And eke the same to honest Lucky,
I wat she is a daintie chuckie,
 As e'er tread clay!
And gratefully, my guid auld cockie,
 I'm yours for ay.
 ROBERT BURNS

Fair, fat and forty

Source: SAINT RONAN'S WELL (Chapter 7)
Author: Sir Walter Scott (1771-1832)
First published: 1824
Type of work: Novel

Context: The inhabitants of the new hotel at the watering place of St. Ronan's Well are so devoured by curiosity about the artist, Francis Tyrrel, a lodger at Meg Dods' inn a few miles away from St. Ronan's, that they invite him to dinner and the post-prandial activities that enliven the evenings and the resort. After dinner, during the serving of tea and cake, various conversations take place; one recorded at considerable length is between the bachelor Dr. Quackleben and a newcomer to the establishment, Mrs. Blower, the widow of a sea captain. The doctor adds a bit of elixir he carries with him in a flask to Mrs. Blower's tea; the addition of his remedy both improves the taste of the tea and elevates Mrs. Blower's spirits. After the two have discussed the methods of various doctors, Mrs. Blower confides to Dr. Quackleben, to whom she applies a variety of names, that she is a lonely widow whose former husband had left her in very comfortable financial circumstances. The doctor's interest in the fair lady is perceptibly quickened. Scott's expression is an inversion of John O'Keeffe's earlier "fat, fair, and forty." (A carrack is a large ship, or galleon.)

. . . Lady Penelope, the presiding goddess of the region, watchful over all her circle, was not long of observing that the Doctor seemed to be suddenly engaged in close communication with the widow, and that he had even ventured to take hold of her fair plump hand, with a manner which partook at once of the gallant suitor, and of the medical adviser.

"For the love of Heaven," said her ladyship, "who can that comely dame be, on whom our excellent and learned Doctor looks with such uncommon regard?"

"**Fair, fat, and forty,**" said Mr. Winterblossom; "that is all I know of her,—a mercantile person."

"A carrack, Sir President," said the chaplain, "richly laden with colonial produce, by name the Lovely Peggy Bryce—no master—the late John Blower of North Leith having pushed off his boat for the Stygian Creek, and left the vessel without a hand on board."

"The Doctor," said Lady Penelope, turning her glass towards them, "seems willing to play the part of pilot."

"I dare say he will be willing to change her name and register," said Mr. Chatterly.

The fair humanities of old religion

Source: THE PICCOLOMINI; OR, THE FIRST PART OF WALLENSTEIN (Act II, sc. ii)
Author: Samuel Taylor Coleridge (1772-1834)
First published: 1800
Type of work: Historical drama

Context: This play is a translation of Schiller's play in German, which was based on a life of Wallenstein, the Duke of Friedland, hero of the Thirty Years' War. Wallenstein, fearful that he may lose his place as the commander of great armies, plots to make his senior officers pledge their loyalty to him alone, and not to the emperor. One officer, Wallenstein fears, may see through the plot; that officer is Lieutenant-General Octavio Piccolomini. To secure the older Piccolomini, Wallenstein uses his daughter, Princess Thekla, who falls in love with the general's son, Max Piccolomini, a colonel of cuirassiers. The two young persons are unaware of the plotting about them; they see only their newly discovered love, found when Max Piccolomini escorts Wallenstein's wife and daughter to the military camp. On the evening of their arrival at the camp, Princess Thekla and Max Piccolomini have a chance to be together, an opportunity arranged for them by Countess Tertsky, the girl's aunt. Princess Thekla tells her aunt and Max of a visit she has just made to the tower where Baptista Seni, an astrologer consulted by her father, consults the stars. Max Piccolomini, a realistic young soldier, states that he will no longer doubt the power of astrology, for love has opened his eyes to something more than "this visible nature, and this common world." He goes on to relate his new-found views:

MAX PICCOLOMINI
For fable is Love's world, his home, his birth-place;
Delightedly dwells he 'mong fays and talismans,
And spirits; and delightedly believes
Divinities, being himself divine.
The intelligible forms of ancient poets,
The fair humanities of old religion,
The Power, the Beauty, and the Majesty,
That had their haunts in dale, or piny mountain,
Or forest by slow stream, or pebbly spring,
Or chasms and wat'ry depths; all these have vanished.
They live no longer in the faith of reason!
But still the heart doth need a language, still
Doth the old instinct bring back the old names. . . .

The fair, the chaste, and unexpressive she

Source: AS YOU LIKE IT (Act III, sc. ii, l. 10)
Author: William Shakespeare (1564-1616)
First published: 1623
Type of work: Dramatic comedy

Context: Safe in the Forest of Arden, the fugtive Orlando has time to remember his love for Rosalind. Daughter of Duke Senior, who has spent many pleasant years of exile in the Forest, Rosalind is now herself a fugitive from court and is in disguise as a young man, having adopted the name Ganymede. Her presence is unknown both to her father and her lover. Orlando festoons the trees of the forest with poems in praise of Rosalind, despite his insistence that she is indescribable, "unexpressive":

ORLANDO

Hang there my verse, in witness of my love,
And thou thrice-crowned queen of night survey
With thy chaste eye, from thy pale sphere above,
Thy huntress' name, that my full life doth sway.
O Rosalind, these trees shall be my books,
And in their barks my thoughts I'll character,
That every eye, which in this forest looks,
Shall see thy virtue witnessed every where.
Run, run, Orlando, carve on every tree
The fair, the chaste, and unexpressive she.

Fair weather cometh out of the north

Source: JOB 37:22
Author: Unknown
First transcribed: c.900-500 B.C.
Type of work: Religious saga

Context: Job, a righteous and God-fearing man of the land of Uz, is put to the test by Satan, with the acquiescence of God. First Satan takes away Job's prosperity and kills Job's seven sons and three daughters. Then Satan visits physical misery on Job, in the form of boils that cover his body from crown to sole. Still Job does not curse God, but neither does he blame himself; he maintains that he is a good man, as he is, and that he has not sinned in any way to justify such miseries and unhappiness. When Eliphaz, Bildad, and Zophar come to visit Job, however, they maintain that he must have done something to deserve his miseries. When the three friends, who give little or no comfort to Job, have finished, Elihu, a fourth man, speaks up. Elihu, too, maintains that God never afflicts a man without cause; he tells Job that God always hears a submissive cry, but that He

273

sends adversity to a man either as a discipline or as a warning. He tells Job that God does great things that mere human beings cannot comprehend. He reminds Job that God causes the snow and the rains, as He causes the winds to blow and the seasons to move in their cycle. And he ends with a terrible warning for Job:

> Hearken unto this, O Job: stand still, and consider the wondrous works of God.
> Dost thou know when God disposed them, and caused the light of his cloud to shine?
> Dost thou know the balancings of the clouds, the wondrous works of him which is perfect in knowledge?
> How thy garments are warm, when he quieteth the earth by the south wind?
> Hast thou with him spread out the sky, which is strong, and as a molten looking glass?
> Teach us what we shall say unto him; for we cannot order our speech by reason of darkness.
> Shall it be told him I speak? if a man speak, surely he shall be swallowed up.
> And now men see not the bright light which is in the clouds: but the wind passeth and cleanseth them.
> **Fair weather cometh out of the north:** with God is terrible majesty.

False, fleeting, perjured Clarence

Source: KING RICHARD THE THIRD (Act I, sc. iv, l. 55)
Author: William Shakespeare (1564-1616)
First published: 1597
Type of work: Historical drama

Context: King Edward the Fourth has sent his brother, George, Duke of Clarence, to the Tower of London, where he will be murdered. Responsible for Clarence's imprisonment is Richard, Duke of Gloucester, the brother of the king and the imprisoned duke. Richard, later to be King Richard the Third, is plotting to remove all obstacles on his path to the throne, and he has persuaded the king that a man whose name begins with "G" will murder the king's sons. Suspicion has fallen, as Richard expected it to fall, on George, the Duke of Clarence, who earlier turned on the Earl of Warwick, his father-in-law, to help King Edward to the English throne. While in prison in the Tower of London, the Duke of Clarence has a terrible dream, in which he sees himself shoved overboard from a ship to his death by his brother Richard. In the dream he sees himself arriving in Hell, having passed over the River Styx in Charon's boat. He dreams he meets the Earl of Warwick, who curses him, and then the ghost of Edward, Prince of Wales, son of Henry the Sixth, whom Clar-

274

ence killed after the Battle of Tewksbury. Prince Edward's ghost also cries out for revenge in Hell. Clarence relates the dream to his keeper at the Tower of London.

CLARENCE

. . . Then came wandring by,
A shadow like an angel, with bright hair
Dabbled in blood; and he shrieked out aloud,
Clarence is come; **false, fleeting, perjur'd Clarence,**
That stabbed me in the field by Tewksbury:
Seize on him, Furies, take him unto torment!
With that, methought, a legion of foul fiends
Environed me, and howled in mine ears
Such hideous cries, that with the very noise
I trembling waked, and for a season after,
Could not believe but that I was in hell,
Such terrible impression made my dream.

Falsehood has a perennial spring

Source: SPEECH ON AMERICAN TAXATION
Author: Edmund Burke (1729-1797)
First published: 1774
Type of work: Political speech

Context: In the second part of his address to Parliament on American taxation, Edmund Burke, who was a foe to its wrongful imposition and a friend to the American Colonies, gives a history of the subject in America. He points out that at the time of the first American Revenue Act, in 1764, the colonists did not object to port duties and that statements made in Parliament itself showed that the colonists had not entered into controversy with the British government on the first excuse, that the colonists had actually been pushed into rebellion by the actions of Parliament. Burke goes on to point out that several falsehoods about the Americans had been widespread, in addition to the lie that they had been looking for controversy. Burke specifically mentions the false story that George Grenville, the author of the Stamp Act, had proposed to the Colonies that they tax themselves and that they had subsequently refused. Burke then proceeds to dispose of another false report— that no one in Parliament had known of the colonists' dislike for port duties:

Thus, Sir, I have disposed of this falsehood. But **falsehood has a perennial spring.** It is said, that no conjecture could be made of the dislike of the Colonies to the principle. This is as untrue as the other. After the resolution of the House, and before the passing of the Stamp Act, the Colonies of Massachusetts Bay and New York did send remonstrances, objecting to this mode of Parliamentary taxation. What was the consequence? They were suppressed; they were put under the table, notwithstanding an Order of Council to the contrary, by the Ministry which composed the very Council that had made the Order: and thus the House proceeded to its business of taxing without the least regular knowledge of the objections that were made to it. . . .

Familiarity begets boldness

Source: THE ANTIQUARY (Act I)
Author: Shackerley Marmion (1603-1639)
First published: 1641
Type of work: Dramatic comedy

Context: With the inconsistent spelling of the seventeenth century, an English dramatist published his first play in 1632 under the name of Schackerley Marmyon, Master of Arts. By the time *The Antiquary* appeared, in 1641, its author was given as Shackerly Mermion, Gent. Actually, the name of the ancient Lancaster family was Shakerly. The dramatist was born in Northampton, in January, 1602 (Old Style). After the usual free-school education, he was sent to Wadham College, out of which he came as gentleman commoner, with a Master of Arts degree in 1624. Lacking a family fortune, for his father was a spendthrift, Shackerley tried the army in the Low Countries, but he found promotion slow, so he returned to England and enlisted in a cavalry troop raised by his friend Sir John Suckling, in 1638, for service against the Scotch Covenanters. However, he became ill during the campaign and returned to London, where he died. His writing, done at intervals, began with two plays, *Holland's Leaguer* (1632), and *A Fine Companion* (1633). A graceful legend of *Cupid and Psyche or An Epic Poem of Cupid and His*

Mistress (1637), on which his poetic fame chiefly rests, was followed by a third play, *The Antiquary* (1641), in imitation of Ben Jonson. A fourth comedy, *The Crafty Merchant or the Soldier'd Citizen,* sometimes attributed to him, was never printed. *The Antiquary* "performed by His Majesty's Servants at the Cock-Pit," was highly admired by Sir Walter Scott and others as one of England's best early dramatic attempts. Scott reprinted it in his *Ancient British Dramas,* as did several other compilers of early plays. The setting of the play is given as Pisa, with the Duke of Pisa as one of the main characters, but the dramatist apparently confused Pisa with Venice, because he mentions "The Rialto" in the first act and "canals" in the third. In the List of Characters he also carelessly called Aemelia "wife to Gasparo" and Lucretia "daughter to Gasparo," where the play shows them as part of the family of elderly Lorenzo. But as Horace observed, even Homer nodded on occasion. The play starts with Lionell, nephew of the wealthy Antiquary Veterano, welcoming Petrutio, Gasparo's stupid son, who is sure his excellent qualities will bring him success at court. Lionell offers, in return for the loan of a hundred ducats, to help him, but now Petrutio is interested only in Lionell's page boy, actually his sister Angelia disguised. Petrutio meets his father in company with Lorenzo, who is seeking a husband for his daughter Lucretia. The fop is not interested in marriage. He declares: "I have chosen Honor as my Mistress upon whose wings I will mount up to heaven where I will fix myself a constellation for all this underworld of mortals to wonder at me." Meanwhile, the Duke of Pisa tells his courtier Leonardo that in order to know his subjects, he has decided to follow the example of Cato, who mingled with the crowds at the Spring Festival to Flora. In Cato's case, his appearance at a public theater amid a licentious festival involving nude women interrupted the spectacle. So the Duke will disguise himself in "mean coverture," or lowly clothing. "Vulgar" refers to the common people. Leonardo suggests that while disguised, they visit the Antiquary, sure to be an excellent companion if he is as expert at wines as at history. At the end of the play, the Duke finds Lionell impersonating him, but arranging justice and happiness for everyone so well that the Duke confirms his decrees. In the first act, planning his walk in disguise among his subjects, the Duke and Leonardo talk. The courtier warns, as many from Aesop and Shakespeare to Mark Twain have done, that "familiarity breeds contempt."

DUKE

. . . I am determin'd to lay by all ensigns of my Royalty for awhile, and walk abroad under a mean coverture. Variety does well; and 't is a great delight, sometimes, to shroud one's head under a coarse roof, as under a rich canopy of gold.

LEONARDO

But what's your intent in this?

DUKE

I have a longing desire to see the fashions of the vulgar; which, should I affect in mine own person, I might divert them from their humors. The face of greatness would affright them, as Cato did the Floralio from the theatre.

LEONARDO

Indeed **familiarity begets boldness.**

DUKE

'T is true, indulgence and flattery take away the benefit of experience from Princes, which ennobles the fortunes of private men.

277

Famous, calm, and dead

Source: A GRAMMARIAN'S FUNERAL (Line 27)
Author: Robert Browning (1812-1889)
First published: 1855
Type of work: Dramatic monologue

Context: The subtitle "Shortly after the revival of learning in Europe" gives the key to this dramatic monologue. It is spoken by one of a group of pupils of the dead grammarian who, with his fellow-students, is carrying the body of his master to burial at the top of a mountain. The pupil describes his late master as a man who has devoted his entire life to scholarship—to the study of the grammatical structure of the Greek language, at that time newly returned to Europe after centuries during which it had been known only in fragments. The grammarian had sacrificed a lifetime to this study; neither illness nor age had halted his work. Now that he is dead, his pupils feel that only burial on a mountain-top, amid the storms and lightnings, is fitting for such a devoted scholar. The poem contains one of Browning's favorite themes: that the important aspect of life is what we *try* to do, not what we accomplish. The man of small mind aims at a low mark and easily attains it. The really great man aims at an impossible goal. This goal he can never reach; yet in his effort to do so, he goes far beyond the reach of the small man. So it was with the dead grammarian: he had tried to master all of the subtleties of the Greek language. He had failed, yet he had been an inspiration to his pupils to whom he had passed on his love of learning for its own sake. So the speaker, who is leading the burial procession, comments:

. . .

Leave we the unlettered plain its herd and crop;
    Seek we sepulture
On a tall mountain, citied to the top,
    Crowded with culture!
All the peaks soar, but one the rest excels;
    Clouds overcome it;
No! yonder sparkle is the citadel's
    Circling its summit.
Thither our path lies; wind we up the heights:
    Wait ye the warning?
Our low life was the level's and the night's;
    He's for the morning.
Step to a tune, square chests, erect each head,
    'Ware the beholders!
This is our master, **famous, calm, and dead,**
    Borne on our shoulders.

Fan spread and streamers out, and a shoal of fools for tenders

Source: THE WAY OF THE WORLD (Act II, sc. ii)
Author: William Congreve (1670-1729)
First published: 1700
Type of work: Dramatic comedy

Context: Mrs. Fainall, formerly the mistress of Mirabell, discusses her situation with Mirabell. When she merely hated her husband, she could tolerate him, but now she despises him and cannot stand him. Mirabell replies that she should have just enough disgust for her husband to give her a relish for her lover. Mirabell explains that he had her marry to save her reputation, as it seemed possible that she might have a child. A better man than her husband should not have been sacrificed to the occasion, and a worse one would not have served the purpose. They then discuss an intrigue they are setting afoot to place Mrs. Fainall's mother, Lady Wishfort, in a compromising position. They are discussing the lady's character when Mrs. Millamant, who loves Mirabell, enters with Witwoud, one of her admirers, and Mincing, her maid. Apparently she makes a rather stately and impressive entrance, for Mirabell likens her to a full-rigged ship; she comes, he says, full sail, with her fan spread and her streamers out, like the ship with its canvas unfurled and all the flags flying:

MRS. FAINALL
Here's your mistress.
[*Enter* MRS. MILLAMANT, WITWOUD, *and* MINCING.]

MIRABELL
Here she comes, i'faith, full sail, with her **fan spread and streamers out, and a shoal of fools for tenders;** ha, no, I cry her mercy!

MRS. FAINALL
I see but one poor empty sculler; and he tows her woman after him.

Fans turn into falchions in fair hands

Source: DON JUAN (Canto I, stanza 21)
Author: George Gordon, Lord Byron (1788-1824)
First published: 1819 (Cantos I and II)
Type of work: Satiric poem

Context: Lord Byron, after selecting "our ancient friend Don Juan" as the protagonist for his satiric epic poem, "begin[s] with the beginning" and goes on to describe the young hero's parents, Don Jóse and Donna Inez, true Gothic aristocrats of Spain without tint of alien blood. Though the

279

learned and witty Donna Inez is virtuous beyond comparison with the saints, she is insipid (as all such perfection must be) as was the garden before the fall, and Don Jóse, a true son of Eve and "a mortal of the careless kind" goes straying after other fruits, never dreaming that she cares. But Donna Inez, for all her merits, has "a devil of a spirit" and repays neglect (the sin to try even a saint!) by getting her lord into many a scrape. And

> This was an easy matter with a man
>   Oft in the wrong, and never on his guard;
> And even the wisest, do the best they can,
>   Have moments, hours, and days, so unprepared,
> That you might "brain them with their lady's fan;"
>   And sometimes ladies hit exceeding hard,
> And **fans turn into falchions in fair hands**
> And why and wherefore no one understands.

> 'Tis pity learned virgins ever wed
>   With persons of no sort of education,
> Or gentlemen, who, though well born and bred,
>   Grow tired of scientific conversation;
> I don't choose to say much upon this head,
>   I'm a plain man, and in a single station,
> But—Oh! ye lords of ladies intellectual,
> Inform us truly, have they not hen-peck'd you all?

Farewell, rewards and fairies!

Source: FAREWELL TO FAIRIES (Line 1)
Author: Bishop Richard Corbet (1582-1635)
First published: 1647
Type of work: Satirical poem

Context: Corbet, in his later days a bishop in the Church of England, and noted for his wit, touches lightly a problem that to him has weighty overtones. Gone from "merry old England," says the poet, are the fairies and the old superstitions countenanced by the Catholics before the coming of Protestantism to the country. If Corbet is critical of the Roman Church for allowing the remnants of paganism to remain among the peasantry, he seems equally critical of the dour-faced Puritans who stamped out the cult of fairies. The first line of the poem supplied Kipling with the title of one of his most famous books for children (1910)

> **"Farewell, rewards and fairies!"**
> Good housewives now may say,
> For now foul sluts in dairies
> Do fare as well as they,

And though they sweep their hearths no less
  Than maids were wont to do,
Yet who of late for cleanliness,
  Finds sixpence in her shoe?

Lament, lament, old abbeys,
  The fairies lost command;
They did but change priests' babies,
  But some have changed your land;
And all your children sprung from thence
  Are now grown Puritanes;
Who live as changelings ever since
  For love of your domains.

　　　•　•　•

Witness these rings and roundelays
  Of theirs, which yet remain,
Were footed in Queen Mary's days
  On many a grassy plain;
But since of late Elizabeth,
  And later, James came in,
They never danced on any heath
  As when the time hath been.

Fast and furious

Source: TAM O'SHANTER (Line 144)
Author: Robert Burns (1759-1796)
First published: 1791
Type of work: Narrative poem

Context: To persuade Captain Francis Grose (1731?–1791) to sketch Alloway Church, where Burns's father was buried, the poet promised to provide him with a versified ghost story to publish with the picture in *Grose's Antiquities of Scotland* (1791). He finished the poem in twenty-four hours and made an immortal masterpiece. Tam o' Shanter, lazy husband of the shrewish Kate, never came home after market until he had spent all his money in the town tavern, drinking with his crony the Shoemaker Johnny, and the tavern keeper and his ingratiating wife. However, on the day of the story, he finally decides at midnight to dare the furious storm and the night in which "a child might understand/ The Deil (devil) had business on his hand." He rides homeward on Meg, his grey mare, humming a Scotch song, till he comes within sight of Kirk Alloway, about which many frightening stories circulate. He remembers some of the dead people associated with the area. To his amazement, the church is ablaze with light. Too full of liquor to be frightened, because "Wi' usquebae, we'll face the devil," Tammie guides his horse in the direction of the church and cemetery. Here he sees "an unco sight." Warlocks and witches are dancing to the music of hornpipes, jigs, and reels, with Old

281

Nick himself looking on. On the table before him, in place of holy relics, are bones of murderers, tomahawks, bloodstained "scymitars," and weapons used to commit many barbarous crimes. Here are the meanings of some of the dialectal words: Cleekit —joined hands; ilka carlin—every old woman; swat and reekit—sweat and steamed; Coost her duddies to the wark—stripped off her clothes; linket in her sark—danced in her chemise.

As Tammie glowr'd, amaz'd, and curious,
The mirth and fun grew **fast and furious;**
The piper loud and louder blew;
The dancers quick and quicker flew;
They reel'd, they set, they cross'd, they cleekit,
Till ilka carlin swat and reekit,
And coost her duddies to the wark,
And linket at it in her sark!

Fat, fair, and forty

Source: THE IRISH MIMIC, OR BLUNDERS AT BRIGHTON (Act II, sc. iii)
Author: John O'Keeffe (1747-1833)
First published: 1797
Type of work: Farce with music

Context: Called in its time a "contrived piece," *The Irish Mimic* is a musical play put together for light entertainment by an Irish actor and playwright noted for dramatic works of many kinds. His most successful performance was probably *Tony Lumpkin in Town,* produced in 1777. Of his farces, *Wild Oats* had the greatest number of performances. However, it is for a song from his *Merry Sherwood,* "I am a Friar of Orders Gray," that O'Keeffe is chiefly remembered today. A line from his *London Hermit* also survives, though usually misquoted. It announces that general statements are not intended to apply to people hearing them, or as O'Keeffe phrased the assertion: "You should always except the present company." *The Irish Mimic* was intended only for amusement. Farces, unlike comedies, are not to be analyzed for plot or action. Here the audience is supposed to accept a situation in which the two Melcombe ladies, Julia and her Aunt Margaret, can move in society without the realization that there are two of them, and that Julia in regimentals and her aunt in a riding habit might be taken for two young gentlemen. In addition, the story told by Captain Clifford to Mr. Parrots, the Irish Mimic, must seem convincing. To persuade him to whip a rival, he tells of a gentleman who has been insulted by a friend but lacks the spirit to resent the insult himself, but who, dying, will put into his will a legacy of a hundred pounds to anyone who will cane the man "in the public Steine." Part of the complication comes because Clifford tries to spur Mr. Parrots into action by doubting the man's courage. Farces frequently insert characters purely for comic effect, as O'Keeffe did in this play, set at Brighton, England's popular beach resort. It was first performed at the Royal Theatre, Covent Garden, in 1795. Two such characters are Colin, servant to "that voine lady, Miss Melcombe," and his brother Harry, who does not know there are two of the ladies. The chief character is Mr. Parrots, a professional mimic who claims to be able to imitate anybody, and does so in the course of the play, especially in one humorous scene involving Margaret Melcombe and her elderly admirer, Cypress. Since young men admire women "fat, fair and forty," perhaps young women may fall for those men who are "shriveled, sallow, and sixty." In Act II, Parrots comes upon Miss Julia wearing regimentals and talking to Harry.

HARRY

Madam!—Well, ma'am, I've seen variety of lodgings.

JULIA

Hush! How indiscreet!

PARROTS

Madam! I'm sure he did say madam. Oh, oh, this must be the lady Cypress desired me to mimic. Such a beautiful creature, love him! May be so, as the F's, **fat, fair, and forty,** was all the toast of the young men.—Who knows but the S's, shriveled, sallow, and sixty, may become the rage of the young women. [*Aside.*]

JULIA

If Clifford quits Brighton, and carries my aunt off with him, I shall have no occasion to change. [*Exit Harry. Music plays.*]

PARROTS

This Irish music is very fine—Pray, sir, how do you like Planxty Connor?

JULIA

I don't know any such person!

PARROTS

Pardon—Why Sir, it's—'Pon my soul she is a pretty little fellow! Drest herself up for some frolic, I suppose. —When a lady is inclin'd for fun, the gentleman should take half the business on himself.

283

The fatal gift of beauty

Source: CHILDE HAROLD'S PILGRIMAGE (Canto IV, stanza 42)
Author: George Gordon, Lord Byron (1788-1824)
First published: 1818 (Canto IV)
Type of work: Narrative poem

Context: Byron's *Childe Harold's Pilgrimage* was written and published piecemeal. The poet finished the first two cantos in 1812, and reaped instant glory. Canto III, generally considered the best, with its references to Bonaparte and the Battle of Waterloo, was published in 1816, but Canto IV did not get into print until 1818. Byron wrote it during his stay in Venice in 1817, where gossip reported him living licentiously, yet he had the time to write this canto, the narrative poems *Beppo* and *Mazeppa,* and to begin his famous *Don Juan.* Canto IV is prefaced by a letter to John C. Hobhouse, (1786–1869), who had traveled with Byron on the trip through the Mediterranean that had inspired the first canto. In the preface, Byron declares that Harold the Pilgrim no longer exists for him. His poem has now become his own personal reactions. The canto begins with the famous lines, "I stood in Venice on the Bridge of Sighs,/ A palace and a prison on each hand." Originally he had intended to discuss contemporary Italian Literature and Manners, but the discussion would have made the composition much too long. He sees about him too many great writers who will leave their mark upon their country's literature. So instead, he writes of the loveliness of storied Venice, whose gondoliers used to sing verses by Tasso. The changes in the city remind him of the changes in himself. He pauses to remark that, though he has traveled far and learned many languages, he wants to die in England and be remembered there. Then back to Venice whose history he learned as a child through the plays of many of the world's dramatists. His thoughts expand to include all of Italy. He thinks of Petrarch's tomb in Arqua, and of the "Bards of Hell and Chivalry," that is, Dante and Ariosto. Their homeland whose beauty attracted all the world has, for that reason, lost some of its power and glory, for those attracted to it have sapped its power and wealth. So he exclaims in Stanza 42:

> Italia! oh, Italia! thou who hast
> **The fatal gift of beauty,** which became
> A funeral dower of present woes and past,
> On thy sweet brow is sorrow plough'd by shame,
> And annals graved in characters of flame.
> Oh, God!, that thou wert in thy nakedness
> Less lovely or more powerful, and couldst claim
> Thy right, and awe the robbers back, who press
> To shed thy blood and drink the tears of thy distress.

284

A faultless monster which the world never saw

Source: AN ESSAY ON POETRY (Line 231)
Author: John Sheffield (1648-1721)
First published: 1682
Type of work: Verse essay

Context: Sheffield was Earl of Mulgrave and later Duke of Buckinghamshire and a member of that group of witty courtly poets which frequented the court of Charles II during the Restoration period. Other members of the group included Sedley, Dorset, Charles Cotton, and the notorious Rochester. The poetry of this group of young noblemen was highly polished and elegant if, at times, somewhat superficial and erotic. Verse was a popular form for the "essay" of criticism in this period, and as Sheffield neared the end of this survey of aesthetic theory he commented that the proper imitation of the classics was appropriate in figures of speech as well as in other features of poetry:

> Their beauties imitate, avoid their faults:
> First, on a plot employ thy careful thoughts;
> Turn it, with time, a thousand several ways;
> This oft, alone, has given success to plays.
> Reject that vulgar errour (which appears
> So fair) of making perfect characters;
> There's no such thing in nature, and you'll draw
> **A faultless monster, which the world ne'er saw.**
> Some faults must be, that his misfortune drew,
> But such as may deserve compassion too.

Fear is the parent of cruelty

Source: SHORT STUDIES ON GREAT SUBJECTS, SERIES III ("Party Politics")
Author: James Anthony Froude (1818-1894)
First published: 1882 (Series III)
Type of work: Political essay

Context: Froude was an English historian of considerable stature, who conceived of history as a great drama; his treatment of British history therefore emphasizes the personal element, and incidents are recounted in a stirring and dramatic manner. His most substantial accomplishment is his *History of England from the Fall of Wolsey to the Defeat of the Spanish Armada.* He also wrote a lengthy biography of Carlyle and a historical novel. His *Short Studies on Great Subjects* include a large variety of essays on various topics. In one of these, "Party Politics," he expresses concern over what he fears is the end of party government. Both parties intend to continue in the same spirit and along the same lines of progress; the only differences between them pertain to the rate at which changes shall take place. As conservatism weakens, it ensures its own doom, talented and ambitious men will join the successful faction, and even when the people desire a change, the materials for a conservative government will no longer exist. Froude then considers the nature of progress, or motion, and points out that it can mean movement toward either growth or decay. He compares expedient social change with the device that captains of slave-ships used to escape their pursuers. They sawed through the bulkheads of their own ships; this trick made the craft more flexible and thus faster. They were safe so long as the wind was behind them, but if they met a head wind the vessel would fall apart and sink. Liberal statesman, in Froude's opinion, act in much the same fashion; for this reason their work can be only destructive in the long run. Froude is suspicious of democracies. "Popular governments have hitherto uniformly glided into democracies, and democracies as uniformly perish of their own excess. If they escape a violent end by faction, they die of a disease which they cannot escape. Men are made by nature unequal." He then considers the necessity of organization, cohesion, and leadership:

. . . If work is to be productive, the wise must direct and the fool must obey; and as the business of life cannot stand still till the fool is convinced of his folly by argument, direction must take the form of command. Thus gradually the continent of human occupation is trodden into roads, which experience proves to lead most directly to the desired end. Experience teaches slowly, and at the cost of mistakes . . . at any given time the beaten track is safer for the multitude than any independent course which originality may strike out for itself; and if a person who fancies that he is not one of the multitude chooses to act in another direction, he is regarded with natural distrust. In one instance in a thousand he may be right, and if he has the courage to persevere he will earn an exceptional place for himself in the honour of his kind. But the presumption is against him, and penalties are fitly imposed on eccentricity in proportion to the disturbance which it threatens.

As it has been with practice, so it has been with opinion. Surrounded by invisible forces, their destination and their origin alike concealed behind a veil, yet liable at any moment to accidents by which their lives, their fortunes, their happiness might be affected for good or ill, men began early to speculate on the nature of the powers which seemed to envelope their existence. They gave rein to their fears and to their fancy. . . . Ignorance is the dominion of absurdity. **Fear is the parent of cruelty.** Ignorance and fear combined have made the religious annals of mankind the most hideous chapters in history. . . .

Fell death's untimely frost

Source: HIGHLAND MARY (Stanza 3)
Author: Robert Burns (1759-1796)
First published: 1799
Type of work: Song

Context: The year 1786, when Burns was twenty-seven years old, was a most important one for the poet. His poems, written in rapid succession, produced such a body of original work—natural, forcible, and picturesque, and also quaint, sarcastic, humorous, and tender—as had not appeared since the time of Shakespeare. Yet for Burns, misfortunes were also piling up. In 1784, he had met "Bonie Jean" (Jean Armour), and on his side, the acquaintanceship had ripened into passion. Her father had forbidden their marriage. In the spring of 1786 he learned she was about to become a mother. He sent her a written acknowledgment of marriage, a document that by the laws of Scotland made their connection legal. He also wrote a poem beginning "Thou's welcome, wean (child)" and addressed "To His Illegitimate Child." But Mr. Armour still refused to recognize a marriage. He burned the document. Then Burns decided to emigrate as bookkeeper to the estate of Dr. Douglas, in Jamaica. To raise the nine pounds necessary for the voyage, he arranged for the publication of all the poems he had written and tossed into the drawer of his table. About then he became acquainted with Mary Campbell, once servant in the family of Gavin Hamilton and then a dairy maid. They fell in love. She returned to her parents in Argyleshire in May, 1786, to get ready for the marriage, after a tender farewell in which they plighted troth on the banks of the Ayr. While Burns was working on the 600-copy edition of his poems, Mary died. The poet was reticent about her and occupied himself with the preparation of a second edition, at the suggestion of Dr. Blacklock. People thought he had put Mary out of his mind, but years later a number of heartfelt songs proved how much she had meant to him and how deeply and affectionately he remembered her. Besides two songs "To Mary in Heaven," beginning "Thou lingering star with less'ning ray/ That lov'st to greet the early morn," and "To Mary," declaring "could aught of song declare my pains. . ./ The Muse should tell, in labour'd pains/ O Mary, how I love thee," Burns wrote four impassioned stanzas to be sung to the tune of *Katherine Ogie*. He remembers the "banks and braes, and streams around/ The castle of Montgomery" where he "took the last fareweel/ O' my sweet Highland Mary." In the final two stanzas he describes the scene:

Wi' monie a vow, an' lock'd embrace,
  Our parting was fu' tender;
And, pledging aft to meet again,
  We tore oursels asunder;
But oh! **fell death's untimely frost,**

287

That nip't my flower sae early!
Now green's the sod, and cauld's the clay,
That wraps my Highland Mary!

O pale, pale now, those rosy lips,
I aft hae kiss'd sae fondly!
And closed for ay the sparkling glance,
That dwelt on me sae kindly!
And mould'ring now in silent dust,
That heart that lo'ed me dearly!
But still within my bosom's core
Shall live my Highland Mary.

A fellow almost damned in a fair wife

Source: OTHELLO (Act I, sc. i, l. 22)
Author: William Shakespeare (1564-1616)
First published: 1622
Type of work: Dramatic tragedy

Context: In the opening scene of the play—in conversation with Roderigo —Iago berates Othello, his military superior, for failure to promote him to second-in-command. Instead, the lieutenancy has been awarded to Cassio, a young Florentine whom Iago denounces as bookish and inexperienced. In his tirade against this new appointee, Iago makes a remark about Cassio's wife which has frequently puzzled readers of the play. "Damned in a fair wife" reflects, of course, a proverbial attitude that a beautiful wife is a source of trouble for her husband. But Shakespeare does not provide Cassio a wife in the play. Perhaps he had originally intended to do so and failed to delete this line when he decided otherwise; in the Italian work by Geraldio Cinthio which served as Shakespeare's source, the captain is indeed married, though not cuckolded. Or perhaps Iago is making a snide remark about the courtesan Bianca and her unsuccessful matrimonial purusit of the lieutenant. In any case, the immediate context is clear. According to Iago, Cassio has neither the experience nor the manliness for his new position. The following lines set the stage for Iago's open declaration of villainy— that he follow Othello but to serve his turn upon him. His subsequent determination to prod Othello into mad jealousy on circumstantial evidence concerning Desdemona's fidelity forms the main action of the plot.

IAGO
• • •
Forsooth, a great arithmetician,
One Michael Cassio, a Florentine,
A fellow almost damned in a fair wife,
That never set a squadron in the field,

288

Nor the division of a battle knows
More than a spinster, unless the bookish theoric,
Wherein the toged consuls can propose
As masterly as he. Mere prattle, without practice
In all his soldiership. But he, sir, had th' election;
And I—of whom his eyes had seen the proof
At Rhodes, at Cyprus, and on other grounds
Christian and heathen—must be be-leed and calmed
By debitor and creditor. This counter-caster,
He, in good time, must his lieutenant be,
And I God bless the mark, his Moorship's ancient.

A fickle thing and changeful is woman always

Source: THE AENEID (Book IV, as translated by John Jackson)
Author: Virgil (Publius Vergilius Maro, 70-19 B.C.)
First transcribed: 29-19 B.C.
Type of work: Epic poem

Context: A true epic is a natural, gradual evolution, about whose author little or nothing is known. So the *Aeneid* (i.e., a poem about Aeneas) is a literary epic, being the result of conscious artistic efforts by Publius Vergilius Maro, product of Rome's Golden Age and friend of its Emperor Augustus. Aeneas, fleeing from burning Troy spends the winter with Queen Dido of Carthage, enjoying her passionate love. Finally details of his delay reach Jove, who has destined Aeneas to found Rome, and he sends his son, Mercury, to order Aeneas to depart. When Queen Dido and her sister Anna beg the Trojan to remain, Mercury again visits him in a vision, to warn him falsely that fickle Dido and her sister are planning to play on his affections and even destroy his ships to prevent his departure. The Greeks are not the only people to have a word for the fickleness of woman. Francis I of France (1494–1547) is supposed to have written with his diamond ring on a window of the Château of Chambord: "Woman often changes; foolish the man who trusts her." The Duke in Verdi's *Rigoletto* sings: "La donna è mobile (Woman is changeable)." As Virgil tells the story:

. . . a vision . . . visited his dreams . . . in all things like to Mercury, voice and color, yellow locks, and the graceful limbs of youth: . . . "Madman, seest not the after-dangers that beset thee? Resolved on death, she is pondering in her heart fell villainy and treachery, and rousing the swirling tide of passion: . . . Anon, thou wilt see the brine a turmoil of shattered timbers, see torches flashing fierce and the strand fervent with fire, if the rays of dawn discover thee tarrying in the land. Up and go!—truce to delay. **A fickle thing and changeful is woman always!**" Thus he said, and mingled with the shadows of night.

289

The final harbor, whence we unmoor no more

Source: MOBY DICK (Chapter 114)
Author: Herman Melville (1819-1891)
First published: 1851
Type of work: Novel

Context: In its search for whales, and with Captain Ahab looking still for Moby Dick, the whaler "Pequod" sails into the relatively calm waters of the Japanese cruising ground. In mild, pleasant weather the boat crews of the whaling-ship seek their prey, often sitting quietly in their frail whale-boats for an hour or more, waiting for whales to rise to the surface. At such times, says Melville, one forgets the tiger heart and remorseless fangs of the ocean, so beautiful and calm it is. On such occasions, "in his whale-boat the rover softly feels a certain filial, confident, land-like feeling towards the sea; that he regards it as so much flowery earth." Even upon Captain Ahab, that tortured soul, the ocean has a soothing effect temporarily. The sea seems almost like land, says Melville, with blue hillsides where play-wearied children sleep in solitude in "some glad Maytime." It is in such a quiet time that a man may think long and deep, to consider not just this life, but the life of his eternal soul, as Melville suggests:

Oh, grassy glades! oh, ever vernal endless landscapes in the soul; in ye,—though long parched by the dead drought of the earthy life,—in ye, men yet may roll, like young horses in new morning clover; and for some few fleeting moments, feel the cool dew of the life immortal on them. Would to God these blessed calms would last. But the mingled, mingling threads of life are woven by warp and woof: calms crossed by storms, a storm for every calm. There is no steady unretracing progress in this life; we do not advance through fixed gradations, and at the last one pause:—through infancy's unconscious spell, boyhood's thoughtless faith, adolescence' doubt (the common doom), then scepticism, then disbelief, resting at last in manhood's pondering repose of If. But once gone through, we trace the round again; and are infants, boys, and men, and Ifs eternally. Where lies **the final harbor, whence we unmoor no more?** In what rapt ether sails the world, of which the weariest will never weary? Where is the foundling's father hidden? Our souls are like those orphans whose unwedded mothers die in bearing them: the secret of our paternity lies in their grave, and we must there to learn it.

A fine puss-gentleman that's all perfume

Source: CONVERSATION (Line 284)
Author: William Cowper (1731-1800)
First published: 1782
Type of work: Essay in verse

Context: Having listed many deterrents to good conversation, such as sound and fury in place of logic, and the smoking of a pipe that not only slows up the story-telling but drives the fair sex from the room, Cowper continues his 908-line discussion of the gift of conversation with attention to another of his pet hatreds, a highly perfumed fine gentleman. His mind travels from the civet out of which perfumes are made to the civet cat from which that secretion is obtained. Accordingly, he calls such persons "puss-gentlemen." Their heavy perfume sickens and even kills some people. The "raree shows" referred to, were peep shows or carnivals, frequented by the unwashed rabble.

I cannot talk with civet in the room,
A fine puss-gentleman that's all perfume;
The sight's enough—no need to smell a beau—
Who thrusts his nose into a raree show?
His odoriferous attempts to please
Perhaps might prosper with a swarm of bees;
But we that make no honey, though we sting,
Poets, are sometimes apt to maul the thing.
'Tis wrong to bring into a mixed resort
What makes some sick, and others à-la-mort,—
An argument of cogence, we may say,
Why such a one should keep himself away.

Fine words butter no parsnips

Source: A LEGEND OF MONTROSE (Chapter 3)
Author: Sir Walter Scott (1771-1832)
First published: 1819
Type of work: Novel

Context: One evening in the decade of the 1640's, when the Royalists of England were fighting the Roundheads, the Earl of Menteith and two servants are traveling up a Scottish glen when a single completely armed man rides towards them. After challenges have been exchanged, the earl says that he is a Royalist and asks the newcomer, Dugald Dalgetty, which side he is on. Dalgetty does not know as yet. He, however, recounts his services on the Continent as a mercenary soldier with various forces: with the Swedes, under Gustavus, the Lion of the North; with Walter Butler's

291

Irish Regiment, under Wallenstein; with the Spanish; and with the States of Holland. Sometimes he got his full pay and sometimes he did not; but whether he did or not, he usually managed to do well enough by plundering to keep himself satisfied. When Menteith says that he cannot see why Dalgetty does not embrace the cause of King Charles I, he is treated to a discourse on slogans. "Caeteris paribus" is Old Latin for "Other things being equal."

"Ye speak reasonably, my lord," said Dalgetty, "and *caeteris paribus,* I might be induced to see the matter in the same light. But, my lord, there is a southern proverb,—**fine words butter no parsnips.** I have heard enough, since I came here, to satisfy me, that a cavalier of honor is free to take any part in this civil embroilment whilk he may find most convenient for his own peculiar. Loyalty is your pass-word, my lord—Liberty, roars another chield from the other side of the strath—the King, shouts one war-cry— the Parliament roars another—Montrose for ever, cries Donald, waving his bonnet—Argyle and Leven, cries a south-country Saunders, vaporing with his hat and feather—Fight for the bishops, says a priest, with his gown and rochet—stand Stout for the Kirk, cries a minister, in a Geneva cap and band.—Good watchwords all—excellent watchwords. Whilk cause is the best I cannot say. But sure I am, that I have fought knee-deep in blood many a day for one that was ten degrees worse than the worst of them all."

Fingers were made before forks

Source: POLITE CONVERSATION (Dialogue II)
Author: Jonathan Swift (1677-1745)
First published: 1738
Type of work: Satire

Context: English satirist Jonathan Swift, noting that the art of conversation is dying, attempts to enliven it by giving examples of "polite conversation," incidentally filled with clichés, appropriate for ladies and gentlemen at tea, dinner, or other social occasions. At a dinner at the home of Lady Smart, the following dialogue ensues when Miss Notable asks Colonel Atwit for a fritter:

MISS NOTABLE
Pray, colonel, send me some fritters.
                    [*Colonel takes them out with his hand.*]

COLONEL ATWIT
Here, miss; they say, **fingers were made before forks,** and hands before knives.

292

Methinks the pudden is too much boil'd.

Oh! madam, they say, a pudden is poison when it's too much
boil'd.

Miss, shall I help you to a pigeon? Here's a pigeon so finely
roasted, it cries, Come eat me.

No, sir; I thank you.

A finished gentleman from top to toe

Source: DON JUAN (Canto XII, stanza 84)
Author: George Gordon, Lord Byron (1788-1824)
First published: 1823-1824 (Cantos XII-XIV)
Type of work: Satirical poem

Context: The parts of *Don Juan* appeared at intervals. Canto I was written in September, 1818 and published with Canto II in 1819; III, IV, and V were printed in 1821; the next nine appeared in groups of three in 1823; XV and XVI were published in March, 1824, and the unfinished Canto XVII, that went to Greece with Byron, was not printed until 1903. After a love affair with the married Donna Julia, a young friend of his mother, Don Juan is sent on a tour of Europe in search of an education in morals. Shipwrecked, he is found by Haidée, the lovely daughter of a pirate and slave-dealer (instead of by the fisherman's daughter as in *Don Juan Tenorio,* a Spanish version). After an amorous interlude, her father ships him to a slave market, and Haidée dies of grief. Sold to the Sultana, the youthful Don Juan is compelled to dress as a dancing maiden to conceal his sex from the Sultan. However, remembering his former sweetheart, Juan refuses to become the Sultana's lover. He escapes, when the armies of Catherine of Russia beseige Ismail. His general bravery and his deed in saving a ten-year-old girl from slaughter by the Cossacks (an actual event of the seige but performed by the Duc de Richelieu), give Don Juan such a reputation that he is chosen to carry news of the victory to the Empress in Russia. In St. Petersburg, with new worlds to conquer, Don Juan quickly becomes a favorite of the Empress. When he is taken ill, Catherine sends him on a diplomatic mission to England which opens another area to the satirical shafts of the poet. As a young, unmarried man, polished and knowledgeable about fashionable etiquette, Juan becomes very popular. Many English ladies make love to him. He is shown the sights of London and introduced to the social world. He also meets "a Prince," actually the Prince Regent, afterward George IV, and about him writes the laudatory stanza quoted below. So slight a thread cannot fill the many stanzas of the long poem. Byron often digresses. He commends Wellington (called Villainton by the French); he excoriates the ministers of England, except Canning; he is ironic about the chastity of English women; he attacks the holiness of the Holy Roman Empire, and criticizes the poetry of numerous contemporaries. As narrator, he introduces many of his own personal likes and dislikes. He even devotes one stanza, number 41 of Canto X, to a rhymed pharmaceutical prescription. But though there are many pages in the poem, there is hardly a dull one.

There, too he saw (whate'er he may be now)
A Prince, the prince of princes at the time,
With fascination in his very bow,
    And full of promise, as the spring of prime.
Though royalty was written on his brow,
    He had *then* the grace, too, rare in every clime,
Of being, without alloy of fop or beau,
A finish'd gentleman from top to toe.

The first fine careless rapture

Source: HOME-THOUGHTS, FROM ABROAD (Line 16)
Author: Robert Browning (1812-1889)
First published: 1845
Type of work: Lyric poem

Context: Though it is widely believed that "Home-Thoughts, from Abroad" was written during Browning's first visit to Italy in 1838, W. C. DeVane said that it was probably written in England during April, 1845. (*A Browning Handbook,* 1935, pp. 147–148.) Regardless of place and date of composition, though, the poem is suffused with the poet's love of the sights and sounds of an English spring. In the first stanza he longs to be in England "Now that April's there," to see the tiny leaves "Round the elm-tree bole" and hear the chaffinch sing. In the second stanza he remembers the full spring of May, and at the end he contrasts the gaity of English buttercups with a "gaudy melon-flower" symbolic of spring in Italy. Stanza two follows:

And after April, when May follows,
And the whitethroat builds, and all the swallows!
Hark, where my blossomed pear-tree in the hedge
Leans to the field and scatters on the clover
Blossoms and dewdrops—at the bent spray's edge—
That's the wise thrush; he sings each song twice over,
Lest you should think he never could recapture
The first fine careless rapture!

294

And though the fields look rough with hoary dew,
All will be gay when noontide wakes anew
The buttercups, the little children's dower
—Far brighter than this gaudy melon-flower!

First follow nature

Source: ESSAY ON CRITICISM (Part I, l. 68)
Author: Alexander Pope (1688-1744)
First published: 1711
Type of work: Satire

Context: Alexander Pope, in his poetic *Essay on Criticism,* warns that to be a bad critic is far worse than to be a bad poet. He notes that few men are born with true taste, and that of these most are led astray by poor education. Two cardinal rules exist for the critic: first, follow nature; second, study the classics. In suggesting nature as a guide for judgment, the poet says:

First follow nature, and your judgment frame
By her just standard, which is still the same:
Unerring nature, still divinely bright,
One clear, unchanged, and universal light,
Life, force, and beauty, must to all impart,
At once the source, and end, and test of art;
Art from that fund each just supply provides;
Works without show, and without pomp presides:
In some fair body thus th' informing soul
With spirits feeds, with vigour fills the whole,
Each motion guides, and every nerve sustains;
Itself unseen, but in th' effects remains.
Some, to whom Heaven in wit has been profuse,
Want as much more, to turn it to its use;
For wit and judgment often are at strife,
Though meant each other's aid, like man and wife.
'Tis more to guide, than spur the muse's steed;
Restrain his fury, than provoke his speed:
The winged courser, like a generous horse,
Shows most true mettle when you check his course.

The first lion thought the last a bore

Source: BOMBASTES FURIOSO (Scene IV)
Author: William Barnes Rhodes (1772-1826)
First published: 1822
Type of work: Burlesque tragic opera

Context: People looking at the short and thick-set Mr. Rhodes, plodding about London, saw nothing in him to indicate humor. There was no twinkle in his eyes. He did his business as Chief Teller in the Bank of England in a serious way. However, in his leisure time, he collected manuscripts of dramas and attended theatrical performances in company with a fellow bank clerk, a tall, gaunt gentleman who ardently admired Siddons and Kemble. Together they beheld Thalia and Melpomene in all their glory at Covent Garden. Between the acts, Rhodes amused himself with extemporaneous parodies on speeches that shortly before had "drowned the stage with tears." Not that he loved Shakespeare less, but he loved burlesque more. And so there came into existence the one-act burlesque tragedy *Bombastes Furioso,* sometimes called *Artaxominous the Great,* performed at the Theatre Royal, London, about 1803, with a noteworthy cast that included Liston as General Bombastes, Liston's diminutive wife as the attractive Distaffina, Mathews as the King, and Taylor as Minister of State Fusbos. The lyrics included in the work are parodies of well-known songs, using familiar melodies. In addition to this work, Rhodes published a mediocre volume of Epigrams, and also supposedly completed two dramatic pieces that were neither performed nor published. The boasting and bombastic soldier provided humor in many a medieval drama under the name of Miles Glorioso or Miles Furioso. Here he is called General Bombastes, commander of the army of cigar-smoking King Artaxominous of Utopia. According to the stage directions, the general wears "a general's military suit—jack boots—comic powdered wig and pigtail—long sword—small cocked hat and plume." The dialog is in a variety of meters. The play opens with His Majesty, in pain after a night of drinking and smoking, uttering such majestic lines as "Get out of my sight, or I'll knock you down." Nevertheless, Minister Fusbos lingers long enough to announce the return of General Bombastes with rich booty after a successful campaign. The king, however, is more concerned wih his problem of how to replace Queen Griskinissa with the charming Distaffina. Upon being consulted, she confesses she loves Bombastes, but a handful of gold coins persuades her to forget the general. Their conversation is interrupted by the sound of the approaching Bombastes. The king flees to a closet, unfortunately leaving his well-known tricorn in sight. At such evidence of Distaffina's inconstancy, furious Bombastes determines to die. To save himself the necessity of suicide, he goes to a woods, fastens his boots to a tree, and displays above them a universal challenge.

"Who dares this pair of boots displace
Must meet Bombastes face to face,"
Thus do I challenge all the human race.

King Artaxominous appears and knocks down the boots with the declaration:

Where'er thou art, with speed prepare to go
Where I shall send thee—to the shades below!

Bombastes answers his roar with the

296

fable of a lion, and is topped by the king's reply. Thereupon he kills the King of Utopia. Into the woods comes Fusbos, and in a duel put to a duet, he slays the regicide. Distaffina then joins Fusbos in a lament, interrupted by the resurrected corpses, and all unite in a jolly final quartet. Here is the fable of the lions:

BOMBASTES
So have I heard on Afric's burning shore,
A hungry lion give a grievous roar;
The grievous roar echoed along the shore.

ARTAXOMINOUS
So have I heard on Afric's burning shore
Another lion give a grievous roar,
And the first lion thought the last a bore.

BOMBASTES
Am I then mocked? Now by my fame I swear
You shall soon have it—There!   [*They fight.*]

ARTAXOMINOUS
Where?

BOMBASTES
There,—and there.

The first smith was the first murderer's son

Source: THE TASK (Book V, l. 219)
Author: William Cowper (1731-1800)
First published: 1785
Type of work: Meditative poem in blank verse

Context: Cowper's descriptions of nature in Miltonian blank verse with their re-creation of the sights and sounds of the country anticipated what was later to be called Romanticism. This poem became immediately popular, as did his technique. He used the same meter later in his translations of Homer (1791). Shortly afterward his old melancholia, for which he had several times spent periods in insane asylums, came upon him, and he wrote very little from then until his death. A frosty morning entices the poet to take a walk. He wonders where the song birds have gone, and whether the earthworm is safe under the cold sod. The sight of a frozen water fall recalls to him the Ice Palace of the Russian Empress, Catherine the Great, who ruled from 1762 to 1796. He thinks of her amusements, including war. That reminds him of "the first artificer of death," Tubal-cain, six generations after Cain, who killed his brother.

297

The Bible refers to Tubal-cain as "the forger of every cutting instrument of brass and iron." (Genesis 4:22) Vulcan was the Roman fire god and blacksmith. A falchion is a curved, medieval broadsword.

Cain had already shed a brother's blood;
The Deluge washed it out, but left unquenched
The seeds of murder in the breast of man.
Soon, by a righteous judgment, in the line
Of his descending progeny was found
The first artificer of death: the shrewd
Contriver who first sweated at the forge,
And forced the blunt and yet unbloodied steel
To a keen edge, and made it bright for war.
Him, Tubal named, the Vulcan of old Times
The sword and falchion their inventor claim,
And **the first smith was the first murd'rer's son.**

A flea in his ear

Source: EUPHUES, THE ANATOMY OF WIT
Author: John Lyly (1554?-1606)
First published: 1579
Type of work: Prose romance

Context: "A flea in his ear" is apparently a traditional English expression, meaning either to take umbrage at a speech by someone else or to be highly surprised. An occurrence of the phrase is in *Pilgrimage of the lyf of the manhode* (c. 1430): "And manye oothere grete wundres which been fleen in myne eres" (II, xxxix); here the expression means to astonish, but in *De Lisle's Legendarie* (1577) "Sending them away with fleas in their eares, vtterly disappointed of their purpose" (Bvj), it means to be annoyed. John Lyly was the first writer of much note to employ the phrase. In his novel *Euphues, the Anatomy of Wit* Lucilla, a rather light Neapolitan lady, has been the love of Philautus, a pleasure-loving young man of the city of Naples. Philautus introduces a new acquaintance, Euphues, a young scholar from Greece, to Lucilla, and immediately Euphues woos her to such effect that she disdains Philautus. By the time that Philautus has been excluded from her consideration, her father, Ferardo, who has been absent from town, returns and endeavors to effect a marriage between Philautus and his daughter, who treats him with great contempt and refuses to marry him. In the quotation below Ferardo prepares to examine Lucilla to discover why she has so completely changed her mind since the time of his departure from the city. While the interrogation is in progress Philautus stands as though with a flea in his ear, the expression at this point evidently meaning that he is dazed by Lucilla's complete denial of affection for him. After Lyly, Robert Armin (*fl.* 1608)

298

used the expression in *A Nest of Ninnies* (1608): "The fellow knowing himselfe faulty, put up his wrongs, quickly departed, and went to work betimes that morning with a flea in his ear." The quotation from Lyly is as follows:

> Ferardo, being a grave and wise gentleman, although he were thoroughly angry, yet he dissembled his fury, to the end he might by craft discover her fancy, and whispering Philautus in the ear (who stood as though he had **a flea in his ear**), desired him to keep silence until he had undermined her by subtlety, . . .

The floor lay paved with broken hearts

Source: GRATIANA, DANCING AND SINGING (Stanza 3)
Author: Richard Lovelace (1618-1657)
First published: 1649
Type of work: Lyric poem

Context: Gay cavaliers of the court of Charles I cultivated the art of light verse, elegant but superficial, addressed to sweethearts whose identity was concealed behind poetic names. Yet some poets also exhibited a serious side, maintaining devotion to the king even at the cost of imprisonment and exile. The poetry of one of the most important of them, Richard Lovelace, exhibits both tendencies. In *To Lucasta, Going to the Wars*, he set out to fight for his king, anticipating death in battle. His poem to Gratiana concerns merely an amorous conflict.

> Each step trod out a Lover's thought
> And the ambitious hopes he brought,
>   Chained to her brave feet with such arts,
> Such sweet command, and gentle awe,
> As when she ceased, we sighing saw
>   **The floor lay pav'd with broken hearts**
>
> So did she move, so did she sing
> Like the Harmonious spheres that bring
>   Unto their rounds their Music's aid;
> Which she performed in such a way
> As all the enamoured world will say
>   The Graces danced, and Apollo played.

The flowery way that leads to the broad gate and the great fire

Source: ALL'S WELL THAT ENDS WELL (Act IV, sc. v, ll. 56-57)
Author: William Shakespeare (1564-1616)
First published: 1623
Type of work: Dramatic comedy

Context: Bertram, son of the Countess of Rousillon, has rudely rejected Helena as a wife. Forced to marry her by the king's command, he sends her home unkissed and himself renounces his nation to serve the Duke of Florence. In subsequent battles the young count distinguishes himself, but the pining Helena, whose true love will not allow her to remain idle, follows him on a pilgrimage to St. Jaques le Grand. She allows word to be sent both to her husband and to his mother that she has died on the journey. The countess, when she receives this news, is grief-stricken; "If she had partaken of my flesh, and cost me the dearest groans of a mother, I could not have owed her a more rooted love." Lavache, a clown in the Rousillon household, attempts to relieve her sorrow with saucy and impertinent dialogue, by describing bawdily the fool and his bauble, and by averring that—though he serve the Prince of Darkness and though he love a good fire—he has no desire to serve at the Devil's court. But his tricks now begin to jade. Such humor is inappropriate to the occasion, and the fool is peremptorily dismissed by the countess. But, not to be denied, a few lines later the fool reenters to announce the arrival home of the count, her son, with a velvet patch (scar) on his face. He is attended by—and here Lavache gets his final sarcastic gibes at the pomposity and flamboyancy of the aristocrats—". . . a dozen of 'em, with delicate fine hats, and most courteous feathers, which bow the head and nod at every man." His speech about the "great fire" is as follows:

> LAVACHE
> I am a woodland fellow sir, that always loved a great fire; and the master I speak of ever keeps a good fire. But sure he is the prince of the world, let his nobility remain in's court. I am for the house with the narrow gate, which I take to be too little for pomp to enter. Some that humble themselves may, but the many will be too chill and tender, and they'll be for **the flowery way that leads to the broad gate and the great fire.**

A fool must now and then be right, by chance

Source: CONVERSATION (Line 96)
Author: William Cowper (1731-1800)
First published: 1782
Type of work: Meditative poem

300

Context: This poem was written during the first months of the poet's association with Lady Austen, who encouraged Cowper to extend himself as a poet, telling him that he was capable of writing about any subject he chose. In *Conversation* Cowper suggests that the ability to be a good conversationalist is a gift from the Deity, rather than an art to be learned. The suggestion is not surprising, inasmuch as Cowper was a highly religious man. He notes, however, that a person must be willing to learn, in order to cultivate the heaven-sent gift. He is also of the opinion that talking is not necessarily conversation: "Words learn'd by rote a parrot may rehearse, / But talking is not always to converse." Language, Cowper goes on to say, is a "sacred interpreter of human thought" which few respect or use as carefully as they should. Particularly, he maintains, we should not use the gift of language for adulterous purposes, either in youth or age. In a verse paragraph near the beginning of the poem Cowper asks help of whatever powers there may be who govern human speech:

> Ye pow'rs who rule the tongue, if such there are,
> And make colloquial happiness your care,
> Preserve me from the thing I dread and hate,
> A duel in the form of a debate:
> The clash of arguments and jar of words,
> Worse than the mortal brunt of rival swords,
> Decide no question with their tedious length,
> For opposition gives opinion strength,
> Divert the champions prodigal of breath,
> And put the peaceably disposed to death.
> Oh thwart me not, Sir Soph, at ev'ry turn,
> Nor carp at ev'ry flaw you may discern,
> Though syllogisms hang not on my tongue,
> I am not, surely, always in the wrong;
> 'Tis hard if all is false that I advance,
> **A fool must now and then be right, by chance;**
> Not that all freedom of dissent I blame,
> No—there I grant the privilege I claim.

Fools are my theme, let satire be my song

Source: ENGLISH BARDS AND SCOTCH REVIEWERS (Line 6)
Author: George Gordon, Lord Byron (1788-1824)
First published: 1809
Type of work: Satiric poem in couplets

Context: In January, 1808, the *Edinburgh Review,* one of the most influential of literary journals, published a very unfavorable review of Byron's *Hours of Idleness.* The poet believed it the work of the *Review's* founder, Francis Jeffrey (1773–1850), who had blasted Wordsworth's *Excursion* in a devastating criticism beginning, "This will never do!" Later Henry

Peter, Baron Brougham (1778–1868), who afterward became Lord Chancellor, was revealed to have written the article. Previously Byron had written a short satire titled "British Bards," in which he expressed his low opinion of a number of current writers: "simple" Wordsworth because of his commonplace themes and sometimes prosy language; "Obscure" Coleridge; a n d "verbose" Southey. It was set up in type but never offered for sale, because of the poet's hesitation. However, the harsh words of the *Edinburgh Review* decided Byron to revise it, broaden the concept to include the Scotch critic he blamed for the article, and publish it anonymously, in 1,070 lines. Eight months later he reprinted it under his own name. Then in 1810 and 1811 he published other versions, with an additional ninety lines. Finally a fifth attempt had been set in type when Byron began to have doubts about his indiscriminate satire, and he tried to suppress it. But a few copies got out, and the definitive version, included in his complete work, uses this last form. Byron's complaint is that it is silly to expect sensible literary reviews from critics. He calls Jeffrey a "self-constituted judge of poesy." He devotes more than a hundred mocking lines to him, and also makes comment on many other contemporaries now practically forgotten. Though in later years Byron expressed regret at having shot barbed arrows so indiscriminately, many of his judgments are still acceptable today. At the conclusion of the poem, he says he can endure the opinions of the critics, but comes nearer the truth in his boast that he can "break him on the wheel he meant for me." The poem begins with a defense of his "grey goose quill" that he is picking up again to express an uncommon theme. William Thomas Fitzgerald was for thirty years the poetaster who read an original and boring ode at the annual banquet of the Literary Fund. The first six lines of the poem declared:

Still must I hear?—shall hoarse Fitzgerald bawl
His creaking couplets in a tavern hall,
And I not sing, lest, haply, Scotch reviews
Should dub me scribbler and denounce my muse?
Prepare for rhyme—I'll publish, right or wrong:
Fools are my theme, let satire be my song.

Footprints on the sands of time

Source: A PSALM OF LIFE (Stanza 7)
Author: Henry Wadsworth Longfellow (1807-1882)
First published: 1838
Type of work: Lyric poem

Context: This nineteenth century poem is in striking contrast to much of the defeatist, pessimistic verse of the twentieth century. Its highly optimistic message is that this is a real world in which we live and that we lose it if we spend our time in vain repinings about what might have been

302

or wishful thinking of what may be in the future. We are living in the here and now, and our duty to ourselves is to live each day so fully that we accomplish something that will leave an imprint on the world. We should not merely endure life until death releases us so that we can go to our graves. There is so much to do in the world, and we individually have so little time in which to do it, that we should act in such a manner as to accomplish something worthy every day. The lives of the great should inspire us to such a degree that we ought to make the effort to leave our mark on the world, a mark which may in the future encourage someone else to great achievement. The whole idea of the poem, that here is a world in which we can do fine things if only we put our whole souls into the effort, is, of course, utterly abhorrent to twentieth century paternalism.

> Trust no Future, howe'er pleasant!
> Let the dead Past bury its dead!
> Act,—act in the living Present!
> Heart within, and God o'erhead!
>
> Lives of great men all remind us
> We can make our lives sublime,
> And, departing, leave behind us
> **Footprints on the sands of time;**
>
> Footprints, that perhaps another,
> Sailing o'er life's solemn main,
> A forlorn and shipwrecked brother,
> Seeing, shall take heart again.
>
> Let us, then, be up and doing,
> With a heart for any fate;
> Still achieving, still pursuing,
> Learn to labor and to wait.

For God! for the Cause! for the Church! for the Laws!

Source: THE BATTLE OF NASEBY (Line 19)
Author: Thomas Babington Macaulay (1800-1859)
First published: 1824
Type of work: Narrative poem

Context: This first of Macaulay's two "Songs of the Civil War" (The English, not the American Civil War), was supposedly written by a sergeant in the regiment of Henry Ireton (1611–1651), a general in the Puritan revolution. On June 14, 1645, the Parliamentarians under Fairfax and Cromwell defeated the Royalists under Charles I and his nephew Prince Rupert, born in Germany, at the decisive Battle of Naseby, in Northamptonshire, England. Macaulay's swinging lines, so effective in re-creating ancient Rome, are just as stirring when he writes about battles and events in the history of his own land. In this poem, the sergeant describes the enemy under King Charles, "the man of blood with his long essenced hair" in contrast to the close-cropped and unperfumed Roundheads. He also speaks of Prince Rupert (1619–1682), Count Palatine of the Rhine and grandson of James I of England. Because of his bravery he won the name of "The Mad Cavalier." Then the narrator turns to his own army:

> Like a servant of the Lord, with his Bible and his sword,
>   The General rode along us to form us to the fight,
> When a murmuring shout broke out, and swell'd into a shout,
>   Among the godless horsemen upon the tyrant's right.
>
> And hark! like the roar of the billows on the shore,
>   The cry of battle rises along their charging line!
> **For God! for the Cause! for the Church! for the Laws!**
>   For Charles King of England and Rupert of the Rhine!

For one restraint, lords of the world besides

Source: PARADISE LOST (Book I, l. 32)
Author: John Milton (1608-1674)
First published: 1667
Type of work: Epic poem

Context: Milton begins *Paradise Lost* with the statement of his theme, man's disobedience to God and the coming of death into the world. Throughout the poem the idea is developed that the death is both physical and spiritual. The idea of the introduction of physical death derives from Genesis 3: 19 and 3: 22, where it is contained both in the curse laid on Adam after he had eaten the forbidden fruit though allowed all the rest, and in the fact that he must be evicted from the garden so that he cannot eat of the tree of life and regain his lost immortality. Milton says that a greater Man will come and restore us; that is, Christ will come down and do away with the necessity for spiritual death. Milton then continues that he is going to do things never before attempted in either prose or poetry; among other things, he will justify the ways of God to man. What is meant here is that he will make clear or explain God's ways, which are sometimes difficult of understanding for the ordinary person. When he has done this, he then makes a direct invocation of the heavenly Muse:

> Say first, for heaven hides nothing from thy view
> Nor the deep tract of hell, say first what cause
> Moved our grandparents in that happy state,
> Favored of heaven so highly, to fall off

From their Creator, and transgress his will
For one restraint, lords of the world besides?
Who first seduced them to that foul revolt?
Th' infernal serpent; he it was, whose guile
Stirred up with envy and revenge, deceived
The mother of mankind, what time his pride
Had cast him out from heaven, with all his host
Of rebel angels, by whose aid aspiring
To set himself in glory above his peers,
He trusted to have equalled the most high,
If he opposed. . . .

For 'tis some virtue, virtue to commend

Source: TO SIR GODFREY KNELLER (Line 42)
Author: William Congreve (1670-1729)
First published: 1710
Type of work: Laudatory epistle in verse

Context: William Congreve, Restoration playwright and wit, gives a new twist to the often-debated superiority of the pen over the sword. He compares the pen to the paint brush in a poem to the fashionable painter of his time, Godfrey Kneller, who, as Gottfried Kniller (1646–1723) came to England in 1675 after having studied art in Amsterdam, Rome, and Venice. Following the death of the court painter of Charles II, Pieter Van der Faes (1618–1680), he joined the royal circle. His predecessor had been knighted as Sir Peter Lely, from a lily over the door of the house where his father was born; the new court painter was renamed Sir Godfrey Kneller. By means of an army of apprentices, Kneller turned out an enormous number of portraits of famous people, including the well-known "Ten Beauties of the Court of William III." His period extended from Charles II to George I, with a brief visit to the court of Louis XIV. Dryden had also accorded Kneller poetic tribute when Congreve wrote. The latter begins his poem with an acknowledgment that Kneller's brush can produce better likenesses of people than can his quill pen. He has been looking at the artist's portrait of L——Y——, using an abbreviation common in English literature, though the real name could probably have been easily discovered by anyone acquainted with Kneller's productions. Though he has often tried, says Congreve, to "trace some image of the much-lov'd fair," only the painter could reproduce her in a way that spoke to the heart. Not only does he catch her likeness, but he "paints her mind." To most people, recognition does not come during their lifetime. "Fame due to vast desert is kept in store, Unpaid, till the deserver is no more." However, Kneller's genius has been recognized during his lifetime, especially by the connoisseurs, and Congreve wants to join them. As Polonius said about virtue in *Hamlet,* "Assume a virtue if you have it not," so there is some virtue in recognizing qualities even if you do not possess

305

them. In the first four and last eight lines of the poem, Congreve writes:

I yield, O Kneller, to superior skill,
Thy pencil triumphs o'er the poet's quill:
If yet my vanquish'd Muse exert her lays,
It is no more to rival thee, but praise.

. . .

Ev'n Dryden has immortalized thy name;
Let that alone suffice thee, think that fame.
Unfit I follow where he led the way,
And court applause by what I seem to pay.
Myself I praise, while I thy praise intend,
For 'tis some virtue, virtue to commend;
And next to deeds which our own honor raise,
Is to distinguish them who merit praise.

For tyme y-lost may not recovered be

Source: TROILUS AND CRISEYDE (Book IV, stanza 184, l. 1283)
Author: Geoffrey Chaucer (c. 1343-1400)
First transcribed: 1380-1386
Type of work: Narrative poem

Context: As Chaucer got his story of Troilus and Criseyde, involved in the twelfth century B.C. siege of Troy, from Benôit and Boccaccio, so Shakespeare borrowed from Chaucer and Robert Henryson (1430–1506). And as Shakespeare transferred the local color from Troy to the days of the late Renaissance, so he modernized his heroine's name to Cressida. The Criseyde of Chaucer is a Trojan widow, attracted by a gallant young warrior who rides past her house to do battle with the Greeks besieging Troy. When her uncle Pandarus tells her that the young hero is dying of love for her, though she suspects there is nothing honorable about his intentions, she allows herself to attend a dinner with him, and with all the ceremony of a medieval court of love, gives him permission to adore her. Next her pandering uncle ma-neuvres her into spending the night at his house, where he brings the lovers together, without much resistance from her. Afterward she even gives Troilus a brooch as token of their eternal love. Book IV shows how eternal it was. In a battle, some of the Greek leaders are captured, including Antenor. Calchas, a Trojan prophet who has fled to the Greeks, arranges that Antenor will be released on condition that Criseyde, his daughter, be allowed to leave Troy and join him in the Greek camp. In the part from which this quotation comes, Criseyde and Troilus spend the last night together, and once more she promises to remain true, and to rejoin him shortly. However, her Greek escort, Diomedes, is too attractive. The change of affection of this girl of old Troy demonstrates that Greek women were as fickle as a Roman woman

306

was proclaimed to be by the Duke of Mantua in *Rigoletto*. She gives Diomedes another of her brooches. Troilus, seeing it, tries to kill her new sweetheart on the battlefield, only to fall beneath the sword of the mighty Achilles. Chaucer does not chide or criticize her; rather, in his well-rounded characterization, he shows that he understands her. As a result, he has produced a very early example of what we now call the psychological novel. In the bedroom scene, she promises:

> For dredelees within a week or two
> I shall ben here! . . .

> For which I wol not make long sermoun,
> **For tyme y-lost may not recovered be;**
> But I will gon to my conclusioun
> (And to the best, in ought that I can see).
> And for the love of God, for-yeve it me
> If I speke ought against your hertes reste,
> For trewely, I speak it for the beste.

For what can war but endless war still breed?

Source: SONNET XV ("On the Lord General Fairfax at the siege of Colchester,' Line 10)
Author: John Milton (1608-1674)
First published: 1694
Type of work: Sonnet

Context: This is one of the four sonnets by Milton not published during the poet's lifetime; the text is from the Cambridge Manuscript of Milton's poems. Sir Thomas Fairfax was early one of the most important of the Puritan generals in the Civil War. He won decisive victories over the royalist forces at Marston Moor on July 2, 1644, and at Naseby on June 14, 1645. He captured Colchester in August, 1648, after a siege of seventy-five days. When the march of events passed what Fairfax considered the point of moderation, he resigned his command of the Parliamentary armies, yielding to Oliver Cromwell. In this poem the poet urges the general to turn his energies to the problems of peace.

. . .

> Thy firm unshak'n vertue ever brings
> Victory home, though new rebellions raise
> Thir Hydra heads, & the fals North displaies
> Her brok'n league, to impe their serpent wings,
> O yet a nobler task awaites thy hand;
> **For what can Warr, but endless warr still breed,**
> Till Truth, & Right from Violence be freed,
> And Public Faith cleard from the shamefull brand

307

Of Public Fraud. In vain doth Valour bleed
While Avarice, & Rapine share the land.

Forever most divinely in the wrong

Source: LOVE OF FAME, ON WOMEN (Satire VI, l. 106)
Author: Edward Young (1683-1765)
First published: 1725-1728
Type of work: Satirical poem

Context: In this poem Young satirizes various forms of female behavior. The first person to meet his censure is Lavinia, who is constant in her attendance at church; as silence is more than she can bear, she talks away to God: but when women are proud of praying well, Satan himself will summon them to church. Drusa receives her visitors while she is still in bed; when she wishes to rise, she requests them to turn their backs on her while she dresses. Flavia is not on good terms with her former lover, but supports him for old time's sake; she, apparently faithful, maintains the brood of children born to her by other men than her husband. Amasia scorns restraint and is not as good as she might be. Lucia married an idiot, but a rich one. Wisdom is the only maker of happiness, but she is likened to a practitioner of fine needlework: at least she works in gold. The poet then arrives at Tullia:

> If Tullia had been blest with half her sense,
> None could too much admire her excellence:
> But since she can make error shine so bright,
> She thinks it vulgar to defend the right.
> With understanding she is quite o'er-run;
> And by too great accomplishments undone:
> With skill she vibrates her eternal tongue,
> **For ever most divinely in the wrong.**

Fortunate isle, the abode of the blest

Source: THE AENEID (Book VI, as translated by John Jackson)
Author: Virgil (Publius Vergilius Maro, 70-19 B.C.)
First transcribed: c. 29-19 B.C.
Type of work: Epic poem

Context: The *Aeneid,* written to give Rome an origin suited to her glory, portrays the adventures of her founder, Aeneas, son of Venus and hero of the Trojan War, as he seeks to establish a settlement in Italy. Reaching Italy after a tempestuous voyage from Troy, Aeneas is conducted by a Sybil to the land of the dead, where he eventually meets his father in the Elysian Fields

308

and learns of his own great destiny. Approaching the *fortunate isle, abode of the blest,* Aeneas performs the prescribed rites and places the Golden Bough on the threshold.

This at length performed and the service of the goddess discharged, they came to the realms of joy—the pleasant lawns of **the Happy Groves,** and the **seats of the Blest.** Here an ampler ether invests the plains in radiance, and they know their own sun and their own stars. Part by their limbs in the verdant lists and, in sportive conflect, wrestle on the yellow sand; part tread the dance and sing. . . .

Fortune's fool

Source: ROMEO AND JULIET (Act III, sc. i, l. 141)
Author: William Shakespeare (1564-1616)
First published: 1597
Type of work: Dramatic tragedy

Context: At a masked ball in Verona, Romeo of the Montague family falls in love with Juliet of the rival Capulet family. The next day Romeo and Juliet are secretly married, hoping to end the feud of the Montague and Capulet families, who would never have condoned the marriage if permission had been sought. Just after the marriage Romeo, who is determined to keep peace, refuses to draw his sword on Juliet's insulting kinsman, Tybalt, until Tybalt slays Mercutio, Romeo's quick-tempered friend and defender. Incited, Romeo kills Tybalt, is warned by his companion Benvolio to flee the wrath of the prince, and exclaims that he is "fortunes's fool."

BENVOLIO

Romeo away, be gone.
The citizens are up, and Tybalt slain.
Stand not amazed, the Prince will doom thee death,
If thou art taken. Hence, be gone, away.

ROMEO

O I am **fortune's fool!**

Founded upon a rock

Source: MATTHEW 7:25
Author: Unknown (traditionally Matthew the Apostle)
First transcribed: c.75-100
Type of work: Gospel

Context: Of the discourses by Jesus which have come down to us, that traditionally known as the Sermon on the Mount is regarded as among the greatest. Matthew quotes a version of the full text in Chapters 5, 6, and 7. He records in Chapter 4 that after Jesus began to gather His disciples He went about Galilee, preaching the gospel and healing the sick, and that His fame spread all over Syria. Great multitudes from the surrounding country followed Him, and when He saw how large their number was He took His disciples up onto a mountain and instructed them in the gospel He wished them to help Him spread. The Sermon on the Mount is an admirable survey and exposition of the basic principles of Christianity. Beginning with the Beatitudes, Jesus continues with an exposition of moral law, emphasizing inner motivations rather than external codes of conduct. He stresses forgiveness of others, even to the point of loving one's enemies, and He illustrates righteousness in various ways. He provides His followers with a model prayer; this, He says in reference to the Lord's Prayer, embodies all that a prayer should be. He then stresses the importance of spiritual considerations over material things. After warning His disciples against base and hypocritical motives and the ease with which they can be rationalized, He states the Golden Rule. This very basic guide to conduct is then illustrated with a number of practical applications. Jesus points out that His way to salvation requires something of those who follow it and warns against false prophets and the barren lives to which they would lead us. Most of Jesus' other sermons are extensions of the rules, maxims, and principles stated in the Sermon on the Mount; and His life was an effort to exemplify them. He concludes with a striking parable drawn from His work as a carpenter. Anything we build, concrete or symbolic, material or spiritual, must have a solid and enduring basis or it is nothing.

Not every one that saith unto me, Lord, Lord, shall enter the kingdom of heaven; but he that doeth the will of my Father which is in heaven.

Many will say to me in that day, Lord, Lord, have we not prophesied in thy name? and in thy name have cast out devils? and in thy name done many wonderful works?

And then will I profess unto them, I never knew you: depart from me, ye that work iniquity.

Therefore whosoever heareth these sayings of mine, and doeth them, I will liken him unto a wise man, which built his house upon a rock:

And the rain descended, and the floods came, and the winds blew, and beat upon that house; and it fell not: for it was **founded upon a rock.**

And every one that heareth these sayings of mine, and doeth them not, shall be likened unto a foolish man, which built his house upon the sand:

And the rain descended, and the floods came, and the winds blew, and beat upon that house; and it fell: and great was the fall of it.

And it came to pass, when Jesus had ended these sayings, the people were astonished at his doctrine:

For he taught them as one having authority, and not as the scribes.

France, famed in all great arts, in none supreme

Source: TO A REPUBLICAN FRIEND ("Continued," Line 4)
Author: Matthew Arnold (1822-1888)
First published: 1849
Type of work: Sonnet

Context: In 1848, the year that Arnold wrote this poem to Arthur Hugh Clough, the overthrow of the French monarchy marked the beginning of a series of revolutions that spread through Europe. At the time liberals like Clough optimistically forecast that an age of equality and freedom was being ushered in, but Arnold had reservations. By nature melancholy and in philosophy a determinist, Arnold does not believe that political revolutions inaugurate ages of peace; instead, he believes that the cry for freedom will be again stifled by tyrants' greed. France had already demonstrated the course of revolutions when a Napoleon stepped in after the monarchy fell; yet France was being praised for repeating its own bloody history. Rather than copy the French, the liberals should, Arnold believes, emulate the English, who had successfully endured ages of tyranny to evolve into a constitutional government; such evolution requires patience, but it is bloodless and more "artistic" than the violent French way of seeking immediate ends.

. . . when I muse on what life is, I seem
Rather to patience prompted, than that proud
Prospect of hope which France proclaims so loud—
France, famed in all great arts, in none supreme;

Seeing this vale, this earth, whereon we dream,
Is on all sides o'ershadow'd by the high
Uno'erleap'd Mountains of Necessity,
Sparing us narrower margin than we deem.

Freedom, and not servitude, is the cure of anarchy

Source: SPEECH ON MOVING HIS RESOLUTIONS FOR RECONCILIATION WITH THE COLONIES
Author: Edmund Burke (1729-1797)
First published: 1775
Type of work: Political Speech

Context: America had no more capable or articulate defender in the English Parliament than Burke. When Parliament considered harsh and repressive measures of taxation and military suppression for the unrest in the Colonies, Burke spoke vehemently in protest. Such measures, he argued, could only be costly and temporary if successful, and they could very well be unsuccessful. He urged instead an act of redress and conciliation such as had been offered to Ireland, Wales, and Chester. He quoted at length from the petition of the citizens of Chester in the reign of Henry VIII and cites that benefits that have been derived from Parliament's acceptance of it:

> What did parliament with this audacious address?—Reject it as a libel? Treat it as an affront to government? Spurn it as a derogation from the rights of legislature? Did they toss it over the table? Did they burn it by the hands of the common hangman? They took the petition of grievance, all rugged as it was, without softening or temperament, unpurged of the original bitterness and indignation of complaint; they made it the very preamble to their act of redress; and consecrated its principle to all ages in the sanctuary of legislation.
>
> Here is my third example. It was attended with the success of the two former. Chester, civilized as well as Wales, had demonstrated that **freedom, and not servitude, is the cure of anarchy;** as religion, and not atheism, is the true remedy for superstition. . . .

Freedom and Whisky gang thegither

Source: THE AUTHOR'S EARNEST CRY AND PRAYER (Last stanza)
Author: Robert Burns (1759-1796)
First published: 1786
Type of work: Political protest

Context: Robert Burns, oldest of the seven children of a farmer who spelled his name Burnes, was born in a cottage that blew down a week after his birth. From his father he inherited brains, general superiority, and a tendency to hypochondria. His wit, love of humor, and lyrical ability came from his mother. He was educated in a small school and later by his father, but his acquaintance with Scotch legends and tales of ghosts and devils came from an old lady, Betty Davidson. When Burns was sixteen, the family moved to a larger community. Here the poet attended dancing school, courted the ladies, and soon became acquainted with taverns and, as he said, "scenes of swaggering riot." He also enjoyed adventures with smugglers who frequented the bare and deeply coved coasts, and took a liking to Scotch whisky. Speaking for all who shared his taste, Burns uttered what is called in the 1793 edition "A Simple Poet's Prayer." It is addressed to "The Right Honourable and Honourable the Scotch Representatives in the House of Commons," in protest

312

against the excise laws which he declares favor "the blackguard Smuggler" and the "chuffie Vintner (Fatfaced Wine Seller)" who get wealthy because of the duty charged on whisky. In a later edition, a signed footnote states that the poem "was wrote before the act anent the Scotch Distilleries of Session 1786; for which Scotland and the author return their most grateful thanks." Apparently his plea, or the general Scotch protest, brought a reduction in taxes, which, in 1789, he could accept appointment as exciseman, to help collect. The poem begins with his appeal addressed to the sober and serious representatives of the boroughs and shires on behalf of his Muse, now hoarse from screeching prosaic verse:

> Ye Irish Lords, ye Knights and Squires,
> Who represent our brughs and shires,
> An' doucely manage our affairs
>   In Parliament,
> To you a simple Bardie's prayers
>   Are humbly sent.

He wants them told that "Scotland an' me's in great affliction/ E'er sin' they laid that curst restriction/ On Aquavitae." He provides a new rhyme for "whisky," "pliskie," meaning a trick, as he declares that ever since they "play'd her that pliskie," she's "like to rin red-wud (stark mad) about her Whisky." In the Postscript, Burns concedes that the half-starved slaves in warmer climes may drink their wine, unenvied by Scotland who "blythe an' frisky/ Eyes her free-born martial boys/ Tak aff their Whisky." And in conclusion, Burns writes:

> Sages their solemn een may steek,
> An' raise a philosophic reek,
> An' physically causes seek,
>   In clime an' season;
> But tell me Whisky's name in Greek.
>   I'll tell the reason.
>
> Scotland, my auld, respected Mither!
> Tho' whyles ye moistify your leather,
> Till whare ye sit, on craps o' heather,
>   Ye tine your dam:
> **Freedom and Whisky gang thegither!**
>   Tak aff your dram!

Freely they stood who stood, and fell who fell

Source: PARADISE LOST (Book III, l. 102)
Author: John Milton (1608-1674)
First published: 1667
Type of work: Epic poem

Context: Milton begins the third book with an address to God as light, and says that he has just worked his way up through the darkness of chaos from hell, where the rebelling Satan and his hosts had been hurled when they lost the battle in heaven. He then reflects upon his blindness, mentioning other blind poets and some blind philosophers. As the acquisition of knowledge on his part is wholly closed to him through the agency of sight, he will have to depend upon his mind: inner light will have to take the place of external light. Milton then turns his attention to God, enthroned in the empyrean; He looks down on earth, where the newly created man and woman live in joy and love in the solitude of the garden. He sees Satan, weary from his arduous journey through chaos, ready to land on the earth to begin the attempt to ruin mankind. God addresses His Son, telling Him that Satan has come to seduce mankind; he will succeed in his attempt, but his revenge will rebound upon himself. He will succeed in perverting mankind, because man will disobey the one command that has been given to him:

> So will fall
> He and his faithless progeny: whose fault?
> Whose but his own? ingrate, he had of me
> All he could have; I made him just and right,
> Sufficient to have stood, though free to fall.
> Such I created all th'ethereal powers
> And spirits, both them who stood and them who failed;
> **Freely they stood who stood, and fell who fell.**
> Not free, what proof could they have given sincere
> Of true allegiance, constant faith or love,
> Where only what they needs must do, appeared,
> Not what they would? What praise could they receive?
> . . .

Freely we serve, because we freely love

Source: PARADISE LOST (Book V, ll. 538-539)
Author: John Milton (1608-1674)
First published: 1667
Type of work: Epic poem

Context: After Adam and Eve have performed their morning devotions, they see through the trees the glorious shape of Raphael approaching them. Adam tells Eve to prepare a meal; Eve does so by collecting all kinds of fruits and pressing out unfermented grape juice. Adam bids Raphael welcome and offers him what Eve has prepared; for a while they talk, and then Raphael explains that angels require food, just as man does. Milton is here considering the angels as a link between God and man in the great chain of being, and therefore composed of rarefied matter instead of pure spirit. Raphael further explains that the angels have all the

314

senses that man has. Finer fruits grow in heaven than on earth, but Raphael will by no means spurn the earthly produce: all things proceed from God, and they are all good until perverted. He explains gradations of being and says that man functions by means of reason and some intuition, the angels by intuition and some reason. He says that man may, through ascending certain steps, become ethereal if he remains obedient. Adam wants to know how he and Eve can possibly become disobedient. Raphael explains that as they are at the moment happy, let them thank God, Who made them so; if they remain happy, they will be so only through obedience: they were made perfect, but not immutable; their wills are free to do whatever they wish, as is true of the angels.

> Our voluntary service He requires,
> Not our necessitated, such with Him
> Finds no acceptance, nor can find, for how
> Can hearts, not free, be tried whether they serve
> Willing or no, who will but what they must
> By destiny, and can no other choose?
> Myself and all th'angelic host that stand
> In sight of God enthroned, our happy state
> Hold, as you yours, while our obedience holds;
> On other surety none; **freely we serve,**
> **Because we freely love,** as in our will
> To love or not; in this we stand or fall:
> And some are fallen, to disobedience fallen,
> And so from heaven to deepest hell; O fall
> From what high state of bliss into what woe!

· · ·

A friend may well be reckoned the masterpiece of nature

Source: FRIENDSHIP
Author: Ralph Waldo Emerson (1803-1882)
First published: 1841
Type of work: Moral essay

Context: Friends, says Emerson, cannot be bought, cannot be looked for; they come unsought with the gift of kindliness and affection that produces a metamorphosis in the world. Indeed, says Emerson, "Let the soul be assured that somewhere in the universe it should rejoin its friend, and it would be content and cheerful alone for a thousand years." Friendship, suggests the essayist, is a gift of God, and "like the immortality of the soul, is too good to be believed." With a friend we may be sincere, for one of the two elements of friendship is truth. One may indeed, says Emerson, think aloud in the presence of a friend, putting aside "even those undermost garments of dissimulation, courtesy, and second thought." The other element of friendship, as Emerson sees it, is tenderness. But it is in

315

his discussion of truth as one of the two qualities of friendship that the quotation appears. He says that a man in solitude is sincere, but that except when we are with friends, hypocrisy appears whenever other persons are present. Ordinarily we "parry and fend the approach of our fellow-man by compliments, by gossip, by amusements, by affairs."

Emerson says he once knew a man who "under a certain religious frenzy" put off the drapery of social graces and spoke to the conscience of every person he met; and people thought the man must be insane. Eventually, however, the man's sincerity was met by equal sincerity, and that situation is unusual in the world:

> . . . But to most of us society shows not its face and eye, but its side and its back. . . . Almost every man we meet requires some civility—requires to be humored; he has some fame, some talent, some whim of religion or philanthropy in his head that is not to be questioned, and which spoils all conversation with him. But a friend is a sane man who exercises not my ingenuity, but me. My friend gives me entertainment without requiring any stipulation on my part. A friend therefore is a sort of paradox in nature. I who alone am, I who see nothing in nature whose existence I can affirm with equal evidence to my own, behold now the semblance of my being, in all its height, variety, and curiosity, reiterated in a foreign form; so that **a friend may well be reckoned the masterpiece of nature.**

From a single crime know the nation!

Source: THE AENEID (Book II, as translated by John Jackson)
Author: Virgil (Publius Vergilius Maro, 70-19 B.C.)
First transcribed: 29-19 B.C.
Type of work: Epic poem

Context: Publius Vergilius Maro, heir to a prosperous family of Northern Italy, and born a few decades before the end of Rome's Golden Age, received an excellent education and the friendship of some of Rome's most cultured and powerful leaders. Through their urging, he began at the age of forty to compose an epic Homeric poem honoring Rome and his friend, the Emperor Augustus. In the story, Aeneas, fleeing from Troy, was driven by storms to Carthage, the city favored by his enemy Juno. Venus, to befriend him, made Queen Dido fall in love with him. During a welcoming feast, the queen urged Aeneas to tell of his adventures. In Book II he commences his account of the fall of Troy, at the moment when the Danaans, or Greeks, have sailed away, leaving on the shore, "with Pallas' celestial skill to aid, a horse, mountain-huge, and interwove the flanks with hewn pine—an offering, they feigned for their safe return." Inside were "weaponed soldiery," a treacherous trick, contrary to fair fighting, that destroyed the reputation for honor and chivalry of the Greek warriors who had taken part in the ten years' siege. While the Trojans are debating what to do with the horse, a prisoner is brought before them. He tells them that the Greeks had built the wooden horse, so big that it could not be moved, intending it to remain on the shore while they go home to make sacrifices, after which they will return and conquer Troy. The destruction of the city can be averted only if the Phrygians (Trojans) get the wooden horse inside their city. In this way Virgil describes the arrival of the treacherous bearer of the false prophecy about the horse, a young warrior who says he is the escaped victim of the sacrifice demanded by the gods. Achaea, actually land around the Gulf of Corinth, here stands for all of Greece. Its Greek inhabitants, descended from the mythical Danaus, were sometimes called Danaans. Indicative of their well-known treachery, says Aeneas, is this episode of the Trojan horse. This same treachery occasioned another well-known expression, "I fear the Greeks, even though they bring gifts."

But, lo, in the meantime came a band of Dardan shepherds, dragging to their king, amid clamorous outcry, a youth whose hands were bound behind him. A stranger, he had thrown himself of free will in their path, that he might compass this very end and leave Troy naked before Achaea. . . . Now harken to Danaan guile, and **from a single crime know the nation!** For, as he stood in full view, unweaponed, confused, and swept his gaze round the Phrygian lines, "Alas!" he cried, "what land, what sea, now shall give me haven? . . . I have no place amid the Greeks, and the very Trojans, no less, prove foes and cry for the penalty of blood!"

From each according to his abilities, to each according to his needs

Source: CRITIQUE OF THE GOTHA PROGRAM
Author: Karl Marx (1818-1883)
First published: 1891
Type of work: Economic essay

Context: Marx is best known today, of course, as the creator of the philosophical basis of modern communism. In 1875 representatives of the two German workers' organizations met at Gotha and combined to form a single organization. The new union announced its socialistic policies and goals in an elaborate statement known as the Gotha Program. Marx regarded the entire proceeding as a useless waste of energy which should have been diverted to action rather than to talk, and he considered the statement to be vague, ambiguous, and worthless ("Every step of real movement is more important than a dozen programs"). Sick though he was, Marx wrote a searching and ruthlessly severe commentary on the program statement in which he dissected every ambiguity and vagary. The Gotha Programmers had proposed that all wealth derived from labor should be equally divided among the workers who produced it; Marx pointed out that different workers produced differing amounts and had differing needs; therefore, some other method of distribution would be necessary:

> In a higher phase of communist society, after the enslaving subordination of the individual to the division of labour, and therewith also the antithesis between mental and physical labour, has vanished; . . . after the productive forces have also increased with the all-round development of the individual, and all the springs of cooperative wealth flow more abundantly—only then can the narrow horizon of bourgeois right be crossed in its entirety and society inscribe on its banners: **From each according to his ability, to each according to his needs!**

From the cradle to the grave

Source: THE PARISH REGISTER (Part III, "Burials")
Author: George Crabbe (1754-1832)
First published: 1807
Type of work: Didactic poem

Context: Crabbe was an early exponent of realism. He disliked intensely the old pastoral, rustic poetry which idealized village life and doted on rural simplicity; he was at the same time completely opposed to the developing school of romanticism, which treated the same subject in more dramatic and sentimental terms. His first major work, *The Village,* is a satirical reply to Goldsmith's *The Deserted Village;* in it and in the works that followed it, he recreates in poetry the lives and condition of the poor with stark and unflinching bluntness. It is true that he tends to exaggerate the misfortunes of these people into a picture of unrelieved agony at times, but this comes from his determination to tell their story without any coating of romance. In *The Parish Register,* as in his other poems of like nature, he surveys the inhabitants of a rural area and draws their portraits both realistically and psychologically. He characterizes them in a variety of ways: an epigrammatic comment, a skeletonized biography, or a revealing speech. This poem is a chain of connected tales; it begins with a number of births, follows the people through their lives, and ends with their death and burial. In the opening lines Crabbe announces that "The year revolves, and I again explore/ The simple annals of my parish poor." The first story under "Baptisms" is that of a girl whose child is born out of wedlock; its father, a sailor, is killed at sea. The youthful mother is abused by all and cast out by her father. Other stories follow: of those who long for children and cannot have them, and of others who have too many; of children wanted and unwanted; of ignorance, and of strange

318

names conferred on children for incomprehensible reasons. The poem then traces out some of the lives thus inauspiciously begun, and in the third section, "Burials," brings them to a cheerless end. Crabbe begins "Burials" with the following lines:

> There was, 'tis said, and I believe, a time
> When humble Christians died with views sublime;
> When all were ready for their faith to bleed,
> But few to write or wrangle for their creed;
> When lively Faith upheld the sinking heart,
> And friends, assured to meet, prepared to part;
> When Love felt hope, when Sorrow grew serene,
> And all was comfort in the death-bed scene.
>   Alas! when now the gloomy king they wait,
> 'Tis weakness yielding to resistless fate;
> Like wretched men upon the ocean cast,
> They labour hard and struggle to the last;
> 'Hope against hope,' and wildly gaze around,
> In search of help that never shall be found:
> Nor, till the last strong billow stops the breath,
> Will they believe them in the jaws of Death!
>   When these my Records I reflecting read,
> And find what ills these numerous births succeed;
> What powerful griefs these nuptial ties attend,
> With what regret these painful journeys end;
> When **from the cradle to the grave** I look,
> Mine I conceive a melancholy book.

From the great deep to the great deep

Source: IDYLLS OF THE KING ("The Coming of Arthur," Line 410)
Author: Alfred, Lord Tennyson (1809-1892)
First published: 1869
Type of work: Narrative poem

Context: Young King Arthur presumes to seek the hand of fair Guinevere, only child of King Leodgran, who has requested and received Arthur's help in repelling both the Saxon invaders and the beast prevalent in the desolate countryside torn by petty native kings and weak Roman rulers. Bellicent, daughter of Ygerne and Gorlois, tells Leodgran of legends of the mysterious lineage of Arthur: (1) he is the son of Ygerne and Gorlois, (2) he is the son of Ygerne and King Uther, who killed Gorlois and took his wife, and (3) before his death Bleys, master of Merlin (a magician who reared Arthur), told Bellicent that on the night of the death of Uther, who wept because he had no heir, Merlin and Bleys beheld a fiery dragon-winged ship sail down from heaven, leaving a baby, whom they hailed as heir to Uther, and who is the youthful King

319

Arthur. Confronted by this riddle,   riddles:
Merlin had answered Bellicent in

> "Rain, rain, and sun! a rainbow in the sky!
> A young man will be wiser by and by;
> An old man's wit may wander ere he die.

> "Rain, rain, and sun! a rainbow on the lea!
> And truth is this to me, and that to thee;
> And truth or clothed or naked let it be.

> "Rain, sun, and rain! and the free blossom blows:
> Sun, rain, and sun! and where is he who knows?
> **From the great deep to the great deep** he goes."

Full fathom five

Source: THE TEMPEST (Act I, sc. ii, l. 396)
Author: William Shakespeare (1564-1616)
First published: 1623
Type of work: Tragi-comedy

Context: Duke Prospero of Milan, his throne usurped by his evil brother Antonio, lives in exile on an island with his daughter Miranda and with a spirit, Ariel, and a savage, Caliban, enthralled by his powers as a sorcerer. At Prospero's behest Ariel causes a storm in which the passengers and crew of a ship, Antonio and other noblemen of Milan and Naples, are cast into the sea and then are allowed to reach Prospero's island safely. Disguised as a water nymph, Ariel, singing, bewitches young Prince Ferdinand, bringing him to Prospero and Miranda. Ariel's words—"Full fathom five thy father lies"—Ferdinand construes to mean that his father has drowned. One stanza of Ariel's song goes:

> ARIEL *sings.*
> **Full fathom five** *thy father lies,*
> *Of his bones are coral made.*
> *Those are pearls that were his eyes,*
> *Nothing of him that doth fade*
> *But doth suffer a sea-change*
> *Into something rich and strange.*
> *Sea-nymphs hourly ring his knell:*
> *[Burden within. Ding-dong.]*
> *Hark, now I hear them—Ding-dong bell.*

320

The further off from England the nearer is to France

Source: ALICE'S ADVENTURES IN WONDERLAND (Chapter 10)
Author: Lewis Carroll (Charles Lutwidge Dodgson, 1832-1898)
First published: 1865
Type of work: Imaginative tale for children

Context: Out rowing in 1862 with the three daughters of his dean, the Rev. Charles Dodgson, instructor in Mathematics of Christ Church College, Oxford, entertained the girls with a fantastic story whose heroine he named Alice, for little Alice Liddell. Later he wrote the story out for her, and still later, in 1865, he had it published. Into this story of another Alice, falling down a rabbit hole into a world of the unusual, the learned Oxford don packed adventures for children, and humor and whimsies for adults. A number of parodies of well-known poems are also slipped in. The wider the knowledge of the reader, the more he will get out of this tale on two levels. Some literary people boast of reading it at least once a year, as musicians like periodically to listen to Mozart, to keep their thoughts in tune. Leaving a world of reality for one where she can grow tall or small at will, and where a cheshire cat can fade away to only his grin, Alice goes on her adventures amid puns and parodies. She hears of the minnows in a "school of fish," learning Laughing and Grief, instead of Latin and Greek, after a grounding in Reeling and Writhing, with Drawling and Stretching for extras in Arts. Here under the instruction of a tortoise ("So-called because he taught us," the Gryphon explains), they study ten hours the first day, nine the next, then eight, and less and less'n lesson, all the time; they learn poems. " 'Tis the Voice of the Sluggard," has been transformed into " 'Tis the Voice of the Lobster." She hears "Twinkle, twinkle, little bat,/ How I wonder where you're at." "Beautiful Snow" becomes "Beautiful Soup, so rich and green," and Alice herself recites to the Caterpillar: "You are old, Father William," based on a serious poem, "The Old Man's Comforts," by Robert Southey. The Duchess sings the unforgettable "Speak roughly to your little boy,/ And beat him when he sneezes." At the Lobster-Quadrille, Alice hears the longest poem. The Mock Turtle, who was once a real Turtle, sings and dances, with tears streaming from his eyes, a nonsense poem about the whitings walking on the sand with a porpoise. "Every fish going on a journey," as the Mock Turtle explains in an aside, "should go with some purpose." The first and last stanzas—with the snail in the second stanza protesting that they are being thrown too far into the sea—go like this:

"Will you walk a little faster?" said a whiting to a snail,
"There's a porpoise close behind us, and he's treading on my tail.
See how eagerly the lobsters and the turtles all advance!
They are waiting on the shingle—will you come and join the dance?

Will you, wo'n't you, will you, wo'n't you,
    will you join the dance?
Will you, wo'n't you, will you wo'n't you,
    wo'n't you join the dance?"

        .   .   .

"What matter it how far we go?" his scaly friend replied.
"There is another shore, you know, upon the other side.
The further off from England the nearer is to France.
Then turn not pale, beloved snail, but come and join the
dance.
Will you, wo'n't you, will you, wo'n't you,
    will you join the dance?
Will you, wo'n't you, will you, wo'n't you,
    will you join the dance?"

The gadding vine

Source: LYCIDAS (Line 40)
Author: John Milton (1608-1674)
First published: 1637
Type of work: Elegiac pastoral poem

Context: Lycidas is an elegy, but the basic subject is Milton, and not the dead person; the poem was written for a volume of verse in honor of Edward King, a Cambridge University student drowned in the Irish Sea. He was not an intimate friend of Milton, and the poem, in its elegiac features, is conventional rather than impassioned; it follows the pattern of the tradition of the classical pastoral elegy. Milton begins his poem by indicating, by references to laurel, myrtle, and ivy, that he is much concerned about his own poetical fame. He then announces that Lycidas, or Edward King, is dead; he says that Lycidas was also a poet, although King's productions were only a few mediocre Latin verses. Milton indicates that he and King were fellow shepherds, that is, students at Cambridge; he refers to their feeding their sheep in the hills, although the region around Cambridge is remarkably flat. ("Gadding" means wandering.) The poet describes their taking their flocks afield, the music of the oaten pipe, the dancing of the satyrs and fauns—but there has been a change:

But O the heavy change, now thou art gone,
Now thou art gone, and never must return!
Thee shepherd, thee the woods, and desert caves,
With wild thyme and **the gadding vine** o'ergrown,
And all their echoes mourn.
The willows and the hazel copses green
Shall now no more be seen,
Fanning their joyous leaves to thy soft lays.
As killing as the canker to the rose,
Or taint-worm to the weanling herds that graze,

322

Or frost to flowers, that their gay wardrobe wear,
When first the white-thorn blows,
Such, Lycidas, thy loss to shepherd's ear.

A gallant company

Source: THE SIEGE OF CORINTH (Prologue, l. 3)
Author: George Gordon, Lord Byron (1788-1824)
First published: 1816
Type of work: Narrative poem

Context: Evidence of the change in public feeling toward Byron's poetry over a century and a half can be found in the modern attitude toward his group classified as "Tales, Chiefly Oriental." At their publication, they were bought and read by thousands. With their flow of life and magnificent egotism, they represented the revolutionary side of Byron's character, his passion for vivid color and exotic adventure. Works by Shelley and Keats were rated considerably below them by most contemporaries. But with the passing of time, a better knowledge of the East and an increasing sophistication brought realization of the falsity and melodrama of their rhetoric, and nowadays few read them. First came *The Giaour* (1813) about a female slave thrown into the sea for infidelity, and her revenge by her Venetian lover. Then *The Bride of Abydos* (1813) and *The Corsair* (1814) followed. In 1816, Byron published *The Siege of Corinth,* based on history. However, while history does tell of an explosion of 600 barrels of gunpowder in the Turkish camp, the explosion is considered an accident and not an act of vengeance by an outraged father. And Francesca and her renegade lover do not appear on the pages of the history books. The narrator begins the Prologue of his story in 1810, sitting on "Acro-Corinth's brow," the hill from which Corinth could best be seen. He recounts what happened to that city a century earlier when the Turks, who held most of Greece under Sultan Achmet (or Ahmed) III (1673–1736), were determined to capture Morea and the Ionian Islands from the Venetians. The Sultan thought it necessary first to capture the fortified city of Corinth. The protagonist in this thirty-three stanza story told in rhymed couplets of varied meters, is "Alp, the Adrian renegade," once Lanciotto, a Venetian gentleman but now wearing the turban, and eager to capture Corinth because of his love for Francesca, daughter of its governor, Minotti. As Alp paces under the walls against which an attack will soon be made, he sees a shadowy figure beside him, his Francesca, who begs him to give up his treason and return to the side of Venice. When indignantly he refuses to change loyalties again, "He turned, but she is gone! nothing is there but the column stone." Had she been real, or a ghost, or only a figment of his imagination? "Hath she sunk in the earth, or melted in air?/ He saw not—he knew not—but nothing is there." The next morning Corinth falls. Into the city dashes Alp. He finds Minotti and demands to

323

know the whereabouts of Francesca. The grieving father reports her death the previous night. While Alp is reeling from the fatal news, a shot from a nearby church slays the renegade. Minotti hastens to the church. When the Paynim host tries to capture it, "Old Minotti's hand/ Touched with the torch, the train." and the holy building, with friend and foe inside, is destroyed. The Prologue begins:

In the year since Jesus died for men,
Eighteen hundred years and ten,
We were **a gallant company,**
Riding o'er land and sailing o'er sea.
Oh, but we went merrily!
         •   •   •
Whether we lay in the cave or the shed,
Our sleep fell soft on the hardest bed.
         •   •   •
Fresh we woke upon the morrow.
    All our thoughts and words had scope,
    We had health, and we had hope,
Toil and travel, but no sorrow.

The game is never lost till won

Source: TALES OF THE HALL ("Gretna Green," Line 334)
Author: George Crabbe (1754-1832)
First published: 1819
Type of work: Narrative poem

Context: The Reverend George Crabbe, an early exponent of realism, disliked intensely the old rustic and pastoral poetic convention that idealized village life; he was equally averse to the newer and oversentimentalized approach of romanticism. His revolt took the form of a harsh, starkly cheerless view of rural existence and of those who endured it. At times his reaction to sentimentality is such that the lives he depicts are sagas of unrelieved anguish—an equally unrealistic point of view. His first major work was *The Village,* a satirical reply to Goldsmith's *The Deserted Village,* which emphasizes the condition of the poor. This was followed by *The Parish Register,* a chain of connected tales about the lives, from birth to death, of the poor people in Crabbe's parish. *Tales of the Hall* deals with life on a somewhat higher level of society, but the lives of its characters are for the most part unenviable. The poem is a loosely woven biography of Richard, a man whose older brother George has acquired the Hall at Binning and invited him there. Into this biography are woven the stories of various people who live at the Hall or visit there, or whose lives impinge upon those of George and Richard. In Book XV, entitled "Gretna Green," Richard meets an old friend who seems cool and distant; he asks George why this should be so. George obliges with the story of James Belwood, a young man who wed un-wisely. Belwood is both weak and self-indulgent, and the girl he married, Clara, is a spoiled local beauty. To him she is but an expensive new toy; and her only desire is to be envied by other women. He had met her at a school conducted by her father. The inevitable quarrel arises; she wishes to visit her parents and he objects. The parents, meanwhile, are consumed by misgivings. The mother, feeling her daughter is a mere captive, upbraids the father. He replies, truthfully enough, that it was she who encouraged the match:

> "Had you o'erawed and check'd them when in sight,
> They would not then have ventured upon flight—
> Had you"—"Out, serpent! did you not begin?
> What! introduce, and then upbraid the sin?
> For sin it is, as I too well perceive:
> But leave me, woman, to reflection leave;
> Then to your closet fly, and on your knees
> Beg for forgiveness for such sins as these."

> "A moody morning!" with a careless air
> Replied the wife—"Why counsel me to prayer?
> I think the lord and teacher of a school
> Should pray himself, and keep his temper cool."

> Calm grew the husband when the wife was gone—
> **"The game,"** said he, **"is never lost till won:**
> 'Tis true, the rebels fly their proper home,
> They come not nigh, because they fear to come;
> And for my purpose fear will doubtless prove
> Of more importance and effect than love, ..."

Gates of ivory

Source: THE ODYSSEY (Book XIX, ll. 657-658, as translated by Alexander Pope)
Author: Homer (c.850 B.C.)
First transcribed: Sixth century B.C.
Type of work: Epic poem

Context: Odysseus, disguised as a beggar, finally returns to his home in Ithaca after his long absence in the Trojan War and his subsequent travels. Penelope, his wife, in questioning the dirty man before her concerning her husband's chances of returning, asks for an interpretation of a dream that she has had in which an eagle kills her twenty geese. Odysseus explains that the eagle clearly represents her husband and the geese the suitors who have plagued the seeming widow. Penelope, however, doubts the optimism of the interpretation and comments on dreams that issue from the gate of ivory and those from the gate of horn:

Hard is the task, and rare, the queen rejoin'd,
Impending destinies in dreams to find;
Immured within the silent bower of sleep,
Two portals firm the various phantoms keep:
Of ivory one; whence flit, to mock the brain,
Of winged lies a light fantastic train:
The gate opposed pellucid valves adorn,
And columns fair incased with polish'd horn:
Where images of truth for passage wait,
With visions manifest of future fate.
Not to this troop, I fear, that phantom soar'd,
Which spoke Ulysses to his realm restored:
Delusive semblance!

A gay deceiver

Source: LOVE LAUGHS AT LOCKSMITHS (Act II)
Author: George Colman, the Younger (1762-1836)
First published: 1803
Type of work: Comic opera

Context: The dramas of a hundred fifty years ago sound artificial to modern readers, and their plots are even more exaggerated. Yet they must have appealed to their contemporaries. The dramatist George Colman (or Coleman) was a successful manager of one of London's most popular theaters, the Haymarket, and some of England's most memorable actors of his time performed there. Of course, *Love Laughs at Locksmiths* is a farce, and farces are supposed to move so fast that spectators have no time to judge their logical development or lack of it. In this play, Lydia, an orphan, has been entrusted to the care of the sister of Vigil, an artist. Vigil maintains guard over her. Yet Frederick Beldare, Captain of Grenadiers, has seen her portrait and has fallen in love. He smuggles a letter to her. The captain's servant, Risk, hearing that Solomon Lob, nephew of Vigil's servant, is coming to London to visit his uncle, schemes to take his place and get into Vigil's house. In the course of the farcical action, Risk interpolates a song about a Captain bold of Halifax who deceived a certain Miss Bailey. Thereupon, she hanged herself. As a ghost, she came back to haunt her betrayer. To exorcise her, he gave her a pound note so that she could secure for herself proper burial. The song has nothing to do with the action of the play. Risk's Captain has honorable intentions in his schemes to get word of his love to Lydia. The second stanza of the song goes:

One night, betimes, he went to rest,
    For he had caught a fever;
Says he: "I am a handsome man,
    But I'm **a gay deceiver.**"

326

His candle, just at twelve o'clock,
Began to burn quite palely;
A ghost stepp'd up to his bed-side,
And said, "Behold Miss Bailey!
Oh! Miss Bailey!
Unfortunate Miss Bailey!"

Gay Lothario

Source: THE FAIR PENITENT (Act V, sc. i)
Author: Nicholas Rowe (1674-1718)
First published: 1703
Type of work: Dramatic tragedy

Context: The Fair Penitent is a domestic tragedy; the playwright in his prologue styles it "A melancholy tale of private woes." It is the story of a young woman who is led astray, the first of Nicholas Rowe's "she-tragedies," plays based on man's inhumanity to woman. The woman of this play is beautiful young Calista, a native of Genoa, who falls in love with Lothario. The immoral Lothario, the archetype of the inconstant lover, steals into Calista's chamber and spends a night with her; but when the girl speaks of marriage, Lothario laughs and leaves her. Despite his treatment, Calista continues to be infatuated with him and is forced to allow an interview with him on her wedding day, after her father has given her in marriage to Alta- mont. Lothario visits her and is discovered by her husband, who has long been Lothario's enemy. In the fight that ensues, Lothario is killed, and Calista, after a scene with her husband and her father, runs out. At the opening of the fifth act of the play, Calista is found in a room hung with black, keeping watch over Lothario's body, which lies on a bier. Though the dead man has ruined her, Calista still loves him. A mournful song is heard, and Calista picks up a devotional book, placed beside her to encourage her penitence. After glancing at it, she throws the book from her, to look at a skull and bones which lie upon a table. From contemplating the bones she turns to the corpse of Lothario, to gaze upon it in awful contemplation:

CALISTA [*throwing away the book.*]
I have more real anguish in my heart
Than all their pedant discipline e'er knew.
What charnel has been rifled for these bones?
Fie! this is pageantry;—they look uncouthly,
But what of that, if he or she that owned 'em
Safe from disquiet sit, and smile to see
The farce their miserable relics play?
But here's a sight is terrible indeed;
Is this the haughty, gallant, **gay Lothario?**

327

That dear perfidious—Ah!—how pale he looks!
How grim with clotted blood, and those dead eyes!

A general flavor of mild decay

Source: THE DEACON'S MASTERPIECE (Stanza 9)
Author: Oliver Wendell Holmes (1809-1894)
First published: 1858
Type of work: Satirical poem

Context: Holmes, who was no admirer of Calvinistic theology, which had played so prominent a role in the history of New England, satirizes the logical structure of the Calvinists in this poem, and, in a way, laughs it out of people's serious thoughts, as it had long since ceased to be a vital force in their lives. Like the fabulous shay, Calvinism had begun in the most logical fashion theologians could devise; no one was ever able to break it down; but like the shay, that logical structure collapsed in importance, leaving the theologians in the dust. The deacon's masterpiece, built of the finest materials for each portion of its structure, lasts for a hundred years; it was finished by its maker on Lisbon Earthquake Day, November 1, 1755, and is still all in one piece on the hundredth anniversary of that date:

> Little of all we value here
> Wakes on the morn of its hundredth year
> Without both feeling and looking queer.
> In fact, there's nothing that keeps its youth,
> So far as I know, but a tree and truth.
>   • • •
> FIRST OF NOVEMBER,—the Earthquake-day—
> There are traces of age in the one-hoss shay,
> **A general flavor of mild decay,**
> But nothing local, as one may say,
> There couldn't be,—for the Deacon's art
> Had made it so like in every part
> That there wasn't a chance for one to start.

A general union of total dissent

Source: A FABLE FOR CRITICS (Line 733)
Author: James Russell Lowell (1819-1891)
First published: 1848
Type of work: Satirical poem

Context: Lowell began *A Fable for Critics,* he says in his first Preface, "to please only myself and my own private fancy." Readers have, for several generations now, been pleased with his humorous satire—pleasant enough, and usually true to the mark, of Emerson, Thoreau, Bryant, Whittier, Hawthorne, Cooper, Poe, and others well known at the time who have slipped, unlike those named, into a literary Limbo. Though his own reputation as a poet has diminished in the decades since his death, Lowell's *Fable,* as well as some selections from *The Biglow Papers,* is still, at least in part, often read. The quotation about "general union of total dissent" is found in Lowell's comments about Theodore Parker, whom he calls the "Orson of parsons":

> Here comes Parker, the Orson of parsons, a man
> Whom the Church undertook to put under her ban
> (The Church of Socinus, I mean),—his opinions
> Being So-(ultra)-cinian, they shocked the Socinians;
> They believed—faith, I'm puzzled—I think I may call
> Their belief a believing in nothing at all,
> Or something of that sort; I know they all went
> For **a general union of total dissent:**
> He went a step farther; without cough or hem,
> He frankly avowed he believed not in them;
> And, before he could be jumbled up or prevented,
> From their orthodox kind of dissent he dissented.
> There was heresy here, you perceive, for the right
> Of privately judging means simply that light
> Has been granted to *me,* for deciding on *you;*
> And in happier times, before Atheism grew,
> The deed contained clauses for cooking you too.

Genius does what it must, and talent does what it can

Source: LAST WORDS OF A SENSITIVE SECOND-RATE POET
Author: Owen Meredith (Edward Robert Bulwer, 1st Earl of Lytton, 1831-1891)
First published: 1868
Type of work: Poetry

Context: The Earl of Lytton played an important part in the British diplomatic world. His father, the first Baron Lytton, is remembered for his novels *Eugene Aram* (1832), *The Last Days of Pompeii* (1834) and *Rienzi* (1835). The son got his early education at Harrow, where he wrote his first poetry at the age of twelve. After Harrow, instead of going on to a university, he was privately educated by tutors, with emphasis on languages, fortunately, because he later represented his country in such places as Paris, Athens, Florence, Vienna, and Madrid. He began as secretary to his uncle in the embassy at Washington, where he wrote most of his poetry, though none was published until 1860. Since it was not appropriate for a diplomat to write poetry, he signed his work "Owen Meredith," a concoction of Christian names of earlier members of his family. In 1874 he achieved a literary reputation with the publication of *Fables in Song*. Then he revised and added poems for two more collections, one in 1885 and a posthumous collection in 1892. In the meantime, he had been Secretary of the British Legation in Copenhagen (1863), British Minister to Lisbon (1872), Viceroy of India (1876–1880), and finally Ambassador to Paris (1887–1891). During his lifetime, critics admired his poetry for its brilliancy of idea, phrase, and description, but complained that such brilliancy eventually became tiring. One critic lamented that, in spite of being appointed Viceroy of India by Disraeli, Lord Lytton is chiefly remembered for his poem *Lucile* (1860), which the critic rated as "a vast, stale, Victorian piece of poetry." Perhaps it lives in memory for the couplet:

> We may live without friends; we may live without books;
> But a civilized man cannot live without cooks.

Considerably different is his "Last Words of a Sensitive Second-Rate Poet," that appeared in Book IX, "Here and There: Romances and Ballads," of his *Chronicles and Characters* (London, 1868). In it, the poet is dying with only his faithful friend, Will, beside him, weary from three days of vigil. The poet thinks of their youth together, their days of girl-courting, and is reminded of one girl who used the poet and left him. But he must not think bitterly of her.

> There can be no space for the ghost of her face down in this
>   narrow room,
> And the mole is blind, and the worm is mute, and there must be
>   rest in the tomb.

In his youth, the poet was optimistic and confident, with hopes of moving the world, though unable himself to stand firm. Now he begs his friend to burn everything he has written. Perhaps he would have been more popular and successful if his poetry had been less melancholic. All he knows is that he has failed, so he waits patiently for death.

> . . . The world, that had paused to listen awhile, because the first
>   notes were gay,
> Pass'd on its way with a sneer in a smile: "Has he nothing fresher
>   to say?
> This poet's mind was a weedy flower that presently comes to
>   nought!"
> For the world was not so sad but what my song was sadder, it
>   thought.
> Comfort me not. For if aught be worst than failure from over-
>   stress
> Of a life's prime purpose, it is to sit down content with a little
>   success.

330

Talk not of genius baffled. Genius is master of man.
Genius does what it must, and Talent does what it can.
Blot out my name, that the spirits of Shakspeare and Milton and
   Burns
Look not down on the praises of fools with a pity my soul yet
   spurns.
And yet, had I only the trick of an aptitude shrewd of its kind,
I should have lived longer, I think, more merry of heart and of
   mind.

Genius is of no country

Source: THE ROSCIAD (Line 207)
Author: Charles Churchill (1731-1764)
First published: 1761
Type of work: Satiric poem

Context: A dissipated clergyman, Churchill won both fame and notoriety as a satiric poet during the last four years of his life. He was associated with and defended John Wilkes, the unscrupulous editor of the *North-Briton.* Much of the harsh and vitriolic nature of Churchill's satire seems to have been formed by this association. In *The Rosciad,* his first important poem, Churchill attacked a number of theatrical personalities with such witty satire that it was at one time regarded as the most important satiric work between those of Pope and Byron. Early in the poem a youth representing Churchill's friend Robert Lloyd speaks forth against the faddish praise of classical culture to the exclusion of native English arts:

> "But more than just to other countries grown,
> Must we turn base apostates to our own?
> Where do these words of Greece and Rome excell,
> That England may not please the ear as well?
> What mighty magic's in the place or air,
> That all perfection needs must center there?
> In states, let strangers blindly be preferr'd;
> In state of letters, Merit should be heard.
> **Genius is of no country,** her pure ray
> Spreads all abroad, as gen'ral as the day:
> Foe to restraint, from place to place she flies,
> And may hereafter e'en in Holland rise."

Gentle dullness ever loves a joke

Source: THE DUNCIAD (Book II, l. 34)
Author: Alexander Pope (1688-1744)
First published: 1728-1743
Type of work: Satiric poem

331

Context: This long, satiric mock-epic describes the establishment of the kingdom of dullness ruled over by the King of the Dunces. In various stages of the revision of the poem over a number of years Pope appointed several different scribblers to the throne of dullness, depending upon whom he was most irritated with at the moment. Dozens of other minor Grub Street scribblers and hacks come under Pope's withering satiric fire in the course of the poem. Book I invokes the Goddess of Dullness, describes her great empire and her college within the city of London, and closes with her proclamation of Cibber, in the 1742 version, as the new King of the Dunces. In Book II the newly proclaimed king is honored with public games and sports, all in satiric imitation of Virgil's *Aeneid*. As this Book opens, the king on his throne is surrounded by admiring spectators:

> Amid that area wide they took their stand,
> Where the tall may-pole once o'er-look'd the Strand;
> But now (so ANNE and Piety ordain)
> A Church collects the saints of Drury-lane.
>   With Authors, Stationers obey'd the call,
> (The field of glory is a field for all.)
> Glory, and gain, th' industrious tribe provoke;
> And **gentle Dulness ever loves a joke.**
> A Poet's form she plac'd before their eyes,
> And bade the nimblest racer seize the prize;
> No meagre, muse-rid mope, adust and thin,
> In a dun night-gown of his own loose skin;
> But such a bulk as no twelve bards could raise,
> Twelve starv'ling bards of these degen'rate days.

The gentle mind by gentle deeds is known

Source: THE FAERIE QUEENE (Book VI, Canto 3, stanza 1)
Author: Edmund Spenser (c.1552-1599)
First published: 1590
Type of work: Allegorical poem

Context: The concept of courtesy is the major theme of Book VI. In the first portion of this book, courtesy is exemplified in the actions of Calidore, the knight of Courtesy. While on his search for the Blatant Beast, Slander, he finds Priscilla weeping beside her wounded knight, Aladine. A lustful knight had attacked the unarmed Aladine while he and Priscilla were making love; she had escaped by hiding quickly. Calidore assures her that their attacker has already been slain by Tristram. Calidore then straps Aladine on his shield; he and Priscilla carry the wounded knight in this manner to the nearby castle of Aldus, Aladine's father. Spenser then comments that Calidore's actions have been an excellent example of true courtesy. The theme of this episode is expressed in Spenser's quotation from Chaucer (*Canterbury Tales,* "Wife of Bath's Tale," 1. 1170):

332

True is, that whilome that good Poet sayd,
The gentle minde by gentle deeds is knowne:
For a man by nothing is so well betrayd,
As by his manners, in which plaine is showne
Of what degree and what race he is growne.
For seldom seene, a trotting Stalion get
An ambling Colt, that is his proper owne:
So seldome seene, that one in baseness set
Doth noble courage shew, with courteous manners met.

The gift of gab

Source: THE OLD NAVY (Stanza 1)
Author: Frederick Marryat (1792-1848)
First published: 1837
Type of work: Sea chantey

Context: A much-quoted poem by Capt. Marryat appears most frequently with its first line as title. It describes a battle between the British and the French, perhaps just such a battle as midshipman Marryat experienced when he ran away from his family in 1806 and shipped aboard the frigate *Impérieuse* under Lord Cochrane (1775–1860), who later fought for Chilean independence. Marryat described another such naval battle in a famous chapter of *The King's Own* (1830). A carronade, getting its name from Carron in Scotland where it was first forged, was a mortar-like cannon, carried on the ship's upper deck for use at short range. "Gab," from Middle English *gabben,* "to mock or talk foolishly," is colloquial for "babbling." Whether it is a gift or a curse depends on whether one is uttering it or listening to it. "Odds bobs" is a euphemism for the oath "God's body!" The poem begins and ends, after the sea-fight, as follows:

The captain stood on the carronade—"First lieutenant," says he,
"Send all my merry men aft here, for they must list to me:
I haven't **the gift of the gab,** my sons—because I'm bred to the
        sea;
That ship there is a Frenchman, who means to fight with we. . . ."
                        •   •   •
Our captain sent for all of us; "My merry men," said he,
"I haven't **the gift of the gab,** my lads, but yet I thankful be;
You've done your duty handsomely, each man stood to his gun;
If you hadn't, you villains, as sure as day, I'd have flogged each
        mother's son.
Odds bobs, hammer and tongs, as long as I'm at sea,
I'll fight 'gainst every odds—and I'll gain the victory!"

Gird up thy loins

Source: JOB 38:3
Author: Unknown
First transcribed: c.900-500 B.C.
Type of work: Religious saga

Context: Job, a good man who enjoys prosperity and many sons and daughters, is said to be a fine example of the God-fearing and God-worshiping man. But Satan says that Job is good only because he has always enjoyed good fortune, that he will turn against God if he is visited by adversity. Responding to Satan's challenge, God permits Satan to take away Job's wealth and to slay his sons and daughters; still Job does not turn against God. Next Satan, with God's agreement, visits physical misery upon Job; still Job refuses to turn against God and curse Him. Job is visited by men who claim that he must have been a great sinner in the past, inasmuch as God does not afflict a man without cause. But Job maintains, truthfully, that he is a good man, that there is no reason for him to receive this treatment as punishment. He is patient and enduring, but he does not understand. Elihu, one of the men who visit him, speaks of God's great power, which controls the winds, the snow, the rain, even the passing cycle of the seasons. He warns Job that man cannot understand God, although God will listen to the cry of the submissive man. He also warns that God will not afflict a man without cause. When Elihu finishes speaking, God Himself, out of a whirlwind, speaks to Job; when Job replies submissively after God is finished, God grants him his well-being and prosperity once again:

> Then the LORD answered Job out of the whirlwind, and said,
> Who is this that darkeneth counsel by words without knowledge?
> **Gird up** now **thy loins** like a man; for I will demand of thee, and answer thou me.
> Where wast thou when I laid the foundations of the earth? declare, if thou hast understanding
> Who hath laid the measures thereof, if thou knowest? or who hath stretched the line upon it?
> Whereupon are the foundations thereof fastened? or who laid the corner stone thereof;
> When the morning stars sang together, and all the sons of God shouted for joy?

Give him a little earth for charity

Source: KING HENRY THE EIGHTH (Act IV, sc. ii, l.23)
Author: William Shakespeare (1564-1616)
First published: 1623
Type of work: Historical drama

334

Context: Cardinal Wolsey, the son of a butcher, has risen in the Church and claims the ear of King Henry VIII. In his duties as Lord Chancellor he has sent far away from Henry all those who oppose his ideas and of whom he is jealous or afraid. He has made himself enormously wealthy, and he even desires to rise to Pope. He sends Buckingham to his death and also rouses Henry against Queen Katharine. She, however, sees through his designs. Henry begins to be conscience-stricken about his marriage to Katharine, his brother's widow. He has met Anne Bullen at a party given by Wolsey and desires to marry her. Wolsey has other plans, but Henry desires Anne and marries her in spite of Wolsey. Through an error, Henry finds papers tallying Wolsey's vast wealth and revealing his desires in the Church. He denounces the cardinal, who, seeing his imminent downfall, only wishes he had been a true churchman. Northumberland arrests him; he goes to the abbey at Leicester, and there, after his overthrow, finds himself, and, as a penitent, dies, forgiven by Katharine.

• • •

KATHARINE
Dids't thou not tell me Griffith, as thou led'st me,
That the great child of honor, Cardinal Wolsey,
Was dead?

• • •

GRIFFITH
He fell sick suddenly, and grew so ill
He could not sit his mule.

• • •

At last, with easy roads, he came to Leicester,
Lodged in the abbey; where the reverend abbot
With all his covent honourably received him;
To whom he gave these words, o, Father Abbot,
An old man, broken with the storms of state
Is come to lay his weary bones among ye;
Give him a little earth for charity.

Give me man as he is <u>not</u> to be

Source: MY FIRST ACQUAINTANCE WITH POETS, BY WILLIAM HAZLITT
Author: Charles Lamb (1775-1834)
First published: 1823
Type of work: Attributed comment

Context: Hazlitt was a harsh and bitter man, badly maladjusted socially, and he quarreled with both enemies and friends; there were many of the former, few of the latter. It appears that he disliked nearly everyone and that the sentiment was repaid in kind. In spite of his social handicap he had a keen mind, was a brilliant essayist, and had a deep appreciation of beauty. He tried first to become a painter, studying in France, and this background made him one of the first aesthetic critics. He was a sensitive

335

man; his reactions to the objects of his literary and dramatic criticism were usually sound and just. Although he later became somewhat estranged from the poets, he was at one time very close to them. His essay, "My First Acquaintance with Poets," reveals the deep respect, even reverence, with which he regarded those he admired. In it he describes his meeting with Coleridge and Wordsworth. The vivid picture he gives of these two great poets at the beginning of their fame is of considerable value in gaining an understanding of them.

Hazlitt tells us that he walked ten miles through freezing mud in January, 1798, to hear Coleridge preach, and that he was transfixed by the power of the man's imagination and imagery; so impressed was he that he arranged a meeting and a visit at the poet's home. He recounts their conversations and his subsequent introduction to Wordsworth. It is evident that these days with Coleridge are unforgettable and that they have furnished an inspiration for the literary life Hazlitt is to undertake.

In a day or two after we arrived at Stowey, we set out, I on my return home, and he for Germany. It was a Sunday morning, and he was to preach that day for Dr. Toulmin of Taunton. I asked him if he had prepared anything for the occasion? He said he had not even thought of the text, but should as soon as we parted. I did not go to hear him,—this was a fault,—but we met in the evening at Bridgewater. The next day we had a long day's walk to Bristol, and sat down, I recollect, by a well-side on the road, to cool ourselves and satisfy our thirst, when Coleridge repeated to me some descriptive lines from his tragedy of *Remorse;* which I must say became his mouth and that occasion better than they, some years after, did Mr. Elliston's and the Drury-lane boards. . . .

I saw no more of him for a year or two, during which period he had been wandering in the Hartz Forest in Germany; and his return was cometary, meteorous, unlike his setting out. It was not till some time after that I knew his friends Lamb and Southey. The last always appears to me (as I first saw him) with a commonplace-book under his arm, and the first with a *bon-mot* in his mouth. It was at Godwin's that I met him with Holcroft and Coleridge, where they were disputing fiercely which was the best—*Man as he was, or man as he is to be.* **"Give me,"** says Lamb, **"man as he is not to be."** This saying was the beginning of a friendship between us, which I believe still continues. . . .

Glad confident morning

.*Source:* THE LOST LEADER (Stanza 2)
Author: Robert Browning (1812-1889)
First published: 1845
Type of work: Lyric poem

Context: "The Lost Leader" is gen-   erally thought of as referring in its first two lines—"Just for a handful of silver he left us,/ Just for a riband to stick in his coat"—to two events in William Wordsworth's life: his acceptance of a pension in 1842 and of the Laureateship in 1843. Whether or not it is associated with Wordsworth's shift from fiery liberalism in youth to staid political conservatism in old age, the whole poem shows Browning's scorn for any desertion of principles for gain. John Greenleaf Whittier's "Ichabod" is a similar poem inspired by Daniel Webster's seeming political opportunism when he supported the Missouri Compromise and the Fugitive Slave Bill in 1850. In "The Lost Leader" Browning's first stanza shows the poet's shock and sense of loss at his leader's apostasy. The closing lines of the second stanza contrast the present symbolic darkness with the brightness of an earlier day:

> Life's night begins: let him never come back to us!
> There would be doubt, hesitation and pain,
> Forced praise on our part—the glimmer of twilight,
> Never **glad confident morning** again!
> Best fight on well, for we taught him—strike gallantly,
> Menace our heart ere we master his own;
> Then let him receive the new knowledge and wait us,
> Pardoned in heaven, the first by the throne!

Gladly would he learn and gladly teach

Source: THE CANTERBURY TALES (Prologue, l. 308)
Author: Geoffrey Chaucer (1343?-1400)
First transcribed: c.1387-1392
Type of work: Collection of tales

Context: The Canterbury pilgrims, having met by chance at the Tabard Inn in Southwark on their way to the shrine of Thomas à Becket at Canterbury, decide to tell tales to make the journey less boring. In the Prologue, Chaucer, to establish the tale-telling framework and to identify the participants of his work, describes vividly his pilgrims. Among the memorable characters is a clerk, or student, noted for his dedication to acquiring and sharing knowledge.

> A CLERK ther was of Oxenford also,
> That unto logyk hadde longe ygo.
> As leene was his hors as is a rake,
> And he nas nat right fat, I undertake,
> But looked holwe, and therto sobrely.
> . . .
> Noght a word spak he moore than was neede,
> And that was seyed in forme and reverence,
> And short and quyk and ful of hy sentence;

337

Sownynge in moral vertu was his speche,
And **gladly wolde he lerne and gladly teche.**

The gladsome light of jurisprudence

Source: INSTITUTES: COMMENTARY UPON LITTLETON (First Institute, Epilogue)
Author: Sir Edward Coke (1552-1634)
First published: 1628
Type of work: Legal commentary

Context: Perhaps remembering his own perplexity as a young legal student preparing to become a lawyer, over the jargon of the profession, Edward Coke took time, after he rose to be the first man to be called Lord Chief Justice of England, to take a second look at one of the principle textbooks. Thomas Littleton (1422–1481) was a jurist whose experiences as Justice of the Assize and Judge of Common Pleas gave him experience from which to compile the earliest treatise on the English Law ever printed (1481), the volume *Tenures,* which provided in legal French a complete coverage of English land laws and which became fundamental in legal education in England. Coke reissued the classic volume with Littleton's French version in one column, a second column with an English rendering of the points of law, and a third column of his own comments, explanations, and clarifications. In his Introduction Lord Coke encouraged the young student by remarking that if he did not understand the point of the original author or the commentator on his first reading, he should try the difficult passage again at a later date. After 749 sections, with commentaries, Coke ended with an Epilogue of encouragement and stimulus. Like any teacher, he comments that he might have provided an index or tables to help students more quickly find some particular section, but he thought they would remember the material better if they compiled their own. Either he had a second thought or someone else took pity on students, because the second edition, in 1633, includes a complete index. Here are Coke's closing words:

I had once intended, for the ease of our Student, to have made a table to these Institutes; but when I considered that Tables and Abridgements are most profitable to them that make them, I have left that worke to every Studious Reader. And for a Farewell to our jurisprudent, I wish unto him **the gladsome light of Jurisprudence,** the loveliness of temperance, the stability of fortitude and the soliditie of Justice.

338

The glass of fashion

Source: HAMLET (Act III, sc. i, l. 161)
Author: William Shakespeare (1564-1616)
First published: 1603
Type of work: Dramatic tragedy

Context: Hamlet, Prince of Denmark, in the position of having to avenge the death of his murdered father, feels himself oppressed by the whole court. Even Ophelia, his love, seems to be a part of the plot against him. Consequently, he berates her in such a vicious manner that when he leaves she can only think that he, the very mirror of the ideal, is mad. Her description of Hamlet as he was before the death of his father is the picture of the idealized Renaissance Prince.

OPHELIA
O what a noble mind is here o'erthrown!
The courtier's, soldier's, scholar's, eye, tongue, sword,
Th' expectancy and rose of the fair state,
The glass of fashion, and the mould of form,
The observed of all observers, quite, quite down,
And I of ladies most deject and wretched,
That sucked the honey of his musicked vows,
Now see that noble and most sovereign reason,
Like sweet bells jangled, out of tune and harsh;
That unmatched form and feature of blown youth
Blasted with ecstasy. O woe is me
T' have seen what I have seen, see what I see.

The glory and the nothing of a name

Source: CHURCHILL'S GRAVE (Line 43)
Author: George Gordon, Lord Byron (1788-1824)
First published: 1816
Type of work: Elegiac poem

Context: Charles Churchill (1731–1764) must have won the admiration of satirical Byron by his biting wit. Though he had died long before Byron's time, his writings, especially his political satires, were still admired. As a young man, son of a Westminster curate, Churchill was refused admittance to Oxford and Cambridge, probably because he had married at the age of seventeen. He tried for the position of postmaster at Merton, but was turned down, allegedly because of lack of a classical training. However, he was ordained a priest in 1756. His was a riotous life. From his acquaintance with the theater and its performers, he published the anonymous *Rosciad* (1761), influenced by Pope's *Dunciad.* In it he lauded Garrick and several of the actresses, but unmercifully criticized many contem-

339

porary actors with such lines as "He mouths a sentence as curs mouth a bone." Divorced in 1761, Churchill led a life of dissipation. He gave up his Church offices in 1763 to write campaign literature for John Wilkes (1727–1797), an English political reformer, the idol of the mobs. Wilkes was expelled from Parliament in 1764 and exiled to France. On his trip to visit his friend, Churchill died in Boulogne of a fever. His body was brought back across the Channel to Dover and buried in St. Martin Cemetery, beneath an inscription: "Life to the last enjoyed, here Churchill lies." About to leave England for the last time, Byron visited his grave. Then he tried to write a poem to him in imitation of Churchill's style, with its beauties and its defects. He also included some touches mocking Wordsworth. At the ill-kept tomb, Byron sees a gardener who tells him he does not know who is buried there. The death happened before the gardener's time, and he cannot read the name. But he does know that strangers come to pay their respects to the dead man and pay to the sexton a few pennies, and that some have said the dead man was the most famous writer of his day. So Churchill has both glory and namelessness. Byron gives the sexton a few silver coins he can scarcely spare, and writes: "Let profane ones smile because my homely phrase the truth would tell." Here is the beginning and the conclusion of the forty-three-line poem.

> I stood beside the grave of him who blazed
> The comet of a season, and I saw
> The humblest of all sepulchres, and gazed
> With not the less of sorrow and of awe
> On that neglected turf and quiet stone . . .

>   .   .   .

> You are the fools, not I—for I did dwell
> With a deep thought, and with a soften'd eye,
> On that Old Sexton's natural homily,
> In which there was Obscurity and Fame,—
> **The Glory and the Nothing of a Name.**

The glory, jest, and riddle of the world

Source: AN ESSAY ON MAN (Epistle II, l. 18)
Author: Alexander Pope (1688-1744)
First published: 1733-1734
Type of work: Philosophical poem

Context: An Essay on Man is a philosophical poem which Pope addressed to Henry St. John, Lord Bolingbroke. The subject of Epistle II of the poem is the nature of man and his place in the universe. Like many of his contemporaries in the eighteenth century, Pope saw man as one link in the great chain of being, holding a middle place in that chain. Since man cannot know or understand the states of being above himself, he should study himself; or, as Pope puts it, "The proper study of mankind is man." In this epistle Pope, following his own advice, examines man and his nature. He sees that man has greatness and power on the one hand, but weakness and ignorance upon the other. He is governed by two principles, self-love and reason, both necessary to his place in the scale of being. Self-love is the principle which motivates man; reason is the principle which restrains him. The first verse paragraph of this epistle celebrates the duality of mankind and shows Pope's reasons for his conclusion that man's proper study is himself, that man should not try to pry into the nature, the knowledge, or the actions of God:

Know then thyself, presume not God to scan:
The proper study of mankind is man.
Plac'd on this isthmus of a middle state,
A being darkly wise, and rudely great:
With too much knowledge for the sceptic side,
With too much weakness for the Stoic's pride,
He hangs between; in doubt to act, or rest;
In doubt to deem himself a god or beast;
In doubt his mind or body to prefer;
Born but to die, and reas'ning but to err;
Alike in ignorance, his reason such,
Whether he thinks too little, or too much:
Chaos of thought and passion, all confus'd;
Still by himself abus'd, or disabus'd;
Created half to rise, and half to fall;
Great lord of all things, yet a prey to all;
Sole judge of truth, in endless error hurl'd:
The glory, jest, and riddle of the world!

Glory of youth glowed in his soul

Source: SONGS OF TRAVEL (XLIV, stanza 2)
Author: Robert Louis Stevenson (1850-1894)
First published: 1896
Type of work: Lyric poem

Context: Robert Louis Stevenson was a gay and radiant personality whose whole life was a courageous battle for health. Scottish by birth, Stevenson was a novelist, short-story writer, essayist, and poet; today he is best known for his tales of adventure and for *A Child's Garden of Verses.* The sense of adventure was keen in Stevenson and helped him through his illnesses, though it was at the same time a contributing factor to them. Suffering in 1873 from exhaustion, he spent some time in southern Europe; while there he met an American lady, Mrs. Osbourne. She was unhappily married. When Stevenson learned in 1879 that she was obtaining a divorce, he went to America to see her. He had little money, and the trip to

California further undermined his health. He married Mrs. Osbourne and they returned to England in 1880. His physical condition was poor; he had tuberculosis and was subject to severe hemorrhages. When he wrote *A Child's Garden of Verses* he was confined to his bed; his right arm was strapped to his side to lessen the danger of hemorrhage, and an eye infection made total darkness necessary. The poems were written with his left hand on large sheets of paper tacked to a board which he had arranged above him. His father died in 1887; he and his wife then moved to America, residing first at Saranac Lake and then at San Francisco. He spent the next few years roaming the South Seas, and settled at Samoa, where he remained until his death. Death was always an imminent possibility to Stevenson, and he was on intimate terms with it. Though he was always outwardly cheerful, an inevitable melancholy must have lurked in him much of the time; it is quite apparent in *Songs of Travel,* a group of poems written mostly in the South Seas between 1888 and 1894. One of these, untitled, speaks for itself:

> Sing me a song of a lad that is gone,
> Say, could that lad be I?
> Merry of soul he sailed on a day
> Over the sea to Skye.
>
> Mull was astern, Rum on the port,
> Egg on the starboard bow;
> **Glory of youth glowed in his soul:**
> Where is that glory now?
> . . .
>
> Give me again all that was there,
> Give me the sun that shone!
> Give me the eyes, give me the soul,
> Give me the lad that's gone!
>
> Sing me a song of a lad that is gone,
> Say, could that lad be I?
> Merry of soul he sailed on a day
> Over the sea to Skye.
>
> Billow and breeze, islands and seas,
> Mountains of rain and sun,
> All that was good, all that was fair,
> All that was me is gone.

Go not, like the quarry-slave at night

Source: THANATOPSIS (Line 77)
Author: William Cullen Bryant (1794–1878)
First published: 1821
Type of work: Lyric poem

342

Context: The well-known 1821 version of "Thanatopsis" is a revision and expansion of a poem written in Bryant's seventeenth year but not published until 1817. The title, meaning "a view of death," was supplied by the editor who published the 1817 version. This earlier poem began, "Yet a few days, and thee,/ The all-beholding sun, shall see no more . . ." (lines 17-18 of the 1821 version) and ended, "And make their bed with thee!"—(line 66 of the 1821 version). The opening lines which Bryant added in 1821 are Wordsworthian in the poet's view of Nature, but the phrasing of much of the poem is marked by eighteenth century "poetic diction" resembling that in the poems of the "graveyard" poets—Edward Young, Robert Blair, and Thomas Gray—whom Bryant had read and enjoyed in youth. In "Thanatopsis" Bryant says to the reader who may now and then muse on the fact that he will someday die: when such thoughts come, listen to the still, comforting voice of Nature. Nature says to man: in a brief time earth, that nourished you, will receive your body which will then be no more than "the insensible rock" or a clod of earth a farmer plows through. Oak roots will "pierce thy mould." Yet when you die you will not rest alone but with the infinite number of others who have lain down in "one mighty sepulchre." Hills, vales, rivers, brooks, ocean—these "Are but the solemn decorations all/ Of the great tomb of man." For ages the heavenly bodies have shone on "the sad abodes of death." Those men who live now "are but a handful" to those who are dead. You shall rest as they do. Though your own passing may be unnoted, "All that breathe/ Will share thy destiny." Through the ages to come you will be joined by infants, youths, men, and women in "the full strength of years," and old people who "Shall one by one be gathered to thy side,/ By those, who in their turn shall follow them." In his later life Bryant was to believe in a personal immortality of the soul and a rejoining of those separated on earth by death. But in "Thanatopsis" there is no hint of this belief. Through the voice of Nature, Bryant counsels man: live so that when death approaches, you will face it not in fear but in the faith that no harm will come to you afterward. Regard death as only an untroubled, but eternal, sleep. This advice is found in the noble lines which close the poem:

So live, that when thy summons comes to join
The innumerable caravan, which moves
To that mysterious realm, where each shall take
His chamber in the silent halls of death,
Thou **go not, like the quarry-slave at night,**
Scourged to his dungeon, but, sustained and soothed
By an unfaltering trust, approach thy grave,
Like one who wraps the drapery of his couch
About him, and lies down to pleasant dreams.

343

Go, tell the Spartans

Source: PALATINE MANUSCRIPT
Author: Simonides of Ceos (556-468 B.C.)
First transcribed: Fifth century B.C.
Type of work: Poetic epitaph

Context: In 480 B.C. Xerxes, seeking revenge for Darius' defeat at Marathon in 490 B.C., invaded Greece. The Pass of Thermopylae was defended by 300 Spartans under their King Leonidas and by 7,500 other Greeks, who held out for three days until a traitor revealed to the Persians a back path. Then many of the Greeks retreated, but Leonidas and his Spartans died trying to hold the pass. A contest was held to choose a fitting inscription for a monument to their memory. It was won by Simonides of Ceos who had beaten Aeschylus for a similar epitaph for those killed at Marathon. He submitted a two-line epigram, a poetic form that sums up a situation or makes some terse or apt comment, or is antithetical. This poetic form, of which Simonides is recognized as the greatest Greek writer, went into Latin literature with Catullus, Martial, and others, where it was often accompanied by a barb of satire, as later in the epigrams of Voltaire. With Alexander Pope and his heroic couplets, it appeared in English literature. The epigram of Simonides was engraved on the monument, which has since disappeared, but the words have survived. Strabo (c.63 B.C.–c. A.D. 21), who saw it on the column, quoted it. So did Herodotus (VII, 228), Cicero, Plutarch, and others. About 90 other epigrams remain of those written by Simonides, greatest Greek lyric poet before the Persian invasion. Many are contained in a tenth century Byzantine Greek anthology found in 1606 in the library of the Counts Palatine. Others have been discovered in an anthology compiled by Maximus Planidus, and printed in Florence in 1484. Literally the two lines declare:

Oh passerby, tell the Lacedaemonians
That we lie here, obeying their orders.

God forbid

Source: ROMANS 3:31
Author: Paul
First transcribed: c.50-60
Type of work: Religious epistle

Context: Paul's letter to the church in Rome was a letter to strangers; he had never visited it and had had no part in its founding. For this reason the epistle is more a treatise on the nature and principles of Christianity than it is a letter. In it his principal purpose is to declare to all men the

344

greatness of God's mercy through Christ, and to persuade them that salvation depends on faith in the grace of God, as it is expressed through Christ. His primary consideration in the first eight chapters of the epistle is the problem which lies in convincing members of the Jewish faith. In his own missionary work he has found them extremely resistant to his teachings, and now he lists every objection he can think of which they might have, answering each in turn. This portion of the epistle was probably intended to be a handbook containing material for use in obtaining conversions, and Paul doubtless hoped that converted Romans would gain a deeper insight into Jewish ideology from it. He begins the epistle by stating his qualifications and his gospel, reminding his readers that God offers salvation to all who believe in this gospel regardless of their origin. God, he adds, is angered by sin; here Paul enumerates a number of examples. His next major point is that all men are sinners and that mere observance of outward requirements will not help them unless their purity is internal and genuine. In Chapter 3 he goes on to say that observance of the law is good, but that faith in God is more important: by observance of laws alone man cannot hope for salvation. Faith in the gospel of redemption through Christ will save men without the law, and the law will be given meaning by it. Laws differ with men, but Christ's doctrine applies to all. In the fourth, sixth, and thirty-first verses, Paul emphasizes his point with the expression, "God forbid." The last is perhaps most effective.

But now the righteousness of God without the law is manifested, being witnessed by the law and the prophets;

Even the righteousness of God which is by faith of Jesus Christ unto all and upon all them that believe: for there is no difference:

For all have sinned, and come short of the glory of God;

Being justified freely by his grace through the redemption that is in Christ Jesus:

Whom God hath set forth to be a propitiation through faith in his blood, to declare his righteousness for the remission of sins that are past, through the forbearance of God;

To declare, I say, at this time his righteousness: that he might be just, and the justifier of him which believeth in Jesus.

Where is boasting then? It is excluded. By what law? of works? Nay: but by the law of faith.

Therefore we conclude that a man is justified by faith without the deeds of the law.

Is he the God of the Jews only? is he not also of the Gentiles? Yes, of the Gentiles also:

Seeing it is one God, which shall justify the circumcision by faith, and uncircumcision through faith.

Do we then make void the law through faith? **God forbid:** yea, we establish the law.

345

God is always for the big battalions

Source: LETTER TO FRANÇOIS LOUIS HENRI LERICHE (February 6, 1770)
Author: Voltaire (François Marie Arouet, 1694–1778)
First published: 1785–1789, in *Oeuvres Completes de Voltaire*
Type of work: Personal letter

Context: Voltaire, the outspoken champion of freedom, was a master of the effective phrase. In some cases the thought did not originate with him, but was transformed by his own inspiration into an epigram of such forceful insight that, once read, it cannot be forgotten. At other times he might use a popular expression, but in such a way that it was given a new freshness and permanence. Voltaire's correspondence was enormous; but this ability seldom failed him, and even in a short letter dashed off in a hurry it frequently stands out. The lines are direct and pungent: they bite into the mind. The note which follows is a good example. It was written to M. Leriche, *Receveur des Domaines* at Besançon, when Voltaire was seventy-six years of age and living in exile near Geneva. His violent criticisms of Christianity and priestcraft had made it unsafe for him to live in France, but his creative activities continued unabated, and his influence upon the thought of his time did not lessen. Voltaire had long since learned how to achieve a maximum of communication through economy of means. In this letter he replies to a well-wisher who has evidently switched political parties or schools of thought in an effort to get away from attitudes which disgust him and to find something more acceptable. Voltaire warns him that he is not likely to find it. In a letter written October 18, 1677, Roger de Rabutin, Comte de Bussy (1618–1693) had remarked, "God is generally for the big squadrons against the little ones (*Dieu est d'ordinaire pour les gros escadrons contre les petits*)." Bussy-Rabutin, as he is commonly known, was a member of the French lesser nobility; a notorious rake, whose licentious sketches of the ladies of the court (*Histoire Amoureuse des Gaules*) landed him in the Bastille, he was gifted with considerable literary power. Voltaire, however, expresses the same thought far more effectively (*dieu est toujours pour les gros bataillons*):

6th February 1770

You, sir, have left the Welsh for the Welsh. You will find these stubborn barbarians everywhere. The number of the sages will always be small. It is true that it is growing; however, its increase is nothing in comparison with that of blockheads, and unfortunately it is said that **God is always for the big battalions.** Men of integrity must close ranks and stay under cover: it is impossible for their little band to attack this party of fanatics in the open.

I have been very ill: I have been near death all winter: it is because of this, sir, that I am so late in answering. I am nonetheless touched by your remembrance. Continue your friendship toward me: that will console me for my ills and for the stupidities of the human race.

Receive the assurances, . . .

God is the perfect poet

Source: PARACELSUS (Part II)
Author: Robert Browning (1812-1889)
First published: 1835
Type of work: Poetic drama

Context: In this long poetic drama, Browning's second publication, the poet turns to the German Renaissance in order to dramatize the aspirations and failures of the famous Paracelsus, alchemist, fraud, and last great practitioner of the occult sciences. In the beginning of this remarkable work, Paracelsus decides that he is tired of teaching, and he tells his friend Festus that he aspires to know all things. Believing that knowledge is the result of experience, and rejecting the soul, he hopes to know infinitely in order to overthrow God, but, as Festus warns, his search is doomed from the beginning because he ignores love that springs from the soul. At his lowest moment of failure, however, he meets the wild-eyed Aprile, a poet who has attempted to love infinitely. While the poet has not the knowledge to discriminate between different kinds of beauty, the alchemist can see no beauty at all because he has become a monster that does not know love. Paracelsus realizes that they are "halves of one dissevered world," but before he can learn Aprile's secret, the poet dies, leaving in the cold alchemist the desire to love. The quotation comes from Aprile's dying vision of the goal he had sought and his discovery that by not learning what the alchemist offers he has failed.

APRILE
Ha! go you ever girt about
With phantoms, powers? I have created such,
But these seem real as I.

PARACELSUS
Whom can you see
Through the accursed darkness?

APRILE
Stay; I know,
I know them: who should know them well as I?
White brows, lit up with glory; poets all!

PARACELSUS
Let him but live, and I have my reward!

347

Yes; I see now. **God is the perfect poet,**
Who in his person acts his own creations.
Had you but told me this at first! . . .

God is thy law, thou mine

Source: PARADISE LOST (Book IV, l. 637)
Author: John Milton (1608-1674)
First published: 1667
Type of work: Epic poem

Context: The angels keep watch over the garden, but Satan enters it by overleaping the wall. Uriel tells Adam that he will seek out the alien spirit the next morning; he then slides down a sunbeam to the sun, which has descended below the earth. Evening comes on, and all the birds and beasts go to their beds except the nightingale, which sings throughout the night. Adam tells Eve that all things seek their rest; other creatures, except man, are idle through the day, as they have no specific duties to perform; therefore they need rest less than does man, who has his daily work, either physical or mental; it is this duty that dignifies man above the beasts. Adam says that he and Eve will have to be up at dawn to perform their pleasant work in the garden. He adds that there is more work than they can do to cultivate the garden, as there is a wanton growth that they have to hold in check; also they have to clean up the dropped blossoms and gums so that they can tread at ease. Meanwhile, night bids them take their rest. Eve, calling Adam her "author," since she was created from his rib, says that as God commands Adam, so man commands woman.

Those blossoms also, and those dropping gums,
That lie bestrown unsightly and unsmooth,
Ask riddance, if we mean to tread with ease;
Meanwhile, as Nature wills, night bids us rest.
To whom thus Eve with perfect beauty adorned.
My author and disposer, what thou biddest
Unargued I obey; so God ordains,
God is thy law, thou mine; to know no more
Is woman's happiest knowledge and her praise.
With thee conversing I forget all time,
All seasons and their change, all please alike.
Sweet is the breath of morn, her rising sweet,
With charm of earliest birds; pleasant the sun
When first on this delightful land he spreads
His orient beams, on herb, tree, fruit, and flower,
Glist'ring with dew. . . .

God keeps a niche in heaven to hold our idols

Source: FUTURITY (Lines 8-9)
Author: Elizabeth Barrett Browning (1806-1861)
First published: 1844
Type of work: Sonnet

Context: This sonnet is typical of Elizabeth Barrett Browning in that it reflects her theme of social consciousness. In beginning the poem "O beloved voices," she is addressing the people who have already died or broken off "in the middle of that song we sang together softly." These people with whom she "sang" are those who tried, along with Mrs. Browning, "to enrich the poor world with the sense of love." Though these companions have now died, the poetess reaffirms her faith in an afterlife and in the fact that she will meet her "idols" in heaven. She goes on to state that these "idols" will be especially recognized by God and "glorified."

> And O belovèd voices, upon which
> Ours passionately call, because ere-long
> Ye brake off in the middle of that song
> We sang together softly, to enrich
> The poor world with the sense of love, and witch
> The heart out of things evil,—I am strong,
> Knowing ye are not lost for aye among
> The hills with last year's thrush. **God keeps a niche**
> **In heaven to hold our idols;** and albeit
> He brake them to our faces, and denied
> That our close kisses should impair their white,
> I know we shall behold them raised, complete,
> The dust swept from their beauty,—glorified
> New Memnons singing in the great God-light.

God the first garden made, and the first city, Cain

Source: THE GARDEN (Stanza 3)
Author: Abraham Cowley (1618-1667)
First published: 1668
Type of work: Ode

Context: Disappointed with his lack of success in life, Abraham Cowley retired from what he termed "the tumult and business of the world" to become one of the best essayists of his time. His essays often contain poetry, sometimes his own, which becomes an integral part of the essay. His poem entitled "The Garden" is really part of such an essay, the first part of which is an epistle to John Evelyn, Cowley's friend and fellow member of the Royal Society, who had dedicated his *Kalendarium Hor-*

349

tense to Cowley. In the prose portion of Cowley's essay, as well as in the poetical portion, the writer displays the epicureanism so often associated with the neoclassical period. He begins by saying, "I never had any other desire so strong and so like to covetousness as that one which I have always had, that I might be master at last of a small house and a large garden. . . ." As a typical neoclassical epicurean, Cowley believed a quiet country life taken up with books, a garden, and domestic tasks was far the best for man. He points out that God gave man a garden even before He gave man a wife. He goes on to say that it was out of His wisdom that God placed man in the Garden of Eden:

> For God, the Universal Architect,
>   'T had been as easy to erect
> A Louvre or Escurial, or a tow'r
> That might with Heav'n communication hold,
> As Babel vainly thought to do of old:
>   He wanted not the skill or pow'r;
>   In the world's fabric those were shown,
> And the materials were all His own.
> But well He knew what place would best agree
> With innocence, and with felicity:
> And we elsewhere still seek for them in vain.
> If any part of either yet remain,
> If any part of either we expect,
> This may our judgment in the search direct;
> **God the first Garden made, and the first city, Cain.**

A godly righteous and sober life

Source: THE BOOK OF COMMON PRAYER (Page 6)
Author: Traditional; translated and arranged by Archbishop Cranmer (1489–1560)
First published: 1549
Type of work: Prayer of confession

Context: The Order for Daily Morning Prayer, the first service in the Book of Common Prayer, is a direct descendent of *Matins,* one of the services in the medieval system of daily devotions known as the Canonical Hours or Daily Offices. These Offices were in turn developed out of customs of regular instruction, prayer, and praise in practice in the early Church and beyond these from the devotional practices of pious Jews at the time of the birth of Christ. Morning Prayer begins in a penitential mood. After a series of opening sentences of Biblical origin which set the theme of the service to come, the faithful are reminded, in the *Exhortation,* that no converse with God can be fitting or profitable until the worshiper has laid bare his disobediences to God's will and has sought reconciliation with His love. The minister beseeches the congregation to go with

350

him to the very "throne of the heavenly grace" and there humbly to confess their sins in the words of the *General Confession*—called "general" because it is said by the minister and all the people together, and refers not only to individual shortcomings but to the guilt of the whole community of believers. Based in general on St. Paul's analysis of sin in Romans 7:8–25, the prayer asserts that the essence of sin is self-assertion and asks that the penitent sinner be restored to the spiritual health which he has forfeited by his offenses against God's holy laws.

Almighty and most merciful Father; we have erred, and strayed from thy ways like lost sheep. We have followed too much the devices and desires of our own hearts. We have offended against thy holy laws. We have left undone those things which we ought to have done; And we have done those things which we ought not to have done; And there is no health in us. But thou, O Lord, have mercy upon us, miserable offenders. Spare thou those, O God, who confess their faults. Restore thou those who are penitent; According to thy promises declared unto mankind in Christ Jesus our Lord. And grant, O most merciful Father, for his sake; That we may hereafter live **a godly, righteous, and sober life,** To the glory of thy holy Name. Amen.

The Gods are just, and of our pleasant vices make instruments to plague us

Source: KING LEAR (Act V, sc. iii, ll. 170-171)
Author: William Shakespeare (1564-1616)
First published: 1608
Type of work: Dramatic tragedy

Context: The subplot of *King Lear,* that of Gloucester and his two sons, Edgar and Edmund, parallels the story of Lear and his three daughters. Edmund, the bastard son, convinces his father by a forged letter that Edgar, the legitimate son, is, in truth, planning to murder his father. When Edmund's treachery has, among other things, cost Gloucester his eyes, Edgar confronts his brother and they fight. Dying, Edmund confesses his evil designs, and Edgar comments on Gloucester's pleasant begetting of the bastard son.

EDMUND
What you have charged me with, that have I done,
And more, much more; the time will bring it out.
'Tis past, and so am I. But what art thou
That hast this fortune on me? If thou'rt noble,
I do forgive thee.

351

EDGAR
Let's exchange charity.
I am no less in blood than thou art, Edmund;
If more, the more th' hast wronged me.
My name is Edgar, and thy father's son.
The gods are just, and of our pleasant vices
Make instruments to plague us.
The dark and vicious place where thee he got
Cost him his eyes.

God's finger touched him and he slept

Source: IN MEMORIAM (Part LXXXV, stanza 5)
Author: Alfred, Lord Tennyson (1809-1892)
First published: 1850
Type of work: Elegy

Context: This elegy was written as a monument to Arthur Henry Hallam, a young man of extraordinary promise and an intimate friend of Tennyson, who died suddenly in Vienna at the age of twenty-two. The poem records Tennyson's slow spiritual progress from his initial depth of personal sorrow to the gradual healing of grief through a sense of spiritual contact with Hallam in a wider love of God and humanity. Section LXXXV is one of the important spiritual turning points of the elegy: from despair to renewed hope. The section looks in both directions, giving a résumé of the earlier grief and showing the stage at which Tennyson has arrived and how he seeks new friendships even though he cannot replace the old. A look at what might have been if Hallam had lived to marry the poet's sister, Emily, only stirs the old bitterness and threatens the poet's "low beginning of content." His friend, Edmund Lushington, asks what sort of life he now leads—if his great sorrow has dimmed or sustained his faith in God; if the loss of Hallam has drained his capacity for love. As he begins to answer these questions, Tennyson admits how deeply Hallam's death has affected him:

My blood an even tenor kept,
    Till on mine ear this message falls
    That in Vienna's fatal walls
God's finger touched him, and he slept.

The great Intelligences fair
    That range above our mortal state,
    In circle round the blessed gate,
Received and gave him welcome there;
       • • •

But I remain'd, whose hopes were dim
    Whose life, whose thoughts were little worth,

352

To wander on a darken'd earth,
Where all things round me breathed of him.

God's gifts put man's best dreams to shame

Source: SONNETS FROM THE PORTUGUESE (Sonnet 26)
Author: Elizabeth Barrett Browning (1806-1861)
First published: 1850
Type of work: Sonnet

Context: In the octave of this autobiographical love sonnet, Mrs. Browning portrays her companions during her years of invalidism as being "visions" rather than actual people. She says that these images satisfied her for a while. But the "visions" began to fade as years passed, and her senses began to dull from lack of contact with people. Then her lover, Robert Browning, whom she married in 1846, came into her life "to be . . . what they seemed." He fulfilled the greatest dreams of her "soul" and gave even more soul satisfaction than her visions. Thus, she reflects, "God's gifts put man's best dreams to shame."

I lived with visions for my company
Instead of men and women, years ago,
And found them gentle mates, nor thought to know
A sweeter music than they played to me.
But soon their trailing purple was not free
Of this world's dust, their lutes did silent grow,
And I myself grew faint and blind below
Their vanishing eyes. Then THOU didst come—to be,
Belovèd, what they seemed, Their shining fronts,
Their songs, their splendors (better, yet the same,
As river-water hallowed into fonts),
Met in thee, and from out thee overcame
My soul with satisfaction of all wants:
Because **God's gifts put man's best dreams to shame.**

God's soldier be he

Source: MACBETH (Act V, sc. ix, l. 13)
Author: William Shakespeare (1564-1616)
First published: 1623
Type of work: Dramatic tragedy

Context: In the final act of the drama, Macbeth, who has usurped the crown of Scotland and established himself as a bloody tyrant, is besieged in his castle at Dunsinane by an English army under the command of Siward, Earl of Northumberland. Macbeth, however, feels secure by

353

reason of the promises given him by the three witches that he cannot be defeated "until/Great Birnam wood to high Dunsinane hill/Shall come against him," and that "none of woman born" can harm him. The first of these assurances is destroyed when Malcolm, rightful heir to the Scottish throne, orders each soldier in the English army to hew a branch from the trees in Birnam wood and carry it before him so that the size of the attacking forces may be concealed. As a result of this stratagem, the watchers on the castle walls are given the impression that the forest is indeed moving towards "high Dunsinane hill." In a last desperate attempt, although he has grown weary of life, Macbeth orders a sortie, and the battle is joined. The first of his enemies to confront him is young Siward, son of the English commander, who is killed in a hand-to-hand fight with the usurper. When the old earl receives this news, he is concerned only with knowing whether his son fought and died bravely, as a soldier should. His conversation with Ross is as follows:

ROSS

Your son my lord, has paid a soldier's debt.
He only lived but till he was a man,
The which no sooner had his prowess confirmed
In the unshrinking station where he fought,
But like a man he died.

. . .

SIWARD
Had he his hurts before?

ROSS

Ay, on the front.

SIWARD
Why then, **God's soldier be he.**
Had I as many sons as I have hairs,
I would not wish them to a fairer death.
And so his knell is knolled.

The gods themselves cannot recall their gifts

Source: TITHONUS (Line 49)
Author: Alfred, Lord Tennyson (1809-1892)
First published: 1860
Type of work: Dramatic monologue

Context: Tithonus was the husband of Aurora, goddess of the dawn, and the son of Laomedan, King of Troy. He asked his wife to grant him immortality, but he neglected to ask also for eternal youth. She granted his wish, and the results were disastrous. While Aurora remained immortally young and lovely, Tithonus became withered and ugly. In this poem he laments his immortality, wishing that he had never tried to transcend the bounds of what was intended for mortal men. He alone is set apart, unable to participate in the cycle of life:

> The woods decay, the woods decay and fall,
> The vapors weep their burthen to the ground,
> Man comes and tills the fields and lies beneath,
> . . .
> Me only cruel immortality
> Consumes. . . .

However, his desire for the beautiful Aurora has not waned, and he is all the more desolate when he reflects upon his present impotence. He asks Aurora:

> Let me go; take back thy gift.
> Why should a man desire in any way
> To vary from the kindly race of men,
> Or pass beyond the goal of ordinance
> Where all should pause, as is most meet for all?
> . . .
> Why wilt thou ever scare me with thy tears,
> And make me tremble lest a saying learnt,
> In days far-off, on that dark earth, be true?
> **"The Gods themselves cannot recall their gifts."**

Goes to grass

Source: THE KNIGHT OF THE BURNING PESTLE (Act IV, sc. v, l. 107)
Author: Francis Beaumont (1585?-1616)
First published: 1613
Type of work: Dramatic comedy

Context: Before the play gets well started, a citizen grocer and his naïve wife speak up to the actors to say that they want a different play from the one scheduled. What is more, they want their apprentice, Ralph, to take a part in it. Throughout the course of the play they interject their comments and interrupt the action. After Ralph is admitted to the cast, two plots develop: one has to do with Jasper, apprentice to the merchant Venturewell, and his love for Venturewell's daughter. Intertwined in this plot are the affairs of the Merrythought family. Old Merrythought, Jasper's father, who lives a happy life of eating, drinking, and singing, with no thought about how to provide these pleasures, is left alone by the departure of Mistress Merrythought, who is disgusted with her husband's improvidence. Ralph, taking to himself a squire and a dwarf, wanders the world as a knight errant, bent on righting wrongs and rescuing dis-

355

tressed damsels. Finally he abandons his role as a knight and appears as a May-lord, giving a long speech about his own antecedents and the glories of the spring. Among other features of that season, little fishes spawn, snails creep out of their shells, streams become warm, and steeds go out to pasture.

RALPH

The lords and ladies now abroad, for their disport and play
Do kiss sometimes upon the grass, and sometimes in the hay;
Now butter with a leaf of sage is good to purge the blood;
Fly Venus and phlebotomy, for they are neither good;
Now little fish on tender stone begin to cast their bellies,
And sluggish snails, that erst were mewed, do creep out of their
  shellies;
The rumbling rivers now do warm, for little boys to paddle;
The sturdy steed now **goes to grass,** and up they hang his saddle;
The heavy hart, the bellowing buck, the rascal, and the pricket,
Are now among the yeoman's peas, and leave the fearful thicket;
And be like them, O, you, I say, of this same noble town,
And lift aloft your velvet heads, and slipping off your gown,
With bells on legs, and napkins clean unto your shoulders tied,
With scarfs and garters as you please, and "Hey for our town!"
  cried,
March out. . . .

The golden bowl

Source: ECCLESIASTES 12:6
Author: Unknown
First transcribed: c.250-200 B.C.
Type of work: Religious confession

Context: This quotation is the title of a novel by Henry James wherein the breaking of a golden bowl symbolizes the end of a strained family relationship. The writer of Ecclesiastes, the preacher, speaks of the futility of this life, where everything—wisdom, pleasure, labor, hope, and desire—ends with death and the grave. Even before death, in this life, the wicked prosper and the righteous suffer; the ways of God are beyond human understanding. All one can do, "the conclusion of the whole matter," is to "Fear God, and keep his command- ments: for this is the whole duty of man." Particularly in youth, says the preacher, must man remember his creator and rejoice in life as youth knows it. He warns that old age and death inevitably come to every generation, and he remarks upon the end of life, when every man must fear the judgment of God upon his actions, when life and its infirmities become a burden, and when the mourners will soon be in the street. The days of this life are short, but the days in the grave, our "long home," are long and many. Of death itself the writer of Ecclesiastes writes symbolically, noting it comes in many ways: as the loosening of a cord, the breaking of a bowl, the breaking of a pitcher, or the breaking of a wheel at a cistern:

> Or ever the silver cord be loosed, or **the golden bowl** be broken, or the pitcher be broken at the fountain, or the wheel broken at the cistern.
> Then shall the dust return to the earth as it was: and the spirit shall return unto God who gave it.
> Vanity of vanities, saith the preacher; all is vanity.

Good Americans, when they die, go to Paris

Source: THE AUTOCRAT OF THE BREAKFAST-TABLE (Chapter VI)
Author: Oliver Wendell Holmes (1809-1894)
First published: 1858
Type of work: Essay

Context: The Autocrat of the Breakfast-Table purports to be a series of monologues delivered by a persona who does not identify himself otherwise than by admitting that he dominates the conversation at the breakfast table of his Boston boarding house. His audience is composed of such people as the landlady, the landlady's daughter, the divinity student, the young girl attending finishing school, the schoolmistress, the old man, and the brash young man. The subject of discussion at the beginning of Chapter VI of *The Autocrat* is the bright sayings of the Seven Wise Men of Boston. The first is by Benjamin Franklin: "He that has once done you a kindness will be more ready to do you another than he whom you yourself have obliged." Another saying, this by the Historian, probably John Lothrop Motley, is, "Give us the luxuries of life, and we will dispense with its necessaries." This one leads up to the following, which may be by Thomas Appleton:

> To these must certainly be added that other saying of one of the wittiest of men:—
> **"Good Americans, when they die, go to Paris."**
> —The divinity-student looked grave at this, but said nothing.
> The schoolmistress spoke out, and said she didn't think the wit meant any irreverence. It was only another way of saying, Paris is a heavenly place after New York or Boston.

A good book is the purest essence of a human soul

Source: SPEECH IN SUPPORT OF THE LONDON LIBRARY
Author: Thomas Carlyle (1795-1881)
First delivered: 1840
Type of work: Speech

357

Context: The greatest library in London, and one of the greatest in the world, is of course the British Museum. Its holdings, however, do not constitute a lending collection for the general reader but a research collection for the scholar. In 1840 Thomas Carlyle had finished his great work on the French Revolution and was beginning his study of Oliver Cromwell. He felt the need, for himself and for the citizens of London, for the establishment of a general lending library. He marshaled all of his influence among persons of political or financial importance and pushed the project to fruition. His contributions included plans, enthusiasm, and one powerful speech. Today the London library stands as one of his finest monuments. In his speech he emphasized the need of the common people of London for a library:

> We will leave the British Museum standing on its own basis, and be very thankful that such a Library exists in this country. But supposing it to be managed with the most perfect skill and success, even according to the ideal of such an Institution, still I will assert that this other Library of ours is requisite also. In the first place by the very nature of the thing, a great quantity of people are excluded altogether from the British Museum as a reading room. Every man engaged in business is occupied during the hours it is kept open; and innumerable classes of persons find it extremely inconvenient to attend the British Museum Library at all. But granting that they all could go there, I would ask any literary man, any reader of books, any man intimately acquainted with the reading of books, whether he can read them to any purpose in the British Museum? A book is a kind of thing that requires a man to be self-collected. He must be alone with it. **A good book is the purest essence of a human soul.** How could a man take it into a crowd, with bustle of all sorts going on around him? The good of a book is not the facts that can be got out of it, but the kind of resonance that it awakens in our own minds.

Good digestion wait on appetite

Source: MACBETH (Act III, sc. iv, l. 38)
Author: William Shakespeare (1564-1616)
First published: 1623
Type of work: Dramatic tragedy

Context: Three witches intercept Macbeth and Banquo along a heath and disclose to the warriors that Macbeth will rise in power until finally he becomes king, but that the heirs of Banquo will eventually receive the throne. Driven by his own ambition and that of his wife, Macbeth murders King Duncan of Scotland and usurps the throne. Since Banquo and his son Fleance stand in the way of the new king, Macbeth plans a banquet to which they will be invited, secretly hiring assassins to murder them before the banquet takes place. After the guests have assembled, one of the murderers draws Macbeth aside and informs him that Banquo has been killed but that Fleance has escaped. The whispered conversation between Macbeth and the murderer lasts so long a time that Lady Macbeth, in order to allay any suspicion on the part of the guests, has to remind her husband that he has forgotten his duties as a host.

LADY MACBETH
My royal lord,
You do not give the cheer. The feast is sold
That is not often vouched, while 'tis a-making,
'Tis given with welcome. To feed were best at home;
From thence, the sauce to meat is ceremony,
Meeting were bare without it.
[*Enter* GHOST OF BANQUO *and sits in* MACBETH'S *seat.*]

MACBETH
Sweet remembrancer!
Now **good digestion wait on appetite,**
And health on both.

LENNOX
May't please your Highness sit.

MACBETH
Here had we now our country's honour roofed,
Were the graced person of our Banquo present; . . .

A good face is a letter of recommendation

Source: THE SPECTATOR (No. 221)
Author: Joseph Addison (1672-1719)
First published: November 13, 1711
Type of work: Essay

Context: In the five hundred and fifty-five regular issues of the *Spectator,* Joseph Addison and Richard Steele brought popular essay journalism to a height of perfection never achieved before and seldom since. For a large middle-class reading public they created an interest in public affairs, literary and dramatic criticism, public morality, and manners. In this essay Addison, behind the mask of Mr. Spectator, amuses himself in an editorial vein by discussing with great mock seriousness the importance of the Latin motto which appeared at the beginning of each issue of the periodical. This selection from a great classical author, he says, is the "good face" which recommends the essay for the day:

359

It was a saying of an ancient philosopher, which I find some of our writers have ascribed to Queen Elizabeth, who perhaps might have taken occasion to repeat it, that **a good face is a letter of recommendation.** It naturally makes the beholders inquisitive into the person who is the owner of it, and generally prepossesses them in his favour. A handsome motto has the same effect. Besides that, it always gives a supernumerary beauty to a paper, and is sometimes in a manner necessary when the writer is engaged in what may appear a paradox to vulgar minds, as it shows that he is supported by good authorities, and is not singular in his opinion.

A good honest and painful sermon

Source: DIARY (17 March, 1661)
Author: Samuel Pepys (1633-1793)
First published: 1825
Type of work: Diary

Context: From January, 1660, until eye trouble forced him to stop, after May, 1669, an impoverished clerk in London, Samuel Pepys, kept a daily record of his activities, important as well as trivial. Set down in shorthand, the Diary was not completely deciphered and published until 1893. It begins at the time of the Restoration of Charles II to the throne of the Stuarts, when Pepys became a minor clerk in the Admiralty. Before he died, he had twice served as Secretary of the Admiralty and was recognized as the foremost naval authority in England. His Diary covers only nine of the seventy years of his life, including, however, the end of his period of poverty and the beginning of his ability to engage in his favorite diversions, wine and the theater. He was also associating with important people. William Batten, an obscure but excellent seaman, had been knighted and made a rear admiral by Prince Charles for defecting from Parliament and taking his ship, the *Constant Warwick,* to Holland. After the Restoration, Batten was made Commissioner of the Navy and a member of Parliament for Rochester. Here are entries for three days of March, 1661. *The Spanish Curate* was a play by Beaumont and Fletcher. A "chine of beef" is a cut containing part of the backbone. Apparently a sermon, like medicine, must be distasteful to accomplish results.

16th. To Whitefriars, and there saw "The Spanish Curate," in which I had no great content.

17th. (Lord's Day). At church in the morning a stranger preached **a good honest and painful sermon.** My wife and I dined upon a chine of beef at Sir W. Batten's, so to church again. Then to supper at Sir W. Batten's again, where my wife by chance fell down and hurt her knees exceedingly.

18th. This morning early Sir William Batten went to Rochester, where he expects to be chosen Parliament-man. This day an ambassador from Florence was brought into the town in state. . . .

Good order is the foundation of all good things

Source: REFLECTIONS ON THE REVOLUTION IN FRANCE
Author: Edmund Burke (1729-1797)
First published: 1790
Type of work: Political treatise

Context: Burke, one of the greatest political philosophers England has ever produced, steadfastly defended traditional and established rights and privileges throughout his long tenure in Parliament. In the French Revolution, which gained much sympathy in England, he saw a gross and danger-ous perversion of the normal, grad-ual, and orderly evolution of political concepts. Toward the end of this trea-tise he speaks out strongly against the violence and chaos of revolutionary measures and expresses his sympathy for order and regulation:

. . . To keep a balance between the power of acquisition on the part of the subject, and the demands he is to answer on the part of the State, is a fundamental part of the skill of a true poli-tician. The means of acquisition are prior in time and in arrange-ment. **Good order is the foundation of all good things.** To be enabled to acquire, the people, without being servile, must be tractable and obedient. The magistrate must have his reverence, the laws their authority. The body of the people must not find the principles of natural subordination by art rooted out of their minds. They must respect that property of which they cannot partake. . . .

The good received, the giver is forgot

Source: EPISTLE TO LORD HALIFAX (Line 40)
Author: William Congreve (1670-1729)
First published: 1710
Type of work: Epistle in verse

Context: When Congreve was driven from Ireland to England by the Revo-lution, he determined to become a writer. During an illness, he wrote his first play, *The Old Bachelor* (per-formed 1693). When he read it to the players, he pronounced English so badly that the play was almost re-jected. Its successful production won for him the patronage of Charles Montagu (1661–1715), first Earl of Halifax, a wit and patron of such lit-erary men as Addison and Steele. Halifax made Congreve one of the commissioners for leasing coaches, then got him a place in the Pipe-office, and finally nominated him in the Customs House service at six hun-dred pounds a year. Congreve dedi-cated to Halifax his next comedy, *The Double Dealer.* Eventually he gave up playwriting, angry at the re-ception given some of his plays, and he retired to private life, writing poetry and engaging in conversation with his many friends. However, Lord Halifax had given him his start, and he was not one to be ungrateful, so he prefaced his collection of verse with a poetic letter to his patron, flattering him by the statement that the earl might well have been so great a poet that England could have competed with Greece. Unfortunately for literature, he said, Lord Halifax was too busy encouraging other literary men, and founding the Bank of England (1694), and serving as First Lord of the Treasury, to be able to devote time to his own writing. In fact, he is chiefly remembered for a parody on Dryden's *Hind and the Panther* (1687) which he and Matthew Prior wrote the same year under the title *The Town and the Country Mouse.* The reference in Congreve's poem is to Homer whose place of birth was claimed by seven cities of Greece. Halifax was a product of all of England.

> O had your genius been to leisure born,
> And not more bound to aid us than adorn!
> Albion in verse with ancient Greece had vy'd,
> And gain'd alone a fame which, there, seven states divide.
> But such, ev'n such renoun, too dear had cost,
> Had we the patriot in the poet lost.
> A true poetic state we had deplor'd
> Had not your ministry our coin restor'd . . .
>
> · · ·
>
> How oft a patriot's best laid schemes we find
> By party cross'd, or faction undermin'd.
> If he succeed, he undergoes this lot,
> **The good receiv'd, the giver is forgot.—**
> But honors, which from verse their source derive,
> Shall both surmount detraction, and survive:
> And poets have unquestion'd right to claim,
> If not the greatest, the most lasting name.

Good sense, which only is the gift of heaven

Source: MORAL ESSAYS (Epistle IV, l. 43)
Author: Alexander Pope (1688-1744)
First published: 1731-1735
Type of work: Satiric poem

Context: Pope's fourth epistle of the *Moral Essays* was addressed to Richard Boyle, the Earl of Burlington; the poem's topic is "Of the Use of Riches." Pope admires the earl for what he is doing with his wealth: "You shew us, Rome was glorious, not profuse,/ And pompous buildings once were things of Use./ Yet shall, my Lord, your just, your noble rules/ Fill half the land with Imitating-Fools." It is those who have wealth, but not taste, that Pope wishes to correct; too often, he thinks, people of wealth and noble birth abuse the word "taste." In the use of riches, says the poet, the "first principle and foundation" is good sense, as it is in everything: to spend one's wealth is not enough in itself. Good sense, he says, is almost worth all the seven branches of knowledge, and fortunately this quality, he adds, is possessed by the Earl of Burlington. If one does not have the quality, however, not even such a great architect as Inigo Jones, or such a landscape and garden designer as Le Nôtre, of France, can give it:

Oft have you hinted to your brother Peer
A certain truth, which many buy too dear:
Something there is more needful than Expence,
And something previous even to Taste—'tis Sense:
Good Sense, which only is the gift of Heaven,
And though no Science, fairly worth the seven:
A Light, which in yourself you must perceive;
Jones and Le Nôtre have it not to give.

Good wine needs no bush

Source: AS YOU LIKE IT (Epilogue)
Author: William Shakespeare (1564-1616)
First published: 1623
Type of work: Dramatic comedy

Context: The play ends with two restorations and four marriages. The usurper Duke Frederick is converted to a life of religion and returns the crown to Duke Senior, who has spent many happy years of exile in the Forest of Arden; Oliver, who had tyrannized over his brother, Orlando, decides to retire as a shepherd to the Forest of Arden and turns over house and estate to Orlando. Orlando marries Rosalind, daughter of Duke Senior; Oliver marries Celia, daughter of Duke Frederick; the court jester Touchstone marries the rustic Audrey; the shepherd Silvius marries the shepherdess Phebe. Finally, after a closing dance, Rosalind makes a curtain speech, asking for the audience's applause, and alluding to the fact that female roles in Shakespeare's day were played by boys in women's dress: "If I were a woman. . . ." The comment reminds the audience that the boy actor has, in the play proper, performed the part of a woman disguised as a man. Rosalind suggests that if the play were a good one, it would scarcely need an apologetic epilogue, just as "good wine needs no bush"—that is, a good vintner would need no bush of evergreen hung over his door to draw trade, such bushes being the common sign on the wine trade. A good product needs no advertisement.

. . .

If it be true that **good wine needs no bush,** 'tis true that a good play needs no epilogue. Yet to good wine they use good bushes; and good plays prove the better by the help of good epilogues. What a case am I in then, that am neither a good epilogue, nor cannot insinuate with you in the behalf of a good play. I am not furnished like a beggar, therefore to beg will not become me. My way is to conjure you, and I'll begin with the women. I charge you, o women, for the love you bear to men, to like as much of the play as please you. And I charge you, o men, for the love you bear to women—as I perceive by your simpering, none of you hates them—that between you and the women the play may please. If I were a woman, I would kiss as many of you as had beards that pleased me, complexions that liked me, and breaths that I defied not. And I am sure, as many as have good beards, or good faces, or sweet breaths, will for my kind offer, when I make curtsy, bid me farewell.   [*Exeunt.*]

A grain of manhood

Source: SAMSON AGONISTES (Line 408)
Author: John Milton (1608-1674)
First published: 1671
Type of work: Dramatic tragedy

Context: The hope of deliverance of Israel from her enemies according to prophecy pronounced before his birth, Samson is betrayed by his beloved Dalila, and captured and blinded by the Philistines. On the feast day of Dagon, when the Philistines honor their god for allowing Samson to fall into their hands, the blind strong man, resting from his toil as he sits on the steps of the Gaza prison, is visited first by Danites, men of his tribe who form a chorus for the drama, and then by Manoa, his father. Refusing to accept the excuses offered him by his friends and father, Samson says he deserves his punishment because of his folly in loving Dalila and in revealing to her the secret of his strength. Samson recounts his shame:

> At times when men seek most repose and rest,
> I yielded, and unlock'd her all my heart,
> Who with **a grain of manhood,** well resolv'd
> Might easily have shook off all her snares:
> But foul effeminacy held me yok't
> Her Bond-slave; O indignity, O blot
> To Honour and Religion! servil mind
> Rewarded well with servil punishment!
> The base degree to which I now am fall'n,
> These rags, this grinding, is not yet so base
> As was my former servitude, ignoble,

364

Unmanly, ignominious, infamous,
True slavery, and that blindness worse then this,
That saw not how degenerately I serv'd.

The grand instructor, Time

Source: LETTER TO SIR H. LANGRISHE (May 26, 1795)
Author: Edmund Burke (1729-1797)
First published: 1844
Type of work: Open letter

Context: Burke was born in Ireland, and although his entire adult life was spent in England he took an active interest in Irish affairs throughout his life. As a member of Parliament he frequently defended the Irish, and he always felt the Anglican domination of the millions of Irish Catholics constituted a sort of tyranny. In 1792 he had published an open letter to Sir Hercules Langrishe which had helped persuade Parliament to extend some degree of legislative franchise to the Catholics. Three years later Langrishe again spoke in defense of the Irish Catholics, and again Burke responded with a sympathetic open letter:

Your speech on the Catholic question I read with much satisfaction. It is solid; . . . and it ought, on the spot, to have produced that effect which its reason, and that contained in the other excellent speeches on the same side of the question, cannot possibly fail (though with less pleasant consequences) to produce hereafter. What a sad thing it is, that **the grand instructor, Time,** has not yet been able to teach the grand lesson of his own value, and that, in every question of moral and political prudence, it is the choice of the moment which renders the measure serviceable or useless, noxious or salutary!

A grand memory for forgetting

Source: KIDNAPPED (Chapter 18)
Author: Robert Louis Stevenson (1850-1894)
First published: 1886
Type of work: Novel

Context: David Balfour, a Scots lad who is shipped off to enforced labor in the American Colonies by a rascally uncle, is rescued by a Jacobite adventurer named Alan Breck, a Highlander. The two make their way ashore on the Scottish coast and fall into a series of adventures and narrow escapes. A man named Glenure is killed by an unknown murderer, and the blame falls on David Balfour and Alan Breck. The two, pursued by

365

the sheriff and a detachment of British soldiers, escape by speed and cunning. When they are safe, David Balfour finds himself thinking that Alan Breck had a hand in the murder, as an act of revenge. The older man assures the boy that he had no part in the act, but Breck knows who the murderer is. However, like the good Highlander he is, he has used himself and the boy to draw the authorities off on a wild-goose chase. David has difficulty understanding the Highland mind and its workings, but his friend is persuasive:

> ". . . And do you know who did it?" I added. "Do you know that man in the black coat?"
> "I have nae clear mind about his coat," said Alan, cunningly, "but it sticks in my head that it was blue."
> "Blue or black, did ye know him?" said I.
> "I could nae just conscientiously swear to him," says Alan. "He gaed very close by me, to be sure, but it's a strange thing that I should just have been tying my brogues."
> "Can you swear that you don't know him, Alan?" I cried, half angered, half in a mind to laugh at his evasions.
> "Not yet," says he; "but I've **a grand memory for forgetting, David.**"

The grand, old, fortifying classical curriculum

Source: FRIENDSHIP'S GARLAND (Part I, letter vi)
Author: Matthew Arnold (1822-1888)
First published: 1871
Type of work: Humorous letters

Context: Matthew Arnold, caught in the Victorian world of shifting values, believed firmly in the continuity of human experience and, above all, in the transcendent emotional values transmitted to his generation by the Christian ideals which had prevailed in the centuries past. Thus, as a patient mediator between the old and the new, he devoted himself to the articulation of the values of the past in language that would be contemporary and meaningful. Between 1866 and 1870 he contributed a series of humorous epistles to the *Pall-Mall Gazette* which, along with the essay *My Countrymen,* previously appearing in *Cornhill Magazine,* was published as *Friendship's Garland.* Expressive of the same social and ethical doctrines as the earlier *Culture and Anarchy,* this essay sets forth with light mockery the "Conversations, Letters, and Opinions of the late Arminius, Baron von Thunder-Ten-Tronckh" concerning his observations on the English scene. At one point Arminius questions the training and intelligence of two magistrates, "Viscount Lumpington" and "Reverend Esau Hittall," the latter recommended highly by his uncle, a prelate:

366

. . . "But I want to know what his nephew learnt [in his education]," interrupted Arminius, "and what Lord Lumpington learnt at Eton." "They followed," said I, **"the grand, old, fortifying classical curriculum."** "Did they know anything when they left?" asked Arminius. "I have seen some longs and shorts of Hittall's," said I, "about the Calydonian Boar, which were not bad. But you surely don't need me to tell you, Arminius, that it is rather in training and bracing the mind for future acquisition,—a course of mental gymnastics we call it,—than in teaching any set thing, that the classical curriculum is so valuable. . . . But for my part I have always thought that their both getting their degree at last with flying colours, after three weeks of a famous coach for fast men, four nights without going to bed, and an incredible consumption of wet towels, strong cigars, and brandy-and-water, was one of the most astonishing feats of mental gymnastics I ever heard of."

The grand Perhaps

Source: BISHOP BLOUGRAM'S APOLOGY (Line 190)
Author: Robert Browning (1812-1889)
First published: 1855
Type of work: Dramatic monologue

Context: Bishop Blougram entertains at dinner a young writer who has questioned the bishop's faith and belief and the manner in which he lives. The bishop, who is modeled on Cardinal Wiseman, who reviewed the poem and found it very bad, begins the explanation of his life by saying that this dinner will be the writer's chief claim to fame in time to come, even though he insists that he despises the bishop for his luxurious manner of living and his lack of belief in the Catholic dogmas. The bishop contends that this feeling of the writer's is mere envy, and likens life to a long voyage on a ship: some of the passengers have well-equipped staterooms and others bare cells, but those who have the bare cells could, if they exerted themself, have comfortable quarters. The bishop admits that he cannot always believe in all the dogmas of the Church—any more than the writer can. Belief and disbelief come and go. But occasionally, when in a period of disbelief, the man experiences something that makes him tend towards belief; *perhaps*—the grand Perhaps—there is a truth in the dogmas. Browning here uses the term in a somewhat similar way to the manner Rabelais, according to Peter Anthony Motteux, who first translated Rabelais into English, is supposed to have used it. According to Motteux, Rabelais, when dying, said, "I am going away in search of a great perhaps."

367

How can we guard our unbelief,
Make it bear fruit to us?—the problem here.
Just when we are safest, there's a sunset-touch,
A fancy from a flower-bell, some one's death,
A chorus-ending from Euripides,—
And that's enough for fifty hopes and fears
As old and new at once as Nature's self,
To rap and knock and enter in our soul,
Take hands and dance, there, a fantastic ring,
Round the ancient idol, on his base again,—
The grand Perhaps! We look on helplessly.
There the old misgivings, crooked questions are—
This good God,—what He could do, if He would,
Would, if He could—then must have done long since:
If so, when, where, and how? some way must be,—
Once feel about, and soon or late you hit
Some sense, in which it might be, after all.
Why not, "The Way, the Truth, the Life"?

The grand style

Source: ON TRANSLATING HOMER ("Last Words")
Author: Matthew Arnold (1822-1888)
First published: 1861
Type of work: Literary essay

Context: Matthew Arnold, like so many of his contemporaries, was caught in the agonizing throes of the intense religious and social transition of the Victorian era. Yet, unlike Newman on the one hand—who rejected the present and took refuge in the dogma of the past—and Huxley on the other—who rejected the past and became an ardent disciple of the New Science—Arnold accepted the modern age with full recognition of its scientific bias and worldly preoccupations. He saw and felt the social crudeness and the spiritual dislocation of his society, but he had a firm faith in the instincts and ideals which the human race had developed. Thus, in the work of his later life, he became a prophet of a new religion, culture—"the best that has been thought and said in the world." Through proper education he would envision a cultured middle-class cognizant of the values of human dignity as they have been articulated in the great aesthetic creations of the past. In 1860, as Professor of Poetry at Oxford, he delivered a series of three lectures in which, as he described it, "I shall try to lay down the true principles on which a translation of Homer should be founded." Among other matters, his lectures criticized a recent translation of the *Iliad* by Francis W. Newman, who printed a rebuttal to the charges. Arnold replied to Newman with an additional lecture, dealing primarily with the style and tone proper to the cultural values of the Greek epic:

. . . Nothing has raised more questioning among my critics than these words, "noble, **the grand style.**" People complain that I do not define these words sufficiently, that I do not tell them enough about them. "The grand style, but what is the grand style?" they cry; some with an inclination to believe in it, but puzzled; others mockingly and with incredulity. Alas! the grand style is the last matter in the world for verbal definition to deal with adequately.

. . .

I think it will be found that the grand style arises in poetry, "when a noble nature, poetically gifted, treats with simplicity or with severity a serious subject." I think this definition will be found to cover all instances of the grand style in poetry which present themselves.

The grasshopper shall be a burden

Source: ECCLESIASTES 12.5
Author: Unknown
First transcribed: c. 250-200 B.C.
Type of work: Religious confession

Context: The preacher in Ecclesiastes warns against vanity; all of this life is sheer vanity, he says: "Vanity of vanities . . . vanity of vanities; all is vanity." The search after wisdom or pleasure, fame or wealth, leads but to the grave for each and every generation. He sees that the worthy are defeated, and that the wicked prosper in this life. But some peace we may have, he suggests, and he advises that we subscribe to charity, duty, and faith. These will bring some measure of peace, even though in this life man is condemned never to understand the ways of God. To obey God, not to understand Him, is the lot of man: "Let us hear the conclusion of the whole matter: Fear God, and keep his commandments: for this is the whole duty of man. For God shall bring every work into judgment, with every secret thing, whether it be good, or whether it be evil." The writer of Ecclesiastes advises the young person to rejoice in his youth, but also to remember God the Creator and the judgment of life that must come. The time will come, he warns, when the spirit of man must return to the Creator:

And the doors shall be shut in the streets, when the sound of the grinding is low, and he shall rise up at the voice of the bird, and all the daughters of musick shall be brought low;
Also when they shall be afraid of that which is high, and fears shall be in the way, and the almond tree shall flourish, and **the grasshopper shall be a burden,** and desire shall fail: because man goeth to his long home, and the mourners go about the streets:

. . .

Then shall the dust return to the earth as it was: and the spirit shall return unto God who gave it.

Vanity of vanities, saith the preacher; all is vanity.

A great empire and little minds go ill together

Source: SPEECH ON MOVING HIS RESOLUTIONS FOR RECONCILIATION WITH THE COLONIES
Author: Edmund Burke (1729-1797)
First published: 1775
Type of work: Political speech

Context: As a member of the English Parliament Burke defended the American Colonies with great vigor and vehemence when that body considered harsh taxation and military suppression in response to unrest. England, he argued, was a great country and could well afford to be magnanimous in this instance as she had with such beneficial results in the cases of Ireland, Wales, and Chester. Conciliation, he insisted, would produce more loyal colonists; but he recognized that the narrow politicians would not understand his arguments:

> All this, I know well enough, will sound wild and chimerical to the profane herd of those vulgar and mechanical politicians, who have no place among us; a sort of people who think that nothing exists but what is gross and material; and who therefore, far from being qualified to be directors of the great movement of empire, are not fit to turn a wheel in the machine. But to men truly initiated and rightly taught, these ruling and master principles, which, in the opinion of such men as I have mentioned, have no substantial existence, are in truth everything, and all in all. Magnanimity in politics is not seldom the truest wisdom; and **a great empire and little minds go ill together.** If we are conscious of our situation and glow with zeal to fill our place as becomes our station and ourselves, we ought to auspicate all our public proceedings on America with the old warning of the church, *Sursum corda* (Lift up your hearts)!

Great griefs I see medicine the less

Source: CYMBELINE (Act IV, sc. ii, l. 243)
Author: William Shakespeare (1564-1616)
First published: 1623
Type of work: Tragi-comedy

Context: Imogen's husband, Posthumus, who has been banished by King Cymbeline and the queen, sends for her to meet him. Actually, he

370

plans to have her slain by the faithful Pisanio, because through the treachery of an Italian, Iachimo, he believes her to be a strumpet and untrue to him. Pisanio, who knows she is virtuous, cannot bring himself to kill her, but sends her on her way dressed as a man and carrying pills, given to him by the deceitful queen, supposedly to aid her in time of sickness. She meets two woodsmen and their father Belarius. They give her shelter, and being tired and ill she takes the pills and falls into a deathlike coma. Her hosts, meanwhile, have gone out to hunt, only to meet the revenge-thirsty Cloten, the queen's son, who wants to kill Posthumus and rape Imogen for spurning him for Posthumus. The woodsman Guiderius, challenged, beheads Cloten. Arviragus, his brother, finds Imogen and believes her to be dead. The brothers forget Cloten in their grief over the disguised Imogen, but Belarius entreats them to remember that he was a queen's son and that his body deserves respect.

BELARIUS

Great griefs I see medicine the less, for Cloten
Is quite forgot. He was a Queen's son, boys;
And though he came our enemy, remember
He was paid for that. Though mean and mighty rotting
Together have one dust, yet reverence,
That angel of the world, doth make distinction
Of place 'tween high and low. Our foe was princely,
And though you took his life as being our foe,
Yet bury him as a Prince.

Great is Diana of the Ephesians

Source: ACTS 19:34
Author: Unknown (traditionally Luke)
First transcribed: 60-150 (probably c.80-90)
Type of work: Religious history and tradition

Context: The Acts of the Apostles is the only contemporary account of the early Christian Church and its beginnings which remains to us. Although Acts and the third Gospel were evidently written by the same person, there is some doubt that he was actually Luke the physician; in any case, Luke probably provided much of the material. Acts is an epic recital of the apostles' lives, and forms a stirring record of the faith and moral courage that were required to build a new and independent religion. Luke begins with the Resurrection and the commission which Jesus laid upon His apostles, then proceeds with the history of their missionary work in Asia Minor, Syria, Jerusalem, and other portions of the Roman Empire. Chapters 15 through 28 follow the career of Paul, who moves from one place to another and preaches the gospel to people who are often deeply hostile to it. Crossing Syria, he wanders through Greece; he gathers a few

371

converts along the way and is occasionally the excuse for riots. One of these occurs at Thessalonica, where ruffians are persuaded or hired to create scenes of disorder. The Christians are blamed for the uproar, and Paul's congregation takes him to Berea. Here he gains some converts; but the hecklers follow from Thessalonica, and he moves on to Athens. In the latter city he preaches his new doctrine to curious philosophers and wins additional converts, though not many. From Athens he goes to Corinth, where he works as a tentmaker and on the Sabbath argues Scripture in the synagogue. Here he is brought to judgement and released. Later wanderings take him to Ephesus. After more than two years in the city his work makes itself felt: the converts multiply, and the worship of Diana in her great temple enters upon a decline. A riot follows, and Luke's account of it gives us an excellent case study of agitation and the genesis of civil disorder. The confusion and uproar are rendered vividly.

And the same time there arose no small stir about that way.

For a certain man named Demetrius, a silversmith, which made silver shrines for Diana, brought no small gain unto the craftsmen;

Whom he called together with the workmen of like occupation, and said, Sirs, ye know that by this craft we have our wealth.

Moreover ye see and hear, that not alone at Ephesus, but almost throughout all Asia, this Paul hath persuaded and turned away much people, saying that they be no gods, which are made with hands:

So that not only this our craft is in danger to be set at nought; but also that the temple of the great goddess Diana should be despised, and her magnificence should be destroyed, whom all Asia and the world worshippeth.

And when they heard these sayings, they were full of wrath, and cried out, saying, **Great is Diana of the Ephesians.**

And the whole city was filled with confusion: and having caught Gaius and Aristarchus, men of Macedonia, Paul's companions in travel, they rushed with one accord into the theatre.

And when Paul would have entered in unto the people, the disciples suffered him not.

And certain of the chief of Asia, which were his friends, sent unto him, desiring him that he would not adventure himself into the theatre.

Some therefore cried one thing, and some another: for the assembly was confused; and the more part knew not wherefore they were come together.

Great joys, like griefs, are silent

Source: HOLLAND'S LEAGUER (Act V, sc. i)
Author: Shackerley Marmion (1603-1639)
First published: 1632
Type of work: Dramatic comedy

372

Context: In 1624 an English dramatist who spelled his name in various ways came penniless out of the university because his father had squandered the family fortune. One way to earn a living was to fight with Gustavus Adolphus' army in the Lowlands, but Marmion thought promotion and wealth lay too far in the future, so after brief service, he put aside his pike and returned to London to make a living with his pen. His first attempt at drama, *Holland's Leaguer,* was often performed, according to the published copy, "with great applause by Prince Charles his servants, at the private house in Salisbury Court." The "Holland" has no connection with the country of Marmion's military service, but was the name of a "leaguer," or brothel in London's Holland Street, in Blackfriars. In cataloguing a copy of the play's first edition for sale, Bernard Quaritch called it "Holland's Leaguer, or a historical discourse of the life and action of Dona Britanica Hollandia, the arch-mistris of the wicked women of Eutopia, wherein is detected the notorious sinne of Pandarisme and the execrable life of the luxurious Impudent." A later commentator, Geneste, summarized the plot: "The Lord Philautus is self-conceited to the last degree; he is en-couraged in his folly by Ardelio, his steward and parasite. Philautus is brought to his sober senses by Faustina. She turns out to be his sister. The bulk of the play consists of an underplot with comic characters; the fourth act passes chiefly before a brothel, which is repeatedly called the Leaguer and sometimes a castle or fort. Trimalchio and Caprito, two gulls with the tutor of the latter are taken up [arrested] by a pretended constable and watchman, as they are coming from the Leaguer." The use of names like Philautus [lover of himself] and Trimalchio bear witness to the author's classical training. "Snarl," as one of the characters is called, comes from the practice of bestowing names according to characteristics. The names of actors appearing in the roles are given in the 1632 edition, but none can be found in lists of players of the period. Philautus was performed by William Browne, and Richard Godwin was Faustina, the sister. At the beginning of the final act, Philautus, back from the war, talks with Faustina whom he does not recognize, and with his acquaintance Fidelio, who is engaged to her. Philautus thanks her for showing him his follies. Fidelio supplies the explanation.

FIDELIO
But, when you know the author of your freedom,
You'll thank her more.

PHILAUTUS
Why, who is it?

FIDELIO
Your sister.

373

PHILAUTUS

Who? Not Faustina? She told me so indeed,
Her name was Faustina . . . I knew her not;
I am glad there is a scion of our stock
Can bear such fruit as this, so ripe in virtue.
Where have you lived recluse? You were betrothed
To one Fidelio, but crossèd by your father;
I have heard good reports of the gentleman.

FAUSTINA

I never knew you flatter any man
Unto his face before.

PHILAUTUS
Unto his face?

Where is he?

FIDELIO
My name's Fidelio.

PHILAUTUS

I am transported, ravished! Give me leave,
God Gods, to entertain with reverence
So great a comfort. First let me embrace you.
Great joys, like griefs, are silent. Loose me now
And let me make you fast. Here join your hands
Which no age shall untie.

Great men are the guide-posts and landmarks in the state

Source: SPEECH ON AMERICAN TAXATION
Author: Edmund Burke (1729-1797)
First published: 1774
Type of work: Political speech

Context: Edmund Burke made this address in the hope of quieting the antagonism that had arisen between Great Britain and the American colonies because of the duty imposed by Parliament on tea imported into America. The second part of the speech delineates the history of taxation in the American Colonies, with particular emphasis on the events from 1763 to 1774. In relating the account of taxation in the Colonies, Burke was led inevitably to recite the positions taken by various prime ministers in Great Britain, including Charles Townshend. In addition to commenting on the events of the ministries, Burke also, and consciously, speaks about the characters of the ministers themselves. Following his comments about the character of Charles Townshend, he makes these observations:

374

I beg pardon, sir, if, when I speak of this and of other great men, I appear to digress in saying something of their characters. In this eventful history of the revolutions of America, the characters of such men are of much importance. **Great men are the guide-posts and landmarks in the state.** The credit of such men at court, or in the nation, is the sole cause of all the public measures. It would be an invidious thing (most foreign, I trust, to what you think my disposition) to remark the errors into which the authority of great names has brought the nation without doing justice, at the same time, to the great qualities whence that authority arose. The subject is instructive to those who wish to form themselves on whatever excellence has gone before them.

The great ones eat up the little ones

Source: PERICLES, PRINCE OF TYRE (Act II, sc. i, ll. 31-32)
Author: William Shakespeare (1564-1616)
First published: 1609
Type of work: Tragi-comedy

Context: Pericles, Prince of · Tyre, has gone to the court of Antiochus, King of Antioch, to woo his daughter. The hand of the princess can, however, be won only by the man who solves a riddle propounded by her father. The failure to do so brings death to the suitor. Pericles is able to solve the riddle; but in so doing, he uncovers the terrible secret of incest between Antiochus and his daughter. The king knows that Pericles has discovered this secret and resolves upon the prince's death, but Pericles escapes from Antioch and returns to Tyre. But even in his own palace he is not safe from the vengeance of Antiochus, and he is advised by a faithful nobleman, Helicanus, to travel incognito until Antiochus either forgets his anger or dies. Pericles accepts the advice and starts on a voyage, just in time to escape Thaliard, an agent sent by Antiochus to murder him. The prince stops for a while at Tarsus; but he is not safe even there, so he resumes his voyage. His ship is wrecked in a storm, and Pericles is the only survivor. As he wanders by the seashore, he meets three fishermen who are discussing the storm and the shipwreck and the dangers of the sea. Their comments on the struggle for survival among the fish are a satirical description of the struggle among men, even among such rulers as Antiochus and Pericles:

PATCH-BREECH
. . . Master, I marvel how the fishes live in the sea.

FIRST FISHERMAN
Why, as men do a-land; **the great ones eat up the little ones.** I can compare our rich misers to nothing so fitly as to a whale; 'a plays and tumbles, driving the poor fry before him, and at last devours

375

them all at a mouthful. Such whales have I heard on a th' land, who never leave gaping till they've swallowed the whole parish, church, steeple, bells and all.

PERICLES [*aside*]

A pretty moral.

Great princes have great playthings

Source: THE TASK (Book V, l. 177)
Author: William Cowper (1731-1800)
First published: 1785
Type of work: Meditative poem in blank verse

Context: This quotation appears in the fifth book of *The Task,* entitled "The Winter's Morning Walk." *The Task* is a long poem, fitting the taste of the time in which it was written. The structure of the poem is discursive and rambling, so that it can contain meditative passages on all sorts of subjects, as well as many remarkable descriptions of nature. In "A Winter's Morning Walk," the poet discusses many topics: the foddering of cattle, man's slavish nature, the respective merits of martyrs and patriots, the Bastille, the whimsical effects of frost at a waterfall, the perishable nature of human institutions, and, among others, the amusements of monarchs. In this passage the poet speaks of war itself as one of the amusements of kings, and he decries the fact that kings can spoil the world by making war. Wise subjects, Cowper comments, would not allow monarchs to "make the sorrows of mankind their sport." The verse paragraph in which the quotation appears is this:

> **Great princes have great playthings.** Some have play'd
> At hewing mountains into men, and some
> At building human wonders mountain-high.
> Some have amused the dull sad years of life
> (Life spent in indolence, and therefore sad)
> With schemes of monumental fame, and sought
> By pyramids and mausolean pomp,
> Short-lived themselves, t'immortalize their bones.
> Some seek diversion in the tented field,
> And make the sorrows of mankind their sport.
> But war's a game, which, were their subjects wise,
> Kings should not play at. Nations would do well
> T'extort their truncheons from the puny hands
> Of heroes, whose infirm and baby minds
> Are gratified with mischief, and who spoil,
> Because men suffer it, their toy the world.

376

The great refusal

Source: THE DIVINE COMEDY, INFERNO (Canto III, l. 60, as translated by
Henry Wadsworth Longfellow)
Author: Dante Alighieri (1265-1321)
First transcribed: c.1314
Type of work: Christian allegory

Context: Dante, in the first chamber of hell, sees the trimmers, or those who did nothing, either good or bad. Here are found the legions of the angels who took neither God's nor Satan's side during the war in heaven. Among these neutral folk, Dante sees the man who through cowardice made "the great refusal." Although there are a few critics who hold this person to be Esau, the great majority consider him to be Pierro Morrone, who was taken from his hermitage when he was eighty years of age and was made pope in 1294. He assumed the name of Celestine V and resigned but five months after he assumed the papal office; he was succeeded by Boniface VIII, to whom Dante ascribes much of the evil of the times. The abdication of Celestine V caused great wonder and wide contemporary comment even as far away as Iceland.

> And I, who looked again, beheld a banner,
>   Which, whirling round, ran on so rapidly,
>   That of all pause it seemed to me indignant;
> And after it there came so long a train
>   Of people, that I ne'er would have believed
>   That ever Death so many had undone.
> When some among them I had recognised,
>   I looked, and I beheld the shade of him
>   Who made through cowardice **the great refusal.**
> Forthwith I comprehended, and was certain,
>   That this the sect was of the caitifi wretches
>   Hateful to God and to his enemies.
> These miscreants, who never were alive,
>   Were naked, and were stung exceedingly
>   By gadflies and by hornets that were there.

The greater the man the greater courtesy

Source: IDYLLS OF THE KING ("The Last Tournament," Line 628)
Author: Alfred, Lord Tennyson (1809-1892)
First published: 1871
Type of work: Narrative poem

Context: "The Last Tournament" is the transitional poem of the *Idylls,* depicting the degeneration of a great civilization. Here is seen the passing of honor, loyalty, and purity. The Tournament of Dead Innocence, the last tournament held at Arthur's court, occurs on a wet and windy autumn day. The weary, disillusioned Lancelot presides. Tristram, just returned from his marriage in Brittany, wins the prize of innocence, a ruby carcanet. Instead of taking the prize to his wife, Iseult of the White Hands, Tristram carries it to his paramour, Queen Iseult, the wife of Mark of Cornwall. Tristram finds Queen Iseult alone at Tintagel castle. She warns him that her husband plans to kill him by guile, perhaps by an ambush or poison. Iseult accuses Tristram of infidelity to her in his marriage to Iseult of Brittany. His lack of honor would stir her hate, she tells him, if she were not married to Mark, compared to whom all men seem noble. Tristram seeks to mollify her, claiming that he loved only the name of his new bride, not her person: "patient, and prayerful, meek,/ Pale blooded, she will yield herself to God." In the give and take of the argument, Tristram angers Queen Iseult. She strikes back, comparing Tristram unfavorably with Lancelot, his old companion in knightly deeds of purity and honor, who has himself fallen into adulterous ways of late:

> Then Tristram, ever dallying with her hand,
> "May God be with thee, sweet, when old and gray,
> And past desire!" a saying that anger'd her.
> " 'May God be with thee sweet when thou art old
> And sweet no more to me!' I need Him now.
> For when had Lancelot utter'd aught so gross
> Even to the swineherd's malkin in the mast?
> **The greater the man the greater courtesy."**

The greater the power, the more dangerous the abuse

Source: SPEECH ON THE MIDDLESEX ELECTION
Author: Edmund Burke (1729-1797)
First published: 1808
Type of work: Parliamentary address

Context: In 1768 one John Wilkes was elected to the House of Commons for Middlesex. At the time of his election he was still outlawed by a court conviction, for, as something of a demagogue, he had been in difficulty in 1764 over political publications. As a result of his unsavory past, in which pornography also figured, the House of Commons voted to expel Wilkes as morally unfit to serve in Parliament. His constituency reelected him four times. Three of those times he was expelled; on the fourth occasion the House of Commons declared his opponent duly elected, contrary to the actual vote of the people. Although he had no regard for John Wilkes, Edmund Burke spoke up in Parliament in opposition to the action of the House, an action he declared to be unconstitutional. As usual, Burke was speaking as a conservative who believed that order and liberty could be had only by limiting personal and group action to what is within the law. For the House of Commons to deviate from their constitutional powers was, in Burke's view, a threat to the whole fabric of the British system of government. And so he spoke against that action to his fellow members of the House of Commons:

> . . . The substance of the question is, to put bounds to your own power by the rules and principles of law. This is, I am sensible, a difficult thing to the corrupt, grasping, and ambitious part of human nature. But the very difficulty argues and enforces the necessity of it. First, because **the greater the power, the more dangerous the abuse.** Since the Revolution, at least, the power of the nation has all flowed with a full tide into the House of Commons. Secondly, because the House of Commons, as it is the most powerful, is the most corruptible part of the whole Constitution. Our public wounds cannot be concealed; to be cured they must be laid open. . . .

The greatest clerks are not the wisest men

Source: THE CANTERBURY TALES ("The Reeve's Tale," Line 4054)
Author: Geoffrey Chaucer (1343?-1400)
First transcribed: c.1387-1392
Type of work: Collection of tales

Context: In the fabliau "The Reeve's Tale," Chaucer tells the story of the outwitting of a dishonest miller by two students from Cambridge, who have determined that all of the grain of their college sent to be ground shall be returned. When the young men declare that they will watch the grinding of the grain, the miller, certain of his ability to steal a portion of it, muses on their caution and finally quotes a proverb of the time.

> This millere smyled of hir nycetee,
> And thoghte, "Al this nys doon but for a wyle.
> They wene that no man may hem bigyle,
> But by my thrift, yet shal I blere hir ye,
> For al the sleighte in hir philosophye.
> The moore queynte crekes that they make,
> The moore wol I stele whan I take.
> In stide of flour yet wol I yeve hem bren.
> **"The gretteste clerkes been noght the wisest men, . . ."**

The greatest fool may ask more than the wisest man can answer

Source: LACON (Volume I, number 322)
Author: Charles Caleb Colton (1780?-1832)
First published: 1820
Type of work: Aphoristic commentary

Context: An English clergyman, sportsman, and wine merchant, educated at Eton and Kings College, Cambridge, Colton occupied his spare time by collecting two volumes of aphorisms. He had previously published what was called a "sermon," under the title *Plain and Authentic Narrative of the Sampford Ghost* (1810). He had also embarked on a work that he called *Hypocrisy: a Satire in Three Books* (1812), of which only one volume appeared. In 1820, Colton completed the first volume of *Lacon, or Many Things in Few Words addressed to Those who Think,* named from the trait of brevity of Laconian Sparta, that gave the word "laconic" to the English language. The book enjoyed such a sale that the first year saw six editions, and so, in 1822, volume II came out. The Reverend Mr. Colton was a man of many talents, but despite his early inclination toward the Church, few of his gifts fitted him to become a member of the clergy. Though unconnected with the army, he liked to appear in military attire. Hoping to better his estate, he frequently gambled, once winning as much as 25,-000 louis at a session in the Palais Royal, only to go bankrupt through speculation in Spanish bonds. He was forced to flee to America to escape his creditors. Later he returned to France where, unwilling to submit to a surgical operation for a cancer, he committed suicide. Stating his ambition "to combine profundity with perspicacity, wit with judgment, solidity with vivacity, truth with novelty, and all of them with liberality," he collected 578 paragraphs, the result of his reading and reflection. He said that by addressing his work to "those who think" he could increase the number of purchasers, "since every individual flatters himself that he is one of that number." The success of the book, not only in England where it first appeared, but in the United States where the first of many editions appeared in 1824, proved him right. Most of the maxims, Colton declared, are founded on two simple truths; that men are the same and that the passions are the powerful and disturbing forces, the greater or the less prevalence of which gives individuality to character. Some of the maxims are only a few lines long; others occupy several pages of the small book in which they were printed. For instance, here are two examples. The first is a thought that has certainly entered the minds of many students at examination time.

322

Examinations are formidable, even to the best prepared, for **the greatest fool may ask more than the wisest man can answer.**

323

It is better to have recourse to a quack, if he can cure our disorder, although he cannot explain it, than to a physician, if he can explain our disease, but cannot cure it. In a certain consultation of physicians in a kingdom, they all differed about the nature of an intermittent, and all of them were ready to define the disorder. The patient was a king. At length an empiric, who had been called in, thus interposed: Gentlemen, you all seem to differ about the nature of an intermittent, permit me to explain it: an intermittent, gentlemen, is a disorder which I can cure, and which you cannot.

The greatest of faults is to be conscious of none

Source: HEROES AND HERO-WORSHIP ("The Hero as Prophet")
Author: Thomas Carlyle (1795-1881)
First published: 1841
Type of work: Moral essay

Context: Having shown the first hero to have been Odin, made into a god, Carlyle, in the second of his series of six lectures "On Heroes, Hero-Worship, and the Heroic in History," considers "The Hero as a Prophet." After the transformation of some Norse thinker and man of genius into the Teutonic god Odin, development came next among the Arabs. Men, now more sophisticated, were no longer willing to concede God-like qualities to their leaders; all they would grant was that the leaders were prophets, God-inspired. Basically every great man, as he comes from the hand of Nature, has similar qualities. Odin, Luther, Dr. Johnson, Burns, "are all originally of the same stuff." They are all "men of genius," the Soul of a man actually sent down from the skies with a God's-message for us. As example of a prophet, "we have chosen Mahomet, not as the most eminent, but as the one we are freest to speak of." Carlyle says that he is willing to call Mahomet a true Prophet, since 180,000,000 men during 1,200 years have listened to him. That fact could not have happened unless he had been sincere. His words as a prophet were unlike any other man's words,—direct from the Inner Fact of Things. And his rude message was a real one, an earnest, confused voice from the unknown Deep. Perhaps he had faults, but Carlyle goes on:

. . . Neither can the faults, imperfections, insincerities even, of Mahomet, if such were never so well proved against him, shake the primary facts about him.

On the whole, we make too much of faults; the details of the business hide the real center of it. Faults? **The greatest of faults,** I should say, **is to be conscious of none.** Readers of the Bible above all, one would think, might know better. Who was called there "the man according to God's own heart?" David, the Hebrew King, had fallen into sins enough; blackest crimes; there was no

381

want of sins. . . . David's life and history, as written for us in those Psalms of his, I consider to be the truest emblem ever given of a man's moral progress and warfare here below. . . .

Greet as angels greet

Source: TO LUCASTA, GOING BEYOND THE SEAS (Line 18)
Author: Richard Lovelace (1618-1657)
First published: 1649
Type of work: Lyric poem

Context: Since the Puritans did not approve of poetry, much of the verse of the seventeenth century was written by men of the king's party. These Cavalier Poets wrote gay, clever, but superficial poems, in which they paid court to sweethearts or boasted of their own triumphs. After Robert Herrick (1591–1674), the best of the group were Sir John Suckling (1609–1642), Richard Lovelace, and others. Lovelace was renowned for his physical beauty as well as for his loyalty to Charles I. For carrying to Parliament a protest in favor of his monarch, he was imprisoned in 1648, where he wrote his celebrated "To Althea from Prison." From prison he also published his verses in a volume called *Lucasta.* In it appeared the well-known "To Lucasta, Going to the Wars." It was formerly believed that the lady Lucy Sacheverell, concealed behind her poetic name "Lux casta" (Chaste Light), inspired these poems. "To Lucasta, Going Beyond the Seas," was written as Lovelace was about to depart for France, in 1646, to serve with Louis XIV. The lines seemed prophetic, for—so it was thought—hearing he had died at Dunkirk fighting, the "Chaste Lucy" quickly married his rival and probably never thought of him again until they met, as he foresaw, in heaven as disembodied spirits. More modern scholars, however, feel that a member of the family of Sir Charles Lucas was the lady to whom the poems were addressed. These are the last two stanzas.

Though seas and land betwixt us both,
Our faith and troth,
Like separated souls,
All time and space controls;
Above the highest sphere we meet,
Unseen, unknown, and **greet as angels greet.**

So then we do anticipate
Our after fate,
And are alive in the skies,
If thus our lips and eyes
Can speak like spirits unconfined
In heaven, their earthly bodies left behind.

Grief is itself a medicine

Source: CHARITY (Line 159)
Author: William Cowper (1731-1800)
First published: 1782
Type of work: Verse essay

Context: Having in the first part of this poem discussed charity or love of one's fellow men, comparing Capt. Cook in the South Seas with Hernán Cortez in Mexico, Cowper indicates how commerce links nations together. Then he talks of art, music, and literature which "thrive most/ Where Commerce has enriched the busy coast." He notes the reciprocal effect of trade upon people and the growth of charity as they learn and teach. But the slave-trade is a most cruel and inhuman commerce, causing endless pain and unendurable sorrow, that no amount of patience can make bearable.

> Oh, most degrading of all ills, that wait
> On man, a mourner in his best estate!
> All other sorrows virtue may endure,
> And find submission more than half a cure;
> **Grief is itself a medicine,** and bestowed
> T' improve the fortitude that bears the load,
> To teach the wanderer, as his woes increase,
> The path of wisdom, all whose paths are peace;
> But slavery!—Virtue dreads it as her grave. . . .

The guardian Naiad of the strand

Source: THE LADY OF THE LAKE (Canto I, stanza 17, l. 24)
Author: Sir Walter Scott (1771-1832)
First published: 1810
Type of work: Narrative poem

Context: When the stag at eve had drunk his fill, he had made his bed in a wood in Glenartney, but with the dawn a hunt begins. A hundred hounds and mounted riders pursue the stag all day. Finally only one rider and two hounds are still in the chase. At evening, when it seems that the stag is cornered and will have to stand at bay, it eludes the hounds and slips off into safety in the wildest part of the Trosachs. When this event occurs, the huntsman's gallant gray horse falls to the ground and dies. The hunter then blows the horn to recall the hounds, which limp back to him, slow, crippled, and sullen. The hunter finds himself upon the shore of Loch Katrine; the scenery is so beautiful that it seems like a fairy dream rather than reality. He enjoys the view for a while and imagines what a magnificent site it would be for a nobleman's or proud churchman's tower, a lady's bower, or a cloister. As, however, he is hopelessly lost in strange territory, he blows his hunting horn again to see if help might be forthcoming. The blast of the horn causes a little skiff to issue from a bay. The occupant of the boat, a young woman of exceeding beauty, comparable only to a Greek deity, actually the Lady of the Lake, like the guardian Naiad of the shore, pauses to listen to the echoes of the horn.

. . .

The boat had touched this silver strand,
Just as the Hunter left his stand,
And stood concealed amid the brake,
To view this Lady of the Lake.
The maiden paused, as if again
She thought to catch the distant strain.
With head upraised, and look intent,
And eye and ear attentive bent,
And locks flung back, and lips apart,
Like monument of Grecian art,
In listening mood, she seemed to stand,
The guardian Naiad of the strand.

Gunpowder, printing, and the Protestant religion

Source: CRITICAL AND MISCELLANEOUS ESSAYS, (Vol. I, "State of German Literature")
Author: Thomas Carlyle (1795-1881)
First published: 1827
Type of work: Book review

Context: Because of his knowledge of the German language, unusual among the British, and his familiarity with its literature and philosophy, Carlyle was frequently asked by editors to review books in German. In 1827, the editor of the *Edinburgh Review* sent him four books by Franz Horn that Carlyle bracketed in a single article in issue No. 92, in 1827. It was reprinted in the first volume of his collected essays. One title was a single volume, *Outlines for the history and Criticism of Polite Literature in Germany during the Years 1790–1818* (Berlin, 1819). The other, in three volumes, was *The Po-* *etry and Oratory of the Germans from Luther's Time to the Present* (Berlin, 1822–1824). As was his custom, Carlyle used the books as the basis for his own essay on the subject. But he was sufficiently faithful to his duties as reviewer to comment that the author's poor arrangement made the studies more a sketch of poets than of poetry. He also objected to Horn's belief that no mortal can be a poet unless he is a Christian, and criticized the author's affected style that forced epigrams like a "perpetual giggle." He remarked that the books were written in a style of "witty and conceited mirth." Johannes Kepler

384

(1571–1630), whom he mentions, was a German mathematician and astronomer, and Baron Gottfried Leibnitz (1646–1716) was a universal genius excelling in philosophy and mathematics. After his brief, preliminary comment, Carlyle gets to his essay.

But our chief business at present is not with Franz Horn, or his book. . . . We have a word or two to say on that strange Literature itself; concerning which our readers probably feel more curious to learn what it is, than with what skill it has been judged of.

Above a century ago, the Père Bouhours propounded to himself the pregnant question: *Si un Allemand peut avoir de l'esprit?* Had the Père Bouhours bethought him of what country Kepler and Leibnitz were, or who it was that gave to mankind the three great elements of modern civilisation, **Gunpowder, Printing, and the Protestant Religion,** it might have thrown light on his inquiry. Had he known the *Nibelungen Lied,* and where *Reinecke Fuchs* and *Faust* and *The Ship of Fools* . . . took its rise, . . . who knows but what he might have found, with whatever amazement, that a German *could* actually have a little *esprit,* or perhaps something even better? . . .

Had I but served my God, with half the zeal
I served my King

Source: KING HENRY THE EIGHTH (Act III, sc. ii, ll. 455-456)
Author: William Shakespeare (1564-1616)
First published: 1623
Type of work: Historical drama

Context: Ambitious and wealthy Cardinal Wolsey, long a favorite and influential adviser of King Henry the Eighth, has lost the king's favor because of two errors: he has withdrawn his assistance to Henry VIII in getting a divorce when it has become obvious that the king intends to marry Anne Bullen, only a lady-in-waiting, instead of making a politically judicious alliance with France, and he has inadvertently allowed a statement of his personal wealth to reach the attention of the king. Wolsey, stripped of his power and his wealth by his liege, talks to Cromwell, his only remaining friend:

WOLSEY
• • •
There take an inventory of all I have,
To the last penny, 'tis the King's. My robe,
And my integrity to heaven, is all
I dare now call mine own. O Cromwell, Cromwell,
**Had I but served my God, with half the zeal
I served my King,** he would not in mine age
Have left me naked to mine enemies.

CROMWELL
Good sir, have patience.

WOLSEY
So I have. Farewell
The hopes of Court, my hopes in heaven do dwell.

Hail, Imperator, those about to die salute thee

Source: LIVES OF THE CAESARS (Book V, "The Deified Claudius")
Author: Suetonius (Gaius Suetonius Tranquillus, c. 70-c. 140)
First transcribed: c. 120
Type of work: Biography

Context: Suetonius, Roman biographer, collected trivia to make his writing interesting as well as informative. Almost all of his *Concerning the Lives of the Caesars* has been preserved, as well as many fragments of an even larger collection of biographies, *Concerning Famous Men.* Book V of the former is devoted to the Deified Claudius, and Part 21 describes the shows Claudius sponsored for the populace. He restored Pompey's Theatre, damaged by fire, and gave magnificent games at the Vatican Circus. They included chariot racing, with bull baiting between every five races, panther hunts, and gladiator shows. In his account, Suetonius includes one of Claudius's feeble attempts at humor that misfired. After the combatants in the arena shouted the traditional: "Ave Imperator, morituri te salutant," they pretended to understand his "Aut non," as meaning that they need not risk their lives in the fight. As Suetonius describes the episode Claudius sponsored:

> . . . representations in the Campus Martius of the storming and sacking of a town in the manner of real warfare, as well as of the surrender of the Kings of the Britons, and presided clad in a general's cloak. Even when he was on the point of letting out the water from Lake Fucinus, he gave a sham sea-fight first. But when the combatants cried out: **"Hail, Imperator, those about to die salute thee,"** he replied: "Or not," and after that, all of them refused to fight, maintaining that they had been pardoned.

Hail, wedded love

Source: PARADISE LOST (Book IV, l. 750)
Author: John Milton (1608-1674)
First published: 1667
Type of work: Epic poem

Context: Uriel, one of the heavenly guards, indicates to Adam that an alien spirit may have made his way from hell to earth, but promises to seek him out next morning; he then departs by sliding down a sunbeam to the sun, which has sunk beneath the world. Adam explains to Eve that all things must rest at night, especially man, who has specific duties to perform which distinguish him from the lower animals, which idle through the day with no ordained work to do. Adam and Eve have to keep the growth of the garden under control and keep their paths unencumbered. Eve says that whatever Adam commands is law to her, as God is law to Adam. Whenever she is with Adam, she forgets everything but him. She then praises the glories of the garden in which they live. Adam explains to her the stellar virtue that is shed alike on them and on the millions of unseen spirits that walk the earth. They then go to their bower, which is adorned with flowers; it is closed to the entrance of all the lower animals, which stand in awe of man. Adam praises God, Who made all things, and refers to the fact that a race is to come from them to fill the earth:

> This said unanimous, and other rites
> Observing none, but adoration pure
> Which God likes best, into their inmost bower
> Handed they went; and eased the putting off
> These troublesome disguises which we wear,
> Straight side by side were laid, nor turned, I ween,
> Adam from his fair spouse, nor Eve the rites
> Mysterious of connubial love refused:
> Whatever hypocrites austerely talk
> Of purity and place and innocence,
> Defaming as impure what God declares
> Pure, and commands to some, leaves free to all.
> Our Maker bids increase, who bids abstain
> But our destroyer, foe to God and man?
> **Hail, wedded love,** mysterious law, true source
> Of human offspring, sole propriety,
> In paradise of all things common else.

. . .

Half seas over

Source: THE TRAGEDY OF TRAGEDIES; OR, THE LIFE AND DEATH OF TOM THUMB THE GREAT (Act I, sc. ii, l. 19)
Author: Henry Fielding (1707-1754)
First published: 1730
Type of work: Burlesque tragic drama

Context: Henry Fielding, certainly one of the great comic writers of all time, is probably best known for *Tom Jones,* but before he was a novelist he was a dramatist. Most of his dramas are farces, several containing biting

387

satire of contemporary political figures. *Tom Thumb,* however, is a parody of the absurdly bombastic heroic tragedy of the Restoration and early eighteenth century. Here Fielding burlesques not only hundreds of verbal absurdities from serious tragedies, but he also appends a set of comic footnotes by "H. Scriblerus Secundus," extending the burlesque to criticism as well. The play concerns the doings at the court of King Arthur and his queen, Dollallolla, "a woman entirely faultless, saving that she is a little given to drink, a little too much a virago towards her husband, and in love with Tom Thumb." Thumb, the miniature hero, loves the princess Huncamunca, who loves both him and Lord Grizzle. The play opens with a celebration because Thumb is returning from defeating the giants and brings as a captive their queen, Glumdalca, who has fallen in love with Tom and with whom the king immediately falls in love. In the second scene the king is proclaiming the celebration when the courtier, Doodle, brings a petition:

KING

Petition me no petitions, Sir, to-day;
Let other hours be set apart for business.
To-day it is our pleasure to be drunk,
And this our queen shall be as drunk as we.

QUEEN

(Though I already **half seas over** am)
If the capacious goblet overflow
With arrack punch—'fore George! I'll see it out:
Of rum, and brandy, I'll not taste a drop.

KING

Though rack, in punch, eight shillings be a quart,
And rum and brandy be no more than six,
Rather than quarrel you shall have your will.

Hand open as day

Source: KING HENRY THE FOURTH: PART TWO (Act IV, sc. iv, ll. 31-32)
Author: William Shakespeare (1564-1616)
First published: 1600
Type of work: Historical drama

Context: Clearly death is near for King Henry IV, who has known ill-health and civil strife. The ailing king is surrounded by several close followers, including his sons Thomas of Clarence and Humphrey of Gloucester. Addressing Clarence, the king inquires about his eldest son and heir Prince Henry and commands Clarence, whom the prince loves the most of all his brothers, to appreciate this affection, to act as a go-between for

Prince Henry and his brothers, and to   Prince of Wales:
acknowledge certain qualities of the

KING HENRY
. . .

How chance thou art not with the Prince thy brother?
He loves thee, and thou dost neglect him, Thomas.
Thou hast a better place in his affection
Than all thy brothers, cherish it my boy,
And noble offices thou mayst effect
Of mediation after I am dead,
Between his greatness and thy other brethren.
Therefore omit him not, blunt not his love,
Nor lose the good advantage of his grace,
By seeming cold, or careless of his will,
For he is gracious, if he be observed.
He hath a tear for pity, and a **hand**
Open as day for melting charity,
Yet notwithstanding, being incensed, he's flint,
As humorous as winter, and as sudden
As flaws congealed in the spring of day. . . .

A happy bridesmaid makes a happy bride

Source: THE BRIDESMAID (Line 4)
Author: Alfred, Lord Tennyson (1809-1892)
First published: 1872
Type of work: Sonnet

Context: During the wedding service the bridesmaid wept so hard that she could not see. Her sister, the bride, told her not to weep for her, as a happy bridesmaid makes a happy bride. Love himself came down between the couple at the altar and laughed at the bridesmaid, repeating what the bride had said. The speaker of the poem suddenly learns an important truth: that it was tenderness of heart that made the bridesmaid dissolve into tears. He presses her hand and his is pressed in return, and he knows that henceforth the single life is not for him. The bridesmaid was Emily Sellwood, whom Tennyson married in 1850. The wedding that inspired the poem was that of the poet's brother Charles in 1836.

O bridesmaid, ere the happy knot was tied,
Thine eyes so wept that they could hardly see;
Thy sister smiled and said, "No tears for me!
A happy bridesmaid makes a happy bride!"
And then, the couple standing side by side,
Love lighted down between them full of glee,
And over his left shoulder laughed at thee,

389

"O happy bridesmaid, make a happy bride."
And all at once a pleasant truth I learned,
For while the tender service made thee weep,
I loved thee for the tear thou couldst not hide,
And prest thy hand, and knew the press returned,
And thought, "My life is sick of single sleep;
O happy bridesmaid, make a happy bride!"

A happy child of earth

Source: RESOLUTION AND INDEPENDENCE (Stanza 5)
Author: William Wordsworth (1770–1850)
First published: 1807
Type of work: Didactic poem

Context: After 1800 a note of disillusionment began to appear in Wordsworth's poetry, and this note is quite obvious in "Resolution and Independence," the sentimentality of which made it fair game for the parodists Edward Lear and Lewis Carroll. The poem had its origin in an experience encountered by the poet and his sister in one of their walks in the Lake District: a meeting with an old leech-gatherer, badly crippled by an accident yet eking out a living at his difficult trade. The poet's conversation with the old man—which occupies the second half of the poem—is the sentimental part that became the butt of the parodists. But from this conversation with a man whom Wordsworth described as "carrying with him his own fortitude, and the necessities which our unjust state of society has laid upon him," the poet derived both inspiration and comfort. In the earlier and more cheerful section of the poem, Wordsworth describes a heavy storm at night that ended in a beautiful morning. The poet, in his familiar vein, then tells of his identification with nature and his happiness in it. Yet he is keenly aware that after such moments of joy comes a corresponding dejection of mind, during which the sensitive man is conscious of the tragedies that life will inevitably bring to him. It is in this realization that he writes, in the early part of the poem:

But, as it sometimes chanceth, from the might
Of joy in minds that can no further go,
As high as we have mounted in delight
In our dejection do we sink as low,
To me that morning did it happen so;
And fears, and fancies, thick upon me came;
Dim sadness—and blind thoughts, I know not, nor could
    name.

I heard the skylark warbling in the sky;
And I bethought me of the playful hare:
Even such **a happy child of earth** am I;

390

Even as these blissful creatures do I fare;
Far from the world I walk, and from all care;
But there may come another day to me—
Solitude, pain of heart, distress, and poverty.

Happy is the city which in time of peace thinks of war

Source: ANATOMY OF MELANCHOLY (Partition II, sec. 3, memb. 6)
Author: Robert Burton (1577-1640)
First published: 1621-1651
Type of work: Essays

Context: The only published work by Robert Burton, after a lifetime of scholarly labor, was *The Anatomy of Melancholy,* a pseudoscientific and philosophic treatise on human happiness. It went into a number of revisions, beginning in 1624. The title page of the first printing gave as the author's name "Democritus, Jr." But a note to the reader revealed the real identity of the author. Partition II discusses remedies for the various causes of melancholy. For instance, a philosophic look at the situation can cure discontent. In the next Member, Burton declares that the best cure for most of man's other passions and feelings is foresight and preparedness. Meditate ahead of time about what is likely to come! He preaches the doctrine of preparedness both by man and by a nation against the woes of life that are bound to occur. Then the calamity will be less painful and troublesome. He cites classical authors, Virgil and Seneca, to prove his point. The couplets that in Burton's original appeared in Latin, have been translated into English.

No labor comes at unawares to me,
For I have long before cast what may be.   (Virgil)

'T is not the first, this wound so sore;
I have suffered worse before.   (Seneca)

The Commonwealth of Venice in their Armoury have this inscription, **Happy is the city which in time of peace thinks of war;** a fit Motto for every man's private home, happy is the man that provides for a future assault. . . .

Hard is to teach an old horse amble true

Source: THE FAERIE QUEENE (Book III, Canto 8, stanza 26)
Author: Edmund Spenser (c. 1552-1599)
First published: 1590
Type of work: Allegorical poem

391

Context: Florimell, beset by a villainous forester in the woods, escapes his clutches and flees, eventually taking refuge in the hut of a witch and her loutish son. The son becomes enamored of Florimell, who decides to fly before his love becomes too violent for her to control. She therefore decamps early one morning. The witch, upon discovering her departure, sets on her trail a savage beast much like a hyena; the beast pursues her until her horse falls from weariness on the seashore. Florimell had thought to drown herself in the sea to escape being devoured by the beast, but finding a small boat occupied by an old sleeping fisherman drawn up on the shore, she enters it and poles her way out into the water. The beast does not follow; instead, it eviscerates her horse. Florimell's movement of the boat wakes the old fisherman, who at first is dazed by her beauty. The old man finally becomes fully awake and leers horribly at Florimell; although aged, he begins to feel the stirrings of foul lust. He leaps at her, but she scornfully repulses his madness. He, however, pays scant attention to her rebuff. Today we say: You can't teach an old dog new tricks.

> But he, that neuer good nor maners knew,
> Her sharpe rebuke full litle did esteeme;
> **Hard is to teach an old horse amble trew.**
> The inward smoke, that did before but steeme,
> Broke into open fire and rage extreme;
> And now he strength gan adde vnto his will,
> Forcing to doe, that did him fowle misseeme:
> Beastly he threw her downe, ne cared to spill
> Her garments gay with scales of fish, that all did fill.

Hark! the Gaul is at her gates!

Source: BOADICEA (Line 20)
Author: William Cowper (1731-1800)
First published: 1782
Type of work: Ode

Context: The happy youth of William Cowper, was followed by long years of mental disorganization, some of them spent in an insane asylum. Between attacks, he wrote simple, but popular, poetry and many letters that are among the most brilliant in English literature. Following one attack, he was sent to the country, to the home of the Reverend William C. Unwin. As a therepeutic measure, Mrs. Unwin suggested that Cowper resume poetry writing and complete a volume. It was published when he was fifty years old. One poem was "Boadicea," an ode to the heroine of the last British uprising against the Romans, about A.D. 60. In this poem when Queen Boadicea asks advice, a Druid foretells the invasion of Italy by Alaric I in 410, and others that would cause the downfall of Rome. He also prophesies the coming of later Italians, famous for music or, like Dante, renowned for words, not arms. He concludes by predicting the future greatness of Britain. Says the Druid:

> Rome shall perish—write that word
> In the blood that she has spilt;
> Perish, helpless and abhorred,
> Deep in ruin as in guilt.
>
> Rome, for empire far renowned,
> Tramples on a thousand states;
> Soon her pride shall kiss the ground,—
> **Hark! the Gaul is at her gates!**
>
> Other Romans shall arise,
> Heedless of a soldier's name.
> Sounds, not arms, shall win the prize,
> Harmony the path to fame.

The harlot's cry from street to street

Source: AUGURIES OF INNOCENCE (Line 115)
Author: William Blake (1757-1827)
First published: 1863
Type of work: Poetic fragment

Context: In the first half of *Auguries of Innocence* Blake attacks man's cruelty to the various creatures with which he shares the earth—wild and domestic animals and birds, even insects. The poem, a series of couplets never polished by Blake and remaining in manuscript at his death, contains many comments of aphoristic nature; those concerning human relationships are often telling. For example, "A truth that's told with bad intent/ Beats all the Lies you can invent;" or "Tools were made & Born were hands." Blake's attention, in the last half of the poem, is directed to man's cruelty to his own species. He lists certain unsavory human characteristics and habits—slander, envy, jealousy, avarice, and lies. He speaks of the beauty of holiness and of the innocence of little children. He turns from this subject, however, to his basic purpose of depicting human cruelty, and castigates those who beat children. Horrified at the existence of such people as beggars and soldiers, he considers both an insult to the heavens. The meager belongings of the poor and labor's small reward are more to be valued than the wealth of nations. Blake then devotes a number of lines to what he seems to consider the worst crime of all: sowing doubt in the minds of the young. Doubt is evil enough in itself, but to mock the beliefs of children is unspeakable. Throughout the poem he implies that if men could only see what is holy and reverence it, many of the sorrows they are born to would cease. Although *Auguries of Innocence* is the outcry of a devout and compassionate man, there is a sort of grim humor in the following excerpt:

A Riddle or the Cricket's Cry
Is to Doubt a fit Reply
The Emmet's Inch & Eagle's Mile
Make Lame Philosophy to smile.
He who Doubts from what he sees
Will neer Believe, do what you Please.
If the Sun & Moon should doubt
They'd immediately Go out
To be in a Passion you Good may do
But no Good if a Passion is in you.
The Whore & Gambler by the State
Licencd build that Nation's Fate
The Harlot's cry from Street to Street
Shall weave Old Englands winding Sheet. . . .

A harmless necessary cat

Source: THE MERCHANT OF VENICE (Act IV, sc. i, l. 55)
Author: William Shakespeare (1564-1616)
First published: 1600
Type of work: Dramatic comedy

Context: Antonio's friend, Bassanio, seems to have lost heavily in commercial investments, and Antonio goes to the rich and usurious Jew, Shylock, to borrow enough money to save his friend. Shylock, pretending a jest, persuades Antonio to pledge a pound of his flesh nearest his heart as surety for the loan. When Antonio's investments seem to miscarry, Shylock appears to demand his due, and when the case comes up in the court of justice, the Duke, as judge, instructs Shylock to show mercy to Antonio. The Jew insists that he have his due and refuses to explain his cruelty:

SHYLOCK
. . .
You'll ask me why I rather choose to have
A weight of carrion flesh, than to receive
Three thousand ducats. I'll not answer that,
But say it is my humour; is it answered?
What if my house be troubled with a rat,
And I be pleased to give ten thousand ducats
To have it baned. What, are you answered yet?
Some men there are love not a gaping pig;
Some that are mad if they behold a cat;
And others when the bagpipe sings i' th' nose,
Cannot contain their urine; for affection,
Mistress of passion, sways it to the mood
Of what it likes or loathes. Now for your answer.
As there is no firm reason to be rendered
Why he cannot abide a gaping pig;

394

Why he—**a harmless necessary cat;**
Why he—a woollen bag-pipe; but of force
Must yield to such inevitable shame,
As to offend himself being offended;
So can I give no reason, nor I will not,
More than a lodged hate, and a certain loathing
I bear Antonio, that I follow thus
A losing suit against him. Are you answered?

Hast thou named all the birds without a gun?

Source: FORBEARANCE (Line 1)
Author: Ralph Waldo Emerson (1803-1882)
First published: 1842
Type of work: Philosophical poem

Context: The question the poet asks is one of a series in the poem which results in a poetic definition of the man who is noble of soul. Emerson wrote this line, of course, at a time when both amateur birdwatchers and professional ornithologists still clung to the notion that the identification of a bird was truly done, as they said, only down the barrel of a shotgun. Emerson, ahead of his time, and in keeping with his idea that the crea- tures and things of Nature are best seen in their environment, suggests that the good man simply observes the bird, as he observes the wild wood-rose and leaves it on its stalk. Such a person, adds Emerson, is the kind who has courage and knows how to respect nobility of character, and as such is the sort of man the poet will value as a friend. The quotation is the opening line of the poem:

Hast thou named all the birds without a gun?
Loved the wood-rose, and left it on its stalk?
At rich men's tables eaten bread and pulse?
Unarmed, faced danger with a heart of trust?
And loved so well a high behavior,
In man or maid, that thou from speech refrained,
Nobility more nobly to repay?
O, be my friend, and teach me to be thine!

Hath not a Jew eyes?

Source: THE MERCHANT OF VENICE (Act III, sc. i, ll. 57-58)
Author: William Shakespeare (1564-1616)
First published: 1600
Type of work: Dramatic comedy

Context: Shylock, a wealthy Jew of Venice, lends Bassanio three thou-

395

sand ducats to aid in his quest of the hand of the fair Portia. Antonio, "the merchant of Venice," agrees to stand bond for Bassanio and promises Shylock a pound of his flesh if, by chance, his many ships fail to produce the expected revenue. With apprehension Salanio and Salerio, friends of Bassanio, note the failure of one after another of Antonio's vessels. Hence they query Shylock.

SALERIO

Why I am sure, if he forfeit, thou wilt not take his flesh, what's that good for?

SHYLOCK

To bait fish withal. If it will feed nothing else, it will feed my revenge. He hath disgraced me, and hindered me half a million, laughed at my losses, mocked at my gains, scorned my nation, thwarted my bargains, cooled my friends, heated mine enemies, and what's his reason? I am a Jew. **Hath not a Jew eyes?** Hath not a Jew hands, organs, dimensions, senses, affections, passions? Fed with the same food, hurt with the same weapons, subject to the same diseases, healed by the same means, warmed and cooled by the same winter and summer, as a Christian is? . . .

A haunt of ancient peace

Source: THE PALACE OF ART (Line 88)
Author: Alfred, Lord Tennyson (1809-1892)
First published: 1842
Type of work: Allegorical poem

Context: As a young man, Tennyson was torn between writing poetry that was merely beautiful and sensual and becoming a poet who was regarded as a profound ethical teacher. Under the influence of the Cambridge Apostles, a society of earnest and sincere college students, he came to see that the best poetry was moral and the best qualities in men become ignoble unless they are shared. In this poem, he describes the type of poetry that he had earlier written for his own pleasure and shows how the beauty becomes sterile and finally terrifying as the poet turns more and more from other men and from his social role; when the poet is compelled to leave his selfish world of art and to enter the world of men, he is able to purge his guilt and to discover the true nature of humble but morally sound poetry and beauty. The rich imagery of the poem is a description of art, the soul's "lordly pleasure-house," and is presented as a series of individual pictures of the different parts of the palace where the soul can wander in its selfish loneliness. The quotation comes from the description of the rooms, each fitted to create a particular mood.

396

Full of great rooms and small the palace stood,
　　All various, each a perfect whole
From living Nature, fit for every mood
　　And change of my still soul.
　　　　　　　·　·　·
And one, an English home—gray twilight pour'd
　　On dewy pastures, dewy trees,
Softer than sleep—all things in order stored,
　　A haunt of ancient Peace.

Have a care of the main chance

Source: HUDIBRAS (Part II, Canto 2, l. 502)
Author: Samuel Butler (1612-1680)
First published: First and second parts, 1663; third part, 1678
Type of work: Burlesque poem

Context: Much of the Second Part of Hudibras deals with a whipping. In his attempt to ridicule the Dissenters, Presbyterians, and others who fought against the Royalists in the civil war between Cromwell and Charles I, Butler wrote a satirical poem about two representative Puritans, the knight Sir Hudibras, and his squire Ralpho. As they are obnoxious, hypocritical, and absurd, the author implies, so were the enemies of royalty. If he expected to be rewarded by Charles II, who had been restored to the throne four years before the poem was published, apparently he was disappointed, for Butler complained several times about how poorly he had been rewarded for his services to the crown. In one of the few bits of action in this loquacious composition, the knight is captured by an enraged populace, angered by his crusade against what he considers sin, and is put into the stocks. A wealthy Widow, whom Hudibras would like to marry, hears of his plight and in a visit convinces him that whipping should be part of courtship. She will get him freed if he will swear an oath to accept a lashing. Because of approaching night, the beating will be postponed till the next day. Then come nearly five hundred lines of argument between the knight and his squire about whether he must keep his oath. Ralpho thinks the idea of a beating is heathenish, and insists that oaths are taken only to be broken. "Quoth Ralpho, Honor's but a word/ To swear by only in a Lord;/ In other men 'tis but a huff/ To vapor with, instead of proof." The followers of Cromwell often broke their oaths, even the leader himself, when he kept Charles I in close confinement, and explained, "The Spirit would not let me keep my word." Later, when his followers broke faith and murdered the king, they protested that "they could not resist the motions of the Spirit." Besides, the knight and his squire decide that if three Jews, according to Scripture, can free another Jew from his obligations, surely two Christians can. With many proverbs, like those of his Spanish counterpart, Sancho Panza, Ralpho tells Hudibras to seize his opportunity. "The main chance" was a common phrase for a long time as something to keep one's eyes on. However, Hudibras suggests that perhaps he ought to beat Ralpho, to avoid the need for a lie. His servant, with his eye on the main chance, insists that the spirit of their oath requires that he beat his master. But no one beats anybody. The servant hurries to the Widow to warn her that Hudibras is going to lie to her about his beating.

> Y'had best (quoth Ralpho), as the Ancients
> Say wisely, **Have a care o' th' main chance,**
> And Look before you ere you leap;
> For As you sow, y'are like to reap;
> And were y'as good as George-a-Green,
> I should make bold to turn agen;
> Nor am I doubtful of the issue
> In a just quarrel, and mine is so.

He bears the seed of ruin in himself

Source: MEROPE (Line 856)
Author: Matthew Arnold (1822-1888)
First published: 1858
Type of work: Dramatic tragedy

Context: Polyphontes slays Cresphontes, the King of Messenia, and two of the latter's sons, to seize the throne of Messenia. He also makes the widow of Cresphontes, Merope, his unwilling wife. Merope sends away her surviving infant son, Aepytus, her third child by Cresphontes, to be reared in safety by his grandfather and Laias, her brother. Twenty years pass, and Aepytus grows to manhood. Accompanied by the uncle who reared him, the young man returns to Messenia to avenge the deaths of his father and brothers, and to make his claim to the kingdom. He goes to the royal palace and asks to see Polyphontes, the usurper. Given an interview by the king, Aepytus passes himself off as an Arcadian nobleman who has come to Messenia as a messenger to bring news of Aepytus' death. Polyphontes, eager to learn of the death of the young man who has a better right than he to the throne of Messenia, asks how Aepytus met his death. The disguised Aepytus says that he died while hunting, that while chasing a stag Aepytus followed the beast into the waters of a lake and was swept to his death by a swift current. He ends by saying that the king of Arcadia bade him bring the news, hoping that the death of the young man would end the suspicion between the Arcadian and Messenian kingdoms:

AEPYTUS
He to thee sends me on, in one thing glad,

398

While all else grieves him, that his grandchild's death
Extinguishes distrust 'twixt him and thee.
But I from our deplored mischance learn this:
The man who to untimely death is doom'd,
Vainly you hedge him from the assault of harm;
He bears the seed of ruin in himself.

He found it inconvenient to be poor

Source: CHARITY (Line 189)
Author: William Cowper (1731-1800)
First published: 1782
Type of work: Verse essay

Context: Having talked about the humane treatment of savages by Captain Cook during his explorations in the Pacific, in contrast to the inhumane treatment of Montezuma and his Indians in Mexico by Cortez, Cowper discusses commerce as one means of knitting the world more closely. However, the slave trade reveals no charity, or love of one's fellow men, but only cruelty. He castigates those who trade in slaves to work the sugar plantations. The fact that slavery brings them money, he says, is no more an excuse than for a burglar to break into a house because he is poor. Only those blinded by greed see no wrong in it.

Canst thou, and honored with a Christian name,
Buy what is woman-born, and feel no shame?
Trade in the blood of innocence, and plead
Expedience as a warrant for the deed?
. . .
So may the ruffian, who with ghostly glide,
Dagger in hand, steals close to your bedside:
Not he, but his emergence forced the door,
He found it inconvenient to be poor.
Had God then given its sweetness to the cane
Unless his laws be trampled on—in vain?
Built a brave world, which cannot yet subsist,
Unless his right to rule it be dismissed?
Impudent blasphemy! So folly pleads,
And, avarice being judge, with ease succeeds.

He giveth his beloved sleep

Source: PSALMS 127:2
Author: Unknown
First transcribed: c. 400-200 B.C.
Type of work: Religious poetry

399

Context: Psalm 127 is a brief expression of man's complete dependence upon God, and is put with deceptive simplicity. The poet emphasizes that God must be a part of everyday undertakings if they are to have any meaning. A house built without spiritual considerations is a sterile and disappointing place, a mere shelter; when faith enters into the construction, integrity and meaning are embodied in it. The poet then elaborates his point: there is little use in guarding a city, he continues, unless there is the firm belief that God is guarding it too. Implied but not stated is the point that if we are convinced that God is *not* guarding the city we immediately become ineffectual protectors. Lack of faith in the undertaking, whatever its nature, is destructive to accomplishment. There is much hard labor in life, but there is comfort even in this fact; for man was not made to spend all his time thus, and the Lord has provided him with rest, that he may have relief from toil. The lines may also have another meaning: that men are prone to fretfulness and worry, and dwell upon their sorrows; and that God has provided comfort and forgetfulness in the form of sleep. In the last half of the poem, the psalmist takes up one of the most important of God's many blessings. Children, he tells us, are a heritage from God and his reward to man. Not only are they the joy of their father; they are his strength in time of need, upholding and supporting him. They give him recognition and honor. The man who has many children is fortunate, for in addition to the devotion they give, they will be his defense against his enemies.

Except the LORD build the house, they labour in vain that build it: except the LORD keep the city, the watchman waketh but in vain.

It is vain for you to rise up early, to sit up late, to eat the bread of sorrows: for so **he giveth his beloved sleep.**

Lo, children are an heritage of the LORD: and the fruit of the womb is his reward.

As arrows are in the hand of a mighty man; so are children of the youth.

Happy is the man that hath his quiver full of them: they shall not be ashamed, but they shall speak with the enemies in the gate.

He has joined the great majority

Source: SATYRICON (Section 42)
Author: Petronius (died c. 66)
First transcribed: c. 60
Type of work: Prose satirical romance

Context: Titus Petronius Arbiter was a favorite and intimate of Nero; he served as leading authority on matters of style and taste in the latter's court and thereby earned for himself an unsavory reputation. In Nero's court vice was a fine art: the "arbiter of elegance" was an authority on the

400

subject and doubtless assisted his emperor in creating new forms of it. Tigellinus, another expert in debauchery, saw Petronius as a possible rival and decided to eliminate him. This act was done by playing on the emperor's love of cruelty; Tigellinus persuaded him to charge Petronius with treason, and Nero doubtless thought the whole thing a hilarious joke. Petronius, knowing full well the emperor's inventive genius regarding forms of death, committed suicide rather than wait for execution. His chief work, *The Satyricon,* is a satire on the social life of the time and a disturbing view of the decadence to which Rome had sunk. The first portion of the work is an elaborate account of Trimalchio's banquet. Trimalchio is a vulgar, newly-rich freedman who loves ostentation and has the means to satisfy his desires. The guests are overwhelmed with a little too much of everything—sumptuous surroundings, the very latest advances in sanitary and other facilities, an almost endless meal. Petronius has a considerable gift for vivid and picturesque writing: after reading the mottoes on the walls, taking part in the orgy, and listening to scraps of incidental chatter among the guests, we feel we have actually been in attendance. Seleucus, in his anecdote about a funeral, says of the departed: *"Tamen abiit ad plures."* This is variously interpreted by translators, ranging from the matter-of-fact "Well, he is gone," to the sententious *"He has joined the great majority."* The following version, however, is much truer to the witty spirit of the original:

> Seleucus took up the tale and said: "I do not wash every day; the bathman pulls you to pieces like a fuller, the water bites, and the heart of man melts away daily. But when I have put down some draughts of mead I let the cold go to the devil. Besides, I could not wash; I was at a funeral to-day. A fine fellow, the excellent Chrysanthus, has breathed his last. It was but the other day he greeted me. I feel as if I were speaking with him now. Dear, dear, how we bladders of wind strut about. We are meaner than flies; flies have their virtues, we are nothing but bubbles. And what would have happened if he had not tried the fasting cure? No water touched his lips for five days, not a morsel of bread. **Yet he went over to the majority.** The doctors killed him—no, it was his unhappy destiny; a doctor is nothing but a stop to conscience. Still, he was carried out in fine style on a bier covered with a good pall. The mourning was very good too—he had freed a number of slaves—even though his own wife was very grudging over her tears. I daresay he did not treat her particularly kindly. But women one and all are a set of vultures. It is no use doing anyone a kindness; it is all the same as if you put your kindness in a well. But an old love pinches like a crab."

He has no hope who never had a fear

Source: TRUTH (Line 298)
Author: William Cowper (1731-1800)
First published: 1782
Type of work: Verse essay

Context: Only God's grace, says the religious Cowper whose occasional mental disorganization and mania of persecution several times caused his confinement to insane asylums, can lead man safely on his journey through life. So he will learn the truth. Such a journey need not be mournful. A saint is not necessarily a Niobe, "all tears." "True piety is cheerful as the day," and Cowper also points out that the only chains of a free-born Christian are "the golden ones of love." A man who is sure has no need of hope. Only to one in uncertainty is fear created and hope necessary. The average man, conscious of his misdeeds, may well fear that his sins will never receive forgiveness. On that account, he will not accept God's promise. He may feel, too, like turning from the Bible, despite the assurance: "The remedy you want I freely give/ The book shall teach you; read, believe, and live!" Such a disbeliever, however, may actually be more fortunate than his fellow who is so sure about the reward for his exemplary existence that he does nothing to insure his future life in heaven. For both of them, the poet has some advice.

Come then—a still, small whisper in your ear—
He has no hope who never had a fear;
And he that never doubted of his state,
He may perhaps—perhaps he may—too late.

He has shook hands with time

Source: THE BROKEN HEART (Act V, sc. ii)
Author: John Ford (1586-1639?)
First published: 1633
Type of work: Dramatic tragedy

Context: At a dance Calantha learns from Armostes that by her father's death, just occurred, she is now Queen of Sparta. Within a few moments she also learns, from Bassanes, that his wife is dead, and from Orgilus that Ithocles, a favorite, has been murdered. Calantha takes all this news calmly; when Orgilus boasts that it was he who murdered Ithocles, for revenge, she coolly tells him that he must die, with the mode of execution his own choice. Orgilus chooses to be his own executioner by cutting his veins. He props himself upon a staff and cuts the veins in one arm; then he asks Bassanes, as a favor, to cut the veins in the other arm. As he stands with his life running out, he recalls that Tecnicus, moved by the power of Apollo, has foretold that revenge would prove its own executioner. Even to the moment of his death Orgilus retains his courage and his presence of mind:

ORGILUS
So falls the standard
Of my prerogative in being a creature!
A mist hangs o'er mine eyes, the sun's bright splendour
Is clouded in an everlasting shadow:
Welcome, thou ice, that sitt'st about my heart!
No heat can ever thaw thee.

[*Dies.*]

NEARCHUS
Speech hath left him.

BASSANES
He has shook hands with time; his funeral urn
Shall be my charge: remove the bloodless body.
The coronation must require attendance;
That past, my few days can be but one mourning.

He in twelve, found truth in all, but one

Source: KING RICHARD THE SECOND (Act IV, sc. i, ll. 170-171)
Author: William Shakespeare (1564-1616)
First published: 1597
Type of work: Historical drama

Context: Richard II, who has banished Henry Bolingbroke on charge of treason and has seized his inheritance on the death of John of Gaunt, father of Bolingbroke and uncle of the king, returns to England from the Irish wars. Bolingbroke, who has invaded England to claim his inheritance, confronts Richard with turncoat accusers and demands a confession of guilt and finally the crown itself from the monarch. The Duke of York, weak and aged uncle of both Richard and Henry Bolingbroke, announces the abdication of Richard and the accession of Bolingbroke, as Henry IV, to the throne. Richard, summoned before the new king, claims that the accusers assembled here have previously pledged to him their allegiance even as the traitor Judas had originally pledged his faith to Christ:

RICHARD
. . . Yet I well remember
The favours of these men: were they not mine?
Did they not sometime cry all hail to me?

403

So Judas did to Christ: but **he in twelve,**
Found truth in all, but one; I, in twelve thousand, none.
God save the King! Will no man say, amen?
Am I both priest, and clerk? Well then, amen.
God save the King, although I be not he,
And yet, amen, if heaven do think him me.
To do what service am I sent for hither?

He is the freeman whom the truth makes free

Source: THE TASK (Book V, l. 733)
Author: William Cowper (1731-1800)
First published: 1785
Type of work: Meditative poem in blank verse

Context: Persuaded to take a walk by the beauty of a frosty winter morning, the English poet Cowper writes pictures in blank verse of the loveliness of the countryside, then digresses into a consideration of royalty, its amusements and diversions, and its likelihood to take itself so seriously as to believe the world made for its use. That idea leads the poet to a consideration that a king is only a human being, and therefore has no right to expect other humans to "bear his burdens" and "sweat in his service." With King George III in mind, about whom he had previously written in admiration, here Cowper continues in further tribute to him for lacking the qualities of a tyrant. "We love the king/ Who loves the laws, respects his bounds,/ And reigns content within them; him we serve/ Freely and with delight, who leaves us free." However, the only true liberty, the one that cannot be taken away, regardless of who tries, is "the liberty of heart, derived from heaven." The reference to mighty Samson who cast off his fetters, is obvious. The reference to knowing the truth and the truth shall make you free, is also Biblical. "Confederate" is taken in its literal meaning, "joined together."

He is the freeman whom the truth makes free,
And all are slaves beside. There's not a chain
That hellish foes, confederate for his harm,
Can wind around him, but he casts it off
With as much ease as Samson his green withes.

He makes a solitude and calls it—peace!

Source: THE BRIDE OF ABYDOS (Canto II, XX, l. 67)
Author: George Gordon, Lord Byron (1788-1824)
First published: 1813
Type of work: Narrative poem

This "Turkish Tale" by Lord Byron has as chief character one of the "Byronic heroes," satiated with pleasure and with civilized society. Though deeply loving a woman, he tries to suppress all tender feeling, along with an equal feeling of guilt for some youthful sin. Byron's half-dozen similar poems take place in the romantic Orient. This one by its title localizes the story on the Dardanelles. Zuleika, daughter of Pasha Giaffir, is supposed to marry the son of Bey Oglou, but suddenly Selim, long thought to be her brother and the Pasha's cowardly son, reveals himself in romantic fashion as leader of a band of pirates who believe it is human nature to prey on their enemies. Only when the foes are wiped out can peace come. Madly in love with her, Selim urges her to flee with him. He promises that "the spoils of nations shall bedeck her," and paints their joys, promising, in words that echo the phrase of Tacitus: "When they make a wilderness, they call it peace":

> To sooth each sorrow; share in each delight,
> Blend every thought, do all—but disunite!
> Once free, 't is mine our horde again to guide;
> Friends to each other, foes to aught beside;
> Yet there we follow but the bent assign'd
> By fatal Nature to man's warring kind;
> Mark! where his courage and his conquests cease!
> **He makes a solitude, and calls it—peace!**

He passed the flaming bounds of place and time

Source: PROGRESS OF POESY (III, 2, l. 4)
Author: Thomas Gray (1716-1771)
First published: 1757
Type of work: Pindaric ode

Context: Charles Dickens once declared, apropos of the slim output of poetry by Gray: "No other poet ever gained a place among the immortals with so small a volume under his arm." But Gray wrote chiefly for himself and his friends. Publication occurred only at their insistence or at the demands of booksellers. Spenser, Dryden, and Milton were his models, but his study of Greek, when few of his countrymen were interested in that language, provided the stanza form of his greatest work, "Progress of Poesy," originally called "Ode in the Greek Style." Having traced the progress of poetry from Greece to Italy and to Shakespeare in England, Gray refers in the second stanza of Part III to John Milton (1608–1674), and to his flight of poetry in *Paradise Lost*. Gray considers him almost on a par with Shakespeare, and since he wrote of Heaven and Hell, and of times past and future, Grey declares that Milton was not limited in his choice of themes by place or time.

Nor second He, that rode sublime
   Upon the seraph-wings of Ecstasy,
   The secrets of th' Abyss to spy,
     He pass'd the flaming bounds of Place and Time;
   The living Throne, the sapphire-blaze,
   Where Angels tremble, while they gaze,
   He saw; . . .

He serves me most, who serves his country best

Source: THE ILIAD (Book X, l. 201, as translated by Alexander Pope)
Author: Homer (c.850 B.C.)
First transcribed: Sixth century, B.C.
Type of work: Epic poem

Context: Temporarily beaten by the Trojans, as Jupiter wills, the Greeks petition Achilles to return to the fighting to help them. But Achilles, still angry over the staining of his honor by Agamemnon, who demanded the girl Briseis as his prize, refuses to rejoin the fighting to help his fellows-in-arms. Agamemnon, when he is told of Achilles' refusal, is quite disturbed by the seriousness of his situation and, with the help of other Greek leaders, awakens the warriors, lest they be surprised during the night by an attack from the Trojans. Nestor, an aged and wise Greek king, is one who goes about the camp helping Agamemnon alert the Greek forces. He wakens, among others, Diomed, who says that such activity during the night ill fits the advanced age of Nestor, who ought to be allowed to rest. But Nestor replies to Diomed that the situation is so grave that despair has overtaken the Greek camp, that everyone, including such an old man as himself, must be alert and active; but Nestor also tells Diomed he may take over waking the others:

My friend, (he answered,) generous is thy care;
These toils, my subjects and my sons might bear;
Their loyal thoughts and pious loves conspire
To ease a sovereign and relieve a sire:
But now the last despair surrounds our host;
No hour must pass, no moment must be lost;
Each single Greek, in this conclusive strife,
Stands on the sharpest edge of death or life:
Yet, if my years thy kind regard engage,
Employ thy youth as I employ my age;
Succeed to these my cares, and rouse the rest;
He serves me most, who serves his country best.

He shall not live; look, with a spot I damn him

Source: JULIUS CAESAR (Act IV, sc. i, 1. 6)
Author: William Shakespeare (1564-1616)
First published: 1623
Type of work: Dramatic tragedy

Context: Julius Caesar has paid the debt of ambition. Returning to Rome amidst great glory following his victory over Pompey, he was hailed by many of the common people as emperor, and his growing ambition was reflected in his being offered the crown on three occasions by his colleague Mark Antony at the feast of Lupercalia. The very thought that Caesar might accept the crown and thus subordinate the law of the Republic to the rule of a single man motivates dissension in Brutus, an idealist who loves Caesar as a man but loves his country more. Consequently, Brutus joined with others of less lofty motivation in a conspiracy to slay Caesar on his way to the Forum during the Ides of March. Following the murder the city, of course, is thrown into political turmoil as factions in defense both of the rebels and the slain Caesar begin to emerge. Antony, Octavius, and Lepidus organize the major opposition to Brutus and his followers. As is the case with any civil war, families and friends are divided in allegiance. Antony, Octavius, and Lepidus, in a council of state, consider those—friend or foe alike—who must be destroyed for the sake of the cause:

ANTONY
These many then shall die; their names are pricked.

OCTAVIUS
Your brother too must die; consent you Lepidus?

LEPIDUS
I do consent.

OCTAVIUS
Prick him down, Antony.

LEPIDUS
Upon condition Publius shall not live,
Who is your sister's son, Mark Antony.

ANTONY
He shall not live; look, with a spot I damn him.
But Lepidus, go you to Caesar's house.
Fetch the will hither, and we shall determine
How to cut off some charge in legacies.

407

LEPIDUS
What, shall I find you here?

OCTAVIUS
Or here, or at the Capitol.

He shared in the plunder, but pitied the man

Source: PITY FOR POOR AFRICANS (Stanza 11)
Author: William Cowper (1731–1800)
First published: 1800
Type of work: Satirical ballad

Context: William Cowper was the last English poet who belonged to what has been called the cult of simplicity; most of his work consists of quiet meditation and reflection, together with vivid though tranquil descriptions of rural life and the countryside. His Calvinism, although it comforted him, was also a source of despair and was a major factor in the attacks of insanity from which he suffered. He was trained in the law, and was called to the bar in 1754. He fell in love with his cousin but emotional stress brought on a breakdown and he was forbidden to see or marry her. Another breakdown occurred in 1763, while he was preparing for an examination, and he attempted suicide. A lengthy convalescence followed, after which he retired to the country and lived with friends, first at Huntingdon and later at Olney. He never married. He had written some verse in his youth but did not turn seriously to the writing of poetry until he was fifty; the first volume, *Poems,* appeared in 1782. His greatest work, *The Task,* was published three years later. Its theme, a sofa, had been suggested to him by his friend Lady Austen. Cowper expanded the theme into a long and tranquil poem on the beauties of the winter countryside, the simple pleasures and routines of daily life, and his own meditations on human existence and the outside world. Another collection of poems was published in 1798; his other works include an edition of Milton and a translation of Homer. He wrote a number of hymns. Little of his spiritual and emotional suffering appears in his work, though he moralizes frequently. He had a sweet disposition and a good though quiet sense of humor; one of his humorous poems, "John Gilpin's Ride," was enormously popular and is still famous. He was also satirical upon occasion; an example, "Pity for Poor Africans," comments both on the frailty of human nature and upon the evils of slavery: decent people react to the latter as does the boy invited to rob a poor man's orchard:

They spoke, and Tom pondered—"I see they will go;
Poor man! what a pity to injure him so!

408

Poor man! I would save him his fruit if I could,
But staying behind will do him no good.

"If the matter depended alone upon me,
His apples might hang till they dropped from the tree;
But since they will take them, I think I'll go too;
He will lose none by me, though I get a few."

His scruples thus silenced, Tom felt more at ease,
And went with his comrades the apples to seize;
He blamed and protested, but joined in the plan;
He shared in the plunder, but pitied the man.

He stands the shadow of a mighty name

Source: THE CIVIL WAR (*Pharsalia*) (Book I, l. 257)
Author: Lucan (39-65)
First transcribed: c. 54-65
Type of work: Epic poem

Context: Pharsalia, Lucan's epic account of the civil war in Rome, depicts the struggle for power between Caesar and Pompey, though many other historic figures appear in the poem. Cato, for instance, the incompetent chief of the opposition party when Caesar returns to Rome because of internal affairs, stands as an old soldier, enjoying the plaudits of his past. Rowe's translation reads:

Victorious Caesar by the gods was crown'd,
The vanquish'd party was by Cato own'd.
Nor came the rivals equal to the field;
One to increasing years began to yield,
Old age come creeping in the peaceful gown,
And civil functions weigh'd the soldier down;
Disus'd to arms, he turn'd him to the laws,
And pleased himself with popular applause;
With gifts and liberal bounty sought for fame,
And lov'd to hear the vulgar shout his name;
In his own theatre rejoic'd to sit,
Amidst the noisy praises of the pit.
Careless of future ills that might betide,
No aid he sought to prop his failing side,
But on his former fortune much rely'd.
Still seem'd he to possess, and fill his place;
But stood the shadow of what once he was.

He still remembered that he once was young

Source: THE ART OF PRESERVING HEALTH (Book IV, l. 227)
Author: John Armstrong (1709-1779)
First published: 1744
Type of work: Didactic poem

Context: John Armstrong, a physician, wrote *The Art of Preserving Health* in four books: Air, Diet, Exercise, and The Passions. Book IV, on The Passions, is a treatment of those internal factors that influence health, the first three books being on externals. After, however, stating that the passions should be kept in moderation, the author treats the subject of love. An unfortunate result of disappointed love is often the resort to inordinate wine-drinking. Armstrong by no means advocates total abstinence from wine, as he has high regard for the virtues of port, champagne, Burgundy, and Rhine wine; but he does deplore drunkenness. While intoxicated, a person can say a word that will lose a friend; he can perform a deed that will haunt him to the grave. Drink will cause the means, the health, the talents to decay and will produce a brutishness that will cause a man to be unrecognizable to those who know him. The author then says that he will give precepts for a happy life, enunciated by a certain virtuous old man:

> How to live happiest; how avoid the pains,
> The disappointments, and disgusts of those
> Who would in pleasure all their hours employ;
> The precepts here of a divine old man
> I could recite. Though old, he still retained
> His manly sense, and energy of mind.
> Virtuous and wise he was, but not severe;
> **He still remembered that he once was young;**
> His easy presence checked no decent joy.
> Him even the dissolute admired; for he
> A graceful looseness when he pleased put on,
> And laughing could instruct. Much had he read,
> Much more had seen; he studied from the life,
> And in th' original perused mankind.
> • • •

He that first cries out stop thief, is often he that has stolen the treasure

Source: LOVE FOR LOVE (Act III, sc. iv)
Author: William Congreve (1670-1729)
First published: 1695
Type of work: Dramatic comedy

410

Context: Samuel Johnson, who had little admiration for Congreve as a dramatist, considered *Love for Love* a comedy closely allied to life, and with more real manners than his previous attempts. It was performed under the direction of Thomas Betterton to open the New Theatre. Johnson admired the regularity of versification (which is almost entirely in the prologue and epilogue) and commented that there is in it "more bustle than sentiment." The plot is busy and intricate, and the events hold the attention of the audience but more because it is perplexed with stratagems and amused with noise than entertained with any real delineation of character. It was Congreve's third play, written by a dramatist not yet twenty-five. In an attack on the English stage in 1698 the Non-conformist clergyman, Jeremy Collier, with plays like this in mind, used the adjective "licentious." It is true that its chief theme is the intimate relation between men and women, but actually Restoration drama, written between 1660 and 1700, deals rather coldly with human love and lust. Following the Puritanical era, people were trying to readjust their values. One defender of the plays commented that scenes in *Pericles* and *Romeo and Juliet* go farther in that direction than anything in the Restoration drama that was trying to cure excess, to exaggerate in order to laugh vice out of existence. Like most Restoration comedies, *Love for Love* has an involved plot, though less so than Congreve's two preceding attempts. It makes an excellent acting vehicle. Wealthy Sir Sampson Legend has two sons, the sailor Ben and a spendthrift gallant, Valentine, now deeply in debt. He is in love with Angelica, an heiress, niece of the astrologer Foresight. Sir Sampson sends his steward to urge Valentine to sign over his inheritance to the favorite Ben (the first realistic sailor in English literature), in return for four thousand pounds in cash to pay his bills. Foresight, learning of the offer, schemes for a marriage between Ben and his silly, awkward daughter, Prue (the first country hoyden in English drama). Sampson approves, but Ben, home from a three years' sea voyage, finds greater charm in Mistress Frail, sister of the second Mrs. Foresight, and well-named because of her easy virtue. Scandal, Valentine's friend, who wants to preserve Valentine's inheritance, enlists the help of a half-witted beau, Tattle. Valentine pretends madness to avoid signing the release, but confesses the truth to Angelica, now courted by Sampson to provide a new heir whom the old man can manipulate. But she marries Valentine, and Tattle is fobbed off on the frail Mistress Frail. Ben is left without the money and Prue without a husband. But the ending convinces Foresight and Sir Sampson that they are "illiterate old fools." In the third act, Scandal has pretended a knowledge of astrology to hoodwink Foresight and make love to his young wife. In one of those frank conversations of Restoration comedy, he confesses his designs upon her. He tells her that some women are virtuous, as men are valiant, because of fear. But faced with pleasure, women should regard Honor as a public enemy and Conscience a domestic thief. In reply, she confesses that she is not entirely displeased with him, but adds:

411

MRS. FORESIGHT

You have a villainous Character; you are a Libertine in Speech, as well as Practice.

SCANDAL

Come, I know what you wou'd say,—you think it more dangerous to be seen in Conversation with me, than to allow some other Men the last Favor; you mistake, the Liberty I take in talking, is purely affected, for the service of your Sex. **He that first cries out stop Thief, is often he that has stol'n the Treasure.** I am a Jugler, that act by Confederacy; and if you please, we'll put a Trick upon the World.

. . .

MRS. FORESIGHT

Oh, fie—I'll swear you're impudent.

SCANDAL

I'll swear you're handsome.

He that is not with me is against me

Source: MATTHEW 12:30
Author: Unknown (traditionally Matthew the Apostle)
First transcribed: c. 75-100
Type of work: Gospel

Context: In Chapter 12 of his Gospel, Matthew tells of a time when Jesus and His disciples go abroad on the Sabbath day and walk among the cornfields. The disciples are hungry; they are picking the grains of corn and eating them. The Pharisees, always eager to trap Jesus, point out that it is not lawful to do such an act on the Sabbath. Jesus replies by reminding them that David took bread from the altar on the Sabbath when he and his companions were hungry, and tells the Pharisees that mercy is more important than sacrifice. "The Son of man," He informs them, "is Lord even of the sabbath day." A man with a withered hand approaches and the Pharisees, in another effort to trap Jesus, ask Him whether it is lawful to heal on the Sabbath. Jesus points out that if any of them had a sheep which fell into a pit on the Sabbath, the sheep would be pulled out —and that surely a sheep is less important than a man. He then heals the cripple and sends him away rejoicing. The Pharisees are infuriated; their laws have been turned upon them in a most uncomfortable way, and it seems this opponent has an answer for everything they bring against Him. All too frequently His answers leave them with none of their own. They retire from His presence and hold a conference, trying to plan some way to destroy Him. While they are doing so, Jesus quietly goes forth among the multitudes that follow Him and as He heals them requests that they not make Him known. Matthew links this episode to

412

one of the prophecies of Isaiah: that the Servant (that is, Messiah) will teach the new religion quietly and gently that it may spread across the earth. The Pharisees' next move is to accuse Jesus of being in league with Beelzebub; in His reply He states firmly that in man's acceptance of Christ, there is no middle ground.

Then was brought unto him one possessed with a devil, blind and dumb: and he healed him, insomuch that the blind and dumb both spake and saw.

And all the people were amazed, and said, Is not this the son of David?

But when the Pharisees heard it, they said, This fellow doth not cast out devils, but by Beelzebub the prince of devils.

And Jesus knew their thoughts, and said unto them, Every kingdom divided against itself is brought to desolation; and every city or house divided against itself shall not stand:

And if Satan cast out Satan, he is divided against himself; how then shall his kingdom stand?

And if I by Beelzebub cast out devils, by whom do your children cast them out? therefore they shall be your judges.

But if I cast out devils by the Spirit of God, then the kingdom of God is come unto you.

Or else how can one enter into a strong man's house, and spoil his goods, except he first bind the strong man? and then he will spoil his house.

He that is not with me, is against me; and he that gathereth not with me, scattereth abroad.

Wherefore I say unto you, All manner of sin and blasphemy shall be forgiven unto men: but the blasphemy against the Holy Ghost shall not be forgiven unto men.

He that strives to touch the stars, oft stumbles at a straw

Source: THE SHEPHEARDES CALENDER (July, ll. 99-100)
Author: Edmund Spenser (c. 1552-1599)
First published: 1579
Type of work: Pastoral eclogue

Context: The Shepheardes Calender was Spenser's first poetical work of any note; it is a series of unconnected pastoral idyls unified only by the device of giving each one the name of a month. The language is consciously archaic, imitative of Chaucer's work, although the spelling and the grammar often depart from strict Middle English usage. There is also a great deal of alliteration, which Chaucer avoids. The argument of the eclogue is conducted by Thomalin, a good shepherd, and Morrell, a proud and ambitious goatherd. Morrell tells Thomalin to ascend the mount upon which he is seated, but Thomalin replies that he has no desire to climb. Morrell thereupon recites the names of a number of saints and other holy

413

men who have dwelt on mounts, but Thomalin still refuses to leave his accustomed ground. The eclogue probably was written to show the virtue of the Protestant clergy, represented by Thomalin, as contrasted with the proud Catholic divines, as represented by Morrell; Spenser himself was an ardent Protestant. Says the quoted proverb: The nearer to the church, the farther from God. When in the eclogue Morrell says that hills are nearer heaven than are the lowlands, Thomalin replies:

> Syker, thou speakes lyke a lewde lorrell,
>   Of Heauen to demen so:
> How be I am but rude and borrell,
>   Yet nearer wayes I knowe.
> To Kerke the narre, from God more farre,
>   Has bene an old sayd sawe.
> And **he that striues to touch the starres,**
>   **Oft stombles at a strawe,**
> Alsoone may shepheard clyme to skye,
>   That leades in lowly dales,
> As Goteherd prowd that sitting hye,
>   Vpon the Mountaine sayles.

He thought I thought he thought I slept

Source: THE ANGEL IN THE HOUSE (Book II, canto viii, prelude 3, "The Kiss")
Author: Coventry Patmore (1823-1896)
First published: 1856
Type of work: Lyric poem

Context: Although condemned today because of its monotony and bathos, Patmore's sequence of odes and various stanzas was immensely popular when it was published, earning the author the honorific title "Poet Laureate of Nuptial Love." Unlike most poets who write of either courtship or adultery, Patmore celebrated the state of marriage with an ardor that has become quaint in the cynicism of the twentieth century. By combining erotic passion and the code of domestic virtue popular a century ago, he develops the theme that marriage is the route to spiritual truth. In bursts of Platonism, Christianity, and mid-Victorian sentiment, he shows that love within an ideal marriage is a way to God, thereby making marriage a sacred state in which Honoria, the wife, is a guiding angel to Felix, leading him through the commonplace incidents of life to a final apotheosis. In the quotation, which comes from the final part of the courtship, Honoria speaks to a friend who saw Felix kiss her; as a proper young lady she cannot let him know that she was awake for such would be a sign of immodesty.

414

"I saw you take his kiss!" " 'Tis true."
"O, modesty!" " 'Twas strictly kept:
He thought me asleep; at least, I knew
He thought I thought he thought I slept."

He was a bold man, that first ate an oyster

Source: POLITE CONVERSATION (Dialogue II)
Author: Jonathan Swift (1667-1745)
First published: 1738
Type of work: Satire

Context: Since, says Swift, noted satirist and Dean of St. Patrick's Cathedral in Dublin, the art of conversation is dying in England, with aplomb he takes it upon himself in his three-dialogue work entitled *Polite Conversation* to enlighten his countrymen by the examples of the conversation of the characters in the work. At the home of Lady Smart oysters are served as an appetizer before dinner, and the following conversation ensues:

LADY SMART
Ladies and gentlemen, will you eat any oysters before dinner?

COLONEL ATWIT
With all my heart. [*Takes an oyster.*] **He was a bold man, that first eat an oyster.**

LADY SMART
They say, oysters are a cruel meat, because we eat them alive: Then they are an uncharitable meat for we leave nothing to the poor; and they are an ungodly meat, because we never say grace.

MR. NEVEROUT
Faith, that's as well said, as if I had said it myself.

He was a rake among scholars and a scholar among rakes

Source: AIKIN'S LIFE OF ADDISON
Author: Thomas Babington Macaulay (1800-1859)
First published: July, 1843
Type of work: Biographical essay and book review

Context: Even while writing the *History of England,* which was to be his masterpiece, Lord Macaulay was always willing to take time out for essay reviews of new books for the *Edinburgh Review. The Life of Joseph*

415

Addison in two volumes had just been published by Macaulay's own London firm, Longmans. Its author, Miss Lucy Aikin (1781–1864) had published three earlier historical studies. At the request of the publisher, Macaulay had looked over some of the proof of the Addison volume and had indicated to the elderly author about forty errors. Her bitter reception of his criticism provoked Macaulay, and his essay began with a rebuke for her many examples of carelessness. Of course, to discuss the life of Addison, Sir Richard Steele, who was his associate in the publication of the news sheets, *The Tatler* (1709) and *The Spectator* (1711) had to be mentioned. Unlike Addison, who had lived a life of sobriety, Steele left Oxford to join the army, where he earned a bad reputation for his life of excesses. The news sheets, containing something of interest for both men and women, included essays on customs, social notes, news from the war, and comments on life and philosophy. Macaulay says that one who, like Steele, crossed the barriers and could interpose Latin phrases from Horace into gossip from the Coffee Houses and from even lower circles of London society, was a logical writer for the three-times-a-week *Tatler,* since he combined the knowledge of a scholar with the experiences of a dissolute man. "Rake" is a shortened form of "rakehell," "one who explores evil." "Intelligence" means "news." Lord Macaulay commented about Sir Richard Steele thus:

. . . He was not ill qualified to conduct the work which he had planned. His public intelligence he drew from the best sources. He knew the town and had paid dear for his knowledge. He had read much more than the dissipated men of that time were in the habit of reading. **He was a rake among scholars and a scholar among rakes.** His style was easy and not incorrect; . . . His writings have been well compared to those light wines which, though deficient in body and flavor, are yet a pleasant small drink, if not kept too long or carried too far.

He wears the rose of youth upon him

Source: ANTONY AND CLEOPATRA (Act III, sc. xiii, ll. 20-21)
Author: William Shakespeare (1564-1616)
First published: 1623
Type of work: Dramatic tragedy

Context: The vast Roman empire is ruled by Antony, Octavius Caesar, and Lepidus, a shaky triumvirate, filled with friction and disputes of power. Antony, enamored of Cleopatra, the bewitching Queen of Egypt, makes such a fool of himself that he loses his power in the empire to young Caesar. Antony attempts to negotiate a treaty with Caesar. Caesar refuses to consider his bargain, but does agree to a bargain sought by Cleopatra—that she be granted the crown of the Ptolemies—on the con-

416

dition that she have Antony beheaded. In his extremity, Antony, deriding his opponent for youthfulness and cowardice, vowing that he will challenge Caesar to a duel, conveys to Cleopatra the message that she must send his head to Caesar in exchange for the power she seeks.

ANTONY
. . .
To the boy Caesar send this grizzled head,
And he will fill thy wishes to the brim
With principalities.

CLEOPATRA
That head, my lord?

ANTONY
To him again, tell him **he wears the rose**
Of youth upon him; from which the world should note
Something particular. His coin, ships, legions,
May be a coward's, whose ministers should prevail
Under the service of a child as soon
As i' th' command of Caesar. I dare him therefore
To lay his gay comparisons apart,
And answer me declined, sword against sword,
Ourselves alone. . . .

He who turns and runs away, lives to fight another day

Source: DE FUGA IN PERSECUTIONE (On Flight in Persecution, 10)
Author: Tertullian (160-240)
First transcribed: Third century
Type of work: Moral and ethical treatise

Context: In answer to Fabius, who asks whether or not the Christian should flee from persecution, Tertullian replies with this treatise in which he sets forth the responsibilities of the persecuted. After examining the demands of God on those who would be soldiers of Christ, the writer comes to the conclusion that those who have received Him as Lord will not choose the broad way of flight from their persecutors but the narrow way of suffering for His sake. However, Tertullian admits that there are those who, rather than obey the exhortations of God, would argue themselves out of standing fast by applying to themselves from the ancient worldly wisdom of the Greeks, a proverb that is found again in English in rhymed form as early as the seventeenth century.

But some, paying no attention to the exhortations of God, are readier to apply to themselves that Greek versicle of worldly wis-

417

dom, **"He who fled will fight again;"** perhaps also in the battle to flee again. And when will he who, as a fugitive, is a defeated man, be conqueror? A worthy soldier he furnishes to his commander Christ, who, so amply armed by the apostle, as soon as he hears persecution's trumpet, runs off from the day of persecution. I also will produce in answer a quotation taken from the world: "Is it a thing so very sad to die?" He must die, in whatever way of it, either as conquered or as conqueror. But although he has succumbed in denying, he has yet faced and battled with the torture. I had rather be one to be pitied than to be blushed for. More glorious is the soldier pierced with the javelin in battle, than he who has a safe skin as a fugitive.

He would love, and she would not

Source: PHYLLIDA AND CORYDON (Line 8)
Author: Nicholas Breton (1545?-1626?)
First published: 1591
Type of work: Pastoral poem

Context: Nicholas Breton was a versatile poet, from an old Essex family. His birthdate has only recently been ascertained. He probably attended Oxford, since some of his work was published there. His most ambitious volume was *The Wil of Wits* (1580), but he also wrote considerable satirical and romantic poetry. His sympathy with country life and rural scenery may be found in his pastoral lyrics, in which he shows a delicate and refined touch. In his period, Breton was classified among the greatest writers of all time. Suckling, the Cavalier poet, linked his name with that of Shakespeare. Lyrics about shepherds, or a nymph and a shepherd, courting in the Spring, were very common at the beginning of the seventeenth century. Generally, as in this poem, by convention they were given Greek-sounding names, yet most of them acted no differently from young people today with more modern names. This universality is one reason why this poem still survives, reprinted in twentieth century anthologies. Sometimes the names are written Phillida and Coridon.

In the Merry month of May,
In a morn by break of day,
Forth I walk'd by the wood-side,
Whenas May was in his pride;
There I spièd all alone,
Phyllida and Corydon.
Much ado there was, God wot!
He would love, and she would not.
She said, never man was true:
He said, none was false to you.
He said, he had loved her long,
She said, love should have no wrong.

418

Corydon would kiss her then:
She said, maids must kiss no men
Till they did for good and all;
Then she made the shepherd call
All the heavens to witness truth:
Never loved a truer youth.
Thus with many a pretty oath—
Yea and nay, and faith and troth,
Such as silly shepherds use
When they would not love abuse,
Love which had been long deluded
Was with kisses sweet concluded:
And Phyllida with garlands gay,
Was made the Lady of the May.

Heads I win, tails you lose

Source: CROKER PAPERS (III, 61)
Author: John Wilson Croker (1780-1857)
First published: 1884
Type of work: Letter

Context: John Wilson Croker, a British politician and author, and member of Parliament between 1807 and 1832, took part, as a contributor to the *Quarterly Review,* in frequent literary feuds, such as his attack on Keats' *Endymion,* in 1818. His many writings were collected after his death. During the debates about the Corn Laws in England in 1846, Sir Robert Peel wanted to repeal them gradually, establish Free Trade, and help reduce the cost of living. One of his opponents was Lord Granby, son of the Duke of Rutland, who resigned his government post to oppose the repeal. His father wrote to Croker, who also was opposed to the total repeal of the Laws. The letter is dated Belvoir Castle, January 25, 1846. The duke begins by thanking Croker for his good opinion of his son's speech. He also talks about the "mess" in which England finds itself in India with its call for soldiers to fight the Sikhs. Then in mentioning the unfairness of the French position, he speaks of a game, or a phrase in it, which leaves the speaker the winner, no matter how the coin falls. The expression, at least, is still used among children. Here is the final paragraph of the letter:

Périer [Périer is Auguste Casimir Périer (1811-1878), a French politician and Minister.] has sent in the French Corn Protecting Duties, which seem very stringent. If they close their arms to us, while we open ours to them, we shall play at a game which a sharper once played with a dupe, intituled, **"Heads I win, and tails you lose."** I cautiously avoid forming my final opinion on the

419

whole subject till the measure is in the House of Lords in the shape of a Bill.

> Ever, my dear Croker, Most truly yours,
> Rutland.

A healthy hatred of scoundrels

Source: LATTER-DAY PAMPHLETS (Number 2, "Model Prisons")
Author: Thomas Carlyle (1795-1881)
First published: 1850
Type of work: Essay of social criticism

Context: The Victorian Age, bringing the world closer together, also increased the difficulties of the lower classes. Some writers, like Carlyle, thought such progress would prove suicidal in the end. He was sick about the sordid lives of the workers in the factories, and the additional crimes occurring with increasing poverty. Since he had known poverty as a child in Scotland, he was sympathetic with the plight of the poor, and began writing attacks on current social evils. His trouble—as one critic pointed out —was that, as a philosopher, he had no system. Some of his conclusions about the social order have proved impractical and dangerous. He believed in a strong paternalistic government because of his sympathy with the unprotected poor, and was convinced that because society changes, it ought to do so intelligently, directed by its best men, "its Heroes." His essay on "Model Prisons" was written following a visit with a friend to an exemplary or model prison in London. There, he says, twelve hundred prisoners are housed in clean buildings where they are well fed and given opportunity to learn in good schools under intelligent teachers. By the "Methods of Kindness," the Captain of the prisoners is training thieves and murderers to do nothing. Yet Carlyle asserts that this system is the worst investment of benevolence that human ingenuity can devise. It is impossible to bestow benevolence on an unworthy man without withdrawing it from a worthy recipient. Around the collection of attractive buildings cluster hundreds of dingy, poor, and dirty dwellings, where nonsinners, not yet a part of the "Devil's regiment," are forced to live. If Carlyle were doing the job, he would sweep the scoundrels somewhere out of the way, and provide good food and good teachers for those who were not criminally inclined. He declares himself sick of the "sugary, disastrous jargon of philanthrophy, the reign of love, the new era of universal brotherhood, that provides, not a Paradise to the well-deserving, but a Paradise to all-and-sundry." It operates under the guise of religion. Then he goes on to say:

Not the least disgusting feature of this Gospel according to the Platform is its reference to religion, and even to the Christian Religion, as an authority and mandate for what it does. Christian Re-

420

ligion? Does the Christian or any religion prescribe love of scoundrels, then? I hope it prescribes **a healthy hatred of scoundrels;** —otherwise what am I, in Heaven's name, to make of it? Me, for one, it will not serve as a religion on those strange terms. Just hatred of scoundrels, I say; fixed, irreconcilable, inexorable enmity to the enemies of God; this, and not love for them, and incessant whitewashing, and dressing and cockering of them, must, if you look into it, be the backbone of any human religion whatsoever.

Hearts of oak

Source: HEART OF OAK (Stanza I)
Author: David Garrick (1717-1779)
First published: 1759
Type of work: Song lyric

Context: The phrase "hearts of oak" is an ancient one and traditionally denotes strength, stoutness of heart, toughness, and unyielding determination. It occurs in Aristophanes' *The Wasps* (422 B.C.): "We'll summon our hearts of oak"; Horace uses a related expression; it appears in the anonymous *Old Meg of Herefordshire* (1609), "Here is a dozen of yonkers that have hearts of oake at fourscore yeares." Cervantes employed the term in *Don Quixote de la Mancha* in 1615 ("Soul of fibre and heart of oak") and Susanna Centlivre, in the epilogue to her play *The Cruel Gift* (1717) asks, "Where are the rough brave Britons to be found/ With Hearts of Oak, so much of old renowned?" More familiar than these, perhaps, are two songs which both contain the expression. One, by David Garrick, appeared in 1759; the other, by Samuel James Arnold, in 1811. Garrick was a great actor who also possessed considerable literary ability; Arnold (1774–1852) was a British dramatist who wrote and produced popular operas. One of these, *The Americans,* contains a song entitled "The Death of Nelson;" the music for it was composed by the famous tenor John Braham, whose rich and powerful voice could span nearly three octaves. He wrote part or all of the music for many operas in which he performed. "The Death of Nelson" became a well-known popular song and so remained for many years. In it appear the following lines: "Our ships were British oak,/ And hearts of oak our men." The song by Garrick, however, has probably enjoyed a wider fame. It was set to music by William Boyce (c.1710–1779), one of England's finest native composers, and was first performed in *The Harlequin's Invasion, or A Christmas Gambol,* given at Drury Lane Theatre on December 31, 1759. This festive affair included a pantomime by Garrick. The song achieved immediate fame, becoming one of England's great national airs and ranking in popularity with "Rule, Britannia." To this day it remains a standard patriotic number. The first and last stanzas are given below; the chorus as quoted for the first stanza is the original. The second chorus quoted is a variant, and perhaps more familiar version:

421

Come, cheer up, my lads! 'tis to glory we steer,
To add something more to this wonderful year:
To honor we call you, not press you like slaves;
For who are so free as the sons of the waves?
   Heart of oak are our ships,
   Heart of oak are our men,
    We always are ready:
    Steady, boys, steady!
We'll fight and we'll conquer again and again.

     . . .

Britannia triumphant, her ships sweep the sea;
Her standard is Justice—her watchword, "Be free."
Then cheer up, my lads! with one heart let us sing,
"Our soldiers, our sailors, our statesmen, our King,"
   Hearts of oak are our ships,
   Hearts of oak are our men,
    We always are ready,
    Steady, boys, steady,
We'll fight and will conquer again and again.

Heaven first taught letters for some wretch's aid

Source: ELOISA TO ABELARD (Line 51)
Author: Alexander Pope (1688-1744)
First published: 1717
Type of work: Poetic monologue

Context: Pope is here giving verse form to John Hughes' translation of the letters of the famous medieval lovers. Abelard was the learned clergyman, philosopher, and theologian who fell in love with the daughter of a friend. The intensely passionate love affair was discovered by the authorities, who confined Abelard to a monastery and Eloisa to a convent. The present poem supposes that after many years separation Eloisa accidentally comes upon a letter written by Abelard to a friend in which he recounts his misfortune. This letter reawakens in Eloisa the old emotions, and she speaks to herself as if she were addressing her lost lover:

   Yet write, oh write me all, that I may join
Griefs to thy griefs, and echo sighs to thine.
Nor foes nor fortune take this pow'r away.
And is my Abelard less kind than they?
Tears still are mine, and those I need not spare,
Love but demands what else were shed in pray'r;
No happier task these faded eyes pursue,
To read and weep is all they now can do.
   Then share thy pain, allow that sad relief;
Ah more than share it! give me all thy grief.
Heav'n first taught letters for some wretch's aid,

422

Some banish'd lover, or some captive maid;
They live, they speak, they breathe what love inspires,
Warm from the soul, and faithful to its fires,
The virgin's wish without her fears impart,
Excuse the blush, and pour out all the heart,
Speed the soft intercourse from soul to soul,
And waft a sigh from Indus to the Pole.

Heaven has no rage like love to hatred turned

Source: THE MOURNING BRIDE (Act III, sc. ii)
Author: William Congreve (1670-1729)
First published: 1697
Type of work: Dramatic tragedy

Context: The Mourning Bride, first performed at the New Theatre, where Congreve's *Love for Love* brought up its curtain for the first time two years before, was Congreve's only tragedy, but except for Shakespeare's work it was the most frequently performed of any English tragedy for a century. It gains part of its effect from the dramatist's choice of blank verse to tell its improbable story. Few read it today but fewer will fail to recognize the line spoken by Almeria, Princess of Granada, first played by the famous Mrs. Bracegirdle, as the curtain rises: "Music has Charms to soothe a savage Breast," and, she adds, "to soften rocks, or bend a knotted oak." The Spanish scene was popular with Restoration theatre-goers because the complicated plots of Spain provided a model for intrigues. Dryden, driven by financial necessity, devoted twenty years to turning out plays for "The Merry Monarch," Charles II and his successors. In selecting themes he hoped would be popular, he wrote *The Conquest of Granada* (1669), *The Spanish Friar* (1691), and *Don Sebastian* (1690). So Congreve, eager for a comeback after an unpopular play, chose a situation used in scores of plays and stories of Spain, the reappearance of someone shipwrecked and thought lost forever. The decision of critics was that while the tragedy engaged the attention, pleased the ear, and charmed the eye, it never touched the heart. Yet Mrs. Sarah Kemble Siddons (1775–1831) increased her Shakespearean reputation with the role of Zara, and other actresses delighted in it. Actors, however, were not so happy about the chief male character, Osmyn-Alphonso. Though given lines to start Act II: "How rev'rend is the face of this tall pile . . . and shoot a chillness to my trembling heart," which Samuel Johnson called the most poetical image in the English language, neither Garrick nor Kemble could bring the part to life. From audiences, it had a mixed reception at first. Here was the most important comic writer of his era offering a tragedy. Dryden, at the first night, declared himself enraptured, but he must have had trouble following the plot. Some years before the play begins, Almeria, daughter of King Manuel of Granada, fell in love with Alphonso, a noble

423

subject of King Anselmo of Valencia. They were married aboard a ship just before it wrecked on an African shore. As the play starts, Manuel returns after a victorious war with captives, Queen Zara and Osmyn, a nobleman who turns out to be Alphonso. Complications begin. Almeria must conceal the identity of her restored husband. Zara, in love with Osmyn, must let King Manuel think she loves him, to save herself and Osmyn; and Osmyn must pretend to love Zara to save himself and Almeria. Meanwhile, the king's favorite, the villainous Gonzalez, schemes for a marriage between his son Garcia and Almeria, to win the throne. The denouement of this typical Elizabethan "drama of blood" is swift and simple. Everybody discovers the secrets of the others. The king takes Osmyn's place in prison to catch Zara. Gonzalez gets there first and stabs the disguised king. Zara finds the body and, thinking it Osmyn, drinks poison. Almeria enters, and seeing the double tragedy, is about to drink the same potion when Alphonso and his retinue appear to provide a happy ending. Though an abrupt change of tone, it helped the popularity of the play. In the dramatic close of Act III, Zara has one of the fine poetic speeches that gave actresses of the early eighteenth century their big moments. Having left Osmyn in his dungeon and preparing to sacrifice and scheme for his release, Zara returns and finds him embracing Almeria.

ZARA

Vile and ingrate! too late thou shalt repent
The base injustice thou hast done my love.
Yes, thou shalt know, spite of thy past Distress,
And all those ills which thou so long hast mourn'd;
Heav'n has no Rage like Love to hatred turn'd,
Nor Hell a Fury like a Woman scorn'd.

The heavenly rhetoric of thine eye

Source: LOVE'S LABOUR'S LOST (Act IV, sc. iii, l. 60)
Author: William Shakespeare (1564-1616)
First published: 1598
Type of work: Dramatic comedy

Context: Berowne enters this scene with a paper in his hand which is a second poem he has written for his love. While he stands in the park, the king enters, also holding a paper. As the king begins reading, unaware of the other's presence, Berowne realizes that he also is reading a love poem. But as the king is considering sending the poem to his love, he hears Longaville approaching and quickly steps out of sight. Longaville is carrying a paper with a love poem which he too begins reading aloud. Each man expresses doubt that his poem is an effective expression of his passion. The first line of Longaville's poem asks, "Did not" the alluring and expressive eyes of his lover lead him to break his vow not to associate with women. He goes on to explain that he did not break his vow, because his love is a goddess; it is an earthly woman to whom his vow applies.

Did not **the heavenly rhetoric of thine eye,**
  'Gainst whom the world cannot hold argument,
Persuade my heart to this false perjury?
Vows for thee broke deserve not punishment.
A woman I forswore, but I will prove,
  Thou being a goddess, I forswore not thee.
My vow was earthly, thou a heavenly love.
  Thy grace being gained cures all disgrace in me.
Vows are but breath, and breath a vapour is.
  Then thou, fair sun, which on my earth dost shine,
Exhalest this vapour-vow; in thee it is.
  If broken then, it is no fault of mine:
If by me broke, what fool is not so wise
To lose an oath to win a paradise?

Heaven's gift takes earth's abatement

Source: ONE WORD MORE (IX, Line 73)
Author: Robert Browning (1812-1889)
First published: 1855
Type of work: Dedicatory epilogue

Context: Browning wrote this poem as an epilogue to dedicate a volume of poetry to his wife, Elizabeth Browning. In it, he discusses the importance of a private existence for the artist apart from his public personage. "God be thanked, the meanest of his creatures/ Boasts two soulsides, one to face the world with,/ One to show a woman he loves her!" The poet wishes he could turn to a new medium to express his love for a woman as did Dante, who painted to honor Beatrice, or as did Rafael, who wrote a century of sonnets for his love. These evidences of love are more precious to other lovers than are all the masterpieces that the artists created in their fields. An artist wishes, at least once, to be only a man and to be judged for the joy of his love and not by the critical standards applicable to his public performance. There follows a lengthy comparison between the poet and the prophet. Both Moses and the poet live with heaven-sent gifts which, at times, they may wish to ignore but cannot:

. . . no artist lives and loves, that longs not
Once, and only once, for one only
(Ah the prize!), to find his love a language
Fit and fair and simple and sufficient—

425

Using nature that's an art to others,
Not, this one time, art that's turned his nature.

    • • •

So to be the man and leave the artist,
Gain the man's joy, miss the artist's sorrow.

Wherefore? **Heaven's gift takes earth's abatement!**
He who smites the rock and spreads the water,

    • • •

Even he, the minute makes immortal,
Proves, perchance, but mortal in the minute,
Desecrates, belike, the deed in doing.

The heavens themselves blaze forth the death of princes

Source: JULIUS CAESAR (Act II, sc. ii, l. 31)
Author: William Shakespeare (1564-1616)
First published: 1623
Type of work: Dramatic tragedy

Context: In his home in Rome, Julius Caesar arises early, and, still in his nightgown, discusses with Calphurnia, his wife, whether to go to the Senate as he has intended, since this is the Ides of March, the day against which a soothsayer has warned him. Calphurnia pleads with him to stay at home, recounting the ominous events of the night reported by a watchman —in addition to thunder and lightning, a lion has whelped in the street, graves have opened for the dead to escape, fiery soldiers have battled in the clouds, raining blood upon the Capitol, and the streets have been filled with the sounds of horses whinnying, of the dying groaning, and of ghosts shrieking. Caesar, contending that the portents of the night are directed at all the world as much as at him, continues the discussion:

CAESAR
What can be avoided
Whose end is purposed by the mighty gods?
Yet Caesar shall go forth; for these predictions
Are to the world in general, as to Caesar.

CALPHURNIA
When beggars die, there are no comets seen;
The heavens themselves blaze forth the death of princes.

426

The heir of all ages, in the foremost files of time

Source: LOCKSLEY HALL (Line 178)
Author: Alfred, Lord Tennyson (1809-1892)
First published: 1842
Type of work: Dramatic monologue

Context: Locksley Hall is Tennyson's first poem of social protest; but it is also an interesting prophecy of the world to come, all the more remarkable when the date of its composition is considered. As the poem opens, the poet stands on the beach near his home, Locksley Hall. He is bidding farewell to the scenes of his boyhood, where he had ranged the moors and beaches, "nourishing a youth sublime/ With the fairy tales of science, and the long result of Time." Here he had glimpsed the wonders of the future; here also he had loved his cousin Amy. She, obeying the customs of the day, had abided by the decision of her parents and married a country gentleman they had chosen for her. The forsaken poet calls her shallow-hearted, "Puppet to a father's threat, and servile to a shrewish tongue." The forecast he gives of her married life is bleak and pitiless: "thou shalt lower to his level day by day,/ What is fine within thee growing coarse to sympathize with clay./ As the husband is, the wife is: thou art mated with a clown,/ And the grossness of his nature will have weight to drag thee down./ He will hold thee, when his passion shall have spent its novel force,/ Something better than his dog, a little dearer than his horse." Torturing himself in this fashion, and feeling it would be better if she were dead, the poet foresees that she will in time be ignored or tolerated by her husband, but will be compensated in some measure by a child. The poet feels he "must mix with action, lest I wither by despair." He yearns for the past, but cannot recapture it: "Knowledge comes, but wisdom lingers, and I linger on the shore,/ And the individual withers, and the world is more and more." He thinks of renouncing civilization completely, going to some island in the South Seas and taking a savage wife who will "rear my dusky race." But even as he considers this course, he knows he cannot follow it:

Iron-jointed, supple-sinew'd, they shall dive, and they shall run,
Catch the wild goat by the hair, and hurl their lances in the sun;

Whistle back the parrot's call, and leap the rainbows of the brooks,
Not with blinded eyesight poring over miserable books—

Fool, again the dream, the fancy! but I *know* my words are wild,
But I count the grey barbarian lower than the Christian child.

I, to herd with narrow foreheads, vacant of our glorious gains,
Like a beast with lower pleasures, like a beast with lower pains!

Mated with a squalid savage—what to me were sun or clime?
I the heir of all the ages, in the foremost files of time—

I that rather held it better men should perish one by one,
Than that earth should stand at gaze like Joshua's moon in Ajalon!

Heirs of all eternity

Source: LOVE'S LABOUR'S LOST (Act I, sc. i, l. 7)
Author: William Shakespeare (1564-1616)
First published: 1598
Type of work: Dramatic comedy

Context: King Ferdinand of Navarre and his lords in attendance, Berowne, Longaville, and Dumaine, take an oath to forsake courtly pleasures and to devote three years to studying and fasting, thus making of Navarre "a little Academe." Ferdinand suggests that fame will defeat death's devouring disgrace, and make of the scholars "heirs of all eternity."

> KING
> Let fame, that all hunt after in their lives,
> Live registered upon our brazen tombs,
> And then grace us, in the disgrace of death;
> When, spite of cormorant devouring Time,
> Th' endeavour of this present breath may buy
> That honour which shall bate his scythe's keen edge,
> And make us **heirs of all eternity.**
> Therefore, brave conquerors—for so you are,
> That war against your own affections,
> And the huge Army of the world's desires—
> Our late edict shall strongly stand in force.
> Navarre shall be the wonder of the world.
> Our court shall be a little Academe,
> Still and contemplative in living art.

• • •

The Hell within him

Source: PARADISE LOST (Book IV, l. 20)
Author: John Milton (1608-1674)
First published: 1667
Type of work: Epic poem

Context: Satan and other angels, unsuccessful in their attempt to snatch from God the control of Heaven, are cast into the burning lake of Hell. The fallen angels meet in council to discuss making another attempt to gain Heaven, but decide instead to explore an alternate course of ven-

428

geance. Since they have heard of the creation of the Earth, Satan's offer to attempt revenge in this sphere is agreed upon, but as Satan approaches the Garden of Eden and envisions the corruption of the innocence of Adam and Eve, he is torn by doubt and despair:

> . . . horror and doubt distract
> His troubl'd thoughts, and from the bottom stirr
> **The Hell within him,** for within him Hell
> He brings, and round about him, nor from Hell
> One step no more then from himself can fly
> By change of place: Now conscience wakes despair
> That slumbered, wakes the bitter memorie
> Of what he was, what is, and what must be
> Worse; of worse deeds worse sufferings must ensue.
> Sometimes towards Eden which now in his view
> Lay pleasant, his grieved look he fixes sad,
> Sometimes towards Heav'n and the full-blazing Sun,
> Which now sat high in his Meridian Towre:
> Then much revolving, thus in sighs began.

Hence, O hence ye that are uninitiate

Source: THE AENEID (Book VI, as translated by John Jackson)
Author: Virgil (Publius Vergilius Maro, 70-19 B.C.)
First transcribed: 29-19 B.C.
Type of work: Epic poem

Context: Virgil died while making the final revisions of his Homeric epic about Aeneas, the legendary founder of Rome. Augustus Caesar, in whose honor it had been composed, ordered the work preserved. In the early books, Aeneas, who had fled from burning Troy carrying his aged father Anchises, tells the story of his flight to Dido, Queen of Carthage. Warned in a dream by Mercury that the queen intends to keep him in Carthage, Aeneas resumes his journey. At Sicily, Anchises dies and is buried. Finally in Book VI Aeneas reaches the shores of Italy at Cumae, famous for its Sibyl or prophetess. She grants Aeneas the privilege of visiting his father in the underworld, and counsels him about the proper religious cere- monies at the Cavern that marks the descent to Avernus. Proserpine or Persephone, the goddess of fertility, wife of Pluto or Hades, is compelled to remain underground part of each year because of the four pomegranate seeds she had eaten when kidnaped and taken there. Hecate, the moon goddess, is her attendant in the lower world, beyond the River Styx, the realm of the Stygian king. The Furies or Erinyes or goddesses of vengeance are the daughters of Earth or Ura- nius. Night is Earth's sister. When all is ready at the Cavern entrance, about sunrise, the uninitiated, that is, not instructed in the religious myste- ries, are ordered to leave the holy for- est. The Sibyl has provided four black steers and a lamb whose fleece is

429

black. She has been:

> . . . calling the while on Hecate, queen alike in Heaven and Hell. Others set the knife to the throat and caught the warm blood in vessels. Himself, Aeneas, smote with the sword a ewe-lamb of sable fleece to the mother of the Furies and her mighty sister, and to thee, Prosperpine, a barren heifer. Then to the Stygian king he reared altars by night and placed on the flames whole carcasses of bulls, pouring rich oil over the burning flesh. But, lo, about the first rays of the orient sun, earth began to moan under foot, and the ridges of forest to tremble, and hounds seemed to bay through the twilight as the goddess drew nigh. **"Hence, O hence,"** cried the prophetess, **"ye that are uninitiate!** Withdraw ye from all the grove!"** . . .

Hence these tears

Source: THE LADY OF ANDROS (Act I, sc. i)
Author: Terence (Publius Terentius Afer, c. 190-159 B.C.)
First transcribed: Second century, B.C.
Type of work: Dramatic comedy

Context: Andria (The Lady of Andros), Terence's first play, was produced in 166 B.C., when the playwright was on the threshold of his career. In the drama Pamphilus, a young man of good family, is deeply in love with Glycerium, a girl from Andros. Gino, Pamphilus' father, recently returned home, fears that his son, despite the lad's excellent reputation, has fallen in love with Glycerium's sister, the courtesan Chrysis. When the father attends Chrysis' funeral he discovers the truth. His discovery makes him very unhappy, for he wishes Pamphilus to marry another, the daughter of his friend Chremes, a girl with a good dowry and a good family. All turns out well, as it does in comedy, for in the end Glycerium proves to be a long-lost daughter of the same Chremes. In the first scene of Act I, Simo tells his servant, Sosia, how he discovered that his son loves Glycerium. What he learns is given added proof when Pamphilus prevents the girl from throwing herself on her sister's funeral pyre. The quotation, "hinc illae lacrumae" in the original Latin, has been variously translated, as the following context illustrates:

SIMO
. . . In short, out of feeling for him I went to the funeral myself, still without suspicion of anything being amiss.

SOSIA
Bless me, Sir, what do you mean?

430

SIMO

You shall be told. The body was brought out and we followed. Presently among the women in attendance I caught sight of one girl whose figure was—

SOSIA

Not bad, perhaps?

SIMO

—and her face, Sosia, so modest and so charming, it couldn't be beaten. As her grief seemed to me deeper than the others' and her figure was more elegant and ladylike than the others', I went up to the waiting-women and asked who she was. They told me she was Chrysis' sister. It struck me at once. Ha, that's the secret, **that's the source of his tears,** that's his compassion.

Hercules is not only known by his foot

Source: HYDRIOTAPHIA: URN BURIAL (Chapter 3)
Author: Sir Thomas Browne (1605-1682)
First published: 1658
Type of work: Philosophy

Context: This philosophical physician and scientist set out to write a report concerning some forty or fifty Roman funeral urns which were exhumed near Norwich. His speculative nature led him beyond the bounds of a mere scientific treatise to a disquisition on burial customs in general, ranging of course through his vast knowledge of classical literature. In Chapter 3 he discusses not only the effects of burial on the remains discovered but digresses to consider generally the information to be derived from exhumed remains, and reflects upon some classical examples:

. . . When Alexander opened the Tomb of Cyrus, the remaining bones discovered his proportion, whereof urnall fragments afford but a bad conjecture, and have this disadvantage of grave enterrments, that they leave us ignorant of most personal discoveries. For since bones afford not only rectitude and stability, but figure unto the body; it is no impossible physiognomy to conjecture at fleshy appendencies; and after what shape the muscles and carnous parts might hang in their full consistences. A full spread Cariola shews a well-shaped horse behind, handsome formed skulls give some analogy of fleshy resemblance. A critical view of bones makes a good distinction of sexes. Even colour is not beyond conjecture; since it is hard to be deceived in the distinction of Negro's skulls. Dante's characters are to be found in skulls as well as faces. **Hercules is not only known by his foot.** Other parts make out their comproportions, and inferences upon the whole or parts.

431

And since the dimensions of the head measure the whole body, and the figure thereof gives conjecture of the principal faculties; physiognomy outlives our selves, and ends not in our graves.

Herded wolves, bold only to pursue

Source: ADONAIS (Stanza 28)
Author: Percy Bysshe Shelley (1792-1822)
First published: 1821
Type of work: Elegy

Context: In his elegy on the death of John Keats (1795-1821), who died of tuberculosis in Rome at the age of twenty-six years, Shelley severely blames the reviewer of Keats' *Endymion* for inflicting a wound on the spirit of the young poet that led to the bursting of a blood-vessel in his lung and his subsequent death. Shelley says that everything in nature renews itself with the coming of spring: the ants, the bees, the swallows reappear; fresh leaves and flowers deck dead winter's bier; the lizard and the snake awake from their trance: only Adonais, or Keats, cannot come back; he will awake no more. Misery invokes Urania, the mother Muse of Adonais, to arise and go to the mournful place where Adonais lies. She flees to him and begs him to revive to comfort her; in her grief she exclaims that she would gladly die, as he did, but as an immortal she is chained to time and cannot depart from this world. She says that he was defenseless against the world; he should have waited until the time when wisdom and scorn would have made him impervious to envious thrusts. Wolves in bands, with courage only to pursue that which flees from them, the obscene raven, and the vultures dare not attack the Pythian of the age, Lord Byron, who treated his critics with the contempt they deserved in *English Bards and Scotch Reviewers.*

"The **herded wolves, bold only to pursue;**
  The obscene ravens, clamorous o'er the dead;
  The vultures to the conqueror's banner true
  Who feed where Desolation first has fed,
  And whose wings rain contagion;—how they fled,
  When, like Apollo, from his golden bow
  The Pythian of the age one arrow sped
  And smiled!—The spoilers tempt no second blow,
They fawn on the proud feet that spurn them lying low."

Here today and gone tomorrow

Source: THE LUCKY CHANCE, OR AN ALDERMAN'S BARGAIN (Act IV)
Author: Aphra Behn (1640-1689)
First published: 1687
Type of work: Dramatic comedy

Context: Lady Fulbank, who has spent a night with Gayman without his knowing her identity, asks him why he was so quick to leave her at a party the night before. Gayman tells her he loves her and offers a token of his esteem and affection: a ring which she, in her unknown identity gave him while his bedroom companion! When she asks about the ring, telling him she knows he is without money, he tells her that he had it the night before from a female devil who entertained him in a bedroom; he describes the "female devil" as like a "canvas bag full of wooden ladles." Lady Fulbank says to herself that she would be insulted at such a description of herself, except that she knows it is untrue. As they talk, her husband, Sir Cautious, comes in, suspicious that Gayman is about to make (or already has made) him a cuckold. Lady Fulbank leaves, and Gayman tells Sir Cautious about the "female devil." They also argue about money that Gayman has lost through Sir Cautious and a mortgage on his lands. Noysey and Bearjest join them; when Gayman leaves, they speak about him and his way of life, using his real name, Wastall:

SIR CAUTIOUS
Do you know this Wastall, Sir!—[*to Noysey.*]

NOYSEY
Know him sir, Ay too well—

BEARJEST
The World's well amended with him Captain, since I lost my money to him and you at the George in *White Fryars.*

NOYSEY
Ay poor fellow—he's sometimes up and sometime down, as the Dice favour him.—

BEARJEST
Faith and that's pity; but how came he so fine o' th' sudden: but last Week he borrowed eighteen pence of me on his Wast Belt to pay his dinner in an Ordinary.

BELMOUR
Were you so cruel Sir to take it?

433

NOYSEY

We are not all one Mans Children; faith Sir; we are **here to Day and gone to Morrow**—

He's for the morning

Source: A GRAMMARIAN'S FUNERAL (Line 24)
Author: Robert Browning (1812-1889)
First published: 1855
Type of work: Dramatic monologue

Context: This poem is the final tribute of a group of students to their dead master, a Greek scholar. As day breaks, they carry his corpse to the mountain top for burial. Their song catches the spirit of those scholars who thirsted after knowledge in the early Renaissance, but they inadvertently reveal that their master chose Knowledge to the exclusion of Life. This unknowing admission by his students shows that the scholar had, in effect, denied the very premise of Renaissance humanism, which originally motivated his search for knowledge. The students praise their master's choice: "That before living he'd learn how to live—No end to learning." They never realize the implications of his withdrawal from both life and humanity. Triumphantly, they bear him to his resting place, isolated from common man:

> That's the appropriate country; there, man's thought,
> Rarer, intenser,
> Self-gathered for an outbreak, as it ought,
> Chafes in the censer.
> Leave we the unlettered plain its herd and crop;
> Seek we a sepulture
> On a tall mountain, citied to the top,
> Crowded with culture!
> . . .
> Our low life was the level's and the night's;
> **He's for the morning.**
> Step to a tune, square chests, erect each head,
> 'Ware the beholders!
> This is our master, famous, calm and dead,
> Borne on our shoulders.

He's only a pauper, whom nobody owns

Source: THE PAUPER'S DRIVE
Author: Thomas Noel (1799-1861)
First published: 1841
Type of work: Humanitarian poem

Context: Though Thomas Noel, the English poet, published a volume of poetry, *Rhymes and Roundelays,* in 1841, only one of its ˙contents survives today, "Rocked in the Cradle of the Deep," set to music for the delight of a basso profundo. He also included in the volume a melancholic picture of a pauper driven unaccompanied to a churchyard for burial. Only at his death, says the poet, did the poor man make a noise in the world, as the rickety hearse clattered over the cobbles. At only this moment, writes Noel ironically, did he approach gentility, for at last he rode through London streets in a coach. The poet adds a satirical reminder to other bums that they, too, will have their chance to be a "gemman" (gentleman). It is a poem of six stanzas, each of which has as refrain, the quoted line.

There's a grim one-horse hearse in a jolly round trot,—
To the churchyard a pauper is going, I wot;
The road it is rough, and the hearse has no springs,
And hark to the dirge which the mad driver sings:
 Rattle his bones over the stones!
 He's only a pauper whom nobody owns!

O, where are the mourners? Alas! there are none;
He has left not a gap in the world, now he's gone,—
Not a tear in the eye of child, woman, or man,
To the grave with his carcass as fast as you can:
 Rattle his bones over the stones!
 He's only a pauper whom nobody owns!

· · ·

You bumpkins! who stare at your brother conveyed,
Behold what respect to a cloddy is paid!
And be joyful to think, when by death you're laid low,
You've a chance to the grave like a gemman to go.
 Rattle his bones over the stones!
 He's only a pauper whom nobody owns!

High Heaven rejects the lore of nicely-calculated less or more

Source: ECCLESIASTICAL SONNETS (Part III, 43, "Inside of King's College Chapel, Cambridge")
Author: William Wordsworth (1770-1850)
First published: 1822
Type of work: Religious sonnet

Context: One of the most beautiful buildings at Cambridge University is King's College Chapel, a Gothic church commissioned by Henry VI (1422–1461); however, the chapel cost so much to construct that many of the more critical minds, both while it was being built and later, felt that the expense was disproportionate to its use, for rather than being a public place of worship, it was designed only for the students. Wordsworth, being by nature opposed to the type of thought that measures beauty by practicability, had no patience with these critics; though deeply concerned with the plight of his fellow men, he became more and more conservative as he grew older. Seeing religion as a means whereby men can find the stoic endurance that enables them to withstand great suffering, he expresses his belief in the ability of great beauty, especially that of Christian art, to uplift the worshiper. Such beauty cannot be reckoned in money, only in the spiritual peace that comes to the beholder.

> Give all thou canst; **high Heaven rejects the lore**
> **Of nicely-calculated less or more;**
> So deemed the man who fashioned for the sense
> These lofty pillars, spread that branching roof
> Self-poised, and scooped into ten thousand cells,
> Where light and shade repose, where music dwells
> Lingering—and wandering on as loth to die;
> Like thoughts whose very sweetness yieldeth proof
> That they were born for immortality.

Him first, Him last, Him midst, and without end

Source: PARADISE LOST (Book V, l. 165)
Author: John Milton (1608-1674)
First published: 1667
Type of work: Epic poem

Context: Morning comes and Adam wonders to find Eve still asleep, looking as if she had had an unquiet night. He gently wakens her, saying that they have their work to do. Eve says that she has had a disturbing dream. She thought that as she slept, Adam called to her; in trying to find him, she arrived at the tree of prohibited knowledge. By the tree was a figure like the angels that inhabit the garden by day. The spirit wondered why knowledge was so despised that no one ate of the tree. He plucked a fruit and tasted it, much to Eve's horror; he was, however, delighted with the taste; the fruit, he said, makes gods of men. He then urged Eve to eat, as it would make her a goddess. He pressed the food to her mouth so that she had to taste it. The result was that she flew up to the clouds in exultation. The guide disappeared, and Eve sank down and fell asleep. Adam says that he believes the dream to be of evil origin, but evil thoughts can enter the minds of the most pure and leave no spot behind. They go to the field and begin their morning prayer, praising their Maker in umpremeditated song:

> These are thy glorious works, Parent of good,
> Almighty, thine this universal frame,
> Thus wondrous fair; Thyself how wondrous then!

436

Unspeakable, who sit'st above these heavens
To us invisible or dimly seen
In these thy lowest works, yet these declare
Thy goodness beyond thought, and power divine:
Speak ye who best can tell, ye sons of light,
Angels, for ye behold Him, and with songs
And choral symphonies, day without night,
Circle His throne rejoicing, ye in heaven,
On earth join all ye creatures to extol
Him first, Him last, Him midst, and without end.

Him that makes shoes go barefoot himself

Source: ANATOMY OF MELANCHOLY (Democritus Junior to the Reader)
Author: Robert Burton (1577-1640)
First published: 1621-1651
Type of work: Essays

Context: Robert Burton was an amazing early English writer. Born at Lindley, Leicestershire, he entered Brasenose College, Oxford, at the age of sixteen, and after twenty years got his Bachelor of Divinity degree from Christ College. He remained associated with Oxford University until his death, while, at the same time, filling several positions as a clergyman. In thirty years as a scholar he read widely in a variety of fields, striving to become a universal man. In 1621, seven years after getting his B.D. degree, he published the first edition of what he ironically called *The Anatomy of Melancholy,* intending in three Partitions or Parts to analyze the causes, species, symptoms, and cure of melancholia. The first edition was published under the pseudonym of "Democritus Junior," but a final "Note to the Reader," dated "At my Study in Christ Church, Oxon., Dec. 5, 1620," revealed the secret by his signature of Robert Burton. Other editions with corrections and additions appeared during his lifetime, the sixth of which, the last published before his death, was dedicated to his patron, Lord George Berkeley, who got him appointed vicar of Segrave, Leicestershire, in 1630. The original Democritus was the greatest of the Greek physical philosophers. He flourished in the late fifth century B.C., and was known as the "Laughing Philosopher." However, in Burton's description he was "a little wearish old man, very melancholic by nature, and much given to solitariness." And so Burton, as "Democritus Junior," "writ of melancholy by being busy to avoid melancholy." For most of his statements, he quotes some classical author, "serving a warmed-over dish," yet the result inspired Milton, Sterne, Thackeray, and Lamb, while Samuel Johnson declared it was the only book capable of forcing him to get out of bed two hours ahead of time to read it. In

437

the book's hundred-page introduction, the author is led from one topic to another, telling anecdotes and quoting classical and modern authors, making it a pleasure to read, but impossible to summarize afterward. In one paragraph, the author looks about him and wonders how the Democritus of twenty-two centuries earlier would react to cruelties of seventeenth century man. He mentions the slaughter of war, and the difference between punishment accorded a poor sheep stealer, hanged for appropriating the property of others, and the honor given a general who robs a whole province. Then in catalog form, Burton lists some of the sights that would disgust the Greek philosopher. To these sights he adds others, giving an earlier form of our current proverb about cobblers' children going shoeless.

> To see a servant able to buy out his master, him that carries the mace worth more than the magistrate, which Plato absolutely forbids, Epictetus abhors; . . . **him that makes shoes go barefoot himself;** . . . a toiling drudge starve, a drone flourish!

Hireling wolves, whose gospel is their maw

Source: SONNET XVI ("To the Lord General Cromwell, May 1652," Last line)
Author: John Milton (1608-1674)
First published: 1694
Type of work: Sonnet

Context: One proposal made to the Parliamentary Committee for the Propagation of the Gospel was that no one should be allowed to speak from a pulpit who had not been certified by two or more "godly and orthodox ministers." It was in protest to this proposed restriction on freedom of speech, in which Milton believed intensely, that the poet addressed this sonnet to Oliver Cromwell, then General of the Parliamentary armies and soon to be named Lord Protector of the Commonwealth of England. Milton praised first Cromwell's military achievements and then appealed to him to secure the victories of peace and to protect freedom of conscience.

> Cromwell, our cheif of men, who through a cloud
> Not of warr onely, but detractions rude,
> Guided by faith & matchless Fortitude
> To peace & truth thy glorious way hast plough'd,
> And on the neck of crowned Fortune proud
> Hast reard Gods Trophies, & his work pursu'd,
> While Darwen stream with blood of Scotts imbru'd,
> And Dunbarr feild resounds thy praises loud,
> And Worsters laureat wreath; yet much remaines
> To conquer still; peace hath her victories

438

No less renownd then warr, new foes aries
Threatning to bind our soules with secular chaines:
Helpe us to save free Conscience from the paw
Of **hireling wolves whose Gospell is their maw.**

His heart runs away with his head

Source: WHO WANTS A GUINEA (Act I, sc. i)
Author: George Colman the Younger (1762-1836)
First published: 1805
Type of work: Dramatic comedy

Context: Mrs. Elizabeth Inchbald (1753–1821), whose maiden name was Sampson (or Simpson), turned from acting to publishing, not only her own plays and novels, but two valuable collections of plays, *The British Theatre* (1806–1809) and *The Modern Theatre* (1809–1812). She used the original stage prompt-books. It is in volume III of the latter that George Colman's five-act comedy appears, as performed at the Theatre-Royal, Covent Garden. It was immensely popular, running for a long time at its initial appearance, and was later revised as *Jonathan in England* (1829) by the American actor James H. Hackett (1800–1871). A critic in 1839 declared "Colman's comedies satirize past ages whose gentry had more character than at present." Action begins at Heartly's house in Yorkshire, near the coast. The day is supposed to be an object lesson of the superiority of "thinking benevolence" over "haste in charity." The logic of the head is better at making decisions than the sentiment of the heart. The village has suffered a terrible fire that consumed two-thirds of the houses. John Torrent, who has just bought the manor house, has come to town. In the opening conversation, Heartly represents the people eager to help those in need but intending to do so judiciously. By contrast, miserly Hogmore will not take fuel needed for his fireside to warm others. And Torrent is typical of those who have money and are spendthrift in their use of it. Solomon Gundy whose every sentence is scarred by badly-pronounced French, has just appeared with a letter from the new landowner.

SOLOMON
His carriage broke into twenty *morso's*. He wanted to send you a *billy*—no messenger at hand—I've brought it. He gave me a guinea; I called him an angel; he bid me run like a devil; I told him I would; so I have, and there's the contention [*Gives a letter.*]

HEARTLY [*reading the letter.*]
"Dear Heartly, I have just *tumbled* into my estate. Let none of the villagers know who I am till I get to my house. I hate fuss— Don't say I am a rich man. Come to me in the alehouse. JOHN

439

TORRENT."

[*Speaking.*] He arrives just in time to assist his tenants in distress; but I dread his impetuosity, and carelessness of discrimination. Even in haste to make people happy, he defeats his own purpose. **His heart runs away with his head,** and he often produces most harm when he shows most benevolence. I'll wait on the gentleman, Solomon, directly.

His helmet now shall make a hive for bees

Source: POLYHYMNIA ("A Sonnet," Line 7)
Author: George Peele (1558?-1597)
First published: 1590
Type of work: Song lyric

Context: During the reign of Queen Elizabeth I, it became customary to entertain her with a grand military pageant and tournament every seventeenth of November. Feats of arms were performed by noblemen of prowess; music and various tableaux added to the glittering displays of costume and armor. One outstanding feature of the "Triumph at Tylt" for 1590 was a song in honor of Sir Henry Lea, performed by one Mr. Hales. Sir Henry had originated the annual tourney some thirty years before and had competed in it every year; now, because of advancing age, he was retiring from the lists. The lyric for his farewell song was written by George Peele and set to music by John Dowland, eminent English composer. Peele, an English playwright and poet, was the author of numerous dramas, pageants, lyrics for songs in his own plays, and considerable verse celebrating important personages and events. It is likely that he had a part in designing the pageant for the 1590 tournament, in addition to providing a song; in a poem of moderate length, *Polyhymnia,* he describes the event and its participants in laudatory terms. To *Polyhymnia* is appended the song that had been so well received. Entitled simply "A Sonnet," though not written in one of the two regular sonnet forms, it voices the loyal sentiments of a warrior grown old in service to his queen and country:

> His golden locks time hath to silver turn'd;
> O time too swift, O swiftness never ceasing!
> His youth 'gainst time and age hath ever spurn'd,
> But spurn'd in vain; youth waneth by increasing:
> Beauty, strength, youth, are flowers but fading seen;
> Duty, faith, love, are roots, and ever green.
>
> **His helmet now shall make a hive for bees,**
> And, lovers' sonnets turn'd to holy psalms,
> A man-at-arms must now serve on his knees,
> And feed on prayers, which are age his alms:

440

But though from court to cottage he depart,
His saint is sure of his unspotted heart.

And when he saddest sits in homely cell,
  He'll teach his swains this carol for a song,—
"Bless'd be the hearts that wish my sovereign well,
  Cursed be the souls that think her any wrong!"
Goddess, allow this agèd man his right,
To be your beadsman now that was your knight.

His looks do menace heaven and dare the gods

Source: TAMBURLAINE THE GREAT (Part I, Act I, sc. ii, l. 352)
Author: Christopher Marlowe (1564-1593)
First published: 1590
Type of work: Dramatic tragedy

Context: Mycetes, newly crowned as King of Persia, becomes concerned about the raids of Tamburlaine, a former Scythian shepherd, upon his kingdom, as it is rumored that Tamburlaine seeks to rule all of the East. Mycetes sends Theridamas, in command of a thousand cavalrymen, to defeat Tamburlaine and destroy the menace. When news comes to Tamburlaine that the richly clad and armored Persian force is near, he bids Techelles, one of his subordinate leaders, to ask for a parley between the Persian commander and himself. Tamburlaine also bids his men make ready to fight, if the need arises, and to display their treasure so the Persians can see it. Theridamas comes to speak with Tamburlaine, and he is mightily impressed by the Scythian, so much so that he becomes Tamburlaine's ally:

THERIDAMAS
Where is this Scythian *Tamberlaine?*

TAMBURLAINE
Whom seekest thou, Persian? I am Tamburlain.

THERIDAMAS
Tamburlaine? A Scythian Shepheard so imbellished
With Nature's pride, and richest furniture,
His looks do menace heauen and dare the Gods,
His fierie eies are fixt upon the earth,
As if he now devis'd some Strategeme:
Or meant to pierce *Avernas* darksome vaults,
To pull the triple headed dog from hell.

441

His mind his kingdom, and his will his law

Source: TRUTH (Line 406)
Author: William Cowper (1731-1800)
First published: 1782
Type of work: Essay in verse

Context: Maintaining that the basic and only Truth is God's truth, the English poet Cowper believes that a humble cottage-dweller, weaving at her doorway and going to bed at dark, light of heart, knows more about Truth than the recently-deceased French skeptic Voltaire (1694–1778), who scoffed at the Bible. He reflects that many more poor people than those wealthy or learned gain Heaven. It is not that the rich, noble, and thoroughly versed in science are not wanted there, but that in their journey toward Heaven, their possessions are "a dead, preponderating weight." However, Cowper, admits that some rich people, and at least one man who wears a coronet, are seekers after truth. In the latter, he refers to William, second Earl of Dartmouth, a prominent figure in the Evangelistic movement of which Cowper was a part. This thought brings the poet to a consideration of the Biblical question: What is a man? He cites one answer, far from the truth, an answer provided by a man who is proud of his own power and heedless of the God Who made him. He considers himself supreme and, except that he lacks power over the elements, a god-like being, attractive in person and supreme over the world around him.

> But what is man in his own proud esteem?
> Hear him—himself the poet and the theme;
> A monarch, clothed with majesty and awe,
> **His mind his kingdom, and his will his law,**
> Grace in his mien, and glory in his eyes,
> Supreme on earth, and worthy of the skies,
> Strength in his heart, dominion in his nod,
> And, thunderbolts excepted, quite a god!

His six days' work, a world

Source: PARADISE LOST (Book VII, 1. 568)
Author: John Milton (1608-1674)
First published: 1667
Type of work: Epic poem

Context: Raphael was sent down to earth by God to instruct Adam in his duty so that he cannot plead ignorance when he falls from grace, as God knows that he will fall. Adam asks how the world began; Raphael answers that he will instruct him in what he ought to know, but there are some things that the Omniscient keeps hidden. He begins his account

442

by saying that after Lucifer, which was Satan's name while he was still an angel, and his rebel host of angels had been expelled from heaven, God decided to create a new world that would in time fill up the population of heaven that had been diminished by the expulsion of the rebels. It was Milton's belief that if man had not fallen, he would by degrees have ascended over the ages until he became a being like the angels: this idea is the reverse of the process by which the fallen angels regress from spiritual substance to an earthy consistency. Raphael then retells the story of creation as it is given in the first chapter of *Genesis;* Milton's account is, however, much fuller and more elaborate than the Biblical one. He finishes his account by telling Adam that he is to have dominion over all things; all things are for his use except the fruit of the one tree that he is warned not to taste. When God had inspected all His work and had found it good, He ascended to His abode in heaven:

> Up He rode
> Followed with acclamation and the sound
> Symphonious of ten thousand harps that tuned
> Angelic harmonies: the earth, the air
> Resounded, (thou remember'st, for thou heard'st)
> The heavens and all the constellations rung,
> The planets in their stations list'ning stood
> While the bright pomp ascended jubilant.
> Open, ye everlasting gates, they sung,
> Open, ye heavens, your living doors; let in
> The great Creator from his work returned
> Magnificent, **His six days' work, a world;**
> Open and henceforth oft; for God will deign
> To visit oft the dwellings of just men
> Delighted, and with frequent intercourse
> Thither will send his wingéd messengers
> On errands of supernal grace. . . .

His truth is marching on

Source: THE BATTLE-HYMN OF THE REPUBLIC (Stanza 1)
Author: Julia Ward Howe (1819-1910)
First published: 1862
Type of work: Hymn

Context: To a tune usually ascribed to a Southern writer of Sunday School songs, William Steffe, a woman suffragette and social reformer, wrote several patriotic stanzas at the suggestion of James Freeman Clarke (1810–1868). The two were in Washington at the time (1861), watching McClellan's army marching past, singing other words put to that same tune and called *John Brown's Body,* with its stirring refrain of "Glory, Glory, Hallelujah." There is a different story: that Mrs. Howe was inspired to write the patriotic stanzas by watching the 12th Massachusetts Regiment swinging by, on its way to the train, and singing that same song. From chronology, either version can be true. But both show how popular among the soldiers was the melodic ballad about the American abolitionist, John Brown (1800–1859), who tried to capture Harper's Ferry, West Virginia, to get a place for the protection of fugitive slaves. Defeated and captured, he was hanged, but by his martyrdom he attracted many to the defense of the slaves so that his soul went marching on. James T. Fields (1817–1881) gave Mrs. Howe's words their present title when publishing them in the *Atlantic Monthly,* in February 1862. They became immediately popular as a war song. Since they were intended to inspire patriotic fervor, and not as a work of great literature, only a carping critic would notice that "evening dews and damps" was a prosy phrase dragged in by the rhyme and that Christ was not born "in the beauty of the lilies," but in the chill of winter. Here are four of the five stanzas, the third one being omitted.

Mine eyes have seen the glory of the coming of the Lord,
He is trampling out the vintage where the grapes of wrath are
    stored;
He hath loosed the fateful lightning of His terrible, swift
    sword,
        His truth is marching on.
Glory! Glory! Hallelujah!
Glory! Glory! Hallelujah!
Glory! Glory! Hallelujah!
        His truth is marching on!

I have seen Him in the watch-fires of a hundred circling
    camps,
They have builded Him an altar in the evening dews and
    damps;
I can read His righteous sentence by the dim and flaring
    lamps;
        His day is marching on.
        • • •

He has sounded forth the trumpet that shall never call retreat;
He is sifting out the hearts of men before His judgment-seat;
Oh, be swift, my soul, to answer Him! Be jubilant, my feet!
    Our God is marching on.

In the beauty of the lilies Christ was born across the sea,
With a glory in His bosom that transfigures you and me:
As He died to make men holy, let us die to make men free,
    While God is marching on.

444

History is little more than the register of the crimes, follies, and misfortunes of mankind

Source: THE DECLINE AND FALL OF THE ROMAN EMPIRE (Chapter 3)
Author: Edward Gibbon (1737-1794)
First published: 1776-1788
Type of work: History

Context: Perhaps no one in his age was better acquainted with the course of history than Edward Gibbon, whose vast study of Roman history has become a classic work in historiography. And to read that work is to understand the force of Gibbon's comment upon the nature of history; his recitation of the events and personalities of the Roman Empire show the truth of his observation, and Gibbon makes it clear that he has glossed over some of the more lurid and notorious aspects of the Roman story, though he notes in passing that they existed. The chapter in which his comment occurs is entitled "Of the Constitution of the Roman Empire in the Age of the Antonines." The chapter begins with what the writer calls "the obvious definition of a monarchy" and proceeds to narrate the progress of the Roman Empire from Augustus, including an account of how he solidified his position, through the reign of Hadrian, to Titus Antoninus Pius and his successor, Marcus. The two Antonines ruled the Roman world for forty-two years, with, in Gibbon's words, "the same invariable spirit of wisdom and virtue." The comment about the nature of history is found in a paragraph describing the reign of the earlier Antonine:

Titus Antoninus Pius has been justly denominated a second Numa. The same love of religion, justice, and peace, was the distinguishing characteristic of both princes. But the situation of the latter opened a much larger field for the exercise of those virtues. Numa could only prevent a few neighbouring villages from plundering each other's harvests. Antoninus diffused order and tranquillity over the greatest part of the earth. His reign is marked by the rare advantage of furnishing very few materials for **history; which is,** indeed, **little more than the register of the crimes, follies, and misfortunes of mankind.** In private life, he was an amiable as well as a good man. The native simplicity of his virtue was a stranger to vanity or affectation. He enjoyed with moderation the conveniences of his fortune, and the innocent pleasures of society: and the benevolence of his soul displayed itself in a cheerful serenity of temper.

History is past politics, and politics present history

Source: THE GROWTH OF BRITISH POLICY (Volume I, p. xii)
Author: Sir John Robert Seeley (1834-1895)
First published: 1895
Type of work: History

Context: A brilliant product of the classical tripos at Cambridge University in 1857, John R. Seeley soon abandoned the classics for his greater interests in religion and history. His most widely read and remarkable work was *Ecce Homo* (1865), which dealt with the humanity of Christ, appeared anonymously, and provoked stormy replies. Seeley was Professor of Modern History at Cambridge, 1869–1895. From the beginning his lectures stressed the subordination of history to politics. Reflecting the critical scholarship of the "scientific" historians of the late nineteenth century, Seeley disparaged the essentially literary works of Macaulay and Carlyle. The importance of history was its utility as a school for statesmen. Thus, for Seeley historical narrative was of little value without generalizations, and generalizations were primarily important for their application to current political problems. He adopted in his lectures, though he did not formulate, the view that *"history is past politics, and politics present history."* Yet the political history which concerned Seeley most was not the domestic and constitutional themes of most previous British historians but the history of states acting and reacting on an international scale. Seeley's *The Expansion of England* (1883) dealt with the colonial and commercial aspects of Britain's struggle with France, 1688–1815. What was to have been a parallel study of Britain's foreign policy became instead a major survey of the foundations of the British empire from the reign of Elizabeth I to that of William III. *The Growth of British Policy* was published in 1895, the year of his death. Both works reflected and contributed to the enthusiasm for empire which characterized the British mood at the end of the nineteenth century. Seeley, however, apparently did not coin the phrase which is associated with his name, for in the Memoir prefixed to his book G. W. Prothero says:

. . . In his lecture [his Innaugural Lecture at Cambridge] he laid down the lines which he constantly followed throughout the whole tenure of his professorship. Though he did not coin the phrase **"History is past politics, and politics present history,"** it is perhaps more strictly applicable to his own view of history than to that of its author. . . .

446

History is the essence of innumerable biographies

Source: CRITICAL AND MISCELLANEOUS ESSAYS (Vol. II, "On History")
Author: Thomas Carlyle (1795-1881)
First published: 1830
Type of work: Essay

Context: In this essay, first published in *Frazer's Magazine,* No. 10, in 1830, the great historian of the French Revolution and of the six-volume history of Frederick II of Prussia gives his ideas on history. Carlyle begins with the assertion that a talent for history is born in everybody, as our chief inheritance. As we *do* nothing but enact History, so likewise we *say* little but recite it. However, the living, actual History of Humanity consists of far different and more fruitful activities than those recorded in the history books. There is an infinite complexity in the simplest facts that constitute the Experience of Life. And the author points out the pitfalls ahead of Historians who produce Artists in history as well as Artisans in history who labor mechanically, without an eye for the whole, or even knowledge that there is a whole. He comments on some of the different sorts of Historians; the Ecclesiastical Historian, like the Political Historian, spends more time on outward mechanics than on essentials. Other Historians concentrate on separate provinces of human action: Sciences, Practical Arts, or Institutions. Carlyle ends with the expressed hope that a Philosophy of History may some day be evolved. As to the difficulties ahead, he has this to say:

. . . Before Philosophy can teach by Experience, the Philosophy has to be in readiness, the Experience must be gathered and intelligently recorded. . . . let anyone who has examined the current of human affairs, and how intricate, perplexed, unfathomable, even when seen into with our own eyes, are their thousandfold blending movements, say whether the true representing of it is easy or impossible. Social Life is the aggregate of all the individual men's Lives who constitute Society; **History is the essence of innumerable biographies.** But if one Biography, nay, our own Biography, study and recapitulate it as we may, remains in so many points unintelligible to us; how much more must these million, the very facts of which, to say nothing of the purport of them, we know not, and cannot know!

A holiday humour

Source: AS YOU LIKE IT (Act IV, sc. i, ll. 68-69)
Author: William Shakespeare (1564-1616)
First published: 1623
Type of work: Dramatic comedy

Context: Passionately in love with each other, Rosalind and Orlando have never spoken to each other of their love. Both are now in the Forest of Arden, where Rosalind is in disguise as a young man named Ganymede. Orlando does not see through her disguise, and Rosalind wittily takes advantage of the situation. She offers to pose as Rosalind, so that Orlando may know what he is in for. Thus, thinking he is making love to a proxy, Orlando actually woos the genuine Rosalind, who, indeed in a holiday humor, may jest as she pleases. When Orlando is late to a meeting, she tells him she would rather be wooed by a snail, who "brings his destiny with him," that is, the horns the cuckold is proverbially supposed to wear. To Rosalind's vast satisfaction, Orlando replies that "virtue is no horn-maker; and my Rosalind is virtuous." The jest continues:

ROSALIND

Come, woo me, woo me; for now I am in **a holiday humour,** and like enough to consent. What would you say to me now, an I were your very, very Rosalind?

ORLANDO

I would kiss before I spoke.

ROSALIND

Nay, you were better speak first, and when you were gravelled for lack of matter, you might take occasion to kiss.

• • •

The hollow crown

Source: KING RICHARD THE SECOND (Act III, sc. ii, l. 160)
Author: William Shakespeare (1564-1616)
First published: 1597
Type of work: Historical drama

Context: King Richard returns to England from the Irish wars to find that Bolingbroke, his exiled cousin, has returned to England to claim his inheritance seized by Richard on the death of his uncle, John of Gaunt, father of the exiled Bolingbroke, and that the companions of Richard charged with the responsibility of Bristol castle have been executed. The downcast king suggests to his companions that they sit down and talk of the deaths of kings:

RICHARD
. . . For within **the hollow crown**
That rounds the mortal temples of a king
Keeps Death his court, and there the antic sits,

448

Scoffing his state and grinning at his pomp,
Allowing him a breath, a little scene,
To monarchize, be feared, and kill with looks,
Infusing him with self and vain conceit,
As if this flesh which walls about our life,
Were brass impregnable; and humoured thus,
Comes at the last and with a little pin
Bores through his castle wall, and farewell king!
Cover your heads, and mock not flesh and blood,
With solemn reverence; throw away respect,
Tradition, form, and ceremonious duty,
For you have but mistook me all this while.
I live with bread like you, feel want,
Taste grief, need friends; subjected thus,
How can you say to me, I am a King?

Home-keeping hearts are happiest

Source: BIRDS OF PASSAGE (Flight the Fifth. Song, Stanza 1)
Author: Henry Wadsworth Longfellow (1807-1882)
First published: 1878
Type of work: Lyric poem

Context: One of the characteristics that made Longfellow so popular with his audience was his ability to render scenes of contentment and domestic happiness, of comfort and quiet reflection. Such verses can scarcely be otherwise than sentimental, and this effect of sentimentality now finds less favor with critics than it once did. Nonetheless, his easy versification and the graceful melody of his lines possess an undeniable charm. The following brief lyric of three stanzas depicts home as many visualize it: a place where one may find rest and peace, a place of refuge and safety. It may be significant that Longfellow included it in one of his *Birds of Passage* collections, which consist largely of verse tales about far-off times and places. Although he had traveled extensively in Europe, Longfellow enjoyed the comforts of home, and this desire to remain at home naturally increased with advancing age. In this poem he tells us that at home our cares and troubles seem less serious than they do elsewhere, and doubts cease to trouble us; we enjoy a security which those who have cast loose such ties cannot have. There is a soothing, almost drowsy effect in the verses—as though the poet had just returned from a long, weary journey and knows that at last he will sleep in his own bed again:

Stay, stay at home, my heart, and rest;
Home-keeping hearts are happiest,
For those that wander they know not where
Are full of trouble and full of care;
   To stay at home is best.

449

Weary and homesick and distressed,
They wander east, they wander west,
And are baffled and beaten and blown about
By the winds of the wilderness of doubt;
 To stay at home is best.

Then stay at home, my heart, and rest;
The bird is safest in its nest;
O'er all that flutter their wings and fly
A hawk is hovering in the sky;
 To stay at home is best.

Home-made dishes that drive one from home

Source: MISS KILMANSEGG AND HER PRECIOUS LEG ("Her Misery," stanza 1)
Author: Thomas Hood (1799-1845)
First published: 1840-1841
Type of work: Satiric poem

Context: This long narrative poem is both humorous and satirical. The humorously grotesque story of Miss Kilmansegg has a serious interest: the satirization of man's pursuit of wealth. The heroine comes from a long line of persons who have wealth in great quantities. Indeed, Miss Kilmansegg's ancestors owned, among other possessions, geese that laid golden eggs, Colchian sheep with golden fleeces, and the Golden Ass. Miss Kilmansegg is born and reared in a golden atmosphere: everything in her surroundings is gold. But one day her horse, a bay named Banker, runs away while she is riding in London; when horse and rider fall upon the street, Miss Kilmansegg suffers a compound fracture of her right leg; when the leg has to be amputated, she insists upon its being replaced by an artificial leg of gold. Despite her artificial leg, the young woman gets about. She learns how to walk, even how to dance. She is courted by a foreign count and marries him, but, alas, the foreign count proves to be a counterfeit, and Miss Kilmansegg dreams one night she is really married to the Devil. Her misery is compared to all sorts of things, including being forced out of courtesy to eat all sorts of dishes, poorly prepared home-made food and drink, when she is a guest:

Who hath not met with home-made bread,
A heavy compound of putty and lead—
And home-made wines that rack the head,
 And home-made liqueurs and waters?
Home-made pop that will not foam,
And **home-made dishes that drive one from home,**
  Not to name each mess,
  For the face or dress,
 Home-made by the homely daughters?

450

Homesickness for the mud

Source: LE MARIAGE D'OLYMPE (Act I)
Author: Guillaume Victor Émile Augier (1820-1899)
First published: 1854
Type of work: Dramatic tragedy

Context: Émile Augier, a French playwright, was outraged at the romanticists' applause of the younger Alexandre Dumas' *La Dame aux camélias,* known as *Camille* in English. The idea that a prostitute is to be forgiven her filthy life because she has loved deeply, so revolted Augier that he wrote *Le Mariage d'Olympe.* This is the story of a courtesan, Olympe Taverny, who had had a notorious career in Paris; she entraps the innocent and inexperienced young son of a high-born family into marriage and gains wealth and a title. Although Olympe glories in being a wealthy countess, a year's virtuous living in small-town hotels far removed from the gaiety of Paris brings her to the verge of distraction from pure boredom; she has been in the company of no one but her husband, Henri de Puygiron, who is too tame for her tastes. She arranges matters so that she and Henri join the de Puygiron family in Vienna, where she soon enters into an affair with a rich young man of common antecedents, the ultimate end of the affair being her death by shooting at the hands of her husband—a conclusion very different from that of *Camille.* As the play opens, the Baron de Montrichard, the Marquis de Puygiron, and Baudel de Beauséjour are discussing the reported death of Olympe Taverny in California. Montrichard says that times are changing, and that such creatures as Olympe are marrying the sons of good families. The marquis suggests that such women should not be allowed to keep the names they gain by their trickery. Baudel takes a romantic view:

BAUDEL
But, M. le Marquis, suppose the woman in question does not drag her stolen plumage in the gutter?

MARQUIS
I cannot admit the hypothesis, Monsieur.

BAUDEL
Is it not possible that she should like to give up her former life and want to lead a quiet and pure existence—?

MARQUIS
Put a duck on a lake among swans, and you will observe that the duck regrets its mire, and will end by returning there.

MONTRICHARD
Homesickness for the mud!

451

An honest exceeding poor man

Source: THE MERCHANT OF VENICE (Act II, sc. ii, l. 52)
Author: William Shakespeare (1564-1616)
First published: 1600
Type of work: Dramatic comedy

Context: Gobbo, old and blind, stumbles along a street in Venice, searching for his son, Lancelot Gobbo, who is employed by the wealthy Jew, Shylock. Lancelot is also walking along the same street, debating with his conscience whether to quit the service of Shylock in favor of the service of the young gentleman Bassanio. Old Gobbo comes upon Lancelot, but, because he is blind and because Lancelot has matured, does not recognize his son, who jests with his father, suggesting that Gobbo must be seeking "Master Lancelot" rather than a menial.

> GOBBO
> Be God's sonties, 'twill be a hard way to hit. Can you tell me whether one Lancelot that dwells with him, dwell with him or no?
>
> LANCELOT
> Talk you of young Master Lancelot? [*aside.*] Mark me now, now will I raise the waters. —Talk you of young Master Lancelot?
>
> GOBBO
> No master sir, but a poor man's son. His father though I say it is **an honest exceeding poor man,** and God be thanked well to live.
>
> LANCELOT
> Well, let his father be what 'a will, we talk of young Master Lancelot.

An honest man's the noblest work of God

Source: AN ESSAY ON MAN (Epistle IV, l. 248)
Author: Alexander Pope (1688-1744)
First published: 1733-1734
Type of work: Philosophical poem

Context: The fourth, and last, epistle in Pope's *Essay on Man* is a discussion of man's happiness and his struggle to achieve it. Man is destined, says Pope, to search for happiness; he calls the search "our being's end and aim." However, he often fails in this search, but the failure, says Pope, is in himself; he errs in the ways he seeks happiness and so is deprived by his own actions of the felicity intended by God for all. Real happiness, says the poet, can be summed up in three words: "health, peace,

452

and competence." Man's troubles stem from various courses of action, some which Pope examines in detail. Man chases fruitlessly after worldly goods, honor, fame, little guessing that happiness is to be found in virtue. Fame, for example, is not real, but "a fancied life in others' breath." Fame, living in others, is beyond our control, in this life or after death. Pope goes on to examine further the weaknesses of fame:

> All that we feel of it begins and ends
> In the small circle of our foes or friends;
> To all beside as much an empty shade
> An Eugene living, as a Caesar dead;
> Alike or when, or where, they shone, or shine,
> Or on the Rubicon, or on the Rhine.
> A wit's a feather, and a chief a rod;
> **An honest man's the noblest work of God.**
> Fame but from death a villain's name can save,
> As justice tears his body from the grave;
> When what t' oblivion better were resign'd,
> Is hung on high, to poison half mankind.
> All fame is foreign, but of true desert;
> Plays round the head, but comes not to the heart:
> One self-approving hour whole years outweighs
> Of stupid starers, and of loud huzzas.

A hooded eagle among blinking owls

Source: LETTER TO MARIA GISBORNE (Line 208)
Author: Percy Bysshe Shelley (1792-1822)
First published: 1824
Type of work: Verse letter

Context: This poem is a verse letter to Shelley's friend, Maria Gisborne, who is residing at the moment in London; the poet is living in the Gisborne residence in Leghorn. Shelley begins by saying that, like the spider in its web and the silkworm in its cocoon, he sits spinning a cell of rare and subtle thoughts that will, after his death, preserve his memory in the minds of those who love him. He then describes the room in which he is composing his letter: it is crowded with a large number of strange mechanical devices and apparatus for performing experiments in natural philosophy that the poet does not fully comprehend; and there are also books, broken teacups, and all the other odds and ends that accumulate in a man's study. In such a room sits the poet while the elements rage in a thunderstorm outside the house. The poet then falls into reminiscence about the time that Maria and he were together in this region: how they picnicked in the country and how the poet expounded his ideas to Maria. But now Maria is in London, a huge sea that casts up its human wreckage on its shores, but the depths of which contain great treasures, such

453

as William Godwin, the philosopher who did much to shape Shelley's political views and who was, in general, influential in shaping his intellect; and Samuel Taylor Coleridge, whose days of intellectual greatness had passed. Coleridge, he says, is like a captive eagle blindfolded by the falconer's hood and surrounded by a crowd of lesser men who are like a flock of owls. The comparison is between Coleridge, who in his great days, could, like the eagle, stare into the sun of truth, and lesser men, who, like owls, cannot tolerate such bright light.

> You will see
> That which was Godwin—greater none than he
> Though fallen—and fallen on evil times—to stand
> Among the spirits of our age and land,
> Before the dread tribunal of *to come*
> The foremost,—while Rebuke cowers pale and dumb.
> You will see Coleridge—he who sits obscure
> In the exceeding lustre and the pure
> Intense irradiation of a mind,
> Which, with its own internal lightning blind,
> Flags wearily through darkness and despair—
> A cloud-encircled meteor of the air,
> **A hooded eagle among blinking owls—**
> You will see Hunt—one of those happy souls
> Which are the salt of the earth, and without whom
> This world would smell like what it is—a tomb.

Hope thou not much, and fear thou not at all

Source: HOPE AND FEAR (Line 14)
Author: Algernon Charles Swinburne (1837-1909)
First published: 1882
Type of work: Sonnet

Context: Man's life, according to Swinburne, is a progression from the innocence and hope of youth to the corruption and despair of adulthood. Having rebelled against conventional customs and morality, Swinburne found that his fame was more often a notoriety that led to public denouncement than an admiration that led to an acceptance of his works; however, he attempted to live up to his bad reputation, although his weak physical condition turned such dissipation into long, very severe illnesses. By 1879 he was so near to death that only the paternal care of his friend Theodore Watts-Dunton was able to save his life. Under Watts-Dunton's care the wild young man who pursued dissipation to its bitter end became a quiet and conventional old man. In this poem, he describes youth from the vantage point of adulthood; while youth may hope and dream, the adult knows that such hopes will end in disappointment when the individual finally faces reality, an inevitable loss of dreams that no one should fear.

Then, when the soul leaves off to dream and yearn,
May truth first purge her eyesight to discern
　　What once being known leaves time no power to appal;
Till youth at last, ere yet youth be not, learn
　　The kind wise word that falls from years that fall—
　　"Hope thou not much, and fear thou not at all."

Hopeless grief is passionless

Source: GRIEF (Line 1)
Author: Elizabeth Barrett Browning (1806–1861)
First published: 1844
Type of work: Sonnet

Context: In this sonnet, Elizabeth Barrett Browning contrasts two reactions to death. On one hand, men without the experience or knowledge of death "Beat upward to God's throne in loud access/ Of shrieking and reproach." But the reaction of the "deephearted man" is compared to a "monumental statue set/ In everlasting watch and moveless woe." This "deephearted man" knows that anguish is pointless. Thus Mrs. Browning's contention is that "hopeless grief is passionless" and that there is no escape from it.

I tell you **hopeless grief is passionless;**
That only men incredulous of despair,
Half-taught in anguish, through the midnight air
Beat upward to God's throne in loud access
Of shrieking and reproach. Full desertness,
In souls as countries, lieth silent-bare
Under the blanching, vertical eye-glare
Of the absolute heavens. Deep-hearted man, express
Grief for thy dead in silence like to death—
Most like a monumental statue set
In everlasting watch and moveless woe
Till itself crumble to the dust beneath.
Touch it; the marble eyelids are not wet:
If it could weep, it could arise and go.

Horribly stuffed with epithets of war

Source: OTHELLO (Act I, sc. i, l. 14)
Author: William Shakespeare (1564-1616)
First published: 1622
Type of work: Dramatic tragedy

Context: Iago, at the opening of the　play, complains to Roderigo that

455

Othello, his military commander, has passed over him in naming the second-in-command. Thus, Cassio ". . . must his lieutenant be,/ And I God bless the mark, his Moorship's ancient." Here are the seeds of rancor which will shortly produce Iago's devastating hatred for the Moor and his bride Desdemona. These seeds spring from the perennial competition between the enlisted man with long years of service and practical experience and the young officer commissioned after a relatively brief period of specialized training. Iago, much of his twenty-eight years spent in the military is now to be commanded by "one Michael Cassio, a Florentine," "a great arithmetician, . . . that never set a squadron in the field," one who knows nothing of the "division of a battle" except by "bookish theoric." "Mere prattle, without practice is all his soldiership." Iago's failure to receive this promotion is all the more galling because he has actively sought it; he personally had secured the good offices of various important men of the city to speak to Othello in his behalf. But to no avail, for the Moor rebuffs them, according to Iago, with the specious bombast of military rhetoric. In the remaining portion of the scene, Iago, in order to gain a measure of revenge upon Othello, persuades Roderigo to go with him to Brabantio—Desdemona's father—in an attempt to destroy the Moor's recent marriage.

IAGO

   . . . Three great ones of the city,
In personal suit to make me his lieutenant,
Off-capped to him—and by the faith of man,
I know my price, I am worth no worse a place.
But he, as loving his own pride and purposes,
Evades them, with a bombast circumstance,
Horribly stuffed with epithets of war,
And in conclusion,
Nonsuits my mediators. For certes, says he,
I have already chose my officer.

• • •

How beautiful upon the mountains

Source: ISAIAH 52:7
Author: Isaiah
First transcribed: c.800-200 B.C.
Type of work: Religious prophecy and exhortation

Context: Chapter 52 is one of several in which the poet foretells, or seems to foretell, the coming of the Messiah. Early Christian scholars were convinced that this coming is the proper interpretation of the lines and that Isaiah prophesied accurately the life and ministry of Jesus and the growth of the Church. Later scholarship puzzled over these passages and considered several Jewish leaders of the period, to whom Isaiah might have assigned the role of deliverer. More recently scholarship has tended to the opinion that a true Messiah, as later exemplified by Christ, is what Isaiah does refer to. Chapter 40 serves as a prelude, announcing that the suffering of Israel will presently end and that at last the glory of God will descend upon its people. In Chapter 42 Isaiah describes one he calls the Servant, who has been prepared by the Lord, and who will bring God's religion to the people that it may be spread abroad in the world; his coming will be quiet and without fanfare; his teaching will be gentle. In Chapter 49 another of these evangelistic hymns announces the Servant and portrays him speaking to the nations and explaining his mission to them; in the following chapter he describes his own suffering and the strength that upholds him in it. Chapter 52 begins with Isaiah's jubilant announcement that Babylonian oppression is at an end; Jerusalem the holy city will no longer be defiled by the unclean. In the words of the Lord, the people have sold themselves into captivity for nothing, and will be redeemed in the same way; for they have been oppressed without just cause in the past. Past suffering has paid for present folly. The people return from exile and Jerusalem, in celebration, arrays itself as a bride. A herald now proclaims that God is king and that His kingdom will endure forever.

How beautiful upon the mountains are the feet of him that bringeth good tidings, that publisheth peace; that bringeth good tidings of good, that publisheth salvation; that saith unto Zion, Thy God reigneth!

Thy watchmen shall lift up the voice; with the voice together shall they sing: for they shall see eye to eye, when the LORD shall bring again Zion.

Break forth into joy, sing together, ye waste places of Jerusalem: for the LORD hath comforted his people, he hath redeemed Jerusalem.

The LORD hath made bare his holy arm in the eyes of all the nations; and all the ends of the earth shall see the salvation of our God.

Depart ye, depart ye, go ye out from thence, touch no unclean thing; go ye out of the midst of her; be ye clean, that bear the vessels of the LORD.

For ye shall not go out with haste, nor go by flight: for the LORD will go before you; and the God of Israel will be your rearward.

Behold, my servant shall deal prudently, he shall be exalted and extolled, and be very high.

As many were astonished at thee; his visage was so marred more than any man, and his form more than the sons of men:

So shall he sprinkle many nations; the kings shall shut their mouths at him: for that which had not been told them shall they see; and that which they had not heard shall they consider.

How far that little candle throws his beams

Source: THE MERCHANT OF VENICE (Act V, sc. i, l. 90)
Author: William Shakespeare (1564-1616)
First published: 1600
Type of work: Dramatic comedy

Context: The heiress Portia, wife of Bassanio, returns to her home, Belmont, after disguising herself as a wise young judge and freeing Antonio, benefactor of Bassanio, from the forefeiture of Shylock's wicked bond —the payment of a pound of flesh since Antonio's ships had failed to come to port. As Portia and her handmaiden, Nerissa, near Belmont, Portia speaks.

PORTIA
That light we see is burning in my hall.
How far that little candle throws his beams,
So shines a good deed in a naughty world.

NERISSA
When the moon shone we did not see the candle.

PORTIA
So doth the greater glory dim the less.
A substitute shines brightly as a king
Until a king be by, and then his state
Empties itself, as doth an inland brook
Into the main of waters. . . .

How ill white hairs become a fool and jester

Source: KING HENRY THE FOURTH: PART TWO (Act V, sc. v. l. 52)
Author: William Shakespeare (1564-1616)
First published: 1600
Type of work: Historical drama

Context: With King Henry IV dead, the responsibilities of the crown have fallen upon his eldest son, the carousing and reckless youth, Prince Henry. The new monarch, now Henry V, wastes no time in letting it be known that he is changed. When his old drinking companion, the roguish Sir John Falstaff, approaches the new king in a "public place," expecting a boon, Henry casts him off in the following speech:

KING HENRY THE FIFTH
I know thee not old man, fall to thy prayers.
How ill white hairs become a fool and jester.

458

I have long dreamed of such a kind of man,
So surfeit-swelled, so old, and so profane;
But being awaked, I do despise my dream.
Make less thy body hence, and more thy grace,
Leave gormandizing, know the grave doth gape
For thee thrice wider than for other men.
Reply not to me with a fool-born jest,
Presume not that I am the thing I was;
For God doth know, so shall the world perceive,
That I have turned away my former self,
So will I those that kept me company.

• • •

How long a time lies in one little word

Source: KING RICHARD THE SECOND (Act I, sc. iii, l. 213)
Author: William Shakespeare (1564-1616)
First published: 1597
Type of work: Historical drama

Context: At the lists of Coventry preparations are complete for the joust between Henry Bolingbroke and Thomas Mowbray to settle with swords a dispute which King Richard II has not settled with arbitration— Bolingbroke and Mowbray have each accused the other with treason against his liege. Just as the trumpets sound, Richard motions the combatants to return to their seats and to hear his decree that the joust is forbidden, and exile is pronounced as punishment for the offending knights, Bolingbroke for ten years, and Mowbray for life. Richard, noting the saddened countenance of his revered uncle, John of Gaunt, father of Bolingbroke, in a word reduces the sentence for Bolingbroke from ten to six years:

RICHARD
Uncle, even in the glasses of thine eyes
I see thy grieved heart. Thy sad aspect
Hath from the number of his banished years
Plucked four away. [*to* BOLINGBROKE.] Six
    frozen winters spent,
Return with welcome home from banishment.

BOLINGBROKE
How long a time lies in one little word.
Four lagging winters and four wanton springs,
End in a word; such is the breath of kings.

459

How much more elder art thou than thy looks

Source: THE MERCHANT OF VENICE (Act IV, sc. i, l. 251)
Author: William Shakespeare (1564-1616)
First published: 1600
Type of work: Dramatic comedy

Context: In a Venetian court Portia, the fair bride of Bassanio, in disguise as a young judge, rescues Antonio, Bassanio's friend, from the fate of having the venomous Jew, Shylock, cut one pound of his flesh as forfeiture of a bond which the merchant Antonio has stood for Bassanio to aid in his suit of Portia. As the trial begins, Shylock interprets the words of the judge to mean that, according to the bargain, Shylock may rightfully claim the heart of Antonio. Antonio demands to hear the sentence, Portia speaks, and Shylock, joyously assuming that he has won the case, pronounces the wisdom of the youthful justice.

ANTONIO
Most heartily I do beseech the court
To give the judgment.

PORTIA
Why then thus it is,
You must prepare your bosom for his knife.

SHYLOCK
O noble judge, o excellent young man!

PORTIA
For the intent and purpose of the law
Hath full relation to the penalty,
Which here appeareth due upon the bond.

SHYLOCK
'Tis very true. O wise and upright judge,
How much more elder art thou than thy looks.

How pleasant it is to have money, heigh ho!

Source: DIPSYCHUS (Part II, sc. ii)
Author: Arthur Hugh Clough (1819-1861)
First published: 1862
Type of work: Satiric poem

Context: This poetic dialogue, like so much of Clough's poetry, illustrates his love of melancholy and his religious conflicts. In the poem we find a

460

Faustian hero, with some touches of Lord Byron, speaking on a series of occasions with a somewhat Satan-like spirit. The poem, begun in 1850, while Clough was in Venice, was left unfinished at the time of his death. Echoes of the poetry of both Byron and Goethe abound in it. The Spirit of the dialogue, though at times Satanic, seems more often to be rather the worldly common-sense, while the figure of Dispsychus tends to speak for the poet's idealism; in a sense the dialogue is autobiographical, for Clough himself struggled inwardly, torn between idealism and worldliness. In this section of the poem the Spirit and Dipsychus converse as they slide along the Grand Canal in Venice; the smooth passage of the craft causes Dipsychus to lament that life cannot go as unvexed as their gondola; he decries the struggles over "quarrels, aims, and cares,/ And moral duties and affairs." After some exchange of comments about its being a pity that the gondoliers do not enjoy life more, the Spirit speaks up on behalf of the enjoyment of life, his speech going on through a dozen verses. At the end of each verse he comments (and one thinks of Iago's advice to Roderigo before they leave Venice, "Put money in thy purse.") in a refrain about the advantages of ready wealth:

SPIRIT

As I sat at the café, I said to myself,
They may talk as they please about what they call pelf,
They may sneer as they like about eating and drinking,
But help it I cannot, I cannot help thinking,
   How pleasant it is to have money, heigh ho!
How pleasant it is to have money.

I sit at my table *en grand seigneur,*
And when I have done, throw a crust to the poor;
Not only the pleasure, one's self, of good living,
But also the pleasure of now and then giving.
   So pleasant it is to have money, heigh ho!
   So pleasant it is to have money.

How the world wags

Source: AS YOU LIKE IT (Act II, sc. vii, l. 23)
Author: William Shakespeare (1564-1616)
First published: 1623
Type of work: Dramatic comedy

Context: His throne usurped by his brother, a Duke of France lives a peaceful, rustic life in exile with a group of followers in the Forest of Arden. However, one of his lords, Jaques, who does not become adapted to the silvan life, weeps when a deer is shot for food and wanders off alone. The Duke searches all day for his doleful companion, but, when Jaques finally appears, he is in a gay mood because of a fool he met in the

461

forest. He repeats the dialogue for the   Duke and his lords:

JAQUES
. . .

Good morrow, fool, quoth I. No sir, quoth he,
Call me not fool till heaven hath sent me fortune.
And then he drew a dial from his poke,
And looking on it, with lack-lustre eye,
Says very wisely, it is ten o'clock:
Thus we may see, quoth he, **how the world wags**
'Tis but an hour ago since it was nine,
And after one hour more, 'twill be eleven;
And so from hour to hour we ripe, and ripe,
And then from hour to hour we rot, and rot;
And thereby hangs a tale. . . .

The huntsmen are up in America

Source: THE GARDEN OF CYRUS (Chapter 5)
Author: Sir Thomas Browne (1605-1682)
First published: 1658
Type of work: Philosophy

Context: Browne, in his five-chapter tract, *The Garden of Cyrus,* has two particular interests: ancient gardens with special interest in the garden of King Cyrus, and the power of five or the quincunx. The quincunx, notes Browne, appears frequently in the arrangement of gardens, as well as in the formations of nature (leaves with five sections, hands and claws with five digits, are examples), a power recognized by both pagan and Christian cultures. As he concludes his treatise the hour is midnight and, rather than "act our Antipodes" or the inhabitants of the opposite side of the globe, he brings his work to a close:

Though Somnus in Homer be sent to rouse up Agamemnon, I find no such effects in these drowsy approaches of sleep. To keep our eyes open longer, were but to act our Antipodes. **The huntsmen are up in America,** and they are already past their first sleep in Persia. But who can be drowsy at that hour which freed us from everlasting sleep? or have slumbering thoughts at that time, when sleep itself must end, and as some conjecture all shall awake again.

I accept the Universe

Source: COMMENT TO THOMAS CARLYLE (as reported by D. A. Wilson)
Author: Margaret Fuller (Ossoli) (1810-1850)
First spoken: 1846
Type of work: Biographical anecdote

Context: A minor New England writer of the nineteenth century, Margaret Fuller was a homely, brilliant, talkative eccentric who edited the transcendentalist magazine *The Dial* and published several books. In the summer of 1846 she traveled to Europe with a family named Spring, sending back gossipy letters which were published in the New York *Tribune*. Among the famous people she met was Thomas Carlyle, in whose home she visited. Emerson had recommended her to Carlyle as "this wise, sincere, accomplished, and most entertaining of women." Carlyle was later to write to Emerson that he had found her a "high-soaring, clear, enthusiast soul" and to his brother John Carlyle that she was "a strange, *lilting* lean old maid, not nearly such a bore as I had expected." Margaret's most famous reported remark is, "I accept the Universe!" To this, Carlyle is supposed to have said, "By god! she'd better" or "Gad! she'd better!" D. A. Wilson, one of Carlyle's biographers, believes that Carlyle's remark was made in Margaret's presence during a visit that Jane and Thomas Carlyle made to Margaret and her friends the Springs. Says Wilson:

It may have been on the same night that Margaret perorated picturesquely, to the admiration of all her listeners but one,—**"I accept the Universe!"**

"Gad, you'd better!" said Carlyle.

I am a feather for each wind that blows

Source: THE WINTER'S TALE (Act II, sc. iii, l. 154)
Author: William Shakespeare (1564-1616)
First published: 1623
Type of work: Tragi-comedy

Context: King Leontes of Sicilia, falsely accusing his wife, Hermione, great with child, of adultery with his friend Polixenes, King of Bohemia, brutally sentences her to imprisonment. A daughter, born to Hermione in prison, is carried by Paulina, a lady-in-waiting of Hermione and wife of Antigonus, to Leontes with the hope that seeing his baby will cause the jealous monarch to reprieve his wife. Beholding the child, Leontes commands that she be burned to death, but then, weakening, commands Antigonus to bear the baby to some desert and abandon her. Recognizing his indecision, Leontes says:

I am a feather for each wind that blows.
Shall I live on, to see this bastard kneel,
And call me father? Better burn it now,
Than curse it then. But be it; let it live.
It shall not neither. [*To* ANTIGONUS.] You sir, come
        you hither;
You that have been so tenderly officious
With Lady Margery, your midwife there,
To save this bastard's life—for 'tis a bastard,
So sure as this beard's gray—what will you adventure
To save this brat's life?

ANITIGONUS
        Any thing, my lord,
That my ability may undergo, . . .

I am a part of all that I have met

Source: ULYSSES (Line 18)
Author: Alfred, Lord Tennyson (1809-1892)
First published: 1842
Type of work: Lyric poem

Context: Following Dante (*Inferno*, XXVI), Tennyson imagines Ulysses many years after his return home to Ithaca from the Trojan War. Though aged he is restless and he longs to set out with a band of mariners on a voyage of exploration and adventure like those he remembers from past years. He will leave his son Telemachus, a prudent administrator, to govern the kingdom in his absence. "He works his work," says Ulysses, "I mine." Though the whole poem is a dramatic monologue addressed to his mariners before the voyage begins, the first half seems more a soliloquy in which Ulysses muses on his present boredom with "an aged wife" and the dull business of ruling "a savage race,/ That hoard, and sleep, and feed, and know not me." This existence is a waste of time, it seems, to a man who, though old, would still drink "Life to the lees." Then he reviews his past and proudly recalls his travels and his fame:

All times I have enjoyed
Greatly, have suffered greatly, both with those
That loved me, and alone; on shore, and when
Through scudding drifts the rainy Hyades
Vexed the dim sea. I am become a name;
For always roaming with a hungry heart
Much have I seen and known—cities of men
And manners, climates, councils, governments,
Myself not least, but honored of them all—

464

And drunk delight of battle with my peers,
Far on the ringing plains of windy Troy.
I am a part of all that I have met; . . .

I am a Roman citizen

Source: IN VERREM (II, v, lvii, 147)
Author: Marcus Tullius Cicero (106-43 B.C.)
First transcribed: 70 B.C.
Type of work: Denunciatory oration

Context: In the summer of 70 B.C., Cicero prosecuted Gaius Verres for extortion, misgovernment, and oppression. During his three years as Governor of the Sicilian people, Verres had used all sorts of legal trickery to avoid a fine and the loss of his Roman citizenship. The trial and verdict were tied up with the passage of a bill to take the complete control of criminal courts away from the Senate, and to give it only a third of the total vote. The criminal confessed his guilt by flight from Rome, and the bill passed. Cicero's second speech against Verres occupies five books. Close to its conclusion, he describes the governor's schemes for enriching himself. He would order the crews of ships arriving at Syracuse seized and flung into a prison called The Stone Quarries. Their claims to Roman citizenship ("Civis Romanus sum"), that granted them the right to be tried in Roman courts, did no good. The governor maintained that they were really fugitives from the army of Sertorius, in revolt, or traders with Mediterranean pirates, and confiscated their possessions, which he kept. Cicero tells about the situation:

These methods presently crowded the prison with honest traders; and then those things began to happen of which you have heard from Lucius Suettius, a Roman knight and most excellent man, and of which you shall hear from others likewise. There, in that prison, guiltless Roman citizens were most shamefully strangled. Now at last the cry, **"I am a Roman Citizen,"** the famous appeal that has so often brought men help and rescue among savage races in the furthest corners of the earth, was to hasten the affliction and increase the agony of these men's death. . . .

I am never merry when I hear sweet music

Source: THE MERCHANT OF VENICE (Act V, sc. i, l. 69)
Author: William Shakespeare (1564-1616)
First published: 1600
Type of work: Dramatic comedy

465

Context: Lorenzo, friend of Bassanio, and his bride Jessica, daughter of the Jew Shylock, talk tenderly on a moonlit night along the avenue to Belmont, home of the heiress Portia and her husband Bassanio. Though messengers inform the pair of the return of Portia and Bassanio, Lorenzo and Jessica delay the preparations for the home-coming of the master and mistress of the house. Lorenzo orders music, commenting that on such a night the soul can almost hear the harmony of the spheres. In a light mood, Lorenzo greets the musicians, but Jessica replies that she is not merry when she hears sweet music.

LORENZO
• • •

Come ho, and wake Diana with a hymn,
With sweetest touches pierce your mistress' ear,
And draw her home with music. [*Music plays.*]

JESSICA
I am never merry when I hear sweet music.

LORENZO
The reason is, your spirits are attentive. . . .

I am not arguing with you—I am telling you

Source: THE GENTLE ART OF MAKING ENEMIES
Author: James McNeill Whistler (1834–1903)
First published: 1890
Type of work: Literary record

Context: James McNeill Whistler was often stung to the quick by opinions other artists, art critics, and the general public expressed about his work, as the famous libel suit he brought against John Ruskin testifies. Among the comments which prompted a reply from Whistler was an article that appeared in *The World of London* on December 8, 1880. In that article an anonymous writer belittles an exhibition of twelve etchings by Whistler, saying that the etchings are of slight workmanship and "unimportant dimensions," without either value of originality. The unknown writer says that the etchings are like the sketches, unfinished, such as every artist brings back from a visit to Venice. These comments called forth the following reply from Whistler:

A PROPOSAL
Atlas, *mon bon, méfiez-vous de vos gens!* Your art gentleman says that Mr. Whistler exhibits twelve etchings, "slight in execution and unimportant in size." Now the private assassin you keep, for us, need not be hampered by mere connoisseurship in the perpe-

466

tration of his duty—therefore, *passe,* for the execution—but he should not compromise his master's reputation for brilliancy, and print things that he who runs may scoff at.

Seriously, then, my Atlas, an etching does not depend for its importance, upon its size. **"I am not arguing with you—I am telling you."** As well speak of one of your own charming *mots* as unimportant in length!

Look to it, Atlas. Be severe with your man. Tell him his "job" should be "neatly done." I could cut my own throat better; and if need be, in case of his dismissal, I offer my services.

I am not in the giving vein to-day

Source: KING RICHARD THE THIRD (Act IV, sc. ii, l. 119)
Author: William Shakespeare (1564-1616)
First published: 1597
Type of work: Historical drama

Context: Richard, having determined to "prove a villain" and to secure for himself the throne of England at any cost, finds the Duke of Buckingham a convenient and profitable ally in his schemes. Following the execution of his brother George, Duke of Clarence, and the death of his brother Edward IV, Richard uses the ambitious Buckingham to create dissension between powerful nobles such as Lord Hastings and Earl Rivers. When the Lord Mayor of London and a representative group of citizens are persuaded to request that Richard assume the protectorate following the king's death, again it is Buckingham who directs the scene, planting men in the crowd who call for Richard at various times and himself describing the holy devotion of Richard as the Duke of Gloucester is disclosed studying the Scripture. As Richard's desire to gain full control grows more desperate, he informs Buckingham that he "would be king," that he would have "the bastards [Edward's sons] dead." Buckingham's hesitation in agreeing to carry out this act is fatal, for Richard perceives in it a moral squeamishness which renders him useless as a henchman. A few lines later Buckingham, requesting the earldom he had earlier been promised, is rebuffed in a despotic fit of whimsicality which illustrates graphically the tenuousness of Richard's favor and foreshadows the ultimate fate which awaits Buckingham:

BUCKINGHAM
My lord, your promise for the earldom—

RICHARD
Richmond! When last I was at Exeter,
The mayor in courtesy showed me the castle,
And called it Rougemont, at which name I started,
Because a bard of Ireland told me once

467

I should not live long after I saw Richmond.

BUCKINGHAM

My lord—

RICHARD

Ay, what's a clock?

BUCKINGHAM

I am thus bold to put your Grace in mind
Of what you promised me.

RICHARD

Well, but what's a clock?

BUCKINGHAM

Upon the stroke of ten.

RICHARD

Well, let it strike.

BUCKINGHAM

Why let it strike?

RICHARD

Because that like a Jack thou keep'st the stroke
Betwixt thy begging and my meditation.
I am not in the giving vein to-day.

BUCKINGHAM

Why then resolve me whether you will or no.

RICHARD

Thou troublest me, I am not in the vein.

I am not the less human for being devout

Source: TARTUFFE (Act III, sc. iii)
Author: Molière (Jean Baptiste Poquelin, 1622-1673)
First published: 1669
Type of work: Tragi-comic drama

Context: The hypocritical Tartuffe makes rapid progress in undermining the happy home of Orgon, his gullible friend. Having already attempted to get himself married to Orgon's daughter Mariane, Tartuffe, in Act III, reveals his designs also upon Orgon's beautiful wife Elmire. He pretends

468

that his love of God has led him to love Elmire, one of God's most beau- tiful creations, and in a long, flatter- ing speech he declares this love:

ELMIRE

The declaration is most gallant, but, to tell the truth, it is a bit surprising. I think you should better guard your heart, and reflect a little on such a design. A devout man like you, one who is everywhere called. . . .

TARTUFFE

Ah! **I am not the less human for being devout;** and when one sees your heavenly allurements the heart surrenders, and does not reflect. I know that such language from me appears strange; but, Madam, after all, I am no angel; and if you condemn the avowal I have made, you must blame your own lovely charms. . . .

I am Sir Oracle

Source: THE MERCHANT OF VENICE (Act I, sc. i, l. 93)
Author: William Shakespeare (1564-1616)
First published: 1600
Type of work: Dramatic comedy

Context: Antonio, "the merchant of Venice," confesses to his friends, Salerio and Salanio, that he is plagued with sadness, not over his trading business, since his fortune rests with many vessels, nor over his love affairs. Salerio and Salanio, having tried in vain to cheer Antonio, leave when Antonio is joined by his close friend, Bassanio, and his companions, Lorenzo and Gratiano. Gratiano, noted for his loquaciousness, also tries to convince Antonio to leave off his sadness, pointing out the folly of those who vainly feign wisdom by a dour countenance:

GRATIANO

There are a sort of men whose visages
Do cream and mantle like a standing pond,
And do a wilful stillness entertain,
With purpose to be dressed in an opinion
Of wisdom, gravity, profound conceit,
As who should say, **I am Sir Oracle,**
And when I ope my lips, let no dog bark!

I appeal unto Caesar

Source: ACTS 25:11
Author: Unknown (traditionally Luke)
First transcribed: 60-150 (probably c.80-90)
Type of work: Religious history and tradition

Context: In The Acts of the Apostles we have the only extant contemporary account of the Christian Church in its beginning and early growth. Acts was evidently written by the same person who wrote Luke; he may or may not have been Luke the physician. In any case it is probable that Luke supplied much of the author's information. The book is a memorable record of hardship and devotion to an ideal, and it records the evolution of Christianity from a sect of Judaism to an independent religion. The story of Paul and his missionary work is given in Chapters 15 through 28. His travels in Syria, Greece, Asia Minor and Israel are covered. He faces many difficulties, and is twice the focal point of riots, in Thessalonica and Ephesus. At length he feels he must go to Jerusalem, and, in spite of warnings, makes the journey. Arrived there, he goes to the temple and is recognized and accused by people who have seen him in Asia Minor. Manhandled by a mob, he is turned over to the centurions. Asking the captain for leave to speak, he tells the people how he became a Christian; they are not receptive, and he is saved from a scourging only because he is a Roman citizen. He is released the next day and examined before his accusers. Another scene of disorder results, and the captain is forced to return Paul to prison in order to save his life. On the following day forty of the Pharisees swear to kill him the next time he is brought before them. The captain, warned, sends Paul under guard to Felix, Roman governor in Cæsarea. The latter postpones judgment, and presently Ananias and his elders appear with an orator named Tertullus who accuses Paul again. Judgment is again postponed; Paul is well treated but confined to the premises. Eventually Felix's term of office expires, and his successor, Festus, inherits the prisoner. The accusations are renewed, and Paul is once more commanded to appear before the seat of judgment.

And when he had tarried among them more than ten days, he went down unto Cæsarea; and the next day sitting on the judgment seat commanded Paul to be brought.

And when he was come, the Jews which came down from Jerusalem stood round about, and laid many grievous complaints against Paul, which they could not prove.

While he answered for himself, Neither against the law of the Jews, neither against the temple, nor yet against Cæsar, have I offended any thing at all.

But Festus, willing to do the Jews a pleasure, answered Paul, and said, Wilt thou go up to Jerusalem, and there be judged of these things before me?

Then said Paul, I stand at Cæsar's judgment seat, where I ought

470

to be judged: to the Jews have I done no wrong, as thou very well knowest.

For if I be an offender, or have committed any thing worthy of death, I refuse not to die: but if there be none of these things whereof these accuse me, no man may deliver me unto them. **I appeal unto Cæsar.**

Then Festus, when he had conferred with the council, answered, Hast thou appealed unto Cæsar? unto Cæsar shalt thou go.

And after certain days king Agrippa and Bernice came unto Cæsarea to salute Festus.

And when they had been there many days, Festus declared Paul's cause unto the king, . . .

I awoke, and behold it was a dream

Source: THE PILGRIM'S PROGRESS (Part I)
Author: John Bunyan (1628-1688)
First published: 1678
Type of work: Religious allegory

Context: The narrator of this dream allegory has witnessed, in his dream, the long and arduous struggles of Christian to overcome the snares and deceits of temptation in his journey to the Heavenly City. Finally, at the end of Part I, Christian and his companion, Hopeful, reach the gate where they are met by shining angels, who first describe and then admit them to the heavenly Jerusalem. Shortly thereafter, Ignorance, who had accompanied Christian and Hopeful on a portion of their journey, assisted by Vain-hope, approaches the gate. The gatekeepers do not admit him; instead, they demand from over the gate to see his certificate which would merit him admission. But Ignorance has no certificate. The dreamer's final vision is of the terrible fate of Ignorance:

So they told the King, but he would not come down to see him, but commanded the two Shining Ones that conducted Christian and Hopeful to the City, to go out and take Ignorance, and bind him hand and foot, and have him away. Then they took him up, and carried him through the air to the door that I saw in the side of the hill, and upt him in there. Then I saw that there was a way to hell, even from the gates of heaven, as well as from the City of Destruction. So **I awoke, and behold it was a dream.**

I awoke one morning and found myself famous

Source: LETTERS AND JOURNAL OF LORD BYRON (Chapter 14)
Author: Thomas Moore (1779-1852)
First published: 1830
Type of work: Biography

Context: Thomas Moore, the Irish poet and writer of sentimental songs, the best remembered of which are "The Last Rose of Summer" and "Believe Me, If All Those Endearing Young Charms," was one of Byron's closest friends. It was to him that Byron, in a characteristically impulsive and indiscreet gesture, had given the MS of His Memoirs to do with as he pleased. Moore, who was chronically in debt, had assigned the MS to the publisher Murray for two thousand guineas. Shortly after the news of Byron's death had reached England, at a meeting in London attended by those concerned with the fate of the Memoirs, the MS was burned; and, for better or for worse, whatever Byron may have said about his own life vanished forever. Because of the notoriety—in fact, scandal—associated with the late poet, no sooner was he dead than inaccurate and highly-colored biographical notes began to appear. Moore, who had known Byron intimately, made the first attempt to write a biography that was factually accurate and that was based upon careful research. In spite of the opposition of many of the poet's other friends, he completed the work in 1830; and it still remains a cornerstone in any study of Byron's life. The quotation above sprang from the phenomenal success of the first two cantos of "Childe Harold," which appeared in March of 1812. Within three days the first edition had been sold out. Byron had already created a commotion with "English Bards and Scotch Reviewers" in 1809; now he was suddenly the most talked-about poet in England. Moore's account of the effect of the new poem is as follows:

. . . never did there exist before, and it is most probable, never will exist again, a combination of such vast mental power and surpassing genius, with so many other of those advantages and attractions, by which the world is, in general, dazzled and captivated. The effect was, accordingly, electric;—his had not to wait for any of the ordinary gradations, but seemed to spring up, like the palace of a fairy tale, in a night. As he himself briefly described it in his Memoranda,—**"I awoke one morning and found myself famous."** The first edition of his work was disposed of instantly; and, as the echoes of its reputation multiplied on all sides, "Childe Harold" and "Lord Byron" became the theme of every tongue. . . .

I can suck melancholy out of a song, as a weasel sucks eggs

Source: AS YOU LIKE IT (Act II, sc. v, ll. 11-12)
Author: William Shakespeare (1564-1616)
First published: 1623
Type of work: Dramatic comedy

Context: Duke Senior, exiled by his usurping brother, is, together with his followers, having a thoroughly pleasurable time in the paradisal Forest of

Arden. "Sweet are the uses of adversity," says the Duke. One of his followers, however, seems constitutionally unable to take pleasure in anything, unless it is in his own melancholy; he is the "melancholy Jaques." After one of the Duke's men, Lord Amiens, sings a verse of the delightful song, "Under the greenwood tree," Jaques begs him to continue:

JAQUES
More, more, I prithee more.

AMIENS
It will make you melancholy Monsieur Jaques.

JAQUES
I thank it. More, I prithee more. **I can suck melancholy out of a song, as a weasel sucks eggs.** More, I prithee more.

AMIENS
My voice is ragged. I know I cannot please you.

JAQUES
I do not desire you to please me, I do desire you to sing. Come, more; another stanzo. . . .

I care not two-pence

Source: THE COXCOMB (Act V, sc. i)
Authors: Francis Beaumont (1585?-1616) and John Fletcher (1579-1625)
First published: 1647
Type of work: Dramatic comedy

Context: Of the thirty-four plays making up the First Folio of the plays of Beaumont and Fletcher, scholars believe Fletcher to be part or complete author of all but two. "Judicious Beaumont" helped with a maximum of ten—the best among them—and another Elizabethan master of stagecraft, Philip Massinger (1583–1640), collaborated in so many that his name should have appeared among the authors. Most critics agree that Beaumont was certainly a collaborator in *The Coxcomb,* performed by the King's Men (Shakespeare's group), at the Blackfriars Theatre, London, in October, 1612. The next year Beaumont married, moved to his country estate, and gave up playwriting, as had Shakespeare by this time. Fletcher continued by himself and with Massinger to supply the King's Men with dramas until the plague killed him in 1625. Massinger wrote plays until he died, when, according to tradition, he was buried in the same grave as Fletcher. The Stuart world of the mid-seventeenth century considered Fletcher the master of comedy, and the poet Beaumont excellent in Tragedy. *The Coxcomb* is all comedy, but with examples of excellent poetic speeches along with its prose. Its plot is complicated and improbable, but to its audiences "good theatre" and a chance to laugh were more important than a credible plot. Antonio, the foppish Coxcomb, has just returned to his wife, Maria, from several years of travel with his companion, Mercury, who has become bored with him. Mercury is smitten by Maria but decides to run away to escape temptation. However, Antonio assures him that friendship is more valuable than a wife's love, and if Maria and Mercury love each other, Antonio will not stand in their way He even disguises himself as an Irish servant to carry to her a false love letter from Mercury. The wife pierces the disguise, orders her servants to beat and lock up her husband, and goes searching for Mercury. Mercury brings her to his mother's house about the time that the continued absence of Antonio, helped by his babbling while disguised as a servant, has created the suspicion that Maria and Mercury murdered Antonio. In search of them come Antonio's kinsman, Curio, and a Justice whose description by the dramatist as "a shallow one," indicates his descent from Shakespeare's Justice Shallow of *Henry IV* and *The Merry Wives of Windsor*. In Act V, the Justice comes to the house where Mercury and Maria are lodging. His bumbling language confirms Curio's comment that he had sought out the Justice as the nearest official, though certainly not the wisest one.

JUSTICE

It shall not be i' faith friend, here I have it,
That one Antonio a Gentleman, I take it so,
Yes, it is so, a Gentleman is lately thought to
Have been made away, and by my faith, upon a
Pearls ground too, if you consider; well, there's
Knavery in't, I see that without spectacles . . .

. . .

And now I have consider'd, I believe it.

CURIO

What Sir?

JUSTICE

That he was murdered.

CURIO

Did you know him?

JUSTICE

No.

CURIO

Nor how it is suppos'd.

474

No, nor **I care not two-pence,** those are toys, and yet I verily believe he was murder'd, as sure as I believe thou art a man, I have never fail'd in these things yet, w'are a man that's beaten to these matters, experience is a certain conceal'd thing that fails not. . . .

I did not weep, they wept

Source: THE DIVINE COMEDY, INFERNO (Canto XXXIII, ll. 46-47, as translated by H. F. Cary)

Author: Dante Alighieri (1265-1321)

First transcribed: c.1314

Type of work: Christian allegory

Context: Dante's great poem takes its name from the poet's definitions of tragedy and comedy. To Dante, a tragedy begins with pleasant scenes and ends in those of a painful or terrible nature; comedy begins painfully and ends in happiness. Thus, for his poem which begins with the terrible scenes of Hell and ascends through Purgatory to the glory of Paradise, he chose the title *Divine Comedy.* At the midway point of his life (that is, in his thirty-fifth year), the poet finds himself in a dark wood; here he meets the Roman poet Virgil, who offers to conduct him through the underworld. Beatrice, Dante's ideal of womanhood, will then accompany the poet through Purgatory and Paradise. Dante and Virgil accordingly begin their journey; as they progress Dante singles out for description the various great criminals of history. The crimes and corresponding punishments increase in horror as the two travelers progress from one circle to the next. The ninth and lowest circle of Hell is reserved for traitors; it is divided into four rounds, in which the sufferers are buried to various depths in solid ice. The first of these rounds, called Caïna, contains those who have betrayed their kindred; the second round, Antenora, those who have betrayed their country. In crossing this round, Dante encounters a spirit who is engaged in gnawing at the skull of another imprisoned with him, and expresses curiosity. The spirit is that of Count Ugolino, leader of one of three factions seeking control of Pisa in the thirteenth century. He and the Archbishop Ruggieri, leader of a second faction, had combined forces in order to destroy the remaining party. The archbishop then betrayed Ugolino. Ultimately the latter, with two sons and two grandsons, was shut up in the tower and killed by starvation; priests were not allowed to enter, even after he repented, and he died unshriven. Now the spirits of Ugolino and Ruggieri are prisoned together in the ice for eternity, and Ugolino tears at the skull of the archbishop. Ugolino tells Dante of his suffering in the tower:

475

```
                                    . . . When I awoke,
        Before the dawn, amid their sleep I heard
        My sons (for they were with me) weep and ask
        For bread. Right cruel art thou, if no pang
        Thou feel at thinking what my heart foretold;
        And if not now, why use thy tears to flow?
        Now had they waken'd; and the hour drew near
        When they were wont to bring us food; the mind
        Of each misgave him through his dream, and I
        Heard, at its outlet underneath lock'd up
        The horrible tower: whence, uttering not a word,
        I look'd upon the visage of my sons.
        I wept not: so all stone I felt within,
        They wept: and one, my little Anselm, cried,
        'Thou lookest so! Father, what ails thee?' Yet
        I shed no tear, nor answer'd all that day
        Nor the next night, until another sun
        Came out upon the world. When a faint beam
        Had to our doleful prison made its way,
        And in four countenances I descried
        The image of my own, on either hand
        Through agony I bit. . . .
```

I do not choose to run

Source: PRESS REPORT
Author: Calvin Coolidge (1872-1933)
First published: August 2, 1927
Type of work: Presidential statement

Context: The taciturnity of the thirtieth President of the United States caused him to be nicknamed "Silent Cal," and during his presidency many of the jokes about him played upon his habit of wasting no words. His most famous remark was made in answer to the question of whether he would run for a second full term. As vice-president, he had finished out the term of President Harding, who had died in 1923; he had then been elected to one full term as president on his own. The written statement which Coolidge issued to the press on August 2, 1927, read: "I do not choose to run for President in nineteen twenty-eight." Though many people for a while thought the statement equivocal, Coolidge meant what he said. The Republicans then chose Herbert Hoover who won the election overwhelmingly against the Democratic candidate, Alfred E. Smith.

I do not choose to run.

I do not know the method of drawing up an indictment against a whole people

Source: SPEECH ON CONCILIATION WITH AMERICA (March 22, 1775)
Author: Edmund Burke (1729-1797)
First published: 1775
Type of work: Parliamentary address

Context: When he gave this speech in the House of Commons, Edmund Burke believed that it was possible to frame legislation which would end the distrust of the American colonists and bring peace between The Colonies and Great Britain. He points out that he is not searching for anything but simple peace, and that he is speaking with good intentions and genuine simplicity of heart. He states that the number of persons living in the American Colonies has been growing rapidly, and he cites the extent of the trade between The Colonies and Great Britain, illustrating its growth between 1704 and 1772. He suggests that to use force on the colonists will be but temporary and uncertain in its results; that the American colonists are the descendants of Englishmen, "not only devoted to liberty, but to liberty according to English ideas, and on English principles," and he notes that one Englishman is the unfittest person in the world to try to argue another Englishman into slavery. He tries to make the point that the British government, in any attempt to conciliate the Americans, must be willing to admit past mistakes and must cease to regard rebellious colonists as criminals:

At this proposition I must pause a moment. The thing seems a great deal too big for my ideas of jurisprudence. It would seem to my way of conceiving such matters, that there is a very wide difference in reason and policy, between the mode of proceeding on the irregular conduct of scattered individuals, or even of bands of men, who disturb order within the state, and the civil dissensions which may, from time to time, on great questions, agitate the several communities which compose a great empire. It looks to me to be narrow and pedantic, to apply the ordinary ideas of criminal justice to this great public contest. **I do not know the method of drawing up an indictment against a whole people.** . . . I hope I am not ripe to pass sentence on the gravest public bodies, intrusted with magistracies of great authority and dignity, and charged with the safety of their fellow-citizens, upon the very same title that I am. I really think, that for wise men this is not judicious; for sober men, not decent; for minds tinctured with humanity, not mild and merciful.

I dreamt that I dwelt in marble halls

Source: THE BOHEMIAN GIRL (Act II, "The Gipsy-Girl's Dream")
Author: Alfred Bunn (1796?-1860)
First published: 1843
Type of work: Operatic aria

Context: One aria in Michael William Balfe's *The Bohemian Girl,* with a libretto by Alfred Bunn, is known to millions of listeners who have never attended a performance of the opera and who know none of the remaining music in it. The aria is sung in Act II by Count Arnheim's daughter Arline, who was abducted as a child by Devilshoof, a gipsy chieftain, and who has lived with a gipsy band for twelve years. Waking from a deep sleep, Arline reveals a beautiful dream she had to Thaddeus, an exiled Pole who has joined the gipsy band and has fallen in love with Arline. Having saved her from a fierce stag shortly before her abduction, Thaddeus knows her identity, but she herself does not learn it until after her gipsy marriage to her rescuer. The first stanza of the aria reads:

> **I dreamt that I dwelt in marble halls,**
>   With vassals and serfs at my side,
>   And of all who assembled within those walls,
>   That I was the hope and the pride.
>   I had riches too great to count—could boast
>   Of a high ancestral name;
>   And I also dreamt, which pleased me most,
>   That you loved me still the same.

I find the medicine worse than the malady

Source: LOVE'S CURE; OR, THE MARTIAL MAID (Act III, sc. ii)
Author: John Fletcher (1579-1625)
First published: 1647
Type of work: Dramatic comedy

Context: Fernando de Alvarez, during a twenty-year enforced absence from his wife Eugenia, has reared their daughter Clara as a boy and later as a soldier. At home, Eugenia has reared her son Lucio as a girl. When Alvarez returns from his long exile he brings the mannish Clara who must now learn to be a woman, just as effeminate Lucio must be taught to be a man. Piorato, a swordsman, is to aid in the curing of Lucio's womanish character. He informs Alvarez's steward Bobadilla of the method he once used to develop manhood in a cowardly milksop. He starved him before a loaded table until he drew a knife to cut meat. Then he dieted him on special food and drink, and rigorously trained him in the use of gun and sword. Bobadilla wonders if perhaps Piorato could use a reverse kind of training to cure him of an ailment. The idea is, of course, more familiar to us in the words of Francis Bacon, "The remedy is worse than the disease."

BOBADILLA

Could you not cure one, sir, of being too rash
And over-daring?—there now's my disease—
Fool-hardy, as they say? for that in sooth
I am.

PIORATO

Most easily.

BOBADILLA

How?

PIORATO

To make you drunk, sir,
With small beer once a-day, and beat you twice,
Till you be bruis'd all over; if that help not,
Knock out your brains.

BOBADILLA

This is strong physic, signior,
And never will agree with my weak body:
I find the medicine worse than the malady,
And therefore will remain fool-hardy still.

•   •   •

I had a soul above buttons

Source: SYLVESTER DAGGERWOOD (Scene x)
Author: George Colman the Younger (1762-1836)
First published: 1795
Type of work: Farce

Context: Sylvester Daggerwood or New Hay at the Old Market is a one-act picture of London theatrical life written by George Colman (or Coleman) a graduate of Christ College, Oxford, and King's College, Aberdeen. He took over management of the Haymarket Theatre when his father, another playwright, went mad. At the beginning of this farce, Fus-tian, a writer of tragedies, and Daggerwood, a strolling player of the Dunstable Company, sit in the manager's office at the Haymarket Theatre, looking for employment. The skit recounts the difficulties in mounting a theatrical performance, and ends with a song. Fustian seeks details about Daggerwood, whom he takes for some rustic barnstormer. He gets an autobiographical answer. Daggerwood feels himself born for something above a commercial or manufacturing life. He is an artist, though an improverished one. He laments the fact that his wife stutters and therefore cannot help him in a stage career. As for his possessions, he says he has three shirts, and:

DAGGERWOOD

Children too young to make a *debut*—except my eldest, Master Apollo Daggerwood; a youth of only eight years old; who has twice made his appearance in Tom Thumb, to an overflowing and brilliant barn—house, I mean—with unbounded and universal applause.

FUSTIAN

Have you been long upon the stage, Mr. Daggerwood?

DAGGERWOOD

Fifteen years since I first smelt the lamp, Sir. My father was an eminent Button-Maker at Birmingham; . . . but **I had a soul above buttons,** and abhorred the idea of mercenary marriage. I panted for a liberal profession—so ran away from my father, and engaged with a travelling company of Comedians.

I had had an affair with the moon

Source: A SENTIMENTAL JOURNEY THROUGH FRANCE AND ITALY ("The Monk. Calais")
Author: Laurence Sterne (1713-1768)
First published: 1768
Type of work: Travel miscellany

Context: In 1765 Sterne traveled through France and Italy; his decision to describe the journey from a "sentimental" point of view probably resulted from his previous account of a stay in France (in *Tristram Shandy*). The present work was intended to reach four volumes; but Sterne completed only two, dying a little less than a month after their publication. His style is best described as chaotic. An effervescent person, Sterne seems in his writings to have approached all aspects of life gleefully. There is little continuity or progress to his books; they are gossipy, haphazard, funny, at times hilarious. They are also full of surprises, vivid snapshots, color and variety. They digress, as Sterne intended: to him digression was an art, and it is obvious that he delighted in it. *A Sentimental Journey* begins with a conversation between Yorick (Sterne) and a gentleman who has been to France and as a result is an immeasurably superior person. Yorick decides that if a mere twenty miles can make that much difference he may as well go himself—so he grabs up his

480

portmanteau and departs. In no time at all he is in Calais and enjoying an excellent dinner. The wine is outstanding; Yorick's heart swells with love for his fellow man. He finds himself overflowing with benevolence and generosity. He kicks his portmanteau: mere possessions are paltry things. Taking out his purse, he wishes he had someone to share it with. His wish is unexpectedly granted, as is told below; but be it said to Yorick's credit that he later repents of his sudden change of heart and actually does reward the supplicant. To return: Yorick, glowing with wine and his own burgeoning humanity, has just declared himself King of France and wants to present his portmanteau to the first beggar who desires it:

I had scarce uttered the words, when a poor monk of the order of St. Francis came into the room to beg something for his convent. No man cares to have his virtues the sport of contingencies —or one man may be generous, as another man is puissant—*sed non quo ad hanc*—or be it as it may—for there is no regular reasoning upon the ebbs and flows of our humours; they may depend upon the same causes, for aught I know, which influence the tides themselves—'twould oft be no discredit to us, to suppose it was so: I'm sure at least for myself, that in many a case I should be more highly satisfied, to have it said by the world, **"I had had an affair with the moon,** in which there was neither sin nor shame," than have it pass altogether as my own act and deed, wherein there was so much of both.

But be this as it may. The moment I cast my eyes upon him, I was predetermined not to give him a single sous; and accordingly I put my purse into my pocket—button'd it up—set myself a little more upon my center, and advanced up gravely to him: there was something, I fear, forbidding in my look: I have his figure this moment before my eyes, and think there was that in it which deserved better.

I have a kind of alacrity in sinking

Source: THE MERRY WIVES OF WINDSOR (Act III, sc. v, l. 14)
Author: William Shakespeare (1564-1616)
First published: 1602
Type of work: Dramatic comedy

Context: As the play progresses, Sir John Falstaff sees himself as a great lover and decides to have affairs with the wives of both Master Ford and Master Page in order to get at the family purses. The two ladies talk and discover that Falstaff has sent each identical love notes. The two are not at all interested in his propositions, but they decide to have some fun at the fat knight's expense. Of course, neither husband is told what is being planned, but an informer tells both of them that the wives are going to be unfaithful and thereby cuckold the two men. After the two ladies plot their scheme, Mistress Ford decides the meeting time and sends word to Falstaff. Master Ford is also informed of the rendezvous by one of Sir John's followers. Mistress Ford and Mistress Page had plotted for Mistress Page to come in just after Falstaff arrives, and Mistress Ford would hide him in a dirty clothes basket. Mistress Ford had previously instructed two servants to carry out the basket and dump Falstaff into the river. Not only does Mistress Page appear but also Master Ford and several of his friends; thus Falstaff is doubly ready to hide in the laundry basket. Being so obese, he of course sinks rapidly to the river bottom when dumped by the servants.

FALSTAFF
. . .

. . . The rogues slighted me into the river with as little remorse, as they would have drowned a bitch's blind puppies, fifteen i' th' litter; and you may know by my size, that **I have a kind of alacrity in sinking.** If the bottom were as deep as hell, I should down. I had been drowned, but that the shore was shelvy and shallow. A death that I abhor. For the water swells a man; and what a thing should I have been, when I had been swelled! I should have been a mountain of mummy.

I have not slept one wink

Source: CYMBELINE (Act III, sc. iv, l. 102)
Author: William Shakespeare (1564-1616)
First published: 1623
Type of work: Tragi-comedy

Context: Imogen, daughter of King Cymbeline, marries Posthumus against the wishes of the king and her stepmother, who wants her to marry the latter's son, Cloten. Cymbeline banishes Posthumus, who, in Italy, makes a bet with an Italian, Iachimo, on the purity and faithfulness of the wife from whom he is forcibly separated. Through treachery on the part of the Italian, Posthumus is led to believe that Imogen has been untrue to him. Posthumus has ordered, by letter, his servant Pisanio, to kill her. Pisanio, however, knows of Imogen's faithfulness and the suffering she has gone through for her husband. He reveals to her his orders, and she, feeling life is worthless if Posthumus believes her to be an adultress, pleads with Pisanio: "I draw the sword myself. Take it, and hit/ The innocent mansion of my love, my heart."

. . .

IMOGEN
. . . Where's thy knife?
Thou art too slow to do thy master's bidding

When I desire it too.

PISANIO
O gracious lady,
Since I received command to do this business,
I have not slept one wink.

IMOGEN
Do't and to bed then.

PISANO
I'll wake mine eyeballs out first.

I have nothing to declare except my genius

Source: COMMENT TO CUSTOMS OFFICERS (as reported by Frank Harris)
Author: Oscar Wilde (1856-1900)
First spoken: 1881
Type of work: Biographical anecdote

Context: No one ever characterized the Dublin-born wit Oscar Wilde as a modest person. Friends continually quoted his boasting, sometimes with a basis in fact. Said E. F. Benson: "How like was his talk to the play of a sunlit fountain." Once, along with an invitation to dinner, the host expressed uncertainty about what would be served. "Oh, anything," Wilde assured him. "I have the simplest tastes. I am always satisfied with the best." About his writing, he declared: "Would you like to know the grand drama of my life? It is that I have put my genius into my life—I have put only my talent into my works." One of his most-quoted quips came at the end of his voyage to New York in 1881 to lecture and press for a production of his drama *Vera.* As his friend Frank Harris described the episode:

It was on the cards that he might succeed in his new adventure. The taste of America in letters and art is still strongly influenced, if not formed, by English taste, and, if Oscar Wilde had been properly accredited, it is probable that his extraordinary gift of speech would have won him success in America as a lecturer.

His phrase to the Revenue Officers on landing: **"I have nothing to declare except my genius,"** turned the limelight full upon him and excited comment and discussion all over the country. But the fuglemen of his caste whose praise had brought him to the front in England were almost unrepresented in the States, and never bold enough to be partisan. . . .

I have set my life upon a cast

Source: KING RICHARD THE THIRD (Act V, sc. iv, l. 9)
Author: William Shakespeare (1564-1616)
First published: 1597
Type of work: Historical drama

Context: Richard III, a deformed hunch-back, has usurped the throne of England by hypocrisy, dissemblance, and murder. The Earl of Richmond, later King Henry VII, leads a revolt against the villainous king, in which the opposing armies meet at Bosworth Field. In desperation Richard vainly seeks a replacement for his slain horse. In a final speech, directed to a supporter, before his death at the hand of Richmond, Richard refuses to withdraw from the fray, saying that the die that determines his fate has already been cast, and he will await his fortune:

RICHARD
Slave, **I have set my life upon a cast,**
And I will stand the hazard of the die.
I think there be six Richmonds in the field;
Five have I slain to-day instead of him.
A horse, a horse, my kingdom for a horse!
[*Exeunt.*]

I have taken all knowledge to be my province

Source: LETTER TO LORD BURGHLEY (1592)
Author: Sir Francis Bacon (1561–1626)
First published: 1734
Type of work: Personal letter

Context: Famous English philosopher and statesman Francis Bacon was appointed Lord Chancellor under James I in 1618 and was created Baron Verulam in 1618 and Viscount St. Albans in 1621. These were the crowning political and social achievements for a man who possessed unquestioned abilities and a rather crass determination to exploit them. Without doubt he was one of the most brilliant men of his day. He carried on scientific and philosophic investigations and planned to reorganize the epistemological systems of his time on an experimental inductive basis. He was stubbornly opposed to reasoning from authority and the syllogistic quibbling to which the Scholastic philosophy had declined in the early seventeenth century. Much of his philosophic work was written in Latin, most significant of which are *Novum Organum* and *De Augmentis Scientiarum*. In literature he is, of course, best known for his essays. At the age of thirty-one ("I wax somewhat ancient; one and thirty years is a great deal of sand in the hour-glass"), in good health, and with as-

484

piring ambitions, he writes in 1592 to Lord Burghley to request a place and opportunity for service to his lordship and the crown:

> Again, the meanness of my estate doth somewhat move me: for though I cannot accuse myself that I am either prodigal or slothful, yet my health is not to spend, nor my course to get. Lastly, I confess that I have as vast contemplative ends, as I have moderate civil ends: for **I have taken all knowledge to be my province;** and if I could purge it of two sorts of rovers, whereof the one with frivolous disputations, confutations, and verbosities, the other with blind experiments and auricular traditions and impostures, hath committed so many spoils, I hope I should bring in industrious observations, grounded conclusions, and profitable inventions and discoveries; the best state of that province.

I hear America singing

Source: LEAVES OF GRASS ("I hear America Singing," Line 1)
Author: Walt Whitman (1819-1892)
First published: 1860
Type of work: Lyric poem

Context: When *Leaves of Grass* was first published, it met with a storm of abuse due in part to the originality of Whitman's style; his poems were a radical departure from previous metrical conventions. Cast in the form of inspired chants, they are not quite blank verse but a verse-prose combination, exciting and full of vitality. Whitman's ideal was to depict America in its entirety, as he saw it, leaving out nothing and glossing nothing over. He loved the common man and had toured the country on foot, working his way from place to place as carpenter and builder. He felt an intense personal relationship to all Creation—to God, to nature, to mankind, to life itself. This idealist who vowed to be a realist found his work despised. He dealt with social and moral topics with a freedom unknown in the 1850's, and to many his work was at best shocking, at worst depraved. It was only gradually that he was recognized for the original genius that he was. Whitman's vitality and enthusiasm, and his ability to see the individual elements of his vast subject with objective and comprehensive clarity and so to present them, are qualities for which he is widely appreciated today, as is the rugged beauty of his lines. In the first portion of *Leaves of Grass,* a number of poems are given under the general heading "Inscriptions," a suggestive and appropriate term; all are brief and intense, and each is in its way a tribute to some aspect of life. The poem entitled "I Hear America Singing" is the eighteenth of these. In it Whitman celebrates his love for the workingman, which he frequently reemphasizes throughout his poetry; at the same time he gives a vivid picture of a young and bustling country, enthusiastically building itself toward greatness.

> I hear America singing, the varied carols I hear,
> Those of mechanics, each one singing his as it should be blithe
>   and strong,
> The carpenter singing his as he measures his plank or beam,
> The mason singing his as he makes ready for work, or leaves off
>   work,
> The boatman singing what belongs to him in his boat, the deck-
>   hand singing on the steamboat deck,
> The shoemaker singing as he sits on his bench, the hatter singing
>   as he stands,
> The wood-cutter's song, the ploughboy's on his way in the morn-
>   ing, or at noon intermission or at sundown,
> The delicious singing of the mother, or of the young wife at work,
>   or of the girl sewing or washing,
> Each singing what belongs to him or her and to none else,
> The day what belongs to the day—at night the party of young fel-
>   lows, robust, friendly,
> Singing with open mouths their strong melodious songs.

I know a bank where the wild thyme blows

Source: A MIDSUMMER NIGHT'S DREAM (Act II, sc. i, l. 249)
Author: William Shakespeare (1564-1616)
First published: 1600
Type of work: Dramatic comedy

Context: Excitement prevails in Athens over the marriage of Duke Theseus and Hippolyta, his fair captive Queen of the Amazons. Even the fairies of India, including King Oberon and Queen Titania, have come to celebrate. Oberon and Titania, however, argue over a changeling boy that Titania refuses to give to Oberon. Vowing vengeance, Oberon sends Puck to secure a love potion that will make Titania fall foolishly in love with whatever her eyes behold, even a beast. As Puck appears with the herb, Oberon says:

OBERON

• • •

> **I know a bank where the wild thyme blows,**
> Where oxlips and the nodding violet grows,
> Quite over-canopied with lush woodbine,
> With sweet musk-roses, and with eglantine.
> There sleeps Titania sometime of the night,
> Lulled in these flowers with dances and delight.
> And there the snake throws her enamelled skin,
> Weed wide enough to wrap a fairy in.
> And with the juice of this I'll streak her eyes,

486

And make her full of hateful fantasies.

. . .

I know a hawk from a handsaw

Source: HAMLET (Act II, sc. ii, l. 396)
Author: William Shakespeare (1564-1616)
First published: 1603
Type of work: Dramatic tragedy

Context: Hamlet is playing a very dangerous game. After having been told by his father's ghost that his Uncle Claudius, the present king, is the murderer of his father, Hamlet feigns madness while he feels his way. Two old schoolmates, Rosencrantz and Guildenstern, have been set the task of determining the cause of Hamlet's madness. Hamlet lures them on, teasingly suggesting a number of possibilities. Finally, he almost, but not quite, admits his sanity. The proverb, "I know a hawk from a handsaw," means simply that he still has sense enough to distinguish obvious dissimilarities, and may be intended as an ironic attack on Rosencrantz and Guildenstern, who pretend loyalty and friendship. "Handsaw" is usually explained as a North Country word meaning "heron."

HAMLET
. . .
You are welcome; but my uncle-father, and aunt-mother, are
    deceiv'd.

GUILDENSTERN
In what, my dear lord?

HAMLET
I am but mad north-north-west; when the wind is southerly
I know a hawk from a handsaw.

I know a trick worth two of that

Source: KING HENRY THE FOURTH, PART ONE (Act II, sc. i, ll. 40–41)
Author: William Shakespeare (1564-1616)
First published: 1598
Type of work: Historical drama

Context: King Henry IV, beset with political problems as rebellion breaks out in the north and in the west, is also plagued by what he assumes to be the utter dissipation of his son and heir apparent, Prince Hal. Actually, Hal perceives his role quite clearly; in anticipation of the time when he will

487

ascend the throne, he is determined to mingle with all classes of people in order that his rule might be more efficient. Moreover, there can be no doubt of Hal's affection for his old companion in fun, Falstaff, that "huge bombard of wit." The group of Eastcheap rowdies with whom the Prince consorts plans to rob the king's retainers at Gads Hill. Secretly Hal and Poins have contrived an elaborate scheme to counter-rob the robbers in order to force Falstaff to display his true colors. Effecting the plan awaits now only the confirmation of the specific time the gold will be in transit. This information is to be secured by one of the prince's companions, Gadshill, who has an agreement with the chamberlain of the inn. In the early morning hours Gadshill mingles with the carriers both to gain their confidence and to pick up any information which might be useful to the robbers. But the carriers are a wary lot; quick with an evasive retort, they effectively parry Gadshill's leading questions:

GADSHILL

Good morrow, carriers. What's a clock?

FIRST CARRIER

I think it be two a clock.

GADSHILL

I prithee lend me thy lantern, to see my gelding in the stable.

FIRST CARRIER

Nay by God soft, **I know a trick worth two of that,** i' faith.

GADSHILL

I pray thee lend me thine.

SECOND CARRIER

Ay when? Canst tell? Lend me thy lantern quotha? Marry I'll see thee hang'd first.

GADSHILL

Sirrah carrier, what time do you mean to come to London?

SECOND CARRIER

Time enough to go to bed with a candle, I warrant thee. Come neighbor Mugs, we'll call up the gentlemen; they will along with company, for they have great charge.

I know thee who thou art

Source: PARADISE LOST (Book II, l. 990)
Author: John Milton (1608-1674)
First published: 1667
Type of work: Epic poem

Context: Satan, once the bright angel named Lucifer, has been plunged into Hell after the civil war in Heaven, precipitated by his ambition to rebel against God's authority. Following their fall, Satan and his fellow rebels hold a conclave in Hell to decide what action to take. Some of the fallen angels urge another battle with the heavenly host, to be undertaken with the goal of regaining Heaven; others urge against renewing the combat. A suggestion by Satan is reviewed, a third proposal. It is to search out the world and man, whose creation by God has been prophesied. This course of action is chosen, and Satan himself undertakes the difficult mission. He passes out of Hell to "the hoary deep, a dark/ Illimitable ocean without bound,/ Without dimension, where length, breadth, and height,/ And time and place are lost." Passing through this void, Satan comes to the throne of Chaos, the ruling spirit, who holds court with Night, his consort, and other spirits: Orcus, Ades, Demogorgon, Rumor, Chance, Tumult, Confusion, and Discord. Satan offers to return the newly created universe to its original darkness, if the spirit Chaos will tell him where it is. Chaos replies to Satan:

> . . . him thus the anarch old
> With faltering speech and visage incomposed
> Answered. "**I know thee,** stranger, **who thou art,**
> That mighty leading angel, who of late
> Made head against heaven's king, though overthrown.
> I saw and heard, for such a numerous host
> Fled not in silence through the frighted deep
> With ruin upon ruin, rout on rout,
> Confusion worse confounded; and heaven gates
> Poured out by millions her victorious bands
> Pursuing."

I lisped in numbers, for the numbers came

Source: EPISTLE TO DR. ARBUTHNOT (Line 128)
Author: Alexander Pope (1688-1744)
First published: 1735
Type of work: Satire

Context: According to the advertisement of the first publication of this work, which was written by the poet himself, the epistle is a complaint against persons who had in one way or another attacked Pope, not only

489

through his person, but also through his family and morals. The epistle takes the form of a dialogue between Dr. John Arbuthnot, the poet's friend, and the poet. Arbuthnot, in addition to being Pope's intimate, was physician to Queen Anne and a well-known literary figure of the time. In the dialogue Pope complains that he gets no rest from flatterers, foes, and would-be writers—all of whom besiege his door. The flatterers, he says, are the worst, for what the flatterer intends as praise proves ridicule in its exaggeration. Others, complains Pope, comment ridiculously that he coughs like Horace, has Ovid's nose, and holds his head in illness like Virgil. He goes on, answering a rhetorical question he puts to himself:

> Why did I write? what sin to me unknown
> Dipp'd me in ink, my parents', or my own?
> As yet a child, nor yet a fool to fame,
> **I lisp'd in numbers, for the numbers came.**
> I left no calling for this idle trade,
> No duty broke, no father disobey'd.
> The Muse but serv'd to ease some friend, not wife,
> To help me through this long disease, my life;
> To second, Arbuthnot! thy art and care,
> And teach the being you preserv'd, to bear.

I must be about my Father's business

Source: LUKE 2:49
Author: Unknown (Traditionally Luke the Apostle)
First transcribed: c.80-100
Type of work: Gospel

Context: The authorship of this Gospel is a matter of some dispute. Both Luke and Acts were evidently written by the same man. Some scholars find internal evidence indicating that the writer must have been a physician; and since Luke the physician was a friend and companion of the Apostle Paul, the traditional attribution of this Gospel to him would seem logical. In any case, the author is at some pains in the beginning of the work to indicate that many are writing gospels, and that he has gathered his own material from people still living who were present when many of these events occurred. The rest of Chapter I discusses the various events which foretold the birth of Christ. In the second chapter he tells the story of the Nativity in terms of quiet and moving simplicity; this is the account which is, because of its poetic beauty, most familiar to us. It has long been a favorite passage for use in the celebration of Christmas. Luke then records the significant events that occurred during the infancy of Jesus: circumcision and purification according to the law, the presentation in the Temple, and the prophecies of Simeon and Anna. Simeon was an old man, who had been told by the Holy Ghost that he would see Christ before

490

his death. Led by the Spirit, he enters the Temple and takes the child up in his arms, saying He will be the glory of Israel. Anna, a prophetess, also enters the Temple at this time and confirms what Simeon has said. When all customary religious observances have been completed, Jesus' parents return with him to Nazareth. Luke tells very little more about the childhood of Jesus, save that He was wise beyond his years. He supports this statement with a memorable picture of the group of old scholars, who are delighted with the boy's eagerness and precocity:

And the child grew, and waxed strong in spirit, filled with wisdom: and the grace of God was upon him.

Now his parents went to Jerusalem every year at the feast of the passover.

And when he was twelve years old, they went up to Jerusalem after the custom of the feast.

And when they had fulfilled the days, as they returned, the child Jesus tarried behind in Jerusalem; and Joseph and his mother knew not of it.

But they, supposing him to have been in the company, went a day's journey; and they sought him among their kinsfolk and acquaintance.

And when they found him not, they turned back again to Jerusalem, seeking him.

And it came to pass, that after three days they found him in the temple, sitting in the midst of the doctors, both hearing them, and asking them questions.

And all that heard him were astonished at his understanding and answers.

And when they saw him, they were amazed: and his mother said unto him, Son, why hast thou thus dealt with us? behold, thy father and I have sought thee sorrowing.

And he said unto them, How is it that ye sought me? wist ye not that **I must be about my Father's business?**

I must be cruel only to be kind

Source: HAMLET (Act III, sc. iv, l. 178)
Author: William Shakespeare (1564-1616)
First published: 1603
Type of work: Dramatic tragedy

Context: Confronting his mother, Queen Gertrude, who has joined in an incestuous marriage with his uncle, Hamlet kills the evesdropping Polonius and reproaches his mother for the bestiality of her nature and begs her to repent. For his quickness to kill and his harshness with her, he asks forgiveness and explains the reason for his cruelty.

HAMLET
   . . . Once more good night,
And when you are desirous to be blessed,
I'll blessing beg of you. For this same lord,
I do repent; but heaven hath pleased it so
To punish me with this, and this with me,
That I must be their scourge and minister.
I will bestow him, and will answer well
The death I gave him. So again good night.
I must be cruel only to be kind.
Thus bad begins, and worse remains behind. . . .

I must become a borrower of the night

Source: MACBETH (Act III, sc. i, l. 27)
Author: William Shakespeare (1564-1616)
First published: 1623
Type of work: Dramatic tragedy

Context: Duncan has been murdered, and Macbeth, on the disappearance of Malcolm and Donalbain, sons of the dead king, has been named sovereign. Nature is in a turmoil, but Macbeth has ordered a feast at which he wishes Banquo's presence. Banquo, however, in a short soliloquy, reveals his suspicions of foul play on Macbeth's part. He also reminds himself of the witches' prophecy that he shall be "the root and father/ Of many kings." He has to leave with his son, Fleance, but he hopes to be back in time for Macbeth's festivities. Macbeth has other plans, however, for he is afraid of Banquo and Banquo's knowledge of the old hags' words.

MACBETH
Ride you this afternoon?

BANQUO
Aye, my good lord.

MACBETH
We should have else desired your good advice,
Which still hath been both grave and prosperous,
In this day's council; but we'll take tomorrow.
Is't far you ride?

BANQUO
As far, my lord, as will fill up the time
'Twixt this and supper. Go not my horse the better,
I must become a borrower of the night
For a dark hour or twain.

492

I own the soft impeachment

Source: THE RIVALS (Act V, sc. iii)
Author: Richard Brinsley Sheridan (1751-1816)
First published: 1775
Type of work: Dramatic comedy

Context: In this last scene of Sheridan's play each of the several strands of the plot is unwoven. Captain Absolute is revealed to be also the fictitious "Ensign Beverley," his own rival for the hand of Lydia Languish in marriage. He is accepted in his true identity by her, to be her husband. One of his real rivals, Acres, a bumpkin from the country, refuses to fight a duel with "Ensign Beverley" when he discovers who the "ensign" really is, his old friend Captain Absolute; young Acres gives up any claim he might have for Lydia in marriage, accepting the girl's decision. But Sir Lucius O'Trigger, another rival suitor, refuses to abdicate his suit for Lydia's hand, being a man of action and honor. He produces letters from "Delia," who is, he assumes, really Lydia Languish. However, it turns out that "Delia" is actually Mrs. Malaprop, Lydia's elderly guardian, who has been writing love letters to Sir Lucius. When Sir Lucius produces the letters, Mrs. Malaprop is forced to confess:

MRS. MALAPROP

O, he will dissolve my mystery!—Sir Lucius, perhaps there's some mistake—perhaps I can illuminate——

SIR LUCIUS

Pray, old gentlewoman, don't interfere where you have no business. —Miss Languish, are you my Delia or not?

LYDIA

Indeed, Sir Lucius, I am not. [*Walks aside with Capt. Absolute.*]

MRS. MALAPROP

Sir Lucius O'Trigger—ungrateful as you are—**I own the soft impeachment**—pardon my blushes, I am Delia.

SIR LUCIUS

You Delia—pho! pho! be easy.

MRS. MALAPROP

Why, thou barbarous Vandyke—those letters are mine. —When you are more sensible of my benignity—perhaps I may be brought to encourage your addresses.

Mrs. Malaprop, I am extremely sensible of your condescension; and whether you or Lucy have put this trick on me, I am equally beholden to you. —And, to show you I am not ungrateful, Captain Absolute, since you have taken that lady from me, I'll give you my Delia into the bargain.

I rose the wrong way today

Source: THE TOWN-FOP; OR, SIR TIMOTHY TAWDREY (Act V, sc. i)
Author: Aphra Behn (1640-1689)
First published: 1676
Type of work: Dramatic comedy

Context: Betty Flauntit is a common prostitute who is ambitious to rise in her world. As a first step she has become the kept woman of Sir Timothy Tawdrey, a London fop. Her new status, however, does not prevent her from plying her trade in the bawdy-house kept by Mrs. Driver. Nor does his keeping of Betty Flauntit prevent Sir Timothy from visiting bawdy-houses, including Mrs. Driver's establishment. On the night of his forced marriage to his cousin, Lady Diana, Bellmour escapes from the bridal chamber and, beside himself with grief over being unable to marry Celinda, the girl he loves, goes to Mrs. Driver's place of business with Sir Timothy. Bellmour, emotionally upset, drinks considerably and loses large sums of money to Sir Timothy and the latter's hangers-on. Mrs. Driver, thinking Bellmour an easy mark, sends Betty Flauntit, along with two other girls, when Sir Timothy calls for women. Betty Flauntit expects, one way or another, to make Bellmour her victim. But her intentions are first prevented by Sir Timothy's recognition of her and, later, by the appearance of Charles, Bellmour's younger brother, who comes to rescue the distraught Bellmour from the rogues who are trying to fleece him. To make matters worse for Betty Flauntit, Mrs. Driver tells Sir Timothy that Betty is not being "true" to her lover. Escaping from the bawdy-house when a brawl breaks out, she walks in Covent Garden, musing over her ill luck:

BETTY FLAUNTIT

Sure **I rose the wrong way to day,** I have had such damn'd ill luck every way: First, to be sent for to such a Man as this Bellmour, and, as the Devil wou'd have it, to find my Knight there; then to be just upon the Point of making my Fortune, and to be interrupted by that virtuous Brother of his; then to have a Quarrel happen, that (before I could whisper him in the Ear, to say so much as, Meet me here again—anon) forc'd me to quit the House, lest the Constable had done it for me; then that silly Baud should discover all to my Cully. If this be not ill Luck, the Devil's in't. . . .

494

I saw the iron enter into his soul

Source: A SENTIMENTAL JOURNEY THROUGH FRANCE AND ITALY ("The Captive. Paris")
Author: Laurence Sterne (1713-1768)
First published: 1768
Type of work: Travel miscellany

Context: Yorick (Sterne) has rushed off to France at a moment's notice because he has discovered in conversation that a trip to that country makes one immeasurably superior; as he observes, if a mere journey of twenty miles can accomplish this result, he may as well go. Arrived in France, he proceeds in a leisurely fashion toward Paris; on the road he flirts with women, hires a servant named La Fleur, and has a fine time in an aimless, harmless way. In Paris he is so overcome by a female shopkeeper that he buys several pairs of gloves, all the wrong size; he is blissfully unaware that she may be available for an altogether different kind of relationship. He attends the opera, learns to his astonishment that the French have a ribald sense of humor, and ponders the fact. Two women have been seated in the same box with a clergyman, and the crowd heckles him, enjoining him to keep his hands in the air. Yorick also notes a dwarf who cannot see the stage because a huge German is standing in front of him. French justice triumphs: a Gendarme places the dwarf in front of the German. Wandering about the city later, Yorick flirts with a chambermaid. Then he learns the police are looking for him. It seems that in his haste to leave England he had forgotten that England and France are at war; moreover, he has no passport. In a sudden access of contrition, Yorick decides to turn himself in; but, hearing a voice, he looks around and spies a starling in a cage. The bird is repeating, in English, "I can't get out." Yorick purchases the feathered prisoner and then begins to reconsider his legal duty; he ponders in his mind the horrors of imprisonment. Giving his imagination free rein, he pictures the victim in the cell:

> I beheld his body half wasted away with long expectation and confinement, and felt what kind of sickness of the heart it was which arises from hope deferr'd. Upon looking nearer I saw him pale and feverish: in thirty years the western breeze had not once fann'd his blood—he had seen no sun, no moon, in all that time— nor had the voice of friend or kinsman breathed through his lattice:—his children—
>
> But here my heart began to bleed—and I was forced to go on with another part of the portrait.
>
> He was sitting upon the ground upon a little straw, in the furthest corner of his dungeon, which was alternately his chair and bed: a little calendar of small sticks were laid at the head, notch'd all over with the dismal days and nights he had passed there—he had one of these little sticks in his hand, and with a rusty nail he

was etching another day of misery to add to the heap. As I darkened the little light he had, he lifted up a hopeless eye towards the door, then cast it down—shook his head, and went on with his work of affliction. I heard his chains upon his legs, as he turned his body to lay his little stick upon the bundle. —He gave a deep sigh—**I saw the iron enter into his soul**—I burst into tears—I could not sustain the picture of confinement which my fancy had drawn—I started up from my chair, and called La Fleur—I bid him bespeak me a *remise,* and have it ready at the door of the hotel by nine in the morning.

I seem to tread on Classic ground

Source: A LETTER FROM ITALY (Line 12)
Author: Joseph Addison (1672-1719)
First published: 1703
Type of work: Literary dedication

Context: Having studied Latin and Greek at Queens College, Oxford, Addison was eager to visit the continent. Through the kindness of Lord Chancellor Somers in 1700, he was given a yearly grant of three hundred pounds to spend four years abroad. His first report of activities came in his rhymed *A Letter from Italy,* dedicated to Charles, Lord Halifax, dated Feb. 19, 1701, and published two years later. His travel book, *Remarks* on *Italy* (1705) dedicated to Somers, was an elaboration on the *Letter,* disappointing to readers who wanted a comment on Italian customs and policies, but delightful in its poetic comparison between the Italy he saw and that drawn by classical writers. In the first stanza, the poet comments on the life of retirement enjoyed by Lord Halifax, while Addison is traveling through balmy Italy a land which has inspired so many to write poetry:

> For wheresoe'er I turn my ravished eyes
> Gay gilded scenes and shining prospects rise,
> Poetic fields encompass me around,
> And still **I seem to tread on Classic ground;**
> For here the Muse so oft her harp has strung
> That not a mountain rears its head unsung,
> Renowned in verse each shady thicket grows
> And every stream in heavenly numbers flows.

I shall sleep like a top

Source: THE RIVALS (Act III)
Author: Sir William Davenant (1606-1668)
First published: 1668
Type of work: Tragi-comedy

496

Context: Sir William Davenant or D'Avenant, was the godson of William Shakespeare. Many suspect that he was an actual son of the great playwright, a belief that Davenant made no effort to deny. But, though he was governor of the King and Queen's Company of Players (1635), he could not equal the dramatic skill of his godfather. With John Dryden (1631–1700), he adapted Shakespeare's *The Tempest,* without improving it. He wrote a number of plays by himself before the closing of the English theaters by Cromwell in 1642; and when he returned from exile in France he formed another acting group for his friend, William Beeston. The theater-loving King Charles II knighted him. Davenant wrote both heroic tragedies and Restoration comedies. *The Rivals* has no connection with the more famous comedy of a century later by Richard B. Sheridan (1751–1816). Davenant's play is a drastically changed rewriting of the earlier *The Two Noble Kinsmen* (1613), thought by many to represent the collaboration of Shakespeare and Fletcher, that, in turn was based on "The Knight's Tale," from Chaucer's *The Canterbury Tales.* The characters have been re-christened. Theocles and Philander are both in love with star-crossed Celania, daughter of the Provost of Prince Arcon of Arcadia. Thwarted in her love for Philander, Celania has gone mad. Perhaps with memories of Ophelia, Davenant presents her in the forest, accompanied by her maid, Leucippe, singing a song born of her insanity. She plans to dress like a man and go searching for her absent love. She will ride a stick like a witch, or pause and sleep. But why "like a top?" The phrase was not forced by the rhyme. The rest of it, the nightingale and the hawthorn, is a poetic figure. A spinning top seems motionless, but it does have a humming sound which may, perhaps, give origin to the expression paraphrased as "to sleep sound." But even granting Celania her madness, it is hard to explain her choice of this figure. Here is her song, with its meaningless refrain.

For straight my green gown into breeches I'll make,
And my long yellow locks much shorter I'll take,
   Sing down a, down, down a, down a.
Then I'll cut me a switch, and on that ride about,
And wander and wander till I find him out,
   With a heigh down, down a, down, down a,
O for a hawthorn; like a nightingale
To lean my breast against, or else **I shall sleep like a top.**

I sighed as a lover, I obeyed as a son

Source: AUTOBIOGRAPHY (World Classics edition, p. 83)
Author: Edward Gibbon (1737-1794)
First published: 1796
Type of work: Autobiography

Context: Edward Gibbon spent most   of his life studying and writing. He

497

was a sickly child with a strong scholarly bent; his life was frequently despaired of until he began to show improved health in his sixteenth year. He was the only one of his father's seven children to reach maturity—a good illustration of the mortality rate at that time. Gibbon went to Oxford in 1752 and while there joined the Roman Catholic Church. He felt the courses at Oxford were a waste of time, and his exasperated father sent him to Lausanne to live with a Calvinist minister, M. Pavilliard. Gibbon learned French through necessity and was soon able to think in that language; his writing, from that time on, exhibited a strong French influence. While there he studied the logic of Crousaz, and as a result returned to Protestantism. He pursued his studies avidly and in 1755 traveled about Switzerland. In 1757 he met Voltaire. It was in this year that he met a girl named Suzanne Curchod, daughter of the pastor of Crassier, and fell in love with her. Gibbon's father, who had just remarried, objected to the marriage of his son. Gibbon complied with his father's wishes in the matter, and did not allow himself to fall in love again. Instead, he continued his studies. During the next few years he determined to write a history, but it was some time before he settled on a topic. Finally, in 1772, he began his *Decline and Fall of the Roman Empire,* a monumental work which took him fifteen years to complete. It may be said to be his life's work; all his studies led up to it, and he wrote little else of consequence. He was interested in his own life history, and a curious fact about this interest is that Gibbon wrote no less than six autobiographical sketches or memoirs. After his death, these were carefully edited by Lord Sheffield and published as a single narrative containing what was considered the best material from each. The third memoir, written about 1789, contains the following wistful account of Gibbon's student friendship and first love:

I should be ashamed if the warm season of youth had passed away without any sense of friendship or love; and in the choice of their objects I may applaud the discernment of my head or heart. Mr. George Deyverdun, of Lausanne, was a young Gentleman of high honour and quick feelings, of an elegant taste and a liberal understanding: he became the companion of my studies and pleasures; every idea, every sentiment, was poured into each other's bosom; and our schemes of ambition or retirement always terminated in the prospect of our final and inseparable union. The beauty of Mademoiselle Curchod, the daughter of a country clergyman, was adorned with science and virtue: she listened to the tenderness which she had inspired; but the romantic hopes of youth and passion were crushed, on my return, by the prejudice or prudence of an English parent. **I sighed as a lover, I obeyed as a son;** my wound was insensibly healed by time, absence, and the habits of a new life; and my cure was accelerated by a faithful report of the tranquillity and chearfulness of the Lady herself. Her equal behaviour under the tryals of indigence and prosperity has displayed the firmness of her character. A citizen of Geneva, a rich banker of Paris, made himself happy by rewarding her merit; the genius of her husband has raised him to a perilous eminence; and Madame Necker now divides and alleviates the cares of the first minister of the finances of France.

I 'spect I growed

Source: UNCLE TOM'S CABIN (Chapter 20)
Author: Harriet Beecher Stowe (1811-1896)
First published: 1852
Type of work: Novel

Context: Like all the Beechers of New England, the daughter of the Reverend Lyman Beecher was enthusiastic about religious matters and the improvement of humanity. In 1836, she married Professor Calvin Stowe, and aided runaway slaves through her Cincinnati, Ohio, station of the "Underground Railroad." From these fugitives and from her brothers in New Orleans, she learned of the cruelty of slavery. So she wrote *Uncle Tom's Cabin or Life Among the Lowly,* published serially in an abolitionist newspaper, *The National Era* (June, 1851–April 1852). The work appeared as a novel in 1852 with 300,000 copies sold the first year. Immediately dramatized by G. L. Aikin, and by many others, it was continually performed for almost a century. Though lacking in literary merit, and absurdly sentimental, the novel played an important part in preparing for the American Civil War, and was a powerful factor in preventing the Confederacy from obtaining in Europe full recognition as an independent nation. President Lincoln, meeting her for the first time, exclaimed: "Is this the little woman that sparked this great war?" Topsy, who supplies much of the comedy in the many stage versions, is introduced in Chapter 20. She is an eight-year-old Negress whom St. Clare has bought for Miss Ophelia to educate. Her new mistress starts questioning the slave, whose name may have been suggested by the expression "topsy turvy."

"Have you ever heard anything about God, Topsy?"
The child looked bewildered, but grinned, as usual.
"Do you know who made you?"
"Nobody as I knows on," said the child, with a short laugh.
The idea appeared to amuse her considerably; for her eyes twinkled, and she added.
"I 'spect I grow'd. Don't think nobody never made me."

I stumbled when I saw

Source: KING LEAR (Act IV, sc. i, l. 19)
Author: William Shakespeare (1564-1616)
First published: 1608
Type of work: Dramatic tragedy

499

Context: Believing in the wrong son as King Lear believed in the wrong daughters, the Earl of Gloucester has been betrayed by his bastard, Edmund. Gloucester secretly helps the maddened king and receives a letter telling him that Lear's daughter Cordelia, still faithful despite Lear's banishment of her, is landing at Dover with a French army. All this, Edmund reveals to one of Lear's evil daughters, Regan, and her vicious husband, the Duke of Cornwall. Cornwall blinds Gloucester and turns him out of doors, where he is discovered by his legitimate son, Edgar, falsely denounced by Edmund as a would-be murderer of his father. Edgar has adopted the disguise of a "bedlam beggar," one who is mad or pretends madness to secure charity. Gloucester, who has finally learned the truth about his sons, wishes to be led to the cliffs of Dover in order to commit suicide, and he asks the presumed Bedlamite to lead him. In a speech reminiscent of Oedipus' assertion that he blinded himself because of his disgust with what he could see, Gloucester tells an old retainer that when he had eyes he felt too sure of himself—his "means" made him feel secure; he is better off with his present "defects."

OLD MAN
You cannot see your way.

GLOUCESTER
I have no way, and therefore want no eyes.
I stumbled when I saw. Full oft 'tis seen,
Our means secure us, and our mere defects
Prove our commodities. O dear son Edgar,
The food of thy abused father's wrath;
Might I but live to see thee in my touch,
I'd say I had eyes again.

I was a king in Babylon and you were a Christian slave

Source: ECHOES (xxxvii, to W.A., ll. 3-4)
Author: William Ernest Henley (1849-1903)
First published: 1884
Type of work: Ballad

Context: Crippled by tuberculosis of the bone, this tall English poet on crutches was the model for Long John Silver, of *Treasure Island.* He fought hard, as a critic, against Victorian prudery and in favor of realism. As editor of a magazine, he gave their start to Kipling, Conrad, and Yeats. His own poetry, first collected in *A Book of Verse* (1888), was aggressively masculine. Perhaps "Invictus" from that volume is the best known. His attempt to be "unpoetic" in vocabulary is evident in his Ballad to W.A. (William Archer), number 37 in the division: "Echoes 1872–1889." It is the poem of which the author was proudest. But though even an

500

unimaginative person can understand being "master of my fate" and "captain of my soul," he may not comprehend the theory of transmigration of souls and the parallel existences of the King of Babylon and his Christian slave, described in the five stanzas of this ballad. So he will prefer "Invictus." "Or ever," that is, before the romantic period of chivalry ended, I was King in Babylon and loved a Christian slave. After loving her, I cast her aside, but upon her death, built her a tomb. Now in a new existence, we are together, but there is still a barrier between us. . . . Expressed poetically:

Or ever the knightly years were gone
  With the old world to the grave,
**I was a King in Babylon
  And you were a Christian Slave.**

I saw, I took, I cast you by,
  I bent and broke your pride.
You loved me well, or I heard them lie,
  But your longing was denied.
Surely I knew that by and by
  You cursed your gods and died.

And a myriad suns have set and shone
  Since then upon the grave
Decreed by the King of Babylon
  To her that had been his Slave.

I was all ear

Source: COMUS (Line 559)
Author: John Milton (1608-1674)
First published: 1637
Type of work: Masque

Context: The Earl of Bridgewater's installation as President of Wales was the occasion for the composition of *Comus* and its presentation in the great hall of Ludlow Castle. The earl's daughter and two sons acted leading roles. As the three seek to make their way through a tangled wood, the daughter, known as the Lady, becomes wearied, and the two brothers separate from her to find fruits and berries with which to restore her strength. They become lost in the forest and are met by the attendant Spirit of the Woods, who is disguised as a shepherd. He tells the brothers that they are in the domain of the great sorcerer Comus, son of Bacchus and Circe, who gives wanderers in the forest an enchanted drink that transforms their faces into those of beasts and undermines their reason. The supposed shepherd had listened this very evening to the roar of the wizard's followers that customarily filled the night woods with bar-

501

barous dissonance; he had noted a sudden cessation of the noise which he considered significant. At last he heard a most pleasing sound, a sound which he perceived was the Lady's voice. When he listened intently and discovered that she was in conversation with Comus, he sped through the woods to find the brothers:

At last a soft and solemn breathing sound
Rose like a steam of rich distilled perfumes,
And stole upon the air, that even silence
Was took ere she was ware, and wished she might
Deny her nature, and be never more,
Still to be so displaced. **I was all ear,**
And took in strains that might create a soul
Under the ribs of death; but O ere long
Too well I did perceive it was the voice
Of my most honored lady, your dear sister.
Amazed I stood, harrowed with grief and fear,
And O poor hapless nightingale, thought I,
How sweet thou singest, how near the deadly snare!

I will make a Star-Chamber matter of it

Source: THE MERRY WIVES OF WINDSOR (Act I, sc. i, ll. 1-2)
Author: William Shakespeare (1564-1616)
First published: 1602
Type of work: Dramatic comedy

Context: As the play opens, Robert Shallow, a country justice, is proclaiming that he has been wronged by Sir John Falstaff. Shallow will not be appeased by Parson Hugh Evans, who recognizes that Falstaff is of noble rank and, being on a hunting trip, does not wish to be bothered. But Shallow knows that Falstaff and his men had "beaten" his associates, "kill'd" his deer, and "broke open" his lodge. Thus he says at the first of the play that despite the fact that Sir John is of the nobility, he will take his charges before a court and "make a Star-Chamber matter of it." The Star-Chamber (so called because of the stars on the ceiling of the room where it sat) was a high court exercising very wide powers.

SHALLOW
Sir Hugh, persuade me not. **I will make a Star-Chamber matter of it.** If he were twenty Sir John Falstaffs, he shall not abuse Robert Shallow, Esquire.

502

I will praise any man that will praise me

Source: ANTONY AND CLEOPATRA (Act II, sc. vi, l. 92)
Author: William Shakespeare (1564-1616)
First published: 1623
Type of work: Dramatic tragedy

Context: The rulers of the Roman Empire—Mark Antony, Octavius Caesar, and Lepidus—force the rebellious Pompey to come to terms, and the four prepare to seal their pact by a round of eating and drinking. In the general euphoria that follows, the delightfully shrewd and cynical Enobarbus, friend and officer of Antony, greets an old acquaintance, the equally shrewd and cynical Menas, friend and officer of Pompey. Their conversation is a humorous foil to the dialogue of the four military leaders:

MENAS

. . . You and I have known, sir.

ENOBARBUS

At sea, I think.

MENAS

We have sir.

ENOBARBUS

You have done well by water.

MENAS

And you by land.

ENOBARBUS

I will praise any man that will praise me, though it cannot be denied what I have done by land.

MENAS

Nor what I have done by water.

ENOBARBUS

Yes, something you can deny for your own safety. You have been a great thief by sea.

MENAS

And you by land.

ENOBARBUS

There I deny my land service. But give me your hand Menas, if our eyes had authority, here they might take two thieves kissing.

503

I would fain die a dry death

Source: THE TEMPEST (Act I, sc. i, ll. 71-72)
Author: William Shakespeare (1564-1616)
First published: 1623
Type of work: Tragi-comedy

Context: A ship bearing noblemen of Milan and Naples, encountering a storm produced by the conjuring of Prospero (the rightful Duke of Milan, whose throne has been usurped by his wicked brother Antonio), is wrecked off the coast of the island occupied by Prospero. As the occupants begin their struggle to reach the island, Gonzalo, an old and trusted friend of Prospero, gasps:

GONZALO
Now would I give a thousand furlongs of sea, for an acre of barren ground. Long heath, brown furze, any thing. The wills above be done, but **I would fain die a dry death.**   *[Exit.]*

I would give all my fame for a pot of ale and safety

Source: KING HENRY THE FIFTH (Act III, sc. ii, ll. 13-14)
Author: William Shakespeare (1564-1616)
First published: 1600
Type of work: Historical drama

Context: Henry V, the "mirror of a Christian king," has led his forces into France to press the English claim to the right of the French throne. Having intercepted at Southampton the English traitors Grey, Scroop, and Cambridge, who planned to betray England, he now lays seige to Harfleur in a determined effort to convince Charles VI and the Dauphin of the superiority of the English forces. Henry is destined to succeed in this venture and to annihilate the French in an amazingly successful display of bravery and skillful tactical maneuvering at Agincourt, a battle which will bring French submission and the arranged royal wedding between Henry and the French princess, Katherine. Much of the success of the English forces can be attributed to their stalwart leader, who with "a touch of Harry in the night" moves among his men to encourage their best efforts as men of England. During the battle of Harfleur he urges them "Once more into the breach, dear friends, . . . / Or close the wall up with our English dead." Among the flurry of soldiers and the bravura of battle, a boy comments with touching irony that—despite the thrill of patriotic endeavor—he would willingly be in England, relaxing at the tavern:

BARDOLPH

On, on, on, on, on, to the breach, to the breach, to the breach!

NYM

Pray thee corporal stay, the knocks are too hot; and for mine own part, I have not a case of lives. . . .

PISTOL

· · ·

Knocks go and come; God's vassals drop and die;
And sword and shield,
In bloody field,
Doth win immortal fame.

BOY

Would I were in an alehouse in London! **I would give all my fame for a pot of ale, and safety.**

PISTOL

And I:

If wishes would prevail with me,
My purpose should not fail with me;
But thither would I hie.

I would live to study, and not study to live

Source: LETTER TO KING JAMES I
Author: Sir Francis Bacon (1561-1626)
First published: 1734
Type of work: Personal letter

Context: Bacon, remembered today for his philosophical writings, was an important political figure in his own time. A member of Parliament and a personal friend of James I, a magistrate trained in the legal profession, he acquired an impressive list of titles: Baron of Verulam, Viscount St. Albans, Lord High Chancellor of England. He was careful to attach himself to royal favorites; one was the ill-starred Essex. When the latter attempted rebellion, Bacon helped to convict him. Another such attachment was George Villiers, Duke of Buckingham. This wise relationship brought Bacon numerous royal favors and advancements, until Buckingham's popularity waned. On January 22, 1621, Bacon observed his sixtieth birthday; on January 27, he was made Viscount St. Albans. In March the blow fell: he was charged with accepting bribes from persons who had appeared in his court. Admitting that the charges were true, Bacon nonetheless insisted he had not allowed any gratuities to influence his decisions. Perhaps he had not; however, he had bowed to Buckingham's wishes whenever any of the latter's friends had appeared in court. Early

505

in May he was stripped of his offices, fined forty thousand pounds, and imprisoned briefly in the Tower of London. He was also forbidden to sit in Parliament again and banned from the court. The last two rulings were never lifted entirely; some of the others were eased. Buckingham, still powerful, coveted Bacon's house; Bacon had to sell it to him in order to gain readmission to the court. He now entered upon his retirement, going to live at Gorhambury, and devoted himself to the writing which has won him lasting fame. His *History of Henry VII* was completed in October; he then embarked upon *The Advancement of Learning.* He appealed to the king for mercy, but with little result. In one letter he pleads his case at some length, pointing out his long service and reminding the king of their old friendship. Apparently undated, it was written when Bacon was "a year and a half old in misery;" this statement would seem to indicate that he wrote the letter during the winter of 1622–23. In it he summarizes his troubles, combining politely veiled rebuke with the lavish flatteries demanded by custom, and ends by begging abjectly that he not be reduced to utter destitution:

. . . Therefore as one that hath had the happiness to know your Majestie near hand, I have (most gracious Sovereign) faith enough for a miracle, much more for a grace, that your Majestie will not suffer your poor creature to be utterly defaced, nor blot that name quite out of your book, upon which your sacred hand hath been so oft for new ornaments and additions.

Unto this degree of compassion, I hope God above . . . will dispose your princely heart, already prepared to all piety. And why should I not think, but that thrice noble Prince . . . will help to pull me (if I may use that homely phrase) out of the mire of an abject and sordid condition in my last days. . . .

But, if it may please your Majestie (for Saints, I shall give them reverence, but no adoration, my address is to your Majestie, the fountain of goodness;) your Majestie shall by the grace of God, not feel that in gift, which I shall extremely feel in help; for my desires are moderate, and my courses measured to a life orderly and reserved, hoping still to do your Majestie honour in my way. Only I most humbly beseech your Majestie to give me leave to conclude with those words which necessity speaketh: help me (*dear Sovereign Lord and Master*) and pity me so far, as I that have born a bag, be not now in my age forced in effect to bear a wallet; **nor I that desire to live to study, may not be driven to study to live.** I most humbly crave pardon of a long letter. . . .

An idiot race to honor lost

Source: ON SEEING STIRLING PALACE IN RUINS
Author: Robert Burns (1759-1796)
First published: 1787
Type of work: Epigram

Context: In 1787 Robert Burns temporarily left Edinburgh where he had been lionized as a literary genius, but generally misunderstood, for a trip through the Highlands, perhaps in memory of Highland Mary. His companion was William Nicol, Master of Edinburgh High School, one of his close friends. They visited Felkirk, Stirling, and the nearby field of Bannockburn where Robert the Bruce in 1314 established himself on the Scotch throne by defeating Edward II of England. On their return to Stirling, with a diamond that he had recently purchased, Burns inscribed some treasonable verses on the window pane of the inn. Six weeks later, worried about what he had written, he returned to Stirling and smashed the glass, but he could not blot out the lines. Too many people had seen and copied them. Some of Burns's ancestors had espoused the cause of the Stuarts, a family acting as regents in Scotland as early as the twelfth century. Because of the marriage of James IV of Scotland to Margaret Tudor, eventually James VI of Scotland became James I of England in 1603. After the death of Anne, the last of the Stuarts to rule England, the crown passed to George I of the House of Hanover. However, the Jacobites continued to support various pretenders. Burns himself was not really politically minded. He was a sort of sentimental Jacobite, upheld by his own discontent. While denouncing the rulers of his country, he was really expressing the private ills that he enlarged to include the world. Unfortunately, he was imprudent in his expression of these opinions. He was being feted in Edinburgh and had created a number of enemies. One can see what his detractors, quick to denounce him for his exuberant living, would make of his brief poem about Stirling Palace. Built on the summit of a hill above the city, it had been the birthplace of James II and other rulers. Mary Stuart and James VI were crowned there. It had been damaged during a three-month seige by Edward I in 1304, and further ruined when it was recaptured by the Scots after Bannockburn. The "outlandish race," of course, were the Hanoverians, of another land and another language, and therefore to a Jacobite, even a sentimental one, an "idiot race," and "to honor lost." However, that the better one knew them the more one despised them was certainly poetic license. Here is the entire poem.

Here Stuarts once in glory reign'd,
And laws for Scotland's weal ordain'd;
But now unroof'd their palace stands,
Their sceptre's sway'd by other hands;
The injur'd Stuart line is gone,
A race outlandish fills their throne,
An idiot race to honor lost,
Who knows them best, despise them most.

Idleness is only the refuge of weak minds

Source: LETTERS TO HIS SON (Letter 75)
Author: Philip Dormer Stanhope, Lord Chesterfield (1694-1773)
First published: 1774
Type of work: Personal letter

Context: Lord Chesterfield was determined to train his son Philip to be an accomplished English Gentleman, statesman, and man of the world; and in his letters he spared no pains to give the young man sound advice. Philip, though illegitimate, was loved by his father, and Chesterfield had great hopes for him. However, the boy did not fulfill his father's hopes; he never became a real devotee of the stylized life of grace, manner, and formula that marked the truly polished and successful gentleman. He died young, leaving a wife and two young sons; Chesterfield, who had not known of their existence, was delighted with all three and undertook their support. The letters Chesterfield wrote to Philip deal for the most part with manners and deportment, the various niceties of social usage, and other habits and accomplishments necessary to success. Philip worked for the British government, his work taking him to various places in Europe; Chesterfield corresponded with him voluminously and faithfully, doing his best to smooth Philip's path and to prepare him for whatever situations he might face. In his letter of July 20, 1749, he chides Philip for neglecting to answer a letter from a friend who is not without influence: "Those attentions ought never to be omitted; they cost little, and please a great deal; but the neglect of them offends more than you can imagine. Great merit, or great failings, will make you respected or despised; but trifles, little attentions, mere nothings, either done, or neglected, will make you either liked or disliked, in the general run of the world. . . . Moral virtues are the foundation of society in general, and of friendship in particular; but attentions, manners, and graces, both adorn and strengthen them." He follows this counsel with an inquiry concerning Philip's health, which has been poor; then tells Philip he has sent a letter of thanks to one Mr. Firmian:

. . . I hope you write to him too, from time to time. The letters of recommendation of a man of his merit and learning will, to be sure, be of great use to you among the learned world in Italy; that is, provided you take care to keep up to the character he gives you in them; otherwise they will only add to your disgrace.

Consider that you have lost a good deal of time by your illness; fetch it up now that you are well. At present you should be a good economist of your moments, of which company and sights will claim a considerable share; so that those which remain for study must be not only attentively, but greedily employed. But indeed I do not suspect you of one single moment's idleness in the whole day. **Idleness is only the refuge of weak minds,** and the holiday of fools. I do not call good company and liberal pleasures, idleness; far from it: I recommend to you a good share of both.

If all the pens that ever poets held

Source: TAMBURLAINE THE GREAT (Part I, Act V, sc. i, l. 1942)
Author: Christopher Marlowe (1564-1593)
First published: 1590
Type of work: Dramatic tragedy

Context: Tamburlaine, flushed with many conquests, almost at the zenith of his career in conquering the world he knew, besieges Damascus. This is the city of Zenocrate, the princess Tamburlaine loves. She asks that her father, its ruler, be dealt with kindly, but Tamburlaine refuses, though to refuse causes him sadness, so that he agrees not to put Zenocrate's father to death when the city falls. The ruler of Damascus sends four beautiful young virgins to Tamburlaine, hoping they can persuade him to accept the city's surrender without slaughter and destruction. The great conqueror, melancholy and dressed all in black, receives the four virgins, but he remains unmoved by their appeal; he has them taken out to be killed by a group of charging horsemen and their bodies hung up in sight of the defenders of the city. Even while giving his heartless orders, however, Tamburlaine thinks of his love for Zenocrate and how her pleas for her father, the Sultan of Egypt, cause him emotion:

TAMBURLAINE
. . .
What is beauty saith my sufferings then
If all the pens that ever poets held,
Had fed the feelings of their master's thoughts,
And every sweetnes that suspir'd their hearts,
Their minds, and muses on admired themes:
If all the heavenly Quintessence they still
From their immortall flowers of Poesy,
Wherein, as in a mirror we perceive
The highest reaches of a human wit.
If these had made one Poems' period
And all combin'd in Beauty's worthiness,
Yet should ther hover in their restless heads,
One thought, one grace, one woonder, at the least,
Which into words no virtue can digest.

509

If God choose, I shall but love thee better after death

Source: SONNETS FROM THE PORTUGUESE (Sonnet XLIII, ll. 13-14)
Author: Elizabeth Barrett Browning (1806–1861)
First published: 1850
Type of work: Sonnet

Context: Elizabeth Barrett, an invalid, made the acquaintance of Robert Browning. The two fell in love as soon as they met, and Elizabeth began the composition of a series of love sonnets, which she kept hidden from Robert until after their marriage, in 1846. The name of the cycle, *Sonnets from the Portuguese,* derives from Browning's having called her "his Portuguese," the name having been suggested by her poem "Caterina to Camoens." The sonnets are probably the most impassioned love poetry in English. In Sonnet XLIII, Elizabeth endeavors to list the many ways in which she loves Robert. She loves him to the length and breadth and height her soul can reach and also on the level of every day's quiet need. She loves him purely and passionately. She loves him as she once did her saints, and with the smiles and tears of her whole life. And if God lets her, she will love him more after death than she does while she is living:

How do I love thee? Let me count the ways.
I love thee to the depth and breadth and height
My soul can reach, when feeling out of sight
For the ends of Being and ideal Grace.
I love thee to the level of every day's
Most quiet need, by sun and candlelight.
I love thee freely, as men strive for Right;
I love thee purely, as they turn from Praise.
I love thee with the passion put to use
In my old griefs, and with my childhood's faith.
I love thee with a love I seemed to lose
With my lost saints—I love thee with the breath,
Smiles, tears, of all my life!—and, **if God choose,
I shall but love thee better after death.**

If I were dead, you'd sometimes say, Poor Child!

Source: TO THE UNKNOWN EROS (Book I, "If I Were Dead," Line 1)
Author: Coventry Patmore (1823-1896)
First published: 1877
Type of work: Lyric poem

Context: In this collection of poems, written after several years of silence, Patmore creates his most mysterious and transcendental volume; often obscure because of his dependence on the tradition of Roman Catholic mysticism and frequently banal because of his exaltation of the commonplace, these poems occasionally reveal the insights of a man who understood both the problems and the joys of marriage. The fortunate moments when Patmore leaves philosophy and mysticism to describe the small, everyday moments that all married people encounter give the collection a perennial charm that keeps the heavier elements from dominating the volume; this quotation comes from one of these lighter poems, a short lyric in which the parent, after punishing his child, hears the boy's pathetic cry.

> 'If I were dead, you'd sometimes say, Poor Child!'
> The dear lips quiver'd as they spake,
> And the tears brake
> From eyes which, not to grieve me, brightly smiled.
> Poor Child, poor Child!
> I seem to hear your laugh, your talk, your song.
> It is not true that Love will do no wrong.
> Poor Child!
> And did you think, when you so cried and smiled,
> How I, in lonely nights should lie awake,
> And of those words your full avengers make?

If I were not Alexander, I would be Diogenes

Source: PARALLEL LIVES ("Alexander")
Author: Plutarch (c.45-c.125)
First transcribed: 105-115
Type of work: Biography

Context: After Alexander and his Macedonians had destroyed Thebes and razed it to the ground, he was reconciled with the Athenians and treated them mercifully, possibly to compensate for his savagery toward the Thebans. Afterward, in a general assembly, the Greeks voted to join under Alexander's leadership in an expedition against Persia.

Thereupon many statesmen and philosophers came to him with their congratulations, and he expected that Diogenes of Sinope also, who was tarrying in Corinth, would do likewise. But since that philosopher took not the slightest notice of Alexander, and continued to enjoy his leisure in the suburb Craneion, Alexander went in person to see him; and he found him lying in the sun. Diogenes raised himself up a little when he saw so many persons coming towards him, and fixed his eyes upon Alexander. And when that monarch addressed him with greetings, and asked if he wanted anything, "Yes," said Diogenes, "stand a little out of my sun." It is said that Alexander was so struck by this, and admired so much the haughtiness and grandeur of the man who had nothing but scorn for him, that he said to his followers, who were

511

laughing and jesting about the philosopher as they went away, "But verily, **if I were not Alexander, I would be Diogenes."**

If it be against reason, it is of no force in law

Source: INSTITUTES: COMMENTARY UPON LITTLETON (First Institute, Book I, chapter 10, section 80)
Author: Sir Edward Coke (1552-1634)
First published: 1628
Type of work: Legal commentaries

Context: Lord Coke, who was speaker of the British House of Commons in 1593, made a life-long enemy of Francis Bacon by defeating him for the position of Attorney General, in 1594. He became Chief Justice of the Court of Common Pleas, in 1606, and was the first to be called Lord Chief Justice of England. Like all lawyers Coke got part of his training by poring over legal tomes. One, based on Justinian's "Institutes," was the work of Thomas Littleton (1422–1481), who wrote in French under the title *Tenures* the earliest treatise on English law ever printed (1481). It covered legal procedure dealing with obligations of landholders to their landlords. Though Coke called it "the ornament of Common Law and the most perfect and absolute book that was ever written in any humane Science," he must have found it difficult reading, because when later he published his commentaries on Littleton's treatise, he offered encouragement to other students in his Introduction. "If the Reader does not in one day reach the meaning of our author or our commentaries, let him proceed on some other day, and that doubt will be cleared." Book I deals with "Estates in Lands and Tenements." It is one of four *Institutes of the Lawes of England* written between 1628 and 1644, and it is generally referred to as "Coke Upon Littleton." It was the standard legal text until the nineteenth century. Each page was divided into three columns. One printed the French opinions of Thomas Littleton, the second provided a statement of the law in English, and in the third, Sir Edward Coke, greatest exponent of England's Common Law, explains, interprets, and gives helpful comments for law students. Perhaps his son was one of those for whom he intended it. At least in several sections he starts the comment with "My son." In his interpretation of Section 80 of Chapter 10 (There is a total of 749 sections), Littleton's text is: "And so it is to bee understood, that in divers Lordships, and in divers Manors, there be many and divers customes, in such cases as to take tenements, and as to plead, and as to other things and customes to be done, and whatsoever is not against reason, may well bee admitted and allowed." Coke's comment on the text follows:

This was cautiously set downe, for in respect to the variety of customes in most mannors, it is not possible to set downe any certainty, only this incident inseparable every custome must have, viz., that it be consonant to reason; for how long soever it hath continued, **if it be against reason, it is of no force in law.**

If you are in Rome, live in the Roman style

Source: DUCTOR DUBITANTIUM (Part I, chapter 1, rule 5)
Author: Jeremy Taylor (1613-1667)
First published: 1660
Type of work: Religious guide

Context: The Reverend Jeremy Taylor, son of a churchwarden who was by profession a barber skilled in drugs and surgery, became a brilliant theologian. He was admitted to college at the age of 13, and given a fellowship at Cambridge in 1630, then sent to Oxford for a Master of Arts degree. Though accused of love for the Roman Catholic faith, he did not follow its precepts. He married in 1639, and had three sons. He became chaplain to Charles I, who gave him a Doctor of Divinity degree when he was dispensing honors. Taken prisoner at the fall of the king in 1644, Taylor was soon released. He established a school to earn his living, and wrote tracts and sermons, but because of fear for his safety, his friends urged him to flee to northeastern Ireland. In his study at Portmore in Kilultagh he wrote *Ductor Dubitantium or the Rules of Conscience in all her general Measures, serving as a great Instrument for the Determination of* *Cases of Conscience.* It was in press when Charles II was restored to the throne, so the author foresightedly hastened to insert a dedication "To the Most Sacred Majesty of Charles II." As a result, he was made bishop of Down, Connor, and Dromore. His writings were noted for their logic and casuistry. His *Ductor Dubitantium* draws its contents from many church leaders. Taylor credits St. Ambrose of Milan (340?–397) for the precept quoted in Latin. St. Ambrose was also a bishop, noted for his justice and concern for the common people, and author of a number of sermons based on the Gospel and the Creed. Some of them spurred the conversion of St. Augustine. Taylor's works were collected in three massive volumes of about 2,800 pages, published in London in 1837. In Rule 5, entitled "All Consciences are to walk by the same Rule, and that which is just to one is so to all, in the like Circumstances," Taylor explains:

If all men were governed by the same laws, and had the same interest, and the same degrees of understanding, they would perceive the truth of this conclusion. But men are infinitely differenced by their own acts and relations, by their understandings and proper economy, by their superinduced differences and orders, by interest and mistake, by ignorance and malice, by sects

513

and deceptions; and this makes that two men may be damned for doing two contradictories: as a Jew may perish for not keeping of his sabbath, and a Christian for keeping it, an iconoclast for breaking images and another for worshipping them; for eating and for not eating. . . .

But this variety is not directly of God's making, but of man's. God commands us to walk by the same rule and to this end . . . "to be of the same mind." . . . He that fasted upon a Saturday in Ionia or Smyrna, was a schismatic; and so was he that did not fast at Milan or Rome upon the same day, both upon the same reason; Cum fueris Romae, Romano vivito more **[When you are in Rome, live in the Roman style]** . . . because he was to conform to the custom of Smyrna, as well as that of Milan, in the respective dioceses.

Ignobly vain, and impotently great

Source: PROLOGUE TO MR. ADDISON'S CATO (Line 29)
Author: Alexander Pope (1688-1744)
First published: 1713
Type of work: Dramatic tragedy

Context: With British political feeling heated between Whigs and Tories in 1712, Joseph Addison was prevailed upon to complete his play *Cato,* a drama emphasizing the heroic qualities of Cato, leader of the unsuccessful party opposed to Caesar during the civil war in Rome. Though Pope disliked Addison, he was willing to write the *Prologue* to *Cato* because of the great publicity the play received. Too late, states Pope in the *Prologue,* Rome realizes that the sword of noble Cato is preferable to the conquering sword of Caesar:

Ev'n when proud Caesar 'midst triumphal cars,
The spoils of nations, and the pomp of wars,
Ignobly vain, and impotently great
Showed Rome her Cato's figure drawn in state,
As her dead father's rev'rend image past,
The pomp was darkened, and the day o'ercast,
The triumph ceased,—tears gushed from ev'ry eye;
The world's great victor past unheeded by;
Her last good man dejected Rome adored,
And honored Caesar's less than Cato's sword.

Ignorance is not innocence but sin

Source: THE INN ALBUM (Section V, l. 2262)
Author: Robert Browning (1812-1889)
First published: 1875
Type of work: Poetic dialogue

Context: Like most of the psychological studies of villainy that Browning produced, *The Inn Album* is based to some extent on actual occurrences. In the present instance his chief inspiration was the story of Lord De Ros, a friend of the Duke of Wellington; it had been recounted in Greville's memoirs. Browning adapted this material and added some ideas deriving from the case of the Tichborne Claimant. The plot involves two men. One is a young man who has just inherited a fortune, but who lacks the aristocratic polish and knowledge of the world which would enable him to move easily in a sophisticated society. The other, with whom he has become friendly, is a man of fifty; he has all the refinement and sophistication the young man lacks but is virtually penniless. The young man wants his companion to teach him how to behave in the company to which wealth will admit him; the older man sees the younger as a potential source of funds. As a step toward acquiring the youngster's money, he allows the latter to win at cards and thus indebts himself to the extent of ten thousand pounds. He intends to use the debt as a lever with which to swindle twice its amount from the boy. In an exchange of confidences each man tells the other he has been unhappy in love; the older admits he once seduced and then abandoned a woman, and the younger tells of his love for a girl who would not have him but took a middle-aged rake instead. The drama reaches its climax when the boy discovers that both have been involved with the same woman. She has encountered the older man and is reacting bitterly when the boy intrudes and recognizes her. He denounces both. She tells the boy to renounce his corrupt companion and to marry the cousin who loves him; and she begs the older man to leave, never letting the other girl know "How near came taint of your companionship!" The rake replies ironically that for innocence to be crowned with ignorance is desirable but difficult. She replied:

"Ignorance is not innocence but sin—
Witness yourself ignore what after-pangs
Pursue the plague-infected. Merciful
Am I? Perhaps! the more contempt, the less
Hatred; and who so worthy of contempt
As you that rest assured I cooled the spot
I could not cure, by poisoning, forsooth,
Whose hand I pressed there? Understand for once
That, sick, of all the pains corroding me
This burnt the last and nowise least—the need
Of simulating soundness. I resolved—
No matter how the struggle tasked weak flesh—
To hide the truth away as in a grave
From—most of all—my husband: he nor knows
Nor ever shall be made to know your part,
My part, the devil's part,—I trust, God's part
In the foul matter. Saved, I yearn to save
And not destroy: and what destruction like
The abolishing of faith in him, that's faith

In me as pure and true? . . . 'Tis God
. . .
Must bear such secrets and disclose them . . ."

I'll cross it, though it blast me

Source: HAMLET (Act I, sc. i, l. 127)
Author: William Shakespeare (1564-1616)
First published: 1603
Type of work: Dramatic tragedy

Context: The ghost of Hamlet's father appears twice in the opening scene of the play. After the first appearance, Hamlet's friend, Horatio, wonders what the apparition might mean—"This bodes some strange eruption to our state"—and notes that "In the most high and palmy state of Rome,/ A little ere the mightiest Julius fell,/ The graves stood tenantless, and the sheeted dead/ Did squeak and gibber in the Roman streets." When the ghost reappears, Horatio performs the dangerous act of moving directly into the path of the spirit. In calling upon the ghost to speak, Horatio lists the causes that may force a spirit to return to earth; he seems about to get a response when the cock crows and the ghost stalks away, for, according to ancient belief, ghosts and other walkers in darkness cannot endure the sunlight. The entire scene is extraordinarily dramatic:

HORATIO
. . .

[*Re-enter* GHOST.]
But soft, behold, lo where it comes again.
[GHOST *spreads its arms.*]
I'll cross it, though it blast me. Stay illusion,
If thou hast any sound or use of voice,
Speak to me.
If there be any good thing to be done
That may to thee do ease, and grace to me,
Speak to me.
If thou art privy to any country's fate
Which happily foreknowing may avoid,
O speak.
Or if thou hast uphoarded in thy life
Extorted treasure in the womb of earth,
For which they say you spirits oft walk in death,
[*Cock crows.*]
Speak of it; stay and speak. Stop it Marcellus.

516

I'll eat my head

Source: OLIVER TWIST (Chapter 14)
Author: Charles Dickens (1812-1870)
First published: 1837-1839
Type of work: Novel

Context: Oliver Twist, accompanying the Artful Dodger and Charlie Bates, the thief-trainer Fagin's assistants, is erroneously thought to have picked the pocket of old Mr. Brownlow. He is pursued, captured, and taken to a police station, where, in spite of all that Mr. Brownlow can do, he is sentenced to three months hard labor. He is saved, however, on the evidence of the bookseller at whose stall Mr. Brownlow was reading when the robbery took place. Upon being released, Oliver faints upon the sidewalk and is picked up and carried home by Mr. Brownlow. For weeks he is unconscious with fever; but when he recovers his health, Mr. Brownlow summons him for a talk in his study. Before the talk gets under way there is a visitor:

> At this moment, there walked into the room; supporting himself by a thick stick: a stout old gentleman, rather lame in one leg, who was dressed in a blue coat, striped waistcoat, nankeen breeches and gaiters, and a broad-brimmed white hat, with the sides turned up with green. A very small-plaited shirt frill stuck out from his waistcoat; and a very long steel watch-chain, with nothing but a key at the end, dangled loosely below it. . . . he fixed himself, the moment he made his appearance; and, holding out a small piece of orange-peel at arm's length, exclaimed, in a growling, discontented voice,
>
> "Look here! do you see this! Isn't it a most wonderful and extraordinary thing that I can't call at a man's house but I find a piece of this poor surgeon's-friend on the staircase? I've been lamed with orange-peel once, and I know orange-peel will be my death at last. It will, sir; orange-peel will be my death, or I'll be content to eat my own head, sir!"
>
> This was the handsome offer with which Mr. Grimwig backed and confirmed nearly every assertion that he made. . . . Mr. Grimwig's head was such a particularly large one, that the most sanguine man alive could hardly entertain a hope of being able to get through it at a sitting—to put entirely out of the question, a very thick coating of powder.
>
> "**I'll eat my head,** sir," repeated Mr. Grimwig, striking his stick upon the ground. "Hallo; what's that!" looking at Oliver, and retreating a pace or two.

I'll have a fling

Source: RULE A WIFE AND HAVE A WIFE (Act III, sc. v)
Author: Francis Beaumont (1585?-1616) and John Fletcher (1579-1625)
First published: 1640
Type of work: Dramatic comedy

Context: This play, probably entirely by Fletcher, is on somewhat the same theme as Shakespeare's *Taming of the Shrew,*—wife-taming. Margarita, an exceedingly wealthy and beautiful young woman of Seville, wants to marry a complaisant husband so that she will be free to pursue her amours without damage to her reputation. Altéa, one of her attendants, recommends Leon (who is actually her very knowing brother, in league with her to win Margarita and her wealth), as a simple, unknowing, but handsome young fellow who would admirably serve Margarita's purpose. Margarita has an interview with him and, believing him to be what she desires, marries him and immediately removes for a short time to her country estate. She soon returns to her city house, and immediately preparations are set on foot for a party at which will be present Margarita's admirer, the Duke of Medina. As the arrangements for the party go forward, Leon gives his wife a bit of counsel as to her behavior; she is astonished both at his tone and the tenor of his remarks. The guests, all unaware that Margarita is married, arrive; among them is Cacafogo, a usurer who entertains thoughts of marrying Margarita for her fortune. He muses that winning her would cost him a bit of money, but decides to risk it, to have a fling, as of the dice.

DUKE OF MEDINA
I thank ye, lady. I am bold to visit ye,
Once more to bless mine eyes with your sweet beauty:
'T has been a long night since you left the court,
For, till I saw you now, no day broke to me.

MARGARITA
Bring in the duke's meat!

SANCHIO
She is most excellent.

JUAN DE CASTRO
Most admirable fair as e'er I looked on;
I had rather command her than my regiment.

CACAFOGO
[*aside.*] **I'll have a fling;** 'tis but a thousand ducats,
Which I can cozen up again in ten days,
And some few jewels, to justify my knavery.

518

Say I should marry her, she'll get more money
Than all my usury, put my knavery to it:
She appears the most infallible way of purchase.

I'll put a spoke among your wheels

Source: THE MAD LOVER (Act III, sc. vi)
Author: John Fletcher (1579-1625)
First published: 1647
Type of work: Dramatic comedy

Context: Memnon, a rough soldier, general of the King of Paphos's armies, arrives home after a long absence; he sees the king's sister, Calis, and falls so completely in love with her that he offers his heart to her, an offer she sportively assumes to be literal. Nothing daunted, Memnon makes preparations for delivering it to her. Syphax, also a soldier, sees the princess and also falls madly in love with her; he enlists the aid of Cleanthe, his sister, in the furtherance of his love. She bribes the priestess of Venus to tell the princess on her next visit to the shrine that, to cure the lovesickness that she had contracted for Polydorus, she is to love a man she describes; the man is to be Syphax. Chilax, a merry old soldier, from a position in hiding, hears Cleanthe giving her directions to the priestess and vows to foil the plot; he says that he will put a spoke among her wheels: the imagery is that of thrusting a tough, strong spoke through a pair of wheels and so bringing the vehicle to a halt. This version of the saying gives a clearer picture of what is meant than does the common modern version: "I'll put a spoke in your wheel." Many people in modern times construe this to mean adding a spoke to the construction of a wheel to strengthen it, a meaning not borne out by Fletcher's version.

CLEANTHE

Charge her take the next man she shall meet with,
When she comes out;—you understand me?—

PRIESTESS

Well.

CLEANTHE

Which shall be he attending. This is all,
And easily without suspicion ended;
Nor none dare disobey, 'tis Heaven that does it,
And who dares cross it then, or once suspect it?
The venture is most easy.

PRIESTESS

I will do it.

519

CLEANTHE

As ye shall prosper?

PRIESTESS

As I shall prosper!

CLEANTHE

Take this too, and farewell; but, first, hark hither.

CHILAX

[*aside.*] What a young whore's this to betray her mistress!
A thousand cuckolds shall that husband be
That marries thee, thou art so mischievous.
I'll put a spoke among your wheels.

An ill-favoured thing sir, but mine own

Source: AS YOU LIKE IT (Act V, sc. iv, l. 60)
Author: William Shakespeare (1564-1616)
First published: 1623
Type of work: Dramatic comedy

Context: The Forest of Arden provides refuge to an exiled Duke of France and his followers; to the daughter of the Duke, Rosalind (disguised as the shepherd lad Ganymede) and her cousin and friend, Celia (disguised as the shepherdess Aliena); to Orlando and his cruel brother, Oliver; and to the clown, Touchstone, as well as to a number of native inhabitants of the area. From a general state of confusion, a reconciliation is effected: Rosalind, revealing herself to her father, plans to wed Orlando; Celia intends to marry his repentant brother Oliver; the little shepherdess, Phebe, is reconciled to the love-sick shepherd, Silvius; and even the clown Touchstone, addressing the Duke, announces his intention to marry the goat-girl, Audrey:

TOUCHSTONE

God 'ild you sir, I desire you of the like, I press in here sir, amongst the rest of the country copulatives, to swear and to forswear, according as marriage binds and blood breaks—a poor virgin sir, **an ill-favoured thing sir, but mine own;** a poor humour of mine sir, to take that that no man else will. Rich honesty dwells like a miser sir, in a poor house, as your pearl in your foul oyster.

I'm sickly but sassy

Source: BROTHER RABBIT PRETENDS TO BE POISONED
Author: Joel Chandler Harris (1848-1908)
First published: 1883 in *Nights with Uncle Remus*
Type of work: Short story

Context: The first Uncle Remus stories, supposedly told by an elderly ex-slave in central Georgia to the seven-year-old son of "Miss Sally," appeared in *The Atlanta Constitution* in 1876, where their author, Joel Chandler Harris, was a reporter. Thirty-four of the tales were collected in 1880 into *Uncle Remus, His Songs and His Sayings.* That volume contained the Tar-Baby story and other accounts of the many times that Mr. Rabbit outwitted Mr. Fox. In his Introduction, the author discussed the wide spread of animal stories in folk lore, with the same episode appearing in Planatation tales, in Indian lore, and in anecdotes from the Amazon regions of South America. Three years later appeared another volume, *Nights with Uncle Remus,* containing more stories. In Chapter 50 of this book, called "Brother Rabbit Pretends to be Poisoned," a squinch owl is a screech owl. While the boy is visiting Uncle Remus, hoping to hear a story

> . . . the door opened and Aunt Tempy made her appearance. Her good humor was infectious.
> "Name er goodness!" she exclaimed, "I lef' you all settin' yer, way las' week; I goes off un I does my wuk, un I comes back, un I fin's you settin' right whar I lef' you. Goodness knows I dunner whar you gits yo' vittles. . . ."
> "Yas, Sis Tempy, we er settin' whar you lef' us, en der Lord, he bin a-pervidin'. W'en de vittles don't come in at de do' hit come down the chimbley, en so w'ats de odds? We er sorter po'ly, Sis Tempy, I'm 'bliged ter you. You know w'at de jay-bird say ter der squinch owl: **'I'm sickly but sassy.'** "

The imperial theme

Source: MACBETH (Act I, sc. iii, l. 129)
Author: William Shakespeare (1564-1616)
First published: 1623
Type of work: Dramatic tragedy

Context: Macbeth and Banquo meet the witches who inform them that Macbeth will be Thane of Cawdor and King of Scotland, and that Banquo will beget kings. As the witches vanish, Ross and Angus appear to tell Macbeth of the praises and rewards heaped upon him by King Duncan— one of which is the title of the Thane of Cawdor, stripped from the traitor whom Macbeth had defeated along with Sweno of Norway. Both Macbeth and Banquo are startled at how suddenly the prophecy of the witches comes true. Banquo is dubious of the "instruments of darkness" and their words, for he fears betrayal. Macbeth too is really torn between a feeling of good and evil and cannot understand why he is so stunned and frightened when part of the tidings has already been fulfilled. He becomes deeply absorbed in his own thoughts, which dwell constantly on the last part of the prediction.

MACBETH [*aside*]
               Two truths are told,
As happy prologues to the swelling act
Of **the imperial theme.** . . .
         • • •

This supernatural soliciting
Cannot be ill, cannot be good. If ill,
Why hath it given me earnest of success,
Commencing in a truth? I am Thane of Cawdor.
If good, why do I yield to that suggestion,
Whose horrid image doth unfix my hair,
And make my seated heart knock at my ribs,
Against the use of nature? . . .
         • • •

In black and white

Source: EVERY MAN IN HIS HUMOUR (Act IV, sc. iv, l. 21)
Author: Ben Jonson (1573?-1637)
First published: 1601
Type of work: Dramatic comedy

Context: At a general gathering of most of the characters of the play at the home of Kitely, a cowardly and jealous husband, Oliver Cob, a waterdrawer, falls foul of the braggart soldier, Captain Bobadill, who bitterly resents Cob's derogatory remarks about the smoking of tobacco. So incensed is Bobadill that he roundly beats Cob with a cudgel. Cob repairs to the home of a mad wag of a judge, Justice Clement, to obtain a writ to bind Bobadill to keep the peace. When Justice Clement learns that the quarrel arose over Cob's finding fault with tobacco smoking, he summarily sentences Cob to jail. Cob is horribly frightened, but Justice Clement reprieves him and orders his clerk, Roger Formal, to make out the warrant. Cob returns to his house and tells his wife Tib that Bobadill will pay for the black and blue he administered in the beating, as he has the warrant in his hand, in black and white. Cob admits that the justice put him in great fear for his liberty; he is a fine old fellow, though. Cob then orders his wife to go into the house, lock the door, and admit no one, especially Bobadill:

522

Why, what's the matter, trow!

O, he has basted me rarely, sumptuously! but I have it here **in black and white,** for his black and blue shall pay him. O, the justice! the honestest old brave Trojan in London! I do honor the very flea of his dog. A plague on him though, he put me once in a villainous filthy fear; marry, it vanished away like the smoke of tobacco; but I was smoked soundly first. I thank the devil, and his good angel, my guest. Well, wife, or Tib, which you will, get you in, and lock the door, I charge you let no body in to you, wife; no body in to you; those are my words; not Captain Bob himself, nor the fiend in his likeness. You are a woman, you have flesh and blood enough in you to be tempted; therefore keep the door shut upon all comers.

In every parting there is an image of death

Source: SCENES OF CLERICAL LIFE ("The Sad Fortunes of the Reverend Amos Barton," Chapter X)
Author: George Eliot (Mary Ann Evans, 1819-1880)
First published: 1858
Type of work: Short novel

Context: Amos Barton is one of a group of three short novels, all dealing with the clergy. It traces the career and hardships of Barton during his tenure as curate of Shepperton. Barton is a dedicated man of unprepossessing appearance and is anything but spectacular; he is blessed with a good wife, Milly, and a large family. Their living is meager and genteel poverty their lot. The influential people of the community dislike the clergyman; his sermons are colorless and unpopular, he is a poor teacher, and they fail to see the underlying goodness of the man. He tries vainly to inspire his congregation and the local coal miners, who are a difficult proposition at best. He and his family must borrow money in order to survive, and his wife is not well. A woman, Countess Czerlaski, who passes herself off as a person of means, moves in with the Bartons temporarily and remains for months. Gossip ensues concerning a fancied relationship between Barton and the countess, who is not paying the Bartons any board or helping with any household tasks. The local snobs disapprove of Barton anyway; they feel that he could at least be poor without showing it. Milly is wearing out with the work of caring for her many children, her husband, and her inconsiderate house guest. Eventually the countess is made aware of what is being said about her, and leaves; but the bills she has run up remain, and Milly dies in childbirth. Following this tragedy, the townspeople relent somewhat, but not enough to relieve Barton's suffering. Finally he receives a letter from the vicar: that worthy is coming to Shepperton himself and will reside there. Barton is done out of his curacy, with no prospects of another nearby. The truth is that the vicar wants this post for his own brother-in-law. Barton finds a curacy in a distant county, in a dingy and unattractive manufacturing town, and takes his leave of Shepperton.

> . . . There was general regret among the parishioners at his departure: not that any one of them thought his spiritual gifts preeminent, or was conscious of great edification from his ministry. But his recent troubles had called out their better sympathies, and that is always a source of love. Amos failed to touch the spring of goodness by his sermons, but he touched it effectually by his sorrows; and there was now a real bond between him and his flock.
>
> •   •   •
>
> The sad good-byes had all been said before that last evening; and after all the packing was done and all the arrangements were made, Amos felt the oppression of that blank interval in which one has nothing left to think of but the dreary future—the separation from the loved and familiar, and the chilling entrance on the new and strange. **In every parting there is an image of death.**

In hell they'll roast thee like a herrin'

Source: TAM O'SHANTER (Line 202)
Author: Robert Burns (1759-1796)
First published: 1791
Type of work: Narrative poem

Context: Kirk Alloway was a small church near where Burns spent the last years of his life. As a young man, he had listened to legends of ghosts told him by Betty Davidson, an old lady with the best collection of horror yarns in the surrounding region. In 1789 Burns dug into his memory for some of them. An antiquarian, Captain Francis Grose, was collecting material in the neighborhood for a book to be called *Grose's Antiquities of Scotland*. Burns asked him to sketch the church and cemetery where his father was buried and where he himself expected to have his grave. The author agreed, on condition that Burns would provide him with a legend to be printed along with the sketch. So in one day Burns completed one of his greatest poems, the legend of Tam o' Shanter. Tam is a ne'er-do-well, a drinker who stays away from his nagging wife Kate, on market days, not going home until he has spent most of the money he has taken in. However, on this particular day, eventually he heads homeward through the storm, on his horse Meg. His road leads past Kirk Alloway which, to his amazement, is brightly lighted. Since John Barleycorn gives men courage even to confront the Devil, Tammie spurs his horse close enough that he can look on the revelry. Presided over by Old Nick, warlocks and witches are dancing reels so furiously among the open coffins that

524

the women are discarding their garments. Most of them are so old and ugly that Tam is disgusted, but there is one winsome wench, Nannie, in a cutty sark (short shift), who dances so madly and is so pretty that the onlooker, forgetting the circumstances, calls out, "Well done, Cutty-sark!" Out go the lights! The evil dancers come after Tam, who spurs his horse. Every Scot knows that witches cannot cross a stream of running water, so Tammie heads Meg for the bridge.

Once beyond the key stone, in the middle, he will be safe. But Nannie follows swiftly. At the moment she overtakes Tam, everything except the tail of his horse is beyond the middle of the stream, but she seizes that, and off it comes in the witch's grasp, leaving only a stump. In concluding, Burns appends a moral. Before you take a drink or focus your mind on scantily clad women, pause and remember Tam o' Shanter. Here is the conclusion:

Ah, Tam! ah, Tam! thou'll get thy fairin!
In hell they'll roast thee like a herrin'!

In vain thy Kate awaits thy comin!
Kate soon will be a woefu' woman!
Now, do thy speedy utmost, Meg.
And win the key-stane of the brig . . .
Ae spring brought aff her master hale,
But left behind her ain gray tail;
The carlin claught her by the rump,
And left poor Maggie scarce a stump.
 Now, wha this tale o' truth shall read,
Ilk man and mother's son, take heed;
Whene'er to drink you are inclin'd,
Or cutty-sarks run in your mind,
Think, ye may buy the joys o'er dear,
Remember Tam o' Shanter's mare.

In married life three is company and two is none

Source: THE IMPORTANCE OF BEING EARNEST (Act I)
Author: Oscar Wilde (1856-1900)
First published: 1895
Type of work: Dramatic comedy

Context: In this comedy by the Dublin-born wit Oscar Fingall O'Flahertie Wills Wilde, Jack Worthing is in love with Gwendolen Fairfax, daughter of Lady Bracknell. His friend Algy is Lady Bracknell's nephew. Algy is a bunburyist, that is, he has invented an invalid friend, Bunbury, whose uncertain health calls Algy from London whenever it is desirable to escape one of his aunt's dull parties. Jack, as a means of occasional relief from his soberness as guardian of a young lady, has invented a reprobate brother called Ernest, who lives in London. He tells Algy that upon

525

marriage, he will get rid of Ernest, and advises his friend to kill off Bunbury. Algernon scoffs at the advice.

ALGERNON
Nothing will induce me to part with Bunbury, and if you ever get married, which seems to me extremely problematic, you will be very glad to know Bunbury. A man who marries without knowing Bunbury has a very tedious time of it.

JACK
That is nonsense. If I marry a charming girl like Gwendolen, and she is the only girl I ever saw in my life that I would marry, I certainly won't want to know Bunbury.

ALGERNON
Then your wife will. You don't seem to realise, that **in married life three is company and two is none.**

In nature there is nothing melancholy

Source: THE NIGHTINGALE (Line 15)
Author: Samuel Taylor Coleridge (1772-1834)
First published: 1798
Type of work: A conversation poem

Context: In addition to the many poems by Wordsworth that appeared in *Lyrical Ballads* (1798), which marks the beginning of the English Romantic Movement, there were only two by his friend and collaborator, Coleridge: "The Ancient Mariner," and "The Nightingale," along with fragments of an unpublished drama *Osorio.* The revised edition of 1800 contained a preface by Wordsworth, stating the creed of the romanticists. Breaking with neoclassical theory, they stood for nature worship and—under the influence of Rousseau and Wordsworth's sojourn in France—democracy, and the common man with his simple, natural language. In "The Nightingale," Coleridge speaks to William Wordsworth and his sister Dorothy, and tells them about his infant son, whom he intends to make "Nature's playmate." The baby loves the nightingale's song and the evening star, and once the poet hushed him by taking him to the orchard where he could see the moon. For *Lyrical Ballads,* Wordsworth was supposed to supply nature poems, and Coleridge to deal with the supernatural and exotic, but in this poem, except for a reference to the mysterious ruins of a castle in an unkempt forest, Coleridge writes about nature. He begins with a description of evening and the sinking sun, and suggests that the hikers rest on an old mossy bridge, amid the stillness. The spring shower has ended, and the stars can be dimly seen. This is the hour to hear the song of the nightingale, which Milton called "most musical, most melancholy."

Coleridge, however, protests that it is really a merry bird, hurrying to fill an April night with delicious notes, as if fearing that dawn would soon appear. Its reputation for melancholy came from some unhappy person who transferred his sorrows to the song of the nightingale; and poets, instead of enjoying the sunshine beside a brook, echoed this idea until everybody came to believe that nightingales were melancholy. There is nothing melancholy in nature unless man makes it so.

> And hark! the Nightingale begins its song,
> "Most musical, most melancholy" bird!
> A melancholy bird? Oh! idle thought!
> **In Nature there is nothing melancholy.**
> But some night-wandering man whose heart was pierced
> With the remembrance of a grievous wrong,
> Or slow distemper, or neglected love,
> (And so, poor wretch! filled all things with himself,
> And made all gentle sounds tell back the tale
> Of his own sorrow) he, and such as he,
> First named these notes a melancholy strain.
> And many a poet echoes the conceit; . . .

In such a night stood Dido

Source: THE MERCHANT OF VENICE (Act V, sc. i, ll. 9-10)
Author: William Shakespeare (1564-1616)
First published: 1600
Type of work: Dramatic comedy

Context: Jessica, daughter of the Jew Shylock, and her husband, Lorenzo, friend of Bassanio, talk poetically on a moonlit night along the avenue to Belmont, home of the heiress Portia, recent bride of Bassanio. The lovers are reminded that on a night such as this Dido, Queen of Carthage, holding a willow branch, symbol of unrequited love, waited vainly for the return of her beloved Æneas.

> LORENZO
> **In such a night**
> **Stood Dido** with a willow in her hand
> Upon the wild sea banks, and waft her love
> To come again to Carthage.

> JESSICA
> In such a night
> Medea gathered the enchanted herbs
> That did renew old Æson.

In the brave days of old

Source: LAYS OF ANCIENT ROME ("Horatius," Stanza 31)
Author: Thomas Babington Macaulay (1800-1859)
First published: 1842
Type of work: Narrative poem

Context: "Horatius at the Bridge" is the best-known poem of the volume, *Lays of Ancient Rome.* "In the brave days of old," when schoolboys had to learn poems to recite on Friday afternoon, it was a favorite. Following Livy and Dionysius, it recounts the brave exploit of Rome's legendary hero, Horatius Cocles, who, with two companions, held the Sublician Bridge that connected Rome with the west, against the Etruscan army of Lars Porsena, until the rest of the defenders of the city could destroy the bridge. Horatius then swam to safety back across the Tiber River. For reward, he was given as much land as he could plough in one day. The poem is imagined to have been composed about 360 B.C., concerning events that happened 120 years earlier. It begins: "Lars Porsena of Clusium/ By the Nine Gods he swore/ That the ancient house of Tarquin/ Should suffer wrong no more." Horatius, the Captain of the Gate, offers to keep the bridge, and Spurius Lartius and Titus Herminius volunteer to fight beside him. Stanzas 31 and 32 set the scene:

"Horatius," quoth the Consul,
  "As thou sayest, so let it be."
And straight against that great array
  Forth went the dauntless three.
For Romans in Rome's quarrel
  Spared neither land nor gold,
Nor sons nor wife, nor limb nor life,
  In the brave days of old.

Then none was for a party;
  Then all were for the state;
Then the great man helped the poor,
  And the poor man loved the great:
The lands were fairly portioned;
  Then spoils were fairly sold:
The Romans were like brothers
  In the brave days of old.

In this world a man must either be anvil or hammer

Source: HYPERION (Book IV, chapter 7)
Author: Henry Wadsworth Longfellow (1807-1882)
First published: 1839
Type of work: Novel

Context: The idea that a man is either the smiter or the one smitten is an old one. If he does not assert himself, he will be put upon by others. Some writers have varied the expression, to insist that in his lifetime man plays both parts, and must act in either role to his utmost capacity. In the days of Christian martyrdom, the second century Bishop of Antioch, St. Ignatius Theophorus, told his followers: "Stand like an anvil when it is beaten upon." A later religious poet, George Herbert (1593–1633) advised in *Jacula Prudentum* (1640): "When you are an anvil, hold you still;/ When you are a hammer, strike your fill." More recently the American poet, Edward Markham (1852–1940) wrote in "Preparedness":

"When you are the anvil, bear—/ When you are the hammer, strike." Longfellow, in his longest prose work, *Hyperion,* employed the same figure. Based on the New England poet's trip to Europe in 1835–1836 to study at Heidelberg, *Hyperion* embodied Longfellow's own experiences and even used as heroine Frances Appleton, whom he was to marry five years later. About Paul Flemming (representing Longfellow), the hero of this sentimental romance, the novelist declares in Book I, chapter IV: "One half of the world must sweat and groan, that the other half may dream." In Part IV, a priest, after telling Flemming a story, bids him goodbye with the comment:

"I shall not see you in the morning, so goodby, and God bless you. Remember my parting words. Never mind trifles. **In this world a man must either be anvil or hammer.** Care killed a cat!"

"I have heard you say that so often," replied Flemming, laughing, "that I begin to believe it. But I wonder if Care shaved his left eyebrow after doing the deed, as the ancient Egyptians used to do!"

"Aha! now you are sweeping cobwebs from the sky! Good night! Good night!"

In time we hate that which we often fear

Source: ANTONY AND CLEOPATRA (Act I, sc. iii, l. 12)
Author: William Shakespeare (1564-1616)
First published: 1623
Type of work: Dramatic tragedy

Context: From Cleopatra's love and Egypt's luxury, Antony is recalled to a stern sense of duty as one of the three rulers of the Roman Empire. The Parthians have invaded from the East ("These strong Egyptian fetters I must break"); his wife, Fulvia, is dead ("There's a great spirit gone."); rebellion is afoot in the West. "I must

from this enchanting queen break off," asserts Antony. Cleopatra, however, has other ideas, and we now see her at work. She tells one of her attendants: "See where he is, who's with him, what he does—/ I did not send you. If you find him sad,/ Say I am dancing; if in mirth, report/ That I am sudden sick. Quick, and return."

But one of her ladies-in-waiting thinks Cleopatra is going about her business in the wrong way:

CHARMIAN
Madam, methinks if you did love him dearly,
You do not hold the method to enforce
The like from him.

CLEOPATRA
What should I do, I do not?

CHARMIAN
In each thing give him way, cross him in nothing.

CLEOPATRA
Thou teachest like a fool—The way to lose him.

CHARMIAN
Tempt him not so too far; ywis forbear,
In time we hate that which we often fear.

The Indian Summer of the heart!

Source: MEMORIES (Last stanza)
Author: John Greenleaf Whittier (1807-1892)
First published: 1843
Type of work: Lyric poem

Context: Among Whittier's *Poems Subjective and Reminiscent* appears his "Memories," with its nine stanzas. After several years of academic training, during which he submitted poems to the *Haverhill* (Mass.) *Gazette,* in 1829 he became editor of a Boston magazine, *American Manufacturer,* in which he published both his prose and his poetry. The poems were collected into a volume in 1857. In "Memories," Whittier thinks back, in later years, to a "Beautiful and happy girl" with whom as a child he used to talk and walk. Whittier's biographer says the poem was written in 1841, when the poet was thirty-four years old, and certainly not in the autumn of his life. Indian Summer is said to come in the fall, after the first frost. Whittier is supposed to have hesitated to publish the poem "because it was so personal and near my heart." Most poets think that that is the stuff of which good poetry is made. The final stanza declares:

Thus, while at times before our eyes
  The shadows melt, and fall apart,
And, smiling through them, round us lies
  The warm light of our morning skies,—

530

The Indian Summer of the heart!
In secret sympathies of mind,
In founts of feeling which retain
Their pure, fresh flow, we yet may find
Our early dreams not wholly vain!

An indifference closely bordering on aversion

Source: THE NEW ARABIAN NIGHTS ("The Rajah's Diamond": Story of the
House with the Green Blinds)
Author: Robert Louis Stevenson (1850-1894)
First published: 1882
Type of work: Fantastic tale

Context: There was a wave of interest in things Oriental during the Victorian era, and Stevenson's *New Arabian Nights* probably reflects this. In this book he turns London into a place of fantasy and mystery, where happenings have the strangeness and vivid illogicality of dreams. "The Rajah's Diamond" is a tale, or series of episodes, following a similar sequence entitled "The Suicide Club"; the Bohemian Prince Florizel, a sort of genie-figure, moves through both. The individual episodes are connected by Stevenson's editorial comments, in which he summarizes whimsically the transitions employed by his "Arabian author." The stories are in a sense modern fairy tales. "The Rajah's Diamond" follows the adventures of a fabulous and unlucky gem from one owner to the next, until finally Prince Florizel acts the good angel and disposes of it forever. It had been obtained by foul means and at the cost of many lives by General Vandeleur when he was in India; he has a fortune in diamonds, but his wife bankrupts him and steals the stones, entrusting them to her manservant. He is to convey them to the general's brother, a connoisseur and collector who is also an accomplished jewel thief. The servant is separated from this fortune by a series of misadventures, and the Rajah's diamond gets into the hands of a clergyman, who immediately falls from grace and joins the underworld in an effort to "fence" the stone. He meets with the general's brother, John, who robs him of it; John's daughter subsequently passes it on to young Francis Scymgeour, who has fallen in love with her. Francis has been given an anonymous but generous monthly allowance, presumably from his unknown father; learning part of the plot, he spies on John and his daughter. From a house next door he sees John drug the clergyman. He has deduced that John is actually his own father and is in some sort of trouble, so he rushes to offer his assistance and reveals himself just as John lifts the diamond from his victim's pocket. His reaction to Francis is anything but cordial:

Then a light seemed to break upon Mr. Vandeleur, and he
laughed aloud.

"I see," cried he. "It is the Scrymgeour. Very well, Mr. Scrymgeour. Let me tell you in a few words how you stand. You have entered my private residence by force, or perhaps by fraud, but certainly with no encouragement from me; and you come at a moment of some annoyance, a guest having fainted at my table, to besiege me with your protestations. You are no son of mine. You are my brother's bastard by a fishwife, if you want to know. I regard you with **an indifference closely bordering on aversion;** and from what I now see of your conduct, I judge your mind to be exactly suitable to your exterior. . . ."

Indolent vacuity of thought

Source: THE TASK (Book IV, l. 297)
Author: William Cowper (1731-1800)
First published: 1785
Type of work: Meditative poem in blank verse

Context: Writing at the urging of a friend, Lady Austen, to uphold the superiority of "rural ease and leisure" over London life, for people who sought to live in virtue, Cowper was the first eighteenth century poet to relish country life for its own sake. Being a highly moral person, he abhorred the many opportunities for lapses from virtue in a big city, but in addition, the poet loved the country, its landscape, its activities, and, here, its moments for relaxation. This highly autobiographical work foreshadows the kind of poetry Wordsworth was to write. It is Cowper's greatest poem. Written in blank verse, and containing many digressions, it commences in Book I, called "The Sofa," to trace the history of a place to sit, from the early stool to a luxurious sofa. Then come Book II, "The Time Piece," Book III, "The Garden," and Book IV, "The Winter Evening." Following the arrival of the post, and the reading of the newspaper, comes dinner and later relaxation before a fire in the mirrored drawing room. This pleasure can happen only during "Winter, ruler of the inverted year." Staring at the imaginary pictures in the fireplace, the poet wonders, whenever thoughts enter his lazy, inactive brain, whether there are people "that never felt a stupor, know no pause, nor need one." He sees:

> Trees, churches, and strange visages expressed
> In the red cinders, while with poring eye
> I gazed, myself creating what I saw.
> Not less amused have I quiescent watched
> The sooty films that play upon the bars,
> • • •
> 'T is thus the understanding takes repose
> In **indolent vacuity of thought**
> And sleeps, and is refreshed. . . .

532

Inflaming wine, pernicious to mankind

Source: THE ILIAD (Book VI, 1. 330, as translated by Alexander Pope)
Author: Homer (c. 850 B.C.)
First transcribed: Sixth century, B.C.
Type of work: Epic poem

Context: Book VI of *The Iliad* relates how, for a time, the gods leave the field of battle, and the Greeks prevail over the Trojans. Hector, the Trojan leader, advised by Helenus, the chief seer of the Trojans, leaves his men to return to the city. He has a two-fold purpose in taking this course: he wishes to have his mother, Hecuba, Queen of Troy, take her women to the temple of Minerva, there to offer sacrifice to gain the goddess' help in removing Diomed, a great Greek warrior, from the fighting; he also hopes to persuade Paris, his brother, to return to the battles, where he has not been seen since his own luckless battle with Menelaus. During Hector's absence the fighting abates between the armies, and Homer describes how Diomed, a Greek, and Glaucus, a Trojan, meet and talk between the two forces. Hector, returning to the royal palace in Troy, finds his mother. She embraces her son, who is weary from the fighting, and tells him she will bring him wine, partly to be used as an offering to the gods, and partly to be used as a refreshing drink for Hector. But Hector refuses the wine, saying it is bad for men and should be used rather as an offering to the gods. He asks his mother, since his hands are stained with blood, and he is impure, to go make offering on behalf of Troy to Minerva:

> Far hence be Bacchus' gifts; (the chief rejoin'd:)
> **Inflaming wine, pernicious to mankind,**
> Unnerves the limbs, and dulls the noble mind.
> Let chiefs abstain, and spare the sacred juice
> To sprinkle to the gods, its better use.
> By me that holy office were profaned;
> Ill fits it me, with human gore distain'd,
> To the pure skies these horrid hands to raise,
> Or offer heaven's great Sire polluted praise.
> You, with your matrons, go! a spotless train,
> And burn rich odours in Minerva's fane.

An injury is much sooner forgotten than an insult

Source: LETTERS TO HIS SON (Letter I)
Author: Philip Dormer Stanhope, Lord Chesterfield (1694-1773)
First published: 1774
Type of work: Personal letters

533

Context: In this letter Chesterfield begins by counselling his illegitimate son to try every day to improve his intelligence, as it is the coach in which men ride through the world. He also says that his son is given to laziness, inattention, and indifference, and begs him to cure these faults. If a man wants to succeed in practically anything, he can, with the exception of poetry, which calls for innate ability. In addition to the accomplishments of the mind there are lesser accomplishments necessary for the man who would succeed. He must do such things as dance gracefully and dress well. Above all, he should not be given to fits of absentmindedness when in the company of others. The only minds that can be excused for not paying attention in company are those that are very weak or those which are thinking great thoughts, like Newton's; there are very few of this latter kind of mind. A young man displaying absence of mind in company, especially in a company given to frivolity, is actually insulting those around him by displaying a form of contempt, and there is nothing that offends people more than insults; injuries are much more readily tolerated than contempt; therefore the wise man will flatter his associates by giving ready attention to their little vanities.

> . . . However frivolous a company may be, still, while you are among them, do not show them, by your inattention, that you think them so; but rather take their tone, and conform in some degree to their weakness, instead of manifesting your contempt for them. There is nothing that people bear more impatiently, or forgive less, than contempt; and **an injury is much sooner forgotten than an insult.** If, therefore, you would rather please than offend, rather be well than ill spoken of, rather be loved than hated; remember to have that constant attention about you which flatters every man's little vanity; and the want of which, by mortifying his pride, never fails to excite his resentment, or at least his ill will. . . .

Inquisitorious and tyrannical duncery

Source: THE REASON OF CHURCH GOVERNMENT URGED AGAINST PRELATY (Book II, preface)
Author: John Milton (1608-1674)
First published: 1642
Type of work: Theological tract

Context: During the years that immediately preceded the civil war the spokesmen for the Puritan and Anglican churches engaged in a spirited and often bitter pamphlet war. As perhaps the most articulate representative of the Puritan position, Milton contributed several important pamphlets to his party's campaign. The major differences between these two parties were not concerned with doctrine, or belief, but with discipline, or

534

the government of the Church. Since the conventions of pamphlet war at this time were to attack both the opposition's argument as well as any personalities of importance, Milton frequently found occasion to defend not only Puritanism but himself as well. In Book I of this work he argues that the proper form of church government is prescribed in Scripture and attempts to refute specific arguments advanced by the Anglicans. In Book II he shows in detail how "Prelaty opposeth the Reason and End of the Gospel in three Ways," but first he inserts a preface in which he replies to some personal attacks which had been made against his shortcomings as a poet. His intentions as a poet, he says, contrary to those of the "libidinous and ignorant poetasters" of the other party, have always been to inspire wisdom and virtue.

> . . . And the accomplishment of them lies not but in a power above man's to promise; but that none hath by more studious ways endeavored, and with more unwearied spirit that none shall, that I dare almost aver of myself, as far as life and free leisure will extend; and that the land had once enfranchised herself from this impertinent yoke of prelaty, under whose **inquisitorious and tyrannical duncery,** no free and splendid wit can flourish. Neither do I think it shame to covenant with any knowing reader, that for some few years yet I may go on trust with him toward the payment of what I am now indebted, as being a work not to be raised from the heat of youth, or the vapors of wine; like that which flows at waste from the pen of some vulgar amorist, of the trencher fury of a rhyming parasite; . . .

The insane root that takes the reason prisoner

Source: MACBETH (Act I, sc. iii, ll. 84-85)
Author: William Shakespeare (1564-1616)
First published: 1623
Type of work: Dramatic tragedy

Context: Macbeth and Banquo, generals in the army of Duncan, King of Scotland, pass along a heath near Forres as they return home after successfully putting down a rebellion against their king. Suddenly three witches appear from the gloom and hail the warriors with the prophecy that Macbeth, Thane of Glamis, will receive the titles Thane of Cawdor and king, and that Banquo, though he will not become king, will beget kings. The fateful words spoken, the witches disappear, leaving Macbeth and Banquo stunned and wondering if they have eaten something to make them have visions, possibly the root of hemlock.

BANQUO
The earth has bubbles, as the water has,

535

And these are of them. Whither are they vanished?

MACBETH
Into the air; and what seemed corporal melted,
As breath into the wind. Would they had stayed.

BANQUO
Were such things here, as we do speak about?
Or have we eaten on **the insane root**
That takes the reason prisoner?

MACBETH
Your children shall be kings.

BANQUO
You shall be king.

MACBETH
And Thane of Cawdor too—went it not so?

BANQUO
To the selfsame tune and words.

An institution is the lengthened shadow of one man

Source: SELF-RELIANCE
Author: Ralph Waldo Emerson (1803-1882)
First published: 1841
Type of work: Moral essay

Context: Emerson believed every human being is divine insofar as he has a soul. Every man can be self-reliant, then, in the sense that he can trust his own judgment in all matters. Emerson specifically objects in this essay to the individual's conforming to either customs of the past or the cry of the multitude, when these forces are contrary to his judgment; as Emerson writes, "What I must do is all that concerns me, not what people think." He warns that by his nonconformity to mass opinion the individual arouses antagonism, that the individual must be willing to pay the price for nonconformity, for "the world whips you with its displeasure." Somewhat later in the essay Emerson says that the world always misunderstands the great individual, as they misunderstood such heroes of the past as Pythagoras, Socrates, Jesus, Luther, Copernicus, Galileo, and Newton. But the important thing, says Emerson, is to be true to one's self, not to violate one's own nature. To be true to one's nature is to be great, to avoid "the smooth mediocrity and squalid contentment" of the

536

times. Emerson issues a call for us all to be great in this way, leading other people instead of following. He believes that "Character, reality, reminds you of nothing else; it takes the place of the whole creation." The great person, suggests Emerson, is the man who makes all surrounding circumstances indifferent, is a creator not a user, a leader instead of a follower:

> . . . Every true man is a cause, a country, and an age; requires infinite spaces and numbers and time fully to accomplish his design; and posterity seem to follow his steps as a train of clients. A man Caesar is born, and for ages after we have a Roman Empire. Christ is born, and millions of minds so grow and cleave to his genius, that he is confounded with virtue and the possible of man. **An institution is the lengthened shadow of one man;** as Monachism, of the Hermit Antony; the Reformation, of Luther; Quakerism, of Fox; Methodism, of Wesley; Abolition, of Clarkson. Scipio, Milton called "the height of Rome"; and all history resolves itself very easily into the biography of a few stout and earnest persons.

The insupportable labor of doing nothing

Source: THE SPECTATOR (Number 54)
Author: Sir Richard Steele (1672-1729)
First published: May 2, 1711
Type of work: Essay

Context: Sir Richard Steele was a busy and talented man. After dropping out of Oxford he served for a time in the dragoon and foot guards, but his literary aspirations were uppermost. He wrote a number of successful comedies and soon gained some notice as a playwright. An ebullient, witty person, he was always immersed in moneymaking schemes that kept him destitute. His great and lasting contribution to English literature was his founding, in 1709, of the first real English magazine. This was *The Tatler,* which ran two years. He was joined by Joseph Addison, who collaborated in the project and wrote some of the articles. *The Tatler* ceased publication in January, 1711, and was soon succeeded by the more famous *Spectator,* a daily which ran from March 1, 1711, to December 6, 1712. Of its 555 issues, Addison wrote about 274 and Steele about 240, while guest essayists contributed the remainder. These papers were a reaction to the excesses of the Restoration, and their basic purpose was to popularize morality and temper it with wit. They succeeded admirably in their design, their social criticism being witty, urbane, cheerful; and in addition, the papers are an unsurpassed running commentary on the life of the time, and a high literary standard is always upheld in them. Nearly any subject could be treated, with the exception of politics. A number of fictitious characters appeared in these pages, among them Mr. Spectator, the detached observer of human affairs. One literary device employed was the letters to the editor, nearly all of which were of course written by the authors—a practice not unknown to modern journalism. Steele prints a letter in *The Spectator,* for example, which is supposedly from Cambridge and tells of a new sect of philosophers, The Loungers; their fundamental belief, upon which their whole system is built, is "That Time being an implacable Enemy to and Destroyer of all things, ought to be paid in his own coin, and be destroyed and murdered without Mercy . . . ." Steele offers a general comment:

> I must be so just as to observe I have formerly seen of this Sect at our other University; tho' not distinguished by the Appelation which the learned Historian, my Correspondent, reports they bear at *Cambridge.* . . . The *Lowngers* are satisfied with being merely Part of the Number of Mankind, without distinguishing themselves from amongst them. They may be said rather to suffer their Time to pass, than to spend it. . . . When one of this Order happens to be a Man of Fortune, the Expence of his Time is transferred to his Coach and Horses, and his Life is to be measured by their Motion . . . The chief Entertainment one of these Philosophers can possibly propose to himself, is to get a Relish of Dress . . . When the *Lowngers* leave an Academick Life, . . . [and] retire to the Seats of their Ancestors, they usually join a Pack of Dogs, and employ their Days in defending their Poultry from Foxes: I do not know any other Method that any of this Order has ever taken to make a Noise in the World; but I shall inquire into such about this Town as have arrived at the Dignity of being *Lowngers* by the Force of natural Parts, without having ever seen an University; and send my Correspondent, for the Embellishment of his Book, the Names and History of those who pass their Lives without any Incidents at all; and how they shift Coffee-houses and Chocolate-houses from Hour to Hour, to get over **the insupportable Labour of doing nothing.**

Invention breeds invention

Source: SOCIETY AND SOLITUDE (Chapter 7, "Works and Days")
Author: Ralph Waldo Emerson (1803-1882)
First published: 1870
Type of work: Moral essay

Context: Philosophical idealist though he was, Emerson had a great admiration for what man was able to do with the stuff of this life. Emerson was a canny Yankee, as well as a philosopher, and he found his own century to be "an age of tools." He pities earlier generations for not having known all the contrivances which had come into being by his own time. Man's discoveries, such as "steam and galvanism, sulphuric ether and ocean telegraphs, photograph and spectroscope," Emerson says, "open great gates of a future, promising to make the world plastic and to lift human life out of its beggary to a god-like ease and power." He goes on to sound a litany of products and techniques acquired by man during the first three-quarters of the nineteenth century, and he sees the progress mankind is making to be an unfolding of the work of the Deity; he hints that such progress is a better approach to Deity, who seems to be working through mankind. But Emerson warns, later in the essay, that man must be careful lest machinery, which he sees as aggressive, does not begin to use mankind, instead of mankind's using machinery. But, as Emerson sees it, the technical progress is enthralling:

There does not seem any limit to these new informations of the same Spirit that made the elements at first, and now, through man, works them. Art and power will go on as they have done,—will make day out of night, time out of space, and space out of time.

Invention breeds invention. No sooner is the electric telegraph devised than gutta percha, the very material it requires, is found. The aëronaut is provided with gun-cotton, the very fuel he wants for his balloon. When commerce is vastly enlarged, California and Australia expose the gold it needs. When Europe is over-populated, America and Australia crave to be peopled; and so throughout, every chance is timed, as if Nature, who made the lock, knew where to find the key.

Irrevocably dark, total eclipse without all hope of day!

Source: SAMSON AGONISTES (Lines 81-82)
Author: John Milton (1608-1674)
First published: 1671
Type of work: Dramatic tragedy

Context: Blind Puritan poet John Milton, in writing the dramatic poetic tragedy *Samson Agonistes,* must have felt particular sympathy for Samson, the blind captive strong-man of Israel, as he toiled in the tread mills of the Philistines, the enemy from which, according to prophecy before his birth, he should deliver his people. While the Philistines celebrate the feast of Dagon, their Sea-Idol, Samson, enjoying a brief rest from his labor, sits on the Gaza prison steps in the sunshine and fresh air and bemoans his sad condition, the most tragic phase of which, says Samson, is his blindness:

O loss of sight, of thee I most complain!
Blind among enemies, O worse then chains,
Dungeon, or beggery, or decrepit age!
Light the prime work of God to me is extinct,
And all her various objects of delight

Annull'd, which might in part my grief have eas'd,
Inferiour to the vilest now become
Of man or worm; the vilest here excel me,
They creep, yet see, I dark in light expos'd
To daily fraud, contempt, abuse and wrong,
Within doors, or without, still as a fool,
In power of others, never in my own;
Scarce half I seem to live, dead more than half.
O dark, dark, dark, amid the blaze of noon,
Irrevocably dark, total Eclipse
Without all hope of day!

Is <u>must</u> a word to be addressed to princes?

Source: A SHORT HISTORY OF THE ENGLISH PEOPLE, J. R. GREEN (Chapter 7, sec. VIII, p. 459)
Author: Elizabeth I, Queen of England (1533-1603)
First published: 1874
Type of work: Biographical anecdote

Context: The last years of the great Queen Elizabeth I were gloomy ones. She had always been a lonely figure, and now she grew lonelier. As sometimes happens, she had outlived the age of which she was a part. The statesmen, counselors, and warriors of her younger days had passed on one by one; those who had followed them were waiting for her to go and already intriguing for a place in the reign that would come next. Lord Essex, her favorite, became involved in a mad attempt at revolution and was executed. The old splendor for which her court had been famous gradually declined and at length disappeared; the nobility avoided her. A brilliant woman, imperious, fanciful, not overly scrupulous, she belonged to the Renaissance—and the Renaissance was gone forever. She had always thoroughly enjoyed life as it had been lived in her youth; now she clung to it. Hunting, dancing, joking and coquetting, scolding, she continued her colorful progresses from one country house to another so long as she was able. These old-fashioned displays of pomp and splendor no longer met with general approval, but she finally gave them up only because her health was failing. Green's recital of the events of her last hours paints a haunting and tragic picture:

. . . Her face became haggard, and her frame shrank almost to a skeleton. At last her taste for finery disappeared, and she refused to change her dresses for a week together. A strange melancholy settled down on her: "she held in her hand," says one who saw her in her last days, "a golden cup, which she put often to her lips: but in truth her heart seemed too full to need more filling." Gradually her mind gave way. She lost her memory, the violence of her temper became unbearable, her very courage seemed to forsake her.

She called for a sword to lie constantly beside her, and thrust it from time to time through the arras, as if she heard murderers stirring there. Food and rest alike became distasteful. She sate day and night propped up with pillows on a stool, her finger to her lip, her eyes fixed on the floor, without a word. If she once broke the silence, it was with a flash of her old queenliness. When Robert Cecil asserted that she "must" go to bed, the word roused her like a trumpet. "Must!" she exclaimed; **"is must a word to be addressed to princes?** Little man, little man! thy father, if he had been alive, durst not have used that word." Then, as her anger spent itself, she sank into her old dejection. "Thou art so presumptuous," she said, "because thou knowest I shall die." She rallied once more when the ministers beside her bed named Lord Beauchamp, the heir to the Suffolk claim, as a possible successor. "I will have no rogue's son," she cried hoarsely, "in my seat." But she gave no sign, save a motion of the head, at the mention of the King of Scots. She was in fact fast becoming insensible; and early the next morning the life of Elizabeth, a life so great, so strange and lonely in its greatness, passed quietly away.

Is the wind in that door?

Source: LE MORTE D'ARTHUR (Book VII, chapter 34)
Author: Sir Thomas Malory (1400?-1471)
First published: 1485
Type of work: Medieval romance

Context: The story of Gareth and how he became a Knight of the Round Table is an entertaining and rather typical example of the romantic tales which make up a large part of Arthurian legend. Gareth, brother of Sir Gawaine, desires knighthood and presents himself to King Arthur at the King's annual high feast. He does not reveal his identity, wishing to prove himself first; but he has three requests to make of the king. The first of these is for a year's food and lodging, which Arthur grants with his characteristic generosity. Gareth will not reveal his other two requests until the next high feast, and in Arthur's world there is nothing unusual in this action. He welcomes Gareth to the court and turns him over to Sir Kay the steward, who christens him Beaumains (Fair Hands), mocks him, and puts him to work in the kitchen. He is befriended by Sir Gawaine, who does not recognize him, and by Sir Launcelot, but he serves out his twelve months in the scullery. At the next high feast a damsel, Linet, arrives to tell the king that her lady is besieged by a cruel tyrant and desires that a knight come and rescue her. Gareth then makes his other two requests of Arthur: that he be allowed the adventure and that Sir Launcelot make him a knight. He then accompanies the damsel, who has a sharp tongue and dislikes kitchen boys. After a long series of battles and adventures he at length rescues the lady, Dame Liones, and falls in love with her; his affection is returned. The story culminates in a great tournament held at her castle, attended by Arthur and his knights. Gareth and Gawaine fight an epic battle; the damsel Linet intervenes, telling Gawaine he is fighting his own brother. There is a joyful reunion, and Sir Gareth and Dame Liones are then presented to King Arthur:

> . . . And there the king asked his nephew, Sir Gareth, whether he would have that lady as paramour, or to have her to his wife. My lord, wit you well that I love her above all ladies living. Now, fair lady, said King Arthur, what say ye? Most noble King, said Dame Liones, wit you well that my lord, Sir Gareth, is to me more lever to have and welde as my husband, than any king or prince that is christened; and if I may not have him I promise you I will never have none. For, my lord Arthur, said Dame Liones, wit you well he is my first love, and he shall be the last; and if ye will suffer him to have his will and free choice I dare say he will have me. That is truth, said Sir Gareth; an I have not you and welde not you as my wife, there shall never lady nor gentlewoman rejoice me. What, nephew, said the king, **is the wind in that door?**

It can't be nature, for it is not sense

Source: THE FAREWELL (Line 200)
Author: Charles Churchill (1731-1764)
First published: 1764
Type of work: Satiric dialogue

Context: Charles Churchill, whose early ambitions turned toward an ecclesiastical career ran afoul of love for wine, women, and wrangling, wrote toward the end of his short life a poetic conversation about his proposal to leave Europe and go to India. "P" probably stands for the poet, and "F" for his friend, who questions his decision by asking what could some other part of the world offer as better targets for satire than England, where he can find vice and folly aplenty? The poet says he is tired of hearing repeated protests of love for England, despite her faults. The same patriotic utterance has frequently been voiced in the United States, as, for example, when Commander Stephen Decatur (1779–1820) of the U.S. Navy declared at a banquet in 1815 after defeating the Algerian pirates: "Our country! In her intercourse with foreign nations, may she be always in the right, but our country, right or wrong!" And Senator John J. Crittenden (1787–1863) of Kentucky, with one son in the Northern armies and one in the Confederacy, vowed to stand by his country, right or wrong. The Friend in the poem sees no difference in mankind, whether in England or Japan. In a slight shift of thought, the poet agrees that man is usually partial to the land of his birth. To call all lands alike "may be PHILOSOPHY, but can't be SENSE."

542

However, the friend says that while Nature must receive its due, one should not cloud Reason and argue that the Master Passion for one's country is "fix'd by Nature in the human breast." If one's native land is found by comparison with other places to be a spot of Virtue, Plenty, Honesty in Politics, with sacred Love, and Liberty certain, even a Hottentot would love it. But if the place of one's birth is some barren spot where injustice and slavery exist, nobody would love it, any more than the Devil is enraptured of Hell. However, at the conclusion, the poet gets around to his point. Since Clive and those accompanying him as governor of India had left for the Orient on June 4, 1764, the poet concludes that he will find abundant material for his satires when he reaches India. In saying that a country must offer certain qualities before it will be loved, the Friend declares:

> But if, by Fate's decrees, you owe your birth
> To some more barren and penurious earth,
> Where, ev'ry comfort of this life denied,
> Her real wants are scantily supplied,
> Where Pow'r is Reason, Liberty's a joke,
> Laws never made, or made but to be broke,
> To fix thy love on such a wretched spot . . .
>   •   •   •
> Is Folly which admits not of defence;
> **It can't be Nature, for it is not Sense.**
> By the same argument which here you hold
> (When Falsehood's insolent, let Truth be bold)
> If Propagation can in torments dwell,
> A Devil must, if born there, love his hell.

It is an honest ghost

Source: HAMLET (Act I, sc. v, l. 138)
Author: William Shakespeare (1564-1616)
First published: 1603
Type of work: Dramatic tragedy

Context: One of Hamlet's basic problems is that of the identity of the ghost who nightly walks at Elsinore. Is it the ghost of his father or a tempting demon in disguise? The problem is stated most clearly at the end of Act II: "The spirit that I have seen/ May be a devil, and the devil hath power/ T' assume a pleasing shape; . . ." The question is raised at the first sighting of the ghost by Horatio and the watchmen, and it is reasserted by Hamlet at his first encounter, when he insists that he will speak to it, "Be thou a spirit of health, or goblin damned." But after the ghost tells Hamlet, in private, that he is his father's spirit, that he was murdered by Hamlet's uncle, Claudius, the present king, and that Clau-

543

dius and Hamlet's mother, Gertrude, had earlier committed adultery, Hamlet concludes—though only for the moment—that the ghost is genuine—

"honest"—and tells Horatio and the guard as much, though he refuses to disclose anything further:

HAMLET

. . .

Touching this vision here—
It is an honest ghost, that let me tell you—
For your desire to know what is between us,
O'ermaster't as you may.

. . .

It is better to be a fool than to be dead

Source: VIRGINIBUS PUERISQUE ("Crabbed Age and Youth")
Author: Robert Louis Stevenson (1850-1894)
First published: 1881
Type of work: Familiar essay

Context: Stevenson begins the essay entitled "Crabbed Age and Youth" by suggesting that proverbs are invented for mediocre people, to discourage them from overly ambitious attempts and to console them in their mediocrity. He notes that though they are discredited in practice, proverbs hold their own in theory. They are, he suggests, a fine example of how allowances are made for the illusions of youth, but none for the disenchantment of age; seldom do the young quote proverbs to the older generation; it is the older generation who quote proverbs for the edification of youth. Stevenson says that youth should be given credit for what it is, for having enthusiasm; one cannot, he implies, be worth while without having been a youth, with all the faults of youth. Youth, he says, needs to be considered carefully, just as are experience and maturity. He writes pointedly, "It is as natural and as right for a young man to be imprudent and exaggerated, to live in swoops and circles, and beat about his cage like any other wild thing newly captured, as it is for old men to turn gray. . . ." Stevenson is thus making a case for each age to be true to itself, and to live as is natural to it:

. . . All error, not merely verbal, is a strong way of saying that the current truth is incomplete. The follies of youth have a basis in sound reason, just as much as the embarrassing questions put by babes and sucklings. Their most antisocial acts indicate the defects of our society. When the torrent sweeps the man against a boulder, you must expect him to scream, and you need not be surprised if the scream is sometimes a theory. . . . Generous lads irritated at the injustices of society, see nothing for it but the abolishment of

544

everything and Kingdom Come of anarchy. Shelley was a young fool; so are these cocksparrow revolutionaries. But **it is better to be a fool than to be dead.** It is better to emit a scream in the shape of a theory than to be entirely insensible to the jars and incongruities of life and take everything as it comes in a forlorn stupidity. . . .

It is, but hadn't ought to be

Source: MRS. JUDGE JENKINS (Being the only Genuine Sequel to "Maud Muller," Last line)
Author: Bret Harte (1836-1902)
First published: 1870
Type of work: Parody

Context: "Maud Muller," the well-known poem by John Greenleaf Whittier, tells the story of a farm girl and a judge. The judge rides by on his fine horse and asks for a drink of water; Maud brings it and the judge chats pleasantly with her about the haying and other everyday topics, thanks her, and rides on. Each later daydreams about the other. Maud thinks of the happiness and security she and her family could have, and all the good she might do, if the judge were her husband. The judge thinks of Maud and longs for the life of rural simplicity she represents. Each marries within his own station; the judge weds an ambitious woman who drives him up the ladder of success, and Maud marries a farmhand who gives her a large family. As the years pass, they still think wistfully of each other. Whittier concludes with his oft-quoted observation, "Of all the words of tongue or pen,/ The saddest are these: 'It might have been!' " Harte, exponent of a somewhat more hard-boiled view of life than that of Whittier, parodies the original with something less ideal and perhaps more realistic. He begins by assuming that the judge returns for Maud after all; when he arrives, Maud can only stammer ungrammatically and her father requests a small loan. Her brother is drunk at the wedding, and the rest of the family is drunk afterward. In the spring Maud bears the judge a pair of twins, "And the Judge was blest, but thought it strange/ That bearing children made such a change;/For Maud grew broad and red and stout,/ And the waist that his arm once clasped about/ Was more than he now could span; and he/ Sighed as he pondered, ruefully,/ How that which in Maud was native grace/ In Mrs. Jenkins was out of place. . . ." The judge finds himself wishing, now that it is much too late, that his sons could look less like hay-hands and that his wife were better educated:

Alas for maiden! alas for judge!
And the sentimental,—that's one-half "fudge;"

545

For Maud soon thought the Judge a bore,
With all his learning and all his lore;

And the Judge would have bartered Maud's fair face
For more refinement and social grace.

If, of all words of tongue and pen,
The saddest are, "It might have been,"

Sadder are these, we daily see:
"It is, but hadn't ought to be."

It is certain, because it is impossible

Source: DE CARNE CHRISTI (5)
Author: Tertullian (c. 155-c. 220)
First transcribed: c. 209
Type of work: Religious philosophy

Context: Tertullian, educated in Carthage and in Rome with specialization in law and rhetoric, and later converted to Christianity, was well prepared for his role as defender of the Christian faith. In *De Carne Christi,* Tertullain answers the heretical writings of Marcion, Apelles, Basilides, and Valentinus, who argued that Christ never existed in the flesh. With legalistic logic Tertullain contends that the heresy of his opponents is fallacious because it is the very foolishness, or one may say wisdom, of God that made Him elect to be born as a human, to suffer, and to die:

> There are, to be sure, other things also quite as "foolish" [as the birth of Christ], which have reference to the humiliations and sufferings of God. Or else, let them call a crucified God "wisdom." But Marcion will apply the knife to this [doctrine] also, and even with greater reason. For which is more unworthy of God, which is more likely to raise a blush of shame, that [God] should be born, or that He should die? that He should bear the flesh, or the cross? be circumcised, or be crucified? be cradled, or be coffined? be laid in a manger, or in a tomb? [Talk of "wisdom!"] You will show more of that if you refuse to believe this also. But, after all, you will not be "wise" unless you become a "fool" to the world, by believing "the foolish things of God." . . . And He was buried, and rose again; **the fact is certain, because it is impossible.**

546

It is enough to have perished once

Source: THE AENEID (Book IX, lines 140-141)
Author: Virgil (Publius Vergilius Maro, 70-19 B.C.)
First transcribed: c. 29-19 B.C.
Type of work: Epic poem

Context: Fired by patriotism, Virgil wrote the *Aeneid* to give to Rome an origin suited to her greatness. Aeneas, son of Venus and hero of the Trojan War, encounters difficulties similar to those of Ulysses as he sails from Troy to Italy, but, led on by his destiny, he reaches Italy and overcomes the armies of the inhabitants. The destined union of the Latins and the Trojan invaders is accomplished when the aged King Latinus gives to Aeneas the hand of his daughter Lavinia. Turnus, chief suitor of Lavinia, becomes the arch enemy of Aeneas, and, declaring his intention of fighting until death against the Trojans, exclaims, "It is enough to have perished once." In the translation of Mackail the passage reads:

> . . . In no wise am I dismayed by those divine oracles of doom that the Phrygians insolently advance. Fate and Venus are satisfied, in that the Trojans have touched our fruitful Ausonian fields. I too have my destiny against theirs, to put utterly to the sword the guilty nation who have robbed me of my bride; not the sons of Atreus alone feel that pain, nor may Mycenae alone take arms. **But to have perished once is enough!** . . .

It is hardly necessary to light a candle to the sun

Source: DISCOURSES CONCERNING GOVERNMENT (Chapter II, section 23)
Author: Algernon Sidney (1622-1683)
First published: 1698
Type of work: Political treatise

Context: English Republican leader, grand-nephew of Sir Philip Sidney and son of Robert Sidney, Second Earl of Leicester, Algernon Sidney was wounded at Marston Moor in 1644 while fighting for the Parliamentary side in the Civil War. After the Restoration he was pardoned by Charles II, but upon his return to England he supported the Duke of Monmouth in the affair in which Charles' illegitimate son challenged the right of his uncle, the Duke of York, to be first in the line of succession to the throne. This conspiracy was discovered by the exposure of another one, the Rye House Plot. After an unfair trial under Jeffreys of Wem in which he was condemned without sufficient evidence, Sidney was sentenced to death for treason and executed on Tower Hill. His name was cleared in 1689. His most significant work is *Discourses Concerning Government,* in which he sets forth the philosophy of political self-determination: "God leaves to man the choice of forms in government."

Political power is established for the good of the governed, not for the good of the governor. He maintains that the political structure inevitably decays when absolute power falls into the hands of an individual man. Consequently, no king has the right to confer upon his descendents an automatic guarantee of political authority. It is impossible for a monarch to govern effectively unless his powers are regulated by law. "The contracts made between magistrates and the nations that created them, were real, solemn, and obligatory." Among the imperative duties of government is the encouragement of valiant citizens through the proper recognition of their deeds and accomplishments:

> The same policy that made men valiant and industrious in the service of their country during the first ages, would have the same effect, if it were now in being; and men would have the same love to the public as the Spartans and the Romans had, if there was the same reason for it. We need no other proof of this than what we have seen in our own country, where in a few years good discipline, and a just encouragement given to those who did well, produced more examples of pure, incorruptible, and invincible virtue than Rome or Greece could ever boast. And if more be wanting, they may easily be found among the Swiss, Hollanders, and others: but **it is hardly necessary to light a candle to the sun.**

It is not best to swap horses while crossing the river

Source: REPLY TO A DELEGATION FROM THE NATIONAL UNION LEAGUE (June 9, 1864)
Author: Abraham Lincoln (1809-1865)
First published: 1864
Type of work: Political speech

Context: Between May 4 and June 8, 1864, General Ulysses S. Grant had suffered a number of serious defeats —the Battles of The Wilderness, Spotsylvania, and Cold Harbor, his losses running as high as 55,000 men. Such events, occurring as they did in an election year, could have spelled serious trouble for incumbent President Abraham Lincoln. Moving quickly and before the country had comprehended the full significance of Grant's defeats, the Republican Party (its name changed briefly to National Union Party) met in convention at Baltimore. Lincoln's party had not been solidly behind him; on the contrary, there was considerable opposition to his policies, and the party's more radical element had been giving him trouble. Nonetheless, those meeting at the convention realized that Lincoln had a better chance of winning the election than anyone else they might propose, and he was accordingly nominated for a second term by unanimous vote. Andrew Johnson, War Governor of Tennessee, was named his running mate. Among the various groups lending Lincoln their support was the Union League of America, or National

Union League. This organization had been founded as a secret society during the early days of the war, its purpose being to organize and consolidate loyalty to the Union. Its National Grand Council met in Baltimore at the same time as the National Union convention and stood solidly for Lincoln's re-election. Lincoln, beset by numerous problems, was deeply gratified by the support given him—even though he knew the campaign of 1864 would be a difficult one. His gratitude and relief are evident in his humble, humorous reply to the Union League's delegation:

> . . . I am very grateful for the renewed confidence which has been accorded to me both by the convention and by the National League. I am not insensible at all to the personal compliment there is in this, and yet I do not allow myself to believe that any but a small portion of it is to be appropriated as a personal compliment. That really the convention and the Union League assembled with a higher view—that of taking care of the interests of the country for the present and the great future—and that the part I am entitled to appropriate as a compliment is only that part which I may lay hold of as being the opinion of the convention and of the League, that I am not entirely unworthy to be intrusted with the place which I have occupied for the last three years. But I do not allow myself to suppose that either the convention or the League have concluded to decide that I am either the greatest or best man in America, but rather they have concluded that **it is not best to swap horses while crossing the river,** and have further concluded that I am not so poor a horse that they might not make a botch of it in trying to swap.

It is nought good a sleeping hound to wake

Source: TROILUS AND CRISEYDE (Book III, stanza 110, l. 764)
Author: Geoffrey Chaucer (c. 1343-1400)
First transcribed: 1380-1386
Type of work: Narrative poem

Context: The story of Troilus and Criseyde first appeared in Benôit de Sainte-Maure's *Roman de Troie* (1184), which was supposed to be based on narratives by Dictys of Crete, author of a fourth century work translated from an earlier Greek original, and from Dares the Phrygian, of at latest the fifth century. During the Middle Ages this pair was generally believed to have been present at the siege of Troy. Giovanni Boccaccio (1313–1375) had Benôit in mind in his *Il filostrato* (c.1335–1345); and Chaucer used both Boccaccio's and Benôit's versions. He even employed the Rima royal of seven-line stanzas that Boccaccio used. The time is the Trojan War in the Bronze Age, perhaps 1200 B.C., but the Chaucerian version fills it with the customs of a medieval court of love. For modern tastes, its five books and more than 8,000 lines

549

make its reading a bit tedious, especially with the long soliloquys, speeches, and digressions. Yet it has been called an almost perfectly constructed narrative poem, full of a strange sweetness characteristic of Chaucer, especially in his second period. It is the only long poem he completed. Troilus, one of the sons of King Priam of Troy—Hector was another—is presented in the first stanza of the "Proem"; then the narrator in the other seven stanzas asks the gods for help in telling his tale. As the story starts, Calchas, the Trojan prophet, foresees that the Greeks will be successful in their siege of Troy, so he flees to the winning side, leaving his widowed daughter, Criseyde. During the spring festival, joining the celebration, where she stood out in beauty, she attracts Troilus's eyes.

Smitten with her, yet believing his love hopeless, he goes out to attack the Greeks. However, Pandarus (whose name originated the expression "to pander,") offers to act as go-between, an easy task, since he is Criseyde's uncle. She has seen Troilus riding by on his way from the battlefield. When she learns that he is dying for her, she finds nothing dishonorable in encouraging him. In the third Book, to carry further his scheme, Pandarus invites her to dine with him, assuring her that Troilus is out of Troy. However, when a rain storm forces her to spend the night at the house, he comes into the bedroom by a secret trapdoor. When she suggests she awaken one of her women, Pandarus answers with the fourteenth century equivalent of "Let sleeping dogs lie."

> **It is nought good a sleping hound to wake,**
> Ne yive a wight a cause to devyne,
> Your women sleepen alle, I undertake,
> So that, for hem, the hous men mighte myne;
> And sleepen wolen til the sonne shyne.
> And whan my tale al brought is to an ende,
> Unwist, right as I com, so will I wende.

It is sweet and fitting to die for one's country

Source: ODES (Book III, Ode 2, l. 13)
Author: Horace (65-8 B.C.)
First transcribed: 23-13 B.C.
Type of work: Ode

Context: Horace encourages fortitude and fidelity in the young soldier. The poet cites the honor attached to dying for one's country, at the same time noting that death comes alike to hero and to coward. H. V. Macnaghton translated the passage:

> Let every Roman boy be taught to know
> Constraining hardship as a friend, and grow
>   Strong in fierce warfare, with dread lance and horse

550

Encountering the gallant Parthian foe.

Aye, let him live beneath the open sky
In danger. Him from leagured walls should eye
  Mother and daughter of th' insurgent king,
And she for her betrothed, with many a sigh,

Should pray, poor maiden, lest, when hosts engage,
Unversed in arms he face that lion's rage
  So dangerous to trust what time he gluts
His wrath upon the battle's bloody stage.

**For country 'tis a sweet and seemly thing
To die.** Death ceases not from following
  E'en runaways. Can youth with feeble knees,
That fears to face the battle, scape his wing?

It is the low man thinks the woman low

Source: QUEEN MARY (Act V, sc. ii, l. 251)
Author: Alfred, Lord Tennyson (1809-1892)
First published: 1875
Type of work: Historical drama

Context: During the 1870's there was a reaction against Tennyson's previously unquestioned leadership in British letters, expressed publicly by Swinburne. In those years when his poetry was reaching a relatively indifferent public, Tennyson turned to writing drama, penning three plays concerned with English history: *Queen Mary, Harold,* and *Becket.* Of the three, only the last-named, revised by Sir Henry Irving, had a successful run in the theater. The queen of Tennyson's play is Mary Tudor, daughter of Henry the Eighth, elder half sister of the woman who was to be Elizabeth the First. Mary is portrayed as loving deeply Philip of Spain and fearing, rightfully, that many persons in her kingdom wish to prevent her marriage to the Spanish (and Catholic) monarch. Outside her kingdom, too, Mary learns, through the French ambassador, there is opposition to a union of Spain and England. Despite the opposition, Mary Tudor dotes on Philip, to the point that she falls in trances and sits upon the floor in an unqueenly manner. While the queen is in a trance, Alice, a maid, and Lady Magdalen Dacres, one of the waiting-women, talk to each other:

ALICE
I would I were as tall and strong as you.

LADY MAGDALEN
I seem half-ashamed at times to be so tall.

551

You are the stateliest deer in all the herd—
Beyond his aim—but I am small and scandalous,
And love to hear bad tales of Philip.

LADY MAGDALEN
Why?
I never heard him utter worse of you
Than that you were low-statured.

ALICE
Does he think
Low stature is low nature, or all women's
Low as his own?

LADY MAGDALEN
There you strike in the nail.
This coarseness is a want of phantasy.
It is the low man thinks the woman low;
Sin is too dull to see beyond himself.

It is the nature of all greatness not to be exact

Source: SPEECH ON AMERICAN TAXATION, 1774
Author: Edmund Burke (1729-1797)
First published: 1774
Type of work: Political speech

Context: Edmund Burke was a friend to the American Colonies; he was also a believer in truth and justice. This speech is an example of the man's principles, beliefs, and actions. In it Burke appeals to Parliament to abolish the duty on tea which has created such animosity in America and led to a threat of war. Burke tries to show that there is really no obstacle to repealing the tax, noting that other taxes imposed by the same bill had been repealed already. He further notes that the principle of taxation which some men thought the tea tax represented had been given up by the British government already, citing a letter written by Lord Hillesborough. Turning to the past, Burke then recites the history of taxation in the American Colonies. Coming to George Grenville and the Act of Navigation, he says that this act of Parliament needed to be changed "according to the change of the times and the fluctuation of circumstances." Not to change the act, says Burke, is to fail to realize that great mischief might be done, and the very purpose of the act defeated, by the change in commerce of the American Colonies in the years after the French and Indian War:

After the war, and in the last years of it, the trade of America had encreased far beyond the speculations of the most sanguine imaginations. It swelled out on every side. It filled all its proper channels to the brim. It overflowed with a rich redundance, and breaking its banks on the right and on the left, it spread out upon some places where it was indeed improper, upon others where it was only irregular. **It is the nature of all greatness not to be exact;** and great trade will always be attended with considerable abuses. The contraband will always keep pace in some measure with the fair trade. It should be a fundamental maxim, that no vulgar precaution ought to be employed in the cure of evils, which are closely connected with the cause of our prosperity. . . .

It is the very error of the moon

Source: OTHELLO (Act V, sc. ii, l. 109)
Author: William Shakespeare (1564-1616)
First published: 1622
Type of work: Dramatic tragedy

Context: Because of a plot of vengeance laid by the Machiavellian Iago, Othello, the noble Moor of Venice, smothers his new bride Desdemona, whom he believes to have been unfaithful to him with Cassio, his former friend and lieutenant. The murder, says Othello, is so horrible that one might expect even an eclipse. When Emilia, maid to Desdemona, reports another murder, Othello attributes the acts of man to the irregularity of the moon.

OTHELLO
. . . My wife? My wife—what wife? I have no wife.
O insupportable! O heavy hour!
Methinks it should be now a huge eclipse
Of sun and moon, and that th' affrighted globe
Did yawn at alteration.
•   •   •

[*Enter* EMILIA]
                What's the matter with thee now?

EMILIA
O my good lord, yonder's foul murders done.
•   •   •

OTHELLO
It is the very error of the moon;
She comes more nearer earth than she was wont,
And makes men mad.

553

It matters not how a man dies, but how he lives

Source: THE LIFE OF SAMUEL JOHNSON, LL.D. (For 1769)
Author: James Boswell (1740-1795)
First published: 1791
Type of work: Biography

Context: Once when Boswell and Johnson were alone, Boswell introduced into the conversation the subject of death, which he knew Johnson abhorred. Johnson strenuously denied that any sensible person could be unafraid of death: if one pointed a pistol at a dying man, he would be terror-stricken. Although Johnson had, in his poem *The Vanity of Human Wishes,* written that death was a retreat from the world to a happier existence, he very much disliked the idea of passing on to that joyful state. The trouble is that a man has to give up everything he has to achieve it. In answer to Boswell's query as to whether we cannot fortify our minds against the idea of death, Johnson exclaimed that the important thing was not how a man dies but how he lives:

> . . . To my question, whether we might not fortify our minds for the approach of death, he answered, in a passion, "No, Sir, let it alone. **It matters not how a man dies, but how he lives.** The act of dying is not of importance, it lasts so short a time." He added (with an earnest look), "A man knows it must be so, and submits. It will do him no good to whine."

It must be right: I've done it from my youth

Source: THE BOROUGH (Letter 3, l. 139)
Author: George Crabbe (1755-1832)
First published: 1810
Type of work: Descriptive poem

Context: The Borough is a description of the town and those who inhabit it in the early nineteenth century. The poem consists of a number of "letters," containing descriptions of people, except for the first letter, which is a general picture of the borough. The third letter describes the local clergy, including the vicar and the curate; the quotation is from the portrait of the vicar. Crabbe speaks of the vicar as a man who from his earliest days as a clergyman sought always to offend no one. The poet also says of him: "Fear was his ruling passion." The vicar is never tempted, because he never allows himself near temptation, even in love. His courtship of the one young girl for whom he felt affection was so languid that she turned from him to marry another, realizing that she would always have to take the lead if she were to marry the clergyman. What were the pleasures of such a man? They were simple: "Fiddling and fishing were his arts: at times/ He alter'd sermons, and he aim'd at rhymes;/ And his fair friends, not yet intent on cards,/ Oft, he mused with riddles and charades." In his work the vicar simply dismisses from his mind other sects and their variant views. Crabbe suggests what the vicar stood for:

These were to him essentials; all things new
He deem'd superfluous, useless, or untrue;
To all beside indifferent, easy, cold,
Here the fire kindled, and the wo [*sic.*] was told.
   Habit with him was all the test of truth,
"It must be right: I've done it from my youth."
Questions he answer'd in as brief a way,
"It must be wrong—it was of yesterday."

It's as easy to marry a rich woman as a poor woman

Source: THE HISTORY OF PENDENNIS (Volume I, chapter 28)
Author: William Makepeace Thackeray (1811-1863)
First published: 1848-1850
Type of work: Novel

Context: Arthur Pendennis, after his father's death, is reared by his mother, Helen, with help from Major Arthur Pendennis, the child's uncle. Young Pendennis is something of a snob and tends to follow his uncle, who wants to help the boy rise socially, rather than to follow his mother, who wants to keep her son natural and unspoiled by selfish scheming to rise from the middle-class to the aristocracy. Mrs. Pendennis hopes her son will marry Laura Bell, Mrs. Pendennis' ward, but the snobbery of young Arthur offends Laura's self-respect, even though she loves him and has used a portion of her inheritance to see him through the university. Following Laura's refusal of his suit, young Pendennis goes down to London to study law, to begin a writing career, and to enjoy the social life. One day he is visited by his uncle, Major Pendennis, who inquires if the young man has any new loves and offers this advice to his nephew:

". . . You are heir to a little independence, which everybody fancies is a doosid deal more. You have a good name, good wits, good manners, and a good person—and, begad! I don't see why you shouldn't marry a woman with money—get into Parliament— distinguish yourself, and—and, in fact, that sort of thing. Remember, **it's as easy to marry a rich woman as a poor woman:** and a devilish deal pleasanter to sit down to a good dinner, than to a scrag of mutton in lodgings. Make up your mind to that. A woman with a good jointure is a doosid deal easier a profession than the law, let me tell you. Look out; *I* shall be on the watch for you. . . ."

It's more than a game. It's an institution

Source: TOM BROWN'S SCHOOL DAYS (Part II, chapter 8)
Author: Thomas Hughes (1822-1896)
First published: 1857
Type of work: Reform novel

Context: As a young man of nineteen, Tom Brown spends his last day at Rugby playing cricket against a rival school. It is an important match, and Tom, as befits a senior boy who is a good cricket man, is captain of the Rugby eleven. As the game progresses, he sits with his friend Arthur and a young faculty member who has taken an interest in him. The young master tries to draw an analogy for Tom and Arthur, pointing out that they see much more of the fine technique of cricket than he, because they are interested and have studied it. He goes on to say that Tom, had he spent as much effort on his Greek, could have just as much insight into, say, an Aristophanic comedy like *The Knights* as anyone, and so enjoy his studies much more. Tom takes this observation good-humoredly, as he has learned to like this particular faculty member and has grown up enough to cease regarding his teachers as, at best, friendly enemies. As they watch, the young master learns some of the finer points of the game and comments to Tom and Arthur:

> "Come, none of your irony, Brown," answers the master. "I'm beginning to understand the game scientifically. What a noble game it is, too!"
>
> "Isn't it? But **it's more than a game. It's an institution**," said Tom.
>
> "Yes," said Arthur, "the birthright of British boys old and young, as *habeas corpus* and trial by jury are of British men."
>
> "The discipline and reliance on one another which it teaches is so valuable, I think," went on the master, "it ought to be such an unselfish game. It merges the individual in the eleven; he doesn't play that he may win, but that his side may."
>
> "That's very true," said Tom, "and that's why football and cricket . . . are such much better games than fives or hare-and-hounds, or any others where the object is to come in first or to win for one's self, and not that one's side may win."

It's no fish ye're buying—it's men's lives

Source: THE ANTIQUARY (Chapter 11)
Author: Sir Walter Scott (1771-1832)
First published: 1816
Type of work: Novel

Context: Mr. Jonathan Oldbuck, Ol- denbuck, or Oldinbuck, known also as Monkbarns, from the name of his estate on the northeastern coast of Scotland, is conducting his young friend, Mr. Lovel, along the seashore to visit Sir Arthur Wardour and his daughter, whom Oldbuck and Lovel had been instrumental in saving from drowning in a storm-driven high tide the previous evening. Unknown to Oldbuck, who has a fanatical love for antiquities of all kinds, Lovel, who had risked his life in the rescue, is in love with Miss Wardour, who does all in her power to discourage his ardor. As the two make their way along the shore, Oldbuck and Lovel come upon a very masculine-looking woman sitting before a cottage and mending a fishing net. Thereupon ensues a bargaining session between Oldbuck and the woman for some fish. At first the two are far apart in their bidding and asking, but eventually they agree on a price. She offers her wares in a strident tone: "What are ye for the day" means "what do you want today?"

. . . "What are ye for the day, your honor?" she said, or rather screamed, to Oldbuck; "caller haddocks and whitings—a bannock-fluke and a cock-padle."

"How much for the bannock-fluke and the cock-padle?" demanded the Antiquary.

"Four white shillings and sixpence," answered the Naiad.

"Four devils and six of their imps!" retorted the Antiquary; "do you think I am mad, Maggie?"

"And div ye think," rejoined the virago, setting her arms a-kimbo, "that my man and my sons are to gae to the sea in weather like yestreen and the day—sic a sea as it's yet outby—and get naething for their fish, and be misca'd into the bargain, Monkbarns? **It's no fish ye're buying—it's men's lives.**"

"Well, Maggie, I'll bid you fair—I'll bid you a shilling for the fluke and the cock-padle, or sixpence separately—and if all your fish are as well paid, I think your man, as you call him, and your sons, will make a good voyage."

I've a great fancy to see my own funeral afore I die

Source: CASTLE RACKRENT ("Continuation of Memoirs")
Author: Maria Edgeworth (1767-1849)
First published: 1800
Type of work: Novel

Context: Blessed—or, according to many critics, cursed—by having a father who not only pushed her into writing but also carefully revised her work, Miss Edgeworth presents a strange figure to moderns. With her father she wrote several books on education, a subject that Mr. Edgeworth hoped to reduce to scientifically provable steps, but she was an incurable romantic, not the calculating rationalist that was her father's ideal of the proper female. In strictest secret she wrote this novel and gave it to her father only after it was printed; thus it is unique among her fiction. It is the long monologue of one of her most delightful characters, Thady Quirk, the homely tenant of the Rackrents whose tale he slowly unfolds. Through the creation of this character, Miss Edgeworth often lets her imagination run wild for the sake of comedy. The quotation comes from one of these sections: Thady is describing Sir Condy, the last of the Rackrents, whose triumph was to have his funeral before he died so that he could hear that people said of him at his wake, a triumph that soured because nothing remarkable was said.

> "Thady," says he, "all you've been telling me [about the civil things said of him] brings a strange thought into my head: I've a notion I shall not be long for this world any how, and **I've a great fancy to see my own funeral afore I die.**"

Ivory tower

Source: PENSÉES D'AOÛT (Stanza 3)
Author: Charles Augustin Sainte-Beuve (1804-1869)
First published: 1837
Type of work: Literary criticism

Context: The idea of retiring to a tower, getting away from the world and its temptations, has been frequently expressed since the Syrian hermit Simeon Stylites, who died about 459, spent thirty-five years on top of a tall pillar to escape mankind. What the escape mechanism was made of, did not matter. The "tower of ivory" mentioned in "Song of Solomon" (VII, 4) describing the neck of the poet's sweetheart, was of a different sort—a temptation, not an escape. In the current significance, an ivory tower is an imaginary place in which a recluse can remain aloof from the world. The phrase occurs in the works of many writers. Jules de Gaultier, in the nineteenth century, in his "War and the Destiny of Art," compared "the poet, retired to his Tower of Ivory, isolated, according to his desires, from the world of men" to a lighthouse keeper. Henry James in 1917 started to write a novel *The Ivory Tower*. Thomas Mann (1875–1955), being told in 1937 that his name had been removed from the list of Honorary Doctors of the University of Bonn, said that no one could separate the artistic and intellectual life from the political and social life and isolate himself within the ivory tower of the "culture" proper. It was, however, the literary critic Sainte-Beuve who probably coined the phrase in his poem to Abel François Villemain (1790–1870), French critic and politician, later Minister of Education. It appears in his volume of poems *Pensées d'Août* (*August Thoughts*), published in 1837.

> Hugo, stern partisan,
> . . . fought in armor,

And held his banner high in the midst of the tumult:
He still holds it; and Vigny, more reserved,
Retired before the noon-day, as if in his **ivory tower.**

Jacob's ladder

Source: GENESIS 28:12
Author: Unknown
First transcribed: c. 1000-300 B.C.
Type of work: Religious history and law

Context: Esau comes to hate his brother Jacob because their father, Isaac, says that Esau shall serve Jacob. So great is Esau's hatred that he vows he will kill Jacob. Rebekah, their mother, learning of her older son's vow of hate, arranges with Isaac to send the younger son to Padan-aram, to stay for a time with Rebekah's brother, Laban. When Jacob leaves home his father bids him choose a wife from among the daughters of Laban. Jacob sets out with his parents' blessings and instructions, leaving Beersheba to travel toward Haran. When sunset comes he is upon the road, where he stops, makes a pillow of stones, and falls asleep. During the night he has a dream, in which he sees a ladder reaching to heaven, and he hears the voice of God making a prophesy about him:

And he **[Jacob]** dreamed, and behold a **ladder** set up on the earth, and the top of it reached to heaven: and behold the angels of God ascending and descending on it.

And, behold, the LORD stood above it, and said, I am the LORD God of Abraham, thy father, and the God of Isaac: the land whereon thou liest, to thee will I give it, and to thy seed:

And thy seed shall be as the dust of the earth, and thou shalt spread abroad to the west, and to the east, and to the north, and to the south: and in thee and in thy seed shall all the families of the earth be blessed.

And, behold, I am with thee, and will keep thee in all places whither thou goest, and will bring thee again into this land; for I will not leave thee, until I have done that which I have spoken to thee of.

A jest breaks no bones

Source: THE LIFE OF SAMUEL JOHNSON, LL.D. (For 1781)
Author: James Boswell (1740-1795)
First published: 1791
Type of work: Biography

Context: A group of men who prac- tised law in the lower courts of Edin-

559

burgh had obtained a royal charter, In that document they took great care to have their old designation of "procurator" changed to "solicitor," on the foolish basis that the latter title was more genteel. They quickly made great public use of their new title in advertising their meetings. The group's undue emphasis upon their name, plus the other meanings attached to the words "procurer" and "solicitor," gave rise to at least one instance of ridicule: *The Caledonian Mercury,* a Scottish newspaper, printed a paragraph which made the group the butt of its humor. The Society of Solicitors proceeded to prosecute the publisher of the newspaper, a Mr. Robertson, for damages to their reputation. The court dismissed the original action, but the Society of Solicitors petitioned for a new trial in the Court of Session; for the second trial James Boswell was counsel for the defense. Boswell reports that Dr. Johnson, when told of the whole matter by Boswell, offered the following opinion of the case:

"All injury is either of the person, the fortune, or the fame. Now it is a certain thing, it is proverbially known that **a jest breaks no bones.** They have never gained half-a-crown less in the whole profession since this mischievous paragraph has appeared; and, as to their reputation, What is their reputation but an instrument of getting money? If, therefore, they have lost no money, the question upon reputation may be answered by a very old position,— *De minimis non curat Praetor."*

A joke's a very serious thing

Source: THE GHOST (Book IV, l. 1386)
Author: Charles Churchill (1731-1764)
First published: 1762-1763
Type of work: Satiric poem

Context: Charles Churchill was a dissipated clergyman who won for himself both fame and notoriety as a satiric poet during the last few years of his life. Much of the character of his verse seems to have been determined by his association with the unscrupulous editor of the *North-Briton,* John Wilkes. The story of the Cock Lane Ghost broke in 1762 when William Kent was accused of having committed adultery with and subsequently murdering his sister-in-law, Fanny Lynes. The accusation was made by Richard Parsons, whom Kent had sued for debt, and the evidence was the testimony of Fanny's ghost given through Parsons' daughter as a medium. Kent appealed to the courts to vindicate his character, and a commission including Dr. Samuel Johnson investigated the affair and pronounced it all a fraud. The affair was a very popular butt for satirists, including the dramatists, and Churchill's somewhat rambling comic treatment extends to four books. Book IV rambles even more discursively, if possible, than Book III, digressing frequently into political satire. One of the bitterest attacks is upon Lewis Bruce, as Crape, who had been given a clerical promotion which Churchill had expected to receive:

> Nor think a joke, CRAPE, a disgrace
> Or to my Person, or my place;
> The wisest of the Sons of Men
> Have deign'd to use them now and then.
>
>   .   .   .
>
> Great Use they have, when in the hands
> Of One, like me, who understands,
> Who understands the time, and place,
> The persons, manner, and the grace,
> Which Fools neglect; so that we find,
> If all the requisites are join'd
> From whence a perfect joke must spring,
> **A joke's a very serious thing.**

Keep up appearances

Source: NIGHT (Line 311)
Author: Charles Churchill (1731-1764)
First published: 1762
Type of work: Satirical poem

Context: Those who have never heard of Charles Churchill will be amazed to learn that his volume of poetical works contains more than 450 pages. The son of a minister and himself intended for the Church he spoiled his chances for a scholarship at Cambridge by an early marriage. Life became difficult. Finally he tried writing poetry to provide an income, and especially to help the political career of his friend in Parliament, John Wilkes (1727–1797). The appearance of his *Rosciad* brought criticisms of his "ingenious and cruel satire." Most people attributed its authorship to a trio of Robert Lloyd, the dramatist George Colman the Elder, and Bonnell Thornton. So in the second edition Churchill put his name onto the title page and wrote "The Apology," that started a lasting quarrel with Tobias Smollett, author of an article about it in the *Critical Review*. Then, still apologetic, Churchill addressed another poem to Lloyd, accused of writing the first one. It was of a different style. The income of the *Rosciad* had lessened restraints put by poverty upon an obscure man. Another reason for taking up his pen again was a poem called "Day," written by an army doctor, John Armstrong (1709–1779), stationed with the forces in Germany. Its manuscript reached John Wilkes, with a request that it be corrected and printed. Churchill imagined himself its target, though he had not been writing long enough to be known, and promptly wrote an answer. It was published in January, 1762, a year after the appearance of "Day." Critics did not think highly of it. Its morality was far

561

removed from that of a Christian, and the careless diction was unworthy of the author of the *Rosciad*. He begins it, "When foes insult, and *prudent* friends dispense,/ In pity's strain, the worst of insolence"; then the poet pays his tribute to his friend Lloyd. In the course of the poem, Churchill brings out his own enmity with Smollet who, because he was a surgeon's mate at the siege of Cartagena in 1741, thought he could set himself up as a physician at Bath. Churchill says he himself leads the sort of life that suits him best. He prefers night life. Punning, he declares: "We, our friends, our foes, ourselves, survey,/ And see by NIGHT what fools we are by DAY." He refuses to court those who appear great. He is "too proud to flatter, too sincere to lie,/ Too plain to please, too honest to be great." Then he quotes an ironic tutor "more read in men than books," a "crafty man, demurely sly," who gives this satirical advice to his favorite pupil:

> Would'st thou, my son, be wise and virtuous deem'd,
> By all mankind a prodigy esteem'd?
> Be this thy rule; be what people *prudent* call;
> PRUDENCE, almighty PRUDENCE gives thee all.
> **Keep up appearances;** there lies the test,
> The world will give thee credit for the rest.
> Outward be fair, however foul within;
> Sin if thou wilt, but then in secret sin.
> This maxim's into common favor grown.
> Vice is no longer vice unless 'tis known.
> Virtue indeed may barefac'd take the field,
> But vice is virtue, when 'tis well conceal'd.

The keys of the kingdom

Source: MATTHEW 16:19
Author: Unknown (traditionally Matthew the Apostle)
First transcribed: c. 75-100
Type of work: Gospel

Context: Jesus, having taught the multitudes and displayed for them His divine power by miracles of healing and of feeding four thousand by the Sea of Galilee, moves up to Caesarea Phillippi with His disciples, concentrating upon making the message of His kingdom clear to them in preparation for the time when they must carry on the work of the kingdom after His ascension. Jesus, asking the disciples who men think He is, is told that He is considered to be a prophet, perhaps John the Baptist, Elias, or Jeremias. The Master then asks who the disciples believe He is:

> And Simon Peter answered and said, Thou art the Christ, the Son of the living God.
> And Jesus answered and said unto him, Blessed art thou, Simon

Barjona: for flesh and blood hath not revealed it unto thee, but my
Father which is in heaven.

And I say also unto thee, That thou art Peter, and upon this
rock I will build my church; and the gates of hell shall not prevail
against it.

And I will give unto thee **the keys of the kingdom** of heaven:
and whatsoever thou shalt bind on earth shall be bound in heaven:
and whatsoever thou shalt loose on earth shall be loosed in heaven.

Kill not the moth nor butterfly

Source: AUGURIES OF INNOCENCE (Line 39)
Author: William Blake (1757-1827)
First published: 1863
Type of work: Poetic fragment

Context: Auguries of Innocence, which Blake never revised for publication, is a lengthy series of couplets concerning human cruelty. This poem is somewhat less difficult to follow than much of Blake's later poetry, which became increasingly mystical and obscure as he grew older. Though it is more or less organized, it is disconnected and quite haphazard in places—obviously a rough draft. Many of the statements in it take the form of aphorisms; and Blake may have simply let the poem grow over a period of time, jotting these thoughts down as they occurred to him. Beginning with the infinity that lies in everything and implying the holiness of all life, he cries out against man's cruelty to animals—a cruelty sometimes deliberate, sometimes merely thoughtless. To Blake, God is in all things and in all creatures, and they deserve consideration and respect. Caged birds, starving dogs, misused horses are all seen as an affront to divinity and a curse to man. After a thorough coverage of man's mistreatment of his fellow-creatures, Blake turns his attentions to man's misuse of man. His conclusion appears to be that although man was made for joy and sorrow, and may in some cases be born to a life of misery and suffering, much of this condition could be alleviated by a concern for other things that share life with him. It is interesting to note that the poet's sympathy is not limited to domestic animals and to wild creatures that are hunted for food or sport; he includes insects in his catalog as well, after presenting a number of maxims about the creatures we are more likely to pity:

> The Lamb misusd breeds Public strife
> And yet forgives the Butchers Knife.
> The Bat that flits at close of Eve
> Has left the Brain that won't Believe.
> The Owl that calls upon the Night
> Speaks the Unbeliever's fright.
> He who shall hurt the little Wren

Shall never be belovd by Men.
He who the Ox to wrath has mov'd
Shall never be by Woman lov'd.
The wanton Boy that kills the Fly
Shall feel the Spider's enmity.
He who torments the Chafer's sprite
Weaves a Bower in endless Night.
The Catterpiller on the Leaf
Repeats to thee thy Mother's grief.
Kill not the Moth nor Butterfly
For the Last Judgment draweth nigh. . . .

The king can do no wrong

Source: COMMENTARIES ON THE LAWS OF ENGLAND (Book III, chapter 17)
Author: Sir William Blackstone (1723-1780)
First published: 1765-1769
Type of work: Legal commentary

Context: Sir William Blackstone was a distinguished student both at school and later at Oxford. He was admitted to the English bar in 1746, but his legal practice was not successful; he lacked elocutionary power, and his personality did not fit him for the role of popular advocate. He abandoned his practice and returned to his fellowship at Oxford. Since there was no provision for any courses dealing with the laws and constitution of the country, Blackstone decided to offer a series of lectures on the subject. So successful were these that they gave Oxford a lasting and enviable distinction; the reputation of the school and the courses grew steadily, and as a result one wealthy patron of the university endowed a school of law there. Blackstone was its first professor. He wrote a number of legal works, but the best known of these is his *Commentaries on the Laws of England*. It is the best work of its type written up to that time, and has kept his name alive since; now considered one of the classics of legal literature, it is still studied, consulted, and cited. In this work Blackstone seeks to cover and to explain in plain terms the whole body of British law. This endeavor not only involves the statement and explanation of individual laws, but careful description of important precedents and historic cases. British law had sufficiently matured by Blackstone's time to allow a methodical treatment of it; Blackstone's work is not only methodical and logically arranged, but possesses remarkable clarity, particularly noticeable in areas of complexity. One important aspect of law in England is its definition of monarchy and of the unique position enjoyed by the king. After discussing "the injuries, or private wrongs, that may be offered by one subject to another, all of which are redressed by the command and authority of the king," Blackstone takes up the matter of injuries committed by the royal personage:

564

That **the king can do no wrong** is a necessary and fundamental principle of the English constitution: meaning only, as has formerly been observed, that, in the first place, whatever may be amiss in the conduct of public affairs is not chargeable personally on the king, nor is he, but his ministers, accountable for it to the people; and, secondly, that the prerogative of the crown extends not to do any injury; for, being created for the benefit of the people, it cannot be exerted to their prejudice. Whenever, therefore, it happens that, by misinformation or inadvertence, the crown hath been induced to invade the private rights of any of its subjects, though no action will lie against the sovereign (for who shall command the king?), yet the law hath furnished the subject with a decent and respectful mode of removing that invasion, by informing the king of the true state of the matter in dispute; and, as it presumes that to *know of* any injury and to *redress it* are inseparable in the royal breast, it then issues as of course, in the king's own name, his orders to his judges to do justice to the party aggrieved.

The distance between the sovereign and his subjects is such that it rarely can happen that any *personal* injury can immediately and directly proceed from the prince to any private man; and, as it can so seldom happen, the law in decency supposes that it never will or can happen at all. . . . But injuries to the rights of *property* can scarcely be committed by the crown without the intervention of its officers; for whom the law in matters of right entertains no respect or delicacy, but furnishes various methods of detecting the errors or misconduct of those agents, by whom the king has been deceived and induced to do a temporary injustice.

A king may make a nobleman, but he cannot make a gentleman

Source: LETTER TO WILLIAM SMITH (January 29, 1795)
Author: Edmund Burke (1729-1797)
First published: 1844
Type of work: Personal letter

Context: Burke was born in Ireland, and although his entire adult life was spent in England he took an active interest in Irish affairs throughout his career. As a member of Parliament he frequently defended the Irish, and he always felt the Anglican domination of the millions of Irish Catholics constituted a sort of tyranny. William Smith, a member of the Irish Parliament, had spoken in defense of Irish Catholics, and Burke responded with this encouraging letter:

. . . The divisions which formerly prevailed in the Church, with all their overdone zeal, only purified and ventilated our common faith, because there was no common enemy arrayed and embattled to take advantage of their dissensions; but now nothing but

565

inevitable ruin will be the consequence of our quarrels. I think we may dispute, rail, persecute, and provoke the Catholics out of their prejudices; but it is not in ours they will take refuge. If anything is, one more than another, out of the power of man, it is to *create* a prejudice. Somebody has said, that **a king may make a nobleman, but he cannot make a gentleman.**

The king never dies

Source: COMMENTARIES ON THE LAWS OF ENGLAND (Book I, chapter 3)
Author: Sir William Blackstone (1723-1780)
First published: 1765-1769
Type of work: Legal commentary

Context: When Sir William Blackstone published his *Commentaries on the Laws of England,* he did his country and his profession an important service; he also won lasting fame for himself. The work was not only greatly superior to anything of its kind attempted prior to his time; it also became a legal classic and has remained so to the present day. Blackstone is still consulted, still quoted. Educated in law at Oxford, he failed as a lawyer through lack of the elocutionary and other talents which contribute to popular appeal; he therefore returned to Oxford, taking up his fellowship at the university. Since there was no provision for a course in English law at Oxford, Blackstone offered a series of lectures on the subject. These became so popular, and so increased the reputation of the university, that a School of Law was endowed by a benefactor and Blackstone made its first profes-sor. He produced a number of other legal works, but his commentaries are his major contribution to the literature of the profession. In them he discusses and explains the entire body of English law, doing so with admirable clarity. In Book I he undertakes the complex and often confusing problem of royal succession. He discusses the nature of monarchy, and points out that while lands and thrones are not naturally descendible, "the law has thought proper, for the benefit and peace of the public, to establish hereditary succession" in both. He notes the feudal character of the royal succession and describes some of the problems arising from cases wherein rulers have died without issue. If a question arises because of an heir's physical or mental incapacity, any decision rests jointly with Parliament and the king. In any case, the office is the important point, and succession perpetual:

. . . however the crown may be limited or transferred, it still retains its descendible quality, and becomes hereditary in the wearer of it. And hence in our law **the king is said never to die,** in his political capacity; though, in common with other men, he is subject to mortality in his natural: because immediately upon the natural death of Henry, William, or Edward, the king survives in his suc-

566

cessor. For the right of the crown vests, *eo instanti* (from that instant) upon his heir; either the *haeres natus* (the heir born), if the course of descent remains unimpeached, or the *haeres factus* (the heir appointed), if the inheritance be under any particular settlement. So that there can be no *interregnum* [the space between two reigns]; but, as Sir Matthew Hale observes, the right of sovereignty is fully invested in the successor by the very descent of the crown. And therefore, however acquired, it becomes in him absolutely hereditary, unless by the rules of the limitation it is otherwise ordered and determined. In the same manner as landed estates, to continue our former comparison, are by the law hereditary, or descendible to the heirs of the owner; but still there exists a power, by which the property of those lands may be transferred to another person. If this transfer be made simply and absolutely, the lands will be hereditary in the new owner, and descend to his heir at law: but if the transfer be clogged with any limitations, conditions, or entails, the lands must descend in that channel, so limited and prescribed, and no other.

King of intimate delights

Source: THE TASK (Book IV, l. 139)
Author: William Cowper (1731-1800)
First published: 1785
Type of work: Meditative poem in blank verse

Context: The quotation is from the fourth book of *The Task,* entitled "The Winter Evening," one of the six books, or divisions, of the poem. Cowper, at the suggestion of Lady Austen, began writing about the simple and uneventful life he was living, a life forced upon him by an earlier, severe mental illness. Lady Austen suggested that he undertake the task (whence the title) of writing a blank verse poem about the sofa, which became the subject of Book I of the poem. Book IV relates the simple pleasures of an eighteenth century winter evening spent drinking tea before a fire in the living room, with curtains drawn to keep out the cold. The poet addresses winter and praises it for the quiet family gatherings it brings:

> Thou hold'st the sun
> A prisoner in the yet undawning east,
> Shortening his journey between morn and noon,
> And hurrying him, impatient of his stay,
> Down to the rosy west; but kindly still
> Compensating his loss with added hours
> Of social converse and instructive ease,
> And gath'ring, at short notice, in one group
> The family dispers'd, and fixing thought,
> Not less dispers'd by day-light and its cares.

567

I crown thee **king of intimate delights,**
Fire-side enjoyments, home-born happiness,
And all the comforts that the lowly roof
Of undisturb'd retirement, and the hours
Of long uninterrupted ev'ning, know.

A king's a king, do fortune what she can

Source: THE BARON'S WARS (Book V, stanza 36)
Author: Michael Drayton (1563-1631)
First published: As *Mortimeriados,* 1596; revised as *The Barons' Wars,* 1603
Type of work: Historical poem

Context: The poem treats of the conflict between King Edward II and his nobles, a subject dramatized by Christopher Marlowe in *Edward the Second.* The barons of England, angered at the king's misrule and insulted by the favoritism shown to Piers Gaveston and to members of the Spencer family, revolted under the Mortimers. Even the much neglected but perhaps not too virtuous queen, Isabella, sister of the King of France, fell away from the king and fled to France to raise a military force, the ostensible purpose of which was to insure her rights and those of her son, Prince Edward, afterwards King Edward III. At first the king's forces were successful in the war, but fortune turned against him and he was captured and imprisoned by the barons. The barons forced Edward to abdicate his throne; he did what he had to, insisting, however, that as an anointed king, he was supreme and the barons had no power over him. His protestations did him no good, and he was taken as a close prisoner from one castle to another. Finally he was set upon by a pair of most odious felons named Gurney and Matrevis, who subjected him to a series of indignities, such as wetting him with pond water, shaving his head and beard, clothing him in rags, depriving him of rest and food, and making him ride on a sorry jade. At this point in the poem the poet addresses the murderers and tells them to keep their unhallowed hands off the king, because he had had the spirit of God infused into him; he was still a king, although fortune had dealt severely with him.

Vile traitors, hold off your unhallowed hands,
His brow, upon it majesty still bears;
Dare ye thus keep your sovereign lord in bands?
And can your eyes behold th'anointed tears?
Or if your sight all pity thus withstands,
Are not your hearts yet pierced through your ears?
　　The mind is free, what ere afflict the man,
　　A king's a king, do fortune what she can.

Dare man take that which God himself hath given?
Or mortal spill the spirit by him infused,

568

Whose power is subject to the power of heaven?
Wrongs pass not unrevenged, although excused.
Except that thou set all at six and seven,
Rise, majesty, when thou art thus abused;
　　　　Or for thy refuge, which way wilt thou take,
　　　　When in this sort thou dost thyself forsake?

Kissing don't last: cookery do!

Source: THE ORDEAL OF RICHARD FEVEREL (Chapter 28)
Author: George Meredith (1828–1909)
First published: 1859
Type of work: Novel

Context: Richard Feverel is reared according to System by his father, Sir Austin Feverel. The father's personal System involves choosing a wife suitable for the young man, but Richard is attracted by a girl different from the one his father intends. He falls in love with the pretty seventeen-year-old niece of a neighboring farmer. The girl's name is Lucy Desborough. Young Richard arranges, with the help of a friend, Ripton Thompson, to house Lucy in London with a Mrs. Berry, until the arrangements can be made for them to be married. One day just before the marriage, Richard, Lucy, and Ripton meet an uncle of Richard in the park. Ripton, to hide Lucy's identity, introduces her as his sister. The experience is un- nerving to the three young persons, especially to Lucy. When she returns to her lodgings, she goes to bed, with what Mrs. Berry calls "the flutters." When Lucy recovers after a few hours, she and Mrs. Berry have a chat, during which Mrs. Berry, who was kicked and deserted by her husband, narrates her unhappy marital experiences. She tries to encourage Lucy about her coming marriage, for Lucy worries about marrying so young. Mrs. Berry tells her about an Irish lady who married at fourteen, three years younger than Lucy, adding that the Irish lady was a grandmother by thirty. Lucy asks Mrs. Berry if the Irish lady's husband always loved her, and receives the following answer:

"In his way, my dear, he did," said Mrs. Berry, coming upon her matrimonial wisdom. "He couldn't help himself. If he left off, he began again. She was so clever, and did make him so comfortable. Cook! there wasn't such a cook out of an Alderman's kitchen; no indeed. And she a born lady! That tells ye it's the duty of all women! She had her saying—'When the parlour fire gets low, put coals on the kitchen fire!' and a good saying it is to treasure. Such is man! no use in havin' their hearts if ye don't have their stomachs."

Perceiving that she grew abstruse, Mrs. Berry added briskly: "You know nothing about that yet, my dear. Only mind me and mark me: don't neglect your cookery. **Kissing don't last: cookery do!**

569

A knave's religion is the rottenest thing about him

Source: TIME AND TIDE (Letter VIII)
Author: John Ruskin (1819-1900)
First published: 1867
Type of work: Satirical letters

Context: Ruskin's series of letters, twenty-five of them, were addressed to one Thomas Dixon, a cork-cutter of Sutherland, England. The purpose of the letters which make up *Time and Tide* was to urge the working-people to consider, beyond the right to vote, the reform of laws. The tone of the letters, in which Ruskin's prejudices and usual startling proposals are evident, is a passionate one, making the letters seem much like sermons. Letter VIII is about four possible theories respecting the authority of the Bible. Ruskin begins, however, by stating that the political economy he is trying to teach is founded on *"presumably attainable honesty* in men," while the popular political economy of the times is based on man's supposed regard for himself. Ruskin goes on to ask, rhetorically, what basis there can be for the honesty he believes man can attain. He proceeds to answer the question he has posed:

> . . . my answer is—not in any hesitating or diffident way (and you know, my friend, that whatever people may say of me, I do often speak diffidently; though, when I am diffident of things, I like to avoid speaking of them, if it may be; but here I say with no shadow of doubt)—your honesty is *not* to be based either on religion or policy. Both your religion and policy must be based on *it*. Your honesty must be based, as the sun is, in vacant heaven; poised, as the lights in the firmament, which have rule over the day and over the night. If you ask why you are to be honest—you are, in the question itself, dishonoured. 'Because you are a man,' is the only answer; and therefore I said in a former letter that to make your children *capable of honesty* is the beginning of education. Make them men first, and religious men afterwards, and all will be sound; but **a knave's religion is** always **the rottenest thing about him.**

A knock-down argument

Source: AMPHITRYON (Act I, sc. i)
Author: John Dryden (1631-1700)
First published: 1690
Type of work: Dramatic comedy

Context: For the songs of this comedy, the famous English musician Henry Purcell (1659–1695) composed the music. In the Dedicatory

Epistle, Dryden acknowledged his indebtedness to farces by Plautus and Molière, but the first version was of much earlier Greek origin. Produced at the Theatre Royal, in Drury Lane, in October, 1690, it remained constantly on the boards until Nokes, the original Socia, died in 1696. It has often been revived, as recently as 1922. Mercury and Phoebus open the comedy in Thebes, as they discuss marital complications in Olympus. They are interrupted by the appearance of Jupiter, who demands their assistance. He wants to enjoy Amphitryon's wife, Alcmena, that night, by appearing in the likeness of her husband. He says he will beget a future Hercules to conquer monsters and reform the world. The gods are not impressed. It looks as if Jupiter has set up straw men as an excuse to create someone to knock them down. But at least the pair appreciate Jupiter's honesty.

MERCURY

Ay, brother Phoebus; and our father made all those monsters for Hercules to conquer, and contriv'd all those vices on purpose for him to reform, too, there's the jest on it.

PHOEBUS

Since arbitrary pow'r will hear no reason, 't is wisdom to be silent.

MERCURY

Why, that's the point; this same arbitrary power is **a knockdown argument;** 't is but a word and a blow. Now methinks, our father speaks out like an honest bare-fac'd god, as he is.

Know what thou canst work at

Source: SARTOR RESARTUS (Book II, chapter 7, "The Everlasting No")
Author: Thomas Carlyle (1795-1881)
First published: 1833-1834
Type of work: Philosophical essay

Context: Sartor Resartus, the tailor retailored, is supposedly the life and works of a German scholar, entirely fictional, named Teufelsdröckh. As part of the fiction, Carlyle supposedly edited the contents of six paper sacks, the German's writings, which came into his hands. The quotation above is from the chapter entitled "The Everlasting No," Carlyle's term for a bitter and sweeping rejection of European society and its conventions, to be contrasted with Carlyle's idea of The Everlasting Yea, which is a call to the life of the soul. Carlyle, as the editor for his fictional savant, says that Teufelsdröckh is as great when uttering his nay-saying as at any other point, even so far as this: ". . . perhaps at no era of his life was he more decisively the Servant of God, than even now when doubting his God's

571

existence." While wandering, filled with weariness of the world, Teufelsdröckh suffered. He doubted even the great maxim of Western philosophy, from the lips of Socrates, and echoed by Plato, to "Know thyself." Knocking about the world, viewing the emptiness and hypocrisy of materialism, Teufelsdröckh cannot accept the idealistic philosopher's view. He must change it; he must out of it force some workable command for action, inasmuch as he finds the old command too much to ask of humankind:

> . . . "The painfullest feeling," writes he, "is that your own Feebleness (*Unkraft*); ever, as the English Milton says, to be weak is the true misery. And yet of your Strength there is and can be no clear feeling, save by what you have prospered in, by what you have done. Between vague wavering Capability and fixed indubitable Performance, what a difference! A certain inarticulate Self-consciousness dwells dimly in us; which only our Works can render articulate and decisively discernible. Our Works are the mirror wherein the spirit first sees its natural lineaments. Hence, too, the folly of that impossible Precept, *Know Thyself;* till it be translated into this partially possible one, **Know what thou canst work at.**"

Knowledge by suffering entereth

Source: A VISION OF POETS ("Conclusion")
Author: Elizabeth Barrett Browning (1806-1861)
First published: 1844
Type of work: Narrative poem

Context: Written as a dream-vision wherein truth is encountered, this poem is an allegorical account of the making of a poet and of his relation to the world of ordinary men. Dreaming that he is unable to sleep, the poet sees a beautiful lady riding upon a white horse; she says that she has come "to crown all poets to their worth," a declaration that the poet does not at first understand because he thinks that poets are never praised in life. However sceptical he might be, he finally follows the strange lady to three fountains of which he must drink in order to become a true poet: world's use, world's love, and world's cruelty. The last fountain causes him to swoon, but upon waking he discovers that the forest has turned into a church and an angel stands before the altar. Soon he is joined by a procession of true poets, each with a bleeding heart, and listens to the angel who tells about the Poet-God that all poets worship in their verse. Allegorically the dream-vision is a journey through death and suffering to the knowledge of God and the acceptance of the poet's role as seer; the "Conclusion" not only makes such an interpretation clear but also shows the adoration of the true poet after his death and the faith that his surviving son has in his father's vision.

"But *thou*," I murmured to engage
The child's speech farther, "hast an age
Too tender for this orphanage."

"Glory to God—to God!" he saith,
"KNOWLEDGE BY SUFFERING ENTERETH,
AND LIFE IS PERFECTED BY DEATH."

Knowledge enormous makes a God of me

Source: HYPERION (Book III, l. 113)
Author: John Keats (1795-1821)
First published: 1820
Type of work: Narrative poem

Context: The Titans, the elder gods, have been overthrown by Jupiter and his brothers and sisters, the younger gods. Saturn, formerly the king of the world, dethroned and defeated in open war by his own children, lies stupefied upon the earth. He is visited by Thea, wife of Hyperion, who leads him to a dark, wild, rock-strewn region where many of the other defeated Titans lie in the dejection of defeat. Meanwhile, Hyperion, a Titan not deprived of his ancient office of driving the sun across the sky, finishes his day's work and repairs to his golden palace in the heavens. He is disturbed at the thought that he, as well as the other Titans, may be deposed. He plunges through the black night and arrives at the spot where the other Titans lie. After a catalogue of the Titans not unlike the catalogue of the devils in Book II of *Paradise Lost,* there is a conference similar to the one in *Paradise Lost* where the devils plot how to regain heaven (Book II). Saturn asks for suggestions on how they can war against the gods. The first to answer is Oceanus, who says that what has happened is in accordance with nature. The Titans are neither the beginning nor the end: they have brought forth a more beautiful race than themselves, and it is proper for the young to succeed to the rule. Then Clymene tells that she heard a far more beautiful music than any that the Titans could produce. But Enceladus is all for open war and revenge for the blows the new gods have dealt them. While the Titans debate, Apollo is wandering about the earth in sadness when he meets Mnemosyne, or Memory, and begs her to fill him with knowledge, because enormous knowledge makes a god of him:

O tell me, lonely Goddess, by thy harp,
That waileth every morn and eventide,
Tell me why thus I rave, about these groves!
Mute thou remainest—Mute! yet I can read
A wondrous lesson in thy silent face:

573

Knowledge enormous makes a God of me.
Names, deeds, grey legends, dire events, rebellions,
Majesties, sovran voices, agonies,
Creations and destroyings, all at once
Pour into the wide hollows of my brain,
And deify me, as if some blithe wine
Or bright elixir peerless I had drunk,
And so become immortal. . . .

The laboring mountain scarce brings forth a mouse

Source: ARS POETICA (Line 168, as translated by the Earl of Roscommon)
Author: Horace (65–8 B.C.)
First transcribed: c.13–8 B.C.
Type of work: Critical essay in form of a letter

Context: In an epistle in which Piso is addressed, which is actually a critical essay on how to write poetry, Horace cautions against either too great a flourish or dullness, suggesting that the style must suit the subject. He advises against originality, in which the aspiring poet may falter, concluding that the writer is more likely to produce a pleasing work of art by following closely the work of another writer whom he admires, but with a style suited to his art as a beginning poet, hence avoiding a ridiculously ostentatious poem:

Begin not as th'old poetaster did,
"Troy's famous war, and Priam's fate I sing;"
In what will all this ostentation end?
The lab'ring mountain scarce brings forth a mouse. . . .

Lady bountiful

Source: THE BEAUX' STRATAGEM (Act I, sc. i)
Author: George Farquhar (1677?–1707)
First published: 1707
Type of work: Dramatic comedy

Context: Farquhar's play is a romantic comedy, with satirical intent being secondary. In his Prologue for this play, the author says that satire is "the Business of the Stage" during times of strife or when society is corrupted by sloth, but that in his time, the reign of Queen Anne, there is no need for satire except to point out fools, who grow, like weeds, in the best cultivated fields. At the beginning of the play the romance is introduced; two young gentlemen, Aimwell and Archer, are looking for wealthy young women to marry. The two aptly named suitors come to Litchfield in their search for wealth and love, with Archer disguised as

Aimwell's servant. They stop at an inn owned by Will Bonniface, who tells them how his wife died because she drank some whiskey instead of their own good ale. In telling about his wife the innkeeper mentions Lady Bountiful, the rich and charitable gentlewoman of the locality, who gives of her time and money to help the sick. When asked by Aimwell to tell more about this good woman, Will Bonniface replies:

BONNIFACE
. . . My **Lady Bountyful** is one of the best of Women: Her last Husband Sir Charles Bountyful left her worth a Thousand Pounds a Year; and I believe she lays out one half on't in charitable Uses for the Good of her Neighbors; she cures Rheumatisms, Ruptures, and broken Shins in Men, Green Sickness, Obstructions, and Fits of the Mother in Women;—The King's-Evil, Chin-Cough, and Chilblains in Children; in short, she has cured more People in and about Litchfield within Ten Years than the Doctors have kill'd in Twenty; and that's a bold Word.

A lady in the case

Source: DON JUAN (Canto V, stanza 19)
Author: George Gordon, Lord Byron (1788–1824)
First published: 1821 (Cantos III–V)
Type of work: Satiric poem

Context: While supposedly writing the epic of Don Juan, Byron uses his vehicle for all sorts of digressions, personal reminiscences, tirades against England, and side-slaps at poets. For instance, in Canto IV, commenting on criticisms against licentiousness in his earlier cantos, he says he will skip over certain episodes and "leave them to the purer pages of Smollett, Prior, Ariosto, Fielding." The poem's slender plot follows the adventures of Don Juan, sent by his bluestocking mother on a tour of Europe following discovery of his affair with one of her young married friends, Donna Julia. Sailing from Cadiz to Italy, Juan's ship is wrecked in a storm. After days in a lifeboat without food or water, the young man is washed ashore almost unconscious. He finds a lovely girl bending over him, Haidée, daughter of the island's ruler, the pirate Lambro. Knowing that her father will sell him as a slave, she hides Juan in a cave. Then when Lambro leaves on an expedition, she brings him to her home, lavishes food on him, loads him with jewels, and as a passionate child of Nature, unacquainted with men, gives herself utterly to him. Though trying to think of Donna Julia, he cannot resist Haidée. Interrupting the story for an apostrophe to Greece and a consideration of fame, along with further insults to the Lake Poets, such as a comment that perhaps Homer sometimes nods, but Wordsworth sometimes awakens, Byron returns to the idyl of Juan and Haidée. It is interrupted by the return of her father, the pirate. He discovers Juan, who is wounded resisting capture. As he is taken aboard ship, Haidée loses her mind in grief at her lover's capture, and in the often quoted line, "Whom the gods love, die young," she leaves the story, and Juan never sees her again or knows that she died giving birth to his child. Juan is shipped off to a slave market along with Circassian beauties, Nubians, and others. Byron ends the fourth canto without telling of Juan's fate, "because the Canto has become too long." After a digression about the poet's "passion for the name of Mary," Byron gets back to the slave market where the youthful Juan and a thirty-year-old Englishman are sold to a eunuch from the sultana's palace. She, wanting Juan for a lover, compels him to dress as a dancing maiden, to conceal his sex from the sultan. In a conversation with the Englishman, Juan learns that the man's first wife died, his second one abandoned him, and he ran away from the third. Seeing Juan's pale and melancholic looks, his friend asks about his experiences. Juan replies that he is not deploring his present lot as a slave, for he has borne hardships "which have the hardiest overworn. . . .

> On the rough deep. But this last blow—" and here
> He stopp'd again, and turn'd away his face.
> "Ay," quoth his friend, "I thought it would appear
> That there had been **a lady in the case;**
> And these are things which ask a tender tear,
> Such as I, too, would shed if in your place;
> I cried upon my first wife's dying day,
> And also when my second ran away."

The land of scholars and the nurse of arms

Source: THE TRAVELLER (Line 356)
Author: Oliver Goldsmith (1728–1774)
First published: 1764
Type of work: Descriptive and meditative poem

Context: The poet addresses his work to his brother, who, although poor, has a happy and contented home life. The poet is a traveler in foreign lands, which he characterizes as to their physical features and the nature of their people, from those living in the arctic to those in the tropics. He discovers that the natives of all lands find their own to be the best. Italy, for instance, is blessed with a benign climate that aids in the production of a profusion of fruits and flowers; but the people, though poor, are too much given to a love of luxury; though submissive, they are vain; though grave, they are trifling; though zealous, they are untrue. They suffer greatly from a realization of departed wealth, which produced a host of architectural monuments that still exist to remind them of their past glories. The Swiss, on the other hand, live in a bleak land with a sufficiency of the

576

necessities of life but no luxuries. The people are good and industrious, but lack the graces. France is a country filled with gay and sprightly people, but they pay too much attention to honor. Their desire for honor leads them into lives of vulgar ostentation. Holland, wrested from the sea, is wealthy, but the people are too likely to stoop to unworthy acts in their desire for gold. The result is a land of tyrants and of slaves. Britain is singularly blessed in its climate, and freedom flourishes in the land. The British, however, are too independent and tend to keep themselves apart from others. Because of this tendency there is continual faction, and there is also a general lack of affection; these characteristics may lead to the growth of avarice and the decline of the nation which has for ages been famous for scholarship and military prowess.

> Nor this the worst. As nature's ties decay,
> As duty, love, and honor fail to sway,
> Fictitious bonds, the bonds of wealth and law,
> Still gather strength, and force unwilling awe.
> Hence all obedience bows to these alone,
> And talent sinks, and merit weeps unknown:
> Till time may come, when, stript of all her charms,
> **The land of scholars and the nurse of arms,**
> Where noble stems transmit the patriot flame,
> Where kings have toiled and poets wrote for fame,
> One sink of level avarice shall lie,
> And scholars, soldiers, kings, unhonored die.

Language is fossil poetry

Source: THE POET
Author: Ralph Waldo Emerson (1803–1882)
First published: 1844
Type of work: Moral essay

Context: As a transcendentalist, a philosophical idealist, Emerson believed in an ultimate reality, the Oversoul. As early as 1836, in his essay entitled *Nature,* he gave his theories a form, including his theory of language as symbolism. Words, as he saw them, are more than symbols for specific facts on the present level of existence; he saw them as symbols for symbols, the specific facts in their turn being symbols of transcendental facts, or realities, on a higher level of existence. To the poet, with whom Emerson lodges the responsibility for expression, he gives the opportunity for creating language at both levels. The poet is then the ultimate knower, who helps, by his expression in the medium of language, the rest of mankind to see that the universe is "the externalization of the soul." From this standpoint, of course, the poet is the true scientist, giving the best insight to the ultimate nature of things:

577

By virtue of this science the poet is the Namer, or Language-maker, naming things sometimes after their appearance, sometimes after their essence, and giving to every one its own name and not another's, thereby rejoicing the intellect, which delights in detachments or boundary. The poets made all the words, and therefore language is the archives of history, and, if we must say it, a sort of tomb of the muses. For, though the origin of most of our words is forgotten, each word was at first a stroke of genius, and obtained currency because for the moment it symbolized the world to the first speaker and to the hearer. The etymologist finds the deadest word to have been once a brilliant picture. **Language is fossil poetry.** As the limestone of the continent consists of infinite masses of the shells of animalcules, so language is made up of images or tropes, which now, in their secondary use, have long ceased to remind us of their poetic origin. . . .

The last of all the Romans, fare thee well!

Source: JULIUS CAESAR (Act V, sc. iii, l. 99)
Author: William Shakespeare (1564–1616)
First published: 1623
Type of work: Dramatic tragedy

Context: Brutus, the idealist who would protect the Roman Republic from degenerating into a dictatorship, has joined with Cassius, Casca, and others, who from malice and ill-fed ambition would grasp more power for themselves. As a coalition, they have murdered Julius Caesar and consequently thrown the city into political turmoil. The civil war which has resulted has turned friend against friend and kin against kin. Antony, Octavius, and Lepidus—leaders of the faction which supports the cause of the slain Caesar—gather their forces to do battle with Brutus and his followers on the plains of Philippi. When a parley between the opposing generals produces nothing but mutual recriminations, the battle begins in earnest. Brutus enjoys initial success against Octavius but Cassius' forces are pushed back by Antony, and Cassius, ordering his servant to strike, dies like a Roman. Titinius, following the example of his general, also strikes home with Cassius' sword. Dejectedly observing the scene of self-destruction, Brutus avers that Julius Caesar is mighty yet: "Thy spirit walks abroad, and turns our swords in our own proper entrails." Perhaps anticipating his own moment of self-sacrifice, he pauses to speak a brief eulogy over the bodies of his comrades-in-arms:

Are yet two Romans living such as these?
The last of all the Romans, fare thee well!
It is impossible that ever Rome
Should breed thy fellow. Friends, I owe moe tears
To this dead man than you shall see me pay.

I shall find time, Cassius; I shall find time.
Come therefore, and to Thasos send his body.
His funerals shall not be in our camp,
Lest it discomfort us. Lucilius come,
And come young Cato, let us to the field.
Labeo and Flavius, set our battles on.
'Tis three a clock; and Romans, yet ere night
We shall try fortune in a second fight.

The last rose of summer, left blooming alone

Source: IRISH MELODIES ("The Last Rose of Summer," Lines 1–2)
Author: Thomas Moore (1779–1852)
First published: 1808
Type of work: Song

Context: Thomas Moore was an Irish poet of the romantic period who tried to do for Ireland what Burns had done for Scotland; he wrote graceful lyrics for traditional and ancient airs of his country, working on the project for nearly twenty years. The results, published over a period of time (1807–1834), were entitled *Irish Melodies.* In some cases Moore composed tunes as well as lyrics, but most of the airs were of great age. He had a good voice and sang these compositions on occasion. Modern critics are likely to feel that his work is too often superficial and oversentimental, but it nonetheless retains considerable charm. In his day Moore was, next to Byron, the most popular poet in Britain. A close friend of Byron, he produced a good biography of the latter and at times defended Byron's memory from critics. Other popular works by him were *Lalla Rookh* and *The Loves of the Angels,* works exploiting the currently stylish Orientalism. He wrote one novel, *The Epicurean,* a *History of Ireland,* and some light satire. Moore came to be regarded as the national poet of Ireland, and it is for his Irish songs that he is remembered today; many are still popular old favorites. Among the best known of these are "Believe Me, If All Those Endearing Young Charms"; "The Minstrel Boy"; "The Harp That Once Through Tara's Halls"; and "The Last Rose of Summer." The last-mentioned was used by Friedrich von Flotow (1812–1883), German composer, in his most successful and still popular opera, *Martha;* here it is used as a theme song, occurring several times during the course of the work. First performed in 1844, it still holds a place in light opera repertoire. The poem merely expresses its writer's sadness upon realizing that the last rose of the season is blooming and that it will be a year before he will see roses again. He likens it to human existence, hoping he will not remain solitary to exist in a bleak world after all his friends are gone into death.

579

'Tis **the last rose of summer,**
  Left blooming alone;
All her lovely companions
  Are faded and gone;
No flower of her kindred,
  No rose-bud is nigh,
To reflect back her blushes,
  Or give sigh for sigh.

I'll not leave thee, thou lone one!
  To pine on the stem;
Since the lovely are sleeping,
  Go, sleep thou with them.
Thus kindly I scatter
  Thy leaves o'er the bed
Where thy mates of the garden
  Lie scentless and dead.

So soon may *I* follow,
  When friendships decay,
And from Love's shining circle
  The gems drop away.
When true hearts are withered,
  And fond ones are flown,
O who would inhabit
  This bleak world alone?

The lasting mansions of the dead

Source: THE LIBRARY (Line 101)
Author: George Crabbe (1754–1832)
First published: 1781
Type of work: Descriptive poem

Context: In 1780–1781 George Crabbe was poverty-stricken, and publishers refused him any help. In despair he wrote to Edmund Burke, whom he did not know personally. Burke, moved by the poet's plight and his appeal, sent money and a promise of influence. As a result of the great man's help, *The Library* was published, and, urged by his benefactor, Crabbe became an Anglican clergyman and received the post of curate at Aldeburgh, his native town in Suffolk. In this poem he discusses many topics related to a library, such as the consolation to the mind afforded by books, an author's hope of speaking through his writings to posterity, the arrangement of books on the shelves, the mode of publishing in pamphlet form, books on medicine and law, and the apprehensions suffered by authors. The quotation is from his discussion of how writers speak to later generations through their works. The poet says, "Delightful prospect! when we leave behind/ A worthy offspring of the fruitful mind!" He goes on to comment, however, that all books are not noble products; some works are better guides than others. He observes that people come to a library and its books for many reasons. Some come to escape their griefs, others to feed their curiosity and assuage its hunger, and still others to find inspiration. The poet then speaks of his own feelings about a library:

> With awe, around these silent walks I tread;
> These are **the lasting mansions of the dead:**—
> "The dead," methinks a thousand tongues reply;
> "These are the tombs of such as cannot die!
> Crown'd with eternal fame, they sit sublime,
> And laugh at all the little strife of time."

Laugh all honesty out of fashion

Source: THE DUCHESS OF MALFI (Act I, sc. ii, ll. 116–117)
Author: John Webster (1580?–1625?)
First published: 1623
Type of work: Dramatic tragedy

Context: The opening scene of this play, the most famous of the post-Shakespearean "tragedies of blood," is in the Presence Chamber of the Duchess' palace at Malfi. Her steward, Antonio, has just returned from France. Early in the first act (which in the older editions is not divided into scenes but is so divided in more modern texts) he answers the questions of his friend Delio concerning the three principal characters of the drama: the Duke of Calabria; his brother, the Cardinal; and their sister, the Duchess of Malfi. Of the Cardinal, Antonio paints the portrait of a "melancholy churchman," a licentious, indeed, a thoroughly wicked man, who missed attaining the Papal Crown only because he scattered bribes too lavishly. The Duke is even worse. Antonio says of the Cardinal "Some good he hath done—," and then breaks off when Delio demands to be told of the Duke. He begins:

ANTONIO
The Duke there? A most perverse and turbulent nature.
What appears in him mirth is merely outside;
If he laughs heartily, it is to **laugh**
All honesty out of fashion.

The laughing queen that caught the world's great hands

Source: THE NILE (Line 8)
Author: Leigh Hunt (1784–1859)
First published: 1818
Type of work: Sonnet

Context: James Henry Leigh Hunt is remembered today for only a few graceful poems. In his day he was poet, critic, and essayist; a friend of Keats, Shelley, and Byron, he influenced Keats' early work to some extent. Keats later outgrew the influence and evolved along lines of his own. In 1822 Byron and Shelley invited Hunt to Italy to edit a new quarterly called *The Liberal;* Hunt took his family there, and four issues of the quarterly appeared. However, Byron lost interest in the project and there was a quarrel; he abandoned the Hunts, who were left without resources in a foreign land. When Hunt managed to return home, in 1825, he found a huge demand for material on Byron, and contributed *Lord Byron and Some of His Contemporaries.* Hunt did not falsify anything in this work but he did take the opportunity to get even with Byron for numerous humiliations to which the latter had subjected him. To show the less attractive side of a public idol, particularly a recently deceased one, is always unwise: Hunt bitterly regretted his criticism afterward. He was vilified; Thomas Moore likened him to a dog attacking a dead lion. Hunt continued with his literary efforts and wrote voluminously until his death, enjoying a measure of success. A good journalist and a man who loved beauty, he nonetheless lacked the sensibility and taste that characterize the great poets. Among the few of Hunt's poems which are still felt to be of lasting value is *The Nile,* a picture of the ancient dreaming river and its vanished civilization, a glimpse of Cleopatra, and a sense of the steadily flowing stream of time. The sonnet was composed in competition with Keats and Shelley, each poet writing a sonnet on the same subject. In fairness to the now almost forgotten Hunt, it should be said that his sonnet was the best of the three. The sonnet is as follows:

It flows through old hushed Egypt and its sands,
    Like some grave mighty thought threading a dream,
    And times and things, as in that vision, seem
Keeping along it their eternal stands,—
Caves, pillars, pyramids, the shepherd bands
    That roamed through the young world, the glory extreme
    Of high Sesostris, and that southern beam,
The laughing queen that caught the world's great hands.

Then comes a mightier silence, stern and strong,
As of a world left empty of its throng,
    And the void weighs on us; and then we wake,
And hear the fruitful stream lapsing along

Twixt villages, and think how we shall take
Our own calm journey on for human sake.

Laughter is nothing else but sudden glory

Source: TRIPOS ("Human Nature," Chapter 9, sec. XIII)
Author: Thomas Hobbes (1588–1679)
First published: 1640
Type of work: Philosophical essay

Context: Thomas Hobbes was a philosopher and political scientist, whose best known work, *Leviathan,* is an analysis of government; it is a strongly materialistic interpretation of political institutions. To Hobbes, man is by nature equal, and self-seeking; competition is basic to him. Every man is the natural enemy of every other: therefore, governments are formed that order may be ensured. In the process, every individual contracts with all other individuals, each giving up his rights to the governing person or body. This sacrifice is made in order to achieve survival, security, and happiness for each individual. The contract is a mutual one among the governed, not between subject and ruler. Thus, to Hobbes, the right of the state or of the sovereign is absolute. He believes also in the separation of church and state: the laws of God are internal, those of man are external, and the two do not conflict. To resist one's government is to sin against the laws of God, since these are the laws of nature. Hobbes' metaphysics also reflects his materialism; he considers the entire universe matter, and things of the spirit, including God, are also matter but somewhat less substantial. His system is actually one of mechanics or physics. Hobbes also explored psychology, concluding that all so-called voluntary actions have necessary causes and are therefore both involuntary and inevitable. *Tripos* is a group of his three most important works on this subject; each is a discourse on certain areas of human psychology and motivation. The first takes up the nature of man; the second examines law and the body politic; and the third explores the relationship between freedom and necessity. In the first essay, *Human Nature,* Hobbes begins with a discussion of the senses, the reasoning process, and the passions. Laughter, representative of a passion which has no name, is subjected to a penetrating analysis:

. . . Men laugh often, especially such as are greedy of applause from every thing they do well, at their *own* actions performed never so little beyond their own expectations; as also at their own *jests:* and in this case it is manifest, that the passion of laughter proceedeth from a *sudden conception* of some *ability* in himself that laugheth. Also men laugh at the *infirmities* of others, by comparison wherewith their own abilities are set off and illustrated. Also men laugh at *jests,* the *wit* whereof always consisteth in the

583

elegant *discovering* and conveying to our minds some *absurdity* of *another:* and in this case also the passion of laughter proceedeth from the *sudden* imagination of our own odds and eminency: for what is else the recommending of ourselves to our own good opinion, by comparison with another man's infirmity or absurdity? For when a jest is broken upon ourselves, or friends of whose dishonour we participate, we never laugh thereat. I may therefore conclude, that the passion of **laughter is nothing else but <u>sudden glory</u>** arising from some sudden *conception* of some *eminency* in ourselves, by *comparison* with the *infirmity* of others, or with our own formerly: for men laugh at the follies of themselves past, when they come suddenly to remembrance, except they bring with them any present dishonour. It is no wonder therefore that men take heinously to be laughed at or derided, that is, triumphed over. Laughter *without offence,* must be at *absurdities* and infirmities *abstracted* from persons, and when all the company may laugh together. . . .

Law is a bottomless pit

Source: THE HISTORY OF JOHN BULL (Title-page and Chapter VI of Pamphlet I)
Author: John Arburthnot (1667–1735)
First published: 1712
Type of work: Political satire

Context: The title page of the first edition of the first installment of this work, which was issued as five pamphlets, reads: *Law is a Bottomless-Pit, Exemplify'd in the Case of the Lord Strutt, John Bull, Nicholas Frog, and Lewis Baboon, Who Spent all they had in a Law-Suit.* In 1727 the collection of pamphlets was reprinted in Pope and Swift's *Miscellanies in Prose and Verse as Law is a Bottomless Pit, or, The History of John Bull,* and since that time it has been known as *The History of John Bull.* It is popularly attributed to John Arburthnot, but whether Jonathan Swift (1667–1745) had a hand in it, or whether he wrote it, is a matter of debate. The work is a satire on the situation that prevailed after the death of Charles II of Spain in 1700.

Charles left the Spanish monarchy to Philip of Anjou, grandson of Louis XIV of France. England and Holland feared that the combining of the two monarchies in one family would injure their trade and in 1702 declared war on Spain and France. The first four chapters of the work give the characters of the various contestants. Chapter VI tells of the Dutch and English military successes during 1702–1709. The victories, however, cost huge sums of money, which were supplied by borrowings. The allegory of the lawsuit means the military campaign; Hocus is the leader of the Dutch and English armies, the Duke of Marlborough; John Bull is England; Lord Strutt is Philip of Spain. Chapter VI begins as follows:

Law is a bottomless pit, it is a cormorant, a Harpy, that devours everything; John Bull was flattered by his lawyers that his suit would not last above a year or two at most; that before that time he would be in quiet possession of his business; yet ten long years did Hocus steer his cause through all the meanders of the law, and all the courts; no skill, no address, was wanting; and to say truth, John did not starve the cause; there wanted not yellow-boys to fee counsel, hire witnesses, and bribe juries. Lord Strutt was generally cast, never had one verdict in his favor; and John was promised, that the next and the next would be the final determination; but alas! that final determination, and happy conclusion was like an enchanted island, the nearer John came to it, the further it went from him: new trials upon new points still arose; new doubts, new matters to be cleared; in short, lawyers seldom part with so good a cause till they have got the oyster, and their clients the shell.

Laws, like houses, lean on one another

Source: TRACT ON THE POPERY LAWS (Chapter III, part 1)
Author: Edmund Burke (1729–1797)
First published: 1865–1867
Type of work: Political treatise

Context: Although he was born in Ireland, Burke spent his adult life in England as a member of Parliament. However, he never lost interest in Irish affairs, and in his official capacity he defended Ireland as strongly against oppression as he did the American Colonies. Although his thoughts on religious toleration were not in advance of his age, he did regard the domination of the millions of Irish Catholics by the Anglican church as a kind of tyranny. His attack on the discriminatory laws directed against the Catholics was never completed. In his third chapter he pauses to comment on the processes of making and changing laws:

In the making of a new law it is undoubtedly the duty of the legislator to see that no injustice be done even to an individual: for there is then nothing to be unsettled, and the matter is under his hands to mould it as he pleases; and if he finds it untractable in the working, he may abandon it without incurring any new inconvenience. But in the question concerning the repeal of an old one, the work is of more difficulty; because **laws, like houses, lean on one another,** and the operation is delicate, and should be necessary: the objection, in such a case, ought not to arise from the natural infirmity of human institutions, but from substantial faults which contradict the nature and end of law itself,—faults not arising from the imperfection, but from the misapplication and abuse of our reason.

Lead apes in hell

Source: THE TAMING OF THE SHREW (Act II, sc. i, l. 34)
Author: William Shakespeare (1564–1616)
First published: 1623
Type of work: Dramatic comedy

Context: Bianca, gentle younger daughter of the rich gentleman of Padua, Baptista, is being wooed by several suitors, but Katharine, the shrewish elder daughter is shunned by every eligible man. In a room in Baptista's house Katharine, trying to dis-cover the suitor preferred by Bianca, ties her sister's hands and strikes her. Baptista comes to the rescue of his daughter, who truthfully says she has not fallen in love, while the spiteful and jealous Katharine regales her father:

BAPTISTA
Why how now dame, whence grows this insolence?
Bianca stand aside. Poor girl, she weeps.
Go ply thy needle, meddle not with her.
For shame thou hilding of a devilish spirit,
Why dost thou wrong her, that did ne'er wrong thee?
When did she cross thee with a bitter word?

KATHARINE
Her silence flouts me, and I'll be revenged.
[*Makes for* BIANCA.]

BAPTISTA [*holds her back*]
What, in my sight? Bianca get thee in.
[*Exit* BIANCA.]

KATHARINE
What will you not suffer me? Nay now I see
She is your treasure, she must have a husband;
I must dance barefoot on her wedding-day,
And for your love to her, **lead apes in hell.**
Talk not to me, I will go sit and weep,
Till I can find occasion of revenge.

Lean and slippered pantaloon

Source: AS YOU LIKE IT (Act II, sc. vii, l. 158)
Author: William Shakespeare (1564–1616)
First published: 1623
Type of work: Dramatic comedy

Context: For the sixth of his "seven ages" of man, the "melancholy Jaques" refers to a stock figure of Italian comedy, the Pantaloon, usually an old, lean, gullible dotard, clothed precisely as Shakespeare describes him. Jaques presents his cynical description of the seven ages— the infant, schoolboy, lover, soldier, justice, "pantaloon," and senile dodderer—after his master, the exiled Duke Senior, has pointed out that unhappiness may be found, not only in the Forest of Arden, but in the entire world, the "wide and universal theatre." Jaques replies:

JAQUES
        All the world's a stage,
And all the men and women merely players.
They have their exits and their entrances,
And one man in his time plays many parts,
His acts being seven ages.
      •   •   •
        The sixth age shifts
Into the **lean and slippered pantaloon,**
With spectacles on nose and pouch on side,
His youthful hose, well saved, a world too wide
For his shrunk shank, and his big manly voice,
Turning again toward childish treble pipes
And whistles in his sound.
      •   •   •

Lean, hungry, savage, anti-everythings

Source: A MODEST REQUEST (Line 98)
Author: Oliver Wendell Holmes (1809–1894)
First published: 1849
Type of work: Occasional verse

Context: Holmes wrote this poem on the occasion of the inauguration of President Everett, of Harvard. It humorously recounts a request that comes by mail for him, the poet, to provide a speech, a song, and a toast —all by himself—for the dinner honoring the new college president; the poem includes the poet's responses to the request, done in Holmes' witty fashion. He describes the speaker, looking very red because he is "so very green," embarrassed by the amount of learning in many studies represented by the men at the banquet tables about him. In mimicry of

587

speeches delivered at such functions as the inaugurations of college presidents, Holmes has his speaker give a prophetic utterance about the future of Harvard, punctuated, as he notes, by "three tremendous cheers." The speaker, looking to a splendid future, declaims:

My eye prophetic, as the depths unfold,
Sees a new advent of the age of gold;
While o'er the scene new generations press,
New heroes rise the coming time to bless,—
Not such as Homer's, who, we read in Pope,
Dined without forks and never heard of soap,—
Not such as May to Marlborough Chapel brings,
Lean, hungry, savage, anti-everythings,
Copies of Luther in the pasteboard style,—
But genuine articles,—the true Carlyle;
While far on high the blazing orb shall shed
Its central light on Harvard's holy head,
And Learning's ensigns ever float unfurled
Here in the focus of the new-born world!

A leap into the dark

Source: LETTERS FROM THE DEAD TO THE LIVING (Part I, number 2)
Author: Thomas Brown (1663–1704)
First published: 1702
Type of work: Satire

Context: The son of a well-to-do Shropshire farmer, Tom Brown, as he usually signed himself, was educated at Oxford. He learned five foreign languages, but it was for his audacity and wildness, rather than his ability to learn, that he became known. The Dean of Christ College, Dr. John Fell, once called him on the carpet to expel him, but because of the student's apparent contrition, agreed to let him stay if he could translate an epigram from Martial, beginning: "Non amo te, Sabidi." Brown's impromptu translation became famous.

"I do not love thee, Doctor Fell,
 The reason why I cannot tell,
 But this I know, and know full well,

I do not love thee, Doctor Fell."

He was allowed to remain. He and the dean became friends, and upon Dr. Fell's death, in 1686, Brown wrote his epitaph. Leaving Oxford without a degree, Brown became a political pamphleteer, one of the best of the Grub Street hacks, and the first to pretend to disguise his victims by replacing the vowels in their name by dashes, as in, Sir Th-m-s T-pt-n. Later he became the protégé of Charles Sackville, sixth Earl of Dorset. However, fonder of jokes than of friends, Brown estranged the earl and died in poverty at the age of forty-one, his last years spent largely in low taverns. Much of Brown's work comprised translations, but he also wrote

London Amusements (1700) and just before his death published Letters from the Dead to the Living (1702), of which he composed only a portion. He revised other entries and translated some from the French. The volume begins with "A Letter of News from Mr. Joseph Haines, of Merry Memory, to his Friends at Will's Coffee House." Haines, who died in 1701, was a versatile person who served as Latin secretary to Sir Joseph Williamson, a seventeenth century British diplomat. Then he became a strolling player for whom Dryden and others wrote plays. He turned Catholic when to do so was expedient, during the reign of James II. Will's Coffee House, at the corner of Bow and Russell Streets, was a favorite with Dryden and his fellow wits. In his letter, Haines tells of his arrival in Hell, and his new job as astrologer and dancing teacher to the Devil's sister. He asks for news from the upper world. A reply "An Answer to Mr. Joseph Haines, High German Astrologer, at the Sign of the Urinal and Cassiopea's Chair," reports discussions in Parliament about a war with France, and the publication of *The Life of the Famous Comedian Jo Haynes,* of unknown authorship, in 1701.

. . . our Grub Street pamphleteers advise the shires and boroughs what sort of members to choose; the shires and boroughs advise their representatives what course to steer in parliament; and the senators, no doubt on't, will advise his majesty what ministers to rely on, and how to behave himself in this present conjuncture. . . . We forgot to tell you, Mr. Haines, that since you left this upper world, your life has been written by a brother player, who pretends he received all his memoirs from your own mouth, a little before you made **a leap into the dark,** and really you are beholden to the fellow, for he makes you a Master of Arts at the university, tho' you never took a degree there. That and a thousand stories of other people, he has fathered upon you, and the truth on't is, the adventures of thy life, if truly set down, are so romantic, that few besides thy acquaintance would be able to distinguish between the history and the fable.

Learn'd without sense, and venerably dull

Source: THE ROSCIAD (Line 592)
Author: Charles Churchill (1731–1764)
First published: 1761
Type of work: Satirical poem

Context: Deprived of remunerative church appointments by an early marriage, Churchill turned to poetry to support his wife and children. The success of *The Actor,* a poem by Robert Lloyd (1733–1764) that had been published in 1760, made him decide to turn his many nights in the first row seats in London's theaters into a poem. So he wrote *The Rosciad,* named from the Roman actor Quintus Roscius (126?–62 B.C.), friend of Cicero and regarded as Rome's greatest comic actor. He is mentioned in *Hamlet*. Imitating Pope's *Dunciad* (1728–43), Churchill called his work *The Rosciad*. No publisher would pay him the £20 he asked for it. The best offer was £5, so Churchill published it anonymously at his own expense. He had no need to advertise it. The agonizing cries of the theatrical people attacked made hundreds more troop to the book stores. One reviewer called it a well-written, ill-natured, ingenious, abusive poem. Many were the poets suspected of having been its author, but the second edition that same year, with a rise in price to one-and-six, carried his name to end doubts. The public enjoyed the actors' distress. Too many times, the stage folk had poked fun at audiences! Many said that Churchill's criticisms of the performers were repetitions of those heard in the coffee houses, but they were listened to. Among those attacked, Thomas Davis (1712?–1795) retired from the stage. The poet also handed out praise, especially to Kitty Clive (1711–1785), Jane Pope (1742–1818), Mrs. Pritchard (1711–1769), the great tragic actress Mrs. Cibber (1714–1766), and of course to David Garrick (1717–1779). However, today's readers need an annotated edition of the poem, since many stage people mentioned in its 1090 lines have long been forgotten. The poem starts: "Roscius deceas'd, each high aspiring play'r/ Push'd all his int'rest for the vacant chair." But how to choose the best? In London, says Churchill, the way to succeed on the stage is through bribery. S-T-R opens his house and feeds people; Y-T-S offers laughter and fun; F-TE serves tea. But this time they are to be judged by performance on the stage. They refuse to accept the verdict of any judge. J-HNS-N would be too serious; ST-NE, too gay; and F-KL-N appreciates only his own talent. Finally, Lloyd makes the acceptable suggestion of leaving the decision to Shakespeare and Dr. Johnson. Then begins the procession of the contestants, with description and criticism of each. About one, the poet goes into great detail. Apart from all the rest, comes the great M-RP-Y. This was Arthur Murphy (1727–1805) who played *Othello* at Covent Garden in 1754 and declared the next year that he was unsuited to be an actor. "The Shuffling Trade" is priesthood. About Murphy Churchill comments: "In cold-wrought scenes, the lifeless actor flags./ In passion, tears the passion into rags," then adds:

How few are found with real talents bless'd,
Fewer with Nature's gifts contented rest.
Man from his sphere eccentric starts astray;
All hunt for fame, but most mistake the way.
Bred at ST. OMER'S to the Shuffling trade,
The hopeful youth a Jesuit might have made,
With various readings stor'd his empty skull,
Learn'd without sense, and venerably dull;
Or at some Banker's desk, like many more,
Content to tell that two and two make four,
His name had stood in CITY ANNALS fair,
And PRUDENT DULLNESS mark'd him for a Mayor.

Learning, that cobweb of the brain

Source: HUDIBRAS (Part I, Canto 3, l. 1339)
Author: Samuel Butler (1612–1680)
First published: First and second parts, 1663; third part, 1678
Type of work: Burlesque poem

Context: In satirizing the Presbyterians, Dissenters, and others who under Cromwell, opposed Charles I, to make them appear odious and obnoxious, an English poet combined pictures of contemporaries with quotable lines and much learning. By making one of the characters an enthusiastic Presbyterian Justice with a nose for sin, and the other an ignorant Independent squire, Butler could work unending religious debates into his poem. Indeed, there is more talk than action, and one of the criticisms of the poem is its poverty of incident. Some of the human foibles, too, against which the lively sarcasm is directed, no longer exist. Nevertheless, the style and execution have long been admired. Like *Don Quixote,* after which the poem was modeled, the knight and his squire get the worst of every encounter, though once they do appear successful. In their first sally, they put an end to a gay gathering at a bear baiting and set the fiddler Crowdero into the stocks. But later the vanquished crowd returns, when the crusaders leave the palace of a wealthy Widow, to do battle again. One Amazonian member, Trulla, attacks Hudibras from behind, and he and his squire occupy the stocks instead of Crowdero, to meditate upon their situation. Ralpho, blaming their predicament upon his master's bad conduct, satirizes Sir Hudibras' religion, and that act starts an argument about Synods, neither pertinent nor interesting to modern readers, that lasts 300 lines to the end of the canto. *Hudibras* is not a story to be read in its entirety, but rather to be dipped into. In the religious debate, Ralpho accuses his master of getting his arguments from the Ranters, a sect that denied Heaven and Hell, and insisted that John the Baptist and Christ were impostors, and that people should learn only from God, directly. Ralpho makes an attack on learning until Sir Hudibras stops him with a plea to take it up later. During his attack on the learning that brought them to their present trouble, Ralpho says:

> The self-same cavils then I heard,
> When b'ing in hot dispute about
> This controversy, we fell out;
> And what thou know'st I answer'd then
> Will serve to answer thee agen.
>   Quoth Ralpho, Nothing but th' abuse
> Of human learning you produce,
> **Learning, that cobweb of the brain,**
> Profane, erroneous, and vain;
> A trade of knowledge as replete
> As others are with fraud and cheat; . . .

591

Leave Now for dogs and apes! Man has Forever

Source: A GRAMMARIAN'S FUNERAL (Lines 83–84)
Author: Robert Browning (1812–1889)
First published: 1855
Type of work: Dramatic monologue

Context: In this poem Robert Browning expresses one of his favorite ideas: that man is finest when he strives mightily, no matter what his actual achievements may be. In the poem, a group of disciples are carrying their dead master, a Renaissance grammarian, to his last resting place upon a high mountain at the top of which shines a citadel. The dead master was born with the face of Apollo, but instead of living a life of pleasure and self-gratification, he devoted himself to learning. He wanted to know all that the poets and sages had learned about man, and so he doggedly ground away at his studies. When his disciples first gathered around him, they found him profoundly learned, but they also found him bald and leaden-eyed, with his youthful handsomeness gone. He wanted to eat even the crumbs of intellectual life. He was going to live when he had learned all about life that books could tell him, but not until then. He would learn to live before living, but as there was no end to learning he decided to leave the present moment to the lower animals, who cannot communicate what they learn; man—the race, not the individual—has the ability to communicate, and so he has forever.

> Yea, this in him was the peculiar grace
>   (Hearten our chorus!)
> That before living he'd learn how to live—
>   No end to learning;
> Earn the means first—God surely will contrive
>   Use for our earning.
> Others mistrust and say—"But time escapes!
>   Live now or never!"
> He said, "What's time? **leave Now for dogs and apes!**
>   **Man has Forever.**"
> Back to his book then: deeper drooped his head;
>   *Calculus* racked him:
> Leaden before, his eyes grew dross of lead:
>   *Tussis* attacked him.

Leave us leisure to be good

Source: HYMN TO ADVERSITY (Line 20)
Author: Thomas Gray (1716–1771)
First published: 1753
Type of work: Pindaric ode

Context: After returning from two years in France and Italy, where he wrote only a few poems in Latin, Gray began in 1742 to write poetry in English. In the spring, he completed "Hymn to Adversity," and in the fall began "An Elegy Wrote in a Country Churchyard," for which he is best known. It was not completed until 1750. His noble friend Horace Walpole issued the "Elegy" in a quarto pamphlet in 1751. Walpole was also responsible for the publication the next year of "Hymn to Adversity," with illustrations by Richard Bentley. The poem bears a motto in Greek from Aeschylus: "It profits to learn discretion through suffering," which is reminiscent of Shakespeare's "Sweet are the uses of adversity," from *As You Like It.* Gray's ambitions in life, he says at its conclusion, are to examine himself, learn about others, and "to feel and know myself as a Man." *Paradise Lost* by Milton seems to be the inspiration of part of this Hymn. Addressing the daughter of Jove, who gives a taste of pain to even the proud and frightens away frivolity and temptation which so involve a man that he has little time to practice goodness, Gray writes in the third stanza:

> Scared at thy frown terrific, fly
> Self-pleasing Folly's idle brood,
> Wild Laughter, Noise, and thoughtless Joy,
> And **leave us leisure to be good.**
> Light they disperse, and with them go
> The summer friend, the flattering foe;
> By vain Prosperity received
> To her they vow the truth, and are again believed.

A leper once he lost and gained a king

Source: PARADISE LOST (Book I, l. 471)
Author: John Milton (1608–1674)
First published: 1667
Type of work: Epic poem

Context: In giving a catalogue of the devils in imitation of Homer's catalogue of the ships in Book II of the *Iliad,* Milton makes a reference to Rimmon's losing a leper; the story is told in II Kings 5: Naaman, a famous Syrian general, is a leper. A little captive maid from the land of Israel who waits on Naaman's wife says that he could be cured of his disease if he would consult the prophet in Samaria. The King of Syria sent a letter to the King of Israel, requesting a cure for Naaman's illness. The king, being powerless to effect a cure, was greatly troubled lest the King of Syria was seeking a quarrel with him, but the prophet Elisha took the matter upon himself. He commanded Naaman to wash seven times in the Jordan; this advice greatly angered Naaman, who said that the rivers of Damascus were superior to the Jordan. He was about to return home, but his servants prevailed upon him to follow Elisha's advice. He did so and was cured, and, as a result, became a believer in the one true God. The reference in the quotation to the gaining of a king concerns Ahaz, King of Judah, who allied himself with Assyria and encompassed the total destruction of the kingdom of Israel. "Grunsel," modern "ground sill," is part of a foundation.

> Next came one
> Who mourned in earnest, when the captive ark
> Maimed his brute image, head and hands lopped off
> In his own temple, on the grunsel edge,
> Where he fell flat, and shamed his worshippers:
> Dagon his name, sea monster, upward man
> And downward fish: yet had his temple high
> Reared in Azotus, dreaded through the coast
> Of Palestine, in Gath and Ascalon,
> And Accaron and Gaza's frontier bounds.
> Him followed Rimmon, whose delightful seat
> Was fair Damascus, on the fertile banks
> Of Abbana and Pharphar, lucid streams.
> He also against the house of God was bold:
> **A leper once he lost and gained a king,**
> Ahaz his sottish conqueror, whom he drew
> God's altar to disparage and displace
> For one of Syrian mode, whereon to burn
> His odious offerings, and adore the gods
> Whom he had vanquished.

Let dogs delight to bark and bite

Source: DIVINE SONGS (XVI)
Author: Isaac Watts (1674–1748)
First published: 1720
Type of work: Didactic poem

Context: Isaac Watts, concerned about the importance of proper moral education for young children and convinced that instruction carried by the vehicle of verse was more easily remembered than prose instruction, wrote *Divine Songs.* In Song XVI, the poet notes that it is the nature of dogs to bark and bite and for bears and lions to growl and fight, but children, he says, should follow the example of the Christ child and be gentle as lambs. The poem begins:

> **Let dogs delight to bark and bite,**
> For God has made them so,
> Let bears and lions growl and fight,
> For 'tis their nature too.

But, children, you should never let
  Such angry passions rise:
Your little hands were never made
  To tear each others' eyes.

Let love through all your actions run,
  And all your words be mild:
Live like the Blessed Virgin's Son,
  That sweet and lowly child.

His soul was gentle as a lamb;
  And, as his stature grew,
He grew in favour both with man
  And God his Father too.

Let Grill be Grill and have his hoggish mind

Source: THE FAERIE QUEENE (Book II, Canto 12, stanza 87)
Author: Edmund Spenser (c. 1552–1599)
First published: 1590
Type of work: Allegorical poem

Context: The theme of temperance is paramount in the Book II of the epic. Guyon, the Knight of Moral Reason, assays to destroy the Bower of Bliss and to overthrow its mistress, Acrasie, who represents Intemperance and who prevents man from attaining his best self. Guyon is guided in his effort by the Palmer, who exemplifies the intellectual virtue of Prudence. Guyon attains the proper balance between his natural, rational soul and his physical actions through theoretical education and physical training at Alma's Castle, the House of Temperance. Having attained this balance, Guyon and the Palmer are able to fight their way through the Bower of Bliss where they find Acrasie with her new lover, Verdant. Casting unbreakable nets over the two, Guyon and the Palmer mercilessly destroy the palace and its garden. There they find men whom Acrasie has turned into wild beasts. The Palmer returns these to their former state. Some are shamed, others angry. Grill, who had been turned into a hog, even berates his saviors for rescuing him. Guyon remarks how quickly this man has forgotten the divine grace which ordains all men to a higher end. The Palmer's answer points out that the saving of all men is not within the power of one man; there are those who will resist all attempts to save them and are best left to their own desires.

Said Guyon, "See the mind of beastly man,
That hath so soone forgot the excellence
Of his creation, when he life began,
That now he chooseth, with vile difference,
To be a beast, and lacke intelligence."

595

To whom the Palmer thus, "The donghill kind
Delights in filth and foule incontinence:
Let Grill be Grill, and have his hoggish mind;
But let us hence depart, whilest wether serves and wind."

Let him not boast who puts his armor on

Source: MORITURI SALUTAMUS (Stanza 9)
Author: Henry Wadsworth Longfellow (1807–1882)
First published: 1875
Type of work: Philosophical poem

Context: Longfellow graduated from Bowdoin College in 1825. In October, 1874, he was urged to write a poem for the fiftieth anniversary of his graduating class, the reunion of which was to take place the following summer. Longfellow felt a strong aversion to writing poems for special occasions, and at first said he could not undertake this one. However, an inspiration evidently came to him; it has been suggested that he may have seen a representation of the painting by Gerome which depicts the Roman gladiators hailing Caesar. At any rate, he not only wrote the poem, but read it for the occasion—a performance he very rarely undertook. The poem begins with a translation of its title: " 'O Caesar, we who are about to die/ Salute you!' was the gladiators' cry/ In the arena, standing face to face/ With death and with the Roman populace." Longfellow then describes the natural beauties of the college and its setting, and adds, "we who are about to die,/ Salute you." The college is the same, but he and his companions are one with the vanished past; they are old and their lives are nearly over; the college, however old it may become, will always be the world of youth. The teachers he and his companions knew are all gone save one, to whom Longfellow pays tribute. He then tells of Dante finding his old teacher among the shades and of Dante's reverence for this man who had instructed him in his youth. "To-day," says Longfellow, "we make the poet's words our own." He then applies them to the teachers he and his companions knew: "Nor to the living only be they said,/ But to the other living called the dead,/ Whose dear, paternal images appear/ Not wrapped in gloom, but robed in sunshine here;/ Whose simple lives, complete and without flaw,/ Were part and parcel of great Nature's law." Finally he addresses another generation which still has most of life before it:

And ye who fill the places we once filled,
And follow in the furrows that we tilled,
Young men, whose generous hearts are beating high,
We who are old, and are about to die,
Salute you; . . .

       .   .   .

How beautiful is youth! how bright it gleams
With its illusions, aspirations, dreams!
Book of Beginnings, Story without End,
Each maid a heroine, and each man a friend!
Aladdin's Lamp, and Fortunatus' Purse,
That holds the treasures of the universe!
All possibilities are in its hands,
No danger daunts it, and no foe withstands;
In its sublime audacity of faith,
"Be thou removed!" it to the mountain saith,
And with ambitious feet, secure and proud,
Ascends the ladder leaning on the cloud!

. . .

Let him not boast who puts his armor on
As he who puts it off, the battle done.
Study yourselves; and most of all note well
Wherein kind Nature meant you to excel.
Not every blossom ripens into fruit; . . .

Let joy be unconfined

Source: CHILDE HAROLD'S PILGRIMAGE (Canto III, stanza 22)
Author: George Gordon, Lord Byron (1788–1824)
First published: 1816 (Canto III)
Type of work: Narrative poem

Context: Though the first two cantos of *Childe Harold's Pilgrimage* brought Byron his great fame when published in 1812, it was the third canto, which did not appear until 1816, that is universally considered the finest part of the poem. It begins with words for his daughter Ada, not seen since he angrily left his wife fifteen months after their marriage. Then he ponders the effect of time on his hero who, too proud to be dominated by others, has sought independence in travel. In the course of his wanderings, Harold reaches the battlefield of Waterloo, "the grave of France," where in June, 1815, Wellington ended the power of Napoleon I. Thackeray, too, incorporated the battle into his *Vanity Fair,* but Byron gives it a different twist. He sees the struggle as the effort of enemies of liberty to tear to pieces the eagle of freedom. Though it resulted in the fall of one despot, it gave increased power to many rulers. Napoleon was a composite of mighty ambitions, as well as petty ones, but they were so extreme that they caused the overthrow of a great man. Stanza 21 begins on the eve of the battle, with a well-known line: "There was a sound of revelry by night." It came from the Duchess of Richmond's ball, on the night of the 15th of June. Byron describes the "fair women and brave men" dancing in Brussels, Belgium's capital. Suddenly they hear a cannon shot, "a deep sound strikes like a rising knell." Byron's description of the heedlessness of the gay dancers in the great ballroom and the sudden shock

597

of their realization of the approaching   battle, fills Stanza 22.

> Did ye not hear it?—No; 't was but the wind.
> Or the car rattling o'er the stony street;
> On with the dance! **let joy be unconfined;**
> No sleep till morn, when Youth and Pleasure meet
> To chase the glowing Hours with flying feet—
> But hark!—that heavy sound breaks in once more,
> As if the clouds its echo would repeat;
> And nearer, clearer, deadlier than before!
> Arm! Arm! it is—it is—the cannon's opening roar!

Let them hate, so that they fear

Source: PHILIPPICS (I, 14)
Author: Marcus Tullius Cicero (106–43 B.C.)
First transcribed: 44–43 B.C.
Type of work: Oration

Context: Julius Caesar was assassinated on March 15th, 44 B.C. Three days later the Roman Senate ratified a number of his acts, as presented by Mark Antony, in the interest of public peace and safety. In June of the same year Antony summoned the Senate to the Temple of Concord, where they were held under armed guard, and forced them to ratify a number of apparently fictitious acts of Caesar. Cicero, discouraged by the train of events, left Rome for Greece. He abandoned his trip, however, and returned to Rome on August 31st. The next day, September 1st, Mark Antony attacked Cicero with a speech before the Senate, decrying Cicero's absence. The following day, Cicero went to the Senate to make his reply, which was not only a defense of his own conduct, but an attack on Mark Antony. In this speech, his first *Philippic,* Cicero first tells why he left and why he returned to Rome; he proceeds to protest the honors paid to Julius Caesar's memory, as being impious; he then says he agrees to the ratification of Caesar's acts, but states that mere promises and memoranda are not acts. Most of all, Cicero complains that certain acts of Caesar should not have been ratified because they abrogate positive laws. He then makes an appeal, which is also an attack on Mark Antony and Dolabella, for them to seek real glory, not mere domination of their fellow Romans. In so doing, Cicero uses a line from an old play, Accius' *Atreus,* which is no longer extant; the line, the quotation above, reads in Latin "Oderint, dum metuant."

> What I more fear is this—that, blind to glory's true path, you
> may think it glorious to possess in your single self more power
> than all, and to be feared by your fellow-citizens. If you think so,
> you are totally blind to the true way of glory. To be a citizen dear
> to all, to deserve well of the State, to be praised, courted, loved, is

glorious; but to be feared and an object of hatred is invidious, detestable, a proof of weakness and decay. We see this even in the play: the very man who said **"Let them hate, so that they fear,"** found that it was fatal. Would, Marcus Antonius, you had remembered your grandfather! though of him you have heard much from me, and that very often. Do you think that he would have wished to earn immortality by being feared for his ability to keep an armed guard? To him life, to him prosperous fortune, was equality in liberty with the rest, the first place in honour.

Let there be light

Source: GENESIS 1:3
Author: Unknown
First transcribed: c.1000–300 B.C.
Type of work: Religious history and law

Context: The Book of Genesis, fir y land was created and, book of the Old Testament, gives tl e vegetation and animal Hebrews' version of the creation ssage is one of the most the universe. It describes how Go n the Bible historically, created both heavens and earth ews and Christians, until though the earth was at first withou ent times, believed in the form. It was also without light, bu not as a legend, but as God's Spirit moved upon the waters account of how there and then He created light, dividing he origin of the universe darkness from light, thus creating nkind finds itself. The night and day. The first chapter of esis, one of the books Genesis goes on to describe how the ntateuch, is the first of waters of the firmament were divided of Moses. into the heavens and earth, and then

In the beginning God created th arth.
And the earth was without for darkness was upon the face of the deep. And the .... God moved upon the face of the waters.
And God said, **Let there be light:** and there was light.
And God saw the light, that it was good: and God divided the light from the darkness.
And God called the light Day, and the darkness he called Night. And the evening and the morning were the first day.

Let us be moral. Let us contemplate existence

Source: MARTIN CHUZZLEWIT (Chapter 9)
Author: Charles Dickens (1812–1870)
First published: 1843–1844
Type of work: Novel

Context: The Pecksniff family removes to London, where they put up at the boarding house of Mrs. Todgers. After a highly patronizing visit to Tom Pinch's sister, Ruth, by the Pecksniffs, plans are formed at Todgers' to have the Pecksniff family dine with the resident commercial gentlemen on Sunday afternoon. The dinner is a great success, with speeches, songs, toasts, and a great deal of other drinking. After dinner the ladies retire, and the gentlemen continue drinking until it is time to rejoin them. During the ensuing jollity, Mr. Pecksniff, who contends that he has a mysterious chronic condition, collapses into the fireplace. He is dragged out and put to bed; when he calls for one last drink a young gentleman suggests water, the idea of which arouses Mr. Pecksniff's ire. As the guests leave, Mr. Pecksniff appears at the head of the stairs in a shaky condition and addresses the company. The "voice of the sluggard" is a quotation from Isaac Watts, later parodied by Lewis Carroll.

"My friends," cried Mr. Pecksniff, looking over the banisters, "let us improve our minds by mutual inquiry and discussion. **Let us be moral. Let us contemplate existence.** Where is Jinkins?"

"Here," cried that gentleman. "Go to bed again!"

"To bed!" said Mr. Pecksniff. "Bed! 'Tis the voice of the sluggard; I hear him complain; you have woke me too soon; I must slumber again. If any young orphan will repeat the remainder of that simple piece from Dr. Watts's collection, an eligible opportunity now offers."

Nobody volunteered.

"This is very soothing," said Mr. Pecksniff, after a pause. "Extremely so. Cool and refreshing; particularly to the legs! The legs of the human subject, my friends, are a beautiful production. Compare them with wooden legs, and observe the difference between the anatomy of nature and the anatomy of art. Do you know," said Mr. Pecksniff, leaning over the banisters, with an odd recollection of his familiar manner among new pupils at home, "that I should very much like to see Mrs. Todgers' notion of a wooden leg, if perfectly agreeable to herself."

Let us hob-and-nob with Death

Source: THE VISION OF SIN (Line 74)
Author: Alfred, Lord Tennyson (1809–1892)
First published: 1842
Type of work: Allegorical poem

Context: In this dream-vision, Tennyson, who was greatly concerned with the doctrine of art-for-art's-sake, shows that the poet interested only in immorality and thus turning from the true calling of the soul is consumed by his own desire. The poem is presented in two parts and a cryptic summary. The young poet rides into a drunken orgy in a palace where the sensual music finally becomes so frenzied that his ability to sing is killed. Then the vision shifts to a senile debauch in a ruined tavern where self-inflicted misery leads to the desire to die. Both selfish pathways end in emotional frenzy, not happiness or peace. At the end of the poem Tennyson insinuates that the only way to true art and thus to genuine joy is through God; however, this way is often obscure because the voice of God cannot always be clearly understood. The quotation comes from the tavern scene where the old man sings of his search for sensation and his disillusionment.

> Slip-shod waiter, lank and sour,
>   At the Dragon on the heath!
> Let us have a quiet hour,
>   **Let us hob-and-nob with Death.**
>
> I am old, but let me drink;
>   Bring me spices, bring me wine;
> I remember, when I think,
>   That my youth was half divine.

Let us reason together

Source: ISAIAH 1:18
Author: Isaiah
First transcribed: c.800–200 B.C.
Type of work: Religious prophecy and exhortation

Context: Isaiah lived in times that were tragic for Israel; and though he had no difficulty in seeing that his country was about to be overrun, he was powerless to save it. Israel had split into two nations after Solomon's reign, Israel and Judah. These and the other small nations of western Asia were no match for any really strong aggressor that might arise, and they had descended to intriguing and fighting among themselves. Meanwhile Assyria was growing steadily in strength and ambition. Israel and

Judah were by this time wealthy countries and tempting prizes, and the people had become indolent and corrupt. The leaders of both countries were unable to see any danger in the Assyrians. When the kings of Israel and of the Aramaeans conspired to plunder Judah, the Judean king called on the Assyrians for help. Invasion followed immediately and as a result both Israel and Judah became Assyrian satellites, doomed to pay heavy tribute thereafter. Assyria had of course been ready for some time to extend its sphere of influence, and its leaders were probably both astonished and delighted when they were given an invitation to attack. Isaiah had seen already the evil that a few greedy and blundering rulers were inviting; now he undoubtedly foresaw that this result was only the beginning of a long and bitter oppression. In terms of reproach that betray his exasperation and his sorrow, Isaiah points out the ruin which all this madness has brought about. He tells his people this is just punishment for allowing themselves to become corrupt and for turning away from God. Now their country is desolate and their cities burnt, and their land is devoured by strangers. "Hear the word of the Lord, ye rulers of Sodom," says Isaiah with bitter sarcasm; "give ear unto the law of our God, ye people of Gomorrah." Then he quotes God's willingness to forgive if they will repent:

To what purpose is the multitude of your sacrifices unto me? saith the LORD: I am full of the burnt offerings of rams, and the fat of fed beasts; and I delight not in the blood of bullocks, or of lambs, or of he goats.

When ye come to appear before me, who hath required this at your hand, to tread my courts?

Bring no more vain oblations; incense is an abomination unto me; the new moons and sabbaths, the calling of assemblies, I cannot away with; it is iniquity, even the solemn meeting.

Your new moons and your appointed feasts my soul hateth: they are a trouble unto me; I am weary to bear them.

And when ye spread forth your hands, I will hide mine eyes from you: yea, when ye make many prayers, I will not hear: your hands are full of blood.

Wash you, make you clean; put away the evil of your doings from before mine eyes; cease to do evil;

Learn to do well; seek judgment, relieve the oppressed, judge the fatherless, plead for the widow.

Come now, and **let us reason together,** saith the LORD: though your sins be as scarlet, they shall be as white as snow; though they be red like crimson, they shall be as wool.

If ye be willing and obedient, ye shall eat the good of the land: . . .

Let's have one other gaudy night

Source: ANTONY AND CLEOPATRA (Act III, sc. xiii, l. 184)
Author: William Shakespeare (1564–1616)
First published: 1623
Type of work: Dramatic tragedy

Context: Mark Antony, co-ruler of the Roman Empire, falls in love with Cleopatra, Queen of Egypt. Through a series of circumstances he ends his friendship with Octavius, his fellow-ruler, and the opposing forces of Octavius and Antony meet at the Battle of Actium, in which Antony is defeated. He is defeated because, at a crucial point in the sea-battle, Cleopatra and her fleet desert him. Antony, who can think only of Cleopatra, leaves the fighting to follow her, thus losing the battle, the empire, and his honor. The lovers meet at Alexandria, some time after the battle, in Cleopatra's palace. At this meeting Antony tells Cleopatra that he knows his whole cause is lost; he says, "Alack, our terrene moon/ Is now eclipsed, and it portends alone/ The fall of Antony." Reassured by Cleopatra that she still loves him, Antony recalls his courage, and resolves to try once more, with his land forces, to seek the defeat of Octavius, after a celebration. Cleopatra, in her reply to him, reveals the selfishness that is part and parcel of her nature. She thinks and speaks, not of Antony and his future, but of the fact that the present day is her birthday. The quotation supplied the title of a famous mystery story by Dorothy Sayers.

ANTONY
I will be treble-sinewed, hearted, breathed,
And fight maliciously; for when mine hours
Were nice and lucky, men did ransom lives
Of me for jests. But now I'll set my teeth,
And send to darkness all that stop me. Come,
Let's have one other gaudy night. Call to me
All my sad captains, fill our bowls once more.
Let's mock the midnight bell.

CLEOPATRA
    It is my birthday.
I had thought t'have held it poor. But since my lord
Is Antony again, I will be Cleopatra.

ANTONY
We will yet do well.

Letting I dare not wait upon I would

Source: MACBETH (Act I, sc. vii, l. 44)
Author: William Shakespeare (1564–1616)
First published: 1623
Type of work: Dramatic tragedy

Context: Macbeth, destined to become King of Scotland according to the prophecy of three witches, wavers in his determination to usurp the throne by murdering King Duncan, his liege, his cousin, and his guest for the night. Lady Macbeth chides her husband for his cowardice, comparing him to the cat, in an adage of Heywood, which would like to eat fish, but does not want to get his feet wet.

MACBETH

We will proceed no further in this business.
He hath honoured me of late, and I have bought
Golden opinions from all sorts of people,
Which would be worn now in their newest gloss,
Not cast aside so soon.

      · · ·

LADY MACBETH

    . . . Wouldst thou have that
Which thou esteem'st the ornament of life,
And live a coward in thine own esteem,
Letting I dare not wait upon I would,
Like the poor cat i' th' adage?

Letting the rank tongue blossom into speech

Source: CALIBAN UPON SETEBOS (Line 23)
Author: Robert Browning (1812–1889)
First published: 1864
Type of work: Dramatic monologue

Context: Caliban—a subhuman monster, half man, half beast—is the unwilling servant of the magician Prospero and his daughter, Miranda. (Shakespeare: *The Tempest*) We hear Caliban speaking literally and morally from the bottom of a swamp as he muses on the nature of Setebos, the god of his witch-mother, Sycorax. He identifies Setebos with the aching unpleasantness of cold and therefore believes that it is safer to talk about him in the summer's warmth and safety. The key to Caliban's interpretation is found in the motto that prefixes the poem: "Thou thoughtest that I was altogether such an one as thyself." Thus Caliban attempts to deduce the character of God from the evidence he sees in nature around

604

him and creates a god made in his own image. Caliban believes that Setebos made the world out of spite, envy, listlessness, or sport. Man can only hope that Setebos will tire of this world and ignore it or that Setebos will evolve into a more beneficent god. The opening lines of the poem describe the physical setting and begin Caliban's philosophical musings:

> He looks out o'er yon sea. . . .
>
>   .   .   .
>
> And talks to his own self, howe'er he please,
> Touching that other, whom his dam called God.
> Because to talk about Him, vexes—ha,
> Could He but know! and time to vex is now,
> When talk is safer than in winter time.
> Moreover Prospero and Miranda sleep
> In confidence he drudges at their task;
> And it is good to cheat the pair, and gibe,
> **Letting the rank tongue blossom into speech.**
>
> Setebos, Setebos, Setebos!
> 'Thinketh He dwelleth i' the cold o' the moon.

Liberty consists in doing what one desires

Source: ON LIBERTY (Chapter 5, "Applications")
Author: John Stuart Mill (1806–1873)
First published: 1859
Type of work: Philosophical essay

Context: John Stuart Mill bases the fifth chapter of his essay on liberty on two maxims: the first is that the individual is not accountable to society for those of his actions which concern only himself, and the second is that the individual is accountable to society for those actions which are prejudicial to others, indeed may for those actions be subjected to legal or social punishments. Mill applies these maxims to the concept of free trade, pointing out that restrictions on trade at least endanger, if not destroy, the liberty of the buyer. Any such infringement, or its danger, seems to Mill objectionable. The sale of poisons, he suggests, is an example of how the limits of police powers and the limits of liberty may be open to question. In his discussion he states that while it is the function of government to prevent crime, this preventive action is liable to abuse by officials. He goes on to say that it is a function of public authority to prevent accidents, and it is here that his definition of liberty occurs:

> . . . it is a proper office of public authority to guard against accidents. If either a public officer or any one else saw a person at-

605

tempting to cross a bridge which had been ascertained to be unsafe, and there were no time to warn him of his danger, they might seize him and turn him back without any real infringement of his liberty; for **liberty consists in doing what one desires,** and he does not desire to fall into the river. Nevertheless, when there is not a certainty, but only a danger of mischief, no one but the person himself can judge of the sufficiency of the motive which may prompt him to incur the risk; in this case, therefore, (unless he is a child, or delirious, or in some state of excitement or absorption incompatible with the full use of the reflecting faculty,) he ought, I conceive, to be only warned of the danger; not forcibly prevented from exposing himself to it. . . .

Liberty must be limited in order to be possessed

Source: LETTER TO THE SHERIFFS OF BRISTOL
Author: Edmund Burke (1729–1797)
First published: 1777
Type of work: Political treatise

Context: Edmund Burke wrote to the sheriffs of Bristol, as their representative in the House of Commons, to relate to them some recent acts of the British Parliament and his reasons for not supporting those acts. Burke was a conservative, but he was also a man who thought that human beings come before abstract principles. He earnestly believed that the British government was, for reasons which could not be defended, mistreating the American colonists. He points out in this letter that the colonists want a free government according to their definition. Burke states, in discussing civil freedom, that liberty "is a blessing and a benefit, not an abstract speculation." He goes on to give his opinion that liberty, like all else in life, is unlike a proposition in geometry or metaphysics; that in life we find not simply right and wrong, but many degrees and shades of events. He continues to comment specifically on the nature of liberty and how it can be enjoyed:

. . . The *extreme* of liberty (which is its abstract perfection, but its real fault) obtains nowhere, nor ought to obtain anywhere. Because extremes, as we all know, in every point which relates either to our duties or satisfactions in life are destructive both to virtue and enjoyment. **Liberty, too, must be limited in order to be possessed.** The degree of restraint it is impossible in any case to settle precisely. But it ought to be the constant aim of every wise public council to find out by cautious experiments and rational cool endeavours with how little, not how much, of this restraint the community can subsist. For liberty is a good to be improved, and not an evil to be lessened. It is not only a private blessing of the first order, but the vital spring and energy of the state itself, which has just so much life and vigour as there is liberty in it. . . .

606

Liberty passes into the harshest and bitterest form of slavery

Source: THE REPUBLIC (Book VIII, 569, as translated by Benjamin Jowett)
Author: Plato (427–347 B.C.)
First transcribed: Fourth century B.C.
Type of work: Political philosophy

Context: Plato, Greek philosopher, a disciple of Socrates and teacher of Aristotle, wrote in the form of dialogues in which Socrates through interrogation leads others to perceive the truth. Probably his greatest work, *The Republic* describes the workings of an imaginary ideal state. This first Utopia was based on justice and a division of labor whereby each class in society happily performed the functions and duties for which it was best suited. Under such a system the philosopher ruled, the soldier fought, the worker tended the field—and all enjoyed the fruits of their common labor. Plato's proposal of communism was not based on the assumption that equality *per se* was the highest good, but that only this form of government could insulate man from the temptations and distractions which more extensive public power inevitably generates. Thus, in Book VIII, Socrates, Glaucon, and Adeimantus consider the various features of timocracy, oligarchy, democracy, and tyranny or despotism. In a democracy three classes emerge: the drones or spendthrifts, the orderly or wealthy, and the workers. The desire of the worker to gain the wealth and status of the orderly leads him to raise a protector who, once he has tasted blood, is converted into a tyrant. As long as the tyrant is able to live off the spoils of his rebellion, he rules with tolerance; but, when necessary, he exploits the very parents (the people) who fostered him:

> By heaven, he said, then the parent will discover what a monster he has been fostering in his bosom; and, when he wants to drive him out, he will find that he is weak and his son strong. . . . Then he is a parricide, and a cruel guardian of an aged parent; and this is real tyranny, about which there can be no longer a mistake: as the saying is, the people who would escape the smoke which is the slavery of freemen, have fallen into the fire which is the tyranny of slaves. Thus **liberty,** getting out of all order and reason, **passes into the harshest and bitterest form of slavery.**

Liberty's a glorious feast!

Source: THE JOLLY BEGGARS (Line 299)
Author: Robert Burns (1759–1796)
First published: 1799
Type of work: Cantata

Context: Gossip did its best to obscure the facts of Burns' life. He was falsely described as a debauched drunkard, chiefly by enemies who fought his strong republicanism by slandering him as a man. There is truth in the accusation that he drank a great deal, but drink was a vice of his time, which he developed while being lionized by high society. *The Jolly Beggars,* devoted to the celebration of drinking, takes the form of a cantata, and was started about 1785. This zestful pagan work is at times serious, at times satirical. So little interest did the author have in it that he did not believe it worth publication. In 1793, his friend George Thomson, editor of a six-volume *Select Collection of Scottish Airs for the Voice* (1793–1811), who had heard it mentioned, wrote to Burns for a copy. Burns replied that he had forgotten it and doubted whether a copy existed. However, Thomson tracked it down and it was published in Glasgow in 1799, after Burns' death. It had its inception following a visit by Burns and his friend James Smith to the Change House of Poosie Nansie's in Mauchline, a favorite haunt of vagrants. The cantata begins with the description of the gang of loafers drinking in the tavern. Popular tunes of the day provided the music. One man nearest the fire is a soldier in a ragged red uniform, sitting with his sweetheart. He sings to her a stanza beginning: "I am a son of Mars," and boasting of fighting in Quebec, Cuba, and in Gibraltar where he lost his leg and arm. A Recitativo introduces his doxy, who comments on her love life and her final decision to love the "sodger laddie." Next a Merry Andrew tells of his experiences as a clown, and is followed by a "raucle carlin" (brave old woman), a traveling violinist, a tinker, and finally a poet. If, as the legend goes, this poem is based on an actual experience, the poet may represent Burns himself. Begged for a ballad, he sings stanzas for which the crowd provides the chorus. The tune used was *Jolly Mortals, fill your glasses.*

See! the smoking bowl before us,
   Mark our jovial, ragged ring;
Round and round take up the chorus,
   And in raptures let us sing:

CHORUS
A fig for those by law protected!
Liberty's a glorious feast!
Courts for cowards were erected,
   Churches built to please the priest!

What is title? what is treasure?
   What is reputation's care?
If we lead a life of pleasure,
   'Tis no matter, how or where.
     · · ·

Here's to budgets, bags, and wallets!
Here's to all the wandering train!

608

License they mean when they cry liberty

Source: SONNET XII ("On the Same," Line 11)
Author: John Milton (1608–1674)
First published: 1673
Type of work: Sonnet

Context: Milton, the great poet and Puritan pamphleteer, wrote four tracts in which he argued in favor of a rational attitude toward divorce and the admission of incompatibility as a basis for it. Although he was an important Puritan spokesman, Milton's views on divorce were widely misinterpreted, and on one occasion a Puritan clergyman denounced them in a sermon to Parliament. In this sonnet, concerned with the public reaction to his views, Milton protests that he only advocates the sanity and reasonableness of the classical virtues and that he has been grossly misunderstood, likening his detractors to those rustics of Greek mythology who jeered at the goddess Latona, refusing to allow her to drink from their fountain, and were turned into frogs for their rudeness. He says:

> I did but prompt the age to quit their cloggs
>> By the known rules of antient libertie,
>> When strait a barbarous noise environs me
>> Of Owles and Cuckoes, Asses, Apes and Doggs.
> As when those Hinds that were transform'd to Froggs
>> Raild at Latona's twin-born progenie
>> Which after held the Sun and Moon in fee.
>> But this is got by casting Pearl to Hoggs;
> That bawle for freedom in their senceless mood,
>> And still revolt when truth would set them free.
>> **Licence they mean when they cry libertie;**
> For who loves that, must first be wise and good;
>> But from that mark how far they roave we see
>> For all this wast of wealth, and loss of blood.

Lick the dust

Source: PSALMS 72:9
Author: Unknown
First transcribed: c. 400–200 B.C.
Type of work: Religious poetry

Context: Psalm 72 is a prayer for Solomon, composed in the early days of that monarch's reign. It is the last in a series of Psalms attributed to David, and in it the poet prays for an enlightened, peaceful, and prosperous reign. He begins by asking for righteousness and judgment on the part of the king, and for attention to the needs of the poor. The reign of Solomon, he believes, will usher in a period of great prosperity; nature will

609

flourish and the fields and mountains will be productive. Again he expresses the hope that this king will have compassion upon the poor and that he will protect his people. It has always been customary for poets to praise new rulers and at the same time to mention those standards which they hope the rulers will uphold: any new ruler is to some extent an unknown quantity. But in this case many of the poet's predictions are accurate, for under Solomon the children of Israel will at last become a nation demanding respect from the nations around it. This king, says the poet, will be a strong ruler, destructive to oppressors; there will be a long period of greatness; his coming will be as welcome as the rain. Rain in a parched land is the greatest of blessings. Solomon, says the poet, will rule the known world and his enemies will humble themselves before him; other nations will pay him tribute. Once again the poet expresses the hope that Solomon will show consideration for the poor, who will repay it by praying for him and giving him everlasting fame. The psalm ends with a moving declaration of faith and optimism.

> Give the king thy judgments, O God, and thy righteousness unto the king's son.
> He shall judge thy people with righteousness, and thy poor with judgment.
> The mountains shall bring peace to the people, and the little hills, by righteousness.
> He shall judge the poor of the people, he shall save the children of the needy, and shall break in pieces the oppressor.
> They shall fear thee as long as the sun and moon endure, throughout all generations.
> He shall come down like rain upon the mown grass: as showers that water the earth.
> In his days shall the righteous flourish; and abundance of peace so long as the moon endureth.
> He shall have dominion also from sea to sea, and from the river unto the ends of the earth.
> They that dwell in the wilderness shall bow before him; and his enemies shall **lick the dust.**
> The kings of Tarshish and of the isles shall bring presents: the kings of Sheba and Seba shall offer gifts.
> Yea, all kings shall fall down before him: all nations shall serve him.

The lie that flatters I abhor the most

Source: TABLE TALK (Line 88)
Author: William Cowper (1731–1800)
First published: 1782
Type of work: Essay in verse

Context: In publishing his first collection of poetry, Cowper decided to lead off with the poem "Table Talk," because "it will repel the ordinary reader less than any of the others." He realized that his purpose in writing, to obtain "a monitor's though not a poet's praise" would result in somewhat dull verse. Yet he wrote satires of admonition and sermons in verse, "with a hope to do good." Though "Table Talk" is a dialogue, there seems to be little attempt to differentiate between the two speakers, A and B, and considerable difficulty in discovering the various subjects of their discussion. As far as can be discerned, the main theme is the need of character and integrity in public servants. Beginning with the premise that only the glory built on unselfish principles is admirable, the two speakers agree in admiration of wars fought for justice. This opinion leads to a discussion of the qualities of an ideal king, and what results is obviously a portrait of George III, in which the poet insists that he is speaking sincerely with no purpose of flattery. "The patriotic tribe" uses the word in its eighteenth century political meaning, as Johnson did when saying: "Patriotism is the last refuge of a scoundrel." A patriot was one who upheld the nation, and was opposed to the king or the court. The following is the way B describes the qualities of King George III:

B. His life a lesson to the land he sways;
To touch the sword with conscientious awe,
Nor draw it but when duty bids him draw;
To sheath it in the peace-restoring close,
With joy beyond what victory bestows—
Blest country, when these kingly glories shine,
Blest England, if this happiness be thine!
A. Guard what you say: the patriotic tribe
Will sneer and charge you with a bribe. *B.* A bribe?
The worth of his three kingdoms I defy
To lure me to the baseness of a lie.
And of all lies (be that one poet's boast),
The lie that flatters I abhore the most.
Those arts be theirs who hate his gentle reign,
But he that loves him has no need to feign.

Life is an incurable disease

Source: PINDARIC ODES ("To Dr. Scarborough," Stanza VI)
Author: Abraham Cowley (1618–1677)
First published: 1656
Type of work: Pindaric ode

Context: Abraham Cowley was a precocious man: his first volume of poems was published when he was fifteen. He was given a good education and had received a Cambridge fellowship when he was dispossessed by the Puritan commissioners and left on his own resources. Following his roy-

611

alist friends to Oxford, he entered the service of the king. He then followed the dispossessed Charles II to France. Cowley, however, had the misfortune to be born into a violent era that he could not cope with; he was a mild and unenthusiastic man, and his nature often placed him in dangerous or ridiculous situations. He was assigned to various secret service activities for which he seems to have been utterly unqualified: Charles II suspected him of treason, and Cromwell put him in prison as a spy. He finally retired to a quiet life in the country, where he studied medicine and botany. At the same time he continued to write poetry and essays. He is again unfortunate in that his unfinished Biblical epic *Davideis* is a failure compared to the *Paradise Lost* of John Milton; and his lyrical poems, inspired by Donne, suffer by comparison with the latter's work. Not a true metaphysical poet, Cowley enjoys intricate metaphors and plays on words; he is sometimes quietly witty and exhibits a cheerful pessimism. In 1656 he published his fifteen *Pindaric Odes*. These established his reputation and exerted a considerable influence for a time. The form he developed retains rhyme but in many ways resembles free verse; it does not actually employ the structure of Pindar's work but is strongly reminiscent of it and is rather impressive. The form enjoyed great popularity for many years, especially for ceremonials and dedications. One of Cowley's "pseudo-Pindaric" odes, honoring Dr. Charles Scarborough, provides a memorable tribute. The closing portion is given below:

And this great race of learning thou hast run,
    Ere that of life be half yet done;
    Thou see'st thyself still fresh and strong,
    And like t' enjoy the conquests long.
The first fam'd aphorism thy great master spoke,
    Did he live now he would revoke,
    And better things of man report;
For thou dost make life long, and art but short.

Ah, learned friend! it grieves me, when I think
    That thou with all thy art must die,
    As certainly as I;
And all thy noble reparations sink
Into the sure-wrought mine of treacherous mortality.
Like Archimedes, honourably in vain,
Thou hold'st out towns that must at last be ta'en,
And thou thyself, their great defender, slain.
Let's e'en compound, and for the present live,
'Tis all the ready-money Fate can give;
    Unbend sometimes thy restless care,
    And let thy friends so happy be
    T' enjoy at once their health and thee:
Some hours, at least, to thine own pleasures spare:
Since the whole stock may soon exhausted be,

612

Bestow 't not all in charity.
Let Nature and let Art do what they please,
When all 's done, **life's an incurable disease.**

Life is too short for chess

Source: OUR BOYS (Act I)
Author: Henry James Byron (1834–1884)
First published: 1880
Type of work: Dramatic comedy

Context: Byron, an enormously prolific writer for the British theater, turned out innumerable comedies, farces, and burlesques. One chronological list of his works includes 136 titles. Probably the most popular was the three-act comedy, *Our Boys,* that opened in London on January 16th, 1875, and had an unequaled continuous run, according to the first printed edition, of 1,500 nights. With other works by Byron, it was reprinted among the 165 volumes of Lacy's *Acting Editions of Plays, Dramas, Extravaganzas, etc.* as No. 116 (1880), and by Samuel French in England and the United States. For Baker, in 1915, Frank E. Fowle edited "An Acting Copy, containing all the Gags and Stage Business employed by Professional Actors." Surprisingly, the comedy has few sympathetic characters. Sir Geoffrey Champney is father of washed-out Talbot with yellowish-red hair, for whom he dreams of a career in Parliament. Uncouth Perkyn Middlewick, a retired "butter man," with ridiculous language and a belief that money not only makes the mare go, but activates a whole stable, has a handsomer son, Charley. The two young men are bracketed by Sir Geoffrey as "Our Boys," As the comedy opens, the two fathers are await-ing the return of their sons from a European trip in which only Charley profited. There he meets the heiress Violet Melrose to whom he identifies himself as Mr. Morton. Her penniless cousin, Mary, traveling with her, is attracted by the unattractiveness of Talbot Champney. Sir Geoffrey can scarcely conceal his disapproval of the coarse Middlewick. His sister, Aunt Clarissa, has a kinder attitude, but she is thinking chiefly of the break in the monotony of the manor offered by Talbot's homecoming. Events disappoint her. Complaining that his father would not let him have his fling abroad, like Charley, he scorns an evening of backgammon or chess at home with his aunt. After his taste of life in Paris, he looks forward to the delights of London. Violet and her cousin appear. Violet is angry that Charles lied about his name, and is further disillusioned by a look at her possible father-in-law. To Sir Geoffrey's delight, Mr. Middlewick is no less scornful of "that rich stuck up gal," for Sir Geoffrey anticipates Violet's marriage to Talbot to provide funds for the young man's political career. The second act contains the scene where Sir Geoffrey invites Mr. Middlewick to a game of billiards. He trounces the inexperienced country merchant, whose skill runs to bowl-

613

ing. Middlewick threatens: "He's up to these grand games, but one of these days I'll *loore* him on to *skittles* and astonish him." In the final act, "Our Boys" have left their parents to live in poverty in the big city, but the plotting of Aunt Clarissa and the change of heart of the fathers achieve a happy ending for the young people. Part of the homecoming in Act I includes a scene between Clarissa and Talbot.

AUNT CLARISSA

Talbot, it is so delightful to have you back again. I shall now have such charming evenings with you at chess.

TALBOT

At what?

AUNT CLARISSA

Chess—the king of games.

TALBOT

Do you call that a game? Ha! ha! No, thanks; **life's too short for chess.**

AUNT CLARISSA

Well, well, we'll say backgammon.

TALBOT

I don't mind saying backgammon, but you don't catch me playing backgammon.

AUNT CLARISSA

Well, then, we must even continue our usual cosy evenings. I do my wool work whilst your father reads us the debates. That's our regular evening's program.

TALBOT (*aside*)

They must have had a rollicking time of it. The debates! a dozen columns of dullness filtered through father. Not for Talbot!

The life of man, solitary, poor, nasty, brutish, and short

Source: LEVIATHAN (Part I, chapter 13)
Author: Thomas Hobbes (1588–1679)
First published: 1651
Type of work: Philosophy

Context: When men are not kept in awe by a common power, says English philosopher Thomas Hobbes, a time of war exists for one of three common causes: competition, diffidence, or glory. Describing the conditions during a time of war, he continues:

Whatsoever therefore is consequent to a time of war, where every man is enemy to every man, the same is consequent to the time wherein men live without other security than what their own strength and their own invention shall furnish them withal. In such condition there is no place for industry, because the fruit thereof is uncertain: and consequently no culture of the earth; no navigation, nor use of the commodities that may be imported by sea; no commodious building; no instruments of moving and removing such things as require much force; no knowledge of the face of the earth; no account of time; no arts; no letters; no society; and which is worst of all, continual fear, and danger of violent death; and **the life of man, solitary, poor, nasty, brutish, and short.**

Life's but a walking shadow

Source: MACBETH (Act V, sc. v, l. 24)
Author: William Shakespeare (1564–1616)
First published: 1623
Type of work: Dramatic tragedy

Context: Macbeth, destined to become King of Scotland according to the prophecy he receives from three witches and urged on by his wife in his ambition to obtain the crown, murders King Duncan and seizes the throne. Insecure in his tenure of power, Macbeth commits additional murders. Lady Macbeth, strong in ambition at first, becomes weak from worry over the foul deeds committed by the pair and finally suffers a complete mental and physical collapse, and dies. Macbeth receives word of her death while he watches the advance of an English army commanded by Malcolm, son of the murdered King Duncan. In a well-known speech Macbeth comments on the brevity and futility of life as he sorrows for his dead queen:

MACBETH
• • •

To-morrow, and to-morrow, and to-morrow,
Creeps in this petty pace from day to day,
To the last syllable of recorded time;
And all our yesterdays have lighted fools
The way to a dusty death. Out, out, brief candle!
Life's but a walking shadow, a poor player,
That struts and frets his hour upon the stage,
And then is heard no more. It is a tale
Told by an idiot, full of sound and fury
Signifying nothing.

615

Light thickens, and the crow makes wing

Source: MACBETH (Act III, sc. ii, ll. 50–51)
Author: William Shakespeare (1564–1616)
First published: 1623
Type of work: Dramatic tragedy

Context: Macbeth, told by three witches that he shall become king, and driven by a wicked ambition, slays King Duncan and usurps the throne. One evil act leads to another as Macbeth plans the murder of Banquo and his son Fleance to foil the decree of the witches that the heirs of Banquo shall be kings. As evening approaches and the time draws near for his hired assassins to kill Banquo and Fleance, Macbeth notes the atmosphere of evil in the night, and says to Lady Macbeth:

MACBETH

. . .

  . . . **Light thickens, and the crow**
Makes wing to th' rooky wood.
Good things of day begin to droop and drowse,
Whiles night's black agents to their preys do rouse.
Thou marvel'st at my words; but hold thee still,
Things bad begun make strong themselves by ill.
So prithee go with me.

            [Exeunt.]

A light to lighten the Gentiles

Source: LUKE 2:32
Author: Unknown
First transcribed: c. 80–100
Type of work: Gospel

Context: Scholars are not agreed upon the authorship of this gospel. Though it is evident that Luke and Acts were both written by the same person, there is some doubt that he is actually the physician Luke, friend and companion of the Apostle Paul. Some have found internal evidence, in the form of terminology a medical man would have been likely to use, which lends support to the traditional attribution. In Chapter 1 the author comments upon the large number of people who are writing gospels, and makes it clear that he has been careful to obtain much of his own material from eyewitnesses and others who actually took part in the great drama of Christ's ministry. "Theophilus," to whom he dedicates this book, may have been a Roman official sympathetic to Christianity. Chapter 1 is largely introductory, covering those events which led up to the birth of Jesus. In Chapter 2 he gives what has become the most popular and familiar account of the Nativity, telling it with great tenderness and beauty. Luke's version is that which most frequently forms a part of the celebration of Christmas. When Jesus is eight days of age he is circumcised and is named according to instructions given Mary by the angel of the Lord. After Mary's days of purification according to the law are ended, Jesus is taken to Jerusalem that he may be presented to the Lord in the Temple, and that a sacrifice may be offered. This sacrifice is made according to holy law, and consists of a pair of turtle-doves or young pigeons. While Jesus and his parents are in the Temple, two persons who are inspired with prophecy enter and foretell something of the consolation that this child will bring to his people, and to the other nations of the world. The first of these is Simeon, an old man; the second is Anna, who confirms his words.

And behold, there was a man in Jerusalem, whose name was Simeon; and the same man was just and devout, waiting for the consolation of Israel: and the Holy Ghost was upon him.

And it was revealed unto him by the Holy Ghost, that he should not see death, before he had seen the Lord's Christ.

And he came by the Spirit into the temple: and when the parents brought in the child Jesus, to do for him after the custom of the law,

Then took he him up in his arms, and blessed God, and said,

Lord, now lettest thou thy servant depart in peace, according to thy word:

For mine eyes have seen thy salvation,

Which thou hast prepared before the face of all people;

A light to lighten the Gentiles, and the glory of thy people Israel.

And Joseph and his mother marvelled at those things which were spoken of him.

And Simeon blessed them. and said unto Mary his mother, Behold, this child is set for the fall and rising again of many in Israel; and for a sign which shall be spoken against;

(Yea, a sword shall pierce through thy own soul also,) that the thoughts of many hearts may be revealed.

A light wife doth make a heavy husband

Source: THE MERCHANT OF VENICE (Act V, sc. i, l. 130)
Author: William Shakespeare (1564–1616)
First published: 1600
Type of work: Dramatic comedy

Context: In the early action of the play Antonio, the merchant, borrows money from Shylock, the usurious Jew, in order to save his friend Bassanio, whose ships are long overdue and feared lost. Shylock, pretending a jest, persuades Antonio to pledge the pound of flesh nearest his heart as surety for the loan. Antonio's investments also seem to fail, and Shylock brings his claim to court in order to collect his pound of flesh. At the trial Antonio is saved by a brilliant young lawyer who is, unknown to the men, the girl both have wooed and Bassanio has won, Portia, in disguise. After the trial Portia hurries home, where she meets Lorenzo and Jessica and swears them to secrecy concerning her part in the trial. Bassanio, Antonio, and several of their friends follow close behind:

LORENZO
Your husband is at hand, I hear his trumpet.
We are no tell-tales madam, fear you not.

PORTIA
This night methinks is but the daylight sick;
It looks a little paler: 'tis a day,
Such as the day is when the sun is hid.
            Enter BASSANIO, ANTONIO, GRATIANO, *and* SERVANTS.

BASSANIO
We should hold day with the Antipodes,
If you would walk in absence of the sun.

PORTIA
Let me give light, but let me not be light;
For **a light wife doth make a heavy husband,**
And never be Bassanio so for me.
But God sort all. You're welcome home my lord.

BASSANIO
I thank you madam. Give welcome to my friend.

Like a great sea-mark standing every flaw

Source: CORIOLANUS (Act V, sc. iii, l. 74)
Author: William Shakespeare (1564–1616)
First published: 1623
Type of work: Dramatic tragedy

Context: Having been unjustly banished from Rome and his family, Coriolanus has joined forces with his sworn enemy, Aufidius, and the Volscian army. Under the guidance of Coriolanus, this army scores a number of successes and is soon standing before the gates of Rome. Coriolanus has revenge within his reach; Rome is powerless before him. He who was once Rome's savior is now ready to destroy her. The Senate sends an old friend to persuade Coriolanus to spare the city. Coriolanus refuses: "Wife, mother, child, I know not. My affairs/ Are servanted to others.

Though I owe/ My revenge properly, my remission lies/ In Volscian breasts." The Roman Senators, in a final effort to hold off the doom that threatens the city, send forth the mother, wife, and child, whom Coriolanus has sworn to "know not." Before his mother's logic and appeal, Coriolanus is faced with an impossible choice. If he denies his own flesh, he will destroy his good name for all history; if he spares Rome, he will probably be killed by the Volscians. Volumnia realizes full well what she is asking, and she begins her attack on her son by presenting him his child:

VOLUMNIA
This is a poor epitome of yours,
Which by th' interpretation of full time
May show like all yourself.

CORIOLANUS
The god of soldiers,
With the consent of supreme Jove, inform
Thy thoughts with nobleness, that thou mayst prove
To shame invulnerable, and stick i' th' wars
Like a great sea-mark standing every flaw,
And saving those that eye thee.

Like Niobe all tears

Source: HAMLET (Act I, sc. ii, l. 149)
Author: William Shakespeare (1564–1616)
First published: 1603
Type of work: Dramatic tragedy

Context: Hamlet, Prince of Denmark, bemoans his noble father's death, the usurpation of the throne by Claudius, his base uncle, and the hasty marriage of his mother, Queen Gertrude, to that same uncle. In his first soliloquy, he laments his mother's frailty and notes that although she wept at the funeral like Niobe whose fourteen children were slain by Apollo, she accepted Claudius in a marriage, which, in Hamlet's eyes, is an incestuous relationship.

HAMLET
. . . That it should come to this—
But two months dead, nay not so much, not two—
So excellent a King, that was to this
Hyperion to a satyr, so loving to my mother,
That he might not beteem the winds of heaven
Visit her face too roughly. Heaven and earth,
Must I remember? Why she would hang on him

619

As if increase of appetite had grown
By what it fed on, and yet within a month—
Let me not think on't—frailty, thy name is woman.
A little month or e'er those shoes were old
With which she followed my poor father's body,
Like Niobe all tears, why she, even she—
O God, a beast that wants discourse of reason
Would have mourned longer—married with my uncle,

· · ·

The lilies and languors of virtue

Source: DOLORES (Stanza 9)
Author: Algernon Charles Swinburne (1837–1909)
First published: 1866
Type of work: Lyric poem

Context: Written in praise of a prostitute, this poem shows the soul broken by suffering and passion, half-humorously playing with pleasures even as it fully recognizes its pain. The woman of the poem brings the speaker only sorrow, yet he is unwilling and unable to flee from her. As in many of Swinburne's poems, pleasure and pain, freedom and bondage, suffering and joy are strangely joined so that the soul must experience the full extreme of the one in order to enjoy the other. Dolores, "Our Lady of the Seven Sorrows," is a fitting symbol for the idol of such a philosophy. As a prostitute she is the goddess of self-inflicted pain, a deity who makes men willingly exchange the comforts of virtue for the misery of vice. As a woman she suffers from her own sterile life and makes others suffer by desiring her; she turns virtue into vice and now makes vice into an endless state of suffering for whoever desires her because she forces men to love her but cannot return their love.

Could you hurt me, sweet lips, though I hurt you?
    Men touch them, and change in a trice
The lilies and languors of virtue
    For the raptures and roses of vice;
Those lie where thy foot on the floor is,
    These crown and caress thee and chain,
O splendid and sterile Dolores,
    Our Lady of Pain.

Lilies that fester smell far worse than weeds

Source: SONNET 94 (Line 14)
Author: William Shakespeare (1564–1616)
First published: 1609
Type of work: Sonnet

620

Context: Those people who have within themselves potential greatness or goodness, says the poet, yet who do not excel, are far worse than those with less promise. The final six lines of the sonnet make clear the superiority of a simple, untainted flower or of a simple, untainted person to an infected blossom or a great person, soured by vile deeds, or as the poet states in the closing couplet, decayed lilies smell worse than decayed weeds:

> They that have power to hurt, and will do none,
> That do not do the thing they most do show,
> Who moving others, are themselves as stone,
> Unmoved, cold, and to temptation slow;
> They rightly do inherit heaven's graces,
> And husband nature's riches from expense;
> They are the lords and owners of their faces,
> Others but stewards of their excellence.
> The summer's flower is to the summer sweet,
> Though to itself it only live and die;
> But if that flower with base infection meet,
> The basest weed outbraves his dignity.
> > For sweetest things turn sourest by their deeds;
> > **Lilies that fester smell far worse than weeds.**

A lion among ladies

Source: A MIDSUMMER NIGHT'S DREAM (Act III, sc. i, ll. 31–32)
Author: William Shakespeare (1564–1616)
First published: 1600
Type of work: Dramatic comedy

Context: The celebration of the marriage of Theseus, Duke of Athens, and Hippolyta, fair captive Queen of the Amazons, will take place at the rise of the new moon. Some common craftsmen plan to produce a play based on the story of Pyramus and Thisbe. During a rehearsal fears are voiced that the ladies in the audience will be frightened at the death of Pyramus by his own sword and at the appearance of a lion. The dialogue among the craftsmen proceeds thus:

SNOUT
Will not the ladies be afeard of the lion?

STARVELING
I fear it, I promise you.

BOTTOM
Masters, you ought to consider with yourselves—to bring in, God shield us, **a lion among ladies** is a most dreadful thing. For there is

621

not a more fearful wild-fowl than your lion living; and we ought
to look to't.

SNOUT
Therefore another prologue must tell he is not a lion.

Lips say, "God be pitiful," who never said, "God be praised"

Source: THE CRY OF THE HUMAN (Lines 7–8)
Author: Elizabeth Barrett Browning (1806–1861)
First published: 1844
Type of work: Humanitarian poem

Context: Handicapped by semi-paralysis and confined between 1821 and 1845 in a darkened room, Mrs. Browning was not a self-centered woman; her concern with the suffering of the lower class and with people anywhere in slavery or political oppression enabled her to rise above her own misfortunes to become one of the great poets of social protest. Hearing of children who must go to bed without food and of the increasing wealth of the already prosperous middle class, she attempted to awaken the consciences of her own class, not by advocating particular reforms but by clearly showing the horrible conditions of life that were present in London itself. In this poem she shows how most people have the tenderness to pity the starving children but are blinded by greed until a loved one dies; then the soul discovers the plight of the multitudes and can learn to pray, thus overcoming selfishness. While such a remedy is, perhaps, far-fetched, the poem does clearly portray the need to overcome greed in order to save the poor and also to improve the callous behavior of the thoughtless middle class.

> "There is no God," the foolish saith,
>   But none, "There is no sorrow;"
> And nature oft the cry of faith,
>   In bitter need will borrow:
> Eyes which the preacher could not school,
>   By wayside graves are raised;
> And **lips say, "God be pitiful,"**
>   **Who ne'er said, "God be praised."**
>   Be pitiful, O God.

The little dogs and all, Tray, Blanch, and Sweetheart

Source: KING LEAR (Act III, sc. vi, ll. 65–66)
Author: William Shakespeare (1564–1616)
First published: 1608
Type of work: Dramatic tragedy

622

Context: The aged King Lear, who has foolishly divided his kingdom between Goneril and Regan, his two unloving daughters, and has disinherited Cordelia, the loving and youngest, but blunt, daughter, finds himself cast out by his heirs. Furious, he rushes into the stormy night. His wits gone, Lear is removed by his old friends Gloucester and Kent, Edgar, disguised as a madman, and his faithful fool, to the shelter of a farmhouse, where in a mock trial he charges his daughters.

LEAR

Arraign her first; 'tis Goneril. I here take my oath
before this honourable assembly, she kicked the
poor King her father.

• • •

And here's another whose warped looks proclaim
What store her heart is made on. Stop her there!
Arms, arms, sword, fire! Corruption in the place!
False justicer, why hast thou let her 'scape?

• • •

KENT

O pity! Sir, where is the patience now
That you so oft have boasted to retain?

• • •

LEAR

The little dogs and all,
Tray, Blanch, and Sweetheart, see, they bark at me.

The little foxes, that spoil the vines

Source: THE SONG OF SOLOMON 2:15
Author: Unknown
First transcribed: c.300–200 B.C.
Type of work: Lyric poetry

Context: The *Song of Songs* has been interpreted in many ways over the centuries. Read literally, it is a dialogue of endearments between a young girl and her lover; she is a keeper of the vineyards, he a shepherd. The vivid and striking imagery and great literary power of the work, combined with its freedom of expression, make it one of the great love poems of the ages. It was at one time thought by Jewish scholars to be an allegory symbolizing the love between the Lord and his chosen people, and probably became a part of Scripture for this reason. This view was accepted by some of the early Christian scholars; others thought it an allegory of Christ and His church. The chapter headings of the Authorized King James Version represent the latter opinion. The modern tendency among scholars is to accept the literal interpretation, and to consider the text a single love lyric, or more probably a collection of love songs edited and unified by its original compiler. In chapter 2, the girl recalls a time when her lover came to her house in the evening, spoke through the lattice to her, and begged her to go with him. The young man's ardor paints a vivid, idyllic picture of the springtime and its beauty. When she remains silent he adds another inducement: this is the season when foxes nibble at the young grapevines. By referring to this annual problem of the vineyards he is implying that she should come out and guard them; he of course will assist her. It is easy to imagine the girl smiling at this transparent approach; nonetheless she pledges herself to him, though not aloud. When she finally speaks to her suitor, it is only to tell that disappointed youth she will be happy to see him in the morning.

My beloved is like a roe or a young hart: behold, he standeth behind our wall, he looketh forth at the windows, shewing himself through the lattice.

My beloved spake, and said unto me, Rise up, my love, my fair one, and come away.

For, lo, the winter is past, the rain is over and gone;

The flowers appear on the earth; the time of the singing of birds is come, and the voice of the turtle is heard in our land;

The fig tree putteth forth her green figs, and the vines with the tender grape give a good smell. Arise, my love, my fair one, and come away.

O my dove, that art in the clefts of the rock, in the secret places of the stairs, let me see thy countenance, let me hear thy voice; for sweet is thy voice, and thy countenance is comely.

Take us the foxes, **the little foxes, that spoil the vines:** for our vines have tender grapes.

My beloved is mine, and I am his: he feedeth among the lilies.

Until the day break, and the shadows flee away, turn, my beloved, and be thou like a roe or a young hart upon the mountains of Bether.

A little more than kin, and less than kind

Source: HAMLET (Act I, sc. ii, l. 65)
Author: William Shakespeare (1564–1616)
First published: 1603
Type of work: Dramatic tragedy

Context: Claudius, brother to King Hamlet, has secretly murdered his brother, usurped the throne from its rightful owner, Hamlet, Prince of Denmark, and married immediately his former sister-in-law, Queen Gertrude. Young Hamlet, unaware of the fact that Claudius has killed the noble king, but feeling deeply the difference between the two kings, and the hasty marriage of his mother to his uncle, broods about the court. On his first appearance in the play, Claudius acts the role of the good king by attending to the affairs of state and to the personal affairs of Laertes, the son of his Lord Chamberlain. Then he turns to Hamlet and attempts to show fatherly concern for the unhappy prince, who cannot accept the low Claudius as re-placing his own noble father. He replies to the words of Claudius, in an aside, in words that may be paraphrased as "I am more closely related to you than cousin (step-son), but little like you in nature." However, he may mean in the second part of the phrase that he cannot be kind to his uncle, that he hates the usurper.

CLAUDIUS
Take thy fair hour Laertes, time be thine,
And thy best graces spend it at thy will.
But now, my cousin Hamlet, and my son.

HAMLET [*aside*]
A little more than kin, and less than kind.

A little rebellion, now and then, is a good thing

Source: LETTER TO JAMES MADISON (January 30, 1787)
Author: Thomas Jefferson (1743–1826)
First published: 1829
Type of work: Personal letter

Context: When the United States had won its independence from Great Britain and hostilities had ceased in 1781, the new nation found it necessary to establish firm connections with other countries in regard to trade and commerce. The negotiation of such matters was of great importance to the survival of this country. In 1784 Jefferson was sent to France to join John Adams and Benjamin Franklin in these efforts, succeeding Franklin in 1785 as minister plenipotentiary to the French court. Before he returned to America in 1789 he had succeeded in persuading the French government to remove a number of unjust restrictions on American commerce. These restrictions had imposed hardships on the eastern states, and the people had grown rebellious. In a letter to James Madison written January 30, 1787 Jefferson analyzes the situation with his usual insight, outlines the causes of the unrest, and expresses a hope that the governments of those states will not be too hard on the offenders. "A consciousness of those in power that their administration of the public affairs has been honest," he cautions, "may, perhaps, produce too great a degree of indignation; and those characters, wherein fear predominates over hope, may apprehend too much from these instances of irregularity. They may conclude too hastily, that nature has formed man insusceptible of any other government than that of force, a conclusion not founded in truth nor experience." Jefferson then describes what he considers the three basic forms of government and their characteristics:

> . . . Societies exist under three forms, sufficiently distinguishable. 1. Without government, as among our Indians. 2. Under governments, wherein the will of every one has a just influence; as is the case of England, in a slight degree, and in our States, in a great one. 3. Under governments of force; as is the case in all other monarchies, and in most of the other republics. To have an idea of the curse of existence under these last, they must be seen. It is a government of wolves over sheep. It is a problem, not clear in my mind, that the first condition is not the best. But I believe it to be inconsistent with any great degree of population. The second state has a great deal of good in it. The mass of mankind under that, enjoys a precious degree of liberty and happiness. It has its evils, too; the principal of which is the turbulence to which it is subject. But weigh this against the oppressions of monarchy, and it becomes nothing. *Malo periculosam libertatem quam quietam servitutem.* Even this evil is productive of good. It prevents the degeneracy of government, and nourishes a general attention to the public affairs. I hold it, that **a little rebellion, now and then, is a good thing,** and as necessary in the political world as storms in the physical.

A little water clears us of this deed

Source: MACBETH (Act II, sc. ii, l. 67)
Author: William Shakespeare (1564–1616)
First published: 1623
Type of work: Dramatic tragedy

Context: Macbeth has just murdered Duncan, the King of Scotland. He is in a state of shock, and he has not carried out the plan he and Lady Macbeth had made to put the knife in the hands of the drugged and drunken grooms who guarded the king. Lady Macbeth, who could not kill Duncan herself because he reminded her of her father, goes to complete the plan. She is now the strong one, for her husband can no longer even think of what he has done, much less look at it again. She bolsters herself with brave talk and leaves to set the scene. Meanwhile Macbeth stares at his bloody hands in horror, believing that they can never be cleansed. Lady Macbeth, however, whose hands are now as bloody, berates him as a coward and assures him that merely washing their hands will clear them of murder. A knocking at the gates halts their hurried conversation and sends them to their rooms to pretend sleep.

MACBETH
. . .
Will all great Neptune's ocean wash this blood

626

Clean from my hand? No. This my hand will rather
The multitudinous seas incarnadine,
Making the green one red.

LADY MACBETH
My hands are of your colour; but I shame
To wear a heart so white. [*Knock.*] I hear a knocking
At the south entry. Retire we to our chamber.
A little water clears us of this deed.

.   .   .

Live, and move, and have our being

Source: ACTS 17:28
Author: Unknown (traditionally Luke)
First transcribed: 60–150 (probably c.80–90)
Type of work: Religious history and tradition

Context: The Acts of the Apostles is the only existing account of the beginnings of the Christian Church. It is evident that the writer of Acts and the author of Luke were one and the same, but whether he was actually Luke the physician is not certain. It is likely that if Luke did not write these he was responsible for portions of them. Acts is a biographical and historical record of the various apostles and their work after the death of Jesus; in it can be seen the gradual evolution of Christianity from a branch or sect of Judaism into an independent evangelical faith. Luke begins with the Resurrection and the commission which Jesus lays upon His apostles, then gives an account of their activities in Jerusalem, in Syria and Asia Minor, and in various parts of the Roman Empire. The reader of Acts cannot but be impressed by the religious devotion and moral heroism that it mirrors. This epic account of struggle and suffering, of growth under persecution into an enduring institution, was doubtless written both to provide a record of events and to be an inspiration to its members. Chapters 15 through 28 follow the career of Paul; in Chapter 17 there is an account of his missionary work at Thessalonica. He and Silas stop here, and at the synagogue Paul proclaims his message. He spends three days arguing Scripture with the Jews. A number of ruffians are then persuaded, perhaps hired, to demonstrate against the Christians and incite a riot. The Christians are blamed for the incident; they get Paul out of the city and send him to Berea. Here he is more successful and wins some converts; but the agitators from Thessalonica follow him, and his congregation moves him to Athens, where there are a number of philosophers who, curious about Paul's new doctrine, ask him to tell them about it.

Then Paul stood in the midst of Mars' hill, and said, Ye men of
Athens, I perceive that in all things ye are too superstitious.

627

For as I passed by, and beheld your devotions, I found an altar with this inscription, TO THE UNKNOWN GOD. Whom therefore ye ignorantly worship, him I declare unto you.

God that made the world and all things therein, seeing that he is Lord of heaven and earth, dwelleth not in temples made with hands;

Neither is worshipped with men's hands, as though he needed any thing, seeing he giveth to all life, and breath, and all things;

And hath made of one blood all nations of men for to dwell on all the face of the earth, and hath determined the times before appointed, and the bounds of their habitation;

That they should seek the Lord, if haply they might feel after him, and find him, though he be not far from every one of us:

For in him we **live, and move, and have our being;** as certain also of your own poets have said, For we are also his offspring.

Forasmuch then as we are the offspring of God, we ought not to think that the Godhead is like unto gold, or silver, or stone, graven by art and man's device.

Live we how we can, yet die we must

Source: KING HENRY THE SIXTH: PART THREE (Act V, sc. ii, l. 28)
Author: William Shakespeare (1564–1616)
First published: 1623
Type of work: Historical drama

Context: With his last breath, Warwick, maker of kings, dies in the service of the House of Lancaster. From fast friend of the Duke of York, he becomes foe when the young King Edward marries Lady Grey instead of Bona, sister to the Queen of France. Warwick switches his allegiance to King Henry VI after he is told that Edward, who succeeded his father as usurper of Henry's throne, has married Lady Grey out of lust, thereby making a fool of Warwick, who had gone to France to plead for the hand of the Lady Bona for his king. Edward has no intention of giving up his crown, and Warwick is mortally wounded in battle between the two Houses and their supporters.

WARWICK
. . .

For who lived king, but I could dig his grave?
And who durst smile when Warwick bent his brow?
Lo, now my glory smeared in dust and blood!
My parks, my walks, my manors that I had,
Even now forsake me; and of all my lands
Is nothing left me, but my body's length.
Why, what is pomp, rule, reign, but earth and dust?
And **live we how we can, yet die we must.**